The Enjoyment of Music

ALSO BY JOSEPH MACHLIS

The Enjoyment of Music

An Introduction to Perceptive Listening

Seventh Edition

Standard

JOSEPH MACHLIS

Professor of Music Emeritus,
Queens College of the City University of New York

AND

KRISTINE FORNEY

Professor of Music, California State University, Long Beach

W. W. NORTON & COMPANY

New York · London

Since this page cannot legibly accommodate all the copyright notices, p. 645 constitutes an
   extension of the copyright page.

The text of this book is composed in ITC Garamond with the display set in Zapf Chancery
   Medium.
Composition by NETS.
Manufacturing by R. R. Donnelley, Crawfordsville

Library of Congress Cataloging-in-Publication Data
Machlis, Joseph, 1906–
   The enjoyment of music : an introduction to perceptive listening.
   —7th ed., standard / Joseph Machlis and Kristine Forney.
      p.   cm.
   Includes index.
   1. Music appreciation.   I. Forney, Kristine.   II. Title.
MT6.M134E5   1995
780—dc20   94-28824

ISBN 0-393-96683-6

W. W. Norton & Company, Inc., 500 Fifth Avenue, New York, N.Y. 10110
W. W. Norton & Company Ltd., 10 Coptic Street, London WC1A 1PU

   5 6 7 8 9 0

For Earle Fenton Palmer

Contents

PART ONE
THE MATERIALS OF MUSIC   5

PART THREE
MORE MATERIALS OF MUSIC   183

Unit IX: The Organization of Musical Sounds

Unit X: Focus on Form

PART FOUR
EIGHTEENTH-CENTURY CLASSICISM   205

Unit XI: The Classical Spirit

Unit XII: Classical Chamber Music

Unit XIII: The Classical Symphony

Unit XIV: The Eighteenth-Century Concerto and Sonata

Unit XV: Choral Music and Opera in the Classical Era

PART FIVE
MEDIEVAL AND RENAISSANCE MUSIC   285

PART SIX
THE BAROQUE ERA   351

PART SEVEN
THE TWENTIETH CENTURY   425

Listening Guides

Cultural Perspectives

Preface

The seventh edition of *The Enjoyment of Music* has much to offer its readers. Like the sixth edition, it is available in three formats: the Chronological, the Shorter, and the Standard. The first two formats progress historically from the Middle Ages to the twentieth century; the last adheres to the book's original philosophy, beginning with the accessible and familiar sounds of Romantic music. Certain other features introduced in the sixth edition have been retained as well: the Listening Guides, which supplement the prose descriptions of the primary repertory, the reference listing of Principal Works for each major composer, the discussions of transitions between eras (along with the outline comparisons of the style traits for consecutive eras), and the overall organization by genre rather than by composer.

This new edition is characterized by an increased breadth and diversity of styles presented. While retaining its focus on the classics of Western art music, the book now has taken on a more "international" flavor through consideration of certain world musics and their influence on the Western tradition. This is achieved primarily through the inclusion of twenty-seven Cultural Perspectives, readings scattered throughout the book that offer stimulating and informative discussions of diverse musical styles and practices. These readings delve into the cultures of African Americans and Latin Americans, and into the musics of nearby Canada and Mexico as well as those of the Far East, Africa, and Asia. In each case, the perspective extends to the present day, and often to aspects of popular culture.

Certain new repertory presented in this edition is well suited to demonstrate the interaction of differing musical traditions. New works include Haydn's Symphony No. 100 (*Military*), Dvořák's *New World* Symphony, Ravel's *Songs of Madagascar*, Mahler's *Song of the Earth*, and Ligeti's *Disorder*, from Etudes for Piano, all of which draw their inspiration from what the composers themselves viewed as "exotic" music. Other new works rely on traditional music from the composer's own heritage, such as Haydn's String Quartet, Op. 76, No. 2, Stravinsky's *Petrushka*, Ives's *Fourth of July*, and Copland's *Billy the Kid*.

While the sixth edition made important strides in its coverage of women composers and musicians, the current edition endeavors to achieve a more balanced perspective of the role women have played in music throughout history. Thus, works by five women composers are included in the primary repertory: Hildegard of Bingen's moving liturgical drama *Ordo virtutum*; Elisabeth-Claude Jacquet de la Guerre's French Baroque suite for harpsichord; Clara Schumann's highly virtuosic Scherzo, Op. 10, for solo piano; Ruth Crawford's whimsical song *Rat Riddles*; and Joan Tower's *Petroushskates*, a chamber work that pays homage to Stravinsky. In addition, women performers are discussed throughout the book, some of whom can be directly associated with the primary repertory. These are the famed Singing Ladies of Renaissance Ferrara, for whom Luca Marenzio wrote his madrigal *Cantate Ninfe*; women pianists of the Classical era, including the student for whom Mozart wrote his Piano Concerto in G major, K. 453; and women as interpreters of twentieth-century music, who premiered, among other works, Babbitt's *Phonemena* and Crumb's *Ancient Voices of Children*. Women singers of opera and blues are also discussed, as are the professional opportunities that were available to female musicians in each era.

The opening chapters present the basic concepts and building blocks of music with a broad focus on all styles—Western and non-Western, art and traditional. Musical examples throughout the elements chapters provide a multicultural perspective, and the discussion of instruments and ensembles is not limited to those of Western art music. Vocabulary is reinforced through suggested listening examples (from the accompanying recordings) at the end of each elements chapter. As in the sixth edition, chapters presenting advanced concepts of harmony and form appear later in the book.

Popular music, notably rock, is included for the first time in this edition. There is a thorough survey of the genre, supported by examples from the Byrds and Santana. The contemporary sound of world beat is also discussed, with a listening selection from the South African choral group Ladysmith Black Mambazo. As in the sixth edition, there are chapters on blues and jazz with examples by Louis Armstrong, Duke Ellington, and Gerry Mulligan as well as on musical theater, represented by Rodgers/Hart and Leonard Bernstein.

A number of works discussed—operas and ballets in particular—are available on videocassette, which can enliven and enrich the teaching experience. Many of the operatic selections remain the same in this edition; works newly added include John Gay's *Beggar's Opera*, Leoncavallo's *Pagliacci*, Strauss's *Der Rosenkavalier*, and John Adams's *Nixon in China*. Beyond the realm of opera, several teaching favorites have returned, including Mozart's Symphony No. 40 and Musorgsky's *Pictures at an Exhibition*; early Renaissance styles are illustrated through Dufay's *L'homme armé* Mass and Josquin's motet *Ave Maria . . . virgo serena*; organ music is represented by Bach's chorale prelude on *Ein feste Burg ist unser Gott*; and contemporary music is enhanced through the inclusion of Boulez's *Le marteau sans maître* and Tod Machover's computer composition *Bug-Mudra*.

The book remains eminently readable, preserving the composer biographies—the "story material"—along with quotes from letters and writings that help each composer come alive to the students. With each new edition, the language is modernized, to keep apace with current usage.

The book's design has also been updated, with increased use of color and highlighting. There are more color illustrations than in any previous edition, and for the first time, their scope extends beyond Western culture.

Two recording packages are available with this edition: one contains eight cassettes or CDs, including all the primary repertory discussed in the Chronological and Standard versions; and one contains three cassettes or

CDs and accompanies the Shorter version of the book. New to the package is a CD-ROM disk that allows interactive study—either in the classroom or individually—of twelve of the primary listening selections, representing the full chronological gamut of the text.

We should like to extend our profound thanks to the individuals who were so generous with their assistance: to our editor Claire Brook, for her experienced counsel and dedicated work on this edition, which extended well into her retirement; to Susan Gaustad, for ably copyediting the text and serving as project coordinator; to Michael Ochs and Suzanne LaPlante, for their considerable in-house support, especially with licensing and design elements; to Gyodi Reid, for handling more details than we can enumerate; to Jennifer Atkins, for her capable acquisition of the illustrations; and to David Hamilton, for his expert assistance with the Listening Guides, recording packages, and score anthology.

We also wish to express our sincere appreciation to the many dedicated teachers, including Michael Annicchiarico of the University of New Hampshire and Bryce Rytting of Brigham Young University, who have used *The Enjoyment of Music*, for their helpful comments and suggestions; and to Richard Crawford of the University of Michigan, Gordon Thompson of Skidmore College, and Helen Myers of Trinity College, for their insightful critiques of the Cultural Perspectives included in this new edition.

Joseph Machlis
Kristine Forney

Note on Recordings

Sets of recordings containing the music discussed in this book are available from the publisher. The location of each work in cassette and CD format is indicated in the text by the following symbols:

Cassette   CD

Works that are included in the Norton CD-ROM Masterworks are indicated by the symbol (MW).

(Note: Longer works often include several CD tracks, to facilitate the location of important internal sections. These track numbers, enclosed in a small box, are indicated in the appropriate Listening Guides in the text and in the *Norton Scores* as well.)

Prelude: Listening to Music Today

We are currently experiencing the most radical technological revolution the world has yet known. The age of supertechnology has touched every aspect of our lives, including how and when we listen to music. From the moment we are awakened by our clock radios, our daily activities unfold against a musical background. We listen to music while on the move—in our cars, on planes, or through our headphones while running or biking—or at home for relaxation. We can hardly avoid it in grocery and department stores, in restaurants, in elevators, at the dentist's office, at work. We can experience music in live concerts—at outdoor festivals, rock concerts, jazz clubs, the symphony, the opera—or we can hear it at the movies or on television. The advent of MTV (Music Television) has revolutionized the way we listen to popular music; now it is a visual experience as well as an aural one. This increased dependency on our eyes—one of our more highly developed senses—makes our ears work less actively, a factor we shall attempt to counteract in this book.

The Los Angeles Philharmonic Orchestra performing at the Dorothy Chandler Pavilion. (Photo courtesy of Dana Ross)

Music media too are rapidly changing. The LP record is largely obsolete, cassettes are quickly falling into disuse in favor of CDs, and newer formats are on the way. Video disc players are part of some home stereos, and CD-ROM drives are standard on today's computer systems. In our musical experiences, we have learned to accept new sounds, many produced electronically rather than by traditional instruments. Much of the music we hear on television, at the movies, and from pop music groups is synthetic, produced by instruments that can accurately recreate the familiar sounds of piano, violin, or drums as well as totally new sounds and noises for special effects. Composers too have welcomed the technological revolution; the tools of music composition, formerly a pen, music paper, and perhaps a piano, now more likely include a synthesizer, computer, and laser printer. In short, modern technology has placed at our disposal a wider diversity of music—from every period in history, from every kind of instrument, and from every corner of the globe—than has ever been available before.

Given this diversity, we must choose our path of study. In this book, we will focus on the classics of Western music and pay special attention to the important influences that traditional, popular, and non-Western musics have had on the European and American heritage. The purpose is to expand our listening experience through a heightened awareness of many styles of music. We will also study the uniquely American forms of blues, jazz, and musical theater, as well as rock and contemporary world music. The goal of the book is to place music, whether art or popular, within its cultural context, and to highlight the relationships between different styles. These points are emphasized in the Cultural Perspectives, stimulating and informative texts placed throughout the book that open windows to other cultures and their musics.

The language of music cannot be translated into the language of words. You cannot deduce the actual sound of a piece from anything written about it; the ultimate meaning lies in the sounds themselves. While certain styles are immediately accessible to their audience without explanation, the world of music often brings us into contact with sounds and concepts that are not always so quickly grasped. What, you might wonder, can be said to prepare the nonmusician to understand and appreciate an eighteenth-century symphony, a contemporary opera, or a rock song? A great deal. We can discuss the social

Whitney Houston in concert at the Hollywood Bowl. (Neal Preston; photo courtesy of Nippy, Inc.)

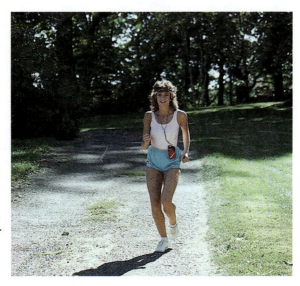

Listening to a favorite tape on her Walkman helps this jogger pass the time. (Jon Fiengersh/ Stock, Boston)

and historical context in which a work was born. We can learn about the characteristic features of the various styles throughout the history of music, so that we can relate a particular piece or style to parallel developments in literature and the fine arts. We can read about the lives and thoughts of the composers who left us so rich a heritage, and take note of what they said about their art. We can acquaint ourselves with the elements out of which music is made, and discover how the composer combines these into any one work. All this knowledge—social, historical, biographical, technical, and analytical—can be interrelated. What will emerge is a total picture of a work, one that will clarify, in far greater degree than you may have thought possible, the form and meaning of a composition.

There are people who claim they prefer not to know anything technical about the music they hear, that to intellectualize the listening experience destroys their enjoyment of music. Yet they would hardly suggest that the best way to enjoy a football game is to know nothing of the rules of the sport. A heightened awareness of musical processes and styles brings listeners closer to the sounds, and allows them to hear and comprehend more.

Some Practical Suggestions

For most of us, it takes practice to become good listeners. Many people "listen" to music as a background to another activity—perhaps studying—or for relaxation. In either case, we are probably not concentrating on the music. The approach set out in this book is intended to develop your listening skills and to expand your musical memory. In order to accomplish this, you should listen to the examples repeatedly, focusing solely on what you are hearing. You will also find it helpful to follow the Listening Guides found throughout the book as you play the music. Since they are outlines, they do not divert your attention from the sounds you hear. The music examples printed in the Listening Guides can be helpful if you follow the general line of the music (see Appendix I, "Musical Notation," and Appendix III, "Using the Listening Guides"). Don't worry if you can't read music; the verbal descriptions of each piece and its sections will tell you exactly what you need to listen for.

It is also important to hear music in live performance. This is your opportunity to try something new and unfamiliar. There are many possibilities available; if you need help finding out about concerts or are unsure of some of the conventions followed in concerts, consult Appendix IV, "Attending Concerts." The goal is to open up a new world of musical experiences for you that you can enjoy for the rest of your life.

You will notice that each historical era begins with a general discussion of the culture, its arts, and its ideas. This should help you integrate the knowledge you have from other disciplines into the world of music and understand that developments in music are very much related to the art, literature, philosophy, religion, and scientific knowledge of the time as well as the social background of the era.

You may be surprised at how technical the study of music can be, and how many new terms you will need to learn. Studying music is not easier than studying other subjects, but it can be more fun. Make use of the Glossary in Appendix II, and note that the most important terms, when introduced in the book, are printed in italics. Some of these terms may be familiar to you from another context ("texture," for example, is a term commonly used to describe a surface or cloth); we will learn to associate these words with different, often more specific, meanings. Others, such as the directions for musical expression, tempo, and dynamics, usually come from a foreign language. We will begin building this vocabulary in the first chapters by breaking music into its constituent parts, its building blocks—its elements. Suggested Listening Examples from the cassettes and CDs accompanying the book appear at the end of each elements chapter, reinforcing the terminology and concepts presented there. We will then analyze how a composer proceeds to shape a melody, how that melody is fitted with accompanying harmony, how music is organized in time, and how it is structured so as to assume logical, recognizable forms. In doing so, we will become aware of the basic principles that apply to all styles of music—classical and popular, Western and non-Western—to music from all eras and countries, and beyond that, to the other arts as well.

*   *   *   *

"To understand," said the painter Raphael, "is to equal." When we come to understand a musical work, we grasp the "moment of truth" that gave it birth and thus become worthy of keeping company with its creator. We receive the message of the music, we recognize the intention of the composer. In effect, we listen perceptively—and that is the one sure road to the enjoyment of music.

PART ONE

The Materials of Music

"There are only twelve tones. You must treat them carefully."—PAUL HINDEMITH

Raoul Dufy *(1877–1953),* The Red Violin (Le violon rouge), *1948.* (Centre Georges Pompidou, Musée National d'Art Moderne, Paris)

UNIT I

The Elements of Music

1

Melody: Musical Line

*"It is the melody which is the charm of music, and it is that which is most
difficult to produce. The invention of a fine melody is a work of genius."*
—JOSEPH HAYDN

Melody is the element that in many musics makes the most direct appeal to the
listener. It is often what moves us emotionally, what we remember and whistle and hum. We know a good melody when we hear it, and we recognize its
power to move us, although we may not be able to explain wherein its power
lies. In some musics, a melody possesses certain specific associations, such as
the time of day that it should be performed or the emotional meaning of its
line. Despite the differences in how melodies sound and interact with the
other aspects of music, all music cultures share the concept of melody as a
musical line.

The Nature of Melody

A *melody* is a succession of single pitches or tones perceived by the mind as a
unity. Just as we hear the words of a sentence not singly but in relation to the
entire thought, so do we perceive the pitches of a melody in relation to each
other. *Pitch* is defined by the highness or lowness of a tone, depending upon   Pitch
the rate of vibration (or frequency)—the faster the vibration, the higher the
pitch. The distance between two different pitches is called an *interval*.   Interval
Intervals may be large or small. The intervals of Western music are familiar to
us, while certain world musics may use intervals so small as to be virtually in-
distinguishable to our ears.

Characteristics of Melody

Melodies may rise and fall with gentle or bold movement, or change slowly, subtly, almost imperceptibly. The melodies of each music culture have their own distinctive character. In some cultures, melody is closely bound to dura- tion—what will be described here as rhythm—and in others, including Western culture, a melody (more popularly called a tune) is nearly inseparable from the sounds that are combined with it. (We will come to know this con- cept as harmony.)

Range

We can describe some characteristics of any melody, regardless of its ori- gin: its range, its shape, and the way it moves. A melody goes up and down, one tone being higher or lower than another. By *range*, we mean the distance between the melody's lowest and highest tones. This can be very narrow, as in the case of a children's song that is easy to sing, or it can be very wide, which is often the case in melodies played on an instrument. The range of a piece is usually described in approximate terms—narrow, medium, or wide.

Shape

Shape is determined by the direction a melody takes as it turns upward or downward or remains static. This movement can be charted on a kind of line graph, resulting in an ascending or descending line, an arch, or a wave, to list a few possibilities.

Conjunct and disjunct movement

Type of movement depends upon whether a melody moves from pitch to pitch in small intervals or by leaps to more distant pitches. Melodies that move principally by small intervals in a joined, connected manner are called *con- junct*, while those that move in disjointed or disconnected intervals are de- scribed as *disjunct*.

Not all melodies can be completely described with these terms, nor do they necessarily remain the same throughout. A melody may begin with a small range and connected tones (that is, conjunct) and, as it develops, ex- pand its range with more disjunct movement.

The Structure of Melody

We can examine the structure of melody in much the same way that we ana- lyze the form of a sentence. A sentence can be divided into its component units or phrases; the same is true for a melody. A *phrase* in music, just as in lan- guage, denotes a unit of meaning within a larger structure. The phrase ends in a resting place or *cadence,* which punctuates the music in the same way that a comma or period punctuates a sentence. The cadence may be either incon- clusive, leaving the listener with the impression that more is to come, or it may sound final, giving the listener the sense that the melody has reached the end. The cadence is where a singer stops to draw breath. An instrumentalist too will breathe at the end of a phrase.

Phrase

Cadence

If the melody is set to words, the text line and the musical phrase will gen- erally coincide. Many folk and popular tunes consist of four phrases that are set to a four-line poem. The first and third lines of the poem may rhyme, as do the second and fourth. This symmetrical type of stanza is reflected in the

Melodic Types

1. Opening of *Shall We Gather at the River* (19th-century American hymn)

Shall we gath-er at the riv - er,   Where bright an - gel feet have trod;____

Range: narrow (4-note span)

Shape: wavelike

Type of movement: conjunct (but with leap at end)

2. Opening of *Joy to the World* (Christmas carol)

Joy   to the world, the Lord is   come.

Range: medium (8-note span)

Shape: descending line

Type of movement: conjunct (no leaps)

3. Opening of *The Star-Spangled Banner* (U.S. national anthem)

Oh,____ say, can you   see,   By the dawn's ear - ly   light,

What so proud - ly we   hailed   At the twi - light's last   gleam - ing?

Range: wide (10-note span)

Shape: wavelike

Type of movement: disjunct (many leaps)

phrase-and-cadence structure of the melody.

An example is the well-known American folk hymn *Amazing Grace*. Its four phrases, both in the poem and the music, are of equal length, and the

Rhyme scheme

rhyme scheme is described *a-b-a-b.* (The *rhyme scheme* of a poem is determined by the similarity in sound of the last syllables or words of each line— here they are "sound," "me," "found," and "see.") The first three cadences (at the end of each of the first three lines) are inconclusive (incomplete), with an upward inflection like a question at the end of the second phrase. The fourth phrase, with its final downward inflection, provides the answer; that is, it gives the listener a sense of finality. One pitch serves as home base, around which the melody revolves and to which it ultimately returns.

The Structure of Melody: Phrasing

Amazing Grace (American hymn)

4 text phrases = 4 musical phrases

A - maz - ing___ grace, how sweet the sound

That saved a___ wretch like me!___

I once___ was___ lost, but now___ am___ found,

Was blind, but___ now I see.___

This same feeling of symmetry and balance can be achieved in melodies that do not rely on words but are played on instruments. Composers can also adapt asymmetrical melodies of irregular phrase length to both vocal and instrumental works. We will hear examples of all these structures in our study of various musical styles.

There is a world of variety possible in forming melodies. Each must be shaped carefully in order to maintain the listener's interest, whether by the composer who plans it out in advance or by the performer who invents it on the spot. What makes a striking effect is a climax, the high point in a melodic line, which usually represents a peak in intensity as well as in range. (Think of the stirring last phrase of *The Star-Spangled Banner,* when the line rises to the words "O'er the land of the free.")

Looking at an Entire Melody

Tune: *Havah nagilah* (Jewish folk dance song)

Translation: Let us rejoice and be happy.
Arise, brethren, with a happy heart.

Opening section (lines 1–2): small range (6 notes), mostly conjunct

Middle section (lines 3–4): smaller range (5 notes), conjunct (one leap near end)

Last section (lines 5–8): begins static (same note), range climbs higher, disjunct (with leaps) at end

We will also hear music that features several simultaneous melodies. Sometimes the relative importance of one over the other is clear, and the added tune is called a *countermelody* (literally, "against a melody"). In other styles, multiple strands of melody can be heard, each of seemingly equal importance.

Countermelody

For much of the music we will study, melody is the most basic element of communication between the composer or performer and the listener. As the twentieth-century composer Aaron Copland aptly put it, "The melody is generally what the piece is about."

Suggested Listening Examples

Conjunct movement, small range—Gregorian chant: *Haec dies*

Mostly conjunct movement, medium range—Mozart: *The Marriage of Figaro* (opening of excerpt)

Disjunct movement, wide range—Schoenberg: *Pierrot lunaire,* No. 18

Symmetrical phrasing—Mozart: *Eine kleine Nachtmusik,* Third Movement

Countermelody—Bach: Cantata No. 80, *A Mighty Fortress Is Our God,* No. 2

2

Rhythm: Musical Time

"In the beginning was rhythm."—HANS VON BÜLOW

Rhythm refers to the orderly movement of music in time. It is the element most closely allied with physical activity and body movement. Since music is an art that exists solely in time, rhythm controls all the relationships within a musical work down to the minutest detail.

The Organization of Rhythm

Beat

Musical time is usually organized in terms of a basic unit of length, known as a *beat*—the regular pulsation heard in most Western styles of music. Some beats are stronger than others; these are known as *accented,* or *strong,* beats. In much of the music we hear, these strong beats occur at regular intervals— every other beat, every third beat, every fourth, and so on—and thus we perceive the beats in groups of two, three, four, or more. These groupings are

Meter and measure

called *meters* and are marked off in *measures,* each containing a fixed number of beats. The first beat of each measure generally receives the strongest accent.

Meter denotes the fixed time patterns within which the music moves. Inside the underlying metrical framework, the rhythm flows freely. Although meter is one aspect of rhythm, it is possible to draw a subtle distinction between them: rhythm refers to the overall movement of music in time and the

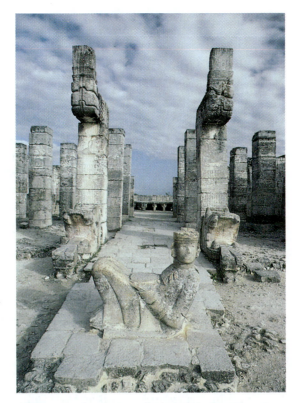

The principles of symmetry and repetition of elements in architecture are comparable to the regular organization of rhythm into meters. The Temple of the Warriors, an eleventh-century structure in Chichén Itza, Yucatán. (Richard Pasly/Stock, Boston)

control of that movement, while meter involves the actual measurement of time. A similar distinction may be drawn in the realm of poetry. For example, the following stanza by Robert Frost is in a simple meter that alternates a strong and weak beat. A metrical reading of this poem will bring out the regular pattern of accented (ˊ) and unaccented (–) syllables:

> Thē wóods āre lóve-lȳ, dárk ānd déep.
> Būt Í hāve próm-īs-és tō kéep,
> Ānd míles tō gó bē-fóre Ī sléep,
> Ānd míles tō gó bē-fóre Ī sléep.

When we read rhythmically, on the other hand, we bring out the natural flow of the language within the basic meter and, more important, the expressive meaning of the words.

Metrical Patterns

Much of Western music draws on simple recurring patterns of two, three, or four beats grouped together in a measure. As in poetry, these meters depend on the regular recurrence of an accent. Simplest of all is a succession of beats in which a strong beat alternates with a weak beat: ONE-two, ONE-two, or, in marching, LEFT-right, LEFT-right. This pattern of two beats to a measure is known as *duple meter* and occurs in many nursery rhymes and marching songs, as well as in other kinds of music.

Duple meter

Triple meter   *Triple meter* is another basic pattern in Western music. It consists of three beats to a measure—one strong beat and two weak—and is traditionally associated with such dances as the waltz and the minuet.

Quadruple meter   *Quadruple meter,* also known as *common time,* contains four beats to the measure, with a primary accent on the first beat and a secondary accent on the third. Although it is sometimes not easy to tell duple and quadruple meter apart, quadruple meter usually has a broader feeling.

Simple meters   Duple, triple, and quadruple meter are regarded as the *simple meters.* Meters in which the basic beat is further subdivided into three are known as

Compound meters   *compound meters.* Most frequent among them is *sextuple meter,* with six beats (two groups of three beats each) to the measure: the primary accent is on the first beat and a secondary accent on the fourth. Marked by a gently flowing effect, this pattern is often found in lullabies.

The following examples illustrate the four basic patterns.

Examples of Simple and Compound Meters

′ = primary accent
⌄ = secondary accent
– = unaccented beat

Duple meter: *Twinkle, Twinkle, Little Star* (children's song)

Accents:	Twín-	klē,	twín-	klē,	lít-	tlē	stár,	____
Meter:	1	2	1	2	1	2	1	2
	Hów	Ī	wón-	dēr	whát	yōu	áre,	____
	1	2	1	2	1	2	1	2

Other examples of duple meter:
> *Yankee Doodle* (American Revolutionary War song)
> *Oh, Susanna* (19th-century American song by Stephen Foster)

Triple meter: *America* (patriotic song)

Mý	cōun-	trȳ	'tís		ōf	thēe,
1	2	3	1	2	3	
Swéet	lānd	ōf	lí-		bēr-tȳ	
1	2	3	1	2	3	
Óf	thēe	Ī	síng.		_____	
1	2	3	1	2	3	

Other examples of triple meter:
> *The Star-Spangled Banner* (U.S. national anthem)
> *Happy Birthday* (traditional American song)
> *Amazing Grace* (American hymn)
> *Cielito lindo* (traditional Spanish song)

Quadruple meter: *America, the Beautiful* (patriotic song)

Ōh,	beaú-	tū-	fŭl	fōr	spá-	ciōus	skĭes,
4	1	2	3	4	1	2	3
Fōr	ám-	bēr	wăves	ōf	gráin,	_____	
4	1	2	3	4	1	2	3
Fōr	púr-	plē	moŭn-	tāin	má-	jēs-	tiĕs
4	1	2	3	4	1	2	3
Ā-	bóve	thē	frŭit-	ēd	pláin,	_____	
4	1	2	3	4	1	2	3

Other examples of quadruple meter:

> *Shall We Gather at the River* (19th-century American hymn)
> *Battle Hymn of the Republic* (American Civil War song)
> *Aura Lee* (folk song, same tune as *Love Me Tender*)
> *Auld Lang Syne* (traditional Scottish song)

Compound (sextuple) meter: *Rock-a-bye Baby* (children's lullaby)

Róck-	ā-	bȳe	bă-	¯	bȳ,	ón	thē	trēe-	tŏp,	¯ ¯
1	2	3	4	5	6	1	2	3	4	5 6
Whén	thē	wīnd	blŏws,	¯	thē	crá-	dlē	wīll	rŏck,	¯ ¯
1	2	3	4	5	6	1	2	3	4	5 6

Other examples of compound meter:

> *Greensleeves* (English folk song)
> *Silent Night* (Christmas carol)
> *Scarborough Fair* (American folk song)

Several additional characteristics of meter should be described. In some cases, a piece will not begin with an accented beat. For example, *America, the Beautiful,* given above under quadruple meter, begins with an *upbeat,* or on the last beat of the measure—in this case, on beat 4. (Notice that the Frost poem cited earlier also begins with an upbeat.) Composers have devised a number of ways to keep the recurrent accent from becoming monotonous. They have used ever more complex rhythmic patterns within the measure, and learned how to vary the underlying beat in different ways. The most common of these procedures is *syncopation,* a term used to denote a deliberate upsetting of the normal pattern of accentuation. Instead of falling on the strong beat of the measure, the accent is shifted to a weak beat or to an *offbeat* (in between the beats). Syncopation has figured in the music of the masters for centuries, and is characteristic of the African-American dance rhythms out of which jazz developed. The examples on the next page illustrate the technique.

Syncopation is only one technique that throws off the regular patterns. A composition may change meters during its course. Indeed, certain twentieth-century pieces shift meters nearly every measure. Another technique is the simultaneous use of two or more rhythmic patterns, such as "two against three"

Upbeat

Syncopation

Syncopation

1. Gently syncopated: *Swing Low, Sweet Chariot* (duple meter)
   (African-American spiritual)

Swing low,_____	sweet		char-		i- ot, _____	
1	2		1		2	

com-in' for to car-ry me			home	_____		
1	2		1		2	

2. Accented and syncopated: *Hello! Ma Baby* (quadruple meter)
   (ragtime song)

Hel-lo!	ma	ba-	by,	Hel-lo!	ma	ho-	ney,
1	2	3	4	1	2	3	4

Hel-lo!	ma	rag-	time	gal._____			
1	2	3	4	1	2	3	4

Polyrhythm

or "three against four." This is called *polyrhythm* (many rhythms), and occurs frequently in the musics of many African cultures as well as in music influenced by those cultures, such as jazz and rock. In the music of some non-Western cultures, the rhythmic organization is even more complex, based on *Additive meter* an *additive meter* or grouping of irregular numbers of beats that add up to an overall larger pattern. For example, a rhythmic pattern of ten beats common in the music of India consists of groupings of 2 + 3 + 2 + 3. We will see that certain folk styles employ similar additive patterns of accents.

Some music moves without a strong sense of beat or meter. We might say *Nonmetric* that such a work is *nonmetric,* as is the case with some early Western music, or that the pulse is veiled or weak, the music moving in a floating rhythm typical of certain non-Western styles.

To sum up: Music is an art of movement in time. Rhythm, the organization of musical movement, permeates every aspect of the musical process. It binds together the parts within the whole: the notes within the measure, the measures within the phrase. Time is the crucial dimension in music, and its first law is rhythm.

Suggested Listening Examples

Nonmetric—Gregorian chant: *Haec dies*

Duple meter—Haydn: Symphony No. 100 in G major (*Military*), Second Movement

Triple meter—Mozart: *Eine kleine Nachtmusik,* Third Movement

Quadruple meter—*Black Magic Woman* by Santana

Compound meter—Jacquet de la Guerre: Suite No. 1, 2nd Gigue

Changing meter––Musorgsky: *Promenade,* from *Pictures at an Exhibition*

> Veiled pulse—Debussy: *Prelude to "The Afternoon of a Faun"*
>
> Polyrhythm—Ligeti: *Disorder,* from Etudes for Piano
>
> Additive patterns—Bartók: *Music for Strings, Percussion, and Celesta,*
> Fourth Movement, opening (accents grouped 2 + 3 + 3)

3

Harmony: Musical Space

"Music, to create harmony, must investigate discord."—PLUTARCH

To the movement of the melody, harmony adds another dimension: depth. It describes the simultaneous happenings in music. Harmony is to music what perspective is to painting—it introduces the impression of musical space. Not all musics of the world rely on harmony for interest, but it is central to most Western styles.

Harmony pertains to the movement and relationship of intervals and chords. We already know that an interval is the distance between any two tones. Intervals can occur melodically—that is, in succession—or simultaneously. When three or more tones are sounded together, a *chord* is produced. *Chord* The intervals from which melodies and chords are built are chosen from a particular *scale,* or collection of pitches arranged in ascending or de- *Scale* scending order. For convenience, the tones of the most frequently used Western scales are assigned syllables, *do-re-mi-fa-sol-la-ti-do*, or numbers, *Syllables* 1-2-3-4-5-6-7-8. Thus the interval *do-re* (1-2) is a second, *do-mi* (1-3) is a third, *do-fa* (1-4) is a fourth, *do-sol* (1-5) is a fifth, *do-la* (1-6) is a sixth, *do-ti* (1-7) is a seventh, and *do-do* (1-8) is an *octave*. As you see from the ex- *Octave* ample on page 19, melody constitutes the horizontal aspect of music, while harmony, consisting of blocks of tones (the chords), constitutes the vertical.

The Function of Harmony

Chords have meaning only in relation to other chords—that is, only as each chord leads into the next. Harmony therefore implies movement and progression. In the larger sense, harmony denotes the overall organization of tones in a musical work in such a way as to achieve order and unity.

The most common chord in Western music is a certain combination of three tones known as a *triad*. Such a chord may be built by combining the *Triad* first, third, and fifth pitches of the scale: *do-mi-sol*. A triad may be built on the second degree (steps 2-4-6, or *re-fa-la*), on the third degree (steps 3-5-7, or *mi-sol-ti*), and similarly on each of the other degrees of the scale. The triad is

Harmony lends a sense of depth to music, as perspective does to painting.
Meindert Hobbema *(1638-1709),* The Avenue, Middelharnis. (Courtesy of the Trustees, National Gallery, London)

a basic formation in our music. In the example on the facing page, the melody of *Old MacDonald* is harmonized by triads. The supporting role of harmony is apparent when a singer or solo instrument is accompanied by piano. As in *Old MacDonald,* the singer presents the melody while an instrument provides the harmonic background. Melody and harmony do not function independently of one another. On the contrary, the melody suggests the harmony that goes with it, and each constantly influences the other.

The Organization of Harmony

Each system of music has set procedures for organizing tones into intelligible relationships; within these various systems, certain tones assume greater importance than others. In Western music, the first tone of the scale, *do,* also *Tonic* called the *tonic* or keynote, serves as a home base around which the others revolve and to which they ultimately gravitate. We observed this principle at work earlier with the tune *Amazing Grace* (p. 10). It is this sense of a home base that helps us recognize when a piece of music ends.

The principle of organization around a central tone, the tonic, is called *Tonality* *tonality.* The particular scale chosen as the basis of a piece determines the identity of the tonic and the tonality. Two different types of scale are commonly found in Western music written between about 1650 and 1900: major and minor. What characterizes these two types are the intervals upon which they are built. We will learn more about the formulation of scales later (see Chapter 34). For the moment, it is sufficient to offer the following observation concerning the differences usually attributed to major and minor scales: music in major may be thought of as bright, while minor sounds more sub-dued. Some people find that minor sounds sadder than major. Indeed, in the nineteenth century, the minor was regarded as more somber than the major. For this reason, a composer would hardly choose a minor tonality for a tri-umphal march or grand finale of a piece. For now, we shall regard major and minor as scale types and tonalities, each with its own unique quality of sound.

Major and minor scales

We make a distinction between notes that belong to a particular scale and tonality and those that do not. The term *diatonic* describes melodies or har-monies that are built from the tones of a major or minor scale; *chromatic* (from the Greek word *chroma*, meaning "color") describes the full gamut of notes available in the octave.

Diatonic and chromatic

Consonance and Dissonance

Harmonic movement, as we shall see, is generated by motion toward a goal or a feeling of resolution. This striving for resolution is the dynamic force in our music. It shapes the forward movement, providing focus and direction. Movement in music receives its maximum impetus from *dissonance*, a com-bination of tones that sounds discordant, unstable, in need of resolution.

Dissonance

Consonance

Dissonance introduces the necessary tension into music. What suspense and conflict are to drama, dissonance is to music. Dissonance finds its resolution in *consonance,* a concordant or agreeable combination of tones that provides a sense of relaxation and fulfillment in music. At their extremes, dissonance can sound harsh, while consonance is more pleasing to the ear. Each complements the other; both are a necessary part of the artistic whole.

In general, music has grown more dissonant through the ages. It is easy to understand why. A combination of tones that sounded extremely harsh when first introduced began to seem less so as the sound became increasingly familiar. As a result, a later generation of composers had to find ever more dissonant harmonies in order to create the same degree of excitement and tension as their predecessors.

Drone

Our notion of harmony is more sophisticated than our approach to melody. Historically, harmony appeared much later—about a thousand years ago—and its development took place largely in the West. In many Far Eastern cultures, it takes a subsidiary role and consists of a supporting sustained tone called a *drone*, against which melodic and rhythmic complexities unfold. This harmonic principle also occurs in certain European folk musics, where, for example, a bagpipe might play the accompanying drone to a lively dance tune.

Our harmonic system has advanced steadily over the past ten centuries, continually adjusting to new needs. Composers have tested the rules as they have experimented with innovative sounds and procedures. Yet their goal remains the same—to impose order upon the raw material of sound, to organize the pitches so that they reveal a unifying idea.

Suggested Listening Examples

Major tonality—Mozart: *Eine kleine Nachtmusik*, Third Movement

Minor tonality—Beethoven: Symphony No. 5, First Movement

Consonance—Handel: *Messiah,* "Hallelujah" Chorus (No. 44)

Dissonance—Ligeti: *Disorder,* from Etudes for Piano

4

Musical Texture

"Ours is an age of texture."—GEORGE DYSON

In writings on music, we encounter frequent references to its fabric, or texture. Such comparisons between music and cloth are not as unreasonable as may at first appear, since the melodic lines may be thought of as so many threads that make up the musical fabric. This fabric may be one of several distinct types.

Types of Texture

The simplest texture is *monophonic,* or single-voiced. ("Voice" refers to an individual part or line, even when we are talking about instrumental music.) Here the melody is heard without either a harmonic accompaniment or other vocal lines. Attention is focused on the single line. Up to about a thousand years ago, the Western music of which we have any knowledge was monophonic.

Monophonic

To this day, much music of the Far and Middle East is largely monophonic. A melody may be accompanied by a variety of rhythm and percussion instruments that embellish it, but interest is focused on the single line rather than on any accompaniment. One type of texture that is found widely outside the tradition of Western art music is based on two or more voices (parts) simultaneously elaborating the same melody, usually in an improvised performance. Called *heterophony,* this technique usually results in a melody combined with an ornamented version of itself. It can be heard too in music derived from African-American sources, such as jazz and spirituals, where improvisation (in which some aspects of the music are created on the spot) is central to performance.

Heterophony

Distinct from heterophony is *polyphony* (or many-voiced texture), in which two or more melodic lines are combined, thus distributing melodic interest among all the parts. Polyphonic texture is based on *counterpoint*. This term comes from the Latin *punctus contra punctum,* "point against point" or "note against note"—that is to say, one musical line set against the other. Counterpoint is the art of combining in a single texture two or more simultaneous melodic lines, each with a rhythmic life of its own.

Polyphony

Counterpoint

In the fourth type of texture, *homophony,* a single voice takes over the melodic interest, while the accompanying voices take a subordinate role. Normally, they become blocks of harmony, the chords that support, color, and enhance the principal part. Here we have a single-melody-with-chords, or homophonic, texture. Again the listener's interest is directed to a single line, but this line is conceived in relation to a harmonic background. Homophonic texture is heard when a pianist plays a melody in the right hand while the left sounds the chords, or when the singer or violinist carries the tune against a

Homophony

harmonic accompaniment on the piano. Homophonic texture, then, is based on harmony, just as polyphonic texture is based on counterpoint.

We have seen that melody is the horizontal aspect of music, while harmony is the vertical. The comparison with the weave of a fabric consequently has validity. The horizontal threads, the melodies, are held together by the vertical threads, the harmonies. Out of their interaction comes a texture that may be light or heavy, coarse or fine.

A composition need not use one texture or another exclusively. For example, a large-scale work may begin by presenting a melody against a homophonic texture, after which the interaction of the parts becomes increasingly polyphonic. So too in a largely homophonic piece, the composer may enhance the effect of the principal melody through an interesting play of countermelodies and counterrhythms in the accompanying parts.

Contrapuntal Devices

Imitation

When several independent lines are combined, composers try to give unity and shape to the texture. A basic procedure for achieving this end is *imitation,* in which a melodic idea is presented in one voice and then restated in another. While the imitating voice restates the melody, the first voice continues with new material. Thus a polyphonic texture is achieved. To the vertical and horizontal threads in musical texture imitation adds a third, the diagonal (see the example on facing page).

Canon and round

The length of the imitation may be brief or may last the entire work. In the latter case, we have a strict type of composition known as a *canon.* (The name

Imitation in a Three-Voice Round

Voice 1:
Row, row, row your boat, Gent - ly down the stream,

Voice 2:
Row, row, row your boat,

Voice 1:
Mer-ri-ly, mer-ri-ly, mer-ri-ly, mer-ri-ly, Life is but a dream.

Voice 2:
Gent - ly down the stream, Mer-ri-ly, mer-ri-ly, mer-ri-ly, mer-ri-ly,

Voice 3:
Row, row, row, your boat, Gent - ly down the stream,

comes from the Greek word for "law" or "order.") The simplest and most popular form of canon is a *round,* in which each voice enters in succession with the same melody. A round is a perpetual canon for singing voices; commonly known examples include the children's songs *Row, Row, Row Your Boat* and *Frère Jacques* (Are You Sleeping?). In the example above, a round begins with one voice, then another voice joins it in imitation, and finally a third voice enters, creating a three-part polyphonic texture.

Contrapuntal writing is marked by a number of devices that have flourished for centuries. *Inversion* is a technique that turns the melody upside down; that is, it follows the same intervals but in the opposite direction. Where the melody originally moved up a third, the inverted version moves down a third. *Retrograde* refers to a statement of the melody backward, beginning with its last note and proceeding to its first. These two techniques can be combined in the *retrograde inversion* of a melody: upside down and backward. *Augmentation* calls for the melody to be presented in longer time values, often twice as slow as the original. Think of it as augmenting or increasing the time it takes to play the melody. The opposite technique is called *diminution*, in which the melody is presented in short time values, thus diminishing the time it takes to be played. These devices are often not easy to hear; they are rather structural means by which composers develop their works.

Inversion

Retrograde

Retrograde inversion
Augmentation

Diminution

Examples of Contrapuntal Devices*

Imitation

Other contrapuntal devices

*Based on a melody from the Sonata for Violin and Piano by César Franck.

Examples of Musical Texture

Monophonic—one melodic line, no accompaniment

Do - mi - ne De - us Rex coe - le - stis De - us Pa - ter o - mni - po - tens

Polyphonic—several melodic lines combined in imitation (separate entries marked with brackets)

Homophonic—one melody, with accompaniment (melody in top part, chords in accompaniment)

Musical Texture and the Listener

Different textures require different types of listening. Although monophonic music is, in principle, the simplest type—with only a single melodic line—it challenges the listener's ability to perceive music on a linear time line. Homophonic music is perhaps the most familiar texture to us today, in that we are accustomed to focusing on the main melody and its subordinate harmonies, and following the interrelation of the two. Indeed, much of the music we have heard since childhood—including many traditional and popular styles—consists of melody and accompanying chords.

Polyphony and heterophony present the most challenging textures. Still, in heterophony, we are generally aware of the principal melody, in spite of the linear fabric that surrounds it. In polyphony, we must be attentive to the independent lines as they flow against one another, each in its own rhythm. With practice and repeated hearings, we will learn to follow the individual voices and to separate each within the contrapuntal web.

5

Musical Form

"The principal function of form is to advance our understanding. It is the organization of a piece which helps the listener to keep the idea in mind, to follow its development, its growth, its elaboration, its fate."
—ARNOLD SCHOENBERG

Form is that quality in a work of art that presents to the mind of the beholder an impression of conscious choice and rational arrangement. *Form* refers, then, to the structure or shape of a work. It is the way the elements of a musical composition have been combined to make it understandable to the listener. In all the arts, a balance is required between unity and variety, between symmetry and asymmetry, activity and repose. Nature too has embodied this balance in the forms of plant and animal life and in what is perhaps the supreme achievement—the human form.

Structure and Design in Music

Our lives are composed of sameness and differentness: certain details are repeated again and again, others are new. Music, regardless of its cultural origin, mirrors this dualism. Its basic law of structure is *repetition and contrast*— unity and variety. Repetition fixes the material in our minds and provides for our need for the familiar. Contrast sustains our interest and feeds our love of change. From the interaction of the familiar and the new, the repeated elements and the contrasting ones, result the contours of musical form. These are to be found in every type of musical work, from the nursery rhyme to the symphony.

One further principle of form that falls between repetition and contrast is *variation,* where some aspects of the music are altered but recognizable. We hear this formal technique when we listen to a new arrangement of a well-

Repetition and contrast

Variation

known popular song. The tune is recognizable, but many features of the known version may be changed.

Form is present in a variety of musical structures. These structures reflect procedures worked out by generations of composers. No matter how diverse the structures, they are based in one way or another on repetition and contrast. The forms, however, are not fixed molds into which composers pour their material. What gives a piece of music its uniqueness is that it adapts a general plan to its own requirements. All faces have two eyes, a nose, and a mouth. In each face, though, these features are found in a wholly individual combination. Similarly, no two symphonies of Haydn or Mozart, no two sonatas of Beethoven, are exactly alike. Each is a fresh and unique solution to the problem of fashioning musical material into a logical and coherent form.

Improvisation

Performers sometimes participate in creating the form of a composition. In works based primarily on *improvisation* (pieces created in performance as opposed to precomposed), such as jazz, rock, and certain non-Western styles, all the elements described above—repetition, contrast, and variation—play a role. Thus, even when a piece is "created" on the spot, a balance of these structural principles is achieved.

Two-Part and Three-Part Form

Binary form

Ternary form

The principles of form may be illustrated through two of the most basic patterns in Western music. Two-part, or *binary*, form is based on a statement and a departure, without a return to the opening section. Three-part, or *ternary*, form extends the idea of statement and departure by bringing back the first section. (In our example below, the pattern of chorus-verse-chorus gives us a ternary form.) Formal patterns can be simply outlined: binary form as **A-B** and ternary form as **A-B-A,** as illustrated in the chart opposite.

Both two-part and three-part forms are common in short pieces such as songs and dances. With its logical symmetry and its balancing of the outer sections against the contrasting middle one, three-part form constitutes a simple, clear-cut formation that is a favorite in architecture and painting as well as music (see illustration on p. 28).

The Building Blocks of Form

Theme

When a melodic idea is used as a building block in the construction of a musical work, we call it a *theme*. The theme is the first in a series of musical situations, all of which must grow out of its basic idea as naturally as does the plant from the seed. The process of spinning out a theme, of weaving and reweaving threads of which it is composed, is the essence of musical thinking. This process of expansion has its parallel in prose writing, where an idea stated at the beginning of a paragraph is embroidered and enlarged upon until all its aspects appear in view. Each sentence leads smoothly into the one that follows. In similar fashion, every measure in a musical work takes up where the one before left off and brings us logically to the next.

Binary and Ternary Form

Binary form: *Yankee Doodle*

Statement—A

Yan - kee Doo - dle   went to town, a - rid - ing on a   po - ny,

Stuck a fea - ther   in his cap and   called it ma - ca - ro - ni.

Departure—B

Yan - kee Doo - dle   keep it up,   Yan - kee Doo - dle   dan - dy,

Mind the mu - sic   and the step and   with the girls be   han - dy.

Ternary form: *Goodbye, Old Paint*

Statement—A

Good - bye, Old   Paint, I'm a - leav - in' Chey - enne, Good -

bye,   Old   Paint, I'm a - leav - in' Chey - enne.   My

Contrast (Departure)—B

foot's in the   stir - rup, my   po - ny won't_   stand,_ I'm a -

leav - in' Chey - enne and I'm   off   to Mon - ta - na. Good -

Repetition—A

bye,   Old   Paint, I'm a - leav - in' Chey - enne,   Good -

bye,   Old   Paint,   I'm a - leav - in' Chey - enne.

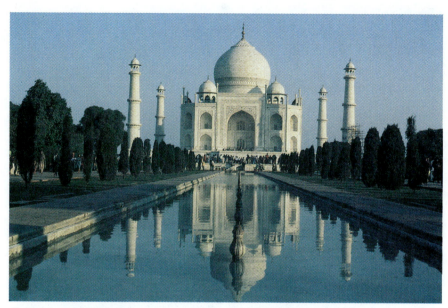

(Left): the Trylon and Perisphere, symbol of New York's World's Fair of 1939, is a visual realization of binary (**A-B**) *form. (Right): the Taj Mahal in Agra, India, one of the world's seven wonders, illustrates that three-part* (**A-B-A**) *form is as appealing to the eye as it is to the ear.* (Bettmann Archive and the Indian Tourist Bureau)

Thematic development

The most tightly knit kind of expansion in music is known as *thematic development*. To develop a theme means to reveal its capacities for growth and bring them to fulfillment. Thematic development is one of the most important techniques in musical composition, demanding of the composer imagination, craftsmanship, and intellectual power. The principle of thematic development—or elaborating or varying a musical idea—is important also to the melody-oriented styles of many Far Eastern and Middle Eastern musics.

In the process of development, certain procedures have proved to be particularly effective. The simplest is repetition, which may be either exact or varied. Or the idea may be restated at another pitch; such a restatement at a *Sequence* higher or lower pitch level is known as a *sequence*.

Motive

Another important technique in thematic development is the breaking up of a theme into its constituent parts, or motives. A *motive* is the smallest fragment of a theme that forms a melodic-rhythmic unit. Motives are the cells of musical growth. Through fragmentation of themes, through repeating and varying motives and combining them in ever fresh patterns, the composer imparts to the musical work the quality of dynamic evolution and growth.

These musical building blocks can be seen in action even in simple songs, such as the popular national tune *America*. In this piece, the opening three-note motive ("My country") is repeated in sequence almost immediately at a different pitch level on the words "Sweet land of." A fine example of a sequence occurs later in the piece: the musical motive set to the words "Land where our fathers died" is repeated beginning on a lower note for the words "Land of the pilgrim's pride."

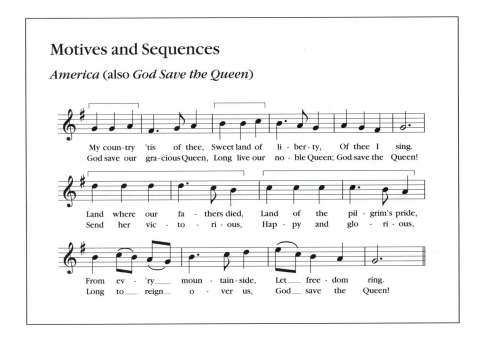

Motives and Sequences

America (also God Save the Queen)

No matter how imposing the dimensions of a composition, each will show the principles of repetition and contrast, of unity and variety, that we have traced here. We will see too that popular and traditional musics from various cultures make use of these same building blocks. One formal practice linked to repetition that can be found throughout much of the world is *call and response*, or responsorial music. Heard in the musics of many African cultures as well as certain Native American and African-American musics, this style of performance is based on a social structure that recognizes a singing leader who is imitated by a chorus of followers. We will study the practice as it occurs in early styles of Western church music (see p. 292). Yet another widely used structural procedure linked to the principle of repetition is *ostinato*, a short musical pattern—melodic, rhythmic, or harmonic—that is repeated persistently throughout a work or a major section of a composition. This unifying technique is especially prevalent in many African musics as well as popular styles such as blues, jazz, and rock.

Call and response

Ostinato

In all its manifestations, our music displays the striving for organic form that binds together the individual tones within a phrase, the phrases within a section, the sections within a *movement* (a complete, comparatively independent division of a large-scale work), and the movements within the work as a whole. As in a novel, the individual words are bound together in phrases, sentences, paragraphs, sections, chapters, and parts.

Movement

It has been said that architecture is frozen music. By the same token, music is architecture floating in time. Form is the structural principle in music. It distributes the areas of activity and repose, tension and relaxation, light and shade, and integrates the many details, large and small, into the spacious structures that are the glory of music.

Suggested Listening Examples

Variation and improvisation—Ellington: *Ko-Ko*

Binary form—Jacquet de la Guerre: Suite No. 1, 2nd Gigue

Ternary form—Handel: *Messiah,* Aria (No. 16)

Motive and thematic development—Beethoven: Symphony No. 5, First
    Movement

Call and response—*That's Why I Choose You* by Ladysmith Black Mambazo

Responsorial singing—Gregorian chant: *Haec dies*

Ostinato—Machaut: *Hareu! Hareu! le feu/Helas!/Obediens*
    Ellington: *Ko-Ko*

6

Tempo and Dynamics

*"The whole duty of a conductor is comprised in his ability to indicate the
right tempo."*—RICHARD WAGNER

The Pace of Music

Tempo

In our musical system, meter tells us how many beats there are in the measure, but it does not tell us whether these beats occur slowly or rapidly. The *tempo,* or the rate of speed, the pace of the music, provides the answer to this vital question. Consequently, the flow of music in time involves both meter and tempo.

Tempo carries emotional implications. We hurry our speech in moments of agitation, our bodies press forward in eagerness. Vigor and gaiety are associated with a brisk pace as surely as despair demands a slow one. In an art of movement such as music, the rate of movement is of prime importance. We respond to musical tempo physically and psychologically. Our pulse, our breathing, our entire being adjusts to the rate of movement and to the feeling brought on by our conscious and subconscious reactions.

Tempo markings

Because of the close connection between tempo and mood, tempo markings indicate the character of the music as well as the pace. It is traditional that tempo markings, along with other indications of expression, are given by composers in Italian. This reflects the domination of Italian music in Europe during the period from around 1600 to 1750, when such performance directions were established. A list of some of the most common tempo markings follows:

Dynamic contrasts in music may be compared to light and shade in painting. **Georges de La Tour** *(1593–1652),* Joseph the Carpenter. (Giraudon/Art Resource, N.Y.)

grave	solemn (very, very slow)
largo	broad (very slow)
adagio	quite slow
andante	a walking pace
moderato	moderate
allegro	fast (cheerful)
vivace	lively
presto	very fast

Frequently encountered too are modifying adverbs such as *molto* (very), *meno* (less), *poco* (a little), and *non troppo* (not too much). Of great importance are the terms indicating a change of tempo. The principal ones are *accelerando* (getting faster) and *ritardando* (holding back, getting slower); *a tempo* (in time) indicates a return to the original pace.

Loudness and Softness

Dynamics denote the degree of loudness or softness at which the music is played. In this area, as in that of tempo, our emotions affect our responses. The main dynamic indications, listed below, are based on the Italian words for loud (*forte*) and soft (*piano*).

Dynamics

| *pianissimo* (**pp**) | very soft |
| *piano* (**p**) | soft |

mezzo piano (***mp***)	moderately soft
mezzo forte (***mf***)	moderately loud
forte (***f***)	loud
fortissimo (***ff***)	very loud

Of special importance are the directions to change the dynamics, either suddenly or gradually. Such changes are indicated by words or signs. Among the most common are the following:

crescendo	(———————)	growing louder
decrescendo or *diminuendo*	(———————)	growing softer
sforzando (***sf***), "forcing"—		
accent on a single note or chord		sudden stress

Tempo and Dynamics as Elements of Musical Expression

The markings for tempo and dynamics contribute to the expressive content of a piece of music. These so-called expression marks steadily increased in number during the late eighteenth and nineteenth centuries, as composers tried to indicate their intentions ever more precisely, until certain twentieth-century composers left few decisions to the performer.

Metronome   If tempo and dynamics are the domain of the composer, what is the role of performers and conductors in interpreting a musical work? Performance directions can be somewhat imprecise—what is loud or fast to one performer may be moderate in volume and tempo to another. Even when composers give precise tempo markings in their scores (using a device known as a *metronome*, which gives the required number of beats per minute), performers have the final say in the tempo that best delivers the message of the music. And for the many styles of music—non-Western, folk, and popular, among others—that do not rely on composer directions or even printed music, the performer takes full responsibility for the interpretation of the music.

Suggested Listening Examples

grave—Purcell: *Dido and Aeneas,* Act III, Dido's Lament

adagio—Beethoven: Piano Sonata in C minor (*Pathétique*), Second Movement

moderato—Brahms: *A German Requiem*, Fourth Movement

allegro—Bartók: *Music for Strings, Percussion, and Celesta*, Fourth Movement

vivace—Stravinsky: *Petrushka*, opening

piano—Copland: *Street in a Frontier Town*, from *Billy the Kid*, opening

forte—Stravinsky: *Petrushka*, opening

crescendo/decrescendo—Brahms: *A German Requiem*, Fourth Movement, opening

UNIT II

Musical Instruments and Ensembles

7

Musical Instruments I

"With these artificial voices we sing in a manner such as our natural voices would never permit."—JOHN REDFIELD

Properties of Musical Sound

Most musical sounds can be described in terms of four qualities or properties: pitch, duration, volume, and timbre. We have seen that *pitch* refers to the relative position—high or low—of a tone in a scale. Pitch is determined by the rate of vibration, measured in frequency (or number of vibrations per second); this factor depends on the length of the vibrating body. Other conditions being equal, the shorter a string or column of air, the more rapidly it vibrates and the higher the pitch. The longer a string or column of air, the fewer the vibrations per second and the lower the pitch. The width, thickness, density, and tension of the vibrating body also affect the outcome. *Duration* depends on the length of time over which the vibration is maintained. We hear tones as being not only high or low but also short or long. *Volume* (dynamics) depends on the degree of force of the vibrations, as a result of which the tone strikes us as being loud or soft.

    The fourth property of sound—known as tone color, or *timbre*—best accounts for the striking differences in the sound of instruments. (The word retains its French pronunciation, tám-br̄.) This is why a note on the trumpet sounds altogether different from the same note played on a guitar or a drum. Timbre is influenced by a number of factors, such as the size, shape, and proportions of the instrument, the material of which it is made, and the manner in which vibration is set up.

Pitch

Duration

Volume

Timbre

Instrument

Register

Music is produced by two basic media—human voices and musical instruments. (An *instrument* is a mechanism that generates musical vibrations and launches them into the air.) One may perform music with either or both, according to one's purpose and the capacities and limitations of each. For each voice type and instrument, there are limits of range, the distance from the lowest to the highest tone, and of dynamics, the degree of softness or loudness beyond which the voice or instrument cannot go. (We describe a specific area in the range of an instrument or voice, such as low, middle, or high, as its *register.*) These and a host of similar considerations determine the composer's and performer's choices.

The Voice as a Model for Instrumental Sound

Vocal ranges

The human voice is the most natural of all musical instruments; it is also one of the most widely used—all cultures have some form of vocal music. Each person's voice has a particular quality or character and range. Our standard designations for vocal ranges, from highest to lowest, are *soprano, mezzo-soprano,* and *alto* (short for *contralto*) for female voices, *tenor, baritone,* and *bass* for male voices.

In earlier eras, Western social and religious customs severely restricted women's participation in public musical events. Thus young boys, and occasionally adult males with soprano- or alto-range voices, sang female roles in church music and on the stage. In the sixteenth century, women singers came into prominence in secular (nonreligious) music. Tenors were most often featured as soloists in early opera; the lower male voices, baritone and bass, became popular soloists in the eighteenth century. In other cultures, the sound of women's voices has always been preferred for certain styles of music; for example, wedding songs are traditionally performed by professional women singers in certain Muslim cultures of northern Africa. Throughout the ages, the human voice has served as a model for instrument builders and players, who have sought to duplicate its lyric beauty and expressiveness on their instruments.

The World of Musical Instruments

Aerophones

Chordophones

The diversity of musical instruments from around the world defies description. Every conceivable method of sound production is used, every possible raw material employed, thus it would be impossible to list or catalog them all here. However, specialists have devised a method for classifying instruments that is based solely on the way their sound is generated. There are four categories in this system. *Aerophones* produce sound by using air as the primary vibrating means. Common instruments in this grouping are flutes, whistles, and horns—in short, nearly any wind instrument. *Chordophones* are instruments that produce sound from a vibrating string stretched between two points. The string may be set in motion by bowing or plucking, so the instruments are as disparate as the violin, harp, guitar, Japanese koto, and Indian sitar.

Aerophone: a European bagpipe, often used in folk music, sounds a sustained drone under the melodic line.

Membranophone: Native Americans playing drums and shaking a gourd rattle (idiophone).

Chordophone: the Japanese koto, a plucked instrument with thirteen strings, is often played with the three-stringed shamisen (right).

Idiophone: the rattles on the African dancer's ankles are one common type of idiophone.

Idiophones   *Idiophones* produce the sound from the substance of the instrument itself. They may be struck, blown, shaken, scraped, or rubbed. Examples of idiophones are bells, rattles, xylophones, and cymbals—in other words, a wide variety of percussion instruments, among others. The fourth category is

Membranophones   *membranophones,* referring to any instrument sounded from tightly stretched membranes. These drum-type instruments can be struck, plucked, rubbed, or even sung into, thus setting the skin in vibration (see illustrations on p. 35).

The next chapter will describe and categorize the instruments used most frequently in Western art music. Throughout the book, however, you will see allusions to various instruments associated with popular and art music cultures around the world and their influence on the Western tradition.

8

Musical Instruments II

"Lucidity is the first purpose of color in music."—ARNOLD SCHOENBERG

The instruments of the Western world—and especially those of the orchestra—may also be categorized in four familiar groups: strings, woodwinds, brass, and percussion. We will see, however, that these categories, or families, of instruments are not entirely homogeneous; that is, all woodwinds are not made of wood, nor do they share a means of sound production. Also, we will see that certain instruments do not fit neatly into any of these convenient categories (the piano, for example, is both a string and percussion instrument).

String Instruments

The string family, like the grouping of chordophones, includes two types of instruments: those that are bowed and those that are plucked. The bowed string family has four principal members: violin, viola, violoncello, and double bass, each with four strings that are set vibrating by drawing a bow across them. The hair of the bow is rubbed with rosin so that it will "grip" the strings. The bow is held in the right hand, while the left hand is used to "stop" the string by pressing a finger down at a particular point, thereby leaving a certain portion of the string free to vibrate. By stopping the string at another point, the performer changes the length of the vibrating portion, and with it the rate of vibration and the pitch.

Violin   The *violin* was brought to its present form by the brilliant instrument makers who flourished in Italy from around 1600 to 1750. Most famous among them were the Amati and Guarneri families—in these dynasties, the secrets of the craft were transmitted from father to son—and the master builder of them all, Antonio Stradivari (c. 1645–1737). Preeminent as a melody instrument, the violin is capable of brilliance and dramatic effect, subtle nuances from soft to loud, the utmost rhythmic precision, and great agility in rapid passages. It has an extremely wide range.

The *viola* is somewhat larger than the violin and is lower in range. Its strings are longer, thicker, heavier. The tone is husky in the low register, somber and penetrating in the high. The viola is an effective melody instrument, and often balances the more brilliant violin by playing a countermelody. It usually fills in the harmony, or it may double another part. One instrument is said to *double* (reinforce) another when it plays the same notes an octave higher or lower.   *Viola*

The *violoncello,* popularly known as *cello,* is lower in range than the viola and is notable for its singing quality, which takes on a dark resonance in the low register. Cellos often carry the melody, they enrich the sound with their full timbre, and together with the double basses, they supply the foundation for the harmony of the string family.   *Violoncello*

The *double bass,* known also as a *contrabass* or *bass viol,* is the lowest of the string instruments of the orchestra. Accordingly, it plays the bass part— that is, the foundation of the harmony. Its deep tones come into focus doubling the cello part an octave lower.   *Double bass*

These four instruments constitute the string section, or what has come to be known as "the heart of the orchestra." This designation indicates the versatility and importance of this section.

Orchestral string instruments can play in many styles and produce many special effects. They are preeminent in playing *legato* (smooth and connected) as well as the opposite quality of tone, *staccato* (short and detached). A special effect, *pizzicato* (plucked), is created when a performer plucks the string with a finger instead of using the bow. *Vibrato* denotes a throbbing effect achieved by a rapid wrist-and-finger movement on the string that slightly alters the pitch. In *glissando,* a finger of the left hand slides along the string while the right hand draws the bow, thereby sounding all the pitches of the scale. *Tremolo,* the rapid repetition of a tone through a quick up-and-down movement of the bow, is associated in the popular mind with suspense and excitement. No less important is the *trill,* a rapid alternation between a tone and the one above it.   *Special effects*

Double-stopping involves playing two strings simultaneously; when three or four strings are played simultaneously, it is called *triple-* or *quadruple-stopping*. In this way the members of the violin family, essentially melodic instruments, become capable of harmony. The *mute* is a small attachment that fits over the bridge, muffling (and changing) the sound. *Harmonics* are crystalline tones in the very high register that are produced by lightly touching the string at certain points while the bow is drawn across the string.

Two plucked string instruments, the harp and the guitar, are also widely used. The *harp* is one of the oldest of musical instruments, and one that has a home in many cultures outside Europe. Its plucked strings produce an ethereal tone. The pedals are used to tighten the strings, hence to raise the pitch. Chords on the harp are frequently played in broken form—that is, the tones   *Harp*

Violinist Anne-Sophie Mutter.
(Photo by M. Jorge Reinhardt)

Violin   Viola   Cello   Double bass

Yo-Yo Ma, cellist.
(Photo © Martha Swope)

Milt Hinton playing the double bass. (Photo
courtesy of Arthur Elgort)

are sounded one after another instead of simultaneously. From this technique comes the term *arpeggio,* which means a broken chord (*arpa* is Italian for "harp"). Arpeggios are created in a variety of ways on many instruments.

The *guitar* too is an old instrument, dating back at least to the Middle Ages, *Guitar* and is probably of Middle Eastern origin. It has always been a favorite solo instrument, and is associated today with folk and popular music as well as classical styles. The standard acoustical guitar (as opposed to electric) is made of wood and has a fretted fingerboard and six nylon strings, which are plucked with the fingers of the right hand or with a pick. The electric guitar, an electronically amplified instrument capable of many specialized techniques, comes in two main types: the hollow-bodied (or electro-acoustic), favored by jazz musicians, and the solid-bodied, used by rock musicians. Related to the guitar are such favorite traditional instruments as the banjo and mandolin.

David Byrne on the electric guitar.
(Courtesy of Warner Brothers)

Narciso Yepes plays the classical guitar.
(Courtesy of Mariedi Anders)

Woodwind Instruments

In woodwind instruments (aerophones), the tone is produced by a column of air vibrating within a pipe that has little holes along its length. When one or another of these holes is opened or closed, the length of the vibrating air column within the pipe is changed. Woodwind instruments are capable of remarkable agility by means of an intricate mechanism of keys arranged to suit the natural position of the fingers.

This is a less homogeneous group than the strings. Nowadays they are not necessarily made of wood, and they employ several different methods of setting up vibration: by blowing across a mouth hole (flute family), by blowing into a mouthpiece that has a single reed (clarinet and saxophone families), or by blowing into a mouthpiece fitted with a double reed (oboe and bassoon families). They do, however, have one important feature in common: the holes in their pipes. In addition, their timbres are such that composers think of them and write for them as a group.

Flute   The *flute* is the soprano voice of the woodwind family. Its tone is cool and velvety in the expressive low register, smooth in the middle, and often brilliant in the upper part of its range. The present-day flute, made of a silver alloy rather than wood, is a cylindrical tube that is held horizontally. It is closed at one end. The player blows across a mouth hole cut in the side of the pipe at the other end. The flute is used frequently as a melody instrument—its timbre stands out against the orchestra—and offers the performer great versatility in *Piccolo*   playing rapid repeated notes, scales, and trills. The *piccolo* (from the Italian *flauto piccolo,* "little flute") is actually the highest pitched instrument in the orchestra. In its upper register, it takes on a shrillness that is easily heard even when the orchestra is playing *fortissimo.*

Oboe   The *oboe* is made of wood. Its mouthpiece is a double reed consisting of two thin strips of cane bound together so as to leave between them an extremely small passage for air. Oboe timbre is generally described as nasal and reedy. The instrument is often associated with pastoral effects and nostalgic moods. The pitch of the oboe is reasonably stable, thus it traditionally sounds *English horn*   the tuning note for the other instruments of the orchestra. The *English horn* is an alto oboe. Its wooden tube is wider and longer than that of the oboe and ends in a pear-shaped opening called a *bell,* which largely accounts for its soft, expressive timbre. The instrument is not well named, for it is neither English nor a horn.

Clarinet   The *clarinet* has a single reed, a small thin piece of cane fastened against its chisel-shaped mouthpiece. The instrument possesses a smooth, liquid tone, as well as a remarkably wide range from low to high and from soft to loud. Almost as agile as the flute, it has an easy command of rapid scales, trills, and *Bass clarinet*   repeated notes. The *bass clarinet* is one octave lower in range than the clarinet. Its rich tone, flexibility, and wide dynamic range make it an invaluable member of the orchestra.

Bassoon   The *bassoon* is a double-reed instrument. Its tone is weighty and thick in the low register, dry and sonorous in the middle, reedy and intense in the upper. Capable of a hollow-sounding staccato and wide leaps that can create a

James Galway, flute virtuoso. (Photo by Brian Davis)

Elaine Douvas, oboist. (Photo courtesy of Lisa Kohler)

Richard Stolzman playing the clarinet in Carnegie Hall.

Bernard Garfield playing the bassoon. (Courtesy of the Philadelphia Orchestra)

Contrabassoon

humorous effect, it is at the same time a highly expressive instrument. The *contrabassoon* produces the lowest tone of the woodwinds. Its function in the woodwind section may be compared with that of the double bass among the strings, in that it supplies a foundation for the harmony.

Saxophone

The *saxophone* is of more recent origin than the other woodwind instruments, having been invented by the Belgian Adolphe Sax in 1840. It was created by combining the features of several other instruments—the single reed of the clarinet, the conical tube of the oboe, and the metal body of the brass instruments. The saxophone blends well with either woodwinds or brass. In the 1920s, it became the characteristic instrument of the jazz band, and has remained a favorite sound in many styles of music today.

Brass Instruments

The main instruments of the brass family (also aerophones) are the trumpet, French horn (generally referred to simply as horn), trombone, and tuba. All these instruments have cup-shaped mouthpieces (except for the horn, whose mouthpiece is shaped like a funnel) attached to a length of metal tubing that flares at the end into a bell. The column of air within the tube is set vibrating by the tightly stretched lips of the player, which act as a kind of double reed. To go from one pitch to another involves not only mechanical means, such as a slide or valves, but also variation in the pressure of the lips and breath. This demands great muscular control. Brass and woodwind instrument players

Embouchure

often speak about their *embouchure,* referring to the entire oral mechanism of lips, lower facial muscles, and jaws.

Trumpets and horns were widely used in the ancient world. The earliest instruments were fashioned from the horns and tusks of animals, which at a later stage of civilization were reproduced in metal. They were used chiefly in religious ceremonies and for military signals. Their tone could be terrifying, as is evidenced by what happened, in the biblical account, to the walls of Jericho.

Trumpet

The *trumpet,* highest in pitch of the brass family, possesses a commanding and brilliant timbre that lends radiance to the orchestral mass. It is often associated with ceremonial display. The trumpet can also be muted, using a pear-shaped device of metal or cardboard that is inserted in the bell, achieving a bright, buzzy sound. Jazz trumpet players have experimented with various kinds of mutes to produce different timbres.

French horn

The *French horn* is descended from the ancient hunting horn. Its mellow resonance lends itself to a variety of uses: it can be mysteriously remote in soft passages and nobly sonorous in loud. The timbre of the horn blends equally well with woodwinds, brass, and strings. Although capable of considerable agility, the horn is often used in sustained, supportive parts. The muted horn has a distant sound. Horn players often "stop" their instrument by plugging the bell with their hand; the result has a somewhat eerie and rasping quality.

Trombone

The *trombone*—the Italian word means "large trumpet"—has a full and rich sound that combines the brilliance of the trumpet with the majesty of the horn, but in a lower range. In place of valves, it has a movable U-shaped slide that alters the length of the vibrating air column in the tube.

Wynton Marsalis, trumpet virtuoso. (Photo courtesy of Nubar Alexanian)

Barry Tuckwell playing the French horn. (Photo by Richard Holt/EMI, Ltd.)

Noreen Harris playing the tuba.

Christian Lindberg, trombonist.

Tuba   The *tuba* is the bass instrument of the brass family. Like the string bass and contrabassoon, it furnishes the foundation for the harmonic fabric. The tuba adds body to the orchestral tone, and a dark resonance ranging from velvety softness to a rumbling growl.

Other brass instruments   Other brass instruments are used in concert and marching bands. Among these is the *cornet,* which has a rounder but less brilliant sound than the trumpet. In the early twentieth century, the cornet was very popular in concert bands; today, however, the trumpet has replaced it in virtually all ensembles. The *bugle* evolved from the military or field trumpet of early times; it has a powerful tone that carries in the open air. Since it is not equipped with valves, it is able to sound only certain tones of the scale, which accounts for the familiar pattern of duty calls in the army. The *fluegelhorn,* much used in jazz and commercial music, is really a valved bugle with a wide bell. The *euphonium* (also known as the *baritone horn*) is a tenor-range instrument whose shape resembles the tuba. And the *sousaphone* is an adaptation of the tuba designed by the American bandmaster John Philip Sousa; it features a forward bell and is coiled to rest over the player's shoulder while marching.

Percussion Instruments

In the percussion family, some instruments are made to sound by striking or shaking—in other words, idiophones, in our world instrument classification. Other instruments, such as the drums, are set vibrating by striking a stretched skin—thus, they are membranophones.

The percussion section of the orchestra is sometimes referred to as "the battery." Its members accentuate the rhythm, generate excitement at the climaxes, and inject splashes of color into the orchestral sound.

Pitched percussion instruments   Percussion instruments fall into two categories: those capable of being tuned to definite pitches, and those that produce a single sound in the realm between music and noise (instruments of indefinite pitch). In the former class are the *timpani,* or *kettledrums,* which are generally used in sets of two or four. The timpani is a hemispheric copper shell across which is stretched a "head" of plastic or calfskin held in place by a metal ring. A pedal mechanism enables the player to change the tension of the head, and with it the pitch. The instrument is played with two padded sticks, which may be either soft or hard. Its dynamic range extends from a mysterious rumble to a thunderous roll. Timpani arrived in western Europe from the Middle East, where Muslims and Turks on horseback used them in combination with trumpets.

Also among the pitched percussion instruments of the orchestra are several of the *xylophone* family; instruments of this general type are used in Africa, Southeast Asia, and throughout the Americas. The xylophone consists of tuned blocks of wood laid out in the shape of a keyboard. Struck with mallets with hard heads, the instrument produces a dry, crisp sound. The *marimba* is a more mellow xylophone of African origin. The *vibraphone* combines the principle of the xylophone with resonators, each containing revolving disks operated by electric motors. Its highly unusual tone is marked by an exaggerated vibrato, which can be controlled by changing the speed of the motor.

This selection of percussion instruments includes (top, left to right): vibraphone, chimes, xylophone, gong, and marimba. (Center): timbales, suspended cymbal, and various percussion accessories. (Bottom): timpani, jazz drum set, concert tom-toms, marching snare drum, concert snare drums, crash cymbals, and bass drum. Instrument identification by Dr. John J. Papastefan, University of South Alabama. (Courtesy of Ludwig Drum Company)

This instrument is featured in jazz groups, and has been used by a number of contemporary composers.

The *glockenspiel* (German for "set of bells") consists of a series of horizontal tuned steel bars of various sizes, which when struck produce a bright metallic sound. The *celesta* resembles a miniature upright piano. It is a kind of glockenspiel that is operated by a keyboard: the steel plates are struck by small hammers and produce a sound like a music box. *Chimes,* or *tubular bells*, consist of a set of tuned metal tubes of various lengths suspended from a frame and struck with a hammer. They are frequently called upon to simulate church bells.

Unpitched percussion instruments

The percussion instruments that do not produce a definite pitch include the *side drum,* or *snare drum,* a small cylindrical drum with two heads stretched over a shell of metal and played with two drumsticks. This instrument owes its brilliant tone to the vibrations of the lower head against taut snares (strings). The *tenor drum* is larger in size, with a wooden shell, and has no snares. The *bass drum,* played with a large soft-headed stick, produces a low heavy sound. The *tom-tom* is a colloquial name given to American Indian or African drums of indefinite pitch. The *tambourine* is a small round drum with "jingles"—little metal plates—inserted in its rim. It is played by striking the drum with the fingers or elbow, by shaking, or by passing the hand over the jingles. Of Middle Eastern origin, it is particularly associated with music of Spain, as are *castanets*, little wooden clappers moved by the player's thumb and forefinger.

The *triangle* is a slender rod of steel bent in the shape of a triangle. It is open at the upper end and, when struck with a steel beater, gives off a bright tinkling sound. *Cymbals* came to the West from Asia Minor during the Middle Ages. They consist of two large circular brass plates of equal size, which when struck against each other produce a shattering sound. The *gong,* or *tam-tam,* is a broad circular disk of metal, suspended in a frame so as to hang freely. When struck with a heavy drumstick, it produces a deep roar. It has found its widest use in the Far East and Southeast Asia, where it is central to the ensemble known as the *gamelan* (see pp. 51, 450).

Other Instruments

Besides the instruments just discussed, several others, especially those of the keyboard family, are frequently heard in solo and ensemble performances.

Piano

The *piano* was originally known as the *pianoforte*, Italian for "soft-loud," which suggests its wide dynamic range and capacity for nuance. Its strings are struck with hammers controlled by a keyboard mechanism. The piano cannot sustain tone as well as the string and wind instruments, but in the hands of a fine performer, it is capable of producing a singing melody. Each string (except in the highest register) is covered by a damper that stops the sound when the finger releases the key. There are three pedals. If the one on the right is pressed down, all the dampers are raised, so that the strings continue to vibrate, producing that luminous haze of sound that composers have used to such advantage. The pedal on the left shifts the hammers to reduce the area of

Pianist André Watts. (Photo by Christian Steiner)

impact on the strings, thereby inhibiting the volume of sound; hence it is known as the "soft pedal." The middle pedal (missing on upright pianos) is the sustaining pedal, which sustains only the tones held down at the moment the pedal is depressed.

The piano is notable for its capacity for brilliant scales, arpeggios, trills, rapid passages, and octaves. It has a wide range from lowest to highest pitch, spanning eighty-eight keys, or semitones. Closely related to this is the *electric piano,* an electronically amplified instrument capable of producing piano-like sounds. The more generic electronic keyboard, commonly used in rock groups, is capable of a number of different sonorities.

The *organ,* once regarded as "the king of instruments," is a wind instru- *Organ* ment; air is fed to its pipes by mechanical means. The pipes are controlled by two or more keyboards and a set of pedals. Gradations in the volume of tone are made possible on the modern organ by means of swell boxes. The organ possesses a multicolored sonority that can easily fill a huge space. Electrically amplified keyboards, capable of imitating pipe organs and other timbres, are commonplace today. A number of sound production methods have been explored, including vibrating metal reeds, oscillators, and, most recently, digital waveform synthesis. (On early organ types and their music, see pp. 315, 410–12.)

The instruments described in this chapter and in the previous one form a vivid and diversified group. To composers, performers, and listeners alike, they offer an endless variety of colors and shades of expression.

Suggested Listening Examples

Instrument families and individual instruments—Britten:
   The Young Person's Guide to the Orchestra (video or recording)

9

Musical Ensembles

Just as there is great variety in musical instruments, so too is there a wide assortment of ensembles or performance groups. Some are homogeneous—for example, choral groups using only voices or perhaps only men's voices; while others are more heterogeneous—for example, the orchestra, which features a wide selection of instruments from the different families. On a global scale, every type of combination is possible.

Choral Groups

Chorus

Choir

Choral music—music performed by many voices in a chorus or choir—is sung around the world, both for religious purposes (sacred music) and for secular (nonspiritual) occasions. Loosely defined, a *chorus* is a fairly large body of singers who perform together; their music is usually sung in several parts. Most often the group consists of both men and women, but the term can also refer to only women's voices or only men's. A *choir* is traditionally a smaller group, often connected with a church or the performance of sacred music. (We will hear an example sung by Ladysmith Black Mambazo, a South African men's choir that often sings religious music.) The standard voice parts in both chorus and choir correspond to the voice ranges described earlier: sopranos, altos, tenors, and basses.

Les Petits Chanteurs de Paris (the Little Singers of Paris), a highly successful touring boys' choir.

In early times, choral music was often performed without accompaniment. This style of singing is known as *a cappella* (meaning "in the church style"). The organ eventually became coupled with the choir in church music, and by the eighteenth century, the orchestra had established itself as a partner of the chorus.

A cappella

There are many smaller, specialized vocal ensembles as well, such as a *madrigal choir* and *chamber choir*. The madrigal choir might perform a cappella secular works, known as *part songs*. The designation "chamber choir" refers to a small group of up to twenty-four singers, performing either a cappella or with piano accompaniment.

Other choral groups

Instrumental Chamber Ensembles

In the Western tradition, *chamber music* is ensemble music for a small group of up to about ten players, with one player to a part, as distinct from orchestral music, in which a single instrumental part is performed by anywhere from two to eighteen players. The essential trait of chamber music is its intimacy.

Many of the standard chamber music ensembles consist of string players. Most common is the string quartet, made up of two violins, viola, and cello. Other popular combinations are the duo sonata (soloist with piano), the piano trio and quartet, the string quintet, as well as larger groups—sextet, septet, and octet. Winds too have standard combinations, especially woodwind and brass quintets. Some of these ensembles are described on page 50.

The Tokyo String Quartet (Peter Oundjian, Kikuet Ikeda, violins; Sadao Harada, viola; and Kazuhide Isomura, cello) enjoys an international reputation. (Photo by Christian Steiner)

Standard Chamber Ensembles

DUO SONATA	Solo instrument and piano		
TRIO			
String trio	Violin 1	or	Violin
	Violin 2		Viola
	Cello		Cello
Piano trio	Piano		
	Violin		
	Cello		
QUARTETS			
String quartet	Violin 1		
	Violin 2		
	Viola		
	Cello		
Piano quartet	Piano		
	Violin		
	Viola		
	Cello		
QUINTETS			
String quintet	Violin 1	or	Violin 1
	Violin 2	(more rarely)	Violin 2
	Viola 1		Viola
	Viola 2		Cello 1
	Cello		Cello 2
Piano quintet	Piano		
	Violin 1		
	Violin 2	} string quartet	
	Viola		
	Cello		
Woodwind quintet	Flute		
	Oboe		
	Clarinet		
	French horn (not a woodwind instrument)		
	Bassoon		
Brass quintet	Trumpet 1		
	Trumpet 2		
	French horn		
	Trombone		
	Tuba		

These chamber music combinations have remained popular well into the twentieth century, alongside new and unusual groupings. We will see that contemporary composers have experimented with combining voice and

Ravi Shankar (center) in a classical Indian ensemble featuring two sitars (long-necked, fretted chordophone) and tabla (a pair of tuned hand drums). (Photo by Alan Koslowski)

small groups of instruments and incorporating electronic elements with live performers. In some cultures, chamber groups combine what might seem to be unlikely timbres to the Western listener—in India, plucked strings and percussion are standard, and in some styles of Chinese music, plucked and bowed strings are normally combined with flutes (a kind of aerophone).

The Orchestra

In its most general sense, the term "orchestra" may be applied to any performing body of diverse instruments—the Japanese ensemble used for court entertainments (called *gagaku*) or the gamelan orchestras of Bali and Indonesia, made up largely of gongs, xylophone-like instruments, and drums. (See illustration on p. 450.) In the West, the term is now synonymous with *symphony orchestra,* an ensemble of strings coupled with an assortment of woodwinds, brass, and percussion instruments.

This orchestra has varied in size and makeup throughout its history, but has always featured string instruments as its core. From its origins as a small, twenty-or-so-piece group, the modern orchestra has grown into an ensemble of more than a hundred players. The performers are divided into the four instrumental families we have studied, and approximately two-thirds of the orchestra consists of string players. The list on page 53 shows the distribution of instruments typical of a large orchestra today.

(Above): the Minnesota Orchestra with its conductor, Edo de Waart, in Orchestra Hall in Minneapolis. (Below): the seating plan of the orchestra.

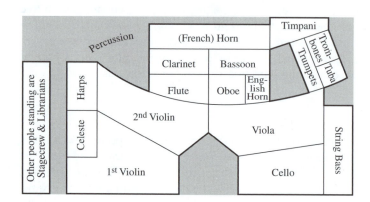

The instruments of the orchestra are arranged to achieve the best balance of tone. Thus, most of the strings are near the front, as are the gentle woodwinds. The louder brass and percussion are at the back. A characteristic seating plan for the Minnesota Orchestra is shown above; this arrangement varies somewhat from one orchestra to another.

Typical Distribution of Orchestral Instruments

Strings	18 first violins divided into two or more groups
	15 second violins
	12 violas
	12 cellos
	9 double basses
	1–2 harps, when needed
Woodwinds	3 flutes, 1 piccolo
	3 oboes, 1 English horn
	3 clarinets, 1 bass clarinet
	3 bassoons, 1 double bassoon
Brass	4–6 French horns
	4 trumpets
	3 trombones
	1 tuba
Percussion	5 players
	1 timpani player (2–4 timpani)
	2–4 on other instruments

Concert, Jazz, and Rock Bands

"Band" is a generic name applied to a variety of ensembles, most of which feature winds and percussion at their core. A band is a much-loved American tradition, whether it is a concert, marching, or military band or jazz or rock ensemble. The earliest wind and percussion groups were used for military purposes. Musicians accompanied soldiers to war, playing their brass and percussion instruments from horseback and their fifes and drums from among the ranks of the foot soldiers to spur the troops on to victory. Concert wind groups originated in the Middle Ages. In northern Europe, a wind band of three to five musicians played each evening, often from the high tower of a local church or city hall. Turkish "Janissary" (military) bands used wind and percussion instruments (see p. 236). From these traditions grew the military bands of the French Revolution and American Civil War. One American bandmaster, John Philip Sousa (1854–1932), achieved worldwide fame with his brass band and the repertory of marches he wrote for it.

Today the *concert band* (sometimes called a *wind ensemble*) ranges anywhere from forty to eighty players or more, and is an established institution in most secondary schools, colleges, and universities and in many communities as well. Modern composers like to write for this ensemble, since it traditionally plays new compositions. The *marching band,* best-known today in the United States, is a popular group for entertainment at sports events and parades. Besides its core of winds and percussion, this group often includes a

Concert band

Marching band

The Indiana University marching band in formation for a football game.

spectacular display of drum majors/majorettes, flag twirlers, and the like.

Jazz band   The precise instrumentation of *jazz bands* depends on the particular music being played, but generally includes a reed section made up of clarinets and saxophones of various sizes, a brass section of trumpets and trombones, and a rhythm section of percussion, piano, and strings, especially double bass *Rock band* and electric guitar. *Rock bands* depend heavily on amplified strings, percussion, and electronically generated sounds.

The Role of the Conductor

When they are playing, Western musicians think about meter in order to keep "in time." Large ensembles such as an orchestra, band, or chorus need the assistance of a conductor in order to perform together. The conductor beats the meter with the right hand in a prescribed pattern that all the musicians in the group understand. These conducting patterns, shown in the diagrams below, further emphasize the strong and weak beats of the measure: beat 1, the strongest in any meter, is always given a downbeat, or a downward motion of the hand; a secondary accent is shown by a change of direction; and the last beat of the measure, a weak beat, is always an upbeat or upward motion, thereby leaving the right hand ready for the downbeat of the next measure.

Basic Conducting Patterns

Duple meter	Triple meter	Quadruple meter	Sextuple meter
↓ ↑ ↓ ↑	↓ → ↑ ↓ → ↑	↓ ← → ↑ ↓ ← → ↑	↓ ← ← → → ↑
1 2 1 2	1 2 3 1 2 3	1 2 3 4 1 2 3 4	1 2 3 4 5 6

The Orchestra in Action

A helpful introduction to the modern orchestra is Benjamin Britten's *Young Person's Guide to the Orchestra,* which was written expressly to illustrate the timbre of each orchestral instrument. The work, composed in 1946, is subtitled *Variations and Fugue on a Theme of Purcell* and is based on a dance tune by Henry Purcell (1659–95), the great composer of seventeenth-century England.

Britten's plan was to introduce the sound of the entire orchestra playing together, then the sonorities of each instrumental family as a group—woodwinds, brass, strings, percussion—and then to repeat the statement by the full orchestra. Once the listener has the theme or principal melody well in mind, the composer features each instrument in the order of highest to lowest in range within each family. Now we encounter variations of the theme, each played by a new instrument with different accompanying instruments. (See Listening Guide 1 for the order of instruments.) Finally, the work closes with a grand fugue, a polyphonic form popular in the Baroque era (1600–1750), which is also based on Purcell's theme. Just as in the variations, the fugue presents its subject, or theme, in rapid order in each instrument. (For a discussion of the fugue, see p. 412.)

Listening Guide 1

 C/S: IA/1   C/S: 1/ 1 - 7

BRITTEN: *The Young Person's Guide to the Orchestra (Variations and Fugue on a Theme of Purcell)*

(Total time: 17:23)

Date of work: 1946

Theme: Based on a dance from Henry Purcell's incidental music to the play *Abdelazar (The Moor's Revenge)*

Form: Theme and variations, followed by a fugue

1   0:00   **I. Theme:** 8 measures in D minor, stated six times to illustrate the instrumental families of the orchestra:

1. Entire orchestra
2. Woodwinds
3. Brass
4. Strings
5. Percussion
6. Entire orchestra

II. Variations: 13 short variations, each illustrating a different instrument or family of instruments

		Variation	Family	Solo Instrument	Accompanying Instruments
2	3:00	1	Woodwinds:	flutes, piccolo	violins, harp, and triangle
		2		oboes	strings and timpani
		3		clarinets	strings and tuba
		4		bassoons	strings and snare drum
3	6:12	5	Strings:	violins	brass and bass drum
		6		violas	woodwinds and brass
		7		cellos	clarinets, violas, and harp
		8		double basses	woodwinds and tambourine
		9		harp	strings, gong, and cymbal
4	10:32	10	Brass:	French horns	strings, harp, and timpani
		11		trumpets	strings and snare drum
		12		trombones, tuba	woodwinds and high brass
5	12:48	13	Percussion:	various	strings

(Order of introduction: timpani, bass drum and cymbals, timpani, tambourine and triangle, timpani, snare drum and wood block, timpani, castanets and gong, timpani, whip, whole percussion section)

6 14:44   **III. Fugue:** Subject based on a fragment of the Purcell theme, played in imitation by each instrument of the orchestra in same order as variations:

Woodwinds: piccolo
flutes
oboes
clarinets
bassoons

Strings: first violins
second violins
violas
cellos
double basses
harp

Brass: French horns
trumpets
trombones, tuba

Percussion: various

7 16:31   Full orchestra at end with Purcell's theme heard over the fugue

The modern orchestra, with its amplitude of tonal resources, its range of dynamics, and its infinite variety of color, offers a memorable experience to both the musician and the music lover. It is clearly one of the wonders of our Western musical culture.

Suggested Listening Examples

Choral groups
    Chorus—Palestrina: *Pope Marcellus* Mass, Gloria
    Choir—Josquin: *Ave Maria . . . virgo serena*
    Men's choir—*That's Why I Choose You* by Ladysmith Black Mambazo
    Madrigal choir—Farmer: *Fair Phyllis*
Chamber music
    String chamber ensemble—Mozart: *Eine kleine Nachtmusik*
    Voice with chamber ensemble (20th century)—
        Schoenberg: *Pierrot lunaire*, No. 18
    Instrumental chamber ensemble (20th century)—
        Tower: *Petroushskates*
Orchestra
    Baroque orchestra—Vivaldi: *Spring,* from *The Four Seasons*
    Classical orchestra—Beethoven: Symphony No. 5, First Movement
    Romantic orchestra—Berlioz: *Symphonie fantastique,* Fifth
        Movement
    Twentieth-century orchestra—Copland: *Billy the Kid*
                                Stravinsky: *Petrushka*
Choir with orchestra—Bach: Cantata No. 80, No. 8
Jazz band—Ellington: *Ko-Ko*
Rock band—*Black Magic Woman* by Santana

10

Style and Function of Music in Society

*"The whole of Africa moves in time to music. We sow seeds to music and
we sing songs to the corn to make it grow and to the sky to make it rain.
Then we reap our harvest to the sound of music and song."*
—ABDULLAH IBRAHIM, SOUTH AFRICAN PIANIST

In every culture, music is intricately interwoven with the lives and beliefs of
its people. This is especially true of many non-Western societies where, just as
in the West, the "classical" exists alongside the "popular," both nourished from
the unbelievably rich store of traditional music that is closely allied with daily
living. Music serves different functions in different societies, though some
basic roles are universal. It accompanies religious and civic ceremonies, it en-
livens work by helping to pass the time, and it provides entertainment
through song and dance. The social organization of any particular culture has
much to do with its musical types and styles. In some cultures, such as in the
Western classical tradition, only a few people are involved with the actual per-

formance of music, while in others, such as that of the African Pygmies, co-operative work is so much a part of society that the people sing as a group, with each person contributing a separate part to build a complex whole.

Genres

Music exists for every conceivable occasion, but the specific occasions celebrated vary from culture to culture. Thus musical *genres,* or categories of repertory, do not necessarily transfer from one culture to the next. In a general sense, dramatic stage works are set to music in many cultures: thus Japanese *noh* drama and Peking opera serve essentially the same social role as opera in the Western world.

Just as the context for music—when, why, and by whom a piece is performed—varies from culture to culture, so do aesthetic judgments of what is beautiful and what is appropriate. For example, preferences in vocal quality vary widely; the Chinese consider a thin, tense tone desirable in their operas, while the Italians prefer a full-throated, robust sound in theirs. Likewise, a cultural preference can change over time, which accounts for the shifting popularity of certain performers and styles.

Oral transmission

Not all music is written down and learned from books or formal lessons. In many lands, music is transmitted through a master-apprentice relationship that lasts many years, while in others, there is no formal instruction; rather, the aspiring musician must learn from watching and listening. Music of most cultures of the world, including some styles of Western popular and traditional music, is transmitted by example or imitation and is performed from memory. The preservation of music without the aid of written notation is referred to as *oral transmission.*

We will focus much of our study on Western art music—that is, the notated music of a cultivated and largely urban society. We often equate art music with "classical" or serious music, for lack of better terms. However, the lines that distinguish art music from other kinds are often blurred. Popular and traditional musics are art forms in their own right: performers of these styles may well be as talented as those that present classical music; and both jazz and rock are considered by many to be American art forms, having already stood the test of time. To confuse these categories further, some composers and performing artists *cross over* from one type of music to another—from jazz to rock, from rock to Western classical—or simply borrow elements of one style to use in another, drawing them ever closer. Later we will hear elements of jazz improvisation in the guitar style of the rock musician Santana and some elements of Western blues combined with a traditional African singing style in the modern choral music of the South African ensemble Ladysmith Black Mambazo (see Chapter 75).

TRANSITION I

Hearing Musical Styles

"A good style should show no sign of effort. What is written should seem a happy accident."—SOMERSET MAUGHAM

The Concept of Style

Style may be defined as the characteristic manner of presentation in any art. We distinguish between the style of a novel and that of an essay, between the style of a cathedral and that of a palace. The word may also indicate the creator's personal manner of expression—the distinctive flavor that sets one artist apart from all others. Thus we speak of the literary style of Dickens or Shakespeare, the painting style of Picasso or Michelangelo, the musical style of Bach or Mozart. We often identify style with nationality, as when we refer to French, Italian, or German style; or with an entire culture, as when we contrast a Western musical style with one of China, India, or some other region.

It is the difference in the treatment of the elements of music that makes one musical work sound similar to or different from another. We have seen that Western music is largely a melody-oriented art based on a particular musical system from which the underlying harmonies are also built. Relatively speaking, rhythm and meter in Western music are based on simpler principles than are melody and harmony. Musics of other cultures may sound foreign to our ears, sometimes "out of tune," because they are based on entirely different musical systems from which they derive their melodic material, and many do not involve harmony to any great extent. One important factor in these differing languages of music is the way in which the octave is divided and scales are produced, an area we will explore in more detail in Chapter 34. Complex rhythmic procedures and textures set some world musics apart from Western styles, while basic formal considerations—such as repetition, contrast, and variation—bring musics of disparate cultures closer. In short, a style is made up of all the factors relating to pitch, time, timbre, and expression, creating a sound that each culture recognizes as its own.

Treatment of elements

Musical Styles in History

Since all the arts change from one age to the next, one very important use of the word "style" is in connection with the various historical periods. The music of each world culture has its own style periods; we are focusing here on the development of Western music. We will find that the concept of style enables us to draw connections between musicians and their time, so that the musical work is placed in its socio-historical frame. No matter how greatly the artists, writers, and composers of a particular era may vary in personality and outlook, when seen in the perspective of time, they turn out to have certain qualities in common. Because of this, we can tell at once that a work of art— whether music, poetry, painting, sculpture, or architecture—dates from the Middle Ages or the Renaissance, from the eighteenth century or the nineteenth. The style of a period, then, is the total art language of all its artists as they react to the artistic, political, economic, religious, and philosophical forces that shape their environment.

Historical periods   Scholars will always disagree as to precisely when one style period ends and the next begins. Each period leads by imperceptible degrees into the following one, dates and labels being merely convenient signposts. The following outline shows the generally accepted style periods in the history of Western music. Each represents a conception of form and technique, an ideal of beauty, a manner of expression and performance attuned to the cultural climate of the period—in a word, a style!

350–600:	Period of the Church Fathers
600–850:	Early Middle Ages—Gregorian chant
850–1150:	Romanesque period—development of the staff in musical notation, about 1000
1150–1450:	Late Middle Ages (Gothic period)
1450–1600:	Renaissance period
1600–1750:	Baroque period
1725–1775:	Rococo period
1750–1825:	Classical period
1820–1900:	Romantic period
1890–1915:	Post-Romantic and Impressionist period
1910– :	Twentieth century

Suggested Listening Examples

Popular music—*Black Magic Woman* by Santana
Crossover—Bernstein: Symphonic Dances from *West Side Story*
Traditional music—*That's Why I Choose You* by Ladysmith Black Mambazo
    (some traditional elements)
For examples of Western art music styles, see individual chapters.

PART TWO

The Nineteenth Century

*"Music is the most romantic of all the arts—one might almost say,
the only genuinely romantic one—for its sole subject is the infinite.
Music discloses to man an unknown realm, a world in which
he leaves behind all definite feelings to surrender himself to an
inexpressible longing."*—E. T. A. HOFFMANN

UNIT III

The Romantic Movement

11

The Spirit of Romanticism

"Romanticism is beauty without bounds—the beautiful infinite."
—JEAN PAUL RICHTER

Historians observe that style in art moves between two poles, the classical and the romantic. Both the classicist and the romanticist strive to express significant emotions and to achieve that expression within beautiful forms. Where they differ is in their point of view. The spirit of classicism seeks order, poise, and serenity as surely as the romantic longs for strangeness, wonder, and ecstasy. Classicists are apt to be more objective in their approach to art and to life. They try to view life sanely and "to see it whole." Romanticists, on the other hand, are apt to be intensely subjective and view the world in terms of their personal feelings. The nineteenth-century German philosopher Friedrich Nietzsche dramatized the contrast between the two through the symbol of Apollo, Greek god of light and measure, as opposed to Dionysus, god of passion and intoxication. Classical and romantic ideals have alternated and even existed side by side from the beginning of time, for they correspond to two basic impulses in human nature: the need for moderation and the desire for uninhibited emotional expression.

The "Classical" and "Romantic" labels are also attached to two important periods in European art. The Classical era held the stage in the last half of the eighteenth century and the early decades of the nineteenth. The Romantic era, stemming from the social and political upheavals that followed the French Revolution, came into full blossom in the second quarter of the nineteenth century.

The French Revolution was the inevitable result of momentous social forces converging. It signaled the transfer of power from a hereditary landholding aristocracy to the middle class, firmly rooted in urban commerce and

French Revolution

63

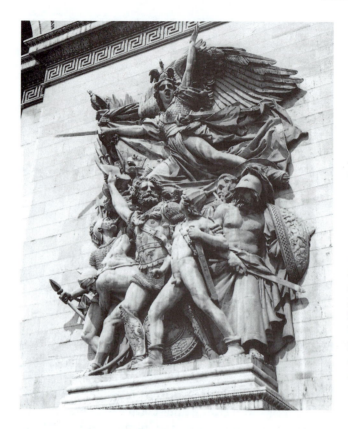

The fervor of the French Revolution inspired this sculpture entitled La Marseillaise (The Departure of the Volunteers of 1792) *by* **François Rude** *(1784–1855). Arc de Triomphe, Paris.*

industry. As in the American Revolution, this upheaval heralded a social order shaped by the technological advances of the Industrial Revolution. The new society, based on free enterprise, emphasized the individual as never before. The slogan "Liberty, Equality, Fraternity" inspired hopes and visions to which few artists failed to respond. Sympathy for the oppressed, interest in simple folk and in children, faith in humankind and its destiny—all these, so intimately associated with the time, point to the increasingly democratic character of the Romantic period.

Romantic writers

The Romantic poets rebelled against the conventional concerns of their Classical predecessors; they were drawn to the fanciful, the picturesque, and the passionate. One of the prime traits of the Romantic arts was their emphasis on an intensely emotional type of expression. In Germany, a group of young writers created a new kind of lyric poetry that culminated in the art of Heinrich Heine, who became one of the favorite poets of Romantic composers. A similar movement in France was led by Victor Hugo, its greatest prose writer, and Alphonse de Lamartine, its greatest poet. In England, the revolt against the formalism of the Classical age produced an upsurge of lyric poetry that reached its peak in the works of Byron, Shelley, and Keats. The new spirit of individualism expressed itself in the Romantic artists' sense of uniqueness, their heightened awareness of themselves as individuals apart from all others. "I am different from all the men I have seen," proclaimed Jean Jacques Rousseau. "If I am not better, at least I am different."

The newly won freedom of the artist proved to be a mixed blessing. Confronted by a bourgeois world indifferent to artistic and cultural values, artists felt more and more cut off. A new type emerged—the artist as bohemian, the rejected dreamer who starved in an attic and through peculiarities of dress and behavior "shocked the bourgeois." Eternal longing, regret for the lost happiness of childhood, an indefinable discontent that gnawed at the soul—these were the ingredients of the Romantic mood. Yet the artist's pessimism was not without its basis in external reality. It became apparent that the high hopes fostered by the revolution were not to be realized overnight. Despite the brave slogans, all people were not yet equal or free. Inevitably optimism gave way to doubt and disenchantment—"the illness of the century."

The artist as bohemian

This state of mind was reflected in the arts of the time. Hugo dedicated *Les Misérables* "to the unhappy ones of the earth." The nineteenth-century novel found its great theme in the conflict between the individual and society. Jean Valjean, the hero of Hugo's novel, Heathcliff in Emily Brontë's *Wuthering Heights,* and Tolstoy's *Anna Karenina* are among the memorable characters who point up the frustrations and guilts of the nineteenth-century world.

Hardly less persuasive was the art of those who sought escape. Some glamorized the past, as did Walter Scott and Alexandre Dumas. A longing for far-off lands inspired the exotic scenes that glow on the canvases of J. M. W. Turner and Eugène Delacroix. The Romantic poets and painters loved the picturesque and the fantastic. Theirs was a world of "strangeness and wonder": the eerie landscape we meet in the writings of Coleridge, Hawthorne, or Poe.

Romantic painters

Romanticism dominated the artistic output of the nineteenth century. It gave its name to a movement and an era, and created a multitude of colorful works that still hold millions in thrall.

Sympathy for the oppressed underscored the essentially democratic character of the Romantic movement. **Honoré Daumier** *(1808–79),* The Third-Class Carriage. (Metropolitan Museum of Art, Bequest of Mrs. H. O. Havemeyer, 1929; The H. O. Havemeyer Collection)

12

Romanticism in Music

"Music is the melody whose text is the world."
—ARTHUR SCHOPENHAUER

Art mirrors the great social forces of its time. Thus Romantic music reflected the profound changes that were taking place in the nineteenth century at every level of human existence.

Improved musical instruments

The Industrial Revolution brought with it not only the means to create cheaper and more responsive musical instruments, but also important technical improvements that strongly influenced the sound of Romantic music. For example, the addition of valves to brass instruments made them much more maneuverable, so that nineteenth-century composers like Wagner and Tchaikovsky could write melodies for the horn that would have been unplayable in the eighteenth century. Several new wind instruments were developed as well, including the tuba and the saxophone. As a result of improved manufacturing techniques, the piano acquired a cast-iron frame and thicker strings, which gave it a deeper and more brilliant tone. If a Romantic piano work by Liszt sounds different from a sonata of the Classical period, it is not only because Liszt's era demanded a different kind of expression, but also because he had at hand a piano capable of effects that were impossible in the earlier period.

The nineteenth-century orchestra offered the composer new instruments and a larger ensemble. Contemporary engraving of an orchestral concert at the Covent Garden Theater, London, 1846.

The Royal Pavilion at Brighton, England (1815–18), with its Islamic domes, minarets, and screens, reflects the nineteenth-century fascination with Eastern culture. Designed by **John Nash** *(1752–1835).*

The gradual democratization of society brought with it a broadening of educational opportunities. New conservatories were established in the chief cities of Europe to train more and better musicians. As a result, nineteenth-century composers could count on instrumental performers whose skill was considerably more advanced than in former times. As music moved from palace and church to the public concert hall, orchestras increased in size, giving composers a more varied and colorful means of expression. This naturally had a direct influence upon the sound. For example, where most eighteenth-century music ranged in dynamic level only from *piano* (soft) to *forte* (loud), the dynamic range of the orchestra in the nineteenth century was far greater. Now the heaven-storming *crescendo*s, the violent contrasts of loud and soft that lend such drama to the music of the Romantics, came into fashion. As orchestral music became more important, the technique of writing for instruments, individually and together—that is, orchestration—became an art in itself. At last the musician had a palette comparable to the painter's, and used it as the painter did—to conjure up sensuous beauty, to create mood and atmosphere, to suggest nature scenes and calm or stormy seascapes.

The development of the orchestra

The desire for direct communication with performers led composers to use a large number of expressive terms intended to serve as clues to their intentions, with the result that a highly characteristic vocabulary evolved. Among the directions frequently encountered in nineteenth-century musical scores are *dolce* (sweetly), *cantabile* (songful), *dolente* (weeping), *mesto* (sad), *maestoso* (majestic), *gioioso* (joyous), *con amore* (with love, tenderly). These and similar terms suggest not only the character of the music but the frame of mind behind it.

Increased expressiveness

The interest in folklore and the rising tide of nationalism impelled

Use of folklore   Romantic musicians to make increased use of the folk songs and dances of their native lands. As a result, a number of national idioms—Hungarian, Polish, Russian, Bohemian, Scandinavian—flourished, opening up new areas to European music and greatly enriching its melody, harmony, and rhythm.

Exoticism   Nineteenth-century exoticism manifested itself, first, in the northern nations' longing for the warmth and color of the south; second, in the West's interest in the fairy-tale splendors of Asia and the Far East. The former impulse found expression in the works of German, French, and Russian composers who turned for inspiration to Italy and Spain. The long list includes Tchaikovsky's *Capriccio italien,* Mendelssohn's *Italian Symphony,* and Chabrier's *España.* One masterpiece in this category is Bizet's *Carmen,* which we shall study later.

The glamour of the East was brought to international attention by the Russian national school. The fairy-tale background of Asia pervades Russian music. Rimsky-Korsakov's orchestrally resplendent *Sheherazade,* Alexander Borodin's opera *Prince Igor,* and Ippolitov-Ivanov's *Caucasian Sketches* are among the many Eastern-inspired works that found favor throughout the world. A number of French and Italian composers also utilized exotic themes: Saint-Saëns in *Samson and Delilah,* Verdi in *Aïda,* and Puccini in *Madame Butterfly* and *Turandot.*

Romantic Style Traits

Singable melody   Even when written for instruments, Romantic melody was eminently singable. The nineteenth century above all was the period when musicians tried to make their instruments "sing." It is no accident that the themes from Romantic symphonies, concertos, and other instrumental works have been transformed into popular songs, for Romantic melody was marked by a lyricism that gave it an immediate emotional appeal. This is evidenced by the enduring popularity of the tunes of Schubert, Chopin, and Verdi, among others. Through innumerable songs and operas as well as instrumental pieces, Romantic melody appealed to a wider audience than ever before.

Expressive harmony   Nineteenth-century music strove for a harmony that was highly emotional and expressive. Under the impact of the Romantic movement, composers such as Richard Wagner sought combinations of pitches more chromatic and dissonant than their predecessors had used.

Expanded forms   The composers of the nineteenth century gradually expanded the instrumental forms they had inherited from the eighteenth. They found that they needed more time to give their ideas expression. A Classical symphony by Haydn or Mozart takes about twenty minutes to play; a Romantic one by Tchaikovsky, Brahms, or Dvořák lasts at least twice that long. As public concert life developed, the symphony became the most important form of orchestral music, comparable to the most spacious form in Romantic literature—the novel. As a result, nineteenth-century composers approached the writing of a symphony with greater deliberation—some would say caution—than their predecessors. Where Haydn wrote more than a hundred sym-

An evening of string quartet music at the Berlin house of Bettina von Arnim, with virtuoso Joseph Joachim playing first violin. Watercolor by **Johann Carl Arnold,** *c. 1855.* (Freies Deutsches Hochstift-Goethemuseum, Frankfurt; photo by Ursula Edelmann)

phonies and Mozart more than forty, Schubert and Dvořák (following the example of Beethoven) wrote nine; Tchaikovsky, six; Robert Schumann and Brahms, four. New orchestral forms emerged as well, including the one-movement symphonic poem, the choral symphony, and works for solo voice with orchestra.

Music in the nineteenth century drew steadily closer to literature and painting—that is, to elements that lay outside the realm of sound. The connection with Romantic poetry and drama is most obvious in the case of music with words. However, even in their purely orchestral music, the Romantic composers responded to the mood of the time and captured with remarkable vividness the emotional atmosphere that surrounded nineteenth-century poetry and painting.

Nineteenth-century music was linked to dreams and passions, to profound meditations on life and death, human destiny, God and nature, pride in one's country, desire for freedom, the political struggles of the age, and the ultimate triumph of good over evil. These intellectual and emotional associations, nurtured by the Romantic movement, brought music into a commanding position in the nineteenth century as a moral force, a vision of human greatness, and a direct link between the artist's inner life and the outside world.

The Musician in Nineteenth-Century Society

The emergence of a new kind of democratic society strongly affected the lives of composers and performers. Concert life began to center on the public concert hall as well as in the salons of the aristocracy and upper middle class. Where eighteenth-century musicians had functioned under the system of aristocratic patronage and had been largely dependent on the favor of royal courts or the nobility, nineteenth-century musicians were supported by the new middle-class audience. Musicians of the eighteenth century belonged to a glorified servant class, which ministered to the needs of a public high above them in social rank. In the nineteenth century, however, musicians met their audience as equals. Indeed, as solo performers began to dominate the concert hall, whether as pianists, violinists, or conductors, they were "stars" who were idolized by the public. Mendelssohn, Liszt, and Paganini were welcomed into the great homes of their time in quite a different way than Haydn and Mozart had been half a century earlier.

The solo performer

Music thrived in the private home and in the public life of most cities and towns as well. Permanent orchestras and singing societies abounded, printed music was readily available at a cost that many could afford, and music journals kept the public informed about musical activities and new works.

With this expansion of musical life, composers and performing artists were called upon to assume new roles as educators. Felix Mendelssohn, active as composer, pianist, and conductor, used his immense prestige to found and direct the Leipzig Conservatory, whose curriculum became a model for music schools all over Europe and America. The Russian composer-pianist Anton Rubinstein performed a similar role as founder of the St. Petersburg Conservatory. Robert Schumann became a widely read critic. Franz Liszt was not only active as a composer and conductor but was also considered the greatest pianist of his time. In later life, he taught extensively and trained a generation of great concert pianists. Richard Wagner directed his own theater at Bayreuth and was thus instrumental in helping the new public to understand his music dramas. Composers everywhere were active in organizing concerts and music festivals, and thereby played a leading role in educating the new public.

WOMEN IN MUSIC

Standard histories of music have largely omitted consideration of women as composers and performers; this circumstance results from insufficient attention to attitudes of the time regarding educational opportunities, the hierarchy of social classes, and the economics of the music professions. Modern scholarship increasingly supports the contributions of women to music through the ages.

Unlike earlier eras, when a handful of women were recognized as virtuoso performers, the society of the nineteenth century saw a substantial number of women make careers as professional musicians. This was now possible through the broadening of educational opportunities, which included the establishment of public conservatories whose doors were open to women. In such schools, women could receive training as singers, instrumentalists, and even composers. Likewise, the rise of the piano as the favored chamber instrument—both solo and with voice or instruments—provided women of the middle and upper classes with a performance outlet that was socially acceptable. There was one area in which women's talents received full expression—

the lyric theater. As opera singers, they performed major roles in dramatic works for the stage.

Yet composition remained largely a man's province. Many men held the view that women lacked creativity in the arts, thereby driving some nineteenth-century women to pursue literary careers under male pseudonyms: George Eliot, George Sand, and Daniel Stern, to name three. However, despite the social pressures against them, some women defied the conventions of their time and made a name for themselves as composers. We shall study the work of one of the best-known of these pioneers: the pianist-composer Clara Schumann.

Women also exerted an important influence as patrons of music or through their friendships with composers. George Sand played an important part in the career of Chopin, as did Carolyne Sayn-Wittgenstein in that of Liszt. Nadezhda von Meck is remembered as the woman who supported Tchaikovsky in the early years of his career and made it possible for him to compose. Also, several women of the upper class presided over musical salons where composers could gather to perform and discuss their music. One such musical center was in the home of the Mendelssohn family, where Fanny Mendelssohn, a respected performer and composer herself, organized concerts that featured works by her more famous brother, Felix.

All in all, women made steady strides in the direction of professional equality throughout the nineteenth century, and thereby laid the foundation for their even greater achievements in the twentieth.

UNIT IV

The Nineteenth-Century Art Song

13

The Romantic Song

"Out of my great sorrows I make my little songs."
—HEINRICH HEINE

The art song met the nineteenth-century need for intimate personal expression. This form came into prominence in the early decades of the century, and emerged as a favored example of the new lyricism.

Types of Song Structure

Strophic form

In the nineteenth century, two main types of song structure prevailed. In *strophic form,* the same melody is repeated with every stanza, or strophe, of the poem. This procedure occurs frequently in folk and popular song. Although the form permits no real closeness between words and music, it sets up a general atmosphere that accommodates itself equally well to all the stanzas. The first may tell of the lover's expectancy, the second of his joy at seeing his beloved, the third of her father's harshness in separating them, and the fourth of her sad death, all being sung to the same tune.

Through-composed form

The other song type, what the Germans call *durchkomponiert,* or *through-composed,* is composed from beginning to end, without repetitions of whole sections. Here the music follows the story line, changing with each stanza according to the text. This makes it possible for the composer to mirror every shade of meaning in the words.

Modified strophic form

There is also an intermediate type that combines features of the other two. The same melody may be repeated for two or three stanzas, with new material introduced when the poem requires it, generally at the climax. This is a *modified strophic form.*

The immense popularity of the Romantic art song was due in part to the emergence of the piano as the universal household instrument. A lithograph by **Achille Devéria** *(1800–57), In the Salon.* (Germanische National-museum, Nuremberg)

The Lied

Despite the prominence of song throughout the ages, the art song as we know it today was a product of the Romantic era. It was created by the union of poetry and music in the early nineteenth century. Among the great Romantic masters of the art song were Franz Schubert, Robert Schumann, Johannes Brahms, and Hugo Wolf. The new genre came to be known throughout Europe by the German word for song—*Lied* (plural, *Lieder*). A Lied is a German-texted solo vocal song with piano accompaniment. Some composers wrote groups of Lieder that were unified by some narrative thread or a descriptive theme; such a group is known as a *song cycle*.

Song cycle

The Lied depended for its flowering on the upsurge of lyric poetry that marked the rise of German Romanticism. Johann Wolfgang von Goethe (1749–1832) and Heinrich Heine (1797–1856) are the two leading figures among a group of poets who, like Wordsworth, Byron, Shelley, and Keats in English literature, cultivated a subjective mode of expression in the short lyric poem. The texts of the Lied ranged from tender sentiment to dramatic balladry; its favorite themes were love, longing, and the beauty of nature.

The popularity of the Romantic art song was furthered by the emergence of the piano as the universal household instrument of the nineteenth century. The piano accompaniment translated the poetic images into music. Voice and piano together infused the short lyric form with feeling, and made it suitable for amateurs and artists alike, for the home and the concert hall.

Cultural Perspective 1

Folk Song and the Lied

What did a Lied composer like Brahms think of as folk song style? What is it that distinguishes folk, or traditional, music from art music? Generally, traditional music is transmitted orally, and is easily sung or played by most people. Usually, a large number of people in one or more social classes or ethnic groups know the song, or a version of it. (In oral transmission, a song may undergo changes as one person learns it from another.) When a folk song is written down, it is captured in just one of its variants, although it may continue in oral as well as written tradition.

What constitutes, for example, German folk song style? Although there are many different regions where songs with German texts may be sung, certain traits are almost always present. Melodies tend to be diatonic (that is, completely within the scale—no chromatic notes added) and set syllabically to the music (one note to each syllable); thus they are easy to sing. Disjunct movement is common, often outlining the chords of the underlying harmony. Many Germanic folk songs as well as dances are in triple meter, and some begin with an upbeat (on the third beat of the measure). Strophic form, with repeated music for each stanza of a poem, is also common in the folk music of many Western cultures.

We can identify some of these same characteristics in actual German (and Austrian) folk songs. Consider one you may have learned as a child: *Ach, du lieber Augustin* (also sung to the English words "Did You Ever See a Lassie"; Example 1).

The text is set with one syllable per note to a weighty "oom-pah-pah" triple meter; the tune has some diatonic leaps that correspond to its accompanying triads. Notice too that the English text requires the addition of pick-up notes that change the opening of the melody. Small differences like these are typical of folk music, and result from oral transmission of words and music. Two other well-known Germanic songs present similar characteristics: *O Tannenbaum (O Christmas Tree*, and also *O Maryland, My Maryland)*; and *Du, du liegst mir im Herzen* (usually sung in German).

Turning to composed works, we can observe that many Romantic Lied composers have copied traits of this traditional style in their art music. Thus not only does Brahms's song *Futile Serenade (Vergebliches Ständchen, LG 3)* fit the characteristics described above, but so does another Lied by Brahms—a piece you have probably heard. Originally published in a set of Five Songs, Op. 49 (1868), *Brahms's Lullaby* (*Wiegenlied*) is set to words from a popular collection of folk song texts titled *The Youth's Magic Horn (Des Knaben Wunderhorn*, c. 1805–8). The melodic line of the lullaby is in the style described earlier—diatonic, disjunct, and outlining a chord. Unlike the earlier example, however, the rhythm of this gently lilting song, to which many babies have been rocked asleep, follows that of the Austrian Ländler, a slow, triple-meter dance that was a precursor to the waltz (Example 2).

Thus a composer wishing to emulate folk music must capture the essence of the style in the melody, rhythms, and harmonies chosen. For Brahms, as well as other composers of the German Lied, this style was their national heritage, and many chose to imitate it. We will see throughout our study of nineteenth- and twentieth-century music that composers of numerous countries and cultures—Poland, Russia, Hungary, and the United States, among others—captivated their audiences through references to traditional music and, in their own way, helped preserve it through their compositions.

Example 1:

Ach,   du lie·ber   Au · gus ·tin,   Au · gus ·tin,   Au · gus · tin
Did you ev · er see a   las · sie,   a   las · sie,   a   las · sie, did you

Example 2:

Gu · ten   A · bend, gut' Nacht,   mit___ Ro · sen   be · dacht___
(Lul · la · by,   and good night,   with___ ro · ses   be · dight___)

These German dancers perform a traditional springtime ceremony in regional costume. The maypole dance, originally a fertility rite, was known throughout ancient Europe, Mexico, Egypt, and India. (Courtesy of German Information Center)

Terms to Note:

traditional music
oral transmission
strophic form

Suggested Listening:

Brahms's *Futile Serenade (Vergebliches Ständchen)* or *Lullaby (Wiegenlied)*
German or Austrian folk songs

14

Schubert and the Lied

"When I wished to sing of love, it turned to sorrow. And when I wished to sing of sorrow, it was transformed for me into love."

Franz Schubert

In the popular mind, Franz Schubert's life has become a romantic symbol of the artist's fate. He was not properly appreciated during his lifetime. He died young. And after his death, he was enshrined among the immortals.

His Life

Early years

Franz Schubert (1797–1828) was born in a suburb of Vienna, the son of a schoolmaster. The boy learned the violin from his father, piano from an elder brother; his beautiful soprano voice gained him admittance to the imperial chapel and school where the court singers were trained. His teachers were astonished at the musicality of the shy, dreamy lad. One of them remarked that Franz "had learnt everything from God."

When his school days were over, young Schubert tried to follow in his father's footsteps, but he was not cut out for the routine of the classroom. He found escape by immersing himself in the lyric poets who were the first voices of German Romanticism. As one of his friends said, "Everything he touched turned to song." The music came to him with miraculous spontaneity. *Erlking,* set to a poem by Goethe, was written in a few hours when he was a teenager. It is one of his greatest songs.

Schubert's talent for friendship attracted a little band of writers, artists, and musicians, who organized a series of evenings at which his newest works were performed. The spirit of these convivial gatherings, known as "Schubertiads," was captured on canvas by the painter Moritz von Schwind (see p. 77). With the encouragement of his friends, Schubert, not yet twenty, left his father's school. In the eleven years that were left him, he held no official position (although he occasionally made half-hearted attempts to obtain one). He lived in alternating states of loneliness and camaraderie, poverty and affluence, hope and despair. And steadily, with an almost superhuman intensity, Schubert produced one masterwork after another.

Schubert was not a practical man of the world. Songs that in time sold in the hundreds of thousands he gave away for the price of a meal. As the years passed, his youthful exuberance gave way to the tragic loneliness of the Romantic artist. "No one understands another's grief," he wrote. Yet he comprehended—and in this he was the Romantic—that his suffering made him receptive to new depths of awareness: "My music is the product of my talent and my misery. And that which I have written in my greatest distress is what the world seems to like best."

Last years

Eventually Schubert perceived that the struggle had been decided against

In this unfinished oil sketch of a "Schubertiade," **Moritz von Schwind** *(1804-71) shows Schubert seated at the piano. Next to him is the singer Johann Michael Vogl, who introduced many of Schubert's songs to the Viennese public.* (Vienna, Schubert-Museum)

him. "It seems to me at times that I no longer belong to this world," he wrote. This was the emotional climate of the magnificent song cycle *Winter's Journey*, in which he introduced a somber lyricism new to music. The long, dark journey—was it not the symbol of his own life? Overcoming his discouragement, he embarked on his last efforts. To the earlier masterpieces was added, in the final year of his life, an amazing group of works that includes the Mass in E flat, the String Quintet in C, the three posthumous piano sonatas, and thirteen of his finest songs.

Even with these outstanding achievements to his credit, he made arrangements to study counterpoint: "I see now how much I still have to learn." When he was already terminally ill, he managed to correct the proofs of the final part of *Winter's Journey.* His dying wish was to be buried near the master he worshipped above all others—Beethoven. His wish was granted.

Schubert was thirty-one years old when he died in 1828. In the memorable words of Sir George Grove, "There never has been one like him, and there never will be another."

His Music

Schubert marks the confluence of the Classical and Romantic eras. His symphonies look back to the eighteenth century in their clear form. But in his Lieder and piano pieces, he was wholly the Romantic. The melodies have a tenderness, a quality of longing that match the Romantic quality of the poetry

Principal Works

More than 600 Lieder, including *Erlkönig* (*Erlking*, 1815) and 3 song cycles, among them *Die schöne Müllerin* (*The Lovely Maid of the Mill*, 1823) and *Winterreise* (*Winter's Journey*, 1827)

9 symphonies, including the *Unfinished* (No. 8, 1822)

Chamber music, including 15 string quartets; 1 string quintet; 2 piano trios and the *Trout* Quintet; 1 octet; various sonatas

Piano sonatas, dances, and character pieces

Choral music, including 7 masses, other liturgical pieces, and part songs

Operas and incidental music for dramas

to which they are set. This magical lyricism prompted the composer Franz Liszt to call him "the most poetic musician that ever was."

Chamber music It was in his chamber music that Schubert revealed his introverted nature. His string quartets, the *Trout* Quintet, the two piano trios, and the String Quintet in C bear the true Schubertian stamp.

Piano works In the impromptus and other short piano pieces, the piano sings with a new lyricism. Here spontaneity and the charm of the unexpected take their place as elements of Romantic art. His piano sonatas were neglected for years, but are now firmly situated in the repertory. Schubert, whose lyric imagination needed room in which to unfold, expanded the form he inherited from his predecessors.

Songs Finally there are the songs, more than six hundred of them. Many were written down at white heat, sometimes five, six, seven in a single morning. Of special interest are the accompaniments: a measure or two conjures up images of the rustling brook, the dilapidated hurdy-gurdy, or the lark "at heaven's gate." Certain of his melodies achieve the universality of folk song. Their eloquence and fresh feeling have never been surpassed. A special place is occupied by two superb song cycles—*The Lovely Maid of the Mill* and *Winter's Journey*, both on poems of Wilhelm Müller.

ERLKING

This masterpiece of Schubert's youth captures the Romantic "strangeness and wonder" of Goethe's celebrated ballad. *Erlking* is based on the legend that whoever is touched by the king of the elves must die.

The eerie atmosphere of the poem is immediately established by the piano. Galloping triplets are heard against a rumbling figure in the bass. This motive pervades the song, helping to unify it. The poem has four characters: the narrator, the father, the child, and the seductive elf (see Listening Guide 2).

The characters are vividly differentiated through changes in the melody, harmony, rhythm, and accompaniment. The child's terror is suggested by clashing dissonance and a high vocal range. The father, calming his son's fears, has a more rounded vocal line, sung in a low range. As for the Erlking, his cajoling is given in suavely melodious phrases.

The song is through-composed; the music follows the unfolding of the narrative with a steady rise in tension—and pitch—that builds to the climax. Abruptly the obsessive triplet rhythm lets up, slowing down as horse and rider reach home. "In his arms the child"—a dramatic pause precedes the two final words—"was dead." The work of an eighteen-year-old, *Erlking* was a milestone in the history of Romanticism.

Listening Guide 2

	C/S: 5A/1	C/S: 5/ 1 – 7
	Sh: 2A/4	Sh: 2/ 20 – 26

SCHUBERT: *Erlking (Erlkönig)*   (4:03)

Date of work: 1815
Form: Through-composed Lied
Text: Narrative poem by Johann von Goethe
Medium: Solo voice and piano
Tempo: Schnell (fast)
Characters: Various, depending on dialogue (performed by one vocalist)
   Narrator: medium range, minor mode
   Father: low range, minor mode; reassuring
   Son: high range, minor mode; frightened
   Erlking: medium range, major mode, coaxing, then insistent

Piano introduction—minor key and rapid repeated octaves in triplets set mood; simulate horse's hooves:

Melody of son's dissonant outcry on "My father, my father":

Mein   Va – ter,   mein   Va – ter,

Text	Translation
	NARRATOR *(minor mode, middle range)*
1 0:00 Wer reitet so spät durch Nacht und Wind?	Who rides so late through night and wind?
Es ist der Vater mit seinem Kind;	It is a father with his child;
er hat den Knaben wohl in dem Arm,	He has the boy close in his arm,
er fasst ihn sicher, er hält ihn warm.	He holds him tight, he keeps him warm.

		FATHER *(low range)*	
		"Mein Sohn, was birgst du so bang dein Gesicht?"	"My son, why do you hide your face in fear?"

SON *(high range)*

"Siehst, Vater, du den Erlkönig nicht? / den Erlenkönig mit Kron' und Schweif?"　　"Father, don't you see the Erlking? / The Erlking with his crown and train?"

FATHER *(low range)*

"Mein Sohn, es ist ein Nebelstreif."　　"My son, it is a streak of mist."

ERLKING *(major mode, melodic)*

|2| 1:29 |

"Du liebes Kind, komm, geh mit mir! / gar schöne Spiele spiel' ich mit dir; / manch' bunte Blumen sind an dem Strand; / meine Mutter hat manch' gülden Gewand."

"You dear child, come with me! / I'll play very lovely games with you. / There are lots of colorful flowers by the shore; / My mother has some golden robes."

SON *(high range, frightened)*

|3| 1:52 |

"Mein Vater, mein Vater, und hörest du nicht, / was Erlenkönig mir leise verspricht?"

"My father, my father, and don't you hear / The Erlking whispering promises to me?"

FATHER *(low range, calming)*

"Sei ruhig, bleibe ruhig, mein Kind; / in dürren Blättern säuselt der Wind."

"Be still, stay calm, my child; / It's the wind rustling in the dry leaves."

ERLKING *(major mode, cajoling)*

|4| 2:14 |

"Willst, feiner Knabe, du mit mir geh'n? / meine Töchter sollen dich warten schön; / meine Töchter führen den nächtlichen Reih'n / und wiegen und tanzen und singen dich ein."

"My fine lad, do you want to come with me? / My daughters will take care of you; / My daughters lead the nightly dance, / and they'll rock and dance and sing you to / sleep."

SON *(high range, dissonant outcry)*

|5| 2:31 |

"Mein Vater, mein Vater, und siehst du nicht dort, / Erlkönigs Töchter am düstern Ort?"

"My father, my father, and don't you see / The Erlking's daughters over there in the / shadows?"

FATHER *(low range, reassuring)*

"Mein Sohn, mein Sohn, ich seh' es genau, / es scheinen die alten Weiden so grau."

"My son, my son, I see it clearly, / It's the gray sheen of the old willows."

ERLKING *(gay, then insistent)*

|6| 3:00 |

"Ich liebe dich, mich reizt deine schöne Gestalt, / und bist du nicht willig, so brauch' ich Gewalt."

"I love you, your beautiful form delights me! / And if you're not willing, then I'll use force."

SON *(high range, terrified)*

|7| 3:10 |

"Mein Vater, mein Vater, jetzt fasst er mich an! / Erlkönig hat mir ein Leids gethan!"

"My father, my father, now he's grasping me! / The Erlking has hurt me!"

NARRATOR *(middle register, speechlike)*

Dem Vater grauset's, er reitet geschwind, / er hält in Armen das ächzende Kind, / erreicht den Hof mit Müh und Noth:

The father shudders, he rides swiftly, / He holds the moaning child in his arms; / With effort and urgency he reaches the court- / yard:

in seinen Armen das Kind war todt.　　In his arms the child was dead.

15
Brahms as a Lied Composer

"It is not hard to compose, but it is wonderfully hard to let the superfluous notes fall under the table."

Johannes Brahms created a Romantic art in the purest Classical style. His veneration for the past and his mastery of musical architecture brought him closer to the spirit of Beethoven than any of his contemporaries.

His Life

Johannes Brahms (1833–97) was born in Hamburg, son of a double-bass player. As a youth of ten, Johannes helped increase the family income by playing the piano in the dance halls of the slum district where he grew up. By the time he was twenty, he had acquired sufficient reputation as a pianist to accompany the Hungarian violinist Eduard Reményi on a concert tour.

Johannes Brahms

His first compositions made an impression on Joseph Joachim, the leading violinist of the day, who made it possible for Brahms to visit the great composer Robert Schumann at Düsseldorf. Schumann recognized in the shy young composer a future leader in the realm of symphonic and chamber music. In his role as music critic, Schumann published in his journal the famous essay entitled "New Paths," in which he named the twenty-year-old "young eagle" as one who "was called forth to give us the highest ideal expression of our time." Brahms was suddenly famous.

Robert and Clara Schumann took the fair-haired youth into their home. Their friendship opened up new horizons for him. Five months later came the tragedy of Schumann's mental collapse. With tenderness and strength, Johannes supported Clara through the ordeal of Robert's illness. (On Robert Schumann as a composer, see Chapter 26.)

Friendship with Schumanns

Robert lingered for two years while Johannes was shaken by the great love of his life. Fourteen years his senior and the mother of seven children, Clara Schumann, herself a fine pianist and composer, appeared to young Brahms as the ideal of womanly and artistic achievement. (We will study Clara Schumann's career in Chapter 19.) What had begun as filial devotion ripened into romantic passion. "You have taught me," he wrote her, "to marvel at the nature of love, affection, and self-denial. I can do nothing but think of you." At the same time, he was torn by feelings of guilt, for he loved and revered Robert Schumann, his friend and benefactor, above all others. He thought of suicide and spoke of himself, as one may at twenty-two, as "a man for whom nothing is left."

This conflict was resolved the following year by Robert's death, but another conflict took its place. Now that Clara was no longer the unattainable ideal, Brahms was faced with the choice between love and freedom. Time and again in the course of his life, he was torn between the two, with the decision always going to freedom. His ardor subsided into a lifelong friendship. Two decades later, he could still write her, "I love you more than myself and more than anybody and anything on earth."

Ultimately, Brahms settled in Vienna, where he remained for the next thirty-five years. During this time, he became enormously successful, the acknowledged heir of the Viennese masters.

This exacting artist had a curiously two-sided nature. He could be morose and withdrawn, yet he loved coarse humor. A bohemian at heart, he craved bourgeois respectability. Behind a rough exterior he hid the tenderness that found expression in his music. Although he complained of loneliness and on occasion fell in love, he was unable to accept the responsibility of a sustained relationship. His motto was "Free—but happy!" "It would be as difficult for me to marry," he explained, "as to write an opera. But after the first experience I should probably undertake a second!"

In early manhood, his mother's death had led him to complete *A German Requiem.* In 1896, the final illness of Clara Schumann gave rise to the *Four Serious Songs.* Her death profoundly affected the composer, already ill with cancer. He died ten months later, at the age of sixty-four, and was buried in Vienna not far from Beethoven and Schubert.

His Music

Brahms was a traditionalist. His aim was to show that new and important things could still be said in the tradition of the eighteenth century. In this he differed from avowed Romantic innovators such as Berlioz, Liszt, and Wagner.

Orchestral music   Brahms's four symphonies are unsurpassed in the late Romantic period for breadth of conception and design, yet their forms draw upon those of earlier

Principal Works

Orchestral music, including 4 symphonies (1876, 1877, 1883, 1884–85); *Variations on a Theme by Haydn* (1873); 2 overtures (*Academic Festival,* 1880; *Tragic,* 1886); 4 concertos (2 for piano, 1858, 1881; 1 for violin, 1878; 1 double concerto for violin and cello, 1887)

Chamber music, including string quartets, quintets, sextets; piano trios, quartets, and 1 quintet; 1 clarinet quintet; sonatas (violin, cello, clarinet/viola)

Piano music, including sonatas, character pieces, dances, and variation sets (on a theme by Handel, 1861; on a theme by Paganini, 1862–63)

Choral music, including *A German Requiem* (1868), *Alto Rhapsody* (1869), and part songs

Lieder, including *Vergebliches Ständchen* (*Futile Serenade,* 1881), *Four Serious Songs* (1896), and folk song arrangements eras. Among his other orchestral works, the *Variations on a Theme by Haydn* and his two concert overtures are frequently heard today. In the two piano concertos and the violin concerto, the solo instrument is integrated into a full-scale symphonic structure.

To a greater degree than any of his contemporaries, Brahms captured the tone of intimacy that is the essence of chamber music style. He is an important figure too in piano music. His three sonatas are works of his youth. His two variation sets, on themes by the Baroque composer George Frideric Handel and the early nineteenth-century composer Nicolò Paganini, represent his top achievement in this field. The Romantic in Brahms also found expression in short lyric piano pieces: the rhapsodies, ballades, capriccios, and intermezzi are among the treasures of the literature. On a more popular level are the *Hungarian Dances* and the set of sixteen waltzes for piano duet.

Chamber and solo music

As a song writer, Brahms stands in the direct line of succession to Schubert and Robert Schumann. His output includes about two hundred solo songs and an almost equal number for two, three, and four voices. The favorite themes are love, nature, and death. Later we will study his finest choral work, *A German Requiem,* written to biblical texts he selected himself. A song of acceptance of death, this work more than any other spread his fame during his lifetime.

Vocal music

The nationalist in Brahms—he spoke of himself as *echt deutsch* (truly German)—inspired his arrangements of German folk and children's songs, as well as the popular tone of many art songs, including the one we will study.

FUTILE SERENADE

The extroverted side of Brahms's personality—robust, delighting in broad humor—can be observed in *Futile Serenade.* It is his version of a lusty folk song from the lower Rhineland (see CP 1 on p. 74).

The four stanzas are set in a modified strophic form (see Listening Guide 3). Following a short piano introduction, the vocal melody outlines the familiar triads and moves in an animated 3/4 time, achieving the directness and naturalness of the folk mood. The opening phrase contains the same little motive repeated three times, each time from a lower note—that is, in sequence.

The relationship of folk song to the dance is emphasized by the regularity of structure: four measures to the phrase, four phrases to the stanza. Yet Brahms introduces a charming asymmetry: the usual four-bar phrase is extended for two bars by repeating the words "mach' mir auf" (let me in). This extension is repeated in every stanza, disrupting the symmetry of the rest.

Remarkable too is the sudden change of color at the third stanza. The melody takes on a plaintive tone as the lover begs: "The night is so cold, so icy the wind." This is achieved by a change from major to minor. The lively accompaniment keeps the song moving and creates a framework for the spirited dialogue.

The folklike character of this song is typical of many of Brahms's Lieder. He wrote Clara Schumann that "songs today have gone so far astray that one cannot cling too closely to one's ideal, and that ideal is folk song."

Listening Guide 3

C/S: 5B/4   C/S: 5/ 47 – 50

BRAHMS: *Futile Serenade (Vergebliches Ständchen)*

(1:41)

Date of work: 1881
Form: Modified strophic Lied
Text: Traditional folklike dialogue, strophic, in 4 verses
Medium: Solo voice and piano
Tempo: Lebhaft und gut gelaunt (lively and good-humored)
Character: Folk song, with dancelike rhythms, in triple meter

Opening vocal melody (3 sequential repetitions of short motive are marked):

Gu - ten   A - bend, mein   Schatz, gu - ten   A - bend, mein   Kind,

		Text	Translation	Key
		HE		
47	0:00	Guten Abend, mein Schatz,	Good evening, my love,	A major
		Guten Abend, mein Kind!	Good evening, my child!	
		Ich komm' aus Lieb' zu dir,	I come out of love for you,	
		Ach, mach' mir auf die Tür!	Ah, open the door for me!	
		Mach' mir auf die Tür!	Open the door for me!	
		Piano interlude (2 measures)		
		SHE		
48	0:23	Mein' Tür ist verschlossen,	My door is locked,	A major
		Ich lass' dich nicht ein;	I will not let you in.	
		Mutter, die rät mir klug,	Mother warned me	
		Wärst du herein mit Fug,	That if I let you in willingly,	
		Wär's mit mir vorbei!	All would be over with me!	
		Piano interlude (2 measures)		
		HE		
49	0:47	So kalt ist die Nacht,	The night is so cold,	A minor
		So eisig der Wind,	The wind is so icy,	
		Dass mir das Herz erfriert,	That my heart is freezing,	
		Mein' Lieb' erlöschen wird;	My love will be extinguished;	
		Öffne mir, mein Kind!	Open up for me, child!	
		Piano interlude (2 measures)		
		SHE		
50	1:10	Löschet dein' Lieb',	If your love is extinguished,	A major
		Lass sie löschen nur!	Just let it go out!	
		Löschet sie immer zu,	Just keep on extinguishing it;	
		Geh' heim zu Bett, zur Ruh',	Go home to bed, to rest!	
		Gute Nacht, mein Knab'!	Good night, my boy!	

UNIT V

The Nineteenth-Century Piano Piece

16

The Piano in the Nineteenth Century

"Provided one can feel the music, one can also make the pianoforte sing."
—LUDWIG VAN BEETHOVEN

The rise in popularity of the piano was an important factor in shaping the musical culture of the Romantic era. All over Europe and America, the instrument became a mainstay of music in the home. It proved especially attractive to the amateur because, unlike the string and wind instruments, it enabled one to play melody and harmony together. The piano thus played a crucial role in the taste and experience of the new mass public.

Hardly less important was the rise of the virtuoso pianist. At first the performer was also the composer; Mozart and Beethoven introduced their own piano concertos to the public, and Franz Liszt first presented his *Hungarian Rhapsodies.* With the developing concert industry, however, a class of virtuoso performers arose whose only function it was to dazzle audiences by playing music others had written.

At the same time, a series of crucial technical improvements led to the development of the modern concert grand piano. By the opening of the twentieth century, the piano recital had come to occupy a central position on the musical scene.

The Short Lyric Piano Piece

The short lyric piano piece was the instrumental equivalent of the song in its projection of lyric and dramatic moods within a compact form. Composers

This beautiful, ornate grand piano was made for the Baroness of Kidderminster by Erard, c. 1840. (Metropolitan Museum of Art, Gift of Mrs. Henry McSweeny, 1959; photo by Sheldon Collins)

adopted new and sometimes fanciful terms for such works. Some titles—"Prelude," "Intermezzo" (interlude), "Impromptu" (on the spur of the moment), for example—suggest free, almost improvisational forms. Many composers turned to dance music, and produced keyboard versions of the Polish mazurka and polonaise, the Viennese waltz, and the lively scherzo. Composers sometimes chose more descriptive titles, such as *Wild Hunt* and *Forest Murmurs* (both by Franz Liszt).

The nineteenth-century masters of the short piano piece—Schubert, Chopin, Liszt, Mendelssohn, Robert and Clara Schumann, and Brahms—showed inexhaustible ingenuity in exploring the technical resources of the instrument and its potential for expression.

17

Chopin and Nineteenth-Century Piano Music

"My life . . . an episode without a beginning and with a sad end."

Frédéric François Chopin (1810–49) has been called the "poet of the piano." The title is a valid one. His art, rooted in the heart of Romanticism, constitutes the golden age of that instrument.

His Life

Chopin, considered the national composer of Poland, was half French. His father had emigrated to Warsaw, where he married a lady-in-waiting to a countess and taught French to the sons of the nobility. Frédéric, who displayed his

Frédéric Chopin

musical gift in childhood, was educated at the newly founded Conservatory of Warsaw. At the age of twenty-one, he left for Paris, where he spent the rest of his career. Paris in the 1830s was the center of the new Romanticism. The circle in which Chopin moved included musicians such as Liszt and Berlioz, and literary figures such as Victor Hugo, George Sand, and Alexandre Dumas the father. The poet Heinrich Heine was his friend, as was the painter Eugène Delacroix. Although Chopin was a man of emotions, he was much influenced by these leading intellectuals of France.

Through the virtuoso pianist Liszt, he met Aurore Dudevant, "the lady with the somber eye," known to the world as the novelist George Sand. She was thirty-four, Chopin twenty-eight when their famous friendship began. Madame Sand was brilliant and domineering; her need to dominate found its counterpart in Chopin's need to be ruled. She left a memorable account of the composer at work:

> His creative power was spontaneous, miraculous. It came to him without effort or warning. . . . But then began the most heartrending labor I have ever witnessed. It was a series of attempts, of fits of irresolution and impatience to recover certain details. He would shut himself in his room for days, pacing up and down, breaking his pens, repeating and modifying one bar a hundred times.

For the next eight years, Chopin spent his summers at Sand's estate at Nohant, where she entertained many of France's prominent artists and writers. These were productive years for the composer, although his health grew progressively worse and his relationship with Sand ran its course from love to conflict, from jealousy to hostility. They parted in bitterness.

According to his friend Liszt, "Chopin felt and often repeated that in breaking this long affection, this powerful bond, he had broken his life." The lonely despair of the Romantic artist pervades his last letters. "What has become of my art?" he wrote during a visit to Scotland. "And my heart, where have I wasted it?"

Chopin died of tuberculosis in Paris at the age of thirty-nine. Thousands joined together at his funeral to pay him homage. The artistic world bid its farewell to the strains of the composer's own funeral march, from his B-flat-minor Piano Sonata.

His Music

Chopin was one of the most original artists of the nineteenth century. His style is so entirely his own that there is no mistaking it for any other. He was the only master of the first rank whose creative life centered about the piano. From the first, his imagination was wedded to the keyboard, and he created a universe within that narrow frame. His genius transformed even the limitations of the instrument—its inability to sustain tone for any length of time—into sources of beauty. Chopin overcame these with such ingenuity that we owe to him, as much as to any individual, the modern piano style. The widely spaced chords in the bass, sustained by pedal, set up masses of tone that encircle the melody. "Everything must be made to sing," he told his pupils. The delicate ornaments

George Sand

Modern piano style

Principal Works

Works for piano and orchestra, including 2 piano concertos

Piano music, including 4 ballades, Fantasy in F minor (1841), *Berceuse* (1844), *Barcarolle* (1846), 3 sonatas, preludes, études, mazurkas, nocturnes, waltzes, polonaises, impromptus, scherzos, rondos, marches, and variations

Chamber music, all including piano; songs

in his music—trills, grace notes, runs—seem magically to prolong the single tones. And all this generally lies so well for the trained hand that the music seems almost to play itself.

Small forms   It is remarkable that so many of his works have remained in the pianist's standard repertory. His nocturnes—night songs, as the name implies—are melancholic. The preludes are visionary fragments; some are only a page in length, several consist of two or three lines. The études crown the literature of the study piece; in these, piano technique is transformed into poetry. The impromptus are fanciful and capricious, and the waltzes capture the brilliance and coquetry of the salon. The mazurkas, derived from a Polish peasant dance, evoke the idealized landscape of his youth.

Larger forms   Among the larger forms are the four ballades. These are epic works of spacious proportions. The polonaises revive the stately processional dance in which Poland's nobles hailed their kings. The Fantasy in F minor and the dramatic scherzos reveal the composer at the peak of his art. The Sonatas in B minor and in B-flat minor are thoroughly Romantic in spirit, as are the Piano Concertos in E minor and F minor.

POLONAISE IN A FLAT

The heroic side of Chopin's style shows itself in the most popular of his polonaises, the one in A flat, Op. 53 (1842). The introduction establishes a dramatic mood against which is set the opening dance theme, a proud melody in a stately triple meter. The octaves for the left hand in the following section approach the limits of what the piano can do. The emotional temperature drops perceptibly after the octave episode; this is Chopin's way of building up tension against the return of the theme, which rounds off the ternary form. A *coda* (Italian for "tail"), a concluding section appended to a form, closes the work. In the hands of a virtuoso, this polonaise assumes a dazzling brilliance; it is the epitome of the grand style. (See the outline in Listening Guide 4.)

Tempo rubato   Important in this piece, as in all of Chopin's music, is the *tempo rubato*—the "robbed time," or "borrowed time," that is so characteristic of Romantic style. In tempo rubato, certain liberties are taken with the rhythm without upsetting the basic beat. As Chopin taught it, the accompaniment—usually the left hand—was played in strict time, while above it the right-hand melody might hesitate a little here or hurry forward there. In either case, the borrowing had to be repaid before the end of the phrase. Rubato, like any seasoning, must be used sparingly. But when it is done well, it imparts to the music a quality of caprice. And it remains an essential ingredient of the true Chopin style.

Listening Guide 4

		C/S: 5A/5	C/S: 5/ 24 — 27
(MW) 📼	💿	Sh: 2A/5	Sh: 2/ 27 — 30

CHOPIN: Polonaise in A flat, Op. 53 (6:16)

Date of work: 1842
Form: **A-B-A′**, with introduction
Genre: Polonaise, a stately triple-meter Polish dance
Medium: Solo piano
Tempo: Alla Polacca e maestoso (like a polonaise and majestic); use of rubato

---

24 0:00 Introduction—dramatic mood established, fast ascending lines build into main theme of **A**

25 0:27 **A** section—stately dancelike theme, in tonic key (A-flat major):

Repeated in louder statement, in octaves

1:57 Brief diversion, features typical polonaise rhythm:

2:13 Main theme stated again; closing cadence chords

26   2:47   **B** section—rapid descending octaves in bass, played staccato (dots); introduces theme in E major (in right hand):

3:52   Lyrical melody, leads back to repeat of **A**

27   5:17   **A'** section—abridged repeat of first section; main theme heard once in loud, dramatic statement

5:45   Coda—animated repetition of opening motive of main theme; dramatic closing chords

PRELUDE IN E MINOR

Chopin's set of twenty-four preludes was clearly inspired by an earlier work: the great *Well-Tempered Clavier* (containing forty-eight preludes and fugues) of the Baroque composer Johann Sebastian Bach. (A prelude and fugue from this collection is discussed in Chapter 62.) Like Bach's preludes, Chopin's display an infinite variety of form and texture but, unlike Bach's, do not serve to introduce anything. The works of Chopin's set are arranged to be played as a cycle, offering contrast, tension, and release; they are, however, frequently played individually as well.

The Prelude in E minor, Op. 28, No. 4 (1839), reveals Chopin's uncanny power to achieve the utmost expressiveness with the simplest means (see Listening Guide 5). The melody hardly moves, unfolding in sustained tones over a succession of chords that change very subtly, usually one note at a time.

The music creates a gently mournful mood that is the essence of Romanticism. Tension builds slowly; there is something inevitable about the

Cultural Perspective 2

Polish Folk Dance and Music

How can modern-day Polish-Americans relate to Chopin's nationalistic music? What is truly Polish about his music? The answers lie in the various dance types of Poland. Let us begin with the polonaise, an example of which we have just studied. Its name implies a Polish origin, and indeed it originally was used to describe a group of Polish dance songs in slow triple meter. Eventually, the polonaise evolved into a festive processional dance popular among the aristocracy; it was this form that Chopin imitated in his piano works, making it a symbol of Polish nationalism in the nineteenth century.

Chopin also wrote in other indigenous dance forms, including the mazurka (and its relative, the oberek) and the krakowiak, a kind of polka from the region of Cracow. All of these were originally rural couple dances that later caught on as ballroom dances. The mazurka and oberek are in a quick triple meter with a strong accent on either the second or third beat of the measure. They were often accompanied by a small bagpipe, which played a drone on the tonic or domi-

nant note of the scale. Chopin's piano mazurkas are close to their folk source in their rhythmic and melodic character. The polka (whose name probably derives from the Polish word for "girl," *polska*) and the krakowiak are in a rapid duple meter with lots of syncopation. "Polkamania" swept nineteenth-century Europe as the dance became a ballroom favorite. Polkas were also popular with military bands and in sheet music form for amateur performers.

Today, the polka remains the best-known of these dance types; it represents a "back to one's roots" music for many Americans. In certain regions of the United States that attracted large numbers of Eastern and Central European immigrants (notably the Midwest and mid-Atlantic states), polkas are still danced to the accompaniment of brass ensembles or accordion bands. With its simple bouncing steps and catchy rhythms and tunes (for example, *The Beer Barrel Polka*, originally titled *Modranska Polka*), the polka is one form of ethnic music that has successfully traveled across cultural boundaries.

Dance, whether it be the stately polonaise or the lively polka, has always been an essential part of Polish life. A wedding scene from a ballet by Karol Kurpinski (1785–1857). (Krakow, Museum Narodowe)

Terms to Note:

polonaise
mazurka (oberek)
polka (krakowiak)

Suggested Listening:

Chopin polonaise or mazurka (Polonaise in A
   flat)
Modern polka band

climax, where the melody, advancing in bold leaps, takes on the character of
a passionate outcry that subsides to a sorrowful *pianissimo* ending. Rarely has
so much been said in a single page. Schumann did not exaggerate when he
said of the Preludes, "In each piece we find in his own hand, 'Frédéric Chopin
wrote it!' He is the boldest, the proudest poet of his time."

Listening Guide 5   C/S: 5A/4   C/S: 5/ 22 – 23

CHOPIN: Prelude in E minor, Op. 28, No. 4   (1:49)

Date of work: 1839
Form: Free
Genre: Prelude (from set of 24)
Medium: Solo piano
Tempo: Largo
Character:
   Melody: simple, conjunct, in right hand only
   Rhythm: regular pulse kept by left-hand chords; much use of rubato
   Harmony: centered on E minor, constantly shifting chords with much chromaticism
   Texture: homophonic, melody with accompaniment
   Form: free, opening repeated with variations

22 0:00   Simple melody, leaps an octave, then con-
           junct, accompanied by rhythmic chords
           with shifting harmonies:

| 23 | 0:50 | Accompaniment stops, tempo rubato, leads into repeat of first melody, which becomes more disjunct, wide-ranging: |
| | 1:11 | *Diminuendo* into closing three chords, marked *pianissimo* |

His countrymen have enshrined Chopin as the national composer of Poland. Yet he is the embodiment of European culture. Despite his homesickness, he spent the whole of his adult life in Paris. Thus Poland was idealized in his imagination as the symbol of that longing that every Romantic artist carries in his heart. Heine, himself an expatriate, understood this when he wrote that Chopin was "neither a Pole, a Frenchman, nor a German. He reveals a higher origin. He comes from the land of Mozart, Raphael, Goethe. His true country is the land of poetry."

18

Franz Liszt and the Rise of the Performer/Composer

"Sorrowful and great is the artist's destiny."

Franz Liszt

As composer, conductor, teacher, and organizer of musical events, Franz Liszt occupied a central position in the artistic life of the nineteenth century. Yet this fabulously successful artist did not escape the Romantic melancholy. "To die and die young," he once exclaimed, "—what happiness!"

His Life

Franz Liszt (1811–86) was born in Hungary, son of a steward in the employ of a wealthy family. A stipend from a group of Hungarian noblemen enabled him to pursue his musical studies in Paris. There he came under the spell of French Romanticism, with whose leaders he, like Chopin, formed close friendships.

The appearance in Paris of the sensational violinist Paganini in 1831 made Liszt aware of the possibilities of virtuoso playing. The new concertgoing public required spectacular soloists. Liszt met the need. He was one of the greatest of pianists—and showmen. An actor to his fingertips, he possessed the

The virtuoso

personal magnetism of which legends are made. Instead of sitting with his back to the audience or facing it, as had been the custom previously, he introduced the more effective arrangement that prevails today. It showed off his chiseled profile, as he crouched over the piano, thundering and caressing the keys. Countesses swooned, while less exalted ladies fought for his snuffbox and tore his handkerchief to shreds. Liszt encouraged these antics as a necessary part of the legend. But behind the facade was a true musician.

The lover

Inseparable from the legend of the pianist was that of the lover. Liszt never married, yet his personal life for the better part of fifty years was marked by unhappy endings to relationships. Important in his intellectual development was his relationship with Countess Marie d'Agoult, who wrote novels under the name of Daniel Stern. They shared an idyllic relationship in Switzerland that lasted for a number of years. Of their three children, Cosima subsequently became the wife of composer Richard Wagner. Liszt and the countess parted in bitterness. She later satirized him in her novels.

The composer

Liszt withdrew from the concert stage at the height of his fame in order to devote himself to composing. In 1848, he settled in Weimar, where he became court conductor to the grand duke. The Weimar period (1848–61) saw the production of his chief orchestral works. As director of the ducal opera house, he was in a position to influence public taste, and he used this power unremittingly on behalf of the "music of the future," as he and Wagner named the type of music that they, along with Berlioz, advocated. At Weimar, Liszt directed the first performances of operas by Wagner and Berlioz and many other nineteenth-century works.

The Weimar period also saw his association with the woman who most decisively influenced his life. Princess Carolyne Sayn-Wittgenstein, wife of a powerful nobleman at the court of the czar, fell in love with Liszt during his

An imaginary gathering painted by **Joseph Dannhauser** *in 1840 shows Liszt at the piano with Marie D'Agoult at his feet. Seated behind him are George Sand and Alexandre Dumas père. Standing are Victor Hugo, Paganini, and Rossini. Looking out upon this improbable assemblage is a marble bust of Beethoven.*

last concert tour of Russia. Shortly thereafter, she came to Weimar to be with him. For years, their home was a center of artistic activity. A woman of domineering will and intellect, the princess assisted Liszt in his later literary efforts. These include a book on Gypsy music and a *Life of Chopin.* Both are eloquent but inaccurate.

In his last years, Liszt sought peace by entering the church. He took minor orders and was known as Abbé Liszt. This was the period of his major religious compositions. At seventy-five, he was received with enthusiasm in England, which had always been reluctant to recognize him as a composer. He journeyed to Bayreuth to visit his daughter, now a widow, and died during the festival of Wagner's works, naming with his last breath the masterpiece of the "music of the future"—Wagner's opera *Tristan and Isolde.*

The cleric

His Music

Liszt's goal was pure lyric expression—projecting a state of soul through "the mysterious language of tone." To give his lyricism free rein, he created the symphonic poem. Here, as in his symphonies and concertos, he based his music on the technique of *thematic transformation.* By varying the melodic outline, harmony, or rhythm of a theme, by shifting it from soft to loud, from slow to fast, from low to high register, from strings to woodwinds or brass, he found it possible to transform its character so that it might suggest romantic love in one section, a pastoral scene in another, tension and conflict in a third, and triumph in the last.

Thematic transformation

Liszt was one of the creators of modern piano technique. The best of his piano pieces, like his songs, are examples of true Romantic lyricism. Characteristic are the colorful *Hungarian Rhapsodies* and the vastly popular *Liebestraum* (Love Dream, c. 1850). In a class apart are his chief works for the piano, the Sonata in B minor and the two piano concertos that date from the 1850s.

Piano pieces

Principal Works

Orchestral music, including symphonic poems (*Les Préludes,* 1848); *Dante Symphony* (1856), *Faust Symphony* (1857); 2 piano concertos; and *Totentanz* (for piano and orchestra, 1849)

Piano music, including *Transcendental Etudes* (1851), Sonata (B minor, 1853), *Hungarian Rhapsodies,* nocturnes, waltzes, ballades, polonaises, and other character pieces; numerous transcriptions of orchestral and opera works for piano

Choral music, including masses, oratorios, psalms, cantatas, and secular part songs

1 opera; songs with piano

WILD HUNT

From the beginning of his career, Liszt was fascinated by the technical possibilities of the piano. Like Chopin, he was drawn to the étude, or study piece, in which a composer confronted a single technical problem. Like Chopin too, he transformed the étude from a dry exercise into a poetic mood piece. In his twelve *Transcendental Etudes,* completed in 1838 and revised thirteen years later, the master did what the title implies. He transcended the limitations of the keyboard and even transformed those limitations into sources of tonal beauty.

The eighth étude, *Wild Hunt (Wilde Jagd)*, is typical; it shows off Liszt's reckless virtuosity, his imaginative use of contrast between the low and high registers of the piano, his dramatic exploitation of massed chords, his fondness for irregular rhythmic accentuations. Marked Presto furioso (very fast and furious) and martellato (hammered), *Wild Hunt* opens *fortissimo* (*fff*). The form is a loose **A-B-A** in which the drama of the opening is contrasted with a calmer melody based on parallel chords that suggest distant hunting horns. (See Listening Guide 6 for an analysis.) Dear to Romantic poets and painters was the image of the supernatural hunt, which Liszt evokes here with the virtuosity that was his alone.

Listening Guide 6   C/S: 5A/6   C/S: 5/ 35 – 37

LISZT: *Wild Hunt (Wilde Jagd)*, Transcendental Etude No. 8   (5:05)

Date of work: 1838, revised 1851
Genre: Etude (study), from *Transcendental Etudes*
Medium: Solo piano
Form: Loose **A-B-A**
Tempo: Presto furioso, martellato (very fast, furious, and hammered)

---

35 · 0:00   **A section—opening idea presents loudly hammered octaves alternating with higher-register chords:**

0:32   Long descending chromatic scale, unison in both hands, leads to return of opening idea

36 1:13 **B** section—chords in irregular rhythm (from opening), now gentler, reminiscent of hunting-horn theme; regular 4-measure phrases:

1:24 Same idea repeated in higher octave

1:47 Lyrical theme, in right hand; regular 4-measure phrases:

1:58 Same theme repeated in higher octave, then much louder

37 3:00 **A** section—return of main idea, marked **pp** (very soft)

3:13 Hunting-like chords of the **B** section return, gradually building in *crescendo*

4:12 Lyrical theme from **B** section returns, more agitated and in high range (right hand)

4:47 Descending fast chords lead to final dramatic close

19

Clara Schumann: Nineteenth-Century Pianist and Composer

*"The practice of [music] is . . . a great part of my inner self.
To me, it is the very air I breathe."*

Clara Schumann (1819–96) is universally regarded as one of the most distinguished musicians of the nineteenth century. She was admired throughout Europe as a leading pianist of the era, but the world in which she lived was not prepared to acknowledge that a woman could be an outstanding composer. Hence her considerable creative gifts were not recognized or encouraged during her lifetime.

Her Life

Clara Schumann

Marriage to Robert Schumann

We caught a glimpse of Clara Schumann's life earlier in connection with Johannes Brahms. Her close association with two great composers put her in the center of the musical life of her time. From her earliest years, she had the clearest possible conception of her goals as an artist and the strength of character to realize them. Clara studied piano from age five, made her first public appearance as a concert artist in Leipzig at age nine, and undertook her first extended concert tour several years later.

The first great crisis in her life came with the violent opposition of Friedrich Wieck, her father and teacher, to her marriage to Robert, but she had the courage to defy him. She then faced the problems of a woman torn between the demands of an exacting career and her responsibilities as a wife and mother. She bore Robert seven children (an eighth died in infancy), yet she managed throughout those years to maintain her position as one of the outstanding concert artists of Europe. Liszt admired her playing for its "complete technical mastery, depth, and sincerity of feeling." Her position was made more difficult by the fact that during her lifetime she was much more famous than her husband. The disparity in their reputations might have led to serious strains between them, were it not for the fact that from the first she dedicated her talents to advancing his music. She gave the first performance of all his important works and also became known as a leading interpreter of the music of Brahms and Chopin.

Clara's life was not an easy one. "What will become of my work?" she wrote after learning she was expecting a fifth child. "Yet Robert says 'children are blessings' and he is right . . . so I have decided to face the difficult time that is coming as cheerfully as possible. Whether it will always be like this, I don't know." Although Clara enjoyed a loving relationship with her husband, life became increasingly difficult. Robert suffered from shifting moods and frequent depressions that eventually led to a complete breakdown. After his death, she

Clara Schumann playing with the virtuoso violinist Joseph Joachim. A chalk drawing by **Adolf von Menzel** (1854).

concertized in order to support herself and her children. Now she in turn was sustained by Brahms's devotion; but their love was transformed into a lifelong friendship.

Clara had the talent, the training, and the background that many composers would envy, but from the beginning of her career she accepted the nineteenth-century attitude toward a woman composer. At twenty, she confided to her diary, "I once believed that I possessed creative talent, but I have given up this idea; a woman must not desire to compose—there has never yet been one able to do it. Should I expect to be the one? To believe this would be arrogant, something which my father once, in former days, induced me to do."

Called the "priestess" by her colleagues, Clara was devoutly serious about her artistic endeavors. Her husband was sympathetic to her creativity, assisting when he could with the publication of her music. But Robert also accepted the prevailing attitudes. "Clara has composed a series of small pieces," he wrote in their joint diary, "which show a musical and tender ingenuity such as she never attained before. But to have children, and a husband who is always living in the realm of imagination, does not go together with composing. She cannot work at it regularly, and I am often disturbed to think how many profound ideas are lost because she cannot work them out."

Clara gave her last public concert at the age of seventy-two, and suc-

Principal Works

Solo piano music, including dances, caprices, romances, scherzos, impromptus, character pieces (*Quatre pièces fugitives,* Op. 15, 1845), variations (including one set on a theme by Robert Schumann, 1854), and cadenzas for Mozart and Beethoven piano concertos

1 piano concerto with orchestra or quintet (1837)

Chamber music, including 1 piano trio (1846) and 3 romances for violin and piano (1855–56)

Lieder, with texts by Burns, Rückert, Heine, and other poets

cumbed to a stroke five years later, in 1896. Her dying wish was to hear her husband's music once more.

Her Music

Clara's output includes many small, intimate works such as songs and piano pieces. There are two large-scale works—a piano concerto and a trio for piano and strings; a number of virtuoso pieces; and, as a gesture of homage to her husband, a set of Variations on a Theme by Robert Schumann.

Her early works leaned toward technical display, which showed off her phenomenal talent. The later ones were more serious and introspective pieces typical of the era in which she lived.

SCHERZO, OPUS 10

Composed in 1838 when Clara was nineteen, the D-minor Scherzo, Opus 10, exemplifies her virtuoso style. It is marked Con passione (with passion), a performance indication typical of the Romantic period. The piece is of the kind that allows pianists to dazzle their public. Clara wrote to Robert from Paris, "It is extraordinary to me that my Scherzo is so well-liked here. I always have to repeat it."

The structure is altogether clear-cut: an impetuous scherzo with two trios or contrasting sections more relaxed in character. (See Listening Guide 7.) Sudden dissonances and *sforzandos* (accents) add to the drama; trills and extended arpeggio figures keep the pianist's fingers busy. The main theme, an exuberant rising figure, builds steadily to the *fortissimo* ending, while the two trios, with their flowing melodic lines, offer the necessary release of tension.

This scherzo displays Clara's creative gift in a most attractive way. It further attests to her extraordinary talents as a virtuoso performer. Forgotten for decades, Clara Schumann has finally received the world recognition long due her.

STUDY SONG!!

Listening Guide 7

C/S: 6A/2   C/S: 6/ 6 – 11
Sh: 2B/1   Sh: 2/ 31 – 36

CLARA SCHUMANN: Scherzo, Op. 10 (4:58)

Date of work: c. 1838
Form: Scherzo with 2 trios
Medium: Solo piano
Tempo: Presto, Scherzo con passione
Key: D minor
Meter: 3/4

---

6 0:00 Introduction—14 measures; trill-like, arpeggiated figures lead to main theme:

7 0:08 Scherzo—very rhythmic, unison rising line; soft, punctuated by **sf** chord, alternates with arpeggiated figure, key of D minor:

Opening theme restated in G minor; return of trill-like figure from introduction followed by loud, dissonant chords

0:36 Scherzo repeated in D minor

1:04 Scherzo varied, opens in D minor; trill figures in left hand, then both hands; becomes more chromatic—*diminuendo* into trio

8   1:30   Trio I—marked *doloroso* (sorrowful), slower; smooth descending melodic lines:

Alternates with rhythmic, accented theme from opening scherzo (4-note rhythm); return to conjunct line, more chromatic; *crescendo* into opening tempo, based on 4-note rhythm

9   2:12   Scherzo returns—*fortissimo*, arpeggiated figures increasingly chromatic and slower, leading to second trio

10   2:41   Trio 2—arched *marcato* (stressed) melody—begins in E-flat major:

Lower pitched melody played rubato, then middle range with rolled chord and 4-note rhythm accompaniment; trill and arpeggio figures lead back to scherzo

11   4:12   Scherzo returns in D minor, builds to loud, fiery close with descending arpeggio and two *fortissimo* chords

UNIT VI

Romantic Program Music

20

The Nature of Program Music

"The renewal of music [is] through its inner connection with poetry."
—FRANZ LISZT

Program music is instrumental music endowed with literary or pictorial associations; the nature of these associations is indicated by the title of the piece or by an explanatory note—the "program"—supplied by the composer. Program music is distinguished from *absolute,* or pure, music, which consists of musical patterns that have no literary or pictorial meanings.

This genre was of special importance in a period like the nineteenth century, when musicians became sharply conscious of the connection between their art and the world about them. It helped them to bring music closer to poetry and painting, and to relate their work to the moral and political issues of their time.

Varieties of Program Music

A primary impulse toward program music derived from the opera house, where the overture was a rousing orchestral piece in one movement designed to serve as an introduction to an opera (or a play). Many operatic overtures achieved independent popularity as separate concert pieces. This pointed the way to a new type of overture not associated with an opera: a single-movement concert piece for orchestra, based on a literary idea, such as Tchaikovsky's *Romeo and Juliet.* This type of composition, the *concert overture,* might evoke a land- or seascape, or embody a poetic or patriotic idea.

The concert overture

Incidental music

Another species of program music, *incidental music,* generally consists of an overture and a series of pieces to be performed between the acts of a play and during the important scenes. The most successful pieces of incidental music were generally arranged into suites, a number of which became vastly popular. (We will study one of the most successful works in this category, Mendelssohn's music for Shakespeare's *A Midsummer Night's Dream.*) Incidental music is still important today; its two very significant offshoots are film music and background music for television.

Program symphony

The passion for program music was so strong that it invaded even the hallowed form of absolute music, the symphony. Thus came into being the *program symphony,* a multimovement orchestral work. The best-known examples are three program symphonies of Berlioz—*Symphonie fantastique, Harold in Italy,* and *Romeo and Juliet*—and two of Liszt, the *Faust* and *Dante* Symphonies.

Symphonic poem

Eventually, the need was felt for a large form of orchestral music that would serve the Romantic era. Toward the middle of the century, this need was fulfilled with the creation of the *symphonic poem,* the nineteenth century's one original contribution to the large forms. It was the achievement of Franz Liszt, who first used the term in 1848. His *Les Préludes* is among the best-known examples of this genre.

A symphonic poem is a piece of program music for orchestra, in one movement, which in the course of contrasting sections develops a poetic idea, suggests a scene, or creates a mood. It differs from the concert overture in one important respect: whereas the concert overture generally retains one of the traditional Classical forms, the symphonic poem is much freer in its structure. The symphonic poem (also called *tone poem*) gave composers the flexibility they needed for a big single-movement form. It became the most widely cultivated type of orchestral program music through the second half of the century.

Program music is one of the most striking manifestations of nineteenth-century Romanticism. This new genre emphasized the descriptive element; it impelled composers to try to express specific feelings; and it proclaimed the direct relationship of music to life.

21

Berlioz and the Program Symphony

*"To render my works properly requires a combination of extreme preci-
sion and irresistible verve, a regulated vehemence, a dreamy tenderness,
and an almost morbid melancholy."*

Hector Berlioz described the prevailing characteristics of his music as passionate expression, intense ardor, rhythmic animation, and unexpected turns.
The flamboyance of Victor Hugo's poetry and the dramatic intensity of Eugène
Delacroix's painting found their counterpart in Berlioz's music. He was the
first great exponent of musical Romanticism in France.

Hector Berlioz

His Life

Hector Berlioz (1803–69) was born in France in a small town near Grenoble.
His father, a well-to-do physician, expected the boy to follow in his footsteps,
and at eighteen Hector was sent away to attend medical school in Paris. The
conservatory and the opera, however, intrigued Berlioz much more than the
dissecting room. The following year, the fiery youth made a decision that horrified his upper middle-class family: he gave up medicine for music.

The Romantic revolution was brewing in Paris. Berlioz, along with Victor
Hugo and Delacroix, found himself in the camp of "young France." Having
been cut off by his parents, he gave music lessons, sang in a theater chorus,
and turned to various musical chores. He fell under the spell of Beethoven and
of Shakespeare, to whose plays he was introduced by a visiting English troupe.
Young Berlioz conceived an overwhelming passion for the actress whose
Ophelia and Juliet excited the admiration of the Parisians. In his *Memoirs,*
which read like a Romantic novel, he describes his infatuation with Harriet
Smithson: "I became obsessed by an intense, overpowering sense of sadness.
I could not sleep, I could not work, and I spent my time wandering aimlessly
about Paris and its environs."

Harriet Smithson

In 1830, Berlioz was awarded the coveted Prix de Rome, which gave him
an opportunity to live and work in the Eternal City. That year also saw the composition of what has remained his most celebrated work, the *Symphonie fantastique.* Upon his return from Rome, he commenced a hectic courtship of
Miss Smithson. There were strenuous objections on the part of both their families and violent scenes, during one of which the excitable Hector attempted
suicide. But he was revived, and they were married.

Now that the unattainable ideal had become his wife, his passion cooled. It
was Shakespeare he had loved rather than Harriet, and in time he sought the
ideal elsewhere. All the same, the first years of his marriage were the most
fruitful of his life. By age forty, he had produced most of the works on which
his fame rests.

In the latter part of his life, Berlioz conducted his music in all the capitals of

Europe. But Paris resisted him to the end. His last major work was the opera *Béatrice et Bénédict,* on his own libretto after Shakespeare's *Much Ado About Nothing.* After this effort, the embittered composer wrote no more. He died at sixty-six, tormented to the end. "Some day," wrote Richard Wagner, "a grateful France will raise a proud monument on his tomb." The prophecy has been fulfilled.

His Music

Berlioz was one of the boldest innovators of the nineteenth century. His approach to music was wholly individual, his sense of sound unique. From the start, he had an affinity—where orchestral music was concerned—for the vividly dramatic or pictorial program.

His works exemplify the favorite literary influences of the Romantic period. *The Damnation of Faust* was inspired by Goethe; *Harold in Italy,* a program symphony with viola solo, and *The Corsair,* an overture, are after Byron. Shakespeare is the source for the overture *King Lear* and for the dramatic symphony *Romeo and Juliet.*

Berlioz's most important opera, *The Trojans,* on his own libretto based on the ancient Roman poet Virgil, has been successfully revived in recent years. His sacred vocal works, including the Requiem Mass and the Te Deum, are conceived on a grandiose scale. This love of huge orchestral and choral forces represents only one aspect of Berlioz's personality. No less characteristic is the tenderness that finds expression in the oratorio *The Childhood of Christ,* the fine-spun lyricism that wells up in his songs, and the sensibility that fills his orchestra with French clarity and grace.

It was in the domain of orchestration that Berlioz's genius asserted itself most fully. His daring originality in handling the instruments opened up a new world of Romantic sound. His scores, calling for a larger orchestra than had

Principal Works

Orchestral music, including overtures *Waverley* (1828), *Rob Roy* (1831), *Le roi Lear (King Lear,* 1831); and program symphonies *Symphonie fantastique* (1830), *Harold en Italie (Harold in Italy,* 1834), *Romeo et Juliette* (1839)

Choral music, including a Requiem Mass (1837), Te Deum (Hymn of Praise, 1849), *La damnation de Faust (The Damnation of Faust,* 1846), and the oratorio *L'enfance du Christ (The Childhood of Christ,* 1854)

3 operas, including *Les Troyens (The Trojans,* 1858) and *Béatrice et Bénédict* (1862)

9 solo vocal works with orchestra

Writings on music, including a treatise on orchestration (1843/55)

Francisco Goya *(1746–1828) anticipated the passionate intensity of Berlioz's music in this painting of the* Witches' Sabbath, *c. 1819–23.* (Museo del Prado, Madrid)

ever been used before, abound in novel effects and discoveries that served as models to all who came after him. Indeed, the conductor Felix Weingartner called Berlioz "the creator of the modern orchestra."

SYMPHONIE FANTASTIQUE

Berlioz wrote his best-known program symphony when he was twenty-seven years old, drawing its story from his personal life. "A young musician of morbid sensibility and ardent imagination, in . . . lovesick despair, has poisoned himself with opium. The drug, too weak to kill, plunges him into a heavy sleep accompanied by strange visions. . . . The beloved one herself becomes for him a melody, a recurrent theme that haunts him everywhere."

The recurrent theme, called an *idée fixe* (fixed idea), that symbolizes the beloved—the basic theme of the symphony—is subjected to variation in harmony, rhythm, meter, tempo, dynamics, register, and instrumental color. These transformations take on literary as well as musical significance. Thus the basic motive, recurring according to the literary program, becomes a musical thread unifying five movements that are diverse in mood and character. (See Listening Guide 8 for theme and analysis.) Following is the composer's own description of each movement. | *Idée fixe*

I. "Reveries, Passions." "[The musician] remembers the weariness of soul, the indefinable yearning he knew before meeting his beloved. Then, the volcanic love with which she at once inspired him, his delirious suffering . . . his religious consolation." The Allegro section introduces a soaring melody—the fixed idea. | *First movement*

II. "A Ball." "Amid the tumult and excitement of a brilliant ball he glimpses the loved one again." The dance movement is in ternary, or three-part, form. In the middle section, the fixed idea reappears in waltz time. | *Second movement*

III. "Scene in the Fields." "On a summer evening in the country he hears two shepherds piping. The pastoral duet, the quiet surroundings . . . all unite to fill his heart with a long absent calm. But she appears again. His heart con- | *Third movement*

Fourth movement

tracts. Painful forebodings fill his soul." The composer described his aim in the pastoral movement as a mood "of sorrowful loneliness."

IV. "March to the Scaffold." "He dreams that he has killed his beloved, that he has been condemned to die and is being led to the scaffold. . . . At the very end the fixed idea reappears for an instant, like a last thought of love interrupted by the fall of the axe." This diabolical march movement exemplifies the nineteenth-century love of the fantastic. The theme of the beloved appears at the very end, on the clarinet, and is cut off by a grim *fortissimo* chord.

⟨ *Fifth movement* ⟩

• very important

V. "Dream of a Witches' Sabbath." "He sees himself at a witches' sabbath surrounded by a host of fearsome specters who have gathered for his funeral. Unearthly sounds, groans, shrieks of laughter. The melody of his beloved is heard, but it has lost its noble and reserved character. It has become a vulgar tune, trivial and grotesque. It is she who comes to the infernal orgy. A howl of joy greets her arrival. She joins the diabolical dance. Bells toll for the dead. A burlesque of the *Dies Irae*. Dance of the witches. The dance and the *Dies Irae* combined."

This final movement opens with a Larghetto (not quite as slow as largo). Berlioz here exploits an infernal spirit that nourished a century of satanic operas, ballets, and symphonic poems. The mood is heightened with the introduction of the traditional religious chant *Dies irae* (Day of Wrath) from the ancient Mass for the Dead (Requiem), heard in the bassoons and tubas (originally written for *ophicleide*, a nineteenth-century brass instrument that is now obsolete). The movement reaches its climax when this well-known melody, now in shorter note values, is combined with the Witches' Dance.

Listening Guide 8

C/S: 5A/2   C/S: 5/ 8 - 12
Sh: 2B/2   Sh: 2/ 37 - 41

BERLIOZ: *Symphonie fantastique,* Fifth Movement   (9:46)

Date of work: 1830

Genre: Program symphony, 5 movements

Program: A lovesick artist in an opium trance is haunted by a vision of his beloved, which becomes an *idée fixe* (fixed idea)

I. "Reveries, Passions"
Largo, Allegro agitato e appassionato assai (lively, agitated, and very impassioned); introduces the main theme, the fixed idea:

II. "A Ball"
Valse, Allegro non troppo (waltz, not too fast); **A-B-A** form, triple-meter dance

III. "Scene in the Fields"
Adagio; **A-B-A** form, 6/8 meter

IV. "March to the Scaffold"
Allegretto non troppo; duple-meter march, in minor mode

V. "Dream of a Witches' Sabbath"

8	0:00	Larghetto—very soft muted strings evoke infernal atmosphere; chromatic scales in strings, low brass, and high woodwinds depict "unearthly sounds, groans, shrieks of laughter"
	1:17	Allegro—fixed idea in high clarinet in transformed version with trills and grace notes ("a vulgar tune, trivial and grotesque"):

Orchestral *fortissimo* signals "howl of joy" at the beloved's arrival.

9	1:21	Fixed idea continues in woodwinds, with bassoons in grotesque accompanying figure
	2:53	"Bells toll for the dead"

Dance tune forecast by its opening motive in violas, followed by foreboding sounds in low brass:

10	3:22	Chant tune *Dies irae* sounded in bassoons and tubas, first slow, then twice as fast in brass:
	3:51	"Burlesque of the *Dies irae*" in strings and woodwinds in altered rhythm; alternates with brass and bells
11	5:15	"Dance of the Witches" ("Ronde du Sabbat")—begins in low strings, builds in fugal setting:

Dance dies out, followed by strange sounds in low strings with fragment of *Dies irae* tune; builds to *fortissimo*

12	8:00	"The dance and the *Dies irae* combined"; strings play dance tune with wood of bows alternating with loud brass statements of *Dies irae;* builds to final cadence

There is a grandeur of line and gesture about the music of Berlioz, an abundance of vitality and invention. He is one of the major prophets of the Romantic era.

22

The Rise of Musical Nationalism

"I grew up in a quiet spot and was saturated from earliest childhood with the wonderful beauty of Russian popular song. I am therefore passionately devoted to every expression of the Russian spirit. In short, I am a Russian through and through!"—PETER ILYICH TCHAIKOVSKY

In nineteenth-century Europe, political conditions encouraged the growth of nationalism to such a degree that it became a decisive force within the Romantic movement. National tensions on the Continent—the pride of the conquering nations and the struggle for freedom of the suppressed ones—gave rise to strong emotions that inspired the works of many creative artists.

The Romantic composers expressed their nationalism in a number of ways. Some based their music on the songs and dances of their people: Chopin in his mazurkas, Liszt in his *Hungarian Rhapsodies,* Dvořák in the *Slavonic Dances.* A number wrote dramatic works based on folklore or the life of the peasantry, such as the German folk opera *Der Freischütz* by Carl Maria von Weber and the Russian fairy-tale operas and ballets of Tchaikovsky and Rimsky-Korsakov. Others wrote symphonic poems and operas celebrating the exploits of a national hero, a historic event, or the scenic beauty of their country. Tchaikovsky's *1812 Overture* and Smetana's *The Moldau* exemplify this trend. Nor were the political implications of musical nationalism lost upon the authorities. Many of Verdi's operas had to be altered again and again to suit the Austrian censor. During the Second World War, the Nazis forbade the playing of Smetana's descriptive symphonic poems in Prague and Chopin's polonaises in Warsaw because of the powerful symbolism behind these works. By associating music with the love of homeland, nationalism enabled composers to give expression to the hopes and dreams of millions of people. The Romantic movement is unthinkable without it.

Russian national school

The foundation for a Russian national school was laid by Mikhail Ivanovich Glinka (1804–57). His dream of a Russian music was taken over by a group of young musicians who were called "The Mighty Five" (or "The Mighty Handful"). Their leader was Mily Balakirev (1837–1910), a self-taught composer who persuaded his four disciples—Alexander Borodin (1833–87), César Cui (1835–1918), Nikolai Rimsky-Korsakov (1844–1908), and Modest Musorgsky (1839–81)—that they would have to free themselves from the influence of German symphony, Italian opera, and French ballet if they wanted to express the Russian soul. Their colleague Peter Ilyich Tchaikovsky (1840–93) was more receptive to European influences. Of all these musicians, Musorgsky and Tchaikovsky are now recognized as Russia's greatest composers.

Modest Musorgsky: His Life and Music

"The artist believes in the future because he lives in it."

Modest Musorgsky

Musorgsky was born in the town of Karevo in the province of Pskov, the son of a wealthy landowner. As a young boy, he learned Russian folk tales from his nurse and studied piano with his mother. In accordance with the family tradition, he prepared for a military career and was commissioned an officer in a fashionable regiment of Guards. At eighteen, he met Balakirev, with whom he studied Beethoven symphonies, and became one of "The Mighty Five."

Early years

As his talents developed, the young officer found his duties tiresome and decided to withdraw from the military so that he could devote his life to music. He resigned his commission when he was twenty-two. At this point, history intervened. The emancipation of the serfs in 1861 proved disastrous to the smaller landowners. Instead of being free to devote himself to his art, the young aristocrat was obliged to seek employment. He established himself in St. Petersburg, where a post in the Ministry of Transport gave him a modest living. Evenings were devoted to musical sessions with his four comrades and his first attempts at composition.

From the start, Musorgsky revealed himself as one who sought a new kind of realism in art: "To trace the finest traits in man's nature—that is the mission of the artist!" Musorgsky at twenty-nine was ready for the great task of his life. His opera *Boris Godunov* revolved around the fascinating figure of the czar (Boris) who had murdered the rightful heir to the throne and was then tormented by guilt. Musorgsky fashioned the libretto himself after the drama by the national poet Alexander Pushkin (1799–1837). When *Boris* was submitted to the Imperial Opera, it was rejected on the ground that it lacked a leading woman's part, whereupon Musorgsky revised the work and added the role of Marina. All obstacles having been overcome, *Boris* was presented in 1874. The critics damned it, but the opera was a great success with the public. Its political implications were not lost on the younger generation, then seething with unrest under the reactionary czarist regime. The choruses depicting the revolt against Czar Boris were soon heard on the streets of St. Petersburg. Despite its success, or because of it, the opera was regarded with suspicion by the official censor, and it was soon dropped from the company's repertory.

Boris Godunov

The withdrawal of *Boris* ushered in a bitter period of Musorgsky's life. He distanced himself from his colleagues of the "Five"; he felt they had sold out for success. He remained alone, a rebel to the end. Moods of exuberant belief in himself alternated with periods of depression. Increasingly his life lost its direction and followed the erratic course of the alcoholic.

To those years of despair belong his greatest songs, the cycles *Sunless* and the *Songs and Dances of Death*. He worked on his other opera, *Khovanshchina,* but left it unfinished. In the last year of his life, when his friends had abandoned all hope of saving him, his fighting spirit enabled him to write, "My motto remains unchanged. 'Boldly on! Forward to new shores! One must give oneself wholly to mankind'!"

Final years

Principal Works

Operas, including *Boris Godunov* (staged 1874), *Khovanshchina* (1880; completed by Rimsky-Korsakov), and *Sorochintsy Fair* (1880; completed by Lyadov and others)

Orchestral music, including a symphonic poem, *Night on Bald Mountain* (*St. John's Night on the Bare Mountain,* 1867)

Piano music, including *Pictures at an Exhibition* (1874; orchestrated by Ravel, 1922)

Choral music and songs, including 3 song cycles: *The Nursery* (1870), *Sunless* (1874), and *Songs and Dances of Death* (1877)

While attending a musical evening, Musorgsky collapsed and was hospitalized, suffering from delirium tremens. His friends rallied to his side, comforting the tragic figure whose image peers out at us in the famous portrait by I. E. Repin, painted at the composer's bedside (see p. 111).

Program music, one of the main currents in the Romantic period, allows music to move closer to poetry and painting. A striking example of this link is Musorgsky's most important instrumental work, *Pictures at an Exhibition,* inspired by an art exhibition.

When composers are immersed in the folk songs of their respective countries, melodies—even if original—often take on a folklike quality. This was especially true of Musorgsky. Whether in *Boris, Pictures at an Exhibition,* or other works, his melodies, while pure Musorgsky, are at the same time completely Russian. He was only twenty when he wrote to his mentor Balakirev, "You know, I have been a cosmopolitan, but now I have experienced a sort of rebirth: I have been brought close to everything Russian."

Many of Musorgsky's works, left unfinished at his death, were completed and edited by his friend Rimsky-Korsakov, among them *Boris Godunov* and the symphonic poem *Night on Bald Mountain.* Although *Boris* conquered the world in Rimsky-Korsakov's version, in recent years the desire grew to hear the opera exactly as Musorgsky wrote it. The original version was finally produced in 1974 at New York's Metropolitan Opera House, a much more somber masterpiece than Rimsky's; it met with enormous success.

Musorgsky left an autobiographical sketch that aptly summarizes his art: "Musorgsky cannot be classed with any existing group of musicians, either by the character of his compositions or his musical views. The formula of his artistic credo may be explained by his view of the function of art: art is a means of communicating with people, not an aim in itself. This guiding principle has defined the whole of his creative activity."

PICTURES AT AN EXHIBITION

Pictures at an Exhibition is a suite of ten short pieces describing an exhibition held in Moscow in 1874 of paintings and drawings by Musorgsky's friend Victor Hartmann. Written for piano solo, the work remains a favorite with

One of the pictures that inspired Musorgsky's Pictures at an Exhibition: **Victor Hartmann's** *drawing for an architectural project,* The Great Gate of Kiev.

concert pianists. But it achieved even wider popularity when the French composer Maurice Ravel, who greatly admired Musorgsky, arranged it for orchestra in 1922. Ravel was one of the great orchestrators of all time, and gave Musorgsky's piece all the rich colors of the virtuoso orchestra.

We will study three movements from the orchestral version. *Promenade,* the opening piece, is said to represent the heavy-set composer walking from one picture to the next at the exhibition. It has a folklike melody, marked *nel modo russico* (in the Russian style) by the composer. The tune, outlining a pentatonic (five-note) scale and set in changing meter, is introduced by solo trumpet and answered by the brass section in Ravel's arrangement. (See Listening Guide 9 for details.)

The middle movements describe a colorful array of subjects taken from Hartmann's artworks: a gnome-like nutcracker, portrayed with disjunct leaps and dissonant harmonies; a troubadour singing in front of a Medieval castle, whose lyrical tune is sounded by the saxophone; children playing in the Tuileries Garden in Paris, set as a scherzo; a whimsical ballet of chicks dancing in their shells; portraits of two Jews, who converse in an animated musical dialogue; the bustling marketplace in the French city of Limoges, complete with shrieks and quarrels; and the catacombs of Paris, whose somber atmosphere is evoked through shifting harmonies and dissonance. These diverse miniatures are unified by recurring statements of the *Promenade* theme.

The ninth movement, *The Hut on Fowl's Legs (Baba-Yaga),* is based on Hartmann's design for a clock shaped like the hut of Baba-Yaga, the witch of Russian fairy tales who grinds up children in her mortar, in which she flies through the woods. Musorgsky created an impetuous scherzo and trio **(A-B-A)** in which the outer sections suggest Baba-Yaga's wild ride, punctuated by clocklike rhythms; the middle part has a properly eerie atmosphere.

The closing movement of the suite is *The Great Gate of Kiev.* This was based on Hartmann's design for a monumental gate in the ancient city of Kiev, a massive stone structure that was never built. Musorgsky's tone poem, based on an old hymn, matches the splendor of the artist's gate. (See illustration on p. 113.) It is a majestic rondo that opens with a processional melody soon adorned with Russian church bells. Kiev, an important center for early Russian church music, had special meaning for anyone as devoted to the culture of Old Russia as was Musorgsky.

Listening Guide 9

	C/S: 6B/1–2		C/S: 6/ 23 – 33
	Sh: 2B/3		Sh: 2/ 42 – 48

MUSORGSKY: *Pictures at an Exhibition,* Three Movements   (10:36)

Date of work: 1874

Genre: Suite

Medium: Solo piano; orchestrated by Maurice Ravel in 1922

Basis: Paintings and drawings by artist Victor Hartmann

Movements of the suite:

Promenade	5. *Ballet of the Chicks in Their Shells*
1. *Gnomus*	6. *Two Jews, One Rich, the Other Poor*
Promenade	Promenade
2. *The Old Castle*	7. *The Marketplace at Limoges*
Promenade	8. *Catacombs*
3. *Tuileries*	9. *The Hut on Fowl's Legs*
4. *Bydlo*	10. *The Great Gate of Kiev*
Promenade	

(Shorter recordings begin with movement 10.)

Promenade: Allegro giusto, nel modo russico (appropriately fast, in the Russian style); changing meter   (1:48)

23	0:00	Pentatonic *Promenade* theme in solo trumpet, answered by brass section; alternating 5/4 and 6/4 meter:

	0:32	Strings enter with theme, then alternate with woodwinds
	1:26	Brass section restates theme, followed by full orchestra to end

---

9. *The Hut on Fowl's Legs:* Allegro con brio, feroce (fast with vigor, fiercely); scherzo and trio (A-B-A), duple meter   (3:20)

24	0:00	A section, scherzo—disjunct and rhythmic; theme grows from 2-note motive in strings and woodwinds, loud and dissonant:

		Forceful brass entry; solo muted trumpet, leads to trio
25	1:09	**B section, trio**—mysterious mood, wavering woodwind line interrupted by 2-note motive in winds and plucked strings; 2-note motive leads back to scherzo
26	2:18	**A section, scherzo**—repeat of opening theme, followed by brass; sweeping upward scales lead directly to next movement

10. *The Great Gate of Kiev:* Allegro alla breve, Maestoso con grandezza (majestically, with grandeur); rondo form, quadruple meter (5:28)

27	0:00	**A**—brass in loud statement, hymnlike, with timpani; repeated with full orchestra:
28	1:03	**B**—woodwinds, soft and modulatory
29	1:37	**A**—brass with opening theme accompanied by sweeping scales in strings, stops abruptly
30	2:12	**B**—return of soft woodwind theme
31	2:47	**C**—accented chords with chimes, wavering string line
32	3:18	**D**—*Promenade* theme in quadruple meter in trumpets and bells (from first movement), accompanied by sweeping string lines:
33	3:53	**A**—statement of opening theme in augmentation (slower) in full orchestra:
	4:16	Wavering strings build to alternation of loud chords and fragments of main theme
	4:56	Final statement—loud and majestic, with percussion (gong and cymbals)

Other Nationalists

In addition to the Russian school, other national groups arose who gave voice to their homelands. In central Europe, Bedřich Smetana (1824–84) and Antonín Dvořák (1841–1904) stand as the founders of the Czech school. Their art was rooted in the songs and dances of their native Bohemia. Smetana's

Bedřich Smetana

Cultural Perspective 3

Folk Tales Set to Music

Each culture's value system is at the heart of its folklore: children learn right from wrong and are prepared for adulthood through folk tales, which are transmitted, like folk music, through oral tradition. We have seen that in *Pictures at an Exhibition,* Musorgsky drew on the folk material of his native land in his portrayal of the witch Baba-Yaga, who, according to Russian legend, lured small children to her hut in the woods, where she ate them and ground their bones in her giant mortar. An equally frightening episode occurs in the famous tale of "Hansel and Gretel," collected by Jakob and Wilhelm Grimm, where the witch's hut was a gingerbread house to which children were attracted and fattened up for her to eat. This German legend formed the basis of an opera by the nineteenth-century composer Engelbert Humperdinck (whose name the contemporary pop singer adopted) and was later included as one of a pastiche of tales told in the popular Stephen Sondheim musical *Into the Woods* (1988).

In addition to Musorgsky, other Russian composers have turned to their native folk traditions for inspiration: these include Nicolai Rimsky-Korsakov, who collected folk songs and wrote several operas based on popular Russian legends, among them *The Golden Cockerel* (1906–7); the early twentieth-century master Igor Stravinsky, who brought life to the Russian fable of *The Firebird* in an exquisite ballet (1910); and his contemporary Sergei Prokofiev, who immortalized the well-known story of *Peter and the Wolf* in a symphonic fairy tale of the same name (1936).

Folklore often transcends national boundaries. The French tales "Sleeping Beauty" and "Cinderella" (both from the 1697 collection of Charles Perrault) were set as Russian ballets (Tchaikovsky's *Sleeping Beauty* in 1890 and Prokofiev's *Cinderella* in 1945); and a fanciful story by the German writer E. T. A. Hoffmann, in an expanded version by French writer Alexandre Dumas, was the basis for Tchaikovsky's most famous ballet, *The Nutcracker* (1892), which we will study in a later chapter.

The theater has traditionally offered a variety of forms through which to retell these stories set as operas, ballets, and musicals.

Bernadette Peters as the witch and Pamela Winslow as Rapunzel in the 1987 Broadway production of Stephen Sondheim's musical Into the Woods. *(© Martha Swope)*

Today, Perrault's "Sleeping Beauty," the Grimms' "Beauty and the Beast," Hans Christian Andersen's "The Little Mermaid," and the Arabian folk tale of "Aladdin" from *The Thousand and One Nights* are often learned from Disney animated films, where their images and songs keep these cultural expressions alive for younger generations.

Suggested Listening:

Tchaikovsky: *Sleeping Beauty* or *The Nutcracker*
Prokofiev: *Peter and the Wolf*
Sondheim: *Into the Woods*

cycle of six symphonic poems, entitled *My Country,* sounds the beauty of Bohemia's countryside and the pomp and pageantry of her legends. Best-known of the series is *The Moldau,* his finest achievement in the field of orchestral music. We will consider Dvořák, who drew inspiration not only from his native land but from America, in a later chapter.

Edvard Grieg

To the international music public, Edvard Grieg (1843–1907) came to represent "the voice of Norway." The nationalist movement of which his music was an expression had a stirring political background. Norway's struggle for independence from Sweden came to a head during the last quarter of the nineteenth century. This cause, to which Grieg was devoted with all his heart, was successful not long before his final illness. His songs and piano pieces attained enormous popularity during his lifetime, and are still current. To the concert public he is best-known for his Piano Concerto and the incidental music for *Peer Gynt.*

Jean Sibelius

As in the case of Smetana and Grieg, the career of Jean Sibelius (1865–1957) unfolded against a struggle for national independence. In the final decades of the nineteenth century, Finland tried to free itself from the yoke of czarist Russia. Out of this ferment flowered the art of Sibelius, which announced to the world that his country had come of age musically. During the 1890s, he produced a series of symphonic poems that captured the spirit of Finnish legends and myths. Best-known of these is *Finlandia* (1899), which occupies the same position in Finland as *The Moldau* does in Czechoslovakia.

Late in the century, musical nationalism came to England in the works of Edward Elgar (1857–1934) and Frederick Delius (1862–1934). Spain produced three important nationalists in Isaac Albéniz (1860–1909), Enrique Granados (1867–1916), and Manuel de Falla (1876–1946). America's musical nationalism, relatively late in flowering, will be discussed in later chapters.

UNIT VII

Absolute Forms in the Nineteenth Century

23

The Romantic Symphony

"A great symphony is a man-made Mississippi down which we irresistibly flow from the instant of our leave-taking to a long foreseen destination."—AARON COPLAND

Earlier we noted that in contrast to program music, absolute music has no non-musical associations provided by the composer, whether of story, scene, or mood. Here the musical ideas are organized in such a way that without any aid from external images, they give the listener a satisfying sense of order and continuity. The larger forms of absolute music range from a sonata for solo instrument to the full-scale symphony.

The Character of the Symphony

A symphony is a large work for orchestra in several parts or movements. (You may remember that a movement is a complete, self-contained part within a larger work.) The movements are contrasted in character, mood, and tempo. Taken together, they form a structural as well as musical entity.

During the Classical period, from around 1750 to 1825, the symphony established itself as the most exalted form of absolute orchestral music. The three Viennese masters at the time—Haydn, Mozart, and Beethoven—carried it to its highest level of significance and formal beauty. They handed down to the composers of the Romantic era a flexible art form that could be adapted to meet the emotional needs of the new age.

In the course of its development, the symphony gained greater weight and importance. By now, the orchestra had vastly increased in size, as had the symphony in length. The nineteenth-century symphonists were not as prolific as their predecessors had been. Instead, their works grew steadily longer and more expansive. Mendelssohn, Robert Schumann, Brahms, and Tchaikovsky each wrote fewer than seven symphonies. All of these were in the domain of absolute music, while Liszt and Berlioz, as we have observed, cultivated the program symphony.

We will get a detailed discussion of symphonic structure in Chapter 37. It will suffice for the present to establish the four-movement form that was standard at the turn of the nineteenth century.

The first movement is generally the most dramatic of the cycle. It is written in what is known as *sonata-allegro* (because the tempo of this movement is almost always Allegro), or first-movement, form. This is a three-part structure: the exposition, or statement; the development; and the recapitulation, or restatement. Sometimes a slow introduction leads into the movement proper. The exposition usually presents two contrasting themes—one strongly rhythmic, one lyrical. There is a transition, or bridge, that leads from the first theme (or theme group) to the second, usually modulating to another key. A codetta completes the exposition. The development is marked by a tremendous increase in tension. Here the composer may break the theme into fragments, recombining them in fresh patterns and revealing them in a new light. In this way, the possibilities of the materials for growth and development are explored. In the recapitulation, we hear again the themes of the exposition, more or less in their original guise but with a wealth of new meaning that they have taken on in the course of the movement. There follows the coda, whose function is to round off the action and to bring the movement to a close.

First movement

The second movement, in contrast with the first, is generally lyrical, set in a slow tempo. It may, however, vary in mood from whimsical, even playful, to tragic and passionate. The tempo marking in most cases is Andante, Adagio, or Largo. This movement may be in three-part (**A-B-A**) or theme and variations form. Other possibilities are indicated in later chapters.

Second movement

Third in the cycle, in the symphonies of the Romantic period, is the strongly rhythmic and excited scherzo, with overtones of humor, surprise, whimsy, or folk dance. "Scherzo" is the Italian work for "jest," but the mood may range from elfin lightness to demonic energy. The tempo marking indicates a lively pace—Allegro molto, Vivace, or the like, in a triple meter. The form is usually a large **A-B-A;** the middle section, known as the trio, is of a somewhat quieter nature. In some symphonies, the scherzo falls second in the cycle.

Third movement

The fourth and last movement of the cycle is of a dimension and character designed to balance the first. The work may draw to a close on a note of triumph or pathos. Frequently, this movement is a spirited Allegro in sonata-allegro form. Some composers experimented with fourth-movement forms: in his Fourth Symphony, for example, Brahms turns to a noble Baroque *passacaglia* (see p. 122) for its closing movement, while the finale of Mendelssohn's Italian Symphony is based on a popular "jumping" dance known as a saltarello. The chart on p. 121 reviews the standard form of the symphony.

Fourth movement

What we have seen here is the barest outline of symphonic form; we will not get a complete picture until after we have heard several representative works. What is important to understand at this point is that the symphony's several movements are concerned with the presentation of abstract musical ideas. These ideas unfold in such a way as to give each movement a quality of logical continuity. The essence of nineteenth-century symphonic style is dramatic contrast and development. It arouses emotion in the listener, but emotion not directed toward any specific image.

Themes and motives, discussed in Chapter 5, figure prominently in any serious discussion of a major musical form. A theme may be a fully rounded melody, or it may be a compact melodic-harmonic-rhythmic kernel that is capable of further growth. It may also be broken down into its constituent fragments, or motives. In the unfolding of a symphony, the theme and its motives might undergo continual development, in the course of which their capacity for growth is explored.

The nineteenth-century symphony holds a place of honor in the output of the era. It retains its hold on the public, and remains one of the most striking manifestations of the spirit of musical Romanticism.

Brahms's Fourth Symphony

Johannes Brahms wrote a total of four symphonies, the first of which was not attempted until he was past forty and at the height of his career. He was fond of saying that it was no laughing matter to compose a symphony after Beethoven. "You have no idea," he told a friend, "how the likes of us feel when we hear the tramp of a giant like him behind us."

The Fourth Symphony, written in 1885, is notable for its somber character and lyrical themes. The first movement, marked Allegro non troppo (not too fast), opens with a long-breathed, heartfelt melody that is truly Brahmsian. Wide leaps give it a distinctive quality and a feeling of might. Second is an Andante moderato (moderately slow) that presents one of Brahms's loveliest tunes, in the mood of gentle resignation that characterizes the master's mature style. The third movement, a scherzo marked Allegro giocoso (fast and playful), is full of high spirits and boundless vigor.

For the last movement of his final symphony, Brahms chose a form that flourished in the Baroque era (1600–1750), the passacaglia (see Listening Guide 10). His choice of an archaic form indicates his strong identification with the past. A *passacaglia* is a composition in a moderately slow triple meter based on a short melody that is repeated over and over again as the basis for continuous variation in the other voices. In the passacaglias of earlier eras, this melody was usually in the bass part while the other voices moved freely about it. Brahms departs from this procedure by having the wind instruments announce the eight-measure theme above the harmonies that accompany it. He then spreads the theme throughout the musical texture so that it sometimes appears in the upper register, other times in the lower register or hidden

Standard Symphony Form

Multimovement work for orchestra
4-movement standard: fast–slow–moderate dance–fast

I. First movement
    Allegro, sonata-allegro form
        Slow introduction (optional)
        Exposition
            Theme 1, rhythmic, home key
            Theme 2, lyrical, contrasting key
            Codetta or closing theme, in contrasting key
        Development—fragmentation or expansion of themes,
           free modulation
        Recapitulation (Restatement)
            Theme 1, home key
            Theme 2, home key
            Coda, affirms home key

II. Second movement
    Slow, lyrical
    Sonata-allegro form, **A-B-A,** or theme and variations

III. Third movement
    Triple meter, dance movement (minuet or scherzo), **A-B-A**;
        sectional, with repeats

IV. Fourth movement
    Allegro or Presto, shorter and lighter than first movement,
        various forms possible

among the middle voices, but always present in one guise or another. Using a comparatively simple tune as a point of departure, Brahms constructs a monumental movement, marked Allegro energico e passionato (an energetic and impassioned Allegro). The constant repetition of the basic melody supplies the element of unity, while the orchestral voices keep changing around it in a series of thirty variations on the tune, followed by a coda. The movement builds with steadily mounting tension that is maintained all the way to the powerful end. The ear is continually challenged by shifting moods, timbres, and lines that bespeak the technical mastery and creative invention of this great master.

Listening Guide 10

BRAHMS: Symphony No. 4 in E minor, Fourth Movement   (10:31)

Date of work: 1885
Movements:

    I. Allegro non troppo; sonata form
   II. Andante moderato
  III. Allegro giocoso (scherzo character)
  IV. Allegro energico e passionato; passacaglia form

FOURTH MOVEMENT: Allegro energico e passionato; 3/4 meter, E minor
Form: Passacaglia (theme with 30 variations), overall **A-B-A** form
    A: minor, fast (theme, variations 1–11)
    B: major, slower (variations 12–15)
    A: tempo I (variations 16–30, coda)

Theme: 8 measures, melody with accompanying chords, ascending scale, then octave leap, returning to starting note:

	Form	Variation	Description
12 0:00	**A**	Theme	Melody with simple chords in winds, adds timpani roll
0:15		1	Timpani rolls, low brass and pizzicato strings answer, *decrescendo* at end
0:31		2	Flowing woodwind melody, theme in low strings
0:46		3	Short, loud, marked notes in strings and winds
1:01		4	Wide-ranging violin melody, chords in low strings
1:17		5	Flowing string melody, theme in double basses
1:32		6	Style similar to variation 5
1:48		7	Dotted, irregular rhythms, loud
2:04		8	Faster motion in violins; first loud, then softer
2:20		9	Style similar to variation 8
2:35		10	Gentle chords alternating between strings and woodwinds; motion slows down
2:53		11	Lilting triplets in strings and woodwinds; descending flute melody leads to new section
13 3:14	**B**	12	Expressive flute solo with string accompaniment; slower tempo
3:56		13	Change to E major; motive exchanged between woodwinds with string accompaniment
4:37		14	Major key; slow chords in low brass, answered by rippling strings
5:17		15	Major key; slow chords in woodwinds and brass; rippling strings; descending flute leads back to
14 6:03	**A** Tempo I	16	Original theme in E minor in brass and woodwinds, answered by strings, *forte*
6:16		17	Tremolos in strings; woodwinds with 2-note motive
6:27		18	French horns, over string tremolos
6:40		19	Staccato melody exchanged between strings and woodwinds

	Variation	Description
6:52	20	Loud, marked triplets in strings and French horns
7:04	21	Rising string glissandos, against trombones
7:18	22	Light, airy, staccato triplets in strings
7:30	23	Loud French horn entry with theme; string accompaniment
7:44	24	Loud brass statement of theme, punctuated by strings
7:58	25	String tremolo melody, punctuated by brass
8:11	26	French horn and woodwind melody; rippling string figure
8:25	27	Slow chords in woodwinds; rippling string figure
8:39	28	Melody in woodwinds against flowing string accompaniment
8:53	29	Melody in woodwinds against pizzicato strings
9:07	30	Loud, syncopated exchange between strings and woodwinds
9:21	Coda	Motion slows; timpani roll; marking of Più Allegro (faster) with original theme in brass and woodwinds; exchange of chords between brass

24

Dvořák as a Symphonist

*"In the Negro melodies of America I discover all that is needed for a great
and noble school of music. These beautiful and varied themes are the
product of the soil. They are American. They are the folk songs of
America, and your composers must turn to them."*

Antonín Dvořák is one of numerous late-Romantic composers who found inspiration in the songs and dances of their native land. He stands alongside Bedřich Smetana as a founder of the Czech national school.

His Life

Antonín Dvořák

Antonín Dvořák (1841–1904) was born in Bohemia (now part of the Czech Republic) and grew up in a village near Prague, where his father kept an inn. For a time, poverty threatened to rule out a musical career. However, the boy managed to get to Prague when he was sixteen. There he mastered his craft and played the viola in the Czech National Theater, under the baton of Smetana. Inspired by the older master, Dvořák wrote his earliest works during this period. These included several symphonies and a song cycle dedicated to one of his students, Anna Cermakova, whom he eventually married.

In 1874, the Austrian government awarded him a stipend, which allowed him to resign his orchestra post and devote himself to composing. He was much encouraged by Brahms, who helped the younger composer find a publisher for his works. By the time he was forty, Dvořák had left behind the financial cares that had plagued his early career. As professor of composition at the Conservatory of Prague, he was able to exert an important influence on the musical life of his country.

The spontaneity and melodious character of his music assured its popularity. By the last decade of the century, Dvořák was known throughout Europe and the United States. In 1891, Jeanette Thurber, who ran the National Conservatory of Music in New York City, invited him to become its director. He received $15,000 a year (a fabulous sum in those days), as compared with the annual $600 he earned in Prague. His stay in the United States was eminently fruitful. He produced what has remained his most successful symphony, *From the New World,* a number of chamber music works, including the *American* Quartet, and the highly lyrical Cello Concerto. Mrs. Thurber wanted him to write an opera on *The Song of Hiawatha;* but although Dvořák already knew and admired Longfellow's poem, the project never materialized. His operas—fourteen in all—were based on European themes.

American visit

Dvořák spent a summer at the Czech colony in Spillville, Iowa, in an atmosphere that suited his simple tastes. Although every effort was made to persuade him to continue at the conservatory, his homesickness overrode all other considerations. After three years, he returned to his beloved Bohemia and spent his remaining years in Prague, in the happy circle of his wife and children, students and friends. He died in his sixty-third year, revered as a national artist throughout his native land.

His Music

Dvořák was a natural musician with a great gift for melody. His style reveals the strong influence of native folk melodies, coupled with a solid craftsmanship that enabled him to shape musical ideas into large forms notable for their clarity.

Dvořák's large output embraced all genres of music. His operas were highly influenced by Smetana, and they have achieved a preeminence as the most strongly national of his country. His symphonies reflect his predeliction for traditional structural procedures, and the *Slavonic Dances* and *Rhapsodies* project a colorful orchestral palette. The Cello Concerto is a crowning achievement in that instrument's repertory. Landmarks among his chamber works include the *Dumky* Piano Trio and the *American* Quartet, so-called for its use of a pentatonic (five-note) scale often associated with Native American music. The time had come for the international language of German Classicism to be enriched by a variety of national styles: Polish, Hungarian, Russian, Czech, and Norwegian. Dvořák was a leader in this historic process.

Having arrived in the United States with an established reputation as a nationalist composer, Dvořák tried to influence his American pupils toward their native heritage. One of his students was Henry T. Burleigh, an African-American baritone and arranger of spirituals. The melodies Dvořák heard from Burleigh appealed to the folk poet in him, and strengthened his convic-

Principal Works

Orchestral music, including 9 symphonies (No. 9, *From the New World,* 1893); symphonic poems; other symphonic works, including *Slavonic Rhapsodies* (1878) and *Slavonic Dances* (orchestrated 1886)

Concertos, including 1 cello concerto (1895)

14 operas, including *Rusalka* (1901) and *Armida* (1904); other incidental music

Choral music, including a cantata (*The Spectre's Bride,* 1884) and a Requiem (1890); masses; oratorio; other sacred choral music, including Stabat mater (1877); part songs and choral arrangements of Czech folk songs

Chamber music, including 14 string quartets (*American,* 1893), 3 string quintets, 6 piano trios (*Dumky,* 1891), 2 piano quartets, and duo sonatas

Keyboard music, including dances and character pieces; music for 2 pianos (*Slavonic Dances,* 1878); organ music

tion that American composers would find their true path only when they had thrown off the influence of Europe and sought their inspiration in the Native American, African-American, and traditional folk songs of their own country. This was the doctrine he taught, and it helped prepare the way for the rich harvest of American works by composers of the next generations.

THE *NEW WORLD* SYMPHONY

Dvořák wrote his Symphony No. 9, subtitled *From the New World,* during his stay in the United States, and it received its first performance in New York in 1893. Czech and American elements intermingle freely in this work. The whole symphony may be seen as a descriptive landscape, evoking the loneliness and openness of the American prairie as well as the composer's longing for his homeland. It is set in a standard four-movement framework, the middle movements of which can be directly linked to the influence of Longfellow's *Song of Hiawatha.* The clearest association is in the third movement, a scherzo, which portrays *Hiawatha's Wedding Feast,* beginning with the *Dance of the Pa-Puk-Keewis,* and a trio that depicts the group of natives who are turned into birds.

We will study the slow movement, a Largo, which the composer associated with a section of the narrative poem called *Hiawatha's Wooing* (see Listening Guide 11). Set in a ternary (**A-B-A**) form, the movement's outer sections loosely portray the travel homeward of Hiawatha and Minnehaha; the mournful middle section, set in a minor key, is supposed to represent Minnehaha's death. The deeply felt English-horn tune that opens the Largo was made famous when sung as a kind of spiritual, set to the words "Goin' Home."

Although Dvořák himself said of the symphony that "the influence of America can be felt to anyone who has 'a nose,'" the listener unacquainted with the composer's intention is as likely to associate this tune with a typically Czech song of longing.

Listening Guide 11

 C/S: 6B/6 C/S: 6/ 43 – 45

DVOŘÁK: Symphony No. 9 in E minor, *From the New World*, Second Movement

(12:07)

Date of work: 1893

Basis: Loosely connected to Longfellow's *Song of Hiawatha*

Movements:

    I. Adagio, Allegro molto; duple meter, E minor
   II. Largo; 4/4 meter, D-flat major
  III. Molto vivace (scherzo and trio, very lively); 3/4 meter, E minor
  IV. Allegro con fuoco (fast, with fire); 4/4 meter, E minor

SECOND MOVEMENT: Largo; A-B-A form, 4/4 meter, D-flat major

A SECTION

| 43 | 0:00 | Opens with slow, chromatic chords in brass |
| | 0:38 | Theme 1—songful and pensive, English horn solo: |

| | 2:07 | Brass and woodwind chords introduce string variation of first theme, followed by English horn, then French horns |

B SECTION (un poco più mosso, moving a little more)

| 44 | 4:26 | New theme—wavering line in flutes and oboes, C-sharp minor |
| | 5:02 | Sustained woodwind theme over plucked "walking" bass line, then heard in strings: |

| | 8:04 | More animated, staccato woodwinds lead to orchestral climax; theme from first movement is heard |

A SECTION (Tempo I)

| 45 | 8:56 | Theme 1 returns—English horn answered by strings, D-flat major, broken up by fermatas |
| | 11:15 | Ends with brass chords, followed by soft, high strings |

Cultural Perspective 4

Dvořák's Influence on African-American Art Music

Is there anything truly American about the Bohemian composer Antonin Dvořák's *New World* Symphony? Dvořák was inspired by traditional music, both of his native Bohemia and of America—specifically, spirituals, Creole tunes and dances, and what he perceived as music of Native Americans. We have already learned about his choice of Henry Wadsworth Longfellow's epic poem *The Song of Hiawatha* as a loose literary program for his *New World* Symphony, and have noted that the two middle movements can be linked with specific sections of the poem. Yet there is little in this symphony that is reminiscent of actual Native American music.

What, then, of Dvořák's professed interest in the traditional music of African Americans? We know that the composer came to love the spirituals sung to him by his student Henry Burleigh (1866–1949), and it is said that Dvořák had a particular fondness for *Swing Low, Sweet Chariot* (a variant of this spiritual can be heard in the first movement of the symphony). The rhythmic syncopations and the particular scale formations used in the *New World* Symphony (the minor mode with a lowered, or flatted, seventh degree) have often been cited as evidence of borrowings from African-American musical styles.

But Dvořák gave much more to American music than he took from it. As a respected teacher, he issued a challenge to American composers to throw off the domination of European music and forge a path of their own, using the "beautiful and varied themes . . . the folk songs of America." Some followed his suggestion, including two of his African-American students. Burleigh published a landmark collection of spirituals arranged in an art music style (*Jubilee Songs of the U.S.A.*, 1916, which included *Deep River*); his goal

was to bring the genre to the concert stage. Will Marion Cook (1869–1944), while a student in Dvořák's composition class, began an opera on *Uncle Tom's Cabin* (Harriet Beecher Stowe's novel about life under slavery), but later turned his efforts to musical theater.

Some African-American composers tried their hands at larger forms of art music that drew from their heritage. One was Robert Nathaniel Dett (1882–1943), who won a prestigious award at Harvard University for his essay "The Emancipation of Negro Music," in which he issued a call to fellow composers to take "Negro themes and fashion from [them] music . . . in choral form, in lyric and operatic works, in concertos and suites and salon music." Florence Price (1888–1953), the first African-American woman to be recognized as a distinguished composer, is believed to have drawn inspiration for her Symphony in E minor (1932) directly from Dvořák's *New World* Symphony. Price's work parallels Dvořák's in a number of ways, including original themes that allude to characteristic African-American rhythms and melodies.

The composer who best rose to this challenge was William Grant Still (1895–1978), whose output exceeds one hundred concert works in a wide variety of genres—symphonies, symphonic poems, suites, operas, ballets, chamber music, choral music, and songs. A nationalist, Still drew musical inspiration from African-American work songs, spirituals, ragtime, blues, and jazz. His *Afro-American* Symphony (1930) is perhaps his best-known work today. Still stated his goal clearly: "I knew I wanted to write a symphony, I knew that it had to be an American work; and I wanted to demonstrate how the blues,

Left: William Grant Still, composer of the Afro-American
Sysmphony. *Right: Henry T. Burleigh, one of Dvořák's students, noted for his collection of spirituals in art-music style.*

so often considered a lowly expression, could
be elevated to the highest musical level."
Although not the first symphonic work written in a jazz or blues style (George Gershwin's
Rhapsody in Blue was premiered in 1924),
Still's symphony was firmly rooted in the
music of his African-American heritage.

Dvořák would surely have welcomed
these examples of musical nationalism,
which were products of an early twentieth-
century movement often referred to as the
Black, or Harlem, Renaissance. Other important manifestations of this movement pro-

moted the music of African Americans; these
included the performance of their works by
major symphony orchestras and choruses,
the stellar careers achieved by some concert
artists (such as singer Marian Anderson, the
leading contralto of her day), and the rising
position of black musicians in the fields of
education and entertainment. Today, the "vali-
dation" of a vernacular music by art music
standards described by William Grant Still is
no longer necessary, since all musics are
coming to be accepted as valuable products
of the culture and people who created them.

Suggested Listening:

Dvořák: *New World* Symphony, Second Movement
Still: *Afro-American* Symphony, First Movement
Spiritual (*Swing Low, Sweet Chariot*)

25

The Romantic Concerto

*"We are so made that we can derive intense enjoyment only from
a contrast."*—SIGMUND FREUD

The Nature of the Concerto

A concerto is a large-scale work in several movements for solo instrument and orchestra. (Occasionally, more than one soloist is involved.) Here the attention is focused upon the solo performer. This circumstance helps determine the style and form. The massive sonorities of the piano, the sweetness of the violin, the dark resonance of the cello may be pitted against the orchestra. This opposition of forces constitutes the essential nature of the concerto.

In its dimensions, the concerto is comparable to the symphony. Most concertos are in three movements: a dramatic Allegro, usually in sonata-allegro form, is followed by a lyrical slow movement and a brilliant finale. In the opening movement, as in the first movement of the symphony, contrasting themes are stated, developed, and restated. In this case, however, the tension is twofold: not only between the contrasting ideas but between the opposing forces—between the solo instrument and the group. Each of the basic themes may be announced by the *tutti* (literally, "all"—that is, the orchestra as a whole) and then taken up by the solo part. Or the soloist may introduce ideas and the orchestra elaborate upon them. In any case, a twofold statement of the themes by the orchestra and the soloist is typical, producing a double exposition within the first-movement form.

Tutti

Second movements continue to present lyrical melodies, often in a loosely structured three-part form. The finales of the Romantic concerto bring to a head the dramatic tension between soloist and orchestra. The soloist is often featured again in a brilliant cadenza that closes the concerto cycle.

A characteristic feature of the concerto is the *cadenza,* a fanciful solo passage in the manner of an improvisation that interrupts the movement. The cadenza came out of a time when improvisation was an important element in art music, as it is today in jazz. The cadenza produces a dramatic effect, as the orchestra falls silent and the soloist launches into a free play of fantasy on one or more themes of the movement. Before the nineteenth century, the performer was usually the composer. With the rise of a class of professional performers who interpreted the music of others but did not invent their own, the art of improvisation declined. Thus the cadenza came to be composed beforehand, by either the composer or the performer.

Cadenza

Virtuosity in the Nineteenth Century

The origins of the Romantic concerto reach back to the late eighteenth century. Mozart and Beethoven, both formidable pianists, performed their con-

In this woodcut from the 1870s, the noted virtuoso Hans von Bülow is seen performing a piano concerto with orchestra in New York City.

certos in public; these works delighted and dazzled their audiences. The concerto thus had to enable performing artists to exhibit their gifts as well as the capacities of the instrument. This element of technical display, combined with appealing melodies, has helped to make the concerto one of the most widely appreciated types of concert music.

Standard Concerto Form

Multimovement work for solo instrument and orchestra
Normally 3 movements: fast–slow–fast

I.   First movement: Allegro
     Concerto form, with two expositions
     Orchestral exposition ⎫ themes presented
     Solo exposition   ⎭
     Development
     Recapitulation
     Cadenza: solo instrument alone
     Coda

II. Second movement: Slow, lyrical
     A-B-A form common

III. Third movement: Very fast
     Sonata or rondo forms popular

As the concert industry developed, ever greater emphasis was placed upon the virtuoso soloist. Technical brilliance became a more and more important element of concerto style. We have noted that nineteenth-century composer-performers such as Paganini and Liszt carried virtuosity to new heights. This development kept pace with the increase in the size and resources of the symphony orchestra. The Romantic concerto took shape as one of the most favored genres of the age. Mendelssohn, Chopin, Liszt, Robert and Clara Schumann, Brahms, and Tchaikovsky all contributed to its literature.

Composers of the concerto often write with a particular artist in mind, and may even consult him or her about the technical peculiarities of the instrument and the artist's own technical resources. The piano concerto of Robert Schumann that we will study was undoubtedly influenced by his wife, one of the finest pianists of the nineteenth century. Brahms consulted Joseph Joachim, the leading violinist of the day, when he wrote his Violin Concerto. And Tchaikovsky wrote his with the virtuoso Leopold Auer in mind; when Auer found the work unplayable, Tchaikovsky turned to another extraordinary violinist, Adolf Brodsky, who gave his monumental Violin Concerto its premiere.

26

Robert Schumann and the Romantic Concerto

"Music is to me the perfect expression of the soul."

The turbulence of German Romanticism, its fantasy and subjective emotion, found its voice in Robert Schumann. His music is German to the core, yet he rose above the national style to make his contribution to world culture.

His Life

Robert Schumann (1810–56) was born in Zwickau, a town in southeastern Germany, son of a bookseller whose love of literature was passed on to the boy. At his mother's insistence, he undertook the study of law, first at the University of Leipzig, then at Heidelberg. The youth daydreamed at the piano, steeped himself in the poetry of Goethe and Byron, and attended an occasional lecture. More and more he surrendered to his passion for music; it was his ambition to become a pianist. At last he won his mother's consent and returned to Leipzig to study with Friedrich Wieck, one of the foremost teachers of the day.

The young man practiced intensively to make up for his late start. Unfortunately, physical difficulties with the fingers of his right hand ended his

Robert Schumann

hopes as a pianist. He then turned his interest to composing, and in a burst of creative energy produced, while still in his twenties, his most important works for piano.

The critic

Schumann was engaged concurrently in an important literary venture. With a group of like-minded enthusiasts, he founded the publication *Die neue Zeitschrift für Musik* (The New Journal for Music). Under his direction, the periodical became one of the most important music journals in Europe.

Marriage to Clara

The hectic quality of this decade was intensified by his courtship of the gifted pianist Clara Wieck. When he first came to study with her father, she was an eleven-year-old prodigy. She was about sixteen when Robert realized he loved her. Friedrich Wieck's opposition to their marriage bordered on the psychopathic. Clara was the supreme achievement of his life, and he refused to surrender her to another. At length, since she was not yet of age, the couple were forced to appeal to the courts against Wieck. The marriage took place in 1840, when Clara was twenty-one and Robert thirty. This was his "year of song," when he produced over a hundred of the Lieder that represent his lyric gift at its purest.

The two musicians settled in Leipzig, pursuing their careers side by side. Clara became the foremost interpreter of Robert's piano works and in the ensuing decade contributed substantially to the spread of his fame. Yet neither her love nor that of their children could ward off his increasing withdrawal

Mental illness

from the world. Moodiness and nervous exhaustion culminated, in 1844, in a severe breakdown. The doctors counseled a change of scene. The couple moved to Dresden, where Robert seemingly made a full recovery. But the periods of depression returned ever more frequently.

In 1850, Schumann was appointed music director at Düsseldorf. But he was ill-suited for public life and was forced to relinquish the post. During a tour of Holland, where Clara and he were warmly received, he began to complain of "unnatural noises" in his head. His last letter to the violinist Joseph Joachim, two weeks before the final breakdown, is a farewell to his art. "The music is silent now . . . I will close. Already it grows dark."

Schumann experienced auditory hallucinations. Once he rose in the middle of the night to write down a theme that he imagined had been brought him by the spirits of Schubert and Mendelssohn. It was his last melody. A week later, in a fit of depression, he threw himself into the Rhine River. He was rescued by fishermen, and Clara had no choice but to place him in a private asylum near Bonn. He died two years later at the age of forty-six.

His Music

Piano pieces

In the emotional exuberance of his music, Schumann is the true Romantic. His piano pieces brim over with impassioned melody, novel changes of harmony, and vigorous rhythms. The titles are characteristic: *Fantasiestücke* (Fantasy Pieces), *Romances, Scenes from Childhood*. He often attached literary meanings to his music, and was especially fond of cycles of short pieces connected by a literary theme or musical motto.

Principal Works

More than 300 Lieder, including song cycles *Frauenliebe und Leben* (*A Woman's Love and Life*, 1840) and *Dichterliebe* (*A Poet's Love*, 1840)

Orchestral music, including 4 symphonies and 1 piano concerto (A minor, 1841–45)

Chamber music, including 3 string quartets, 1 piano quintet, 1 piano quartet, piano trios, and sonatas

Piano music, including 3 sonatas; numerous miniatures and collections, among them *Papillons* (Butterflies, 1831), *Carnaval* (1835), and *Kinderszenen* (*Scenes from Childhood*, 1838); large works, including *Symphonic Etudes* (1835-37) and Fantasy in C (1836-38)

1 opera; incidental music

Choral music

As a composer of Lieder, Schumann ranks second only to Schubert. His favorite theme was love, particularly from a woman's point of view. His favored poet was Heine, for whom he had an affinity like Schubert's for Goethe. Especially notable are several song cycles, the best-known of which are *A Poet's Love,* on poems of Heine, and *A Woman's Love and Life,* on poems of Chamisso. *Lieder*

The four symphonies are thoroughly Romantic in feeling. These works, especially the first and fourth, communicate a lyric freshness that has kept them alive. Typical of the essence of German Romanticism is the opening of the *Spring* Symphony, his first. "Could you infuse into the orchestra," he wrote the conductor, "a kind of longing for spring? At the entrance of the trumpets I should like them to sound as from on high, like a call to awakening." *Symphonies*

PIANO CONCERTO IN A MINOR

In 1841, Schumann composed a *Phantasie for Piano and Orchestra,* which ultimately became the first movement of his celebrated Piano Concerto. He added the second and third movements in 1845.

The first movement, a spacious Allegro affettuoso (fast and with feeling), opens with a brief but dramatic Introduction, followed by the main theme, a haunting melody of great tenderness and an inward quality typical of Schumann. The second theme is not a new idea at all, but an imaginative transformation of the first. A development section features some interesting variations of the theme, which lead to the recapitulation. The cadenza, Schumann's own, is both emotional and introspective. This Allegro achieves a balance between melodic and virtuoso elements. *First movement*

The second movement is an Intermezzo (Interlude) marked Andantino grazioso (a little faster than Andante and graceful), which begins with an inti- *Second movement*

Listening Guide 12

C/S: 5B/1 C/S: 5/ 28 – 34

ROBERT SCHUMANN: Piano Concerto in A minor, Op. 54, First Movement

(14:49)

Date of work: 1841–45
Movements:
  I. Allegro affettuoso; 4/4 meter, A minor
 II. Intermezzo, Andante grazioso (moderately slow, graceful); ternary (**A-B-A**) form, 2/4 meter, F major
III. Allegro vivace; sonata-allegro form, 3/4 meter, A major

FIRST MOVEMENT: Allegro affettuoso (fast and tenderly); 4/4 meter, A minor

EXPOSITION

28 0:00 Brief introduction—orchestral chord and downward-sweeping piano line lead to main theme

0:06 Theme 1—lyrical melody in A minor, heard first in oboe:

0:24 Solo piano statement of theme 1; piano arabesques alternate with lyrical string lines

29 2:27 Theme 2 — derived from first theme, previewed by piano, then heard in C major with clarinet, marked Animato (animated):

3:12 Increasingly animated orchestral treatment of second theme; new motive introduced by oboe:

Piano takes up new motive from second theme

3:59 Closing—triumphal orchestral statement

DEVELOPMENT

30 4:33 Marked Andante expressivo—features tender dialogue between piano and clarinet; sudden shift to Allegro, develops introductory material; modulates and returns to A minor for recapitulation

RECAPITULATION

31 7:47   Theme 1—oboe, in A minor; then in solo piano

32 10:10   Theme 2—clarinet, in A major, with piano arabesques, animated; second motive exchanged between instruments

33 12:00   Cadenza—solo piano, unaccompanied, in improvised style

34 13:50   Coda—Allegro molto; marchlike melody based on theme 1, in A minor:

mate dialogue between piano and strings. Its main idea is derived from a motive of the opening theme of the first movement. The Intermezzo is in a simple three-part form (**A-B-A**); the middle contrasting section features a broad cello line.

The finale is an Allegro vivace (fast and lively) in 6/8 time, a tempo that helps create a sense of vigorous movement conjuring up the outdoors. The movement abounds in elaborate passage work for the solo instrument that demands not only nimble fingers but also an impeccable sense of timing.

Third movement

In this concerto, Schumann achieved the perfect fusion of dramatic and lyric elements. The work is universally regarded as his masterpiece.

UNIT VIII

Choral and Dramatic Music in the Nineteenth Century

27

The Nature of Romantic Choral Music

"In a sense no one is ignorant of the material from which choral music springs. For this material is, in large measure, the epitomized thought, feeling, aspiration of a community rather than an individual."
—PERCY M. YOUNG

The nineteenth century witnessed a broadening of the democratic ideal and an enormous expansion of the musical public. This climate was uniquely favorable to choral singing, an enjoyable group activity involving increasing numbers of amateur music lovers. As a result, choral music played an important part in the musical life of the Romantic era.

Amateur choral groups

Singing in a chorus required less skill than playing in an orchestra. It attracted many people who had never learned to play an instrument or who could not afford to buy one. With a modest amount of rehearsal (and a modest amount of voice), they could take part in the performance of great choral works. The music they sang, being linked to words, was somewhat easier to understand than absolute instrumental music, both for the performers and the listeners. The members of the chorus not only enjoyed a pleasant social evening once or twice a week but also, if their group was good enough, became a source of pride to their community.

Choral music offered the masses an ideal outlet for their artistic energies. It served to relieve, for example, the drabness of life in the English factory towns of the early Victorian period. And it had the solid support of the authorities, who felt that an interest in music would protect the ordinary citizens from the

In the nineteenth century, enormous choral and orchestral forces were frequently used, as in this engraving depicting the opening concert at St. Martin's Hall, London, 1850.

dangerous new ideas that were floating around. This is amusingly illustrated in the constitution of the Huddersfield Choral Society (1836), which stipulated that "no person shall be a member of this Society who frequents the 'Hall of Science' or any of the 'Socialist Meetings,' nor shall the Librarian be allowed to lend any copies of music (knowingly) belonging to this society to any Socialist, upon pain of expulsion."

The repertory centered about the great choral heritage of the past. Nevertheless, if choral music was to remain a vital force, its literature had to be enriched by new works that would reflect the spirit of the time. The list of composers active in this area includes some of the most important names of the nineteenth century: Schubert, Berlioz, Mendelssohn, Schumann, Liszt, Verdi, Brahms, Dvořák. Out of their efforts came a body of choral music that represents some of the best creative efforts of the Romantic period.

Choral forms

Among the main forms of choral music in the nineteenth century were the mass, requiem, and oratorio. We will study these in detail in later chapters. It will suffice now to define them briefly. A *mass* is a musical setting of the most solemn service of the Roman Catholic Church. A *requiem* is a setting of the Mass for the Dead. It takes its name from the opening text: "Requiem aeternam dona eis, Domine" (Give them eternal rest, O Lord). An *oratorio* is a dramatic composition based on a text of religious or serious character, performed by solo voices, chorus, and orchestra. All three forms were originally intended to be performed in church. By the nineteenth century, they had found a wider audience in the concert hall. In addition, a vast literature of secular choral pieces appeared. These works, settings for chorus of lyric poems in a variety of moods and styles, were known as *part songs*—that is, songs in three or four voice parts. Most of them were short melodious works, easy enough for ama-

Part songs

teurs. They gave pleasure both to the singers and to their listeners, and played an important role in developing the new audience of the nineteenth century.

Choral texts

It is important to remember that in choral music, the text is related to the music in a different way than in solo song. The words are not as easy to grasp when a multitude of voices project them. In addition, the four voice parts in the chorus (soprano, alto, tenor, and bass) may be singing different words at the same time. Most important, music needs more time to establish a mood than words do. For these reasons, the practice arose of repeating a line, a phrase, or an individual word over and over again instead of introducing new words all the time. This principle is well illustrated by the choral work *A German Requiem* by Johannes Brahms.

BRAHMS'S REQUIEM

Choral music occupied a prominent position in Brahms's creative output. Some of his works, such as the *Liebeslieder Waltzes,* were extremely popular during his lifetime. He also wrote many motets (sacred or devotional choral works) and a cappella (unaccompanied) part songs. But his greatest choral composition is the Requiem, which psychologically and musically became the central work of his career.

A German Requiem was rooted in the Protestant tradition into which Brahms was born. Its aim was to console the living and lead them to a serene acceptance of death as an inevitable part of life. Hence its gentle lyricism. Brahms chose his text from the Old as well as New Testament, from the Psalms, Proverbs, Isaiah, and Ecclesiastes as well as from Paul, Matthew, Peter, John, and Revelation. Brahms was not a religious man in the conventional sense, nor was he affiliated with any particular church; significantly, Christ's name is never mentioned in the work. Brahms was moved to compose his Requiem by the death first of his teacher and friend Robert Schumann, then of his mother, whom he idolized; but the piece transcends personal emotions and endures as a song of mourning for all humanity.

Written for soloists, four-part chorus, and orchestra, *A German Requiem* is in seven movements arranged in a formation resembling an arch. There are connections between the first and last movements, between the second and sixth, and between the third and fifth; this leaves the fourth movement, the widely sung chorus *How Lovely Is Thy Dwelling Place,* as the centerpiece of the arch.

This movement is based on a verse from Psalm 84 (see Listening Guide 13). The first two lines of the Psalm are heard three times, separated by the two contrasting sections that present the other lines. The form, therefore, is **A-B-A′-C-A′.** The first two sections for the most part move in quarter notes, but the third section (**C**) moves more quickly in a vigorous rhythm, better suiting the line "that praise Thee evermore," with much expansion on "evermore." With the final reappearance of the **A** section, the slower tempo returns. Marked *piano* and *dolce* (soft and sweet), this passage serves as a coda that brings the piece to its gentle and serene close.

Listening Guide 13

C/S: 5B/3
Sh: 2B/4

C/S: 5/ 42 — 46
Sh: 2/ 49 — 53

BRAHMS: *A German Requiem,* Fourth Movement

(5:46)

Date of work: 1868
Genre: Requiem, for Protestant church
Medium: 4-part chorus, soloists, and orchestra
Movements: 7
Language: German

FOURTH MOVEMENT: Mässig bewegt (moderately agitated)

Text: Psalm 84
Form: Rondo (**A-B-A′-C-A′**)
Character: Lilting triple meter, marked *dolce* (sweetly)

Opening melody: clarinets and flutes begin in inversion of first phrase in chorus:

		Text	Translation	Description
42	0:00	Wie lieblich sind deine Wohnungen, Herr Zebaoth!	How lovely is Thy dwelling place, O Lord of hosts!	**A**—flowing, arched melody, SATB homophonic setting, answers orchestral opening, E-flat major; text repeated in Tenors, joined by other voices
43	1:24	Meine Seele verlanget und sehnet sich nach den Vorhöfen des Herrn; mein Leib und Seele freuen sich in dem lebendigen Gott.	My soul longs and even faints for the courts of the Lord; my flesh and soul rejoice in the living God.	**B**—shift to minor, builds fugally with word repetition from lowest to highest voices; sudden accents on first beat of measures, with plucked strings; text repeated, climax on "lebendigen"
44	2:38	Wie lieblich . . . Wohl denen, die in deinem Hause wohnen,	How lovely . . . Blessed are they that live in Thy house,	**A′**—opening returns in E-flat major, new text and varied setting
45	3:49	die loben dich immerdar!	that praise Thee evermore!	**C**—martial quality, faster movement in polyphonic setting
46	4:42	Wie lieblich . . .	How lovely . . .	**A′**—coda-like return, reminiscent of opening; soft orchestral closing, in E-flat major

28

Romantic Opera

"It is better to invent reality than to copy it." —GIUSEPPE VERDI

For well over three hundred years, opera has been one of the most alluring forms of musical entertainment. A special glamour is attached to everything connected with it—its superstar performers, celebrated conductors, extravagant scenic designs, not to mention the glitter and excitement of opening nights.

At first glance, opera would seem to demand that the spectator believe the unbelievable. It presents us with human beings caught up in dramatic situations, who sing to each other instead of speaking. The reasonable question is: how can an art form based on so unnatural a procedure be convincing?

True enough, people in real life do not sing to each other. Neither do they converse in blank verse, as Shakespeare's characters do, nor live in rooms of which one wall is conveniently missing so that the audience may look in. All the arts employ conventions that are accepted by both the artist and the audience. The conventions of opera are more in evidence than those of poetry, painting, drama, or film, but they are not different in kind. Once we have accepted the fact that the carpet can fly, how simple to believe that it can also carry the prince's luggage. Thus the fundamental goal of art is not to copy nature but to heighten our awareness of it.

Opera functions in the domain of poetic drama. It uses the human voice to project the basic emotions—love, hate, jealousy, joy, grief—with an elemental force. The logic of reality gives way on the operatic stage to the power of music over the imagination.

The Components of Opera

An *opera* is a drama that is sung. It combines the resources of vocal and instrumental music—soloists, ensembles, chorus, orchestra, and sometimes ballet—with poetry and drama, acting and pantomime, scenery and costumes. To weld the diverse elements into a unity is a challenge that has attracted some of the best minds in the history of music.

Recitative   Explanations necessary to plot and action are generally presented in a kind of musical declamation known as *recitative.* This disjunct vocal style imitates the natural inflections of speech; its rhythm is curved to the rhythm of the language. Instead of a purely musical line, recitative is often characterized by a fast-paced patter and "talky" repetition of the same note; also by rapid question-and-answer dialogue that builds dramatic tension in the theater. In time, two styles of recitative became standard: *secco,* which features a sparse accompaniment and moves with great freedom, and *accompagnato,* which is accompanied by various instruments and thus moves more evenly.

Recitative gives way at the lyric moments to the *aria* (Italian for "air"), *Aria*
which releases through melody the emotional tension accumulated in the
course of action. The aria is a song, generally of a highly emotional kind. It is
what audiences wait for, what they cheer, what they remember. An aria, because of its tunefulness, can be effective even when removed from its context.
Many arias are familiar to multitudes who have never heard the operas from
which they are excerpted. One formal convention that developed early in the
genre's history is the *da capo aria,* a ternary, or **A-B-A,** form that brings back
the first section with improvised embellishments by the soloist.

An opera may contain ensemble numbers—duets, trios, quartets, quintets, *Ensembles*
sextets, septets—in which the characters pour out their respective feelings.
The chorus is used in conjuction with solo voices, or it may function independently. It may comment and reflect upon the action in the manner of the
chorus in Greek tragedy, or it may be integrated into the action.

The orchestra too supports the action of the opera, setting the appropriate
mood for different scenes. An opera usually begins with an instrumental number, known as the *overture,* which may introduce melodies from arias to *Overture*
come. Each act of the opera normally has an orchestral introduction, and interludes, or *sinfonias* as they were called in Baroque opera, may occur between scenes as well.

The opera composer works with a *librettist,* who writes the text of the
work, creating characters and plot with some dramatic insight and fashioning
situations that justify the use of music. The *libretto,* the text or script of the *Libretto*
opera, must be devised so as to give the composer an opportunity for the diverse numbers—recitatives and arias, ensembles, choruses, interludes—that
have become the traditional features of this art form.

The Development of National Styles

As one of the most important and best-loved theatrical genres of the nineteenth century, opera fostered different national styles in the three leading
countries of musical Europe—France, Germany, and Italy.

In Paris, the opera center of all Europe in the late eighteenth and early nine- *France*
teenth centuries, *grand opera* was all the rage. This new genre, which focused on serious, historical themes and was nourished by the propagandist *Grand opera*
purposes of France's new leaders, suited the bourgeoisie's taste for the big and
the spectacular very well. Complete with huge choruses, crowd scenes, elaborate dance episodes, ornate costumes and scenery, grand opera was as much
a spectacle as a musical event. Giacomo Meyerbeer (1791-1864), a German
composer who studied in Italy, was primarily responsible for bringing grand
opera to Paris. His best-known works in the style are *Robert le diable* (Robert
the Devil, 1831) and *Les Huguenots* (1836), both of which reveal careful attention to the drama as a whole—a blend of social statement, history, and
spectacle with memorable melodies and rich orchestration.

Less pretentious than French grand opera was *opéra comique,* which re- *Opéra comique*

Margrave's Opera House in Bayreuth, 1879. A painting by **Gustav Bauernfeind.**
(Deutsches Theatermuseum, Munich)

quired smaller performance forces, was written in a simpler style, and featured spoken dialogue rather than recitatives. One of the lighter works that delighted Parisian audiences was Jacques Offenbach's (1819–80) *Orphée aux
enfers* (*Orpheus in the Underworld*, 1858), which blended wit and satire into
the popular model. These two genres merged—the spectacle of grand opera
Lyric opera   and the simplicity of opéra comique—to produce *lyric opera*. This hybrid
type featured appealing melodies and romantic drama, and found its greatest
proponent in Georges Bizet, whose *Carmen* is one of the masterpieces of the
French lyric stage (see Chapter 31).

Germany   Nineteenth-century Germany did not have the long-established opera tradition of France and Italy. The immediate predecessor of German Romantic
Singspiel   opera was *Singspiel,* a light or comic drama with spoken dialogue. The first
representative of the German Romantic spirit in opera was Carl Maria von
Weber (1786–1826), whose best-known work is *Der Freischütz* (1821). In this
opera, supernatural beings and mysterious forces of nature intertwined with
the fate of heros and heroines to produce drama featuring simple and direct
melodies, almost folklike, accompanied by expressive timbres and harmonies.
The greatest figure in German opera—and one of the most significant in the
history of the Romantic era—was Richard Wagner, who created the music
drama, a genre that integrated theater and music completely (see Chapter 30).

Italy   Italy in the early nineteenth century still recognized the opposing genres of
opera seria (serious opera) and *opera buffa* (the Italian version of comic

opera), legacies of an earlier period. Important composers of these styles include Gioachino Rossini (1792–1868), whose masterpiece was *Il barbiere di Siviglia* (*The Barber of Seville,* 1816); Gaetano Donizetti (1797–1848), composer of some seventy operas, including *Lucia di Lammermoor* (1835); and Vincenzo Bellini (1801–35), whose *Norma* (1831) is preeminent for its beautiful melodies. These operas marked the high point of a *bel canto* (beautiful singing) style, characterized by florid melodic lines and delivered by voices of great agility and purity of tone. The consummate master of nineteenth-century Italian opera was Giuseppe Verdi, who sought to develop a uniquely national style (see Chapter 29).

Bel canto style

Women in Opera in the Nineteenth Century

Opera was one medium that allowed women musicians a good deal of visibility. Only a few tried their hand at composing them, but those who did were able to see a number of their works produced. The French composer Louise Bertin (1805–77) had several full-scale operas produced at the exclusive Opéra-Comique in Paris, including *Esmerelda* (1836), on a libretto based on Victor Hugo's novel about the hunchback of Notre Dame.

Louise Bertin

Women opera singers were among the most prominent performers of their day, idolized and in demand throughout Europe and the Americas. One such international star was Jenny Lind (1820–87), known as the "Swedish nightingale" and famous for her roles in operas by Meyerbeer, Donizetti, Weber, and Bellini. A concert artist as well, Lind made her American debut in 1850 in a tour managed by circus impresario P. T. Barnum.

Jenny Lind

The famous singer Jenny Lind during a recital at Exeter Hall, London, 1855. (Bettmann Archives)

Maria Malibran

Pauline Viardot

Professional singing was often a family tradition, as was the case with the offspring of the famous Spanish tenor Manuel Garcia. A brilliant teacher, Garcia coached his daughters to stardom. His eldest, Maria Malibran (1808–36), was renowned as an interpreter of Rossini, whose works she sang in London, Paris, Milan, Naples, and New York. A riding accident brought her successful career to a tragic close. Her sister, Pauline Viardot (1821–1910), the youngest daughter of the great Garcia, was highly acclaimed for her great musical and dramatic gifts. Viardot did much to further the careers of French opera composers Charles Gounod, Jules Massenet, and Gabriel Fauré, and sang the premieres of vocal works by Brahms, Robert Schumann, and Berlioz. In 1849, her Paris performance in Meyerbeer's *Le prophète,* in a role created specially for her, prompted Berlioz to write: "Madame Viardot is one of the greatest artists . . . in the past and present history of music." A composer herself, Viardot's intellectual approach to her art did much to raise the status of women singers.

29

Verdi and Italian Opera

"Success is impossible for me if I cannot write as my heart dictates!"

In the case of Giuseppe Verdi, the most widely loved of operatic composers, time, place, and personality were happily met. He inherited a rich musical tradition, his capacity for growth was matched by masterful energy and will, and he was granted a long span of life in which to fully exploit his creative gift.

His Life

Giuseppe Verdi

Early years

Born in a small town in northern Italy where his father kept an inn, Giuseppe Verdi (1813–1901) grew up amid the poverty of village life. His talent attracted the attention of a prosperous merchant in the neighboring town of Busseto, a music lover who made it possible for the youth to pursue his studies. After two years in Milan, Verdi returned to Busseto to fill a post as organist. When he fell in love with his benefactor's daughter, the merchant in wholly untraditional fashion accepted the penniless young musician as his son-in-law. Verdi was twenty-three, Margherita sixteen.

Three years later, he returned to Milan with the manuscript of an opera, which was produced at the opera house of La Scala in 1839 with fair success. The work brought him a commission to write three others. Shortly after, Verdi faced the first crisis of his life. His first child, a daughter, died before he left for Milan. The second, a baby boy, was carried off by fever, a catastrophe followed several weeks later by the death of his young wife. "In a sudden moment of despondency I despaired of finding any comfort in my art and resolved to give up composing," he wrote.

The months passed; the distraught young composer held to his decision. One night he happened to meet the director of La Scala, who insisted that he take home a libretto about Nebuchadnezzar, king of Babylon. With this work, the musician returned to his art. The opera *Nabucco,* presented at La Scala in 1842, was a triumph for the twenty-nine-year-old composer and launched him on a spectacular career.

Italy at this time was in the process of liberating itself from Austrian Hapsburg rule. Verdi from the beginning identified himself with the national cause: "I am first of all an Italian!" In this charged atmosphere, his works took on special meaning for his countrymen. No matter the time or place in which an opera was set, it was interpreted as a symbol of their cause. The chorus of exiled Jews from *Nabucco* became a patriotic song that is still sung today.

Verdi the nationalist

Although he was now a world-renowned figure, Verdi retained the simplicity that was at the core of both the artist and man. He returned to his roots, to an estate at Busseto, where he settled with his second wife, the singer Giuseppina Strepponi. She was a sensitive and intelligent woman who had created the leading roles in his early operas and who was his devoted companion for half a century. After Italy won independence, Verdi was urged to run for election to the first parliament because of the prestige his name would bring the new state. The task conformed to neither his talents nor his inclinations, but he accepted and sat in the Chamber of Deputies for some years.

In these years of public life, he was able to produce one masterpiece after another. He was fifty-seven when he wrote *Aïda.* At seventy-three, he completed *Otello,* his greatest lyric tragedy. In 1893, on the threshold of eighty, he astonished the world with *Falstaff.*

Late years

Verdi's death at eighty-seven was mourned throughout the world. He left the bulk of his fortune to a home for aged musicians he had founded in Milan. Italy accorded him the rites reserved for a national hero. From the voices of thousands who marched in his funeral procession there arose the haunting melody of "Va pensiero sull' ali dorate." It was the chorus from *Nabucco,* which he had given his countrymen as a song of inspiration sixty years before.

His Music

Verdi's music stands as the epitome of Romantic drama and passion. Endowed with an imagination that saw all emotion in terms of action and conflict, he

Principal Works

28 operas, including *Macbeth* (1847), *Rigoletto* (1851), *Il trovatore* (The Troubadour, 1853), *La traviata* (The Lost One, 1853), *Un ballo in maschera* (A Masked Ball, 1859), *La forza del destino* (The Force of Destiny, 1862), *Don Carlos* (1867), *Aïda* (1871), *Otello* (1887), and *Falstaff* (1893)

Vocal music, including a Requiem Mass (1874)

The Egyptian theme of Verdi's opera Aïda *is graphically illustrated on the cover of the score published by G. Ricordi of Milan.*

was able to communicate a dramatic situation with shattering expressiveness. True Italian that he was, he based his art on melody, which to him was the most immediate expression of human feeling. "Art without spontaneity, naturalness, and simplicity," he maintained, "is no art."

Early works

Of his fifteen early operas, the most important is *Macbeth,* his first work based on story material from Shakespeare. There followed in close succession *Rigoletto,* based on Victor Hugo's drama *Le roi s'amuse* (The King Is Amused); *Il trovatore,* derived from a fanciful Spanish play; and *La traviata,* which we will study. In these works, the mature musical dramatist stands revealed.

Middle period

The operas of the middle period are on a more ambitious scale, showing Verdi's attempt to assimilate elements of the French grand opera. The three most important are *A Masked Ball, The Force of Destiny,* and *Don Carlos.* "After *La traviata,*" he declared, "I could have taken things easy and written an opera every year on the tried and true model. But I had other artistic aims."

Final period

These aims were attained in *Aïda,* the work that ushers in his final period (1870–93). *Aïda* was commissioned in 1870 by the ruler of Egypt to mark the opening of the Suez Canal. Delayed by the outbreak of the Franco-Prussian War, the production was mounted with great splendor in Cairo the following year. In 1874 came the Requiem, in memory of Alessandro Manzoni, the novelist and patriot whom Verdi revered as a national artist.

Verdi and Boito

Verdi found an ideal librettist in Arrigo Boito (1842–1918). For their first collaboration, they turned to Shakespeare. Verdi's *Otello* is the high point of three hundred years of Italian lyric tragedy. After its opening night, the seventy-four-year-old composer declared, "I feel as if I had fired my last cartridge. Music needs youthfulness of the senses, impetuous blood, fullness of life." But he disproved his words when six years later (1893), again with Boito, he completed *Falstaff,* based on Shakespeare's *Merry Wives of Windsor*. Fitting crown to the labors of a lifetime, this luminous work ranks with the greatest comic operas.

LA TRAVIATA

La dame aux camelias (The Lady of the Camellias, known on the English stage simply as *Camille*) by the younger Alexandre Dumas, was a revolutionary play in its time, for it contrasted the noble character of a courtesan—a so-called fallen woman—with the rigidly bourgeois code of morals that finally destroys her. With a libretto by Francesco Piave, based on Dumas's play, Verdi's opera—under the title *La traviata* (The Lost One)—quickly won a worldwide audience.

The heroine is Violetta Valéry, one of the reigning beauties of Paris, who already is suffering from the early stages of tuberculosis when the drama begins. She lives for the pleasure of the moment until Alfredo Germont, a young man from a good Provençal family, falls in love with her and offers to take her away from the fast-paced life that is killing her. They go off to a country villa; but their idyllic existence is interrupted by Alfredo's father, a dignified gentleman who appeals to Violetta not to lead his son to ruin and disgrace the family name. She reveals to him that, far from taking money from Alfredo, she has been supporting both of them. As the discussion progresses, the elder Germont is amazed by her dignity. All the same, her immoral past is against her, and he points out to her the futility of a relationship that can never win the approval of God or society. Violetta makes the agonizing decision to leave Alfredo and return to Baron Douphol, whose mistress she was before.

Unaware of his father's intervention and seeking Violetta, Alfredo breaks into a festive party at the home of Violetta's friend Flora. Mad with jealousy and rage, he accuses Violetta of having betrayed him, insults her in the presence of her friends, and is challenged to a duel by the Baron. The last act takes place in Violetta's bedroom. Her doctor friend comes to cheer her up but confides to her maid that she is dying. Left alone, Violetta reads a letter from the elder Germont informing her that the duel has taken place. He has told his son of her great sacrifice; both are coming to ask for her forgiveness. Alfredo arrives. He is followed by his father, who realizes how blind he has been and, filled with admiration for Violetta, welcomes her as his daughter. It is too late. Violetta dies in Alfredo's arms.

We will concentrate on the finale of the second act, which takes place at Flora's party. Alfredo, at the gambling table, has played for huge stakes against the Baron and won a great deal of money. When the guests go to the next room for supper, Violetta remains behind to wait for him. Their scene unfolds against a tense, repetitive rhythm in the orchestra that suggests their agitation. She begs him to leave the party at once; she is terrified of the Baron and fears

A scene from Act II of La Traviata, *performed by the Opera Theater of Saint Louis, with Sheri Greenawald as Violetta and Jon Frederic West as Alfredo.* (Photo by Ken Howard)

that Alfredo will be hurt. Their dialogue exemplifies Verdi's uncanny ability to find the right music for a suspenseful dramatic situation. Unable to reveal to Alfredo that she left him at his father's request, Violetta lets him believe that she threw him over because she loved the Baron. (See Listening Guide 14 for text and analysis.)

At this point, Alfredo throws open the door and summons the guests into the room. He tells them that Violetta squandered all she had upon him, and he allowed her to do so because he thought she loved him. Now he wants to repay her. With the utmost contempt, he hurls at her feet the purse containing his winnings. Violetta faints in Flora's arms, and the guests react with horror at Alfredo's ungentlemanly behavior. Germont arrives in time to witness his son's outburst and is thoroughly ashamed of him.

We hear the great ensemble that crowns the act, with the voices of the principal characters intermingling as each expresses his or her feelings. Alfredo is overwhelmed with remorse, Germont is horrified, the Baron decides that only a duel can wipe out the insult. Flora and her guests (the chorus) sympathize with Violetta, whose voice soars above them in a beautiful passage. Some day, she hopes, Alfredo will learn the truth and understand.

Such an ensemble depends upon an outstanding melody that will guide the ear through the intricate maze of vocal lines. Verdi's great theme soars in a broad curve that imprints itself indelibly upon the mind and—more important—the heart.

Listening Guide 14

 C/S: 6A/1
Sh: 3A/1

 C/S: 6/ [1] – [5]
Sh: 3/ [1] – [2]

VERDI: *La traviata*, Act II, Finale (10:34)

First performance of work: 1853, Venice
Librettist: Francesco Maria Piave
Major characters:
    Violetta Valéry, a courtesan
    Alfredo Germont, Violetta's lover
    Giorgio Germont, Alfredo's father
    Gastone, Viscount de Letorières, a young man-about-town
    Baron Douphol, a rival of Alfredo
    Flora Bervoix, friend of Violetta

(Shorter recordings begin with "Di sprezzo degno," top of p. 152.)

ACT II, SCENE 2: A party at Flora's house in Paris

Opening of Violetta's recitative:

In - vi - ta - to a qui se - guir - mi,   ver - rà des - so?   vor - rà u - dir - mi?

		VIOLETTA
[1] 0:00	Invitato a qui seguirmi,	I've asked him to follow me.
	verrà desso? vorrà udirmi?	Will he come? Will he heed me?
	Ei verrà. Chè l'odio attroce	I think he'll come, for his terrible hatred
	puote in lui più di mia voce . . .	Moves him more than my words . . .
		ALFREDO
	Mi chiamaste? Che bramate?	You called me? What do you want?
		VIOLETTA
	Questi luoghi abbandonate;	You must go,
	un periglio vi sovrasta!	you're in danger!
		ALFREDO
	Ah, comprendo. Basta, basta,	Ah, I see, but that's enough,
	e sì vile mi credete?	so you think I'm a coward?
		VIOLETTA
	Ah no, no, mai!	No, never!
		ALFREDO
	Ma che temete?	What are you afraid of?
		VIOLETTA
	Tremo sempre del barone.	The Baron frightens me.
		ALFREDO
	È fra noi mortal quistione.	It's a question of life and death between us.
	S'ei cadrà per mano mia,	If I kill him,
	un sol colpo vi torria	you'll lose lover and protector
	coll'amante il protettore.	at a single blow.
	V'atterrisce tal sciagura?	Doesn't such a fate terrify you?

VIOLETTA

Ma s'ei fosse l'uccisore!　　But if he should be the killer?
Ecco l'unica sventura　　That's the only thought
ch'io pavento a me fatale.　　that puts the fear of death into me.

ALFREDO

La mia morte! Che ven cale?　　My death? What do you care about that?

VIOLETTA

Deh, partite, e sull'istante!　　Please, go, go at once!

ALFREDO

Partirò, ma giura innante　　I'll go if you will swear
che dovunque seguirai　　that wherever I go
seguirai i passi miei . . .　　you'll follow me . . .

VIOLETTA

Ah! no, giammai!　　No, never!

ALFREDO

No, giammai!　　No, never!

VIOLETTA

Va, sciagurato!　　Go, you are wicked!
Scorda un nome ch'è infamato!　　Forget a name that's without honor!
Va, mi lascia sul momento　　Go, leave me this minute.
di fuggirti un giuramento　　I've made a solemn vow
sacro io feci.　　to fly from you.

ALFREDO

A chi? Dillo, chi potea?　　Who to? Tell me, who could make you?

VIOLETTA

A chi dritto pien n'avea.　　One who had every right.

ALFREDO

Fu Douphol?　　Was it Douphol?

VIOLETTA *(with utmost willpower)*

Si.　　Yes.

ALFREDO

Dunque l'ami?　　Then you love him?

VIOLETTA

Ebben . . . l'amo . . .　　Yes . . . I love him . . .

ALFREDO *(runs furiously to the door and calls)*

Or tutti a me.　　Come here, all of you!

(Everybody enters in confusion.)

ALL

Ne appellaste? Che volete?　　You called us? What do you want?

ALFREDO *(pointing to Violetta, who leans feebly against a table)*

Questa donna conoscete?　　You know this lady?

ALL

Chi? Violetta?　　You mean Violetta?

ALFREDO

Che facesse non sapete?　　But you don't know what she's done.

VIOLETTA	
Ah! taci!	Oh, don't!
ALL	
No.	No.

Opening of Alfredo's solo, expressing anger and bitterness:

Ogni suo aver tal femmina per amor mio sperdea, io cieco, vile, misero,

ALFREDO

2   2:34

Ogni suo aver tal femmina	For me this woman lost all she possessed.
per amor mio sperdea,	I was blind.
io cieco, vile, misero,	A wretched coward,
tutto accettar potea.	I accepted it all.
Ma è tempo ancora!	But it's time now for me
tergermi da tanta macchia bramo,	to clear myself from debt,
qui testimon vi chiamo,	I call you all to witness here
che qui pagata io l'ho.	that I've paid her back!

(With furious contempt he throws a purse at Violetta's feet. She faints into the arms of Flora.)

Choral response to Alfredo's charges against Violetta, sung in unison, delivered forcefully:

Gaston. Oh, in-famia or-ri-bi-le tu commet-te-sti! un cor sen-si-bi-le co-sì uc-ci-de-sti!

Baron, Doctor and Marquis. Oh, in-famia or-ri-bi-le tu commet-te-sti! un cor sen-si-bi-le co-sì uc-ci-de-sti!

ALL

3   3:34

Oh, infamia orribile	What you have done is shameful!
tu commettesti!	So to strike a tender heart!
un cor sensibile	You have insulted a woman!
così uccidesti!	Get out of here!
Di donne ignobile insultatore,	We've no use for you!
di qua allontanati,	We've no use for such as you!
ne desti orror! Va!	Go!

[4] 4:09

GERMONT *(with dignified fire)*

Di sprezzo degno se stesso rende	A man who offends a woman, even in anger,
chi pur nell'ira la donna offende.	merits nothing but scorn.
Dov'è mio figlio?	Where is my son?
Più non lo vedo;	I see him no more
in te più Alfredo	in you, Alfredo,
trovar non so.	no more in you.

Opening of Alfredo's remorseful solo, in response to his father and the crowd:

ALFREDO *(to himself)*

Ah sì! che feci! ne sento orrore!	What have I done? Yes, I despise myself!
Gelosa smania, deluso amore	Jealous madness, love deceived,
mi strazian l'alma, più non ragiono	ravaged my soul, destroyed my reason.
da lei perdono più non avrò.	How can I ever gain her pardon?
Volea fuggirla, non ho potuto.	I would have left her, but I couldn't;
Dall'ira spinto son qui venuto!	I came here to vent my anger,
Or che lo sdegno ho disfogato,	But now I've done so, wretch that I am,
Me sciagurato, rimorso n'ho!	I feel nothing but a deep remorse!

FLORA, GASTONE, THE DOCTOR, THE MARQUIS, THE CHORUS *(to Violetta)*

O quanto peni!	Yes, you have suffered,
Ma pur fa cor!	But take heart!
Qui soffre ognuno del tuo dolor;	Each one of us has shared your pain;
fra cari amici qui sei soltanto	friends are about you to dry the tears
rasciuga il pianto che t'inondò.	you have shed.

GERMONT *(to himself)*

Io sol fra tanti, so qual virtude	I alone know the true devotion
di quella misera il sen racchiude	this poor girl hides within her breast;
io so che l'ama, che gli è fedele;	I know her faithful heart
eppur crudele tacer dovrò!	that's vowed so cruelly to silence.

BARON *(softly to Alfredo)*

A questa donna l'atroce insulto	Your deadly insult to this lady
qui tutti offese, ma non inulto	offends us all, but such an outrage
fia tanto oltraggio, provar vi voglio	shall not go unavenged!
Che il vostro orgoglio fiaccar saprò.	I shall find a way to humble your pride!

ALFREDO

Che feci! Ohimè!	Alas, what have I done?
Ohimè, che feci!	What have I done?
Ne sento orrore!	How can I ever
Da lei perdono più non avrò.	Gain her pardon?

Violetta's melody, vowing her love for Alfredo:

5 6:09

VIOLETTA *(reviving; in a very weak but passionate tone)*

Alfredo, Alfredo, di questo core
non puoi comprendere tutto l'amore,
tu non conosci che fino a prezzo
del tuo disprezzo provato io l'ho.
Ma verrà tempo, in che il saprai
come t'amassi, confesserai . . .
Dio dai rimorsi ti salvi allora!
Ah! Io spenta ancora t'amerò.

Alfredo, how should you understand
all the love that's in my heart?
How should you know that I have proved it
even at the price of your contempt?
But the time will come when you will know,
when you'll admit how much I loved you.
God save you then from all remorse!
Even after death I shall still love you.

*(Germont draws Alfredo with him. The Baron follows him.
Violetta is led by Flora into another room. The others disperse.)*

30

Wagner and the Music Drama

*"The error in the art genre of opera consists in the fact that a means
of expression—music—has been made the object, while the object of
expression—the drama—has been made the means."*

Richard Wagner

Richard Wagner looms as probably the single most important phenomenon in the artistic life of the later nineteenth century. Historians often divide the period into "before" and "after" Wagner. The course of post-Romantic music is unimaginable without the impact of this complex and fascinating figure.

His Life

Early years

Richard Wagner (1813–83) was born in Leipzig, son of a minor police official who died when Richard was still an infant. The future composer was almost entirely self-taught; he had in all about six months of instruction in music theory. At twenty, he abandoned his academic studies at the University of Leipzig and obtained a position as chorus master in a small opera house. In the next six years, he gained practical experience conducting in provincial theaters. He married the actress Minna Planer when he was twenty-three, and produced his first operas at this time. As with all his later works, he wrote the librettos himself. He was in this way able to achieve unity of the musical-dramatic conception beyond anything that had been known before.

Wagner was thirty when his grand opera *Rienzi* won a huge success in Dresden. As a result, he found himself appointed conductor to the king of Saxony. With his next three works, *The Flying Dutchman, Tannhäuser,* and *Lohengrin,* Wagner took an important step from the drama of historical intrigue to the idealized folk legend. He chose subjects derived from Medieval

German epics, displayed a profound feeling for nature, employed the supernatural as an element of the drama, and glorified the German land and people. But the Dresden public was not prepared for *Tannhäuser.* They had come to see another *Rienzi* and were disappointed.

Wagner the revolutionary

The Zurich years

A revolution broke out in Dresden in 1849. Wagner was not only openly sympathetic to the revolutionaries but was involved in their activities. When the revolt failed, he escaped to his friend Liszt at Weimar, where he learned that a warrant had been issued for his arrest. With the aid of Liszt, he crossed the border and found refuge in Switzerland. He settled in Zurich and commenced the most productive period of his career. For four years Wagner wrote no music, producing instead his most important literary works, *Art and Revolution, The Art Work of the Future,* and the two-volume *Opera and Drama,* which sets forth his theories of the *music drama,* as he named his concept of opera. He next proceeded to put theory into practice in the cycle of four music dramas called *The Ring of the Nibelung.* When he reached the second act of *Siegfried* (the third opera in the cycle), he grew tired "of heaping one silent score upon the other," and laid aside the gigantic task. There followed two of his finest works—*Tristan and Isolde* and *Die Meistersinger von Nürnberg.* (In English-speaking countries, many operas are commonly known by their original rather than translated titles. Just as Verdi's *La traviata* is seldom referred to as *The Lost One,* Wagner's *Die Meistersinger* is rarely called *The Mastersingers of Nuremberg,* and his *Götterdämmerung* is not known by its English title, *The Twilight of the Gods.*)

The years following the completion of *Tristan* were the darkest of his life. The musical scores accumulated in his drawer without hope of performance; Europe contained neither a theater nor singers capable of presenting them. At this point, a miraculous turn of events intervened. In 1864, an eighteen-year-old boy who was a passionate admirer of Wagner's music had ascended the throne of Bavaria as Ludwig II. One of the young monarch's most artistically important acts was to summon the composer to Munich, where *Tristan* and *Die Meistersinger* were performed at last. The king then commissioned him to complete the *Ring,* and Wagner took up where he had left off a number of years before.

A theater was planned specifically for the presentation of Wagner's music dramas, which ultimately resulted in the Festival Theater at Bayreuth. And to crown his happiness, the composer found a woman equal to him in will and courage—Cosima, the daughter of his old friend Liszt. She left her husband and children in order to join her life with Wagner's. They were married some years later, after Minna's death.

The Wagnerian gospel spread across Europe, a new art-religion. Wagner societies throughout the world gathered funds to raise the theater at Bayreuth. The *Ring* cycle was completed in 1874, and the four dramas were presented to worshipful audiences at the first Bayreuth Festival in 1876.

One task remained. To make good the financial deficit of the festival, Wagner undertook *Parsifal* (1877–82), a "consecrational festival drama" based on the legend of the Holy Grail. He finished it as he reached seventy. He died shortly after, in every sense a conqueror, and was buried at Bayreuth.

Richard Wagner at Home in Bayreuth: *a painting by* **W. Beckmann,** *1882. To Wagner's left is his wife, Cosima; to his right, Franz Liszt and Hans von Wolzogen.*

His Music

Wagner did away with the old "number" opera with its separate arias, duets, ensembles, choruses, and ballets. His aim was to create a continuous fabric of melody that would never allow the emotions to cool. He therefore evolved an "endless melody" that was molded to the natural inflections of the German language, more melodious than traditional recitative, more flexible and free than traditional aria.

Endless melody

The focal point of Wagnerian music drama is the orchestra. The composer developed a type of symphonic opera as native to the German genius as vocal opera is to the Italian. The orchestra is the unifying principle of his music drama. It floods the action, the characters, and the audience in a torrent of sound that embodies the sensuous ideal of the Romantic era.

The orchestral tissue is fashioned out of concise themes, the *leitmotifs,* or "leading motives"—Wagner called them basic themes—that recur throughout the work, undergoing variation and development as do the themes and motives of a symphony. The leitmotifs carry specific meanings, like the "fixed idea" of Berlioz's *Symphonie fantastique.* They have an uncanny power of suggesting in a few notes a person, an emotion, an idea, an object (the gold, the ring, the sword) or a landscape (the Rhine, Valhalla, the lonely shore of Tristan's home). Through a process of continual transformation, the leitmotifs trace the course of the drama, the changes in the characters, their experiences

Leitmotifs

Principal Works

13 music dramas (operas), including *Rienzi* (1842); *Der fliegende Holländer* (*The Flying Dutchman*, 1843); *Tannhäuser* (1845); *Lohengrin* (1850); *Tristan und Isolde* (1865); *Die Meistersinger von Nürnberg* (The Mastersingers of Nuremberg, 1868); *Der Ring des Nibelungen* (*The Ring of the Nibelung*, 1869–74), consisting of *Das Rheingold* (The Rhine Gold, 1869), *Die Walküre* (The Valkyrie, 1856), *Siegfried* (1876), and *Götterdämmerung* (The Twilight of the Gods, 1876); and *Parsifal* (1882)

Orchestral music, including *Siegfried Idyll* (1870)

Piano music; vocal music; choral music

and memories, their thoughts and hidden desires. As the leitmotifs accumulate layer upon layer of meaning, they themselves become characters in the drama, symbols of the relentless process of growth and decay that rules the destinies of gods and heroes.

Chromatic harmony   Wagner's musical language was based on chromatic harmony, which he pushed to its then farthermost limits. Chromatic dissonance gives Wagner's music its restless, intensely emotional quality. Never before had the unstable pitch combinations been used so eloquently to portray states of soul. The active chord (the dominant, built on the fifth scale degree) seeking resolution in the chord of rest (the tonic, on the first scale degree) became in Wagner's hands the most romantic of symbols: the lonely man—Flying Dutchman, Lohengrin, Siegmund, Tristan—seeking redemption through the love of the ideal woman, whether Senta, Elsa, Sieglinde, or Isolde.

DIE WALKÜRE

The story of *The Ring of the Nibelung* centers on the treasure of gold that lies hidden in the depths of the Rhine River, guarded by three Rhine Maidens. The world is young and does not know the power of gold. Only he who renounces love can gain that power. Alberich the Nibelung, of the hideous race of dwarfs who inhabit the dark regions below the earth, tries to make love to each of the maidens. When they repulse him, he renounces love, steals the treasure, and makes it into a ring that brings unlimited power to its owner. Wotan, father of the gods (for whom our Wednesday, or Wotan's Day, is named), compromises his honor by obtaining the ring through trickery, whereupon Alberich pronounces a terrible curse: may the ring destroy the peace of mind of all who gain possession of it, may it bring them misfortune and death.

   Thus begins the cycle of four dramas—the Tetralogy, as it is known—that ends only when the curse-bearing ring is returned to the Rhine Maidens. Gods and heroes, mortals and Nibelungs, intermingle freely in this tale of betrayed love, broken promises, magic spells, and general corruption brought on by the lust for power. Wagner freely adapted the story from the myths of the Norse sagas and the legends associated with a Medieval German epic, the *Nibelungenlied.*

He wrote the four librettos in reverse order. First came his poem on the death of the hero Siegfried. This became the final opera, *Götterdämmerung,* in the course of which Siegfried, now possessor of the ring, betrays Brünnhilde, to whom he has sworn his love, and is in turn betrayed by her. Wagner then realized that the events in Siegfried's life were shaped by what had happened to him in his youth; the poem of *Siegfried* explained the forces that molded the young hero. Aware that these in turn were determined by forces set in motion before the hero was born, Wagner wrote the poem about Siegfried's parents, Siegmund and Sieglinde, that became *Die Walküre.* Finally, this trilogy was prefaced by *Das Rheingold,* the drama that unleashed the workings of fate and the curse of gold out of which the entire action stemmed.

First performed in Munich in 1870, *Die Walküre* revolves around the twin brother and sister who are the offspring of Wotan by a mortal. (In Norse as in Greek and Roman mythology, kings and heroes were the children of gods.) The ill-fated love of Siegmund and Sieglinde is not only incestuous but also adulterous, for she has been forced into a loveless marriage with the grim chieftain Hunding, who challenges Siegmund to battle. Wotan, father of the gods, is eager for his son to win. But Wotan's wife, Fricka, the goddess of marriage, insists that Siegmund has violated the holiest law of the universe, and that he must die. Although he argues with her, Wotan sadly realizes that even he must obey the law.

Act I

The second act opens with a scene between Wotan and Brünnhilde. She is one of the Valkyries, the nine daughters of Wotan. Their perpetual task is to circle the battlefield on their winged horses, swooping down to gather up the fallen heroes, whom they bear away to Valhalla, where they will sit forever feasting with the gods. Wotan tells Brünnhilde, his favorite daughter, that in the ensuing combat between Siegmund and Hunding, she must see to it that Hunding is the victor. When Brünnhilde comes to Siegmund to tell him of his fate, she yields to pity and decides to disobey her father. The two heroes fight, and Brünnhilde tries to shield Siegmund. At the decisive moment, Wotan appears and holds out his spear, upon which Siegmund's sword is shattered. Hunding buries his spear in Siegmund's breast. Wotan, overcome by his son's death, turns a ferocious look upon Hunding, who falls dead. Then the god rouses himself and hurries off in pursuit of the daughter who dared to defy his command.

Act II

The prelude to Act III is the famous "Ride of the Valkyries," a vivid orchestral picture of the Amazon-like goddesses whirling through the storm on their chargers. On the Valkyries' rock, Brünnhilde rushes in with Siegmund's widow Sieglinde, whom she has carried off from the scene of battle. Sieglinde wants to die, but Brünnhilde hands her the two fragments of Siegmund's sword and tells her she must live to bear his son, who will become the world's mightiest hero. Sieglinde takes refuge in the forest, while Brünnhilde remains to face her father's wrath. Her punishment is severe. She is to be deprived of her godhood, Wotan tells her, and will become a mortal woman. No more will

Act III

Flames leap up around the rock as Wotan, sung by James Morris in the Metropolitan Opera production of Die Walküre, *is silhouetted against the sky.* (Courtesy of Winnie Klotz, Metropolitan Opera)

she sit with the gods, nor will she carry heroes to Valhalla. He will put her to sleep on the rock, and she will fall prey to the first one who finds her. Brünnhilde defends herself. In trying to protect Siegmund, was she not carrying out her father's innermost desire? She begs him to soften her punishment. Let him at least surround the rock with flames, so that only a fearless hero will be able to penetrate the wall of fire. Wotan relents and grants her request.

He kisses her on both eyes, which close at once. Wagner's stage directions are explicit:

> She sinks back with closed eyes, unconscious, in his arms. He gently bears her to a low mossy mound, which is overshadowed by a wide-spreading fir tree, and lays her upon it. He looks upon her and closes her helmet; his eyes then rest on the form of the sleeper, which he now completely covers with the great steel shield of the Valkyrie. He turns slowly away, then again turns around with a sorrowful look. He strides with solemn decision to the middle of the stage and directs the point of his spear toward a large rock.

Striking the rock three times, he invokes Loge, the god of fire. Flames spring up around the rock—and in the music, as the tall figure of the god in his black cloak is silhouetted against the red sky. "Whosoever fears the tip of my spear shall never pass through the fire," he sings, as the orchestra announces the theme of Siegfried, the fearless hero who in the next music drama will force his way through the flames and awaken Brünnhilde with a kiss. (See Listening Guide 15 for text and an analysis.) The curtain falls on as poetic a version of the Sleeping Beauty legend as any artist ever created.

Listening Guide 15

C/S: 5B/2   C/S: 5/ 38 – 41
Sh: 2B/5   Sh: 2/ 54 – 55

WAGNER: *Die Walküre*, Act III, Finale   (11:50)

Date of work: 1856, first performed 1870, Munich

Genre: Opera, second in a cycle of 4, *The Ring of the Nibelung*

Characters:

    Wotan, father of the gods

    Brünnhilde, one of the Valkyries, the favorite of the 9 daughters of Wotan

(Shorter recordings begin with "Loge, hör'!" p. 160.)

38 0:00 Orchestra with "slumber" motive, Langsam (slow):

Opening melody of Wotan's farewell:

Der Au - gen leuchtendes Paar,   das oft ich lächelnd ge - kos't

WOTAN

Der Augen leuchtendes Paar,	That bright pair of eyes
das oft ich lächelnd gekos't,	that often I fondled with smiles
wenn Kampfes lust ein Kuss dir lohnte,	when lust of battle won you a kiss,
wenn kindisch lallend der Helden Lob	when childlike chatter in praise of heroes
von holden Lippen dir floss:	flowed from your dear lips:
dieser Augen strahlendes Paar,	that radiant pair of eyes
das oft im Sturm mir geglänzt,	that often in tempests blazed at me,
wenn Hoffnungssehnen das Herz mir sengte,	when hopeful yearning burned up my heart,
nach Welten wonne mein Wunsch verlangte	when for worldly joy my desires longed
aus wild webendem Bangen:	amid wild weaving fear:
zum letzten Mal	for the last time
letz' es mich heut'	let them delight me today
mit des Lebewohles letztem Kuss!	with farewell's last kiss!
Dem glücklicher'n Manne	May their star shine
glänze sein Stern:	for that happier man:
dem unseligen Ew'gen	for the luckless immortal
muss es scheidend sich schliessen.	they must close in parting.

(He clasps her head in his hands.)

Denn so kehrt der Gott sich dir ab,	For thus the god departs from you,
so küsst er die Gottheit von dir!	thus he kisses your godhead away!

(He kisses her long on the eyes.)

39   4:04   "Magic sleep" motive in woodwinds and harp:

(She sinks back with closed eyes, unconscious, in his arms. He gently bears her to a low mossy mound, which is overshadowed by a wide-spreading fir tree, and lays her upon it. He looks upon her and closes her helmet; his eyes then rest on the form of the sleeper, which he now completely covers with the great steel shield of the Valkyrie. He turns slowly away, then again turns around with a sorrowful look.)

"Slumber" motive is heard again, in brass, then in strings

(He strides with solemn decision to the middle of the stage and directs the point of his spear toward a large rock.)

40   7:11   Forceful trombone passage precedes invocation to Loge:

WOTAN

Loge, hör'! Lausche hieher!	Loge, listen! Harken here!
Wie zuerst ich dich fand, als feurige Gluth,	As I found you first, a fiery blaze,
wie dann einst du mir schwandest,	as once you vanished from me,
als schweifende Lohe;	a random fire;
wie ich dich band, bann' ich dich heut'!	as I allied with you, so today I conjure you!
Herauf, wabernde Lohe,	Arise, magic flame,
umlod're mir feurig den Fels!	girdle the rock with fire for me!

(He strikes the rock thrice with his spear.)

Loge! Loge! Hieher!	Loge! Loge! Come here!

(A flash of flames issue from the rock, which swell to an ever-brightening fiery glow. Bright shooting flames surround Wotan. With his spear he directs the sea of fire to encircle the rock; it presently spreads toward the background, where it encloses the mountain in flames.)

41 8:13 "Magic fire" music is heard in full orchestra:

"Magic sleep" music is heard, followed by "slumber" motive in orchestra

WOTAN

Wer meines Speeres Spitze fürchtet,
durchschreite das Feuer nie!

Whosoever fears the tip of my spear
shall never pass through the fire!

(He stretches out the spear as a spell. He gazes sorrowfully back on Brünnhilde. Slowly he turns to depart. He turns his head again and looks back. He disappears through the fire.)

9:08 Wotan sings "Siegfried" motive to text above, followed by brass, announcing the hero to come:

Orchestral closing with "magic fire" music and "slumber" motive

31

Exoticism in Romantic Opera

"The composer gives the best of himself to the making of a work. He be-
lieves, doubts, enthuses, despairs, rejoices, and suffers in turn."
—GEORGES BIZET

We saw that a yearning for far-off lands was an important component of the Romantic imagination. This tendency found a perfect outlet in opera, whose action could take place anywhere in the world. Composers of such works were not terribly interested in authenticity; their primary concern was to create a picturesque atmosphere that would appeal to audiences. In other words, an exotic setting reflected the imagination of the composer rather than first-hand knowledge of a culture. Whether the action took place in Asia or Africa, the work was in the musical language of the West, but that language was flavored with melodies, harmonies, and rhythms suggestive of the faraway locale.

A prime example is Verdi's *Aïda,* which within the traditional idiom of Italian opera manages to evoke ancient Egypt under the pharaohs. The French composer Camille Saint-Saëns (1835–1921) turned to the Bible for the story of *Samson and Delilah.* Another biblical story inspired the German composer Richard Strauss to write *Salome.* Although the opera was set in ancient Judea, Salome's "Dance of the Seven Veils" centers around a tune reminiscent of a langorous Viennese waltz. Another opera by Strauss, *Elektra,* is a powerful evocation of mythological Greece. The turn-of-the-century Italian master Giacomo Puccini (1858–1924) produced two well-known operas with Asian settings: *Turandot,* based on a legend of ancient China, and *Madame Butterfly,* a romantic drama set in late nineteenth-century Japan.

French composers have always been fascinated by Spain. Thus a number of French orchestral classics describe the colorful peninsula, as does Bizet's wonderful opera *Carmen,* which we will study.

Georges Bizet: His Life and Music

Georges Bizet (1838–75) was born and raised in Paris. A student at the conservatory, he won the highest award of the school, the Prix de Rome, which made possible a three-year stay in the Italian capital. The rest of his career was passed in his native city. The works of his youth were followed by three operas that display the composer's power of evoking exotic atmosphere. *The Pearl Fishers* is a drama of love and ritual in Ceylon (modern-day Sri Lanka). Four years later came *The Fair Maid of Perth* (after Walter Scott's novel), which takes place in a romanticized Scotland, and *Djamileh,* set in Cairo, Egypt. Although none of these operas was an overwhelming success, they established Bizet's reputation as a composer to be reckoned with.

Bizet was then offered the libretto that Henri Meilhac and Ludovic Halévy

Georges Bizet

had fashioned from Prosper Mérimée's celebrated story of Spanish Gypsy life and love. He was ready for his appointed task. The result was the greatest French opera of the century.

Mérimée's tale belonged to a new type of literature, which tried to get closer to the realities of life. His characters—many of them smugglers and bandits—were depicted with an honesty that proclaimed the new realism. The opera softened the naked fury of the original story. But enough remained to disturb the audience that assembled for the opening night on March 3, 1875. The Opéra-Comique was a "family theater" where the bourgeois of Paris brought their wives and marriageable daughters. Passion on the stage was acceptable if it concerned kings and duchesses long dead; Carmen and her unsavory companions were too close for comfort.

The opera was not the fiasco that popular legend makes it out to have been. It did fail, however, to conquer its first audience. But the rumor that the piece was not quite respectable helped give it a run of thirty-seven performances in the next three months, an average of three a week. In addition, the manager offered the composer and his librettists a contract for their next work. *Carmen* was a failure only in Bizet's mind. He had put every ounce of his genius into the score. Its lukewarm reception was a bitter disappointment. His delicate constitution, worn out by months of rehearsals and by the emotional tension surrounding the production, was ill prepared to take the blow. Exactly three months after the premiere, he died of a heart attack, at the age of thirty-seven. His death came just when he had found his mature style.

Carmen was immediately dropped by the Opéra-Comique. Yet within three years, it had made its way to Vienna and Brussels, London and New York. Five years later, it returned to Paris, was received rapturously, and embarked on its fabulously successful career. Today it is one of the best-loved operas of the world.

CARMEN

The power of this lyric drama stems from the impact with which it projects emotions: love, hate, desire. The story line follows one of the most compelling themes literature has to offer—the disintegration of a personality. The action is swift and unfaltering as the characters are carried step by step to their doom. The story centers around Carmen, a beautiful, tempestuous Gypsy girl

Acts I and II

Principal Works

Orchestral music, including incidental music for *L'arlésienne* (The Woman of Arles, 1872) and the Symphony in C (1855)

Operas, including *Les pêcheurs de perles* (*The Pearl Fishers,* 1863), *La jolie fille de Perth* (*The Fair Maid of Perth,* 1867), *Djamileh* (1872), and *Carmen* (1875)

Piano music; vocal music

The Habanera from Act I of the Virginia Opera's 1992 production of Bizet's Carmen. *Carol Sparrow appears in the title role.*

who works in a cigarette factory in Seville, and the simple soldier who falls in love with her. Don José had been planning to marry his childhood sweetheart Micaela, but his desire for Carmen grips him with obsessive force. She tries to lure him into the band of smugglers to which she belongs, but he cannot possibly abandon the respectable life he has known. However, when his superior officer, Lieutenant Zuniga, tries to make love to Carmen, José, mad with jealousy, attacks him. The die is cast; he can no longer return to the barracks. The band of smugglers welcomes the deserter into their midst with a rousing chorus that hails the freedom of their lawless life.

Act III   In a deserted mountain pass that serves as the hideout of the smugglers, José gloomily reflects on his life. His happiness with Carmen was short-lived. As fickle as she is willful, she has tired of him and transferred her affection to the handsome bullfighter Escamillo. She suggests to José that he had perhaps better return to his village. They quarrel. Carmen's friends, Frasquita and Mercédès, open a deck of cards and tell their fortunes. The cards promise to each what her heart desires—to Frasquita a handsome young lover, to Mercédès a rich old husband who will die and leave her his money. Carmen cuts the cards and draws the ace of spades. "Death! I've read it well. First I, then he," she says. Micaela comes looking for José, hoping still to rescue him from his madness. Then the bullfighter arrives, eager to join Carmen. A fight develops between him and the jealous José; they draw knives but are separated. José learns from Micaela that his mother is dying and is persuaded to leave with her. "We will meet again!" he warns Carmen, as the orchestra sounds the motive of fate that runs like a dark thread through the score.

Act IV   The final act takes place outside the bullring in Seville. A festive crowd hails the bullfighters; finally Escamillo enters, with a radiant Carmen on his arm. The crowd accompanies him into the bullring; Carmen remains to face José. Their encounter is tense and volcanic. Each is driven by a basic instinct: José cannot relinquish his love, she cannot surrender her freedom. He begs her to go with him; there is still time to begin again. She refuses. "Then you love me no more?" "No, I love you no more." "But I, Carmen, I still love you!" He reaches the breaking point against the jubilant strains of the chorus in the arena. "For the last time, you fiend, will you come with me?" "No!" He stabs her as the "Toreador Song" rises from the crowd pouring out of the arena. José, dazed, kneels beside her body. The orchestra again sounds the motive of fate.

The libretto is a tightly knit text revolving around a few key words— *l'amour* (love), *le sort* (fate), *jamais* (never), *la mort* (death), all highly singable. Bizet's brilliant orchestration and rhythmic vitality evoke all the warmth and color of Spain. The work remains one of the great examples of nineteenth-century exoticism; its picturesque atmosphere is inescapably romantic. With its spoken dialogue, set to music after Bizet's death by his friend Ernest Guiraud, *Carmen* issued from the tradition of popular opéra comique. But it expanded that tradition with its realism, sensuality, and tragic ending, in the same way that a century later *West Side Story* expanded the conventions of the Broadway musical. Bizet never actually saw Spain. It remained for him a symbol of that distant, unattainable land whose image every artist carries in his or her heart.

Our excerpt is from Act I, set in a square in Seville in front of the cigarette factory (see Listening Guide 16). Soldiers loiter before the guard house. A trumpet offstage announces the changing of the guard; the relieving troop arrives, led by bugle and fife. The newcomers are hailed by a crowd of street boys who strut beside them, pretending to be soldiers too. They sing a snappy march tune in high register, their "Ta ra ta ta" imitating a bugle call. The retiring squad marches offstage, followed by the youngsters, and the march tune dies away in the distance "as soft as possible."

The factory bell rings at noon, and the young men of the town gather to flirt with the girls who are about to come out. They express their anticipation in a short chorus sung in unison. The girls enter smoking cigarettes, which was quite a daring thing to do back in 1875. They blow smoke rings as they sing their chorus to a gentle melody that is in Bizet's suavest manner.

The mood changes as a few agitated measures prepare us for the entrance of Carmen. The scene is set for her aria in the graceful dotted rhythm of a *ha-* *banera,* the Cuban dance-song that originated in Havana and was popular in the early nineteenth century. Based on a descending chromatic scale, the Habanera follows a "verse and chorus" form; at the choral verse, Carmen sings a seductive countermelody on the key word *l'amour.* Carmen's song establishes her character—capricious, tough, and dangerous. "The bird you thought to surprise has spread its wings and flown; love is far away, you may wait for it; when you've given up waiting, it is there!" She throws Don José a flower. He doesn't know it yet, but she has already settled his fate.

It was a German philosopher who discovered in *Carmen* the ideal lyric

Habanera

tragedy. "It is necessary to Mediterraneanize music!" Friedrich Nietzsche declared in an eloquent tribute.

> I envy Bizet for having had the courage of this sensitiveness—which hitherto in the music of European culture had found no means of expression. I know of no case in which the tragic irony that constitutes the kernel of love is expressed with such severity or in so terrible a formula as in the last cry of Don José: "Yes, it is I who killed her—Ah, my adored Carmen!"

Listening Guide 16

C/S: 6A/4   C/S: 6/ 15 – 22

BIZET: *Carmen,* Act I, excerpt

(13:49)

Date of work: 1875, Paris
Libretto: Henri Meilhac and Ludovic Halévy
Basis: Short story by Prosper Mérimée
Principal characters:
    Carmen, seductive cigarette girl
    Don José, a corporal obsessed with Carmen
    Escamillo, vain bullfighter who wins Carmen's love
    Micaela, childhood sweetheart of Don José
    Lieutenant Zuniga, Don José's superior officer, who also desires Carmen

15   0:00   The relieving guard arrives, signaled by a trumpet fanfare, followed by a staccato march tune:

A group of street children follow, singing the march:

A - vec la gar - de mon - tan - te, nous ar - ri - vons, nous voi - là!

Son - ne, trom - pette é - cla - tan - te! Ta ra ta ta, ta ra ta ta.

CHORUS OF BOYS

1:15 Avec la garde montante,	Along with the relief guard,
nous arrivons, nous violà!	here we come, here we are!
Sonne, trompette éclatante!	Let the shrill trumpet sound!
Ta ra ta ta, ta ra ta ta.	Ta ra ta ta, ta ra ta ta.
Nous marchons la tête haute	We come marching, head held high,
comme de petits soldats,	like little soldiers
marquant sans faire de faute,	marching all in step,
une, deux, marquant le pas.	one, two, marching time.
Les épaules en arrière	Shoulders back
et la poitrine en dehors,	and chest thrown out,
les bras de cette manière,	arms like this, held
tombant tout le long du corps.	straight down next to the body.
Avec la garde montante,	Along with the relief guard,
Nous arrivons, nous violà!	here we come, here we are!
Sonne, trompette éclatante!	Let the shrill trumpet sound!
Ta ra ta ta, ta ra ta ta, *etc.*	Ta ra ta ta, ta ra ta ta, *etc.*

(They continue in the same strain.)

Recitative:

MORALES *(to José)*

16 2:23 Une jeune fille charmante	A pretty girl
vient de nous demander	has just been asking us
si tu n'étais pas là!	if you were here!
Jupe bleue et natte tombante.	Blue skirt and long braids!

DON JOSÉ

Ce doit être Micaela.	It must be Micaela.

(The retiring guard departs, accompanied by the children.)

CHORUS OF BOYS

17 2:42 Et la garde descendante	And the retiring guard
rentre chez elle et s'en va.	is returning to barracks and going off duty.
Sonne, trompette éclatante!	Let the shrill trumpet sound!
Ta ra ta ta, ta ra ta ta.	Ta ra ta ta, ta ra ta ta.
Nous marchons la tête haute, *etc.*	We come marching, head held high, *etc.*

ZUNIGA *(to Don José, who is occupied with his equipment)*

18 3:49 C'est bien là, n'est-ce pas,	It's right there, isn't it,
dans ce grand bâtiment	in that big building
que travaillent les cigarières?	that the cigarette girls work?

DON JOSÉ

C'est là, mon officier, et	It is, sir, and
bien certainement on ne vit	you certainly won't find a more
nulle part filles aussi légères.	flighty bunch of females anywhere.

ZUNIGA

Mais au moins sont-elles jolies?	But are they pretty, at least?

DON JOSÉ

Mon officier, je n'en sais rien,	I couldn't say, sir,
et m'occupe assez peu de ces	I'm not much interested in goings-on
galanteries.	of that sort.

ZUNIGA

Ce qui t'occupe, ami,	I know very well what you are
je le sais bien,	interested in, my friend,
une jeune fille charmante	a charming girl
qu'on appelle Micaela—	called Micaela—
jupe bleue et natte tombante.	blue skirts and long braids!
Tu ne réponds rien à cela?	Have you nothing to say to that?

DON JOSÉ

Je réponds que c'est vrai,	I say it's true,
Je réponds que je l'aime!	I say I love her!
Quant aux ouvrières d'ici	As for the local factory girls
quant à leur beauté, les voici!	and their looks, here they come!
Et vous pouvez juger vous-même.	You can judge for yourself.

(José resumes what he is doing and remains completely indifferent to everything that goes on around him. The factory bell rings.)

CHORUS OF MEN *(Tenors)*

19   5:08

La cloche a sonné, nous,	The bell has rung, and we
des ouvrières nous venons	are on the look-out here
ici guetter le retour;	for the factory girls' return.
et nous vous suivrons,	And we shall follow you
brunes cigarières,	dusky cigarette girls
En vous murmurant	murmuring protestations of love,
des propos d'amour!	and making loving proposals.

(Basses)

20   6:30

Voyez-les! Regards impudents,	Just look at them! Impudent glances
mine coquettes!	and flirtatious airs,
fumant toutes, du bout des dents	each with a cigarette dangling
la cigarette.	from her lips.

CIGARETTE GIRLS

Dans l'air nous suivons des yeux	In the air we follow with our eyes
la fumée, qui vers les cieux	the fragrant smoke as it
monte, monte parfumée.	rises to the skies.
Cela monte gentiment à la tête	Sweetly it rises to our heads,
tout doucement,	gently, imperceptibly,
Cela vous met l'âme en fête!	it makes you feel good!
Le doux parler des amants	Lovers' pretty speeches
c'est fumée!	are smoke!
Leurs transports et leurs serments	Their transports and their vows
c'est fumée! *etc.*	are smoke! *etc.*
Oui, c'est fumée, c'est fumée!	Yes, it's smoke, so much smoke!
Dans l'air nous suivons des yeux,	In the air we follow with our eyes,
dans l'air nous suivons la fumée	In the air, we watch the smoke,
qui monte en tournant vers le cieux!	which rises in spirals to the sky!
La fumée, la fumée!	The smoke! The smoke!

CHORUS OF YOUNG MEN

21   8:40

Mais nous ne voyons pas	But we don't see
la Carmencita!	Carmencita!
La voilà! La voilà!	Ah! there she is! Here she comes!

ALL

La voilà! Voilà la Carmencita!	There she is! Here's Carmencita!

> ### CHORUS OF YOUNG MEN
>
> | | |
> |---|---|
> | Carmen! sur tes pas nous nous pressons tous! | Carmen, we all crowd around you |
> | Carmen! sois gentille, | Carmen, be kind, |
> | au moins réponds-nous | at least answer us |
> | et dis-nous quel jour | and say when you will |
> | tu nous aimeras! | love us! |
>
> ### CARMEN
> *(having cast a swift glance in the direction of the oblivious José)*
>
> | | |
> |---|---|
> | Quand je vous aimerai? | When I shall love you? |
> | Ma foi, je ne sais pas! | Upon my word, I don't know! |
> | Peut-être jamais, peut-être demain! | Perhaps never, perhaps tomorrow! |
> | Mais pas aujourd'hui, c'est certain. | But not today, that's certain. |

Opening of Carmen's Habanera, with dancelike rhythmic ostinato in bass:

ALL DETAILS REQUIRED IN EXAM)

Habanera:

22 **9:51**

L'amour est un oiseau rebelle	Love is a rebellious bird
que nul ne peut apprivoiser,	that nobody can tame,
et c'est bien en vain qu'on l'appelle	and it's simply no good calling it
s'il lui convient de refuser.	if it suits it to refuse;
Rien n'y fait, menace ou prière,	neither threat nor prayer will prevail.
l'un parle bien, l'autre se tait;	One of them talks, the other holds his peace.
et c'est l'autre que je préfère;	and I prefer the other one!
il n'a rien dit, mais il me plaît.	He hasn't said a word, but I like him!

CHORUS

L'amour est un oiseau . . .	Love is a rebellious bird . . .

CARMEN

L'amour! L'amour! L'amour!	Love! Love! Love!
L'amour est enfant de Bohème,	Love is a Gypsy,
il n'a jamais connu de loi,	it has never been subject to any law.
si tu m'aimes pas, je t'aime;	If you do not love me, I love you;
si je t'aime, prends garde à toi!	if I love you, take care!

	CHORUS	
11:52	Prends garde à toi! . . .	Take care! . . .
	CARMEN	
	L'oiseau que tu croyais surprendre battit de l'aile et s'envola; l'amour est loin, tu peux l'attendre; tu ne l'attends plus, il est là! Tout autour de toi vite, vite, il vient, s'en va, puis il revient; Tu crois le tenir, il t'évite; Tu crois l'éviter, il te tient!	The bird you thought to surprise has spread its wings and flown; love is far away, you may wait for it; when you've given up waiting, it is there! All around you, quickly, quickly it comes, goes, and comes again. You think you've caught it, it escapes you; you think to escape it, you are caught!
	CHORUS	
	Tout autour de toi . . .	All around you . . .
	CARMEN	
	L'amour! L'amour! . . .	Love! Love! . . .
	CHORUS OF GIRLS	
	L'amour est enfant de Bohème . . .	Love is a Gypsy . . .
	(The factory bell rings a second time. Chattering noisily, the girls enter the premises, *while the townsfolk disperse and the soldiers, all save José, enter the guard house.)*	

Cultural Perspective 5

The Lure of Spain

The French composer Georges Bizet's opera *Carmen* was described in the text as an example of exoticism. But what exactly did Bizet find exotic about this story (based on a tale by French writer Prosper Mérimée) and its Spanish setting? And how does his music for this opera fire the listener's imagination with thoughts of far-off lands?

In *Carmen,* Bizet played on his romanticized concept of Gypsy culture, which he presents through a title character whose moral values—or lack of them—shocked nineteenth-century audiences. The libretto echoes the theme of naturalism, a movement led by French novelist Émile Zola (1840–1902) that focused on the life of the lower classes and their suffering. Carmen and her friends, a band of Gypsy smugglers, fell far short of the standards of middle-class

virtue. But they are seen against the exotic allure of Spain, and Bizet's music invests them with a certain human dignity.

The music for *Carmen* imitates the songs and dances of the Spanish Gypsies, a style often referred to as flamenco. Typical of southern Spain, flamenco music is actually a variety of different dance songs, most performed to the accompaniment of a strummed guitar, with hand clapping, foot stomping, and finger snapping. One type of flamenco music heard in *Carmen* is the seguidilla, a dance in moderate triple meter that is sung to a fixed poetic verse form. Flamenco performances often begin with shouts of encouragement from the audience, followed by a rhapsodic guitar introduction that sets the mood for the dancers. Distinctive features include a hoarse, nasal vocal quality and a

Spanish flamenco dancers, whose performance traditionally includes singing, foot stamping, hand clapping, and finger snapping, accompanied by strummed guitars. (Tourist Office of Spain)

freely melismatic style of singing, both influences of Arabic music in southern Spain. Some styles of flamenco also make use of castanets, a percussion instrument consisting of two shell-shaped pieces of wood clapped together in one hand. Today, flamenco remains a vibrant and spectacular entertainment that reflects the interpenetration of other folk and popular genres.

But Bizet also looked to a more distant locale in his music. Carmen's famous aria—the Habanera, which we studied—is based on a Cuban dance form. A habanera is a slow dance in duple meter whose name reflects its origin in Havana. It gained popularity in the nineteenth century in Europe and Latin America, and had a major influence on the Argentine tango, a dance with sudden rhythmic movements by couples in tight embrace. The tango has enjoyed popularity for some years as a ballroom dance. You may recall the expert demonstration given by Al Pacino in the 1992 film *Scent of a Woman,* where, playing a blind army officer, he guides his partner through this dramatic and intense dance.

Terms to Note:

flamenco	habanera
seguidilla	tango
castanets	

Suggested Listening:

Bizet: Habanera, from *Carmen*
Spanish dance music (flamenco)
Tango music

32

Late Romantic Opera

The Italian operatic tradition was carried on in the post-Romantic era by a group of composers that included Giacomo Puccini, Pietro Mascagni (1863–1945), and Ruggero Leoncavallo, whom we will study. These Italians were associated with a movement known as *verismo* (realism), whose advocates tried to bring into the lyric theater the naturalism of such writers as Émile Zola, Henrik Ibsen, and their contemporaries. Instead of choosing historical or mythological themes, they picked subjects from everyday life and treated them in down-to-earth fashion. The most famous operas in this tradition include *La bohème* (Bohemian Life, 1896) and *Tosca* (1900), both by Puccini; *Cavalleria rusticana* (Rustic Chivalry, 1890) by Mascagni; and *Pagliacci* (The Clowns, 1892) by Leoncavallo. Although a short-lived movement, verismo had counterparts in Germany and France, and it produced some of the best-loved works in the operatic repertory.

Ruggero Leoncavallo: His Life and Music

Leoncavallo (1857–1919) was born in the southern Italian city of Naples, son of a police magistrate. He studied composition at the Naples Conservatory, and then completed a degree in literature at the University of Bologna. His first opera, *I Medici,* about the famous historical family of Florence, was not a success. Having difficulty establishing himself as a composer, Leoncavallo made his living for a time as a café pianist. His second opera, *Pagliacci* (1892), made him famous overnight. He wrote the libretto himself, drawing the plot from one of his father's murder cases. The premiere took place in Milan, under the baton of the great conductor Arturo Toscanini.

Leoncavallo wrote several additional operas, which met with marginal success. He was one of the first composers to become involved with a new medium—the phonograph record—and *Pagliacci* had the honor of being the first opera recorded in Italy (1907).

Leoncavallo belongs to the category of artists who with a single work achieve a huge success that they never again duplicate. To the world, he is the composer of *Pagliacci;* his twenty other stage works are more or less forgotten.

Ruggero Leoncavallo

PAGLIACCI

Commedia dell'arte

Although the action of *Pagliacci* is drawn from a real-life scenario, its characters—a troupe of traveling actors, or "clowns"—look back to the earlier Italian tradition of the *commedia dell'arte.* This was a type of improvised comedy featuring stock characters, popular in the sixteenth and seventeenth centuries.

Principal Works

10 operas, including *Pagliacci* (*The Clowns,* 1892), *I Medici* (1893), *La bohème* (1897), and *Zazà* (1900)

Other vocal works, including 10 operettas (in French, Italian, and English); songs and choruses, including a Requiem

Orchestral works, including a symphonic poem and a ballet

Piano works, including short character pieces and dances

The opera opens with the arrival of the actors in Calabria, in southern Italy. The troupe immediately sets about drumming up an audience for the evening performance. Canio is the middle-aged head of the group. Tonio, a clown, lusts after Canio's beautiful young wife, Nedda, and tries to make love to her. But he fills her with disgust, and she drives him off with a whip. Tonio, rejected, overhears Nedda planning to elope with a handsome young villager, Silvio. Eager for revenge, he reveals the plan to the husband. Canio surprises the lovers and tries to catch Silvio, who escapes. He then beats Nedda to make her name her lover, but she refuses to do so. Heartbroken, Canio puts on his greasepaint and prepares for the evening show. *Act I*

With Act II, the play within the play begins, presenting the stereotyped characters of the commedia dell'arte. Harlequin (Beppe) and Colombina (Nedda) plan to elope, leaving her husband Pagliaccio (Canio) forlorn. He suspects them and catches them in their lovemaking, but Harlequin escapes. Pagliaccio tries to force Colombina into revealing who her lover is. At this point, the fine line in Canio's mind between reality and make-believe snaps, and he can no longer control his feelings. With mounting urgency, he demands the name of her lover. At first the audience thinks Canio is a marvelous actor, but they soon begin to suspect that something is amiss. Beside himself with rage, Canio draws out a knife and chases the frightened Nedda across the stage. As he stabs her to death, Silvio rushes upon him, only to be stabbed as well. Canio, dazed, holds up the dagger and cries, "The comedy is finished!" *Act II*

We will hear Canio's great solo "Vesti la giubba" (Put on your costume) from the end of Act I. He's only a clown, he tells himself. The audience comes for amusement; the show must go on no matter what he feels inside. (See Listening Guide 17 for text.) The conflict between make-believe and reality forms the climax of Leoncavallo's drama.

The selection begins with a short recitative, followed by the famous and poignant aria "Ridi, Pagliaccio" (Laugh, Pagliaccio), colored with the rich harmonic language that marks it distinctly as a late nineteenth-century work. Leoncavallo originally planned *Pagliacci* as a one-act opera. But on opening night, the wild applause after "Vesti la giubba" made him realize that the aria created a climax that made a perfect ending for the first act, while the play within the play could form the second act.

Listening Guide 17

C/S: 6B/7 C/S: 6/ 46 – 47
Sh: 2B/6 Sh: 2/ 56 – 57

LEONCAVALLO: *Pagliacci*, Act I, Canio's Aria (3:34)

Date of work: 1892
Librettist: The composer
Setting: Calabria, in southern Italy
Characters:
   Canio, head of the troupe
   Nedda, his wife
   Tonio, a clown
   Beppe, a clown
   Silvio, a handsome villager

Recitative

CANIO

46 **0:00**

Recitar! Mentre preso dal delirio	Perform! When my head's whirling with anguish,
non so più quel che dico e quel che faccio!	Not knowing what I'm saying or what I'm doing!
Eppurè d'uopo . . . sforzati!	And yet I'll have to force myself!
Bah, sei tu forse un om? Tu se' Pagliaccio!	Bah, can't you be a man? You're a clown!

Opening of recitative, introduced by timpani and sustained chord in strings:

Re - ci - tar! Men - tre pre - so dal de - li - rio

Aria: two sections and postlude, with 4-measure phrases

A section—four 4-measure phrases

47 **0:49**

Vesti la giubba e la faccia infarina.	Put on your costume and paint your face.
La gente paga e rider vuole qua.	Your public pays you and they must be amused.
E se Arlecchin t'invola Colombina,	Even if Harlequin and Colombina betray you,
Ridi, Pagliaccio . . . e ognun applaudirà!	Laugh, clown, be merry . . . and they will all applaud!

Transition—two 4-measure phrases

Tramuta in lazzi lo spasmo ed il pianto;	You must transform your despair into laughter;
in una smorfia il singhiozzo e'l dolor . . . Ah!	And make a joke of your sobbing, your pain . . . Ah!

B section—two 4-measure phrases

2:03

Ridi, Pagliaccio, sul tuo amore infranto!	Laugh and be merry, though your love betrayed you!
Ridi del duol che t'avvelena il cor!	Laugh through the torment that poisons your heart!

Climax of aria (**B** section), marked "in full voice, heart rend-ing":

a piena voce, straziante

Ri - di, Pa - gliac - cio, sul tuo a - mo - re in - fran - to!

Postlude—shifts to triple meter, lush, chromatic chords

Luciano Pavarotti in full costume as Canio for a performance of Pagliacci. (Photo courtesy of Christian Steiner)

Canio's shattering aria has become a staple of the operatic repertory. It was sung and recorded by several generations of famous singers, including the three foremost tenors of our time—José Carreras, Plácido Domingo, and Luciano Pavarotti.

33

Tchaikovsky and the Ballet

"Dancing is the lustiest, the most moving, the most beautiful of the arts, because it is no mere translation or abstraction from life; it is life itself."
—HAVELOCK ELLIS

Ballet—Past and Present

Ballet has been an adornment of European culture for centuries. Ever since the sixteenth century, it has been central to lavish festivals and theatrical entertainments presented at the courts of kings and dukes. Royal weddings and similar celebrations were accompanied by spectacles with scenery, costumes, and staged dancing. This continued during the seventeenth century with the *intermedio* in Italy, the *masque* in England, and the *ballet de cour* in France. Louis XIV himself took part in one as the Sun King. Elaborate ballets were also featured too in the operas of Lully and Rameau.

The eighteenth century saw the rise of ballet as an independent art. French ballet achieved preeminence in the early nineteenth century. Then Russian ballet came into its own, fostered by the patronage of the czar's court. A decisive event in this development was the arrival at St. Petersburg in 1847 of the

Marius Petipa

great choreographer Marius Petipa, who left an unforgettable mark on the art of ballet. He created the dances for more than a hundred works, invented the structure of the classic *pas de deux* (dance for two), and brought the art of staging ballets to unprecedented heights.

Serge Diaghilev

The history of early twentieth-century ballet is identified with the career of Serge Diaghilev (1872–1929), an impresario whose genius lay in his ability to recognize genius. Diaghilev's dance company, the Ballets Russes, which he brought to Paris in the years before the First World War, opened up a new chapter in the cultural life of Europe. He surrounded his dancers—the greatest were Vaslav Nijinsky and Tamara Karsavina—with productions worthy of them. He invited such artists as Picasso and Braque to paint the scenery, and commissioned the three ballets—*The Firebird, Petrushka,* and *The Rite of Spring*—that catapulted the composer Igor Stravinsky to fame. His ballets have served as models for the composers and choreographers who came after.

Ballet is the most physical of the arts, depending as it does upon the leaps and turns of the human body. Out of these movements it weaves an enchantment all its own. We watch with amazement as the ballerinas in their white tutus, accompanied by their male partners, float through the air, seeming to triumph over the laws of gravity. A special glamour attaches to the great dancers—Nureyev, Baryshnikov and their peers—as they hold a worldwide public in thrall. Yet theirs is an art based on an inhumanly demanding discipline. Their bodies are their instruments, which they must keep in top shape in order to perform the gymnastics required of them. They create moments of elusive beauty, but the basis of these is their total control of their muscles. It is this combination of physical and emotional factors that marks the distinctive power of ballet. The dancer transforms the body into a work of art, and it is this transformation that the world eagerly watches.

As our century approaches its end, we see ballet becoming more and more popular in the United States. Regional groups thrive throughout the country, their activities supplemented by visits from the famous European companies—the Bolshoi from Moscow, the Royal Ballet from London, the Paris Opéra Ballet, the Stuttgart and Danish Ballets, among others. This is a many-faceted art, and the number of its devotees is steadily growing. One has only to watch a good performance to understand why.

Peter Ilyich Tchaikovsky: His Life and Music

"Truly there would be reason to go mad were it not for music."

Few composers typify the end-of-the-century mood as does Peter Ilyich Tchaikovsky (1840–93). He belonged to a generation that saw its truths crumbling and found none to replace them. He expressed above all the pessimism that engulfed the late Romantic movement.

Tchaikovsky was born at Votinsk in a distant province of Russia, son of a government official. His family intended him for a career in the government; he graduated at nineteen from the aristocratic School of Jurisprudence in St.

Peter Ilyich Tchaikovsky

Petersburg and obtained a minor post in the Ministry of Justice. At twenty-three, he decided to resign his position and enter the newly founded Conservatory of St. Petersburg. He completed the course there in three years and was immediately recommended by Anton Rubinstein, director of the school, for a teaching post in the new Conservatory of Moscow. His twelve years in Moscow saw the production of some of his most successful works.

Extremely sensitive by nature, Tchaikovsky was subject to attacks of depression aggravated by guilt over his homosexuality. In the hope of achieving some degree of stability, he married a student of the conservatory, Antonina Miliukov, who was hopelessly in love with him. But his sympathy for Antonina soon turned into uncontrollable revulsion, and, on the verge of a serious breakdown, he fled to his brothers in St. Petersburg.

In this desperate hour, a kind benefactress appeared who enabled him to go abroad to recover his health, freed him from his teaching post, and launched him on the most productive period of his career. Nadezhda von Meck, widow of an industrialist, was an overbearing and emotional woman. She lived the life of a recluse in her mansion in Moscow, from which she ran her railroads, her estates, and the lives of her eleven children. Her passion was music, especially Tchaikovsky's. Bound by the rigid conventions of her time and her class, she had to be certain that her enthusiasm was for the artist, not the man; hence she stipulated that she was never to meet the recipient of her patronage.

Nadezhda von Meck

Their correspondence gives us an insight into Tchaikovsky's method of work. "You ask me how I manage the instrumentation," he wrote. "I never compose in the abstract. I invent the musical idea and its instrumentation simultaneously." Madame von Meck inquired if the Fourth Symphony (which he dedicated to her) had a definite meaning. Tchaikovsky replied,

> How can one express the indefinable sensations that one experiences while writing an instrumental composition that has no definite subject? It is a purely lyrical process. It is a musical confession of the soul, which unburdens itself through sounds just as a lyric poet expresses himself through poetry. . . . As the poet Heine said, "Where words leave off, music begins."

Principal Works

8 operas, including *Eugene Onegin* (1879) and *Pique Dame* (The Queen of Spades, 1890)

3 ballets: *Swan Lake* (1877), *The Sleeping Beauty* (1890), and *The Nutcracker* (1892)

Orchestral music, including 7 symphonies (No. 1, 1866; No. 2, 1872; No. 3, 1875; No. 4, 1878; No. 5, 1888; No. 6, *Pathétique*, 1893; *Manfred,* 1885); 3 piano concertos, 1 violin concerto; and symphonic poems and overtures (*Romeo and Juliet,* 1870)

Chamber and keyboard music; choral music and songs

The years covered by the correspondence saw the spread of Tchaikovsky's fame. He was the first Russian whose music appealed to Western tastes, and in 1891 he was invited to participate in the ceremonies that marked the opening of Carnegie Hall in New York. From America, he wrote,

> These Americans strike me as very remarkable. In this country the honesty, sincerity, generosity, cordiality, and readiness to help you without a second thought are extremely pleasant. . . . The houses downtown are simply colossal. I cannot understand how anyone can live on the thirteenth floor. I went out on the roof of one such house. The view was splendid, but I felt quite giddy when I looked down on Broadway. . . . I am convinced that I am ten times more famous in America than in Europe.

In 1893, immediately after finishing his Sixth Symphony, the *Pathétique,* he went to St. Petersburg to conduct it. The work met with a lukewarm reception, owing in part to the fact that Tchaikovsky, painfully shy in public, conducted his music without any appearance of conviction. Some days later, although he had been warned of the prevalence of cholera in the capital, he carelessly drank a glass of unboiled water and contracted the disease. He died within the week, at the age of fifty-three. The suddenness of his death and the tragic tone of his last work led to rumors that he had committed suicide.

"He was the most Russian of us all!" said Stravinsky. In the eyes of his countrymen, Tchaikovsky is a national artist. He himself laid great weight on the Russian element in his music. "I am Russian through and through!" At the same time, in the putting together of his music, Tchaikovsky was a cosmopolitan. He came under the spell of Italian opera, French ballet, German symphony and song. These he joined to the strain of folk melody that was his heritage as a Russian, imposing on this mixture his sharply defined personality.

THE NUTCRACKER

Tchaikovsky had a natural affinity for the ballet. Dances, especially waltzes, are scattered throughout his works, from the rousing waltz of the opera *Eugene Onegin* to the exquisite waltz of the *Serenade for Strings.* His three ballets—*Swan Lake, The Sleeping Beauty,* and *The Nutcracker*—were not immediate successes with the dancers, who complained at first that the rhythms were too complicated to be danced to. Within a few years, however, they had changed their view, and these three ballets established themselves as basic works of the Russian repertory.

The Nutcracker was based on a fanciful story by E. T. A. Hoffmann (the Romantic writer from whom the composer Jacques Offenbach derived his opera *Tales of Hoffmann*). An expanded version by Alexandre Dumas served as the basis for choreographer Petipa's scenario, which was offered to Tchaikovsky when he returned from his visit to the United States in 1891.

Act I   Act I takes place at a Christmas party during which two children, Clara and Fritz, help decorate the tree. Their godfather arrives with gifts, among which is a nutcracker. The children go to bed but Clara returns to gaze at her gift, falls asleep, and begins to dream. (Russian nutcrackers are often shaped like a human head or a whole person, which makes it quite logical for Clara to

Mikhail Baryshnikov in an American Ballet Theater production of The Nutcracker. *(© Martha Swope)*

dream, as she does, that this one was transformed into a handsome prince.) First, she is terrified to see mice scampering around the tree. Then the dolls she has received come alive and fight a battle with the mice, which comes to a climax in the combat between the Nutcracker and the Mouse King. Clara helps her beloved Nutcracker by throwing a slipper at the Mouse King, who is vanquished. The Nutcracker then becomes the Prince, who takes Clara away with him.

Act II takes place in Confiturembourg, the land of sweets, which is ruled by the Sugar Plum Fairy. The Prince presents Clara to his family, and a celebration follows, with a series of dances that reveal all the attractions of this magic realm.

Act II

The mood of the ballet is set by the Overture, whose light, airy effect Tchaikovsky achieved by omitting most of the brass instruments. The *March* is played as the guests arrive for the party, and a snappy little march it is (see Listening Guide 18). "I have discovered a new instrument in Paris . . . ," Tchaikovsky wrote his publisher, "something between a piano and a glocken-spiel, with a divinely beautiful tone, and I want to introduce it into the ballet." The instrument was the *celesta,* whose ethereal timbre perfectly suits the Sugar Plum Fairy and her veils. In the *Trepak* (Russian Dance), the orchestral sound is enlivened by a tambourine. Coffee dances the muted *Arab Dance,* while Tea responds with the *Chinese Dance,* in which bassoons set up an ostinato that bobs up and down against the shrill melody of flute and piccolo. *The Dance of the Toy Flutes* is extraordinarily graceful, and the climax of the ballet comes with the *Waltz of the Flowers,* which has delighted audiences for a century. With its suggestion of swirling ballerinas, this finale conjures up everything we have come to associate with the Romantic ballet.

Listening Guide 18

TCHAIKOVSKY: *The Nutcracker,* Three Dances from Act II (5:09)

Date of work: 1892
Genre: Ballet (from which an orchestral suite was made)
Basis: E. T. A. Hoffmann story, expanded by Alexandre Dumas
Choreographer: Marius Petipa
Sequence of dances in orchestral suite:

March	Chinese Dance
Dance of the Sugar Plum Fairy	Dance of the Toy Flutes
Trepak	Waltz of the Flowers
Arab Dance	

March: **Tempo di marcia viva (lively march); A-B-A form, 2/4 meter, G major** (2:13)

34 0:00   **A** SECTION
Brass announce march theme:

Answered by strings in irregular rhythms:

Alternation of two ideas

35 0:58   **B** SECTION
Short section, featuring staccato runs in woodwinds and strings

36 1:11   **A** SECTION
Brass march theme returns, answered by strings

Dance of the Sugar Plum Fairy: **Andante non troppo; A-B-A form, 2/4 meter** (1:44)

37 0:00   **A** SECTION
Short introduction (4 measures) of pizzicato strings

Main theme introduced by celesta, staccato in high range (heard in dialogue with bass clarinet):

B SECTION

38 0:38 Brief section with arched lines in woodwinds, answered by strings

A SECTION

39 1:10 Solo celesta leads back to main theme, accompanied by plucked strings

Closes with loud pizzicato chord

***Trepak* (Russian Dance): Tempo di trepak, molto vivace (very lively); A-B-A form, 2/4 meter**   (1:12)

A SECTION

40 0:00 Lively dance tune in strings, repeated in full orchestra:

B SECTION

41 0:26 Brief diversion in same rhythmic style, melody in low strings

A SECTION

42 0:46 Return of dance tune, quickens at end, with trumpet fanfare and syncopations

PART THREE

More Materials of Music

"All music is nothing more than a succession of impulses that converge towards a definite point of repose."—IGOR STRAVINSKY

Fernand Léger *(1881-1955),* The City. (Philadelphia Museum of Art, A. E. Gallatin Collection)

UNIT IX

The Organization of Musical Sounds

34

Musical Systems

"Composing is like driving down a foggy road toward a house. Slowly you see more details of the house, the color and slates and bricks, the shape of the windows. The notes are the bricks and mortar of the house."
—BENJAMIN BRITTEN

At the beginning of this book, we learned various elements of music. Now that we have had occasion to hear how these are combined in a number of works, we are ready to consider the materials of music on a more advanced level; specifically, how musical systems are built—in the West and elsewhere.

The Miracle of the Octave

A string of a certain length, when set in motion, vibrates at a certain rate per second and produces a certain pitch. Given the same conditions, a string half as long will vibrate twice as fast and sound an octave higher. A string twice as long will vibrate half as fast and sound an octave lower. When we sound two tones other than the octave together, such as C–D or C–F, the ear hears two distinctly different tones. But when we strike an octave—two notes with the same name, such as C–C or D–D—the ear recognizes a very strong similarity between the two tones. Indeed, if we were not listening carefully, we would almost believe that a single tone was being sounded. This "miracle of the octave" was observed thousands of years ago in many musical cultures, with the result that the octave became the basic interval in music. (An interval, we saw, is the distance and relationship between two tones.)

THE DIVISION OF THE OCTAVE

One important variable in the different languages of music around the world is the way the octave is divided. In Western music, it is divided into twelve equal semitones or half steps; from these are built the two scale types used most frequently, major and minor. These two seven-note scales have constituted the basis of this musical language for nearly four hundred years.

The Formation of Major and Minor Scales

Chromatic scale

The twelve semitones described above constitute what is known as the *chromatic scale*. (You can see these twelve half steps on the piano keyboard, counting from any tone to its octave.) They are duplicated in higher and lower octaves. No matter how vast and intricate a musical work, it is made up of the same twelve tones and their higher and lower duplications. Hence the statement of the composer Paul Hindemith quoted at the beginning of this book: "There are only twelve tones. You must treat them carefully."

Just as in fractions two halves make a whole, so do two half steps equal a whole step. The chart above gives the names of the notes on a piano keyboard. You can see that the black keys are named in relation to their white-key neighbors. When the black key between C and D is thought of as a half step higher than C, it is known as C sharp (♯). When the same key is thought of as a half step lower than D, it is called D flat (♭). And the distance between C and D is a whole step. Similarly, D sharp is the same tone as E flat, F sharp is the same tone as G flat, and G sharp is the same tone as A flat. Which of these names is used depends on the scale and key in which a sharp or flat appears.

Both major and minor scales function within *tonality,* a principle of organization whereby we hear a piece of music in relation to a central tone, the tonic, and a scale or group of notes. When we listen to a composition in the key of C major, we hear a piece built around the central tone C, the major scale on C, and the harmonies formed from that scale.

By a *key,* then, we mean a group of related tones that revolve around the central tone, the tonic, or keynote, to which they ultimately gravitate. This "loyalty to the tonic" is fostered in us by much of the music we hear. Tonality resides in our minds rather than in the tones themselves. It underlies our whole system of relationships among tones as they operate in keys, scales, and the harmonies based on those. Tonality is the basic harmonic principle at work in most Western music written from around 1600 to 1900.

Key

THE MAJOR SCALE

The major scale is probably most familiar to our ears. It has the *do-re-mi-fa-sol-la-ti-do* pattern already mentioned. If you play the white keys on the piano from C to C, you will hear this series. Let us examine it a little more closely.

Looking at the piano keyboard illustrated above, we notice that there is no black key on the piano between E and F (*mi-fa*) and between B and C (*ti-do*). These tones, therefore, are a half step apart, while the others are a whole step apart. Consequently, when we sing the *do-re-mi-fa-sol-la-ti-do* sequence, we are measuring off a pattern of eight tones that are each a whole step apart except tones 3-4 (*mi-fa*) and 7-8 (*ti-do*). (The succession of intervals that form a major scale is summarized in the table on p. 132.) You may find it helpful to sing this scale, trying to distinguish between the half- and whole-step distances as you sing.

Whether the major scale begins on C, D, E, or any other tone, it follows the same pattern in the arrangement of the whole and half steps. Such a pattern is known as a *mode.* Thus all the major scales exemplify the major mode of arranging whole and half steps.

Mode

This scale implies certain relationships based upon tension and resolution. One of the most important of these is the thrust of the seventh tone to the eighth (*ti* seeking to be resolved to *do*). There are others. If we sing *do-re,* we are left with a sense of incompleteness that is resolved when *re* moves back to *do*; similarly, *fa* gravitates to *mi*; *la* descends to *sol.*

1	2	3	4	5	6	7	8
do	*re*	*mi*	*fa*	*sol*	*la*	*ti*	*do*

Most important of all, the major scale defines the two poles of traditional harmony: the tonic *(do)*, the point of ultimate rest; and the fifth note, the dominant *(sol)*, representative of the active harmony. Tonic going to dominant and returning to tonic becomes a basic progression of harmony. It will also serve, we shall find, as a basic principle of form.

THE MINOR SCALE

The minor scale complements and serves as a contrast to the major. It differs from the major primarily in that its third degree is lowered a half step; for example, the scale of C minor has an E flat instead of E. The minor is pronouncedly different from the major in mood and coloring. "Minor," the Latin word for "smaller," refers to the fact that the distinguishing interval C–E flat is smaller than the corresponding interval C–E in the major ("larger") scale.

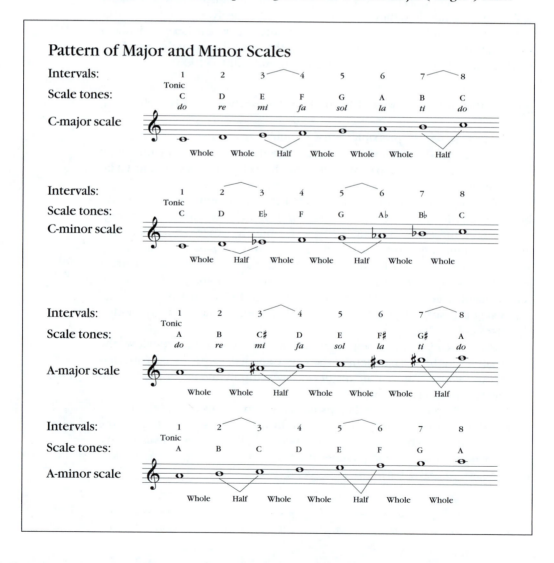

Like the major, the pattern of the minor mode or scale, given in the table opposite, may begin on any of the twelve tones of the octave. In each case, there will be a different group of seven tones out of twelve; that is, each scale will include a different number of sharps or flats. This gives us twelve keys in the major mode and twelve keys in the minor mode.

Chromaticism

When seven tones out of twelve are selected to form a major or minor key, the other five become extraneous in relation to that key and its tonic note. They enter the composition only occasionally, mainly to embellish the melody or harmony. In order for a piece to sound firmly rooted in a key, seven notes of the key should prevail. If the five foreign tones become too prominent in the melody and harmony, the relationship to the key center is weakened, and the key feeling becomes ambiguous. The distinction between the tones that do not belong within the key area and those that do is expressed in the contrasting terms "chromatic" and "diatonic." *Chromatic,* we have noted, refers to the twelve-tone scale, including all the semitones of the octave, whereas *diatonic* refers to music based on the seven tones of a major or minor scale, and to harmonies that are firmly rooted in the key. We can best associate chromatic music with the Romantic era. We have heard already how composers such as Liszt and Wagner explored the possibilities of chromaticism, which charged their music with emotion. We will learn that in contrast, music of the Baroque and Classical eras tended to be largely diatonic, centering more closely around a keynote and its related harmonies.

Chromatic
Diatonic

Other Scale Types

There are many other ways to structure music besides that of the Western musical system. For example, the musical languages of other cultures often divide the octave differently, producing different scale patterns. Among the most common is the *pentatonic,* or five-note, scale, used in some African, Far Eastern, and Native American musics. There are a number of patterns possible in fashioning a pentatonic scale, each with its own unique quality of sound. Thus the scales heard in Japan and China, although both pentatonic, sound quite different from each other. Other scale types include *tritonic,* a three-note pattern found in the music of some African cultures, and a number of other seven-note, or *heptatonic,* scales fashioned from combinations of intervals other than those of than major and minor scales.

Pentatonic scale

Tritonic and heptatonic scales

Some scales are not playable on Western instruments because they employ intervals smaller than our semitone. Such intervals, known as *microtones,* may sound "off-key" to Western ears. One way of producing microtonal music is by inflecting a pitch, or making a brief microtonal dip or rise from the original pitch; this technique, similar to that of the "blue note" in jazz (see Chapter 73), makes possible a host of subtle inflections unknown in Western melody. Microtonal inflections can be sung, and played on a wide variety of string and

Microtones

wind instruments. (There are microtonal inflections indicated in the musical example of Japanese koto music on p. 197.)

The simple ascending and descending order of a scale does not provide the raw material for all melodic conception; in some cultures, the internal pitch relationships and melodic patterns are far more complex than a mere scale. In *Ragas* music of India, for example, the scale formations—called *ragas*—have distinctive forms for their ascent and descent, and certain pitches are heard in only one direction (see example below). These "scales" have extra-musical associations, connected with certain emotions, colors, seasons, times of day, or magical properties. The following example, entitled *Bhimpalasi,* is a raga that is pentatonic (B♭–C–E♭–F–G) as it ascends (with gaps between its notes) and heptatonic as it descends—its downward pattern also turns back up for one note. This is a raga performed in the afternoon, and its use evokes a mood of tenderness and longing on the part of the listener.

North Indian Raga, *Bhimpalasi*

Ascending form:

Descending form:

Thus it is the musical system or structure of a music, and the tones chosen in that system that determine its sound and its character. They are what make Western music sound familiar to us and musics of some cultures sound foreign. They are what make up the world of differing musics, whether classical, popular, or traditional.

35

Aspects of the Major-Minor System

"Form follows function."—LOUIS SULLIVAN

There are several other aspects of the harmonic system we use that make it both flexible and practical. For example, composers can set a work in a new key altogether or shift the tonal center of a work temporarily to another tonality. These principles are known as transposition and modulation.

Transposition

Suppose a certain melody usually begins on G. If you felt that the song lay a little too high for your voice, you might begin on F instead of G and shift all the tones of the melody one step lower. Someone else, who might find that the song was too low, could begin on A and sing each tone of the melody one step higher than it was written. The act of shifting all the tones of a musical composition a uniform distance to a different level of pitch is called *transposition*.

When we transpose a piece, we shift it to another key. We change the level of pitch, the keynote, and the corresponding notes of the scale. But the melody line remains the same because the pattern of its whole and half steps has not changed in the new key. That is why the same song can be published in various keys for soprano, alto, tenor, or bass.

Why does a composer choose one key rather than another? In former times, external factors strongly influenced this choice. Up to around the year 1815, for example, brass instruments were not able to change keys as readily as they are now, since they had no valves. In writing for string instruments, composers considered the fact that certain effects, such as playing on the open strings, could be achieved in one key but not in another. Several nineteenth-century composers even associated a certain emotional atmosphere or color with various keys, a concept not too far removed from the extra-musical meaning found in the ragas of India.

Choice of key

Modulation

If a piece of music can be played in one key as well as in another, why not put all music in the key of C and let people transpose it as needed? Because the contrast between keys and the movement from one key to another is an essential element of musical structure. We have seen that the tones of the key form a group of seven out of twelve, which provides coherence and focus to the music. But this closed group may be opened up, in which case we are shifted, either gently or abruptly, to another area centering on another keynote. Such a change gives us a heightened sense of activity and expressiveness. The process of passing from one key to another is known as *modu-*

lation. There is no way to describe in words something that can be experienced only in the domain of sound. Suffice it to say that the composer has available a number of ways of modulating whereby the listener is "lifted" from one tonal area to another. As the composer Arnold Schoenberg put it, "Modulation is like a change of scenery."

The twelve notes of the Western chromatic scale provide twelve major and twelve minor keys; these may be compared to rooms in a house, with the modulations equivalent to corridors leading from one to the other. We shall see that modulation was a common practice of the Baroque period and was refined as a formal procedure in the Classical era. The eighteenth-century composer as a rule established the home key, shaped the passage of modulation—the "corridor"—in a clear-cut manner, and usually passed to a key area that was not too far away from the starting point. There resulted a spaciousness of structure that was the musical counterpart of the rolling sentences of the eighteenth-century novel and the balanced façades of eighteenth-century architecture, which will be discussed further in Chapter 38.

Nineteenth-century Romanticism, on the other hand, demanded a whipping-up of emotions, an intensifying of all musical processes. In the Romantic era, modulations were more frequent and abrupt. There came into being an emotion-charged music that wandered restlessly from key to key in accord with the need for excitement of the mid- and late-Romantic era.

Active and Rest Chords

Triad
Tonic

Just as melodies have inherent active and rest poles, so do the harmonies built around these tones. The three-note chord, or *triad,* built on the first scale tone is known as the I chord, or the *tonic,* and serves as a point of rest. But rest only has meaning in relation to activity. The chord of rest is counterposed to other chords, which are active. The active chords seek to be completed, or resolved, in the rest chord. This striving for resolution is the dynamic force in our music. It shapes the forward movement, imparting to it direction and goal.

Dominant

The fifth scale step, the *dominant,* is the chief representative of the active principle. We therefore obtain two focal points: the active triad, the V chord, and the tonic chord, to which it seeks to resolve. The triad built on the fourth

Subdominant

scale step (*fa*) is known as the *subdominant.* The movement from the subdominant to the tonic (IV to I) is familiar from the chords traditionally associated with the "Amen" sung at the close of many hymns.

These three triads, the basic ones of our system, suffice to harmonize many a tune. The Civil War song *The Battle Hymn of the Republic* (also known as *John Brown's Body*) illustrates the use of these chords.

Mine eyes have seen the glory of the coming of the Lord,

    I _____

He is trampling out the vintage where the grapes of wrath are stored;

    IV_____ I _____

He has loosed the fateful lightning of His terrible swift sword,

    I _____

His truth is marching on.

I   IV _____ V _____ I

Glory, glory! Hallelujah! Glory, glory! Hallelujah!

I _____ IV _____ I

Glory, glory! Hallelujah! His truth is marching on.

I _____ IV _____ V _____ I

The Key as a Form-Building Element

By marking off an area in musical space with a fixed center, the key provides the framework within which musical growth and development take place. The three main harmonies of the key—tonic (I), dominant (V), and subdominant (IV)—are the focal points over which melodies and chord progressions unfold. Thus the key becomes a prime factor for musical unity.

At the same time, the contrast between keys may further the cause of variety. Composers pitted one key against another, thereby achieving a dramatic opposition between them. They began by establishing the home key. Presently they modulated to a related key, generally that of the dominant (for example, from C major to G major, or from G major to D major). In so doing, they created a tension, since the dominant key was unstable compared with the tonic. This tension required resolution, which was provided by the return to the home key.

Key contrast

The progression or movement from home key to contrasting key and back outlined the basic musical pattern of statement-departure-return. The home key was the anchor, the safe harbor; the foreign key represented adventure. The home key was the symbol of unity; the foreign key ensured variety and contrast.

Focus on Form

36

The Development of Musical Ideas

"I alter some things, eliminate and try again until I am satisfied. Then begins the mental working out of this material in its breadth, its narrowness, its height and depth."—LUDWIG VAN BEETHOVEN

Thinking, whether in words or tones, demands continuity and sequence. Every thought must flow out of the one before and lead logically into the next. In this way is created a sense of steady progression toward a goal. If we were to unite the first phrase of one melody and the second phrase of another, it would not make any more sense than it would if we joined the beginning of one sentence to the end of another from the next page. On the contrary, an impression of cause and effect, of natural flow and continuity, must pervade the whole musical fabric.

This desired impression is achieved in a variety of ways, depending upon the style of the musical work we are examining. In Western music, as we saw, a musical idea that is used as a building block in the construction of a composition is called a *theme,* and its expansion is known as *thematic development.* Conversely, a theme can be fragmented by dividing it into its constituent motives, a *motive* being its smallest melodic unit. A motive can grow, as a germ cell multiplies, into an expansive melody, or it can be treated in sequence, that is, repeated at a higher or lower level. A short, repeated musical pattern—called an *ostinato*—can also be an important organizing feature of a work.

Thematic development is generally too complex a technique to work in short pieces; in these, a simple contrast between sections and a modest expansion of material within one or more sections supplies the necessary continuity. But thematic development does find its proper frame in larger forms of music. In those forms, it provides a clarity, coherence, and logic that are indispensable attributes of this most advanced type of musical thinking.

All the ways of developing thematic material—extension, contraction, reiteration—are as typical of musics around the world as they are of the notated forms of Western art music. We have already seen that much music is improvised, or created spontaneously, by performers. Although it might seem that structure and logic would be alien to this process, this is rarely the case. In jazz, for example, musicians organize their improvised melodies within a highly structured, preestablished harmonic pattern, time frame, and melodic outline that is understood by all the performers. In other cultures, such as those of India and the Middle East, improvisation is a refined and classical art. Yet in each style, the seemingly free and rhapsodic spinning out of the music is tied to prescribed musical material that is manipulated in a lacework of variations.

We can compare how these building blocks of form are treated in examples from two very different music cultures. The first example, from the opening of Beethoven's Symphony No. 5, which we shall study later, illustrates the thematic development of a four-note motive that is repeated in sequence one step lower and then grows into a theme. Here the composer has predetermined the importance and possibilities of his short idea, working out on paper the specific path it will take within the symphony.

The second example comes from the opening of a work entitled *Fuki,* written for voice and Japanese *koto* (a long wooden instrument with thirteen strings and movable frets, played by plucking the strings; see illustration on p. 35). This instrumental excerpt appears to have the regular four-measure phrase structure common in much Western music, but this style of music is more freely conceived and lacks metrical accents. Each phrase of sixteen beats is based on the opening four measures, but no two are identical; rather, a kind of variation form is at work, with each repetition subtly shifting pitches and rhythms, then subdividing beats in dotted figures and adding octave leaps. Note too the use of sequence and the importance of widely disjunct motivic material. (We have already observed variation form in two compositions—Britten's *Young Person's Guide to the Orchestra* and the fourth movement of Brahms's Symphony No. 4—and we will study it as a major structural procedure in the Classical era; see p. 200.) One unique element of the koto selection is the pitch inflections, small dips or rises on a note, used as ornaments to the melody. Since these are difficult to notate precisely in our Western system—the Japanese system is quite different—the inflections are indicated with an arrow up or down. Thus musical processes from distant cultures can sometimes be compared, even when their contexts and resulting sounds are dissimilar.

Suggested Listening Examples:

Improvisation—Ellington: *Ko-Ko*

Thematic development—Beethoven: Symphony No. 5, First Movement

Ostinato—*Black Magic Woman* by Santana

Beethoven: Symphony No. 5 in C minor

Opening of first movement:

Theme based on repetitions of motive:

Theme based on extension of motive:

Fuki, Japanese koto piece

37

The Sonata Cycle

"The history of the sonata is the history of an attempt to cope with one of the most singular problems ever presented to the mind of man, and its solution is one of the most successful achievements of his artistic instincts."—HUBERT PARRY

All music has form; sometimes it is simple, other times complex. In some cases, the form is dictated by considerations outside music, such as a text or an accompanying program.

Absolute music

In *absolute,* or *pure, music,* however, form is especially important since there is no story or text to hold the music together. Here the story is the music itself; its shape, consequently, is of primary concern for the composer, the performer, and the listener. Large-scale works have an overall form that shapes the relations of the several movements and the various tempos in which they are cast. In addition, each movement has an internal form that binds its different sections into one artistic whole. We have already learned two of the simplest forms: two-part, or binary (**A-B**), and three-part, or ternary (**A-B-A**).

We will further examine one of the most important structural procedures of Western art music—sonata cycle, used from around 1750 well into the twentieth century. The term *sonata* (from the Italian *suonare,* "to sound") refers to an instrumental genre for one or two players (a solo or duo sonata), consisting of a series of three or four contrasting movements. *Sonata cycle* refers to a structural plan commonly found in many multimovement genres, including the sonata, concerto, symphony, and string quartet. We have already been introduced to this structure; the following discussion presents the standard form for each movement of these large-scale works.

The First Movement

The most highly organized and characteristic movement of the sonata cycle is the opening one, which is usually in a fast tempo such as Allegro. This is written in what is called *sonata-allegro form* (also known as first-movement form, or simply sonata form). A movement in sonata-allegro form is based on two assumptions. The first is that the music takes on direction and goal if, after establishing itself in the home key, it moves or modulates to another area and ultimately returns to the home key. We may therefore regard sonata-allegro form as a drama between two contrasting key areas. The "plot"—that is, the action and the tension—derives from this contrast, thus providing the framework for a statement, a departure, and a return.

Sonata-allegro form

Second is the assumption that a theme may have its potential released through the development of its components, or motives, as we saw in the previous chapter. Most useful for this purpose is a brief, incisive theme, one that has momentum and tension and lends itself well to creative manipulation. The themes will be stated, or "exposed," in the first section; developed in the second; and restated, or "recapitulated," in the third.

The opening section of sonata-allegro form, the *exposition,* or statement, generally sets forth the two opposing keys and their respective themes. (A theme may consist of several related ideas, in which case we speak of it as a *theme group.*) The first theme and its expansion establish the home key, or tonic. A *transition,* or *bridge,* leads into a contrasting key; in other words, the function of the bridge is to modulate. The second theme and its expansion establish the contrasting key. A closing section rounds off the exposition in the contrasting key. In eighteenth-century sonata-allegro form, the exposition is repeated. Our interest is piqued by the exposition, which brings us from the home key to the contrasting key.

Exposition

The *development* wanders further through a series of foreign keys, building up tension against the inevitable return home. The frequent modulations contribute to a sense of activity and restlessness. At the same time, the composer seeks to reveal the potential of the themes by breaking them into their component motives, recombining them into fresh patterns, and releasing their dormant energies. Conflict and action are the essence of drama. In the development, the conflict erupts, and the action reaches maximum intensity. Emotion is transformed into musical sound and motion. As described earlier, the theme may be modified or varied, expanded or contracted, combined with other motives or with new material. If the sonata-allegro form is in an orchestral work—that is, a symphony—a fragment of the theme may be presented by one group of instruments and imitated by another, thereby changing register and timbre.

Development

When the development has run its course, the tension lets up. A bridge passage leads back to the key of the tonic. The beginning of the third section, the *recapitulation,* or restatement, is in a sense the psychological climax of sonata-allegro form. The first theme appears as we first heard it, in the tonic, proclaiming the victory of unity over variety, of continuity over change.

Recapitulation

The recapitulation follows the general path of the exposition, restating the first and second themes more or less in their original form, but with new and varied twists. Most important of all, in the recapitulation the opposing elements are reconciled, the home key is triumphant. For this reason, the third section differs in one important detail from the exposition: it now remains in the tonic for the second theme, which was originally in a contrasting key. In other words, although the second theme and its expansion unfold in substantially the same way as before, we now hear this material transposed into the home key. There follows the final pronouncement, the *coda,* in the home key. This is fashioned from material previously heard in the closing section, to which new matter is sometimes added. The coda rounds off the movement with a vigorous final cadence.

Coda

The formal procedure just described is summed up in the chart below. The main features outlined there are present in one shape or another in many sonata-allegro movements, yet no two are exactly alike in their arrangement of the material. Each constitutes a unique solution of the problem in terms of

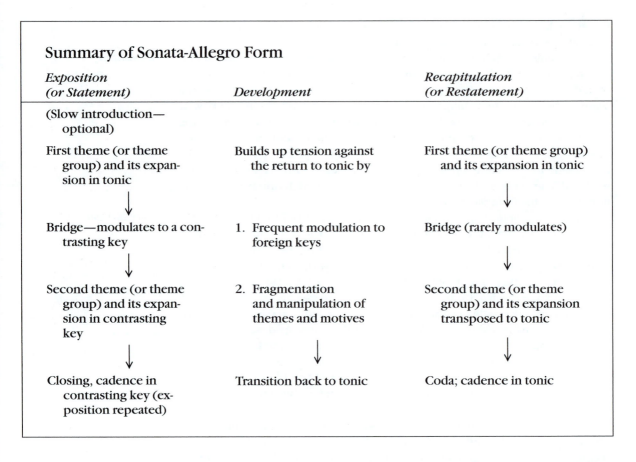

Summary of Sonata-Allegro Form

Exposition (or Statement)	Development	Recapitulation (or Restatement)
(Slow introduction— optional)		
First theme (or theme group) and its expansion in tonic ↓	Builds up tension against the return to tonic by	First theme (or theme group) and its expansion in tonic ↓
Bridge—modulates to a contrasting key ↓	1. Frequent modulation to foreign keys	Bridge (rarely modulates) ↓
Second theme (or theme group) and its expansion in contrasting key ↓	2. Fragmentation and manipulation of themes and motives ↓	Second theme (or theme group) and its expansion transposed to tonic ↓
Closing, cadence in contrasting key (exposition repeated)	Transition back to tonic	Coda; cadence in tonic

character, mood, and relation of forces. Thus what looks on paper like a fixed plan followed by the composer becomes, when transformed into living sound, a supple framework for infinite variety.

The Second Movement

The second is most often the slow movement of the sonata cycle, offering a contrast to the Allegro that preceded it. Frequently, it will be a songful movement that gives the composer an opportunity to present the purely lyrical aspect of the musical art. It is often an Andante or Adagio in **A-B-A** form, a shortened sonata form, or a theme and variations.

Theme and variations   We have seen that variation is an important procedure that is to be found in every species of music. But in one form—*theme and variations*—it is the ruling principle. In this structure, the theme is stated at the outset, so that the audience will know the basic idea that serves as the point of departure. The melody may be of the composer's invention or may be borrowed from another (as Britten did in his *Young Person's Guide to the Orchestra*). The theme is apt to be a small two- or three-part idea, simple in character to allow room for elaboration. There follows a series of variations in which certain features of the original idea are retained while others are altered. Each variation sets forth the idea with some new modification—one might say in a new disguise—through which the listener glimpses something of the original theme.

To the process of variation the composer brings all the techniques of musical embellishment. To begin with, the melody may be varied by the addition or omission of notes or by shifting the melody to another key. *Melodic variation* is a favorite procedure in a jazz group, where the solo player embellishes a popular tune with a series of decorative flourishes. In *harmonic variation,* the chords that accompany a melody are replaced by others, perhaps shifting from major to minor mode. The type of accompaniment may be changed, or the melody may be shifted to a lower register with new harmonies sounding above it. So too the rhythm, meter, and tempo may be varied—*rhythmic variation*—with interesting changes in the nature of the tune. The texture may be enriched by interweaving the melody with new themes or countermelodies. By combining these methods with changes in dynamics and tone color, the expressive content of the theme may be changed. This type of character variation was especially in favor in the nineteenth century.

Melodic variation

Harmonic variation

Rhythmic variation

The Third Movement

In the eighteenth-century symphony, the third movement almost invariably is a *minuet and trio.* Originally, the minuet was a Baroque court dance (see p. 402); its stately 3/4 time embodied the ideal of an aristocratic age. Since dance music lends itself to symmetrical construction, we often find in a minuet a clear-cut structure based on phrases of four and eight measures. (All the same, we shall see that the minuets of Haydn and Mozart reveal an abundance of nonsymmetrical phrases.) In tempo, the minuet ranges from stateliness to a lively pace and whimsical character. As a matter of fact, certain of Haydn's minuets are closer in spirit to folk dance than to the palace ballroom.

Minuet and trio

The custom was to present two dances as a group, the first repeated at the end of the second **(A-B-A).** The one in the middle was originally arranged for only three instruments; hence the name "trio," which persisted even after the customary setting for three was abandoned. The trio as a rule is thinner in texture and more subdued in mood. Frequently in a symphony, woodwinds figure prominently in this section, creating an out-of-doors atmosphere that lends it a special charm. At the end of the trio, we find the words *da capo* ("from the beginning," often abbreviated *D.C.*), signifying that the first section is to be played over again. Minuet-trio-minuet is a symmetrical three-part structure in which each part in turn is a small two-part, or binary, form. The second section may bring back the theme of the first at its close, making a *rounded binary form.* (See chart on p. 202.)

Rounded binary form

The composer indicates the repetition of the subsections with a repeat sign (:‖:). However, when the minuet returns after the trio, the repeat signs are customarily ignored. A *codetta* may round off each section.

In the nineteenth-century symphony, the minuet was displaced by the *scherzo.* This is generally the third movement, occasionally the second, and is

Scherzo

Minuet (**A**)	Trio (**B**)	Minuet (**A**)
‖: a :‖: b-a :‖	‖: c :‖: d-c :‖	a-b-a
or	or	or
‖: a :‖: b :‖	‖: c :‖: d :‖	a-b

usually in 3/4 time. Like the minuet, it is a three-part form (scherzo-trio-scherzo), the first section being repeated after the middle part. But it differs from the minuet in its faster pace and vigorous rhythm. The scherzo is marked by abrupt changes of mood ranging from the humorous or the whimsical to the mysterious and even demonic. In the hands of Beethoven at the turn of the nineteenth century, the scherzo became a movement of great rhythmic drive.

The Fourth Movement

Rondo The Classical sonata and symphony often ended with a *rondo,* which is a lively movement filled with the spirit of the dance. Its distinguishing characteristic is the recurrence of a musical idea, the rondo theme, in alternation with contrasting elements. Its symmetrical sections create a balanced architecture that is satisfying aesthetically and easy to hear. In its simplest form, **A-B-A-B-A,** the rondo is an extension of three-part form. If there are two contrasting themes, the sections may follow an **A-B-A-C-A** or similar pattern.

A more complex rondo form was developed by the Classical masters: the symmetrical or arched formation **A-B-A-C-A-B-A** was most typical. Because the theme is to be heard over and over again, it must be catchy. The rondo figured in eighteenth- and nineteenth-century music both as an independent piece and as a member of the sonata cycle. While eighteenth-century composers were fond of using a rondo for the fourth movement, symphonists in the nineteenth century frequently set the finale as a sonata-allegro, whose spacious dimensions served to balance the first movement.

The Sonata Cycle as a Whole

The four-movement cycle of the Classical masters, as we will find in their symphonies, sonatas, string quartets, and various types of chamber music, became the vehicle for their most important instrumental music. The outline below sums up the common practice of the Classical-Romantic era. It will be helpful provided you remember that it is no more than a general scheme and does not necessarily apply to all works of this kind.

Eighteenth-century composers thought of the four movements of the cycle as self-contained entities connected by key. First, third, and fourth movements

Sonata Cycle: General Scheme

Movement	Character	Form	Tempo
First	Epic-dramatic	Sonata-allegro	Allegro
Second	Slow and lyrical	Theme and variations, sonata form, or **A-B-A**	Andante, Adagio, Largo
Third	Dancelike Minuet (18th century) Scherzo (19th century)	Minuet and trio Scherzo and trio	Allegretto Allegro
Fourth	Lively, "happy ending" (18th century) Epic-dramatic with triumphal ending (19th century)	Sonata-allegro Sonata-rondo Theme and variations	Allegro, Vivace, Presto

were in the home key, with the second movement in a contrasting key. The sonata cycle satisfied composers' need for an extended instrumental work of an abstract nature. It mobilized the contrasts of key and mode inherent in the major-minor system. With its fusion of emotional and intellectual elements, its intermingling of lyricism and action, the sonata cycle may justly claim to be one of the most ingenious art forms ever devised.

PART FOUR

◼

Eighteenth-Century Classicism

"Classicism stands for experience, for spiritual and human maturity which has deep roots in the cultural soil of the nation, for the mastery of the means of expression in technique and form, and for a definite conception of the world and of life; the final compression of the artistic values of a people."—PAUL HENRY LANG

Jacques Louis David *(1748–1825),* Oath of the Horatii *(Le Serment des Horace).* (Louvre, Paris)

UNIT XI

The Classical Spirit

38

Classicism in the Arts

"Music . . . the favorite passion of my soul."—THOMAS JEFFERSON

Classicism can be defined in two ways: in general terms, as pertaining to the highest order of excellence in literature and art; specifically, as pertaining to the culture of the ancient Greeks and Romans. The classical attitude suggests that supreme excellence has been reached in the past and can be attained again through adherence to tradition.

Classicists stress the power of their art as a means of communication rather than as a means of self-expression. For them, a work exists in its own right rather than as an extension of their own egos. This disciplined view encourages the qualities of order, stability, and harmonious proportion that we have come to associate with the Classical style.

The art of the eighteenth century bears the imprint of the spacious palaces and formal gardens, with their balanced proportions and finely wrought detail, that formed the setting for enlightened despotism. In the middle of the century, Louis XV presided over extravagant celebrations in Versailles; Frederick the Great ruled in Prussia, Maria Theresa in Austria, and Catherine the Great in Russia. In such a society, the ruling class enjoyed its power through hereditary right. The past was revered, tradition was prized, and the status quo upheld no matter what the cost.

Enlightened despotism

Before the end of the eighteenth century, Europe was convulsed by the French Revolution (1789–99). The Classical era therefore witnessed both the twilight of the old regime and the dawn of a new political-economic alignment in Europe—specifically, the transfer of power from the aristocracy to the middle class, whose wealth was based on a rapidly expanding capitalism. This drastic shift was made possible by the Industrial Revolution, which gathered

French Revolution

Industrial Revolution

207

The Parthenon, Athens (448–432 B.C.). The architecture of ancient Greece embod-ied the ideals of order and harmonious proportions.

momentum in the mid-eighteenth century with a series of important inven-tions, from James Watt's steam engine and James Hargreaves' spinning jenny in the 1760s to Eli Whitney's cotton gin in the 1790s.

These decades saw significant advances in science. Benjamin Franklin har-nessed electricity, Joseph Priestley discovered oxygen, and Edward Jenner perfected vaccination. There were important events in intellectual life as well, such as the publication of the French *Encyclopédie* (1751–52) and the first edition of the *Encyclopaedia Britannica* (1771).

The American Revolution (1776–83) broke out almost a decade and a half before the French. Its immediate cause was the anger of the colonists at the economic injustices imposed upon them by King George III. Beyond that, however, was a larger vision of human equality and freedom. It was this vision that impelled Thomas Jefferson, principal author of the Declaration of Independence, to incorporate into that epoch-making document the idea that all people have the right to life, liberty, and the pursuit of happiness. These words became fundamental to the democratic faith that has resonated throughout the course of American history.

Intellectual climate   The intellectual climate of the Classical era, consequently, was nourished by two opposing streams. On the one hand, Classical art captured the exquis-ite refinement of a way of life that was drawing to a close. On the other, it caught the first intimations of a new way of life that was struggling to be born. The eighteenth century has been called the Age of Reason; but the opponents of the established order, the philosophers who created the French

Encyclopédie and the Enlightenment—Voltaire, Rousseau, and others—also invoked reason to attack the existing order. Thus these advocates for the rising middle class became prophets of the approaching upheaval.

Eighteenth-century thinkers idealized the civilization of ancient Greece and Rome. They viewed the Greek temple as a thing of beauty, unity and proportion, lightness of grace. Yet here too the revival of interest in classical antiquity meant different things to the opposing camps. To the protagonists of the middle class, Greece and Rome represented city-states that had rebelled against tyrants and thrown off despotism. It was in this spirit that the foremost painter of revolutionary France, Jacques-Louis David, filled his canvases with the symbols of Greek and Roman democracy. In this spirit too, Thomas Jefferson patterned the nation's Capitol, the University of Virginia, and his home at Monticello after Greek and Roman temples. This gave strength to the classical revival in the United States, which made Ionic, Doric, and Corinthian columns an indispensable feature of public buildings well into the twentieth century.

Classical ideals

By the 1760s, there had already appeared a number of works that clearly indicated the new interest in a romantic point of view. In the same decade, Rousseau, the "father of Romanticism," produced some of his most significant writings. His celebrated declaration "Man is born free, and everywhere he is in chains" epitomizes the temper of the time. So too the first manifestation of the Romantic spirit in Germany, the movement known as *Sturm und Drang* (storm and stress), took shape in the 1770s, when it produced two characteristic works by its most significant young writers: the *Sorrows of Young Werther* by Johann von Goethe and *The Robbers* by Friedrich von Schiller. (Goethe, we have seen, became the favorite lyric poet of the Romantic com-

Thomas Jefferson's design for the Rotunda of the University of Virginia at Charlottesville reflects his admiration for classical architecture. (Courtesy of the University of Virginia)

Sir Joshua Reynolds *(1723-92)*
invested his subjects with noble
qualities borrowed from the past.
Jane, Countess of Harrrington.
(Henry E. Huntington Library and
Art Gallery)

posers.) By the end of the century, the atmosphere had completely changed.

Eighteenth-century Classicism, then, mirrored the unique moment in history when the old world was dying and the new was in the process of being born. From the meeting of two historic forces emerged an art of noble simplicity that constitutes one of the pinnacles of Western culture.

39
Classicism in Music

"Ought not the musician, quite as much as the poet and painter, to study
nature? In nature he can study man, its noblest creature."
—JOHANN FRIEDRICH REICHARDT

The Viennese school

The Classical period in music (c. 1750–1825) centers on the achievements of the masters of the Viennese school—Haydn, Mozart, Beethoven, and their successor Franz Schubert. They practiced their art in a time of great musical experimentation and discovery, when musicians were confronted by three challenging problems: first, to explore to the full the possibilities offered by the major-minor system; second, to perfect a large form of absolute instrumental music that would mobilize those possibilities to the fullest degree; and third, having found this ideal form in the sonata cycle, to differentiate between its various types—the solo and duo sonata, trio, quartet, other kinds of chamber music, the concerto, and the symphony.

If by "Classicism" we mean strict adherence to traditional forms, we certainly cannot apply the term to the composers of the Viennese school. They experimented boldly and ceaselessly with the materials at their disposal. It should not surprise us to find that Romantic elements abound in the music of Haydn, Mozart, and Beethoven, especially in their late works.

In consequence, the term "Classicism" applies to the art of the Viennese masters in only one of its meanings: "as pertaining to the highest order of excellence." Those composers solved the problems presented to them so brilliantly that their symphonies and concertos, piano sonatas, duo sonatas, trios, string quartets, and similar works remained unsurpassable as models for all who came after.

Elements of Classical Style

The music of the Viennese masters is notable for its elegant, lyrical melodies. *Lyrical melody* Classical melodies "sang" even when they were intended for instruments. They were usually based on symmetrical four-bar phrases marked off by clear-cut cadences; they moved stepwise or by narrow leaps within a narrow range. Clarity was further provided by repetition and the frequent use of sequence— that is, the repetition of a pattern at a higher or lower pitch. These devices made for symmetrical, balanced structures that were readily accessible to the listener.

Equally clear were the harmonies that sustained these melodies. The chords were firmly rooted in the key and did not change so rapidly as to be confusing. The chords underlined the balanced symmetry of phrases and cadences; they formed vertical columns of sound over which the melody unfolded freely and easily.

The harmony of the Classical period was based on the seven tones of the major or minor scale; in other words, it was largely *diatonic*. This diatonic *Diatonic harmony* harmony gives the music of Haydn, Mozart, and Beethoven its freshness, its feeling of being rooted in the key.

Melody and harmony were powered by strong flexible rhythms that moved *Rhythmic regularity* at a steady tempo. Much of the music was in one of the four basic meters— 2/4, 3/4, 4/4, or 6/8. If a piece or movement began in a certain rhythm, it was apt to stay there until it ended. Classical rhythm worked closely with melody and harmony to make clear the symmetrical phrase-and-cadence structure of the piece. The form unfolded in clearly shaped sections that established the home key, moved to contrasting but closely related keys, and returned to the home key. There resulted the beautifully molded architectural forms of the Classical style, fulfilling the listener's need for both unity and variety.

Folk elements   Despite its aristocratic elegance, music of the Classical era absorbed a variety of folk and popular elements. This influence made itself felt not only in the German dances and waltzes of the Viennese masters but also in their songs, symphonies, concertos, string quartets, and sonatas.

The Patronage System

The culture of the eighteenth century thrived under the patronage of an aristocracy for whom the arts were a necessary adornment of life. Music was part of the elaborate ritual that surrounded the existence of princes, and the center of musical life was the palace.

Eighteenth-century musicians functioned under the system of aristocratic patronage. The social events at court created a steady demand for new works that they had to supply. It is true that in terms of social status musicians were little better than servants, but this was not quite as depressing as it sounds, for in that society virtually everybody was a servant of the prince. The patronage system gave musicians economic security and a social framework within which they could function. It offered important advantages to the great masters who successfully adjusted to its requirements, as the career of Haydn richly shows. On the other hand, Mozart's tragic end illustrates how heavy the penalty was for those unable to make that adjustment.

Women under patronage   Women too found a place as musicians under the patronage system. In Italy and France, professional female singers achieved prominence in opera and in court ballets. Others found a place within aristocratic circles as court instrumentalists and music teachers, offering private lessons to members of the nobility. We will see too that a number of women made their mark as solo instrumentalists, especially on the piano and violin. With the growth of the music trades, especially music printing and publishing, women found more opportunities open to them. Important also was the rise of amateur music making, which allowed women of the middle as well as upper classes an outlet for their talents.

At this time, music was beginning to move from the palace to the public concert hall. The rise of the public concert gave composers a new outlet for performing or conducting their works. Haydn and Beethoven conducted their symphonies at concerts, Mozart and Beethoven played their piano concertos. The public flocked to hear their new works, unlike modern concertgoers, who are mainly interested in the music of the past. The eagerness of eighteenth-century audiences for new music surely stimulated composers to be as productive as possible.

Cultural Perspective 6

Concert Life in America: Then and Now

What kind of music and concerts did people hear in eighteenth-century America? It should not surprise us that British musical tastes and traditions were highly influential. By the 1760s, European-style benefit and subscription concert series were flourishing in major Eastern cities, notably Boston, Charleston, and New York. Typically, a concert was a long affair, lasting three hours or more and featuring a wide variety of music and performers—quite different from modern events focused on a soloist, an orchestra, or a string quartet! Concerts were organized into acts, similar to plays, and frequently closed with a ball where the latest fashionable dances were played. The concert repertory centered on English composers and others popular in England (such as Handel and Haydn). It was rather expensive to attend these events; thus they probably attracted the wealthier and better educated Americans.

Other types of entertainment aimed at a wider spectrum of the American public. Opera was immensely popular in eighteenth-century America. But an evening at the theater then was rather different from what it is today: the performance of an English stage work might well include spoken drama, dance, mime, and even acrobatics. Songs were sometimes borrowed from other operas, and requests might be shouted from the audience, resulting in inserted numbers and encores. (An encore, from the French word for "again," is the repetition of a piece or an extra piece performed in response to audience applause.) At such events, regular concertgoers generally sat in the expensive box seats, while others sat on the main floor in the pit (today called the orchestra section) or in the gallery, farthest from the action. The theater public sometimes became rowdy—in the gallery, there was even drunkenness, gambling, and prostitution going on during the performance—which caused some controversy over the morality of theatrical productions.

Public concert life slackened during the years of the American Revolution (1775–83), but music making continued in the home. Many of America's great patriots were amateur musicians: George Washington played the flute, Thomas Jefferson and Patrick Henry were violinists, and Benjamin Franklin performed on the guitar, harp, and a new instrument called the glass harmonica (this is not a harmonica as we know it, but a set of glass bowls played by running a wet finger around the rim). This instrument became fashionable in Europe as well as America; Mozart wrote a quintet for flute, oboe, viola, cello, and glass harmonica.

Women too were active in amateur music making. The diary of Philip Fithian, an eighteenth-century teacher, describes talents then considered desirable in the educated woman: "She plays well on the Harpsichord, & Spinet; understands the principles of Musick, & therefore performs her Tunes in perfect time . . . she sings likewise to her instrument, has a full, strong voice, & a well-judging Ear."

After the revolution, musical societies, which sponsored professional and amateur concerts alike, sprang up around the country. Typical among these was the Boston Handel and Haydn Society, founded in 1815. As more North American composers were trained, their works were eventually included in the concert repertory along with the European masters.

A scene from an American performance of the dialogue opera The Padlock *(1768) by the British composer Charles Dibdin (1745–1814). This work was popular in New York, Baltimore, and other major American cultural centers.* (New York Public Library)

The United States has sustained a vibrant musical life throughout its history, thanks to such major institutions as the Philharmonic Society of New York (established 1842), the Metropolitan Opera Company (1883), the Chicago Symphony Orchestra (1891), and the San Francisco Symphony Orchestra (1911). Today, symphony concerts and opera performances abound in large and small cities alike, on college campuses and in community forums, alongside rock concerts, Broadway musicals, and a myriad of other programs. The American musical palette continually widens, beckoning new audiences to sample its varied sounds.

Terms to Note:

encore
subscription concert

UNIT XII

Classical Chamber Music

40

Eighteenth-Century Chamber Music Style

"No other form of music can delight our senses with such exquisite beauty of sound, or display so clearly to our intelligence the intricacies and adventures of its design."—SIR WILLIAM HENRY HADOW

Chamber music, as we have seen, is written for small ensembles (two to about ten players), with one player to a part. It is so named for its suitability for performance in a small chamber or salon. In the intimate domain of chamber music, each instrument is expected to assert itself fully, but the style of playing differs from that of the solo virtuoso. Virtuosos are encouraged to display their own personalities; chamber music players function as part of a team.

The Classical era was the golden age of chamber music. Haydn and Mozart, Beethoven and Schubert established the true chamber music style, which is in the nature of a friendly conversation among equals. The central position in Classical chamber music was held by the *string quartet,* which, we have seen, consists of two violins (a first and a second), viola, and cello. Other favored combinations were the *duo sonata*—piano and violin, or piano and cello; the trio—piano, violin, and cello; and the quintet, usually a combination of string or wind instruments, or a string quartet and solo instrument such as the piano or clarinet. (See chart on p. 50.) The age also produced some memorable examples of chamber music for larger groups—sextets, septets, and octets.

Also widely cultivated were types of compositions that stood midway between chamber music and the symphony, their chief purpose being entertainment. Most popular among these were the *divertimento* and the *serenade.*

Divertimento and serenade

In this vignette of amateur music making, from the title page of Joseph Haydn's Trio for Piano or Harpsichord, Violin, and Cello (1798), the keyboard player is, as was common at the time, a woman.

The String Quartet

The string quartet was the most influential chamber music genre of the Classical era. Its four-line texture was viewed as ideal by composers of the era; its focused string timbre poses a special challenge to both composer and listener. In its general structure, the string quartet follows the four-movement scheme of the sonata cycle. The first movement is usually an Allegro in sonata-allegro form. The second is a slow, lyrical movement, often in **A-B-A** or theme and variations form. Third is a moderate dance in minuet and trio form. The fourth is a fast movement, in either sonata-allegro or rondo form. This pattern applies equally to other types of chamber music. The composer adjusts the material to the particular combination of instruments, but the underlying structure is more or less the same.

The movements

The musical texture is woven out of the themes and their motives, and the composer aims to distribute the material among the four instruments. Haydn favored a dense musical texture based on the continual expansion and development of motives, while Mozart was apt to be more lyrical and relaxed. Beethoven and Schubert further expanded the architecture of the quartet, the former through motivic development and the latter through the element of song, which was his special gift. Folk elements abound in Haydn's quartets, while Mozart's exude the elegance of court dances. Beethoven's rousing scherzos replaced the graceful minuet of the Classical era.

Quartet style

Because the string quartet was addressed to a small group of cultivated music lovers, composers did not need expansive gestures here. They could entrust to the string quartet their most private thoughts. In consequence, the final string quartets of Haydn, Mozart, and Beethoven contain some of their most profound and cherished utterances.

HAYDN'S STRING QUARTET, OP. 76, NO. 2 (*QUINTEN*)

Franz Joseph Haydn played a central role in the evolution of the string quartet. His sixty-eight works in this medium form an irreplaceable part of the literature. The late quartets show fanciful key relationships, wanderings from one key to the next, a greater demand of virtuosity from the players, and a texture in which the four instruments share equally.

By the early 1800s, when **Carl Heinrich Arnold** *(1798–1874) made this drawing of* A String Quartet at Spohr's House, *chamber music making in the home was exceedingly popular.*

The six string quartets of Opus 76 were composed in 1797 and published two years later. They came from a period when Haydn was producing one masterpiece after another, marked by freedom and diversity of style. (We will study Haydn's life and works in detail in Chapter 43.) The slow movement of the third quartet of the group consists of a set of variations on a melody Haydn wrote for the emperor's birthday, *Gott erhalte Franz den Kaiser* (God Save the Emperor). The tune became the national anthem of the Hapsburg Empire.

The quartets of this set owe much to the style of Mozart. Indeed, there was much crisscrossing of influences between the styles of Haydn and Mozart; each learned from and in turn influenced the other. Mozart so esteemed his fellow composer that he dedicated a set of six quartets to him in the mid-1780s, called the "Haydn" quartets.

The second string quartet of Haydn's Opus 76, in D minor, is known as the *Quinten*—a term meaning the interval of a fifth—because its opening theme, played by the first violin, has a repeated motive marked by a descending fifth. The first movement is written in a tight, economic style with much imitation between the four instruments. The second movement, a graceful theme and variations, is in D major but switches to D minor in the middle. Third is the minuet, set in a canonic or strictly imitative texture. Its harsh harmonies have caused it to be called the "Witches' Minuet." Even the trio section, which generally relaxes tension, in this instance maintains it.

The Quinten *Quartet*

The fourth movement is a folklike finale in quick tempo and sonata-allegro form (see Listening Guide 19). The first theme, with its strong syncopation, smacks of a Hungarian dance tune. Like many dances, it is stated in two sections, each of which is repeated. The second theme is a gentle duet between

Fourth movement

the two violins, quickly followed by a disjunct idea building to the cadence at the end of the exposition. The movement begins in the home key of D minor, but changes to D major in the recapitulation and remains there until the end. Notable is Haydn's introduction of a triplet rhythm (three notes to the beat instead of two), which gives the closing section, or coda, a sense of climax that leads naturally to the *fortissimo* ending.

Listening Guide 19

C/S: 2B/8   C/S: 2/ 58 – 63

HAYDN: String Quartet, Op. 76, No. 2 (*Quinten*), Fourth Movement   (3:51)

Date of work: 1797
Key: D minor
Movements:
    I. Allegro; sonata-allegro form
    II. Andante o più tosto allegretto; theme and variations form
    III. Menuetto, Allegro ma non troppo; minuet and trio form
    IV. Vivace assai; sonata-allegro form

FOURTH MOVEMENT: Vivace assai; 2/4 meter, D minor/major

EXPOSITION

58   0:00   Theme 1
      a—8 measures, first violin ends with upward sweep, held and repeated:

      b—12 measures, first violin, repeated

    0:32   Transition—denser texture; pedal sustained in cello, 2nd violin has tune; unison writing leads to theme 2

59   0:54   Theme 2—gentle tune in violins, F major:

    1:05   Closing—more animated, disjunct rhythm builds to close over pedal in cello

		DEVELOPMENT
60	1:29	Based on theme 2
		RECAPITULATION
61	2:10	Theme 1—in D minor
62	2:39	Theme 1—in D major, first violin:

63	3:01	Theme 2—returns in D major
		Closing—disjunct, D major
		Coda—quick triplet figures in first violin build to *fortissimo* chords at end

41

Mozart and Classical Chamber Music

"People make a mistake who think that my art has come easily to me. Nobody has devoted so much time and thought to composition as I. There is not a famous master whose music I have not studied over and over."

Something of the miraculous hovers about the music of Mozart. His masterful melodic writing, his elegance of style, and his rich orchestral colors sound effortless. This deceptive simplicity is indeed the art that conceals art.

His Life

Wolfgang Amadeus Mozart (1756–91) was born in Salzburg, Austria, son of Leopold Mozart, an esteemed composer-violinist at the court of the archbishop of Salzburg. He began his career as the most extraordinarily gifted child in the history of music. He first started to compose before he was five, and, with his sister Nannerl, performed at the court of Empress Maria Theresa at the age of six. The following year, his ambitious father organized a grand tour that included Paris, London, and Munich. By the time he was thirteen, the boy had written sonatas, concertos, symphonies, religious works, and several operas.

Mozart reached manhood having attained a mastery of all musical forms. The speed and sureness of his creative power, unrivaled by any other composer, is best described by himself: "Though it be long, the work is complete and finished in my mind. I take out of the bag of my memory what has previ-

Wolfgang Amadeus Mozart

Mozart Family Portrait *(1780–81) by* **Johann Nepomuk della Croce.** *Child prodigies Wolfgang and sister Nannerl are at the keyboard, while Leopold observes them, violin in hand. The portrait of the late Frau Mozart hangs on the wall.* (Internationale Stiftung Museum, Mozarteum, Salzburg)

ously been collected into it. For this reason the committing to paper is done quickly enough."

From patronage to free artist

The decade of the 1770s was a period of relative stability for Mozart, despite the fact that his relations with his patron, the archbishop of Salzburg, were strained. The high-spirited young artist rebelled against the social restrictions imposed by the patronage system. At length, he could endure his position no longer. He quarreled with the archbishop, was dismissed, and at twenty-five established himself in Vienna to pursue the career of a free artist, while he sought an official appointment. Ten years remained to him. These were spent in a struggle to achieve financial security. Worldly success depended on the support of the court. But Emperor Joseph II either passed him by in favor of lesser composers such as Antonio Salieri or assigned him to tasks unworthy of his genius, such as composing dances for the court balls. Of his pay for this work Mozart remarked with bitterness, "Too much for what I do, too little for what I could do."

Marriage to Constanze

In 1782, he married Constanze Weber, against his father's wishes. The step signaled Mozart's liberation from the close ties that had bound him to the well-meaning but domineering parent who strove so futilely to ensure the happiness of the son.

With the opera *The Marriage of Figaro,* written in 1786 on a libretto by Lorenzo da Ponte, Mozart reached the peak of his career. He was commissioned to do another work for the Prague Opera the following year. With da Ponte again as librettist, he produced *Don Giovanni.* A success in Prague, this opera baffled the Viennese public. Of *Don Giovanni* Joseph II declared, "The opera is heavenly, perhaps more beautiful than *Figaro.* But no food for the teeth of my Viennese." Upon which Mozart commented, "Then give them time to chew it." One publisher advised him to write in a more popular style. "In that case I can make no more by my pen," he answered. "I had better starve and die at once." ** *The da Ponte operas*

His final years were spent in poor health, and his creative output slackened. Still, in the last year of his life, he wrote his Clarinet Concerto and, for the Viennese theater, *The Magic Flute.* With a kind of fevered desperation, he turned to his last task, the Requiem, which had been commissioned by a music-loving count who fancied himself a composer and intended to pass off the work as his own. Mozart in his overwrought state became obsessed with the notion that this Mass for the Dead was intended for himself and that he would not live to finish it. A tragic race with time began as he worked feverishly on this masterwork steeped in visions of death. *Last years*

Mozart was cheered in his last days by the growing popularity of *The Magic Flute.* One afternoon, singers from the theater visited the gravely ill composer to sing through the completed movement of his Requiem. He died that same night, December 4, 1791, shortly before his thirty-sixth birthday. His premonition had come true; his favorite pupil, Franz Xavier Süssmayr, completed the work from the master's sketches, with some additions of his own.

His Music

Mozart is preeminent among composers for the inexhaustible wealth of his melodic ideas. His melodies are simple, elegant, and songful. He had a fondness for moderately chromatic harmonies, especially in the development sections of his sonata forms. A born man of the theater, he infused a sense of drama into his instrumental forms, particularly through contrasts of mood ranging from lively and playful to solemn and tragic. His orchestration is richly colorful, his part writing notable for the careful interweaving of the lines.

The Salzburg years saw the completion of a quantity of social music—divertimentos and serenades of great variety, the most famous of which is *Eine kleine Nachtmusik* (1787). In chamber music, he favored the string quartet. The last ten quartets rank with the finest specimens in the literature, among them the set of six dedicated to Haydn, his "most celebrated and very dear friend." Worthy companions to these are the string quintets (set for two violins, two violas, and cello) and the enchanting Quintet for Clarinet and Strings. *Chamber music*

One of the outstanding pianists of his time, Mozart wrote copiously for his favorite instrument. Among his finest solo works are the Fantasia in C minor, K. 475, and the Sonata in C minor, K. 457. (The K followed by a number refers to the catalogue of Mozart's works by Ludwig Köchel, who numbered them all in what he determined to be the order of their composition.) Mozart led the *Piano works*

Principal Works

Orchestral music, including some 40 symphonies (late symphonies: No. 35, *Haffner,* 1782; No. 36, *Linz,* 1783; No. 38, *Prague,* 1786; No. 39, No. 40, and No. 41, *Jupiter,* all from 1788); cassations, divertimentos, serenades, marches, dances

Concertos, including 5 for violin and 27 for piano; concertos for clarinet, oboe, French horn, bassoon, flute, and flute and harp

Operas, including *Idomeneo* (1781), *Die Entführung aus dem Serail* (*The Abduction from the Seraglio,* 1782), *Le nozze di Figaro* (*The Marriage of Figaro,* 1786), *Don Giovanni* (1787), *Così fan tutte* (Women Are Like That, 1790), and *Die Zauberflöte* (*The Magic Flute,* 1791)

Choral music, including 18 masses, the Requiem, K. 626 (incomplete, 1791), and other liturgical music.

Chamber music, including 23 string quartets; string quintets; clarinet quintet; oboe quartet; flute quartet; piano trios and quartets; violin and piano sonatas; and divertimentos and serenades *(Eine kleine Nachtmusik,* K. 525, 1787)

Keyboard music, including 17 piano sonatas and Fantasia in C minor (K. 475, 1785)

Secular vocal music

way in developing one important form: the concerto for piano and orchestra. He wrote more than twenty works for this medium, which established the piano concerto as one of the important genres of the Classical era.

Symphonies   Mozart's symphonies, which extend across his career, tend toward a richness of orchestration, freedom of part writing, and depth of emotion. The exact number of them is difficult to determine. Although four of the forty-one numbered symphonies are probably not by Mozart, newly discovered and reworked compositions bring the number to over fifty. The most important are the six written in the final decade of his life. With these works, the symphony achieves its position as the most significant form of abstract music in this period.

Operas   But the genre most central to Mozart's art was opera. He wrote in the three dramatic styles of his day: *opera buffa,* or comic Italian opera (including *The Marriage of Figaro* and *Don Giovanni*); *opera seria,* or serious Italian opera (including *Idomeneo*); and *Singspiel,* a lighter form of German opera with spoken dialogue (*The Magic Flute*). No one has ever surpassed his power to delineate character in music or his lyric gift, so delicately molded to the human voice. His orchestra, never obtruding upon the voice, becomes the magical framework within which the action unfolds.

EINE KLEINE NACHTMUSIK

Mozartian elegance and delicacy of touch are embodied in the serenade for strings *Eine kleine Nachtmusik,* whose title means "A Little Night Music." Probably the work was intended for a double string quartet supported by a bass. The version we know has four movements—compact, intimate, and beautifully proportioned; originally there were five.

First movement

The first movement is a sonata-allegro form in 4/4 time in G major, and opens in a marchlike manner. The first theme ascends rapidly to its peak, then turns downward at the same rate. The second theme, with the downward curve of its opening measure, presents a graceful contrast to the upward-leaping character of the first. A delightful closing theme rounds off the exposition. As befits the character of a serenade, which is less serious than a symphony or concerto, the development section is brief. The recapitulation follows the course of the exposition and expands the closing theme into a vigorous coda. (See Listening Guide 20 for themes and an analysis of all four movements.)

Second movement

Second is the Romanza, an eighteenth-century Andante that maintains the balance between lyricism and restraint. In this movement, symmetrical sections are arranged in a rondo-like structure. The **A** theme is gracious, a mood that is maintained by the **B** theme. The **C** theme is darker in tone, centers about C minor, and is heard against a restless background of quick notes. The movement is rounded off with a return to the **A** section.

Third movement

The minuet and trio is an Allegretto in G major, marked by regular four-bar phrases set in a rounded binary form. It opens in a bright, decisive manner. The trio presents a contrast with a soaring curve of truly Mozartian melody.

Fourth movement

The last movement, a sprightly Allegro in the home key of G, alternates with an idea in the key of the dominant, D major. We have here a prime ex-

This performing group has all the features of the pre-Classical orchestra, with the leader at a large rectangular harpsichord and the string players and singers distributed on both sides of the garden. Open-Air Orchestra, c. 1790. Engraving by **Giuseppe Servellini.**

Listening Guide 20

C/S: 3B/2–5
Sh: 1B/5–6

C/S: 3/ 31 – 50
Sh: 1/ 46 – 54

MOZART: *Eine kleine Nachtmusik, K.525*   (17:28)

Date of work: 1787
Medium: Double string quartet or chamber orchestra
Movements: 4

(Shorter recordings begin with movement III.)

FIRST MOVEMENT: Allegro; sonata-allegro form, 4/4 meter, G major   (5:27)

EXPOSITION

31   0:00   Theme 1—aggressive, ascending "rocket" theme, symmetrical phrasing, in G major:

Transitional passage, modulating

32   0:45   Theme 2—graceful, contrasting theme, less hurried, in key of dominant, D major:

0:58   Closing theme—insistent, repetitive, ends in D major:

Repeat of exposition

DEVELOPMENT

33   3:06   Short, begins in D major, manipulates theme 1 and closing theme; modulates, and prepares for recapitulation in G major

RECAPITULATION

34   3:39   Theme 1, in G major

35   4:21   Theme 2, in G major

4:34   Closing theme, in G major

5:04   Coda—extends closing, in G major

SECOND MOVEMENT: Romanza, Andante; sectional rondo form, duple meter, C major

(5:48)

| 36 | 0:00 | **A** section—lyrical, serene melody in 2 sections, each repeated (‖:a:‖:b a:‖): |

| 37 | 0:54 | First violin with faster movement at beginning of second section of **A**: |

| 38 | 1:53 | **B** section—more rhythmic movement, varies idea of **a**, brings **a** back at end in 2 sections, each repeated (‖:c:‖:d a:‖): |

| 39 | 2:54 | Return of **a** theme (first time) |

| 40 | 3:22 | **C** section—in C minor, active rhythmic accompaniment; exchanges between violins and cellos; in 2 sections (‖:e:‖: f) |

| 41 | 4:13 | **A** section—return of first section in tonic, without repeats (**a-b-a**)

Coda—3 loud chords extend the idea of **a**

(Shorter recordings begin here.)

THIRD MOVEMENT: Allegretto; minuet and trio form, 3/4 meter, regular 4-measure phrases, G major

(2:06)

| 42 | 0:00 | Minuet theme—in accented triple meter, decisive character, in 2 sections (8 measures each), both repeated: |

| 43 | 0:44 | Trio theme—more lyrical and connected, in 2 sections (8 + 12 measures), both repeated: |

| 44 | 1:41 | Minuet returns, without repeats |

FOURTH MOVEMENT: Allegro; sonata-rondo form, two main themes in alternation, 4/4 meter, G major

(4:07)

EXPOSITION

| 45 | 0:00 | Theme 1—merry, quick-paced theme, symmetrical, 4-measure phrases, each repeated, in G major: |

Transition

| 46 | 0:24 | Theme 2—begins with downward leap, opposite in character to theme 1, in D major: |

	0:39	Theme 1—returns in varied setting as closing
		Exposition repeated
		DEVELOPMENT
47	2:10	Theme 1—modulates through various keys, ends up in G minor
		RECAPITULATION
48	2:39	Theme 2—returns in tonic
49	2:55	Theme 1—in tonic, as closing and extension of cadence
50	3:26	Coda—theme 1 returns as in exposition, in G major

ample of the Classical rondo finale, bright, jovial, and—a trait inseparable from this master—stamped with an aristocratic refinement.

In the music of Mozart, subjective emotion is elevated to the plane of the universal. He is one of the supreme artists of all time.

The Classical Symphony

42

The Nature of the Symphony

"To write a symphony means, to me, to construct a world."
—GUSTAV MAHLER

Historical Background

The central place in Classical instrumental music was held by the symphony, a genre that grew in dimension and significance, as we have seen. With the final works of Mozart and Haydn, it became the most important type of absolute music of the era.

The symphony as it developed in the Classical period had its roots in the Italian opera overture of the earlier part of the century. This was a piece for orchestra in three sections: fast-slow-fast. First played to introduce an opera, these sections eventually became separate movements, to which the early German symphonists added a number of effects that were later taken over by Haydn and Mozart. Among these was the use of a quick, aggressively rhythmic theme rising from low to high register with such speed that it came to be known as a *rocket theme* (such as we heard in the opening of Mozart's *Eine kleine Nachtmusik*). Equally important was the use of drawn-out *crescendo*s slowly gathering force as they rose to a climax. Both these effects are generally credited to composers active at Mannheim, a German city along the Rhine River. With the addition of the minuet and trio, also a Mannheim contribution, the symphony paralleled the string quartet in following the four-movement sonata cycle.

The Classical Orchestra

The Classical masters established the orchestra as we know it today. They based the ensemble on the blending of the four instrumental families. The

227

In this eighteenth-century performance scene, the orchestra is at the rear of the hall, arranged in two tiers, one seated and one standing. Concert in the Shoemakers' Guildhall. **Anonymous** *engraving, 1753, Zurich.* (Zurich, Zentralbibliothek)

heart of this orchestra was the string choir. Woodwinds, used with great imagination, ably assisted the strings. The brass sustained the harmonies and contributed body to the sound mass, while the timpani supplied rhythmic life and vitality. The eighteenth-century orchestra numbered from thirty to forty players. The volume of sound was still more appropriate for the salon than the concert hall.

The orchestra of Haydn and Mozart lent itself to delicate nuances in which each timbre stood out. These composers created a dynamic style of orchestral writing in which all the instruments participated actively. The interchange and imitation of themes among the various instrumental groups assumed the excitement of a witty conversation. The Classical orchestra brought to absolute music a number of effects long familiar in the opera house. The gradual *crescendo* and *decrescendo* established themselves as central elements of the new symphonic style. Also heard were the abrupt alternations of soft and loud, sudden accents, dramatic pauses, the use of tremolo and pizzicato. These and similar devices of operatic music added drama and tension to the Classical orchestral style.

The Movements of the Symphony

First movement The first movement of a Classical symphony is an Allegro in sonata-allegro form, sometimes preceded by a slow introduction, especially in the symphonies of Haydn. Sonata-allegro form, we saw, was based on the opposition of two keys, personified by the contrast between two themes. However,

Haydn sometimes based a sonata-allegro movement on a single theme, which was first heard in the tonic key and then in the contrasting key. Such a movement is referred to as *monothematic.* Mozart, on the other hand, preferred two themes with maximum contrast between them. This contrast was frequently achieved through varied instrumentation; for example, the first theme might be played by the strings and the lyrical second theme by the woodwinds. (See chart on p. 121.)

The slow movement of a symphony is often a three-part form (**A-B-A**), a theme and variations, or a modified sonata-allegro (without a development section). Generally a Largo, Adagio, or Andante, this movement is in a key other than the tonic, with colorful orchestration that often emphasizes the woodwinds. The mood is essentially lyrical, and there is less development of themes here than in the opening movement.

Second movement

Third is the minuet and trio in triple meter, a graceful **A-B-A** form in the tonic key; as in the string quartet, its tempo is moderate. The trio is gentler in mood, with a moderately flowing melody and a prominent wind timbre. Beethoven's scherzo (a replacement for the minuet and trio), also in 3/4 time, is taken at a swift pace.

Third movement

The fourth movement is normally a vivacious finale, an Allegro molto or Presto in rondo or sonata-allegro form that is not only faster but also lighter than the first movement, and that brings the cycle to a spirited ending. It often features themes of a folk-dance character, especially in Haydn's works. (We observed this characteristic in the last movement of Haydn's String Quartet Op. 76, No. 2.) With Beethoven's Fifth Symphony, the fourth movement was transformed into a triumphal finale in sonata-allegro form.

Fourth movement

MOZART'S SYMPHONY NO. 40

Using Symphony No. 40 in G minor by Mozart as a model, we can observe how the movements of a particular composition conform to this general description.

Symphony No. 40 represents the mingling of Classical and Romantic elements that marked the final decades of the eighteenth century. Along with several important works that preceded it, the symphony strikes an emotional tone. (In Vienna, it is known as the *Romantic.*)

The first movement, in sonata-allegro form, opens with an intense theme for the violins that establishes the home key of G minor. It flowers out of a three-note germ motive that is genuinely symphonic in its capacity for growth. A vigorous transitional passage that sustains tension through a steady *crescendo* leads into the contrasting key, the relative major—B flat. The second theme provides an area of comparative relaxation in the fast-paced drive of the movement. The codetta, in which we hear echoes of the basic motive, establishes the cadence in the contrasting key. (See Listening Guide 21.)

First movement

The development concentrates on the three-note motive from the exposition. The music modulates rapidly from one key to the next. Mozart develops his material in a number of ways: by changing the melody, putting it in the bass with a new melody above it, combining motives, expanding them through a descending sequence, or turning them upside down (inversion). The development is crowned by the transition back to the home key, one of those extraordinary passages that only Mozart could have written.

The recapitulation follows the course of the exposition. The transition is expanded and circles about the home key. The second theme is shifted to G minor rather than major, taking on a tender tone. The coda energetically confirms the home key.

Other movements
The second movement, an Andante in E flat, is also in sonata-allegro form. With its graceful embellishments, this movement reflects the courtly refinement of an era that was drawing to a close. The third movement, a minuet and trio in G minor, recaptures the emotional tension of the first; it is remarkable for its vigor and onrush. The finale, Allegro assai (very fast), is a compact sonata-allegro form, abrupt and commanding. The first subject represents the kind of rocket theme that was so dear to the Classical era. This work demonstrates the great artist functioning at the summit of his powers.

Listening Guide 21   C/S: 4A/1 💿 C/S: 4/ 1 – 5

MOZART: Symphony No. 40 in G minor, First Movement   (8:11)

Date of work: 1788
Movements:
    I. Allegro molto; sonata-allegro form, G minor
    II. Andante; sonata-allegro form, E-flat major
    III. Allegro moderato; minuet and trio form, G minor
    IV. Allegro assai; sonata-allegro form, G minor

FIRST MOVEMENT: Molto allegro; sonata-allegro form, 2/4 meter, G minor

EXPOSITION

1   0:00   Theme 1—in G minor, vigorous melody, develops from 3-note motive (marked with brackets), presented in violins:

     0:32   Bridge—vigorous passage, building in a *crescendo;* modulation to key of relative major (B-flat major)

2	0:51	Theme 2—in B-flat major; lyrical, relaxed melody in woodwinds and strings:

| | 1:28 | Codetta—based on 3-note motive from theme 1, leads to cadence in B-flat major that closes exposition |

Exposition repeated

DEVELOPMENT

| 3 | 4:05 | Short, compact section built on 3-note motive in various guises; in new keys, in the bass part (bassoon and low strings), as focus of string and woodwind dialogue, in inversion; returns to tonic of G minor |

RECAPITULATION

| 4 | 5:21 | Theme 1—in G minor |

| 5 | 6:36 | Theme 2—in G minor; minor key gives it new character |

| | 7:19 | Coda—energetic extension of closing, in G minor |

43

Haydn and the Classical Symphony

*"Can you see the notes behave like waves? Up and down they go! Look,
you can also see the mountains. You have to amuse yourself sometimes
after being serious so long."*

The long career of Haydn spanned the decades when the Classical style was being formed. He imprinted upon it the stamp of his personality, and made a contribution to his art—especially to the symphony and string quartet—that in scope and significance was second to none.

His Life

Joseph Haydn (1732–1809) was born in Rohrau, a village in lower Austria, son of a wheelwright. Folk song and dance were his natural heritage. The beauty of his voice secured him a place as chorister in St. Stephen's Cathedral in Vienna, where he remained until he was sixteen. With the breaking of his voice, his time at the choir school came to an end. He then established himself in an attic in Vienna, managed to obtain a dilapidated harpsichord, and set

Joseph Haydn

A modern-day photograph of the Esterháza Palace at Fertód, Hungary. (© Hungarian Travel Company)

himself to master the art of music. He made his living through teaching and accompanying, and often joined the bands of musicians who performed in the streets. In this way, the popular Viennese idiom entered his style along with the folk music he had absorbed in childhood.

Esterházy patronage

Before long, Haydn attracted the notice of the music-loving aristocracy of Vienna. In 1761, when he was twenty-nine, he entered the service of the Esterházys, a family of enormously wealthy Hungarian princes famous for their patronage of the arts. He remained in their service for almost thirty years, the greater part of his creative career. The palace of the Esterházys was one of the most splendid in Europe, and music played a central part in the constant round of festivities there. The musical establishment under Haydn's direction included an orchestra, an opera company, a marionette theater, and a chapel. Haydn's life is the classic example of the patronage system at its best. "My Prince was always satisfied with my works. I not only had the encouragement of constant approval but as conductor of an orchestra I could make experiments, observe what produced an effect and what weakened it, and . . . improve, alter, make additions, or omissions, and be as bold as I pleased."

By the time Haydn reached middle age, his music had brought him fame throughout Europe. After the prince's death, he made two visits to England (1791–92, 1794–95), where he conducted his works with phenomenal success. He returned to his native Austria rich with honors and money. He died in 1809, revered by his countrymen and acknowledged throughout Europe as the premier musician of his time.

His Music

It was Haydn's historic role to help perfect the new instrumental language of the late eighteenth century. His terse, angular themes lent themselves readily to motivic development. Significant too, in his late symphonies, was his ex-

Principal Works

Orchestral music, including over 100 symphonies (6 *Paris* Symphonies, Nos. 82–87, 1785–86; 12 *London,* or *Salomon,* Symphonies, Nos. 93–104, 1791–95); concertos for violin, cello, harpsichord, and trumpet; divertimentos

Chamber music, including some 68 string quartets, piano trios, and divertimentos

Sacred vocal music, including 14 masses (*Mass in Time of War,* 1796; *Lord Nelson* Mass, 1798); oratorios, including *Die sieben letzten Worte* (*The Seven Last Words of Christ,* 1796), *Die Schöpfung* (*The Creation,* 1798), and *Die Jahreszeiten* (*The Seasons,* 1801)

Dramatic music, including 14 operas

Keyboard music, including about 40 sonatas; songs; including folk song arrangements; secular choral music

pansion of the size and resources of the orchestra through greater emphasis on the brass, clarinets, and percussion. It was in his expressive harmony, structural logic, and endlessly varied moods that the mature Classical style seemed to be fully realized for the first time.

As mentioned earlier, the string quartet occupied a central position in Haydn's output; his works are today among the most loved and frequently performed in the repertory. One understands Mozart's remark, "It was from Haydn that I first learned the true way to compose quartets." *String quartets*

Like the quartets, the symphonies—over a hundred in number—extend across Haydn's entire career. Especially popular are the twelve written in the 1790s, in two sets of six, for his appearances in England. Known as the *London* Symphonies (or *Salomon,* after the London impresario who commissioned them), they abound in effects generally associated with later composers: syncopation, sudden *crescendo*s and accents, dramatic contrasts of soft and loud, daring modulations, and an imaginative color scheme in which each choir of instruments plays its allotted part. Of Haydn's symphonies it may be said that they, like his quartets, are the spiritual birthplace of Beethoven. *Symphonies*

Haydn was also a prolific composer of church music. His fourteen masses form the core of this repertory. The prevailing cheerfulness of these works reflects a trusting faith undisturbed by inner torment or doubt. "At the thought of God," he said, "my heart leaps for joy and I cannot help my music doing the same." Among his oratorios, *The Creation,* based on the biblical book of Genesis and John Milton's *Paradise Lost,* attained a popularity second only to that of Handel's *Messiah.* Haydn followed it with another work based on English literature—*The Seasons,* on a text drawn from the Scottish writer James Thomson's celebrated poem of the same name. Completed when the composer was approaching seventy, it was his last major composition. *Church music*

SYMPHONY NO. 100 (*MILITARY*)

Haydn's Symphony No. 100, the *Military,* was one of the twelve works composed for his concerts in London. It was presented in 1794, during his second visit there, and was received enthusiastically by the British public. The nickname attached to the work comes from Haydn's use of instruments associated with Turkish military music—triangle, cymbals, bass drum, and bell tree (also called Turkish crescent). The piece also features a trumpet fanfare, another colorful military effect.

First movement   The first movement opens with a slow introduction, one of Haydn's favorite devices, followed by the traditional Allegro. Also characteristic are the sudden shifts from major to minor, the prominence of the winds, and unexpected turns to remote keys.

Second movement   The second movement, an Allegretto, combines three-part, or ternary, form with a variation technique that presents the theme in an ever-changing guise. The grace and charm are unmistakably Haydn's, as is the easy mastery with which the movement unfolds. (See Listening Guide 22.)

The opening section is based on the alteration of two short phrases, each of which is repeated with varied instrumentation. The next section, set in C minor, features sudden contrasts in dynamics and the addition of the "military" instruments. Most dramatic is a military fanfare on trumpet that ushers in a *fortissimo* chord alien to the key, after which the music resumes its good-humored course. The solo trumpet returns at the end, leading to another *fortissimo* chord, this time victorious.

Third and fourth movements   Third is an elegant minuet and trio, a model of symmetrical structure. The finale, a Presto, combines elements of sonata-allegro and rondo form. In the recapitulation, Haydn surprises the listener with a return of the military instruments heard in the second movement.

Listening Guide 22

| | C/S: 2B/7 | | C/S: 2/ 54 – 57 |
| | Sh: 1B/7 | | Sh: 1/ 55 – 58 |

HAYDN: Symphony No. 100 in G major (*Military*), Second Movement

(6:20)

Date of work: 1794

Medium: Enlarged orchestra, with flute, oboes, bassoons, horns, trumpets, timpani, and strings (also clarinets, triangle, cymbals, and bass drum in certain movements)

Movements:
   I. Adagio-Allegro; sonata-allegro form, 4/4 meter, G major
  II. Allegretto; **A-B-A'** form, 2/2 meter, C major
 III. Moderato; minuet and trio form, 3/4 meter, G major
 IV. Presto; sonata-allegro form, 6/8 meter, G major

SECOND MOVEMENT: Allegretto; A-B-A* form, 2/2 meter, C major

54 0:00   **A** section—C major, binary form (2 sections, each repeated, with varied instrumentation): ‖:**a**:‖:**b a**:‖

a = elegant, arched theme with grace notes; 8 measures, with string and flute:

Repeated with oboes, clarinets, and bassoons

0:33   **b** = 12-measure theme developed from **a,** with strings and flute:

b + **a** phrases repeated with oboes, clarinets, and bassoons

55 1:57   **B** section—C minor, "military" sound, with added percussion (triangle, cymbals, bass drum); begins with loud, C-minor statement of **a;** mixes **a** and **b** themes with sudden dynamic changes:

56 3:10   **A** section—returns to C major, later adds percussion section

    a stated in woodwinds, with pizzicato string accompaniment

    b stated with bowed strings, flutes, and oboes

    a stated with full orchestra and percussion, *forte*

    b varied in woodwinds, against moving bassoon part

    a stated in full orchestra, *forte*

    b varied, full orchestra, soft dynamics

57 5:13   Coda—solo trumpet fanfare, followed by drum roll, leads to *fortissimo* chord in A-flat major; motive from theme **a** repeated until full orchestra closing

Cultural Perspective 7

East Meets West: Turkish Influences on the Viennese Classics

We are all attracted and excited by the new and the mysterious. The public of eighteenth-century Vienna turned to the East to satisfy its appetite for the unusual. Over the centuries, there had been ample opportunities, most of them military, for cultural interaction between the Austrian Hapsburg Empire and the large and powerful Ottoman Empire, of which Turkey was a part. When the dust from their hostile skirmishes had settled, more civil relations were established. Viennese cuisine smacked increasingly of Eastern spices, fashions hinted at an Eastern look, and the city's music took on a distinctly martial sound, derived from the Turkish Janissary, or military, bands.

The Janissary band originated in Turkey in the fourteenth century as an elite corps of mounted musicians composed of players of shawm and bass drum. (We have already noted the introduction of these instruments into western Europe as a result of the Crusades and the establishment of early trade routes.) In the seventeenth century, the trumpet, small kettledrums, cymbals, and bell trees were added to this ceremonial ensemble, producing a loud and highly percussive effect. The Turkish sound captured the imagination of the Viennese masters, who attempted to recreate it in their orchestral and theatrical works. Haydn wrote three "military" symphonies (including No. 100, which we are studying), Beethoven wrote three orchestral works with Turkish percussion, including his monumental Symphony No. 9, and Mozart and Haydn, among others, used this military sound in their operas. The influence was felt even in these composers' piano music; for example, Mozart's appealing Rondo alla turca, from his Sonata in A major.

So popular was this style that some nineteenth-century pianos featured a "Janissary pedal" to add percussive effects.

Although the fascination with Turkish music proved to be a passing fancy, it nevertheless affected the makeup of the Western orchestra by establishing percussion instruments of Turkish origin (bass drum, cymbals, bells) as permanent members of the ensemble. It's hard to imagine an orchestra today without them! The Turkish Janissary ensemble also had a significant impact on the development of the military band in the West and is the direct antecedent of the modern Shriner's band (Ancient Arabic Order of Nobles of the Mystic Shrine), frequently seen in parades today.

Beethoven was fascinated by another Turkish musical tradition—this one a mystical religious ceremony to which he alluded in his incidental music for the stage work *The Ruins of Athens* (1811). The ceremony derives from one of the sects of Islam, that of the Mevlevis, who were famous for their whirling dervish ritual: dancing in a circle with a slow, controlled spinning motion as a part of their religious experience. This ceremony was sung to the accompaniment of flute, lute, and percussion, including kettledrum and cymbals. Beethoven's *Chorus of Whirling Dervishes,* a pale imitation of the original, is an example of exoticism that has been filtered through Western culture. Both the Janissary band and the whirling dervish ceremony are obsolete in modern-day Turkey, except as tourist attractions. The term "whirling dervish"—implying one who twists and turns, like a restless child—has, however, endured in the West.

A Turkish Janissary band featuring mounted players of trumpets (boru), cymbals (zil), cylindrical drums (davul), and kettledrums (kös). Miniature from The Festival Book of Vehbi, *written and illuminated for Ahmed III (r. 1703–30).* (Istanbul, Topkapi Sarayi Museum)

Terms to Note:

Janissary band
whirling dervish

Suggested Listening:

Turkish music (Janissary ensemble)
Mozart: Rondo alla turca, from Piano Sonata
   in A, K. 331
Haydn: Symphony No. 100, *Military,* Second
   Movement
Beethoven: Symphony No. 9, Fourth
   Movement

44

Beethoven and the Symphony in Transition

"Freedom above all!"

Beethoven belonged to the generation that received the full impact of the French Revolution. He created the music of a heroic age and, in accents never to be forgotten, proclaimed its faith in the power of man to shape his destiny.

His Life

Ludwig van Beethoven

Ludwig van Beethoven (1770–1827) was born in Germany, in the city of Bonn, where his father and grandfather were singers at the court of the local prince, the elector Max Friedrich. The family situation was unhappy; his father was an alcoholic, and Ludwig at an early age was forced to support his mother and two younger brothers. At eleven and a half, he was assistant organist in the court chapel, and a year later, he became harpsichordist in the court orchestra. A visit to Vienna in his seventeenth year provided an opportunity to play for Mozart. The youth improvised so brilliantly on a theme given him by the master that Mozart remarked to his friends, "Keep an eye on him—he will make a noise in the world some day."

Early years in Vienna

Beethoven's talents as a pianist took the music-loving aristocracy by storm. He was welcomed in the great houses of Vienna by the powerful patrons whose names appear in the dedications of his works, such as Prince Lichnowsky, Prince Lobkowitz, and Count Razumovsky. In an era of revolution, this young genius came to the "princely rabble," as he called them, forcing them to receive him as an equal and friend. "It is good to move among the aristocracy," he observed, "but it is first necessary to make them respect you."

Beethoven functioned under a modified form of the patronage system. He was not attached to the court of a prince. Instead, the music-loving aristocrats of Vienna helped him in various ways—by paying him handsomely for lessons or presenting him with gifts. He was also aided by the emergence of a middle-class public and the growth of concert life and music publishing. At the age of thirty-one, he was able to write, "I have six or seven publishers for each of my works and could have more if I chose. No more bargaining. I name my terms and they pay." A youthful exuberance pervades the first decade of his career, an almost arrogant consciousness of his strength. "Power is the morality of men who stand out from the mass, and it is also mine!" Thus spoke the individualist in the new era of individualism.

The onset of deafness

Then, fate struck in a vulnerable spot: Beethoven began to lose his hearing. His helplessness in the face of this affliction dealt a shattering blow to his pride: "Ah, how could I possibly admit an infirmity in the one sense that should have been more perfect in me than in others. A sense I once possessed in highest perfection. Oh I cannot do it!" As his deafness closed in on him— the first symptoms appeared when he was in his late twenties—it forced a sense of apartness from other men. Upon the advice of his doctors, he retired in 1802 to a summer resort outside Vienna called Heiligenstadt. A titanic strug- gle shook him, between the destructive forces in his soul and his desire to live and create: "But little more and I would have put an end to my life. Only art . . . withheld me. Ah, it seemed impossible to leave the world until I had pro- duced all that I felt called upon to produce, and so I endured this wretched existence."

Beethoven slowly realized that art must give him the happiness that life withheld. The will to struggle reasserted itself; he fought his way back to health. "I am resolved to rise superior to every obstacle. With whom need I be afraid of measuring my strength? I will take Fate by the throat. It shall not over- come me. O how beautiful it is to be alive—would that I could live a thousand times!" He had stumbled on an idea that was to play a decisive part in nine- teenth-century thought: the concept of art as refuge, as compensation for the shortcomings of reality—art as the ultimate victory over life. "I am the Bacchus who presses out the glorious wine for mankind. Whoever truly un- derstands my music is freed thereby from the miseries that others carry about in them."

The remainder of his career was spent in ceaseless effort to achieve his *Final years* artistic goals. Biographers and painters have made familiar the squat, sturdy figure—he was five foot four, the same height as that other conqueror of the age, Napoleon—walking hatless through Vienna, the bulging brow furrowed in thought, stopping to jot down an idea in his sketchbook; an idea that, be- cause he could not hear its sonorous beauty, he envisioned all the more vividly in his mind. A ride in an open carriage in severe weather brought on an attack of edema that proved fatal. Beethoven died in his fifty-seventh year, famous and revered.

His Music

Beethoven is the supreme architect in music. His genius found expression in the structural type of thinking embodied in the sonata and symphony. The sketchbooks in which he worked out his ideas show how gradually they reached their final shape: "I carry my thoughts within me long," he wrote, "often very long before I write them down. As I know what I want, the funda- mental idea never deserts me. It mounts, it grows in stature. I hear, I see the picture in its whole extent standing all of a piece before my spirit, and there remains for me only the task of writing it down."

His compositional activity fell into three periods. The first reflected the *Three periods* Classical elements he inherited from Haydn and Mozart. The middle period saw the appearance of characteristics more closely associated with the nine- teenth century: strong dynamic contrasts, explosive accents, and longer movements. Beethoven expanded the dimensions of the first movement, es-

Principal Works

Orchestral music, including 9 symphonies: No. 1 (1800); No. 2 (1802); No. 3, *Eroica* (1803); No. 4 (1806); No. 5 (1808); No. 6, *Pastoral* (1808); No. 7 (1812); No. 8 (1812); No. 9, *Choral* (1824); overtures, including *Leonore* (Nos. 1, 2, 3) and *Egmont;* incidental music

Concertos, including 5 for piano, 1 for violin (1806), and 1 triple concerto (piano, violin, and cello, 1804)

Chamber music, including string quartets, piano trios, quartets, 1 quintet, 1 septet, and violin and cello sonatas; serenades and wind chamber music

32 piano sonatas, including Op. 13. *Pathétique* (1806); Op. 27, No. 2, *Moonlight* (1801); Op. 53, *Waldstein* (1804); and Op. 57, *Appassionata* (1805)

1 opera (*Fidelio,* 1805)

Choral music, including *Missa solemnis* (1823)

Songs, including song cycle *An die ferne Geliebte* (To the Distant Beloved, 1816)

pecially the coda, and like Haydn and Mozart made the development section the dynamic center of the form. In his hands, the slow movement acquired a hymnlike character, the essence of Beethovenian pathos. The scherzo became a movement of rhythmic energy ranging from "cosmic laughter" to mystery and wonder. His goal throughout was powerful expression rather than elegance. He enlarged the finale into a movement comparable in size and scope to the first, and ended the symphony on a note of triumph.

In his third period—the years of the final piano sonatas and string quartets—Beethoven used more chromatic harmonies and developed a skeletal language from which all nonessentials were rigidly pared away. This was a language that transcended his time. To someone who asked him if one of his more advanced quartets was music, he replied, "Not for you. For a later time."

Symphonies   The symphony provided Beethoven with the ideal medium by which to address humanity. His nine symphonies are spiritual dramas of universal appeal. They are conceived on a scale too large for the aristocratic salon; they demand the concert hall.

The first two symphonies stand closest to the two Classical masters who preceded him; with his Third Symphony, the *Eroica,* Beethoven achieved his mature style. The work was originally dedicated to Napoleon, who seemed to represent the spirit of revolution and the freedom of man. When the news came that Napoleon had proclaimed himself emperor, Beethoven was disenchanted. "He too is just like any other! Now he will trample on the rights of man and serve nothing but his own ambition." The embittered composer tore up the dedicatory page of the just-completed work and renamed it "Heroic

Symphony to celebrate the memory of a great man."

The Fifth Symphony is popularly viewed as the archetype of the genre. The Seventh rivals it in universal appeal. The Ninth, the *Choral* Symphony, strikes the searching tone of Beethoven's last period. Its finale, in which vocal soloists and chorus join with the orchestra, contains the famous line "Be embraced, ye millions!" The choral movement is a setting of Schiller's *Ode to Joy,* a ringing prophecy of the time when "all men shall be brothers."

Concertos and piano sonatas

The concerto offered Beethoven an ideal form in which to combine virtuosity with symphonic structure. His Violin Concerto displays the virtuosity of the soloist within a much enlarged form, and his five piano concertos went hand in hand with—and in turn encouraged—the rising popularity of the instrument. The piano occupied a central position in Beethoven's art. His thirty-two sonatas are an indispensable part of its literature, whether for the amateur pianist or concert artist. They are aptly called the pianist's New Testament (the Old being *The Well-Tempered Clavier* of Bach).

String quartets

Beethoven wrote a great deal of chamber music, the string quartet being closest to his heart. The six quartets of Opus 18 are the first in a series that extended throughout the whole of his career. His supreme achievements in this area are the last five quartets, which, together with the Grand Fugue, Op. 133, occupied the final years of his life. In these, as in the last five piano sonatas, the master employs a searching, introspective style, far from the exuberance of his youth.

Vocal music

Beethoven also made significant contributions to vocal music. His one opera, *Fidelio,* centers on wifely devotion, human freedom, and the defeat of those who would destroy it. The *Missa solemnis* (Solemn Mass) ranks in importance with the Ninth Symphony and the final quartets. The work transcends the limits of any specific creed or faith. Above the Kyrie of the mass, he wrote a sentence that applies to the whole of his music: "From the heart . . . may it find its way to the heart."

THE FIFTH SYMPHONY

First movement

Perhaps the most popular of all symphonies, Beethoven's Symphony No. 5 in C minor, Op. 67, is also the most concentrated expression of the spirit that we have come to call Beethovenian. The first movement, marked Allegro con brio (lively, with vigor), springs out of the rhythmic idea of "three shorts and a long" that dominates the symphony. It is the most compact and commanding gesture in the whole symphonic literature. The power of the movement springs from the almost terrifying single-mindedness with which this idea is pursued. This dramatic sonata-allegro movement ends with an extended coda in which the basic rhythm reveals a new fund of explosive energy. (See Listening Guide 23.)

Second movement

Beethovenian serenity pervades the second movement, a theme and variations, with two melodic ideas. In the course of the movement, Beethoven exploits his two themes with all the procedures of variation—changes in melodic outline, harmony, rhythm, tempo, dynamics, register, key, mode, and type of accompaniment.

Cultural Perspective 8

The Composer Heard 'Round the World

Ludwig van Beethoven stands today as the most popular composer of art music in the world. What accounts for the universality of this master, whose compositions have endured repeated performances and intense scholarly dissection as well as popular distortion? Clearly, his wide acceptance results from more than the powerful influence that Western culture has exerted globally.

Beethoven's Fifth Symphony was recognized in its day as a masterpiece. Premiered in Vienna (December 2, 1808) at a four-hour concert of his music, the work was immediately hailed by one reviewer, the German composer Johann Friedrich Reichardt, as "a great symphony"—not a typical critic's reaction to new music. Although the general public might not have fully understood the master's works, they revered him nevertheless—some twenty thousand people turned out for his funeral in Vienna!

Beethoven represented the newly emerging "free artist," who lived from the sale of his works rather than the bounty of a single prince. In his lifetime, his music was published from Russia to the United States, and emerging music societies around the globe performed his orchestral and choral compositions. The Philharmonic Society of New York (the oldest continuing orchestra in the United States, founded in 1842) opened its first public program with the "Grand Symphony in C minor (the 5th)" by Beethoven. The nineteenth-century composer Hector Berlioz, on first hearing the master's symphonies in 1828, claimed that "Beethoven opened before me a new world of music, as Shakespeare had revealed a new universe of poetry." Berlioz then convinced his teacher, Jean-François Lesueur, to attend a

performance of the Fifth Symphony at the Paris Conservatory. Lesueur's reaction was immediate: "Let me get out. I must have some air. It's amazing! Wonderful! I was so moved and disturbed that when I emerged from the box and attempted to put on my hat, I couldn't find my head."

The famous opening motive of the Fifth Symphony—three shorts and a long—has inspired a variety of interpretations, the most popular being "fate knocking at the door." During the Second World War, the rhythm was associated with its Morse code meaning of "V" for victory, and transmitted via radio waves over thousands of miles.

Perhaps even more popular is Beethoven's great Ninth Symphony, with its famous choral finale—commonly known as *Ode to Joy*—set to inspirational words of unity among peoples by the German poet Friedrich von Schiller. This musical work has exerted such strong appeal that it has been used as a rallying cry for widely divergent philosophies, including democracy, totalitarianism, and fascism. In Japan, the performance of this piece with a colossal choir is traditional each December 31, to bring the year to a close.

The youth of the rock era first rejected this style of art music, voiced in Chuck Berry's 1956 hit *Roll Over, Beethoven,* but even this vernacular music has succumbed to the timelessness of Beethoven: several disco settings of the Fifth Symphony have been produced, including the popular *Hooked on Classics,* and a karaoke version of the finale of the Ninth Symphony is now available in Japan. (*Karaoke,* a Japanese word meaning "empty orchestra," is a popular nightclub style where customers sing the melody to an accompanying track.) Today, Beethoven's music can

Beethoven's death, unlike Haydn's and Mozart's, did not pass unnoticed. Thousands of people from all walks of life followed his funeral procession to the cemetery. A watercolor by **Franz Stöber.** (Beethoven-Haus, Bonn)

even be heard in commercials and movie soundtracks, further testament to the continued popularity of this ageless musician.

Terms to Note:

Philharmonic
karaoke

Suggested Listening:

Beethoven: Symphony No. 9, Fourth Movement
Hooked on Classics

Third in the cycle of movements is the scherzo, which opens with a rocket theme introduced by cellos and double basses. After the gruff, humorous trio in C major, the scherzo returns in a modified version, followed by a transitional passage in which the basic rhythm of the first movement is sounded by the timpani.

Third movement

The fourth movement, a monumental sonata form, once again brings back the "three shorts and a long." This return of material from an earlier movement gives the symphony its cyclical, or unified, form. At the end of the extended coda, the tonic chord is proclaimed triumphantly by the orchestra again and again.

Fourth movement

Beethoven's career bridged the transition from the old society to the new. His music stems from a relentless struggle for self-realization. It is the expression of a titanic force, the affirmation of an all-conquering will.

Listening Guide 23

C/S: 4B/1–3   C/S: 4/ 32 – 55
Sh: 1B/8   Sh: 1/ 59 – 64

BEETHOVEN: Symphony No. 5 in C minor, Op. 67 (31:55)

Date of work: 1807–8
Movements: 4

FIRST MOVEMENT: Allegro con brio; sonata-allegro form, 2/4 meter, C minor (7:28)

32	0:00	EXPOSITION Theme 1—based on famous 4-note motive, in C minor:

	0:05	Treated sequentially:

	0:43	Expanded from 4-note motive; horns establish key of second theme:

33	0:45	Theme 2—more lyrical, in woodwinds, in E-flat major, heard against rhythm of 4-note motive:

	1:17	Closing—based on 4-note motive
		(Repeat of exposition) DEVELOPMENT
34	2:54	Beginning of development
	3:04	Manipulation of 4-note motive through a descending sequence:

	3:16	Melodic variation, interval filled in and inverted:

| | 4:13 | Expansion through repetition; leads into recapitulation: |

RECAPITULATION

35	4:18	Theme 1—in C minor, brief oboe solo
36	5:14	Theme 2—returns in C major
	5:50	Closing theme
37	5:57	Coda—extended treatment of 4-note motive

(Shorter recordings stop here.)

SECOND MOVEMENT: Andante con moto; theme and variations form, with two themes, 3/8 meter, A-flat major

(10:09)

| 38 | 0:00 | Theme 1—broad, flowing melody, heard in low strings: |

| 39 | 0:53 | Theme 2—upward-thrusting 4-note motive: |

Examples of variations on theme 1

| 40 | 1:58 | Embellished with running sixteenth notes: |

41 3:54 Embellished with thirty-second notes:

42 5:09 Melody exchanged between woodwind instruments:

43 6:43 Melody shifted to minor, more disjunct:

44 8:16 Coda—Più mosso (faster), in bassoon

THIRD MOVEMENT: Allegro; scherzo and trio form, 3/4 meter, C minor   (5:34)

45 0:00 Scherzo theme—rising, rocket theme in low strings:

      0:18 Recurrent rhythmic motive (from opening of first movement):

46 1:58 Trio theme—in C major, in double basses:

      2:28 Trio theme broken up and expanded through sequences:

47 3:29 Scherzo returns, with varied orchestration

48 4:50 Transition to next movement with timpani rhythm from opening 4-note motive:

FOURTH MOVEMENT: Allegro; sonata-allegro form, 4/4 meter, C major   (8:44)

      EXPOSITION
49 5:34 Theme 1—in C major, powerful melody whose opening outlines C-major chord:

50	6:07	Lyrical transition theme, modulating from C to G major:
51	6:34	Theme 2—in G major, vigorous melody with triplets:
	7:00	Codetta—features clarinet and violas, decisive theme:

DEVELOPMENT

52	7:31	Much modulation and free rhythmic treatment; brings back 4-note motive (3 short and a long) from first movement
53	9:12	Brief recurrence of scherzo

RECAPITULATION

54	9:45	Theme 1, in C major
55	10:33	Theme 2, in C major
	10:53	Coda—long extension

The Eighteenth-Century Concerto and Sonata

45

The Classical Concerto

"Give me the best instrument in Europe, but listeners who understand nothing or do not wish to understand and who do not feel with me in what I am playing, and all my pleasure is spoilt."—W. A. MOZART

The Movements of the Concerto

In the early eighteenth century, the word "concerto" implied a mixing together of two disparate elements, such as a soloist and orchestra or a solo group and orchestra. The Classical era shifted the emphasis to the concerto for solo instrument, especially piano or violin, and orchestra.

First movement

The three movements of the Classical concerto follow the pattern fast-slow-fast already established (see Chapter 25). The Classical concerto begins with a first-movement form that adapts the principles of the ritornello procedure (a *ritornello,* developed in the Baroque era, is a recurring musical passage) to those of sonata-allegro form. The movement usually opens with an orchestral exposition or ritornello in the tonic key, often presenting several themes. A second exposition follows for the solo instrument and orchestra, now making the necessary key change to the dominant. The soloist often plays elaborated versions of the themes first heard in the orchestra, frequently adding new material as well. The development offers ample opportunity for solo virtuosic display, in dialogue with the orchestra. The recapitulation brings back the themes in the tonic, played by the soloist and orchestra. A solo cadenza—generally a brilliant improvisation—is normally played near the end of the movement, and a coda brings the movement to a close with a strong affirmation of the home key. First-movement concerto form is sometimes described as a sonata-allegro form with a double exposition.

Second is the slow lyrical movement, generally an Andante, Adagio, or Largo, which features the soloist in songlike melody. This movement is often in a key that lies close to the tonic but contrasts with it. Thus, if the first movement is in C major, the second might well be in F major, four steps above.

Second movement

The finale is normally an Allegro molto or Presto (very fast), usually shorter than the first movement, and often in rondo form or a rondo that has taken over some developmental features of sonata-allegro form. This movement may contain a cadenza of its own that calls for virtuoso playing and brings the piece to an exciting end.

Finale

MOZART'S PIANO CONCERTO IN G MAJOR, K. 453

Mozart played a crucial role in the development of the piano concerto. His concertos were written primarily as display pieces for his own public performances. They abound in the brilliant flourishes and ceremonious gestures characteristic of eighteenth-century music.

The year 1784 was a most prolific one for Mozart as far as piano concertos were concerned—he wrote six. He was then in great demand as a pianist, and this flurry of success was reflected in the happy mood of these works. The Concerto in G major, K. 453, was composed for a student, nineteen-year-old Barbara von Ployer.

A woman performs a keyboard concerto, accompanied by a small orchestra of strings, flutes, and horns. Engraving by **Johann Rudolf Halzhalb** *(1777).*

First movement   The first movement, an Allegro, opens with an orchestral ritornello, followed by the piano with its own exposition, plus a new theme. An orchestral tutti leads to the development section, and the ritornello is heard again in the recapitulation. This concerto, notable for its graceful writing for piano and woodwinds, is usually performed with the cadenza that Mozart wrote. (For analysis, see Listening Guide 24.)

Second movement   There follows an Andante in 3/4, in a kind of double exposition format typical of first movements of concertos. It is most lyrical and marked by true Mozartean sentiment. This Andante is remarkable for its variety of woodwind color.

Third movement   Third is an Allegretto in 2/2, or cut time, set in a theme and variations form. The theme is a graceful, dancelike tune that unfolds in two short phrases, each of which is repeated. This clear-cut, highly symmetrical formation makes the two-part (binary) structure quite apparent to the ear. The five variations that follow set the piano and orchestra in a dialogue of melodic, rhythmic, and harmonic elaborations on the appealing theme. (Mozart was so fond of this tune that he taught it to his pet starling, who consistently got one note and the rhythm wrong.) The movement ends with a Presto coda that introduces new material as well as dazzling piano writing.

Listening Guide 24

C/S: 3A/2–4   C/S: 3/ 4 – 26
Sh: 2A/2   Sh: 2/ 6 – 15

MOZART: Piano Concerto in G major, K. 453   (29:31)

Date of work: 1784
Movements: 3

FIRST MOVEMENT: Allegro; first-movement concerto form, 4/4 meter, G major   (11:30)

ORCHESTRAL RITORNELLO, in G major

4   0:00   Theme 1—refined theme in violins, with woodwind figurations:

0:27   Transitional theme—forceful, in full orchestra

5   0:59   Theme 2—gently undulating theme in violins, answered in woodwinds:

1:40   Closing theme—in full orchestra

SOLO EXPOSITION

[6] 2:08   Theme 1—piano enters with sweep into main theme, decorated, in G major; woodwind accompaniment; scales and arpeggio figurations in piano

2:38   Transition theme—orchestral ritornello; piano with decorative part; modulates to key of dominant

[7] 3:11   Piano theme—introduced by piano alone in D major, then presented in woodwinds:

[8] 4:01   Theme 2—in piano, with string accompaniment

4:57   Closing—decisive, in D major

DEVELOPMENT

[9] 5:16   Virtuosic piano part, references to piano theme, runs and arpeggios against woodwinds; various modulations, leading back to tonic

RECAPITULATION

[10] 6:36   Theme 1—returns in strings, with woodwind accompaniment; piano joins in with decorated version of theme

7:03   Transition theme—forceful, in full orchestra

[11] 7:36   Piano theme, solo, in G major, more decorated, with light orchestral accompaniment

[12] 8:25   Theme 2—in piano, then in woodwinds, now in G major

[13] 9:33   Cadenza—solo piano, variations on earlier themes; ends on dominant

10:49   Closing—final ritornello, in G major

(Shorter recordings stop here.)

SECOND MOVEMENT: Andante; first-movement concerto form, 3/4 meter, C major

(10:26)

ORCHESTRAL EXPOSITION

[14] 0:00   Theme 1—gentle, quiet idea in strings, ends with fermata (hold):

Answer by woodwinds in lyrical dialogue:

15 1:15   Theme 2—alternates *forte* in strings with *piano* in woodwinds, in G major

    1:38   Closing—chromatic line, in strings and woodwinds

            SOLO EXPOSITION
16 1:59   Theme 1—solo piano, in C major; answer in dramatic statement in G minor:

            Idea of theme 2 in alternation of soft and loud statements; woodwind dialogue heard near opening,
            extended by piano

            Closing—chromatic line, extended by piano with cadential trill

            DEVELOPMENT
17 4:10   Theme 1 in G major—in woodwinds; answered by dramatic piano statement reminiscent of solo ex-
            position; short modulatory section, with virtuosic piano line; orchestral *crescendo* brings return to
            C major

            RECAPITULATION
18 5:48   Theme 1—opening in solo piano; answer with *forte,* disjunct theme, E-flat major; woodwind dia-
            logue returns; loud/soft alternating theme returns
19 7:56   Cadenza—solo piano, ends with cadential trill

            Coda—woodwinds play theme 1, which is then decorated in solo piano, followed by soft statement
            of closing theme

            ――――――――――――――――――

            THIRD MOVEMENT: Allegretto, Presto; theme and variations form, 2/2 meter, G major
                                                                                                (7:35)
20 0:00   Theme 1—elegant, dancelike tune in full orchestra; tune in 2 sections (8 measures each), each re-
            peated (‖:a:‖:b:‖)

            a section:

    0:22   **b section:**

21 0:46 Variation 1—solo piano, with melodic ornamentation, each part of tune repeated:

22 1:32 Variation 2—woodwinds introduce each part of theme, repeated by orchestra over piano figurations in triplets

23 2:17 Variation 3—solo woodwind instruments in dialogue, answered by piano; more lyrical than opening

24 3:10 Variation 4—strings introduce theme, now in mysterious mood in minor key; answered by syncopated, chromatic piano line:

25 4:01 Variation 5—loud march in full orchestra, characterized by quick descending pattern at beginning of phrases; answered by piano; transition in piano leads to cadenza

    5:11 Cadenza—solo piano

26 5:19 Coda—Presto tempo; long closing section features new theme and highly virtuosic piano writing; opening theme heard in varied form (piano version shown):

BEETHOVEN'S VIOLIN CONCERTO

As a great public form of musical communication, the concerto interested Beethoven throughout the first and second periods of his creative career. In the third period, when his gaze turned increasingly inward, it disappeared from his output.

The Violin Concerto in D major, dating from 1805, is one of his most lyrical works. It is highly demanding for the solo instrument, showing off its resources brilliantly. In this work, Beethoven greatly expanded the limits of the form and achieved the rich, colorful orchestral writing characteristic of his middle period. At its first performance in 1806, one Viennese critic praised the work and reported that it "was received with exceptionally great applause."

First movement

The opening Allegro ma non troppo (fast, but not too fast) is a huge first-movement concerto form built on a five-note motive first announced by the timpani. Characteristic are the abrupt shifts from major to minor, the lyrical use of the violin's upper register, and the way Beethoven interweaves the solo part with the orchestra. The songful second theme, which moves stepwise up the scale, has been aptly described as heavenly.

Second movement

The second movement, a Larghetto in G major, is set in a theme and variations form. Muted strings establish a serene stillness, with the solo violin weaving a fanciful embroidery over the orchestral part. A short cadenza leads directly into the finale.

Third movement

The last movement is an energetic rondo, growing out of the five-note motive that dominates this entire movement. The main idea alternates with two subsidiary themes. Beethoven achieves a propulsive quality that drives the movement forward with endless gusto. It becomes evident that rondo form, with its indispensable repetitions, is really an outgrowth of the ritornello procedure of the Baroque. This rondo never lets up. On the contrary, it builds tension steadily to the breathtaking coda. (See Listening Guide 25.)

Famous Women Virtuosos of the Eighteenth Century

Since eighteenth-century society deemed it proper that noble and upper-middle-class women study music, many became highly skilled amateurs. Some women were able to make a living as music teachers, and a few attained the status of professional performers. We will soon encounter the successful career of the French harpsichordist/composer Elisabeth-Claude Jacquet de la Guerre, and will learn of the highly acclaimed performances of the all-female orchestra at Venice's Ospedale della Pietà, where the early eighteenth-century composer Antonio Vivaldi taught violin. Several Venetian-trained violinists went on to successful professional careers, including Anna Maria della Pietà, who became a teacher at the Ospedale, where she had studied as a girl, and Maddalena Lombardini, who toured extensively as a soloist. A student of the great violin virtuoso Giuseppe Tartini (1692–1770), Lombardini played his demanding works "with such perfection it is said that she is his descendant." Her violin technique was so excellent that she was sought out to play the newest, most demanding pieces of her day, and she herself composed several violin concertos.

Maria Anna Mozart

Three women in particular—all associated with Mozart—stand out as impressive keyboard players of the late eighteenth century. Maria Anna Mozart (1751–1829), known as Nannerl, was an accomplished pianist who toured extensively with her brother Wolfgang, performing concertos and four-hand piano works. Her father noted that at age twelve, Nannerl was "one of the most skillful players in Europe," able to perform the most difficult works with "incredible precision," and played "so beautifully that everyone is talking about her and admiring her execution." Later, when she retired from profes-

Listening Guide 25

BEETHOVEN: Violin Concerto in D major, Op. 61, Third Movement   (9:30)

Date of work: 1806
Movements:
    I. Allegro ma non troppo; first-movement concerto form, 4/4 meter, D major
    II. Larghetto; theme and variations form, 4/4 meter, G major
    III. Allegro; rondo form, 6/8 meter, D major

THIRD MOVEMENT: Allegro; rondo (A-B-A-C-A-B-A)

24 0:00 **A** section—lilting theme in solo violin, D major:

    Last motive answered by orchestra, repeated 2 octaves higher by violin; full orchestra with theme, now ponderous

  1:07 Transition in solo violin, accompanied first by winds, then strings

25 1:27 **B** section—A major, alternates orchestra and solo violin; virtuosic violin part, punctuated by orchestral chords:

    Trill leads to return of **A**

26 2:21 **A** section—D major, return of main theme by solo violin, repeated in higher range, then in full orchestra; transition based on opening of theme

27 3:14 **C** section—lyrical theme, in G minor, introduced in solo violin:

  3:26 Repeated in bassoon with violin figurations; second part of theme in solo violin, followed by solo bassoon; transition builds on opening 5-note motive

28 4:28 **A** section—D major, solo violin, low range, then high as in opening; repeated in full orchestra, *fortissimo;* transition in solo violin

29	5:59	**B** section—full orchestral statement of second theme alternates with violin figurations, D major; 5-note motive in full orchestra, builds to cadenza
30	7:08	Cadenza—highly virtuosic solo passage, based on opening 5-note motive
31	7:28	**A** section—double basses enter with 5-note motive, solo violin with main theme, gentle statement; main theme heard in oboes in D major; orchestra builds against solo violin scales and arpeggios

sional life to raise a family, her brother wrote several works for her and sent his piano cadenzas to her to try out.

Maria Theresa von Paradis

The career of the blind musician Maria Theresa von Paradis (1759–1808) parallels that of her friend Mozart. An excellent pianist and organist, she was renowned for her remarkable musical memory; she prepared a repertory of some sixty different concertos for an extended European tour (1783–86). Mozart wrote his Piano Concerto in B flat, K. 456, for her in 1784, and her teacher, the court composer Antonio Salieri (1750–1825), wrote his only organ concerto in her honor. She was a composer herself, but many of her works, including two concertos, a piano trio, and a number of sonatas, have been lost.

Barbara von Ployer

The third gifted pianist was Barbara von Ployer, a young student of Mozart's for whom he wrote two concertos, including the G-major work we just studied. Mozart was so proud of his talented student that he invited the composer Giovanni Paisiello (1740–1816) to the premiere of the work. He wrote to his father, "I am fetching Paisiello in my carriage, as I want him to hear both my pupil and my compositions."

The public prominence achieved by these women performers was unusual for the era. However, the many engravings and paintings of the time illustrating music-making scenes make it clear that women were frequent participants in performances in the home, in aristocratic salons, and at court.

46

The Classical Sonata

The Movements of the Sonata

The sonata, as Haydn, Mozart, and their successors understood the term, was an instrumental work for one or two instruments, consisting of a series of contrasting movements. The movements were three or four in number (some-

An eighteenth-century engraving dated 1773, showing a typical violin-piano duo, with a woman at the keyboard. (Paris, Bibliothèque Nationale)

times two) and followed the basic sonata cycle described earlier in the discussions of string quartet, symphony, and concerto.

In the Classical era, the sonata became an important genre for amateurs in the home, as well as for composers appearing in concerts as performers of their own music. The late eighteenth century favored the solo piano sonata as well as sonatas for violin or cello and piano. At first, the piano was heard as the major instrument, with the string instrument acting as accompaniment. Mozart and Beethoven changed this. In their duo sonatas, the two instruments are treated as equal partners. It is the piano sonatas of Beethoven, however, that are most significant in the solo literature for that instrument and epitomize the genre in the Classical era.

BEETHOVEN'S *PATHÉTIQUE* SONATA

The title of the Piano Sonata in C minor, Op. 13—*Pathétique*—was Beethoven's own. Certainly the Beethovenian pathos is apparent from the first chords of the slow introduction (see Listening Guide 26). Marked Grave (solemn), this celebrated opening has something fantasy-like about it, as if Beethoven had captured here the passionate intensity that so affected his listeners when he improvised at the keyboard.

In the movement proper, marked Allegro di molto e con brio (very fast and

First movement

with vigor), Beethoven uses the resources of the instrument most imaginatively: contrasts in dynamics and register, the brilliance of rapid scale passages, the excitement of tremolo, and the power of a slowly gathering *crescendo* allied with the gradual climb in pitch. Very dramatic, just before the end of the movement, is a brief reminder of the slow introduction, followed by a swift cadence in the home key.

Second movement   The second movement is a famous Adagio cantabile (slow and songful), which shows off the piano's ability to sing. The opening theme of this melodious rondo (in **A-B-A-C-A** form) is stated in A-flat major, then repeated an octave higher. It returns after a brief contrasting theme. Insistent triplets increase the tension in a dialogue between the right and left hands of the pianist. The animation continues through the last statement of the memorable theme and a short coda. This hymnlike Adagio combines an introspective character with the quality of strength that Beethoven made his own.

Third movement   The final movement is a rondo, whose principal theme is darkened by the C-minor tonality; this sets it apart from the usually cheerful rondo finales of Haydn and Mozart. The structure is spacious; within it, lyric episodes alternate with dramatic ones. The *Pathétique* has been a favorite for generations. In the hands of a great performing artist, it stands as one of Beethoven's most personal sonatas.

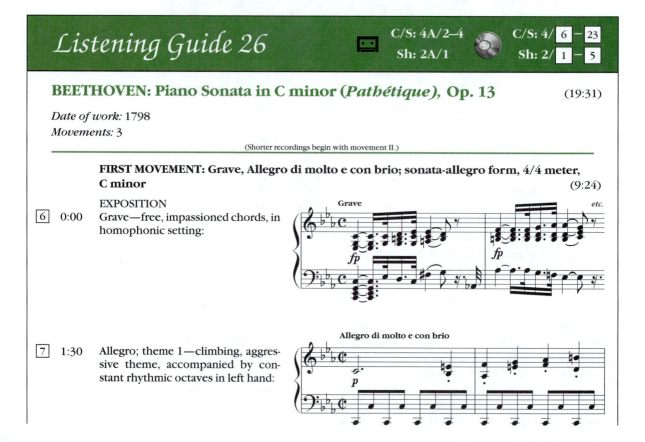

Listening Guide 26

C/S: 4A/2–4   C/S: 4/ 6 – 23
Sh: 2A/1   Sh: 2/ 1 – 5

BEETHOVEN: Piano Sonata in C minor (*Pathétique*), Op. 13   (19:31)

Date of work: 1798
Movements: 3

(Shorter recordings begin with movement II.)

FIRST MOVEMENT: Grave, Allegro di molto e con brio; sonata-allegro form, 4/4 meter, C minor   (9:24)

EXPOSITION
6   0:00   Grave—free, impassioned chords, in homophonic setting:

Grave

fp   *fp*   *etc.*

7   1:30   Allegro; theme 1—climbing, aggressive theme, accompanied by constant rhythmic octaves in left hand:

Allegro di molto e con brio

p

| 8 | 1:59 | Theme 2—lyrical, in E-flat minor, grace notes and crossed hands: |

	2:25	Theme 3—in E-flat major, builds to *crescendo*
	2:44	Codetta—closes exposition with ideas from opening Allegro
		(Exposition repeated)
		Return of Grave
		DEVELOPMENT
9	6:02	Combines opening Allegro and Grave themes:

		RECAPITULATION
10	7:23	Themes 1, 2, and 3 return in C minor
11	8:41	Grave returns, leading to coda (Allegro), like opening

SECOND MOVEMENT: Adagio cantabile; rondo form (A-B-A-C-A), 2/4 meter; A-flat major

(5:52)

| 12 | 0:00 | **A** section—lyrical melody, first in middle range, then repeated up an octave: |

13	1:16	**B** section—a contrasting lyrical melody, modulating, more disjunct:	

14	2:14	**A** section—returns in A-flat major

15	2:52	**C** section—more dramatic, with triplet figures, accents, and arpeggios:	

16	3:51	**A** section—returns in A-flat major, more rhythmically animated, in triplets
		Coda

(Shorter recordings stop here.)

THIRD MOVEMENT: Allegro; rondo form (A-B-A-C-A-B-A), duple meter, C minor   (4:15)

17	0:00	**A** section—quick-paced melody in C minor; its recurrence is the basis for the movement:	

18	0:19	**B** section—modulates to E-flat major, melody moves up and down in arpeggios, then scales; a slower, chordal section, leading to exchange of motive between right and left hands:	

19	1:12	**A** section—in C minor

| 20 | 1:32 | **C section**—modulates to A-flat major, with disjunct theme and syncopated rhythms, motivic exchange between hands: | |

21	2:23	**A section**—in C minor
22	2:38	**B section**—in C major
23	3:22	**A section**—in C minor, final statement

Choral Music and Opera in the Classical Era

47

Sacred Choral Music

"Make a joyful noise to the Lord, all the earth; break forth into joyous song and sing praises."—PSALM 98

Mass, Requiem, and Oratorio

The late eighteenth century inherited a rich tradition of choral music from earlier eras. Among the principal forms of choral art were the *mass,* a musical setting of the most solemn service of the Roman Catholic Church, and the *requiem,* a musical setting of the Mass for the Dead. Both types were originally intended to be performed in church. By the nineteenth century, they had found a much larger audience in the concert hall.

The blending of many voices in a large space such as a church or cathedral could not fail to be an uplifting experience. For this reason, both the Catholic and Protestant churches were patrons of music throughout the ages. Haydn and Mozart made significant contributions to the mass repertory. Haydn's Mass in D minor (*Lord Nelson*) remains one of his most frequently performed works, and Mozart's Requiem, his last composition, quickly established itself as one of the masterpieces of the Classical Viennese school.

Important too was the *oratorio,* a dramatic composition based on a text of religious or serious character for solo voices, chorus, and orchestra. Haydn wrote two oratorios—*The Creation* and *The Seasons,* which attained enormous popularity throughout the nineteenth century and helped build a new audience for these genres.

A performance of Haydn's oratorio The Creation *in the Great Hall of the University of Vienna in 1808, as painted by* **Balthasar Wigand.** (Vienna Historical Museum)

HAYDN'S *LORD NELSON* MASS

Haydn's Mass in D minor (*Lord Nelson*) has no direct connection with the great English admiral Lord Horatio Nelson. Haydn was finishing the work as Admiral Nelson destroyed the French fleet in the harbor of Abukir, Egypt, on August 1, 1798. Haydn first called the work "Mass in a Time of Anxiety," which suggests how involved his country was in the distant war. Two years later, it was performed in the presence of Lord Nelson, at that time a guest of the Esterházys, and came to be known by his name.

Scored for three high trumpets and timpani, solo organ and strings, four vocal soloists (soprano, alto, tenor, bass), and a four-part chorus, the *Lord Nelson* Mass is notable for its heroic tone and freshness of invention. We shall study the Credo, which has one of the longest texts among the movements of the mass. (When Stravinsky, a century and a half later, was asked why the Credo of his mass was so long, he answered, "There is much to believe.") This movement begins as an Allegro con spirito for full chorus. It is cast in the style of a *canon,* in which one vocal line imitates another at a fixed distance throughout a movement. In this case, Haydn pairs sopranos and tenors against altos and basses, who imitate the two higher voices a measure later at the interval of a fifth. It takes a master to handle so intricate a procedure with such grace and ease. (For the full text of this movement, see Listening Guide 27.)

Credo

"Et incarnatus est"   The "Et incarnatus est de Spiritu Sancto" (And was made flesh by the Holy Spirit) is a moving Largo in triple time for soprano, tenor, alto, and bass soloists, with full chorus. Here the sopranos carry the main line, with repetition of text throughout. A homophonic texture in the chorus is integrated with a tightly knit, polyphonic passage for the quartet of soloists. Thus the two types of texture are brought into an artistic unity. Notice the descending vocal line with which Haydn sets the saddest phrase of the text, "Crucifixus etiam pro nobis" (He was also crucified for us).

"Et resurrexit"   The "Et resurrexit" (And He rose again), a Vivace for solo soprano and chorus, begins with an upward-leaping figure in the orchestra whose joy is mirrored in the voices. The chorus unfolds a homophonic texture against an extremely active orchestral background. The soprano soloist enters toward the end with a florid, melismatic expansion of the final word, "Amen." The chorus takes over the expansion of "Amen," and brings the Credo to a powerful conclusion. Haydn's masterful introduction of high trumpets and drums at strategic points gives the movement a sense of glory.

Listening Guide 27

   C/S: 3A/1   C/S: 3/ 1 – 3

HAYDN: *Lord Nelson* Mass, Credo   (9:49)

Date of work: 1798
Medium: 4 soloists, 4-part chorus, orchestra (strings, 3 trumpets, and timpani)
Genre: Mass, setting of the Ordinary

THREE MAIN SECTIONS OF CREDO

I. "Credo in unum Deum," Allegro con spirito

1   0:00   Orchestral opening—unison statement of choral canon theme

Text	Translation	Description
Credo in unum Deum, Patrem omnipotentem, factorem coeli et terrae, visibilium omnium, et invisibilium omnium, et ex Patre natum ante omnia saecula. Deum de Deo, lumen de lumine, Deum verum de Deo vero; genitum, non factum, consubstantialem Patri, per quem omnia facta sunt. Qui propter nos homines et propter nostram salutem descendit de coelis.	I believe in one God, the Father almighty, Maker of heaven and earth, and of all things visible and invisible, born of the Father before all ages. God of God, Light of Light, true Son of God; begotten, not made; of one being with the Father, by Whom all things were made. Who for us men, and for our salvation, came down from heaven.	Choral canon, imitative voices in pairs (ST, AB) Repetition of final phrase of text, ending in unison homophonic statement

Opening canon in chorus, showing voice pairs (ST, AB):

II. "Et incarnatus est," Largo

2 1:52 Orchestral introduction—previews soprano solo line

Text	Translation	Description
Et incarnatus est de Spiritu sancto ex Maria virgine, et homo factus est.	And was incarnate by the Holy Spirit, of the Virgin Mary; and was made man.	Soprano solo, with orchestra
Text repeated		SATB chorus; homophonic setting

Opening of lyrical soprano solo:

Text	Translation	Description
Crucifixus etiam pro nobis sub Pontio Pilato, passus et sepultus est.	He was crucified for us, suffered under Pontius Pilate, and was buried.	Unison chorus, chantlike, on repeated pitch
Text repeated		Soloists in polyphonic settings, alternating with chorus

III. "Et resurrexit," Vivace

3 6:09 Et resurrexit tertia die secundum Scripturas, et ascendit in coelum, sedet ad dexteram Patris. Et iterum venturus est cum gloria, judicare vivos et mortuos; cujus regni non erit finis.   And on the third day He rose from the dead according to the Scriptures; and He ascended into heaven. He sitteth at the right hand of the Father; and He shall come again to judge the living and the dead; and His kingdom shall have no end.   Chorus, polyphonic, then homophonic against active orchestral writing

Et in Spiritum sanctum, Dominum et vivificantem. Qui   And in the Holy Spirit, the Lord and Giver of life, Who with   Choral declamation, on repeated pitch

cum Patre et Filio simul adoratur et conglorificatur, qui locutus est per Prophetas. Et unam sanctam Catholicam et Apostolicam ecclesiam. Confiteor unum baptisma in remissionem peccatorum. Et expecto resurrectionem mortuorum, et vitam venturi saeculi. Amen.	the Father and Son is worshipped and glorified; Who spoke through the prophets. And in one holy, Catholic, and Apostolic church. I acknowledge one baptism for the remission of sins. And I look for the resurrection of the dead, and the life of the world to come. Amen.

Soprano solo, ornamented choral closing and "Amen"

Opening chorus—begins polyphonic, quickly becomes homophonic:

48

Classical Opera

"I had always placed a certain confidence in opera, hoping that from it will rise . . . tragedy in a nobler form."—FRIEDRICH VON SCHILLER

The opera house was a center of experimentation in the Classical era. Opera was the most important branch of musical entertainment and the one that reached the widest public. The music was the point of departure and imposed its forms on the drama.

Opera Types

Opera seria The opera of the early eighteenth century accurately reflected the society out of which it sprang. The prevalent form was *opera seria,* "serious" or tragic Italian opera, a highly formalized genre inherited from the Baroque that occu-

An opera performance at Esterháza. The musician at the harpsichord (far left, bottom) is thought to be Haydn. Anonymous eighteenth-century watercolor. (Theater-museum, Munich)

pied itself largely with the affairs of kings and heroes drawn from the legends of antiquity. Its rigid conventions were shaped by the poet Pietro Metastasio (1698–1782), whose librettos were set again and again throughout the century. Opera seria consisted mainly of a series of recitatives and arias specifically designed to display the virtuosity of star singers to the aristocracy.

However, new winds were blowing in the second half of the century. Increasingly the need was felt for simplicity and naturalness, for an opera that reflected human emotions more realistically. One impulse toward reform came from the operas of Christoph Willibald Gluck, whose achievement in this regard will be recounted later (see p. 421). Another derived from the popular comic opera that flourished in every country of Europe. Known in England as *ballad opera,* in Germany as *Singspiel,* in France as *opéra comique,* and in Italy as *opera buffa,* this lighter genre was the answer of the rising middle class to the aristocratic form it would inevitably supplant.

Comic opera

Comic opera differed from opera seria in several basic ways. It was sung in the language of the audience rather than in Italian, which was the standard language of international opera. It presented lively, down-to-earth plots rather than the remote concerns of gods and mythological heroes. It featured exciting ensembles at the end of each act in which all the characters participated, instead of the solo arias that were the norm in the older style. And it abounded in farcical situations, humorous dialogue, popular tunes, and the impertinent remarks of the *buffo,* the traditional character derived from the theater of buffoons, who spoke to the audience with a wink and a nod in a bass voice. This was a new sound in a theater previously dominated by the artificial soprano voice of the castrato.

As the Age of Revolution approached, comic opera became an important social force whose lively wit delighted even the aristocrats it satirized. Classical opera buffa spread quickly, steadily expanding its scope until it culminated in the works of the greatest dramatist of the eighteenth century: Mozart.

MOZART'S COMIC OPERA *THE MARRIAGE OF FIGARO*

Mozart found his ideal librettist in Lorenzo da Ponte (1749-1838), an Italian-Jewish adventurer and poet whose dramatic vitality matched his own. Their collaboration produced three great operas: *The Marriage of Figaro, Don Giovanni,* and *Così fan tutte* (Women Are Like That).

Da Ponte adapted his libretto for *The Marriage of Figaro* from the play by Pierre-Augustin Caron de Beaumarchais (1732-99), a truly revolutionary work in that it satirized the upper classes and allowed Figaro, the clever and cocky valet of Count Almaviva, to outwit his master. When Louis XVI read the manuscript, he pronounced it detestable and unfit to be seen. It was the liberal friends of the queen, Marie Antoinette, who persuaded the king to allow the play to be produced. Vienna was even more conservative than Paris: the play was forbidden there. But what could not be spoken could be sung. Mozart's opera was produced at the Imperial Court Theater of Vienna in May 1786, and brought him the greatest success of his life.

Da Ponte used all the traditional devices of bedroom farce. Characters are disguised as each other, are led into all sorts of misunderstandings, and are caught in compromising situations they barely manage to wriggle out of. He cut some of Beaumarchais's complications, and as court poet to Emperor

"The Count discovers the Page." Detail of an illustration from the first Paris edition of Beaumarchais's comedy Le Mariage de Figaro, *engraved by* **Jean-Baptiste Liénard,** *1785.*

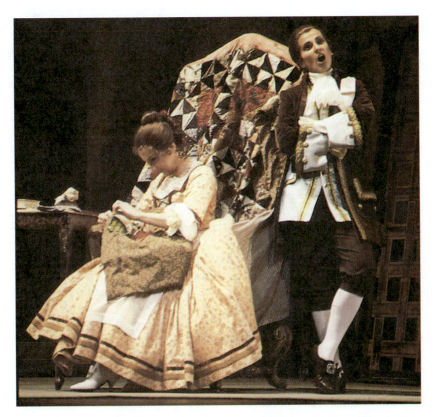

Susanna (seated) and Cherubino in a performance of The Marriage of Figaro *by the New York City Opera.* (Photo © by Martha Swope)

Joseph II, da Ponte was clever enough to know that he must soften the political satire.

Although *The Marriage of Figaro* came out of the rich tradition of popular comic opera, Mozart's genius lifted the genre to another dimension. In place of the stereotyped characters of opera buffa, he created real human beings who come alive through his music, so that we can identify with their emotions. The Count is a likable ladies' man; the Countess is noble in her suffering. Her maid, Susanna, is pert and endlessly resourceful in resisting the advances of her master. Figaro is equally resourceful in foiling the schemes of the Count. And the Countess's page, Cherubino, is irresistible in his boyish ardor and innocence.

In Classical opera, the part of a young man was often sung by a soprano or alto wearing trousers. In Mozart's opera, the soprano voice is ideally suited to Cherubino's romantic idealism. His aria in Act I, "Non so più," establishes his character as a young man in love with love. "I no longer know who I am or what I'm doing," he sings. "Every woman I see makes me blush and tremble." (For the Italian-English text and analysis of the aria, see Listening Guide 28.)

Cherubino's aria is followed by recitative, which we know is the rapid-fire, talky kind of singing whose main function is to advance the plot. Eighteenth-century audiences accepted this change of texture and orchestration just as we today accept, in a Broadway musical, the change from song to spoken dialogue.

The action moves rapidly, with overtones of farce. Cherubino has sung his love song to the Countess in Susanna's room. When the Count arrives to ask Susanna to meet him that night in the garden, Cherubino hides behind a huge armchair. At this point, the music master Basilio, a gossip if ever there was one, arrives looking for the Count, who tries to hide behind the chair. Susanna cleverly places herself between the Count and Cherubino, so that the page is able to slip in front of the chair and curl up in it. Ever resourceful, she manages to cover him with a cloth. With both the front and back of the armchair occupied, Susanna scolds Basilio as a gossip and busybody. At this point, the Count reveals his presence (see illustrations on pp. 268 and 269).

Susanna is aghast that the Count has been discovered in her room. The Count, having overheard Basilio's statement that Cherubino adores the Countess, is angry with the young man. And Basilio thoroughly enjoys the rumpus he has stirred up. The action stops as the three join in a trio in which each expresses his or her emotion. There is quick exchange among the three voices and much repetition of text. The extended structure of this trio ("Cosa sento! Tosto andate") is related to sonata form. No one has ever equaled Mozart's ability to reconcile the demands of a dramatic situation with the requirements of absolute musical form.

The Count pulls the cloth from the chair and discovers Cherubino. Furious, he vows to banish him from the estate. At this point, Figaro arrives with a group of peasants whom he has told that the Count has decided to abolish the "right of the first night," the hated feudal privilege that gave the lord of the manor the right to deflower every young woman in his domain. In their gratitude, the peasants have come to serenade their master, singing, "His great kindness preserves the purity of a bride for the one she loves." Figaro, delighted to have forced the Count's hand, announces his impending marriage to Susanna, and the Count plays along by accepting the tributes of the crowd.

Figaro intercedes for Cherubino with his master, whereupon the Count relents, appoints the page to a captain's post in his regiment, and leaves with Basilio. The complications in the next three acts lead to a happy ending: the Count is reconciled with his wife, and Figaro wins his beloved Susanna.

Two centuries have passed since Mozart's characters first strutted across a stage. They live on today in the opera houses of the world, lifted above time and fashion by the genius of their creator.

Listening Guide 28

C/S: 3B/1   C/S: 3/ 27 – 30
Sh: 2A/3   Sh: 2/ 16 – 19

MOZART: *The Marriage of Figaro (Le nozze di Figaro)*, Act I, Scenes 6 and 7

(10:15)

Date of work: 1786
Genre: Opera buffa (comic opera)
Librettist: Lorenzo da Ponte
Basis: Play by Beaumarchais
Principal characters:
Figaro, servant to Count Almaviva
Susanna, maid to Countess Almaviva
Cherubino, page
Count Almaviva
Countess Almaviva
Basilio, music master
Doctor Bartolo
Marcellina, his housekeeper

ACT I, SCENE 6: Aria, Cherubino

Form: **A-B-A-C**, followed by recitative
A—quick rhythms (in E flat):

Non so   più co-sa son, co-sa fac-cio,

B—more lyrical (in B flat):

So   lo ai   no-mi d'a-mor di di-let-to,

A—return (in E flat)

C—begins quietly, then builds in E flat,
modulates:

Par-lo d'a-mor   ve-glian-do.

CHERUBINO

27 0:00

A Non so più cosa son, cosa faccio, | I don't know what I am, what I'm doing;
or di foco, ora sono di ghiaccio, | first I seem to be burning, then freezing;
ogni donna cangiar di colore, | every woman makes me change color,
ogni donna mi fa palpitar. | every woman I see makes me shake.
B Solo ai nomi d'amor, di diletto, | Just the words "love" and "pleasure"
mi si turba, mi s'altera il petto, | bring confusion; my breast swells in terror,
e a parlare mi sforza d'amore | yet I am compelled to speak of love
un desio ch'io non posso spiegar. | by a force which I cannot explain.
A Non so più cosa son, . . .
C Parlo d'amor vegliando, | I speak of love while waking,
parlo d'amor sognando, | I speak of love while dreaming,
all'acqua, all'ombra, ai monti, | to the water, to shadows, to mountains,
ai fiori, all'erbe, ai fonti, | to the flowers, the grass, and the fountains,
all'eco, all'aria, ai venti, | to the echo, to the air, to the winds

che il suon de'vani accenti,	which carry the idle words
portano via con se.	away with them.
C Parlo d'amor . . .	
E se non ho chi m'oda,	And if there is no one to listen,
parlo d'amor con me!	I'll speak of love to myself!

(Seeing the Count in the distance, Cherubino hides behind the chair.)

CHERUBINO

28   2:50

Ah! Son perduto!	I'm done for!

Recitative: Susanna, Count, Basilio

SUSANNA

Che timor . . . il Conte! Misera me!	I'm afraid . . . the Count! Poor me!

(tries to conceal Cherubino)

COUNT ALMAVIVA *(entering)*

Susanna, tu mi sembri agitata e confusa.	Susanna, you seem to be agitated and confused.

SUSANNA

Signor, io chiedo scusa,	My lord, I beg your pardon,
ma, se mai, qui sorpresa,	but . . . indeed . . . the surprise . . .
par carità, partite.	I implore you, please go.

COUNT

(sits down on the chair and takes Susanna's hand; she draws it forcibly away)

Un momento, e ti lascio. Odi.	One moment, then I'll leave. Listen.

SUSANNA

Non odo nulla.	I don't want to hear anything.

COUNT

Due parole: tu sai che ambasciatore a Londra	Just a word; you know that the king
il Re mi dichiarò;	has named me ambassador to London;
di condur meco Figaro destinai.	I had intended to take Figaro with me.

SUSANNA

Signor, se osassi—	My lord, if I dare—

COUNT *(rising)*

Parla, parla, mia cara,	Speak, speak, my dear,
e con quel dritto ch'oggi prendi su me,	and with that right you have of me today,
finchè tu vivi chiedi, imponi, prescrivi.	as long as you live, you may ask, demand, prescribe.

SUSANNA

Lasciatemi, signor,	Let go of me, my lord,
dritti non prendo,	I have no rights,
non ne vò, non ne intendo.	I do not want them, nor claim them.
Oh me infelice!	Oh, what misery!

COUNT

Ah no, Susanna, io ti vò far felice!	Ah no, Susanna, I want to make you happy!
Tu ben sai quanto io t'amo;	You well know how much I love you;
a te Basilio tutto già disse.	Basilio has told you that already.
Or senti, se per pochi momenti	Now listen, if you would meet me
meco in giardin, sull'imbrunir del giorno,	briefly in the garden at dusk,
ah, per questo favore io pagherei . . .	ah, for this favor I would pay . . .

BASILIO (*outside the door*)

E uscito poco fa.	He went out just now.

COUNT

Chi parla?	Whose voice is that?

SUSANNA

O Dei!	Oh, heavens!

COUNT

Esci, ed alcun non entri.	Go, and let no one come in.

SUSANNA

Ch'io vi lasci qui solo?	And leave you here alone?

BASILIO (*outside*)

Da madama sarà, vado a cercarlo.	He'll be with my lady, I'll go and find him.

COUNT

Qui dietro mi porrò.	I'll get behind here.

(*points to the chair*)

SUSANNA

Non vi celate.	No, don't hide.

COUNT

Taci, e cerca ch'ei parta.	Hush, and try to make him go.

SUSANNA

Ohimè! che fate?	Oh dear! What are you doing?

(*The Count is about to hide behind the chair; Susanna steps between him and the page.
The count pushes her gently away. She draws back; meanwhile the page slips round to the front
of the chair and hops in with his feet drawn up. Susanna rearranges the dress to cover him.*)

BASILIO

Susanna, il ciel vi salvi!	Heaven bless you, Susanna!
Avreste a caso veduto il Conte?	Have you seen his lordship by any chance?

SUSANNA

E cosa deve far meco il Conte?	And what should his lordship be doing here
Animo, uscite.	with me? Come now, be gone!

BASILIO

Aspettate, sentite, Figaro di lui cerca.	But listen, Figaro is looking for him.

SUSANNA (*aside*)

Oh cielo!	Oh dear! Then he's looking for the one
Ei cerca chi, dopo voi, più l'odia.	man who, after you, hates him most!

COUNT (*aside*)

Vediam come mi serve.	Now we'll see how he serves me.

BASILIO

Io non ho mai nella moral sentito	I have never heard it preached that
ch'uno ch'ama la moglie odi il marito,	one who loves the wife should hate the husband;
per dir che il Conte v'ama.	that's a way of saying the Count loves you.

SUSANNA

Sortite, vil ministro dell'altrui sfrenatezza:	Get out, vile minister of others' lechery!

io non ho d'uopo della vostra morale,
del Conte, del suo amor!

                                   I have no need of your preaching
                                   nor of the Count or his lovemaking!

BASILIO

Non c'è alcun male.
Ha ciascun i suoi gusti.
Io mi credea che preferir
doveste per amante,
come fan tutte quante,
un signor liberal, prudente, e saggio,
a un giovinastro, a un paggio.

        No offence meant.
        Everyone to their own taste.
        I thought you would have preferred
        as your lover,
        as all other women would,
        a lord who's liberal, prudent, and wise,
        to a raw youth, a mere page.

SUSANNA

A Cherubino?

        To Cherubino?

BASILIO

A Cherubino! Cherubin d'amore,
ch'oggi sul far del giorno
passeggiava qui intorno per entrar.

        To Cherubino! Love's little cherub
        who early today
        was hanging about here waiting to come in.

SUSANNA

Uom maligno, un'impostura è questa.

        You insinuating wretch, that's a lie.

BASILIO

È un maligno con voi
chi ha gli occhi in testa?
E quella canzonetta,
ditemi in confidenza,
io sono amico,
ed altrui nulla dico,
è per voi, per madama?

        Do you call it an insinuation
        to have eyes in one's head?
        And that little ditty,
        tell me confidentially
        as a friend,
        and I will tell no one else,
        was it written for you or my lady?

SUSANNA *(aside)*

Chi diavol gliel'ha detto?

        Who the devil told him about that?

BASILIO

A proposito, figlia, istruitelo meglio.
Egli la guarda a tavola sì spesso,
e con tale immodestia,
che s'il Conte s'accorge—
e sul tal punto sapete, egli è una bestia—

        By the way, my child, you must teach him
        better. At table he gazes at her so often
        and so wantonly,
        that if the Count noticed it—
        on that subject, as you know, he's quite wild—

SUSANNA

Scellerato! e perchè andate voi
tai menzogne spargendo?

        You wretch! Why do you go around
        spreading such lies?

BASILIO

Io! che ingiustizia!
Quel che compro io vendo,
a quel che tutti dicono,
io non ci aggiungo un pelo.

        I! How unfair!
        That which I buy I sell,
        and to what is common knowledge
        I add not a tittle.

COUNT *(emerging from his hiding place)*

Come! che dicon tutti?

        Indeed! And what is common knowledge?

BASILIO *(aside)*

Oh bella!

        How wonderful!

SUSANNA

Oh cielo!

        Oh heavens!

ACT I, SCENE 7: Terzetto (Trio), Count, Basilio, Susanna

Form: Sonata-type structure, with development and recapitulation

Style: Quick exchange between voices; much text repetition; each character with own emotional commentary

The Count—angry:

Basilio and the Count—comforting Susanna, who has fainted:

	COUNT
29 5:59 Cosa sento! Tosto andate, e scacciate il seduttor!	I heard it all! Go at once, throw the seducer out!
	BASILIO
In mal punto son qui giunto; perdonate, o mio signor.	I have come to an unfortunate moment; forgive me, my lord.
	SUSANNA
Che ruina! me meschina! Son' oppressa dal dolor!	What a catastrophe! I am ruined! Terror grips my heart!
	COUNT
Tosta andate, andate . . .	Go at once, go . . .
	BASILIO
In mal punto . . .	I have come . . .
	SUSANNA
Che ruina!	What a catastrophe!
	BASILIO
. . . son qui giunto;	. . . at an unfortunate moment;
	COUNT
. . . e scacciate il seduttor.	. . . and throw the seducer out.
	BASILIO
. . . perdonate, o mio signor.	. . . forgive me, o my lord.
	SUSANNA
Me meschina! Me meschina! Son' oppressa dal dolor.	I am ruined! I am ruined! Terror grips my heart.
	BASILIO, COUNT *(supporting Susanna)*
Ah! già svien la poverina! Come, oh Dio! le batte il cor.	Ah! The poor girl's fainted! O God, how her heart is beating.

	BASILIO
Pian, pianin, su questo seggio—	Gently, gently on to the chair—
	(taking her to the chair)
	SUSANNA *(coming to)*
Dove sono? Cosa veggio?	Where am I? What's this I see?
Che insolenza! andate fuor.	What insolence! Leave this room.
	BASILIO, COUNT
Siamo qui per aiutarvi, . . .	We're here to help you, . . .
	BASILIO
. . . è sicuro il vostro onor.	. . . your virtue is safe.
	COUNT
. . . non turbarti, o mio tesor.	. . . do not worry, sweetheart.
	BASILIO
Ah, del paggio, quel che ho detto,	What I was saying about the page
era solo un mio sospetto.	was only my own suspicion.
	SUSANNA
È un'insidia, una perfidia,	It was a nasty insinuation,
non credete all'impostor.	do not believe the liar.
	COUNT
Parta, parta il damerino, . . .	The young fop must go, . . .
	SUSANNA, BASILIO
Poverino!	Poor boy!
	COUNT
. . . parta, parta il damerino.	. . . the young fop must go.
	SUSANNA, BASILIO
Poverino!	Poor boy!
	COUNT
Poverino! poverino!	Poor boy! Poor boy!
ma da me sorpreso ancor!	But I caught him yet again!
	SUSANNA
Come?	How?
	BASILIO
Che?	What?
	SUSANNA
Che?	What?
	BASILIO
Come?	How?
	SUSANNA, BASILIO
Come? che?	How? What?
	COUNT
Da tua cugina,	At your cousin's house
l'uscio jer trovai rinchiuso,	I found the door shut yesterday.
picchio, m'apre Barbarina	I knocked and Barbarina opened it
paurosa fuor dell'uso.	much more timidly than usual.

Io, dal muso insospettito,	My suspicions aroused by her expression,
guardo, cerco in ogni sito,	I had a good look around,
ed alzando pian, pianino,	and very gently lifting
il tappeto al tavolino,	the cloth upon the table,
vedo il paggio.	I found the page.

(imitating his own action with the dress over the chair, he reveals the page)

Ah, cosa veggio?	Ah, what do I see?

SUSANNA

Ah! crude stelle!	Ah! wicked fate!

BASILIO

Ah! meglio ancora!	Ah! better still!

COUNT

30   8:53 Onestissima signora, . . .   Most virtuous lady, . . .

SUSANNA

Accader non può di peggio.	Northing worse could happen!

COUNT

. . . or capisco come va!	. . . now I see what's happening!

SUSANNA

Giusti Dei, che mai sarà!	Merciful heaven, whatever will happen?

BASILIO

Così fan tutte . . .	They're all the same . . .

SUSANNA

Giusti Dei! che mai sarà	Merciful heaven! Whatever will happen?
Accader non può di peggio,	Nothing worse could happen!
ah no! ah no!	ah no! ah no!

BASILIO

. . . le belle,	. . . the fair sex,
non c'è alcuna novità,	there's nothing new about it,
così fan tutte.	they're all the same.

COUNT

Or capisco come va,	Now I see what's happening,
onestissima signora!	most virtuous lady!
or capisco, *ecc.*	Now I see, *etc.*

BASILIO

Ah, del paggio quel che ho detto,	What I was saying about the page
era solo un mio sospetto.	was only my own suspicion.

SUSANNA

Accader non può di peggio, *ecc.*	Nothing worse could happen, *etc.*

COUNT

Onestissima signora, *ecc.*	Most virtuous lady, *etc.*

BASILIO

Così fan tutte, *ecc.*	They're all the same, *etc.*

"People often complain that music is too ambiguous, that what they should think when they hear it is so unclear, whereas everyone understands words. With me it is exactly the opposite, and not only with regard to an entire speech but also with individual words. These too seem to me so ambiguous, so vague, so easily misunderstood in comparison to genuine music, which fills the soul with a thousand things better than words."—FELIX MENDELSSOHN

We have studied three great masters of the Viennese Classical school—Haydn, Mozart, and Beethoven. It is clear that certain of Beethoven's characteristics foreshadowed the Romantic style; we have already observed his striking dynamic contrasts, his explosive accents, his expansion of strict Classical form, his hymnlike slow movements, and the overall dramatic intensity of his music.

The music of two other masters reveals them to be the heirs of the Classical tradition—Franz Schubert and Felix Mendelssohn. Born at the very end of the eighteenth century, Schubert followed in a direct line of development from Haydn, Mozart, and Beethoven in his approach to chamber music and the symphony. His songs and piano music, we saw, show him as a true Romantic (see Chapter 14).

The life of Felix Mendelssohn coincided with the first upsurge of Romanticism. His mission was to preserve Classical forms in an age that was turning away from them. At the same time, his interest focused on nature—one of the prime traits of the new Romanticism. His music therefore represents a happy marriage of Classical form and Romantic content.

Felix Mendelssohn: His Life and Music

Felix Mendelssohn (1809–47) was the son of a music-loving banker and grandson of a famous Jewish philosopher, Moses Mendelssohn. His family converted to Protestantism when Felix was still a child. The Mendelssohn home was a meeting place for Berlin intellectuals, their garden house the scene of memorable concerts. Here an orchestra under the direction of the seventeen-year-

Felix Mendelssohn

old Felix performed his Overture to *A Midsummer Night's Dream* for a captivated audience. Felix was not the only musician in the household. His sister Fanny was a gifted pianist and composer as well. (Some of her works were published under her brother's name.)

The youth worshipped the earlier masters. In 1829, at the age of twenty, Felix organized a performance of Bach's *St. Matthew Passion,* which had been neglected since the death of its composer. The event proved to be a turning point in the nineteenth-century revival of Bach's music.

Mendelssohn excelled in a number of roles—as pianist, conductor, organizer of music festivals, and educator. At twenty-six, he was named conductor of the Gewandhaus Orchestra in Leipzig and went on to transform it into the finest in Europe. As an educator, he founded the Conservatory of Leipzig, which raised the standards for the training of musicians. His ten visits to England aroused enormous public enthusiasm.

Mendelssohn's happy life was shattered in 1847 by the death of his sister, Fanny, to whom he was deeply attached. This blow, along with his very demanding musical career, brought on a stroke, from which he died at age thirty-eight.

Of his symphonies, the best-known are the Third (the *Scottish*) and the Fourth (the *Italian*)—mementos of his youthful travels. Both works were begun in 1830, when he was twenty-one. The Concerto for Violin and Orchestra retains its position as one of the most popular ever written. The Octet for Strings, which he wrote when he was sixteen, is much admired, as are the *Songs Without Words,* eight sets of short piano pieces. Mendelssohn was a prolific writer for the voice. The oratorio *Elijah,* one of his best-loved works, represents the peak of his achievement in this category.

Principal Works

Orchestral music, including 5 symphonies (No. 3, *Scottish*, 1842; No. 4, *Italian*, 1833; No. 5, *Reformation*, 1830); concert overtures (*A Midsummer Night's Dream*, 1826; *The Hebrides, or Fingal's Cave*, 1830); 2 piano concertos, 1 violin concerto (1844)

Dramatic music, including 1 opera and incidental music for 6 plays (*A Midsummer Night's Dream*, 1843)

Choral music, including 2 oratorios (*St. Paul*, 1836; *Elijah*, 1846); cantatas, anthems, and part songs

Chamber music, including 6 string quartets, 2 string quintets, piano quartets, 1 octet, and various sonatas

Piano music, including *Songs Without Words* (8 sets, 1829–45); sonatas, fugues, and fantasias

Organ music; solo vocal music, transcriptions and arrangements of Bach, Handel, Mozart, and Beethoven

The popularity of Shakespeare's play A Midsummer Night's Dream *is evident in this fanciful canvas by* **Henry Fuseli** *(1741–1825) entitled* Titania and Bottom, *c. 1790.* (London, Tate Gallery/Art Resource, N.Y.)

AN EARLY ROMANTIC OVERTURE: *A MIDSUMMER NIGHT'S DREAM*

The Overture to Shakespeare's play *A Midsummer Night's Dream* is in Mendelssohn's happiest vein. The mood of elfin enchantment that the youthful composer achieved here was to return again and again in his later years. Four prolonged chords in the woodwinds and horns open the doors to the realm of the fairy king Oberon and his queen, Titania. The fairy music is introduced by the violins in a high register, very lively and very soft, and staccato (short and detached). An energetic transition leads into a second theme, which represents the young lovers in the play. It is a lyrical idea, smooth and flowing, that provides an effective contrast with the fairy music. Third is the noisy dance of the clowns, which is played *fortissimo* in a lively rhythm with wide leaps in the melody to underline its boisterous character. Its last four notes suggest the "hee-haw" of a donkey, since in the play a magic spell fastens an ass's head on Bottom the Weaver (see Listening Guide 29).

These three basic ideas are presented in the first section, developed in a middle section, and restated in the last section—in short, it is in sonata-allegro form. A coda concludes the piece with a mood of quiet farewell. As the young composer explained, "After everything has been satisfactorily settled and the principal players have joyfully left the stage, the elves follow them, bless the house, and disappear with the dawn. So ends the play, and my overture too." This picturesque work is an example of program music—instrumental music with literary or pictorial associations, which we know as a favorite Romantic genre.

In 1842, King Frederick William decided on a production of Shakespeare's comedy at the Royal Theater in Leipzig and suggested to Mendelssohn that he write incidental music for it. Several of these pieces—the Scherzo, Nocturne, and especially the Wedding March—have achieved worldwide popularity and are frequently performed together with the Overture as a suite.

Mendelssohn has remained a favorite with the concertgoing public. His elegant workmanship, melodious charm, and refinement of feeling are qualities that wear well through the ages.

Listening Guide 29

C/S: 5A/3   C/S: 5/ 13 – 21

MENDELSSOHN: *A Midsummer Night's Dream*, Overture   (11:27)

Date of work: 1826

Genre: Orchestral overture; incidental music to play added 1843

Program: Based on Shakespeare's play *A Midsummer Night's Dream*. Plot centers on four groups of characters: courtly party (Theseus and Hippolyta), four young lovers, the fairies (Oberon and Titania, King and Queen), and the clownish tradesmen. Action focuses on pairs of lovers from all groups and transformations brought on by mischievous Puck.

Form: Sonata-allegro form
Exposition—4 themes introduced
Development—themes varied
Recapitulation—main themes return
Coda—closing

13	0:00	Introduction to realm of the fairies—4 long chords in winds
		EXPOSITION: Allegro di molto
	0:21	Fairy theme—soft, lively, high violins playing staccato:

| 14 | 1:06 | Transitional theme—loud, energetic, descending, then ascending line: |

| 15 | 2:07 | Young lovers' theme—lyrical, expressive melody in violins: |

16	2:57	Clowns' theme; magic spell places ass's head on Bottom the Weaver—rhythmic theme, disjunct; wide leap reminiscent of donkey's hee-haw:
	3:18	Closing—based on transitional theme

DEVELOPMENT

17	3:42	Fairy music developed; exchanged between strings in imitation
	5:23	Closes with reminiscence of lovers' theme

RECAPITULATION

18	5:53	Realm of fairies returns—4 chords in winds
	6:17	Fairy music—like opening, light staccato strings
19	7:00	Lovers' theme—lyrical melody
20	7:50	Clowns' theme—active, disjunct
	8:12	Extension of clowns' theme and hee-haw

CODA

21	9:16	Opens with fairy music, followed by transitional theme from exposition, heard slower:
	10:59	Realm of fairies—4 closing chords, like opening

A Comparison of Classical and Romantic Styles

Classical (c. 1750–1825)	*Romantic (c. 1820–1900)*
Haydn, Mozart, Beethoven, Schubert, Mendelssohn	Beethoven, Schubert, Mendelssohn, Clara Schumann, Robert Schumann, Chopin, Liszt, Berlioz, Brahms, Tchaikovsky, Strauss
Symmetrical melody in balanced phrases and cadences; tuneful; diatonic, with narrow leaps	Expansive, singing melodies; wide ranging; more varied, with chromatic inflections
Clear rhythmically, with regularly recurring accents; dance rhythms favored	Rhythmic diversity and elasticity; tempo rubato
Diatonic harmony favored; tonic-dominant relationships expanded, become basis for large-scale forms	Increasing chromaticism; expanded concepts of tonality
Homophonic textures; horizontal perspective	Homophony, turning to increased polyphony in later years of era
Symphony, solo concerto, solo sonata, string quartet	Same large forms, adding one-movement symphonic poem; solo piano works
Opera, mass, solo song	Same vocal forms, adding works for solo voice/orchestra
Ternary form predominant; sonata-allegro form developed; absolute forms preferred	Expansion of forms and interest in continuous forms as well as miniature programmatic forms
Secular music predominant; aristocratic audience	Secular music predominant; middle-class audience
Continuously changing dynamics through *crescendo* and *decrescendo*	Widely ranging dynamics for expressive purposes
Changing tone colors between sections of works	Continual change and blend of tone colors; experiments with new instruments and unusual ranges

String orchestra with woodwinds and some brass; 30-to-40-member orchestra; rise of piano to prominence	Introduction of new instruments (tuba, English horn, saxophone); much larger orchestras; piano predominant as solo instrument
Improvisation largely limited to cadenzas in concertos	Increased virtuosity and expression; composers specify more in scores
Emotional restraint and balance	Emotions, mood, atmosphere emphasized; interest in the bizarre and macabre

PART FIVE

■

Medieval and
Renaissance Music

*"Music was originally discreet, seemly, simple, masculine, and of good
morals. Have not the moderns rendered it lascivious beyond measure?"*
—JACQUES DE LIÈGE

UNIT XVI

The Middle Ages

49

The Culture of the Middle Ages

"Nothing is more characteristic of human nature than to be soothed by sweet modes and stirred up by their opposites. Infants, youths, and old people as well are so naturally attuned to musical modes by a kind of spontaneous feeling that no age is without delight in sweet song."
—BOETHIUS

The relics of the ancient civilizations—Sumer, Babylonia, Egypt—bear witness to a flourishing musical art. In the antique world, religious myth and tradition ascribed divine powers to music. The walls of Thebes rose and those of Jericho fell to the sound of music. David played his lyre to cure the melancholy of Saul. In the temple at Jerusalem, the Levites, who were the musicians, "being arrayed in white linen, having cymbals and psalteries and harps, stood at the east of the altar, and with them a hundred and twenty priests sounding with trumpets" (2 Chronicles 5:12).

Only a few fragments of the music of antiquity have descended to us. The centuries have forever silenced the sounds that echoed through the Athenian amphitheater and the Roman circus. Those sounds and the attitudes they reflected, in Greece and throughout the Mediterranean world, were the foundation out of which grew the music of later ages. They became part of the heritage of the West.

The Middle Ages extended over the thousand-year period between the fall of Rome, commonly set at 476 A.D., and the flowering of the culture of the modern world. The first half of this millennium, from around 500 to 1000 and often referred to as the Dark Ages, should be viewed as a period not of decline but rather of ascent, during which Christianity spread throughout Europe. In this society, all power flowed from the king, with the approval of the church and its bishops. The two centers of power, church and state, were bound to

Early Middle Ages

287

clash, and the struggle between them shaped the next chapter of European history. The modern concept of a strong, centralized government as the guardian of law and order is generally credited to Charlemagne (742–814), the legendary emperor of the Franks in whose domains Roman, Frankish, and Teutonic elements intermingled. This progressive monarch, who regretted until his dying day that he did not know how to write—he regarded the ability as a talent he simply did not possess—encouraged education and left behind him an ideal of social justice that illuminated the "darkness" of the early Medieval world.

The church as patron

The culture of this period was largely shaped by the rise of monasteries. It was the monks who preserved the learning of the ancient world and transmitted it, through their manuscripts, to European scholars. In their desire to enhance the church service, they extensively patronized music. Because of their efforts, the art music of the Middle Ages was largely religious. Women too played a role in the preservation of knowledge and in the cultivation of music for the church, for nuns had an important societal role in this era. One woman stands out in particular, Hildegard of Bingen, head of a monastery in a small town in western Germany. She is remembered today for her writings on natural history and medicine and for her poetry and music for special church services. We will study a religious drama with music by Hildegard in Chapter 50.

Late Middle Ages

The late Middle Ages, from around 1000 to 1400, witnessed the building of the great cathedrals and the founding of universities throughout Europe. Cities emerged as centers of art and culture, and within them the townspeople, the bourgeoisie, were destined to play an ever expanding role in civic life. Developing national literatures played their part in shaping the languages of Europe: the *Chanson de Roland* (c. 1100) in France, Dante's *Divine Comedy* (1307) in Italy, Chaucer's *Canterbury Tales* (1386) in England. These literary landmarks have their counterparts in painting with Lorenzetti's frescoes for the Town Hall in Siena (1338–40) and Orcagna's *Last Judgment* for Florence (c. 1355).

Civic life is the focus of **Ambrogio Lorenzetti's** *(d. 1348?) fresco* Good Government in the City. (Scala/Art Resource, N.Y.)

Cultural Perspective 9

The Changing Face of Patronage

We have identified the early Christian church as a major patron or benefactor of music in the Middle Ages. How did the church's support further the cause of music, and who else championed the art in early times? Who plays this important role today?

In the Medieval era, the leading promoters of music and musicians were the state—that is, the courts of royalty and nobility—and the church. These two institutions offered stable employment to composers, singers, and instrumentalists, keeping them supplied with food, clothing, and work in their chosen field. They were also the principal consumers of, or customers for, music at the time. The church, we will see, had a great need for singers and organists and for newly composed music in its services. Royalty and nobility valued music as a symbol of prestige for their courts, so they engaged the best composers and musicians of the day to entertain them and their guests at banquets, dances, and tournaments. Often, the role of artistic patron was fulfilled by the reigning lady at court, as with French queen Eleanor of Aquitaine (c. 1122–1204) and, later, the Italian noblewoman Isabella d'Este (1474–1539).

Eventually, cities took over a civic role in promoting music—in the Renaissance, they sponsored daily wind band concerts played from the church tower, for example—offering yet more possibilities for employment to aspiring musicians and marking the beginning of a new state-sponsored system of support for the arts. By the sixteenth century, the growing middle class became an important consumer of music, purchasing newly printed books for amateur music making.

Over the centuries, composers and musicians have made a living from these various institutions. We have seen that the eighteenth-century composer Joseph Haydn, for example, enjoyed a rather comfortable life under the patronage of the noble Hungarian Esterházy family. Others, like Mozart, were not well suited to this system, and struggled to survive financially. Beethoven lived off commissions for new works as well as sales of his music to the public.

Today, support for the arts has many faces. Employment possibilities for musicians are much more diverse than they were in earlier times: composers often have positions as professors in colleges and universities, and performers hold paying jobs as church musicians, orchestral or ensemble members, and teachers. Government agencies, such as the National Endowment for the Arts (NEA) and state and regional arts organizations, remain vitally important to the livelihood of modern musicians. Equally vital are the donations of private patrons—many concert halls across the country are named after benefactors who have given large amounts of money for the halls' construction. Even the White House sponsors today's musicians: the inauguration of President Bill Clinton in January 1993 presented an impressive lineup of performers, including soprano saxophonist Kenny G and the rock group Fleetwood Mac.

Corporate patronage has altered the role of the public as supporters of the arts. Now, there is often an intermediary—a record company, concert promoter, or entrepreneur—who provides up-front support for musicians and then capitalizes on the product through sales to the general public. Still, when you purchase a CD of your favorite rock group or buy tickets to their next con-

Court trumpeters announce the arrival of noble visitors in this fifteenth-century illumination from the Chronicles *of* **Jean Froissart.** (Courtesy of British Library, London)

cert, attend a symphony program or see a musical theater production, you are choosing to patronize a particular branch of the art of music. Unlike early times, when only a small fraction of the population could enjoy the arts, people at all levels of today's society can in some way enrich their lives through music. And those actively involved in the music field have responded accordingly, providing an ever-widening array of sounds and experiences for your enjoyment and patronage.

The age of knighthood

This was an era of violence brought on by fervent religious beliefs. Knights embarked on Crusades to conquer the Holy Land. Although feudal society was male-dominated, idealizing as it did the figure of the fearless warrior, women's status was raised by the universal cult of Mary, the mother of Christ, and by the concepts of chivalry that sprang out of the age of knighthood. In the songs of the court minstrels, woman was adored with a fervor that laid the foundation for our concept of romantic love. This poetic attitude found its perfect symbol in the image of the faithful knight who worshipped his lady from afar and was inspired by her to deeds of daring and self-sacrifice.

The Middle Ages, in brief, encompassed a period of enormous ferment and change. Out of its stirrings, faint at first but with increasing clarity and strength, emerged the profile of what we know today as Western civilization.

50

Sacred Music and Religious Drama in the Middle Ages

"When God saw that many men were lazy, and gave themselves only with difficulty to spiritual reading, He wished to make it easy for them, and added the melody to the Prophet's words, that all being rejoiced by the charm of the music, should sing hymns to Him with gladness."
—ST. JOHN CHRYSOSTOM

The early music of the Christian church was shaped in part by Greek, Hebrew, and Syrian influences. It became necessary in time to assemble the ever growing body of music into an organized liturgy. The task extended over several generations but is traditionally associated with the name of Pope Gregory the Great, who reigned from 590 to 604.

Like the music of the Greeks and Hebrews, *Gregorian chant* (also known as *plainchant* or *plainsong*) consists of a single-line melody. In other words, it is monophonic in texture, lacking harmony and counterpoint. Its freely flowing vocal line is subtly attuned to the inflections of the Latin text. Gregorian melody is generally free from regular accent. Its unmeasured flow expresses what may be called prose rhythm in music, or free-verse rhythm, as distinguished from metrical-poetry rhythm such as we find in the regularly accented measures of duple or triple meter.

Gregorian chant

The Gregorian melodies, numbering more than three thousand, formed a body of anonymous music whose roots reached deep into the spiritual life of the people. In melodic style, Gregorian chant avoids wide leaps and dynamic contrasts. Its gentle rise and fall constitute a kind of musical speech. Free from the shackles of regular phrase structure, the continuous, undulating vocal line is the counterpart in sound of the lacy ornamentation of Romanesque art and architecture.

At first the Gregorian chants were handed down orally from one generation to the next. As the number of chants increased, singers needed to be reminded of the general outlines of the different melodies. Thus came into being *neumes*, little ascending and descending signs that were first written above the words to suggest the contour of the melody, and which developed into a musical notation with square notes on a four-line staff (see p. 293).

Neumes

As far as the setting of text is concerned, the melodies fall into three main classes: *syllabic,* with one note sung to each syllable of text; *neumatic,* generally with groups of two to four notes sung to a syllable; and *melismatic,* with a single syllable of text extending over longer groups of notes. The melismatic style, descended from the rhapsodic improvisations of Eastern cultures, became a prominent feature of Gregorian chant and exerted a strong influence on subsequent Western music.

Text settings

From Gregorian chant through Renaissance polyphony, Western music

Modes

used a variety of scale patterns, or *modes.* In addition to major and minor modes, there were others that lacked a strong sense of gravitation to a tonic note. The modes served as the basis for European art music for a thousand years. With the development of polyphony, or many-voiced music, a harmonic system evolved based on these scale patterns. The adjective *modal* thus refers to the type of melody and harmony that prevailed in the early and later Middle Ages. It is frequently used in opposition to *tonal,* which refers to the harmony based on major-minor tonality that came later.

The Mass

The Mass, the most solemn ritual of the Roman Catholic Church, constitutes a reenactment of the sacrifice of Christ. The name is derived from the Latin *missa,* "dismissal" (of the congregation at the end of the service). The collection of prayers that make up the Mass fall into two categories: those that vary from day to day throughout the church year, dependent upon the particular feast celebrated, called the *Proper;* and those that remain the same in every Mass, the *Ordinary.* (A chart of the organization of the Mass with the individual movements of the Proper and Ordinary appears in Chapter 53, p. 325.) The church liturgy is supported by Gregorian melodies for each item of the ceremony. In this way, Gregorian chant was central to the celebration of the Mass, which was and remains today the most important service in the Catholic Church.

Proper and Ordinary

A Gregorian Melody: Haec dies

Gradual

A fine example of Gregorian chant is *Haec dies,* the Gradual from the Mass for Easter Day. *Gradual* is the name of the fourth item of the Proper, or variable part of the Mass. Derived from the Latin word for "steps" (because the melody may have been sung from the steps of the altar), the term was applied to the singing of portions of a Psalm in a musically elaborate, melismatic style. The Gradual is performed in a *responsorial* manner, that is, as a series of exchanges between soloist and chorus in which one answers the other. The solo passage is known as a *verse,* the choral answer is the *response.* The Gradual therefore involves the contrast between two dissimilar bodies of sound, yet it is monophonic in texture.

Responsorial singing

Melismatic setting

    Haec dies opens with a brief introductory passage for a soloist. The choral response occupies the first half of the melody. The second half is the soloist's verse, which is followed by a brief choral conclusion. (See Listening Guide 30 for the text, which is drawn from two Psalms.) The melody moves by step or small leap within a narrow range and consists of a series of tiny motives that grow like cells and expand in a natural process of variation. The way in which certain key words are drawn out over a series of notes is striking. This melismatic treatment emphasizes such important words as "Dominus" (Lord) or "exsultemus" (we will rejoice), setting them apart from the others.

ÆC dí- es, * quam fé- cit Dó-

mi- nus : exsulté- mus,

et lae-té- mur in é- a.

The opening of the chant Haec dies in Gregorian notation.

The Rise of Polyphony: The Notre Dame School

Toward the end of the Romanesque period (c. 850–1150) began the single most important development in the history of Western music: the emergence of polyphony, or the combination of two or more simultaneous melodic lines.

Once several melodic lines proceeded simultaneously, the flexible prose rhythms of single-line music disappeared. Polyphony contributed to the increased use of regular meters, which enabled the different voices to keep together. This music had to be written down in a way that would indicate precisely the rhythm and the pitch, which necessitated a more exact notational system not unlike the one in use today. (For an explanation of our modern notational system, see Appendix I, "Musical Notation," p. 611.)

With the development of a more precise notation, music progressed from being an art of improvisation and oral tradition to one that was carefully planned and preserved. The period of anonymous creation drew to a close, and the individual composer began to be recognized.

Development of notation

This development took shape during the Gothic era (c. 1150–1450), a period that saw the rise of cathedrals with their choirs and organs. The learned musicians, for the most part monks and priests, mastered the art of constructing extended musical works through the various devices of counterpoint discussed earlier (Chapter 4, pp. 22–23). Their prime interest at this point was in the structural combination of musical elements, which explains the derivation of the word "composer" from the Latin *componere,* "to put together."

The earliest kind of polyphonic music was called *organum,* which developed when the custom arose of adding to the Gregorian melody a second voice that ran parallel to the plainchant at the interval of a fifth or fourth above or below. The way was now open for the development of a polyphonic art in which the individual voices moved with ever greater independence, not only in parallel but also in contrary motion. In the forefront of this development were the composers whose center was the Cathedral of Notre Dame in Paris during the twelfth and thirteenth centuries. Their leader, Léonin, lived in the

Organum

Notre Dame school

Léonin

In both architecture and music, the Gothic period saw great advances in the techniques of construction. The Cathedral of Notre Dame, Paris (1163–1235).

latter part of the twelfth century, and is the first composer of polyphonic music whose name is known to us.

It was self-evident to the Medieval mind that the new must be founded on the old. Therefore composers of organum based their pieces on a preexisting Gregorian chant. While the lower voice sang the fixed melody in enormously long notes, the upper voice sang a freely composed part that moved rapidly above it. In such a setting, the chant was no longer recognizable as a melody. Its presence was symbolic, anchoring the new in the old.

In the organum *Haec dies* (see Listening Guide 30), the solo polyphonic sections are answered by choral ones, sung in chant. The faster-moving top *Rhythmic mode* voice sings in a *rhythmic mode*—a fixed pattern of long and short notes that is repeated or varied. Already European music was on its way to the metrical patterns familiar to modern listeners.

The Early Medieval Motet

While Léonin limited himself to polyphony in two parts, his successor Pérotin extended the technique by writing for three and four different voices. Toward *Pérotin* the end of Pérotin's life, musicians began composing new texts for the previously textless upper voices of organum. The addition of these texts resulted in *Motet* the *motet,* the most important form of early polyphonic music. The term "motet" derives from the French word *mot,* referring to the words that were added to the vocal lines. These might present two different Latin texts at the same time, or one voice might sing in Latin, the other in French. The Medieval motet is, then, a vocal composition, either sacred or secular, which may or may not have had instrumental accompaniment.

The early motet illustrates how Medieval composers based their own works on what had been handed down from the past. They selected a fragment of Gregorian chant, such as the *Haec dies,* and, keeping the pitches intact, gave them precise rhythmic values, usually of very long notes that contrasted with the more active movement of the other parts. This served as the structural skeleton of the piece, to which the composer added one, two, or three freely composed countermelodies. (A *countermelody,* as we have noted, is a melody heard against another.) In the motet, a sacred text might be combined with a quite secular—even racy—one. The basic Gregorian theme, hidden among the voices, fused these disparate elements into a unity—if not in the listener's ear, at least in the composer's mind.

Countermelody

The anonymous thirteenth-century motet *O mitissima/Virgo/Haec dies* is in three-part polyphony, built on a bottom voice, the *Tenor* (from the Latin *tenere,* meaning "to hold"), which sounds—either vocally or instrumentally— the notes of the chant *Haec dies.* This part unfolds a repeated rhythmic pattern based on the notes of the chant, in the order long-long-short-long, forming the structural basis for the piece. A repetition of a musical pattern— melodic, rhythmic, or harmonic—is known as an *ostinato.* Above this, musical interest is focused in the two upper parts, which present different Latin poems in praise of the Virgin Mary. These voices are set in a similar rhythm of long and short notes, with the two lines frequently crossing each other in a lively exchange. (See Listening Guide 30.)

Tenor

Ostinato

The motet is in triple meter, which to Medieval listeners symbolized the perfection of the Trinity. The opening and closing sounds as well as the cadences—resting places that punctuate the music—are based on open fifths and octaves, which have a hollow sound to our ears. We will see that these open sounds intrigued later composers such as Debussy, who tried to recapture the essence of Medieval music at the turn of the twentieth century.

Listening Guide 30

(MW) 📼   C/S: 1A/2–4   💿   C/S: 1/ 8 – 10

Sh: 1A/1–3   Sh: 1/ 1 – 3

Chant, Organum, and Motet

GREGORIAN CHANT: *Haec dies*   (2:25)

Text: Psalms 118:24 and 106:1
Chant type: Gradual, from the Proper
Occasion: Easter Sunday
Performance: Responsorial (solo and chorus)
Style: Elaborate and melismatic

		Text	Translation	Performance
8	0:00	Haec dies,	This is the day	Solo intonation
	0:09	quam fecit Dominus	which the Lord hath made;	Choral response
		exsultemus et	we will rejoice and be	
		laetemur in ea.	glad of it.	
	1:13	Confitemini Domino,	O give thanks to the	Solo verse
		quoniam bonus:	Lord, for He is good:	
		quoniam in saeculum	for His mercy	
		misericordia	endureth	
	2:04	ejus.	forever.	Chorus

Solo melisma on "Domino":

2:25 **ORGANUM:** *Haec dies* **(excerpt)**   (3:51)

Date of work: C. 1175

Composer: Notre Dame School of Paris, in style of Léonin

Voices: 2 voices, both with "Haec dies"

Upper voice—freely composed, rhythmic, fast moving, sung melismatically:

Lower voice—contains *Haec dies* chant in long notes:

3:51 **MOTET:** *O mitissima/Virgo/Haec dies*   (4:23)

Date of work: 13th century

Composer: Anonymous

Voices/Text: 3 voices, each with different text

Characteristics: Polyphonic, all voices rhythmic

Basis: Bottom voice (Tenor) with chant notes, very melismatic on 2 words only ("Haec dies")

Text	Translation
	Top Voice
O mitissima Virgo Maria,	O sweetest Virgin Mary,

Posce tuum filium,	beg thy son
Ut nobis auxilium	to give us help
Det et remedium	and resources
Contra demonum	against the deceptions
Fallibiles astucias	of the demons
Et horum nequicias.	and their iniquities.

Middle Voice

Virgo virginum,	Virgin of virgins,
Lumen luminum,	light of lights,
Reformatrix hominum,	reformer of men,
Que portasti Dominum,	who bore the Lord,
Per te Maria,	through thee, Mary,
Detur venia,	let grace be given
Angelo nunciante,	as the Angel announced:
Virgo es post et ante.	Thou art a Virgin before and after.

Bottom Voice
(performed instrumentally on our recording)

Haec dies	This is the day . . .

Motet opening—ostinato pattern bracketed (long-long-short-long):

Life in the Medieval Monastery and Convent

One lifestyle available to men and women in the Middle Ages centered around the church. Life in a cloister (a place for religious seclusion) allowed people to withdraw from secular society to the shelter of monasteries and convents, where they devoted themselves to a variety of interests: prayer, scholarship, preaching, charity, or healing the sick, depending upon the religious order they joined. Others adopted a freer religious way of life; men joined orders of wandering friars who preached to the masses, and women joined lay religious groups devoted to teaching or hospital work. Individuals from all levels of society chose the religious life—members of the aristocracy and the middle class who sought a quiet, contemplative existence, younger sons of the gentry who inherited no land, and young women without marriage prospects.

A life devoted to the church was not an easy one. Some religious orders, such as the Franciscans, required vows of poverty; each new member dis-

Cultural Perspective 10

Influences on the Early Christian Church

How did the early Christians first establish the rituals of their church, and where did their musical practices come from? Since Christianity descended directly from Judaism—Jesus and his followers were, after all, Jews—the early Christians naturally retained some familiar Judaic traditions in defining their religious beliefs and practices. For example, they retained the concept of one God (many religions of the world worship more than one deity) and the general code of moral behavior that governs us today. Christianity also borrowed from Judaism the use of congregational prayer, an appreciation of books, including the biblical texts of the Hebrew Scriptures (Old Testament), and the practice of reading and discussing sacred texts in a public meeting house—the Jewish synagogue or Christian church. Some Hebrew words, such as *Amen* (in truth) and *Halleluiah* (Praise God), are still used in Christian prayer.

Judaism and Christianity are linked musically by the Psalms (the 150 texts from the Old Testament Book of Psalms). Many of these mention singing; "O come, let us sing to the Lord," "O sing to the Lord a new song," and "I will sing of loyalty and justice" are a few opening lines. Although scholars have not yet agreed on precisely when the practice of singing Psalms became part of Jewish and Roman Catholic services, the Psalms eventually gained a respected place in both religions; they were sung during services, at ceremonial meals, and in the home. Some of the Psalms have a refrain of *alleluia;* these were especially important to Jewish practice, where they were sung responsorially by a cantor (a soloist and singing leader) and the congregation. In the Roman Catholic Church,

the recitation of Psalms, more like speaking than singing, became the core of many religious services (the Divine Offices—the daily cycle of services or hours—and, to a lesser extent, the Mass). Here too they were "sung" in a responsorial manner, in alternation between the priest and the other clergy and choir members. We will see later that the practice of singing Psalms was adopted in the services of the Protestant churches during the Reformation and after (see CP 5 on music and religion in the Americas).

Other practices in the early Roman Catholic Church came from the East—the church of Byzantium (or Constantinople, now Istanbul in Turkey), another branch of the Christian church. From this institution came a body of hymns (devotional songs), as well as influential concepts on the formation of melodies and harmonies that shaped the sounds of Western music for centuries. The influence of Byzantium can be seen too in the architecture of some Roman Catholic Churches: perhaps the most famous example is St. Mark's in the great seaport of Venice (see p. 122). Features of Greek music and other Mediterranean cultures were also absorbed into the liturgy of the early Christian church. (For example, the Greek text *Kyrie eleison* was retained as a section of the High Mass.)

You may wonder why the music of the early Christian church—Gregorian chant, as we call it today—was only sung rather than accompanied with instruments. Certainly, in secular (nonreligious) settings, instruments were used with singing and dancing, and the Hebrew Scriptures are full of references to them—psaltery, harp, organ, trumpet, and cymbals, among many others. Yet it was be-

Illuminated initial from Psalm 114 in Hebrew, depicting the exodus from Egypt in which Moses led the Israelites. (From the Kaufmann Haggadah, courtesy of the Library of the Hungarian Academy of Science, Budapest)

lieved by the early Christians that instrumental music did not serve religion and that music lacking a spiritual text might arouse erotic passions in the listener; hence, most instruments were banned from use in the Roman Catholic Church for many years. The organ, an invention of the Greeks, is often associated with church music and was the first instrument to be generally accepted and used in Christian worship.

Some of these conventions have changed today. Texts for devotional music tend to be in the vernacular (the language of the particular region) rather than in the older languages of Hebrew or Latin; thus everyone can understand them. Many styles of music now serve religion, and, generally, whatever moves people spiritually is acceptable, whether it be instrumental or vocal, electronic or acoustic, popular or art, new or old.

Terms to Note:

synagogue	Mass
Book of Psalms	responsorial
cantor	Gregorian chant
Divine Offices	

Suggested Listening:

Gregorian chant (*Haec dies*)
Jewish chant or synagogue music

carded all worldly possessions upon joining. The discipline of the religious life was arduous. A typical day began at 2:00 or 3:00 A.M. with the celebration of daily services, the reading of lessons, and the singing of psalms. Each day in the church calendar had its own ritual and its own order of prayers. The members of the community interspersed their religious duties with work in the fields, in the library, in the workshop. Some produced items that could be sold—wine, beer, cheese, for example—thus bringing in revenue to the order.

In a monastery, the monks sing during the celebration of Mass and an altar boy (left) pulls a bell rope in this fourteenth-century manuscript illumination.

Despite the grueling schedule, many men and women in religious life dedicated themselves to writing and preserving knowledge from earlier times. One such person was Hildegard of Bingen, one of the most remarkable women of the Middle Ages, who was renowned in her day as a poet and prophet.

Hildegard of Bingen and Medieval Religious Drama

Hildegard of Bingen (1098–1171) was the daughter of a noble family, who promised her, as their tenth child, to the service of the church. (This is called a *tithe,* or giving to the church one-tenth of what one has.) She was raised by a religious recluse and took her vows at the age of fifteen. With the death of her teacher, Hildegard became superior of the order, and later founded her own monastery in Rupertsberg, on the Rhine River near Bingen. Her influence grew, so that she was able to found yet another house of her followers. Her miracles and prophecies made her famous throughout Europe; popes, kings, and priests sought her advice on political and religious issues. She was also known for her scientific and medical writings. Although never officially canonized, Hildegard is regarded as a saint by the church.

From childhood, Hildegard experienced visions, which intensified in later life. She was reportedly able to see hidden things and to foretell the future. Moved to record her visions and prophecies, Hildegard completed three collections in manuscript. "The words I speak come from no human mouth; I saw and heard them in visions sent to me. . . . God moves where He wills, and not to the glory of earthly man. . . . I have no confidence in my own capacities— I reach out my hand to God that He may carry me along as a feather borne weightlessly by the wind." A particular vision she had in 1141 was a turning point in her life: "It came to pass . . . that the heavens were opened and a blinding light of exceptional brilliance flowed through my flame." From this moment, she claimed to fully understand the meaning of the Scriptures.

Hildegard also wrote religious poetry with music, which she collected in a volume entitled *Symphony of the Harmony of Celestial Revelations (Symphonia armonie celestium revelationum)*. These works form a liturgical cycle appropriate for singing at different religious feasts throughout the year. Best-known of her works is a play with music entitled *The Play of the Virtues (Ordo virtutum)*. Her musical style was highly original; it resembled Gregorian chant, but unlike most other new music of the time, it did not draw from the existing repertory.

THE PLAY OF THE VIRTUES

The Play of the Virtues is a religious drama sung in verse. This work is the earliest known example of a *morality play,* a drama meant to teach righteous and upright values. Written in Latin poetry full of brilliant imagery and mysticism, this play presents the battle between the Virtues and the Devil for the soul, Anima. Many of the characters are personifications of virtues—among them, Faith, Hope, Charity, Patience, Humility, Chastity, Obedience, Discipline, and Victory. The drama tells how Anima falls to the temptations of the Devil but is saved by the Virtues. The Virtues then engage in a debate with the Devil, each introducing herself with appropriate music and answered by the other Virtues as a group. Having saved another soul, the Virtues rejoice as Victory swoops down on the Devil and ties him up.

Morality play

An abbot, head of a monastery, preaches to a group of Flemish nuns in this miniature from a manuscript dated 1351.

The music for *The Play of the Virtues* consists of eighty-two monophonic, chantlike melodies organized by the repetition of certain musical phrases and motives (see Listening Guide 31). The style is largely neumatic—several notes are sung to each syllable of text—except where a word is emphasized through extension in a melisma. All the parts were sung by women—presumably nuns—except that of the Devil, who was played by a local priest. Hildegard herself appears at the beginning to explain how she came to record her experiences.

Set in a prologue and four scenes, the play reaches its musical high point in the last scene, with the salvation of the soul. The Devil speaks harshly to Anima, who vows to fight him with the help of Victory, Humility, and the other Virtues. Victory sings with a commanding tone in a high range, while Humility's voice soars heavenward in anticipation of the salvation of the lost soul. The chorus of Virtues responds in a simpler unison line of angelic voices, resounding the celestial triumph in a style unique to Hildegard.

Listening Guide 31   C/S: 1A/5   C/S: 1/

HILDEGARD: *The Play of the Virtues (Ordo virtutum)*, Scene 4   (4:31)

Date of work: Mid-12th century
Genre: Religious drama (morality play) with music
Principal characters:
   Anima, a soul
   The Devil
   The Sixteen Virtues (Humility, Knowledge of God, World Rejection, Charity, Celestial Love, Modesty, Hope, Patience, Obedience, Innocence, Discretion, Faith, Discipline, Chastity, Victory, Compassion)
   Hildegard
   Church Elders and Prophets

SCENE 4, beginning

		Text	Translation	Description
			DEVIL	
11	0:00	Quae es, aut unde venis? Tu amplexata es me, et ego foras eduxi te. Sed nunc in reversione tua confundis me—ego autem pugna mea deiciam te!	Who are you? Where are you coming from? You were in my embrace, and I led you out. Yet now you are going back, defying me—but I will fight you and bring you down!	Spoken rather than sung
			REPENTANT SOUL	
12	0:21	Ego omnes vias tuas malas esse cognovi, et ideo fugi a te; modo autem, o illusor, pugno contra te. Inde tu, o regina Humilitas, tuo medicamine adiuva me.	I knew that all your ways were wicked, so I fled you; but now, you deceiver, I'll fight you face to face. Queen Humility, come with your medicine, give me aid.	Sung in neumatic, conjunct style; climaxes near end; with instrumental accompaniment

HUMILITY *(to Victory)*

1:30	O Victoria, quae istum in caelo superasti, curre cum militibus tuis, et omnes ligate diabolum hunc.	Victory, who once conquered this creature in the heavens, run now, with all your warriors, and all of you, bind this devil.	Line opens with two rising leaps; more animated style

VICTORY *(to the Virtues)*

| 1:58 | O fortissimi et gloriosissimi milites, venite et adiuvate me istum fallacem vincere. | Bravest and most glorious warriors, come, help me vanquish this deceitful one! | Middle range, forceful delivery, with organ accompaniment |

VIRTUES

| 13 | 2:31 | O dulcissima bellatrix, in torrente fonte qui absorbuit, lupum rapacem! O gloriosa coronata, nos libenter militamus tecum contra illusorem hunc. | Oh sweetest warrior, in the scorching torrent that swallowed up the voracious wolf! O glorious, crowned one, we'll gladly fight against that deceiver, at your side. | Chorus, singing conjunct line, simpler style |

HUMILITY

| 3:11 | Ligate ergo istum, o virtutes praeclare! | Bind him then, you shining virtues! | More neumatic style with short melismas |

VIRTUES

| 3:27 | O regina nostra, tibi parebimus, et praecepta tua in omnibus adimplebimus. | Queen of us all, we obey— we'll carry out your orders in all things. | Chorus, nearly syllabic |

VICTORY

| 3:48 | Gaudate, o socii, quia antiquus serpens ligatus est. | Rejoice, comrades; the old snake is bound. | High range, more dramatic and melismatic; accompanied by bells |

VIRTUES

| 4:17 | Laus tibi Christe, rex angelorum! | Praise be to you, Christ, King of angels! | Chorus, with melismatic ending on "angelorum" |

Expressive leaps open Humility's soaring line:

Victory's joyful line, set in high range:

51

Secular Music in the Middle Ages

"There are many new things in music that will appear altogether
plausible to our descendants."
—JEAN DE MURIS

Goliard songs

Alongside the learned or art music of the cathedrals and choir schools, there sprang up a popular literature of songs and dances that reflected every aspect of Medieval life. The earliest secular songs that have been preserved were set to Latin texts, which suggests that their origin was in university towns rather than in the villages. Typical are the *Goliard,* or student, songs of the period, many with lewd texts, which express the seize-the-moment philosophy that has always inspired youthful poets. Both poetry and music celebrate the joys of the bottle, the impermanence of love, the beauty of springtime, and the cruelty of fate. Seven hundred years later, the German composer Carl Orff admirably resurrected their spirit in his *Carmina burana*.

Medieval Minstrels

Jongleurs

Minstrels emerged as a class of musicians who wandered among the courts and towns. These were versatile entertainers who played instruments, sang and danced, juggled and showed tricks along with animal acts, and performed plays. In an age that had no newspapers, they regaled their audience with gossip and news. These itinerant actor-singers—called *jongleurs* and, if women, *jongleuresses*—lived on the fringe of society.

Troubadours

Trouvères

Minnesingers

Roles of secular music

On a different social level were the poet-musicians who flourished at the various courts of Europe. They were the *troubadours,* a term applied to both men and women (women were also called *trobairitz*), who lived in the southern region of France known as Provence. Musicians from northern France were called *trouvères*. Both terms mean the same thing—finders or inventors (in musical terms, composers). Troubadours and trouvères flourished in aristocratic circles, numbering among their ranks kings and princes as well as members of the nobility. They either sang their music and poetry themselves or entrusted its performance to other musicians. In Germany, they were known as *Minnesingers,* or singers of courtly love.

Secular music became an integral part of Medieval court life, supplying the necessary accompaniment for dancing, dinner, and after-dinner entertainment. It was central to the ceremonies that welcomed visiting dignitaries, as well as tournaments and civic processions; military music supported campaigns, strengthened the spirit of warriors departing on the Crusades, and greeted them upon their return. Among the royal musicians were Alfonso the Wise of Spain and Richard the Lion-Hearted of England, whose mother, the legendary Eleanor of Aquitaine, presided over a famous court of poet-musicians. Whether in France, Germany, Italy, or Spain, the aristocratic singers

Heinrich von Meissen, called "Frauenlob," or champion of ladies, is exalted by musicians playing drum, flute, shawm, fiddles, psaltery, and bagpipe. Frauenlob was a Minnesinger (singer of courtly love), the German counterpart of the troubadour. (Heidelberg University Library)

were creating a literature that would exert a profound influence upon European culture.

Courtly poetry

The poems of the troubadour and trouvère repertory ranged from simple ballads to love songs, political and moral ditties, war songs, chronicles of the Crusades, laments, and dance songs. They exalted the virtues prized by the age of chivalry—valor, honor, nobility of character, devotion to an ideal, and the quest for perfect love. Like so many of our popular songs today, many of them dealt with the subject of unrequited passion. The object of the poet's desire was generally unattainable, either because of her high rank or because she was already wed to another. This poetry, in short, dealt with love in its most idealized form. The subjects of poems by women were similar to those by men, ranging from the sorrow of being rejected by a lover to the joy of true love, but written from a somewhat different point of view. The songs in praise of the Virgin Mary were cast in the same style and language, sometimes even to the same melodies, as served to express love of a more worldly kind.

Moniot d'Arras and the Trouvère Tradition

Moniot d'Arras (fl. 1213–39) was a monk in the abbey of St. Vaast. His work in his native Arras marked the end of the trouvère tradition. Characteristic is his love song *Ce fut en mai* (It Happened in May). The poem tells of an unhappy lover who finds solace in religious feeling. (See Listening Guide 32.) The music

Cultural Perspective 11

Opening Doors to the East

The Middle Ages was an era of religious wars and exploration, both of which opened doors to the East. Between 1096 and 1217, there were five organized Crusades, military expeditions undertaken by European Christians in an attempt to conquer the Holy Land of Palestine. With money from the pope and promises of forgiveness of sins, thousands of people—men, women, and children, nobility and their servants—journeyed east on a spiritual quest that now seems one of the darkest episodes in the history of Christianity. Along the way, crusaders massacred local people, plundered their riches, and destroyed their artworks. Yet out of these violent episodes came a significant meeting of cultures. The crusading knights learned from the expert military skills and weapons of the Turkish and Moorish warriors, and marveled that their own protective metal armor could be pierced by enemy arrows. The advanced medical and scientific knowledge of the Arab world was imported to Europe, and the Arab number system was adopted in Western commerce and banking. (Until then, Europeans had used Roman numerals—I, II, III, IV, V; today, we primarily use Arabic numerals—1, 2, 3, 4, 5.)

What of the musical interaction of these cultures? Instruments of all kinds as well as music and theoretical ideas were brought back to western Europe. Among the new instruments that gained popularity in the West were bowed and plucked strings, woodwinds, and percussion. For example, the Medieval rebec, a small, violin-like instrument, is derived from the Arab rabab, and the loud, double-reed shawm used for outdoor events is closely related to the Turkish zurna. We have seen that more Turkish instruments

—especially percussion—found their way into Western ensembles in the eighteenth century. Crusaders heard too the sounds of the Saracen military trumpets and drums and soon adopted these as their call to battle. The foundations of our Western system of modes (or scale forms) also felt the influence of Eastern theoretical systems.

In 1271, the Venetian merchant and explorer Marco Polo (1254–1324) made a historic journey to China. Polo was welcomed by the great Kublai Khan, a Mongol ruler who had conquered northern China and further modernized the already highly sophisticated civilization there. The Khan encouraged literature, the arts, and medical research, and established Buddhism as the official state religion. Polo and his entourage were much impressed by this society's technical advances; many, such as the making of gunpowder and the art of printing from movable type, were still unknown in western Europe. The Khan was equally fascinated by his Western visitors, and petitioned the pope—unsuccessfully—to send him one hundred Europeans learned in sciences and the arts so that the Chinese could better understand the ways of the West. Polo's diary describes the importance of music to the Chinese military campaigns: "The Tartars never attack until they hear their commander's drums, but while waiting for the battle to begin, they always play and sing. . . . Anyone present would have heard pipes and other instruments, including a beautiful two-stringed one, all playing while men sang at the tops of their voices."

The information Marco Polo recorded throughout his travels helped open routes for the exchange of commerce (especially silks and spices), arts, and ideas from East to West. It is difficult to imagine, in our modern, jet-set society, with its instantaneous satellite transmissions of sounds and images, how arduous these journeys were (for example, it took Polo four years to travel from Venice to China). Although these early encounters were isolated, they helped immeasurably in the centuries that followed to encourage communication between different nations and cultures. We see the results of this process today in the unprecedented freedom of exchange between different societies, making it possible for students from all regions of the globe to attend schools in foreign countries, and enabling audiences everywhere to enjoy performing artists from distant lands.

Terms to Note:

rebec
shawm
mode

Suggested Listening:

Turkish music (Janissary ensemble; see p. 236)
Medieval dance with shawm (saltarello; see
    p. 315)

is folklike and charming, and makes no attempt to express the unhappiness described in the text. The song is monophonic in texture, consisting of a single line of melody heard against an accompaniment that was improvised.

Medieval instruments   In our recording, the accompaniment is played on a psaltery, a dulcimer, and a vielle. The *psaltery* was a Medieval folk instrument like our zither, consisting of a sound box over which were stretched four or five melody strings and a larger number of accompanimental strings; these were plucked. The *dulcimer* resembled the psaltery, but its strings, instead of being plucked, were struck with little hammers. The *vielle* was an ancestor of the violin.

The poem consists of five stanzas, with an elaborate rhyme scheme (as the Listening Guide makes clear). The melody unfolds in two short sections, each of which is repeated. The overall musical form is *strophic,* with the same melody repeated for every stanza of the poem. A brief instrumental interlude is repeated between the stanzas. The use of a poem based on stanzas dictates the repetition of a musical section. When only one or two lines were repeated at the end of each stanza, the repetition took shape as a musical refrain. Thus music responded to the fixed forms of poetry in the most natural manner, creating an intimate relationship between the words and music.

Listening Guide 32   📼 C/S: 1A/6   💿 C/S: 1/ 14 – 18

MONIOT D'ARRAS: *Ce fut en mai* (Trouvère Song)   (2:37)

Date of work: Mid-13th century
Genre: Chanson, strophic setting of 5 stanzas, each of 12 lines
Musical form: **A-A-B-B** (2 short selections, each repeated)
Rhyme scheme: a-a-b-a-a-b-c-c-b-c-c-b (for each stanza)

Enjoyment of Music Moniot D'Arras *Ce fut en mai*

Text	Rhyme Scheme	Musical Form	Translation
I			
Ce fut en mai	*a*	**A**	In early May
Au douz tens gai	*a*		When skies are gay

14   0:00

	Que la saisons est bele;	*b*		And green the plains and mountains,
	Main me levai	*a*	**A**	At break of day
	Joer m'alai	*a*		I rose to play
	Lez une fontenele.	*b*		Beside a little fountain.
	En un vergier	*c*	**B**	In garden close
	Clos d'aiglentier	*c*		Where shone the rose
	Oi une viele;	*b*		I heard a fiddle played, then
	La vi dancier	*c*	**B**	A handsome knight
	Un chevalier	*c*		That charmed my sight
	Et une damoisele.	*b*		Was dancing with a maiden.

II

15	0:34	Cors orent gent	*a*	**A**	Both fair of face,
		Et avenant,	*a*		They turned with grace
		Et molt très bien dançoient;	*b*		To tread their Maytime measure;
		En acolant	*a*	**A**	The flowering place,
		Et en baisant	*a*		Their close embrace,
		Molt biau se deduisoient.	*b*		Their kisses brought them pleasure.
		Au chief du tor,	*c*	**B**	Yet shortly they
		En un destor,	*c*		Had slipped away
		Doi et doi s'en aloient;	*b*		And strolled among the bowers;
		Le jeu d'amor	*c*	**B**	To ease their heart
		Desus la flor	*c*		Each played the part
		A lor plaisir faisoient.	*b*		In love's games on the flowers.

III

16	1:03	J'alai avant,	*a*	**A**	I crept ahead
		Molt redoutant	*a*		All chill with dread
		Que nus d'aus ne me voie,	*b*		Lest someone there should see me,
		Maz et pensant	*a*	**A**	Bemused and sad
		Et desirrant	*a*		Because I had
		D'avoir ausi grant joie.	*b*		No joy like theirs to please me.
		Lors vi lever	*c*	**B**	Then one of those
		Un de lor per	*c*		I'd seen there, rose
		De si loing com j'estoie	*b*		And from afar off speaking
		Por apeler	*c*	**B**	He questioned me
		Et demander	*c*		Who I might be
		Qui sui ni que queroie.	*b*		And what I came there seeking.

IV

17	1:32	J'alai vers aus	*a*	**A**	I stepped their way
		Dis lor mes maus,	*a*		To sadly say
		Que une dame amoie,	*b*		How long I'd loved a lady
		A cui loiaus	*a*	**A**	Whom all my days
		Sans estre faus	*a*		My heart obeys
		Tot mon vivant seroie,	*b*		Full faithfully and steady,
		Por cui plus trai	*c*	**B**	Though still I bore
		Peine et esmai	*c*		A grief so sore
		Que dire ne porroie.	*b*		In losing one so lovely
		Et bien le sai,	*c*	**B**	That surely I
		Que je morrai,	*c*		Would come to die
		S'ele ne mi ravoie.	*b*		Unless she deigned to love me.

V

18	2:02	Tot belement	*a*	**A**	With wisdom rare,
		Et doucement	*a*		With tactful air,

Chascuns d'aus me ravoie.	*b*		They counseled and relieved me;
Et dient tant	*a*	**A**	They said their prayer
Que Dieus briement	*a*		That God might spare
M'envoit de celi joie	*b*		Some joy in love that grieved me
Por qui je sent	*c*	**B**	Where all my gain
Paine et torment:	*c*		Was loss and pain,
Et je lor en rendoie	*b*		So I, in turn, extended
Merci molt grant	*c*	**B**	My thanks sincere
Et en plorant	*c*		With many a tear
A Dé les comandoie.	*b*		And them to God commended.

Guillaume de Machaut and the French Ars Nova

The breakup of the feudal social structure brought with it new concepts of life, art, and beauty. This ferment was reflected in the musical style that made its appearance at the beginning of the fourteenth century in France and somewhat later in Italy, known as *Ars Nova* (new art). The music of the French Ars Nova shows greater refinement than the *Ars Antiqua* (old art), which it displaced. Writers such as Petrarch, Boccaccio, and Chaucer were turning from the divine comedy to the human; painters would soon begin to discover the beauties of nature and the attractiveness of the human form. So too composers turned increasingly from religious to secular themes. The Ars Nova encompassed developments in rhythm, meter, harmony, and counterpoint that transformed the art.

Its outstanding figure was the French composer-poet Guillaume de Machaut (c. 1300–77). He took holy orders at an early age, became secretary to John of Luxembourg, King of Bohemia, and was active at the court of Charles, Duke of Normandy, who subsequently became king of France. He spent his old age as a canon at the Cathedral of Rheims, admired as the greatest musician of the time.

Machaut's double career as cleric and courtier inspired him to write both religious and secular music. His poetry reveals him as proponent of the ideals of Medieval chivalry—a romantic devoted to the moral and social code of an age that was already finished.

HAREU! HAREU! LE FEU/HELAS!/OBEDIENS

The secular motet came to full flower in the art of Machaut. He expanded the form of the preceding century to incorporate the new developments made possible by the Ars Nova, especially the greater variety and flexibility of rhythm. Characteristic is the motet *Hareu! hareu! le feu/Helas! ou sera pris confors/Obediens usque ad mortem.* Since the three simultaneous parts have different texts, the listener is obviously expected to follow the general idea rather than the individual words. The top voice, the *triplum,* sings a poem on a favorite theme of fourteenth-century verse: the suffering of the lover who is consumed by his desire. At the same time, the middle voice, the *duplum,* sings a different love poem. (See Listening Guide 33 for the texts.)

The lower voice, the *Tenor,* is taken from a plainsong Gradual that refers to Christ, but Machaut chooses only the section that goes with the words "obediens usque ad mortem" (obedient even unto death), a sentiment appropriate to the chivalric love described in the other poems. The notes of this Tenor are arranged in a rhythmic pattern that is stated twelve times—six statements in long notes, then six more in diminution (in notes half as long, which makes the voice move twice as fast).

This procedure identifies *Hareu! hareu! le feu* as an *isorhythmic motet* (*iso* means "the same"), based on a rhythmic ostinato. The slow-moving Tenor was probably played on an instrument. The upper two voices move at a much faster rate, with many rhythmic complexities. This highly stylized art, which delights in structural sophistication, tells us something important about the society for which it was created.

Isorhythmic motet

Listening Guide 33

C/S: 1A/7
Sh: 1A/4

C/S: 1/ 19 – 20
Sh: 1/ 4 – 5

MACHAUT: *Hareu! hareu! le feu/Helas!/Obediens*   (1:54)

Date of work: Mid-14th century

Genre: Isorhythmic motet, 3 voices

Text: 3 different texts (2 French, 1 Latin)

Form: Based on rhythmic ostinato pattern in Tenor voice: short-long-long-long-short. Repetitions of ostinato: 6 in very long notes, 6 in diminution (half as long); played instrumentally.

Ostinato pattern in Tenor:

Opening of motet:

	Form	Text	Rhyme Scheme	Translation
	Long-note ostinato			Triplum Voice
19 0:00	1	Hareu! hareu! le feu, le feu, le feu	*a*	Help! Help! Fire! Fire! Fire!
		D'ardant desir, qu'einc si ardant ne fu,	*a*	My heart is on fire with burning desire

		Qu'en mon cuer a espris et soustenu	a	Such as was never seen before.
	2	Amours, et s'a la joie retenu	a	Love, having started it, fans the flames
		D'espoir qui doit attemprer telle ardure.	b	Withholding all hope of joy that might put out such a blaze.
		Las! se le feu qui ensement l'art dure,	b	Alas, if this fire keeps on burning,
	3	Mes cuers sera tous bruis et esteins,	c	My heart, already blackened and shriveled,
		Qui de feu est ja nercis et teins,	c	Will be burnt to ashes.
		Pour ce qu'il est fins, loyaus et certeins;	c	For it is true, loyal, and sincere.
	4	Si que j'espoir que deviez yert, eins	c	I expect I shall be mad with grief
		Que bonne Amour de merci l'asseure	b	Before gentle Love consoles it
		Par la vertu d'esperance seure.	b	With sound hope.
	5	Car pour li seul, qui endure mal meint;	d	It alone, suffering much Hardship,
		Pitié deffaut, ou toute biauté meint;	d	Is devoid of Pity, abode of all beauty.
		Durtés y regne et Dangiers y remeint,	d	Instead, Harshness rules over it and Haughtiness flourishes.
	6	Desdeins y vit et Loyautez s'i feint	d	Disdain dwells there, while Loyalty is a rare visitor
		Et Amours n'a de li ne de moy cure.	b	And Love pays no heed to it or to me.
		Joie le het, ma dame li est dure,	b	Joy hates it, and my lady is cruel to it.

Diminution of ostinato

[20] 1:14

	1	Et, pour croistre mes dolereus meschiés,	e	To complete my sad misfortune,
	2	Met dedens moy Amours, qui est mes chiés,	e	Love, my sovereign lord,
	3	Un desespoir qui si mal entechiés	e	Fills me with such bitter despair
	4	Est que tous biens a de moy esrachiés,	e	That I am left penniless,
	5	Et en tous cas mon corps si desnature	b	And so wasted in body
	6	Qu'il me convient morir malgré Nature.	b	That I shall surely die before my time.

Long-note ostinato

[19] 0:00

Duplum Voice

	1	Helas! ou sera pris confors	a	Alas, where can I find consolation
		Pour moy qui ne vail nés que mors?	a	Who am as good as dead?
	2	Quant riens garentir ne me puet	b	When my one salvation
	3	Fors ma dame chiere qui wet	b	Is my dear lady,
		Qu'en desespoir muire, sans plus,	c	Who gladly lets me die in despair,
	4	Pour ce que je l'aim plus que nulz,	c	Simply because I love her as no other could

	5		Et Souvenir pour enasprir	*d*	And Memory, in order to keep
			L'ardour de mon triste desir	*d*	My unhappy desire alive,
	6		Me moustre adés sa grant bonté.	*e*	Always reminds me of her great goodness.

Diminution
of ostinato

[20]	1:14	1	Et sa fine vraie biauté	*e*	And her delicate beauty,
		2	Qui doublement me fait ardoir.	*f*	Thereby making me want her all the more.
		3	Einssi sans cuer et sans espoir	*f*	Deprived thus of heart and hope
		4	Ne puis pas vivre longuement,	*g*	I cannot live for long.
		5	N'en feu cuers humeins nullement	*g*	No man's heart can long survive
		6	Ne puet longue duree avoir.	*f*	When once aflame.

Tenor Voice

Obediens usque ad mortem   Obedient unto death.
(played instrumentally).

Early Instruments and Instrumental Music

The fourteenth century witnessed a steady growth in the scope and importance of instrumental music. Though the central role in art music was still reserved for vocal works, instruments gradually found more and more uses. As we have seen, they could play a supporting role in vocal music, doubling or accompanying the singers. Instrumental arrangements of vocal works grew increasingly popular. In dance music, where rhythm was the prime consideration, instruments found their earliest prominence.

Unlike the "learned" vocal music of church and court, instrumental music was rarely written down; rather, it was improvised, much like jazz. We can therefore only speculate about the extent and variety of the instrumental repertory during the late Middle Ages. But our speculation can be guided by an ever growing body of knowledge. Some of the instruments themselves survive, in museums and private collections. Paintings and sculpture contain many representations of instruments—not always reliable in detail, but informative about their use and playing technique. Historical documents, such as court payrolls, tell us about the size and makeup of musical establishments. From these, and from the actual instrumental music that has survived, scholars have reconstructed a remarkable body of information about early instruments.

Improvised music

These old instruments were more limited in range and volume than their modern counterparts; they were, however, well suited to the purposes of the societies that devised them. Thus, while early instruments fell into the same general families as modern ones—strings, woodwinds, brass, percussion, and keyboard—they were also divided into *soft (bas)*, or indoor, and *loud (haut)*, or outdoor, categories according to their use.

The Virgin surrounded by angel musicians performing the motet Ave Regina caelorum *by Walter Frye, the English composer. Accompanying instruments include (counter-clockwise from top left): shawm, harp, portative organ, lute, vielle, recorders, and hammer dulcimer.* Mary, Queen of Heaven *by the* **Master of the St. Lucy Legend,** *c. 1485.* (Samuel H. Kress Collection ©1994, Board of Trustees, National Gallery of Art, Washington, D.C.)

Soft instruments

Among the most commonly used soft instruments were the *recorder,* an end-blown flute with a breathy tone; the *lute,* a plucked string instrument of Middle Eastern origin with a more rounded back than a guitar; the *harp* and *psaltery,* plucked string instruments of biblical fame; and the *rebec* and *vielle,* the two principal bowed string instruments of the Middle Ages.

Loud instruments

The loud category of instruments, used mainly for outdoor occasions such as tournaments and processions, included the *shawm,* an ancestor of the oboe with a loud, nasal tone, and the *slide trumpet,* which developed into the early trombone known as the *sackbut.* Two wind instruments that became increasingly popular in the late Middle Ages do not fit neatly into the categories of loud and soft. The *crumhorn* (crooked horn) is a woodwind instrument shaped like the letter J with a cap over its double reed, making it considerably less raucous than the shawm. The *cornetto* developed from the traditional cow horn but was made of wood; it had a cup-shaped mouthpiece like a brass instrument, with fingerholes like a woodwind. Percussion instruments of the time included a large cylindrical drum called the *tabor* and small drums known as *nakers,* usually played in pairs. Several of these instruments had their origins in the Middle East, and nakers are mentioned in Marco Polo's account of his travels in Asia.

Several types and sizes of organ were already in use in the Middle Ages. *Organs* There were large ones, requiring a team of men to pump their giant bellows and often several more to manipulate the cumbersome slider mechanisms that opened and closed the pipes. At the other end of the scale were *portative* and *positive* organs, miniatures with keyboards and a few ranks of pipes. One type of small organ, the *regal,* took its name from one of the reed stops of the larger organs.

The revival of early music has grown in recent decades, as scholars and performers have endeavored to reconstruct some of the conditions under which early music was performed. A growing number of ensembles specialize in this repertory, and their members have mastered the playing techniques of old instruments. Their concerts and recordings have made the public aware of the sound of these instruments to a degree that was undreamed of fifty years ago. What was once considered esoteric or "scholarly" has now become the regular fare of many music lovers.

AN ANONYMOUS SALTARELLO

Professional instrumentalists of the Middle Ages must have been both skilled and sophisticated, since historical evidence indicates that their earnings were often quite high. However, many of them did not read or write musical notation—they had no need to, for most of their music making was improvised; consequently little of their music has survived. This particular work (see Listening Guide 34) dates from the fourteenth century, when it was among several tunes that were added to the end of a large manuscript of Italian vocal music.

The saltarello is a lively Italian "jumping dance." This early example consists of short sections of varying lengths, alternating in the pattern **A-B-A-C-A-C-A.** Each section is repeated, and new sections use melodic figures from the preceding one. This chainlike construction permits additional repetitions should the dancers have energy for more.

The wild, piercing sound of the shawm (used as the solo instrument in our recording) seems quite appropriate for this energetic, even frenetic dance. Aside from the melody, everything about this performance is conjectural, resting upon the educated guesses of a knowledgeable and sensitive scholar-musician: the tempo; the phrasing; the *embellishment,* or melodic decora- *Embellishment* tion, of the written music; the rhythmic backing by nakers, tabor, and tambourine; the addition of a sustained single note (known as a *drone,* a common feature of folk music around the world). But the results are musically convincing, breathing fresh life into music of which only the skeleton has survived the ravages of time.

Listening Guide 34

 C/S: 1A/8   C/S: 1/ 21 – 23

ANONYMOUS: Saltarello

(1:51)

Date of work: 14th century, Italian
Form: Sectional, with repeats; **A** section as refrain; much embellishment on melodic lines
   (A-B-A-C-A-C-A)
Instrumentation used in recording: Shawm (loud, double-reed instrument), sustaining (drone)
   instrument, and percussion
Character: Fast and lively, leaping dance

21 0:00   **A** section (called *prima pars,* or first part)
           —played twice (recording takes second
           ending each time):

22 0:17   **B** section (*secunda pars,* or second part)—
           short section, played twice:

           A section—played twice

23 0:42   **C** section (*tertia pars,* or third part)—short
           section, played twice (high note is held
           longer than indicated):

    0:56   **A** section—played twice, much embellish-
           ment

    1:12   **C** section—played twice

    1:25   **A** section—played twice, much embellish-
           ment, ends on long, high note

UNIT XVII

The Renaissance

52

The Renaissance Spirit

"I am not pleased with the Courtier if he be not also a musician, and besides his understanding and cunning (in singing) upon the book, have skill in like manner on sundry instruments."
—BALDASSARE CASTIGLIONE

The Renaissance (c. 1450–1600) is one of the most beautiful if misleading names in the history of culture: beautiful because it implies an awakening of intellectual awareness, misleading because it suggests a sudden rebirth of learning and art after the presumed stagnation of the Middle Ages. History moves continuously rather than by leaps and bounds. The Renaissance was the next phase of a cultural process that, under the leadership of the church, the universities, and princely courts, had begun long before.

The Arts in the Renaissance

What the Renaissance does mark is the passing of European society from an exclusively religious orientation to a more secular one; from an age of unquestioning faith and mysticism to one of belief in reason and scientific inquiry. The focus of human destiny was seen to be life on earth rather than in the hereafter. There was a new reliance on the evidence of the senses rather than on tradition and authority. Implied was a new confidence in people's ability to solve their problems and rationally order their world. This awakening found its symbol in the culture of Greek and Roman antiquity. Renaissance society discovered the summit of human wisdom not only in the Church Fathers and saints, as their ancestors had done, but also in Homer and Virgil and the ancient philosophers.

Philosophical developments

317

Historians used to date the Renaissance from the fall of Constantinople to the Turks in 1453 and the emigration of Greek scholars to the West. Today, we recognize that there are no such clear demarcations in history. But a series of momentous circumstances around this time help to set off the new era from the old. The introduction of gunpowder signaled the eventual end of the age of knighthood. The development of the compass made possible the voyages of discovery that opened up a new world and demolished old superstitions. Although the great explorers of this age—Christopher Columbus, Amerigo Vespucci, and Ponce de León, among others—were in search of a new trade route to the riches of China and the Indies, they happened upon the unknown continents of North and South America. During the course of the sixteenth and seventeenth centuries, these new lands became increasingly important to European treasuries and society.

The revival of ancient writings was associated with the humanists, and was spurred by the introduction of printing. This revival had its counterpart in architecture, painting, and sculpture. If the Romanesque found its grand architectural form in the monastery and the Gothic in the cathedral, the Renaissance lavished its constructive energy upon palace and château. The gloomy fortified castles of the Medieval barons gave way to spacious villas that displayed the harmonious proportions of the classical style. (The term "classical" in this context refers to the culture of the ancient Greeks and Romans, whose art embodied the ideals of order, stability, and balanced proportions.) In effect, Renaissance architecture reflected the gracious and reasoned existence that was the great gesture of the age.

So too the elongated saints and martyrs of Medieval painting and sculpture were replaced by the David of Donatello and the gentle Madonnas of Leonardo. Even where artists retained a religious theme, the Mother of Sorrows and the symbols of grief gave way to smiling Madonnas—often posed for by very secular ladies—and dimpled cherubs. The human form, denied for centuries, was revealed as a thing of beauty; also as an object of anatomical study. Nature entered painting along with the nude, and with it an intense preoccupation with the laws of perspective and composition.

Medieval painting had presented life as an allegory; the Renaissance preferred realism. The Medieval painters posed their figures frontally, impersonally; the Renaissance developed psychological characterization and the art of portraiture. Medieval painting dealt in stereotypes; the Renaissance concerned itself with individuals. Space in Medieval painting was organized in a succession of planes over which the eye traveled as over a series of episodes. The Renaissance created unified space and the simultaneous seeing of the whole. It discovered the landscape, created the illusion of distance, and opened up endless vistas upon the physical loveliness of the world.

The Renaissance came to flower in Italy, the nation that stood closest to the classical Roman culture. Understandably, the great names we associate with its painting and sculpture are predominantly Italian: Donatello (c. 1386-1466), Botticelli (1444-1510), Leonardo da Vinci (1452-1519), Michelangelo (1475-1564), Raphael (1483-1520), and Titian (1488-1576). With masters who lived in the second half of the century, such as Tintoretto

*The Renaissance painter preferred realism to allegory and psychological character-
izations to stylized stereotypes. These attributes are exemplified in* Madonna of the
Rocks *by* **Leonardo da Vinci** *(1452–1519).* (National Gallery, London/Art
Resource, N.Y.)

Cultural Perspective 12

When the Old World Meets the New World

Have you ever tried to imagine the reaction of European explorers to the Native American peoples and cultures they encountered on first reaching the New World? And vice versa? Christopher Columbus recorded his impressions in his diary, remarking that the first locals he met were "so peaceful . . . they love their neighbors as themselves; and their discourse is ever sweet and gentle, and accompanied by a smile, and though it is true that they are naked, yet their manners are decorous and praiseworthy."

Europeans found the music of the Native Americans quite foreign to their ears, noting the highly repetitious nature of their songs, the use of vocables (sung syllables that lack literal meaning), and the sometimes high, piercing vocal quality (sung by males in falsetto, a technique by which they can sing above their normal vocal range). The English explorer Captain John Smith (1580–1631) described the instruments he saw among the locals of eastern Virginia.

> For their musicke, they use a thicke cane, on which they pipe as on a Recorder. For their warres, they have a great deepe platter of wood. They cover the mouth thereof with a skin, at each corner they tie a walnut, which meeting on the backside neere the bottome, with a small rope they twitch them togither till it be so tought and stiffe, that they may beat upon it as upon a drumme. But their chiefe instruments are Rattels made of small gourds or Pumpion [pumpkin] shels. Of these they have Base, Tenor, Countertenor, Meane and Trible.

Thus this particular tribe had flute- or whistle-like instruments (of the aerophone category) fashioned from cane, drums made from hollowed trees over which animal skins were stretched (membranophones), and

rattles of widely varying sizes made from gourds or animal horns (idiophones). The use of the latter two categories of instruments was typical of the musics of many Native American nations.

There were many occasions for music making among the Native Americans: their songs told of love and war, the harvest and the hunt, rites of passage (birth, marriage, death), and their deities. Smith had the opportunity to observe ceremonial rituals of one tribe in Virginia. He noted in particular the painted faces of the priests and the singing style he heard: "Their devotion was most in songs in which the chiefe Priest beginneth and the rest followed him." This call-and-response exchange is much like the responsorial singing style we have noted in early church music; it is a style that has developed in the musics of many world cultures.

Unlike some cultural encounters we will observe, relatively little cross influence of styles took place between Native Americans and Europeans during the seventeenth century, perhaps because the two cultures were so profoundly different. The music of Native Americans has been preserved largely through oral tradition within their individual cultures, although some early efforts were made to preserve their music in European notation. In the nineteenth century, some art music composers wrote romanticized settings of what they believed were Native American melodies. For example, the Second Suite for Orchestra by Edward MacDowell (1861–1908) purports to incorporate a harvest song, a war song, and a women's dance of the Iroquois and a love song of the Iowas. Today, of course, there has been a lot of stylistic cross-fertilization. Young Native

Powatans of Virginia in a ceremonial dance, as depicted by the English artist **John White** *in 1585.* (Permission of the Trustees of the British Museum, London)

Americans listen to the same rock and country/western music as youths of European, African, or Asian heritage. Further, a few Native Americans have brought their music to a wider audience; one is flutist R. Carlos Nakai (of Navaho-Ute heritage), whose haunting recordings have captured the imagination of many listeners and who has combined his native musical traditions with those of European art music.

Terms to Note:

vocable	idiophone
falsetto	call and response
aerophone	responsorial singing
membranophone	oral tradition

Suggested Listening:

Native American ceremonial music
Modern Native American music
   (R. Carlos Nakai)

(1518–94) and Veronese (1528–88), we approach the world of the early Baroque.

From the multicolored tapestry of Renaissance life emerge historical figures that have captured the imagination of the world: Lorenzo de' Medici and Ludovico Sforza, Lucrezia Borgia and Isabella d'Este. Few centuries can match the sixteenth for its galaxy of great names. The list includes the scholar-philosopher Erasmus (c. 1466–1536) and the Protestant reformer Martin Luther (1483–1546), the Italian statesman Machiavelli (1469–1527) and the scientist Galileo (1564–1642), the French writer Rabelais (c. 1494–1553) and the Spanish author Cervantes (1547–1616), and the English playwrights Marlowe (1564–93) and Shakespeare (1564–1616).

The human form, denied for centuries, was revealed in the Renaissance as a thing of beauty. David *by* **Donatello** *(c. 1386–1466).* (Scala/Art Resource, N.Y.)

The Renaissance marks the birth of the modern European spirit and of Western society as we have come to know it. In that turbulent time was shaped the moral and cultural climate we still inhabit.

The Musician in Renaissance Society

Musicians as professionals

Musicians of the sixteenth century were supported by the chief institutions of their society—the church, city, and state as well as royal and aristocratic courts. As the influence of the art spread, professional possibilities widened. Musicians could find employment as choirmasters, singers, organists, instrumentalists, copyists, composers, teachers, instrument builders, music printers, and publishers. There was a corresponding growth in a number of basic musical institutions: church choirs and schools, publishing houses, civic wind bands. So too were there increased opportunities for apprentices to study with master singers, players, and instrument builders. A few women can be identified as professional musicians in this era, earning their living as court instrumentalists and singers. We will hear more about a famous ensemble of women vocalists known as the Singing Ladies of Ferrara in Chapter 54.

The rise of the merchant class brought with it a new group of patrons of music. This development was paralleled by the emergence, among the cultivated middle and upper classes, of the amateur musician. When, in the early sixteenth century, the system for printing type was made available to music, printed music books became available—and affordable. This in turn made possible the rise of the great publishing houses, such as Attaingnant in Paris and Susato in Antwerp. As a result, there was a dramatic upsurge of musical literacy.

Renaissance Musical Style

The vocal forms of the Renaissance were marked by smoothly gliding melodies conceived for the voice. The sixteenth century has come to be regarded as the golden age of the *a cappella* style (a vocal work without instrumental accompaniment). Its polyphony was based on a principle called *continuous imitation.* The motives wandered from vocal line to vocal line, the voices imitating one another so that the same theme or motive was heard now in the soprano or alto, now in the tenor or bass. There resulted a close-knit musical fabric capable of the most subtle and varied effects.

A cappella music

Continuous imitation

Most church music was written in a cappella style. Secular music, on the other hand, was divided between purely vocal works and those in which the singers were supported by instruments. The period also saw the growth of solo instrumental music, especially for lute and the keyboard instruments. In the matter of harmony, the Renaissance leaned toward fuller chords. There was a turning away from the parallel fifths and octaves favored by Medieval composers to the more pleasing thirds and sixths; also a greater use of dissonance was linked with the text, although in sacred music this tendency was carefully controlled. The expressive device of *word painting*—that is, making the music reflect the meaning of the words—was much favored. An unexpected, harsh dissonance might coincide with the word "death," or an ascending line might lead up to the word "heavens" or "stars."

Word painting

Polyphonic writing offered the composer many possibilities, such as the use of a *cantus firmus* (fixed melody) as the basis for elaborate ornamentation

Cantus firmus

In the sixteenth century, women played an active role in music making in the bourgeois home. The Van Berchem Family, *credited to* **Frans Floris, 1561.** (Musea Wuyts–Van Campen en Baron Caroly, Lier)

in the other voices. As we have seen, triple meter had been especially attractive to the Medieval mind because it symbolized the perfection of the Trinity. The new era, much less preoccupied with religious symbolism, showed a greater interest in duple meter.

The composers of the Burgundian or Franco-Flemish school were preeminent in European music from around 1450 to the end of the sixteenth century. They came from the southern Lowlands, which is now Belgium, and from the adjoining provinces of northern France and Burgundy. Several among them—Dufay, Ockeghem, and especially Josquin—created the masterpieces of the epoch.

53

Renaissance Sacred Music

"He who does honor and reverence to music is commonly a man of worth, sound of soul, by nature loving things lofty."
—PIERRE DE RONSARD

Music played a prominent part in the ritual of the church. There were several types of music for church services in addition to the monophonic Gregorian chant; these include polyphonic settings of the Mass, motets, and hymns. These were normally based on counterpoint and, especially in the early sixteenth century, on preexistent music. Such works were sung by professional singers, usually churchmen, trained from childhood in the choir schools.

The Early Renaissance Mass

Sections of the Mass

With the rise of Renaissance polyphony, composers concentrated their musical settings on the fixed portion of the Mass that was sung daily, the *Ordinary*. Thus came into prominence the five main sections of the Mass: Kyrie, Gloria, Credo, Sanctus, and Agnus Dei. (Today these sections of the Mass are recited or sung in the language of the country, the *vernacular*.) The opening section, the Kyrie—a prayer for mercy—dates from the early centuries of Christianity, as its original Greek text attests. It is an **A-B-A** form that consists of nine invocations: three of "Kyrie eleison" (Lord, have mercy), three of "Christe eleison" (Christ, have mercy), and again three of "Kyrie eleison." There follows the Gloria (Glory to God in the highest), a joyful hymn of praise that is omitted in the penitential seasons, Advent and Lent. The third movement is the confession of faith, Credo (I believe in one God, the Father Almighty). It includes also the "Et incarnatus est" (And He became flesh), the "Crucifixus" (He was crucified), and the "Et resurrexit" (And He rose again).

Movements and Order of the Mass

Proper (variable portion)	*Ordinary* (fixed portion)
Introit	
	Kyrie
	Gloria
Collect	
Epistle	
Gradual	
Alleluia (or Tract)	
Evangelium	
	Credo
Offertory	
Secret	
Preface	
	Sanctus
	Canon
	Agnus Dei
Communion	
Post-Communion	
	(Ite missa est)

Fourth is the Sanctus (Holy, holy, holy), which concludes with the "Hosanna" (Hosanna in the highest) and the "Benedictus" (Blessed is He Who comes in the name of the Lord), after which the "Hosanna" is repeated as a kind of refrain. The fifth and last part, the Agnus Dei (Lamb of God, Who takes away the sins of the world), is sung three times. Twice it concludes with "miserere nobis" (have mercy on us), and the third time with the prayer "dona nobis pacem" (grant us peace). A summary of the order of the Mass, with its Proper and Ordinary movements, may be found above. (Remember that we studied an example of a Gradual for Easter Sunday, *Haec dies,* in Chapter 50.)

Early polyphonic settings of the Mass were usually based on a fragment of Gregorian chant. This became the cantus firmus, or fixed melody, that served as the foundation of the work, supporting the florid patterns that the other voices wove around it. When used in all the movements of a Mass, the Gregorian cantus firmus helped to weld the work into a unity. It provided composers with a fixed element that they could embellish with all the resources of their artistry.

Of the Masses for special services, the most important is the Mass for the Dead, the *Requiem*, sung at funerals and memorial services. Included are prayers in keeping with the solemnity of the occasion, among them the awesome evocation of the Last Judgment, "Dies irae" (Day of Wrath).

Requiem

The history of the Mass as an art form extends over the better part of eight hundred years. In that time, it garnered for itself some of the greatest music ever written.

*Guillaume Dufay (left)
stands next to a portative
organ, while fellow com-
poser Gilles Binchois holds
a harp. Miniature from* Le
Champion des dames *by*
Martin Le Franc, *dated
1441–42.* (Bibliothèque
Nationale, Paris)

Dufay and the Cantus Firmus Mass

Guillaume Dufay (c. 1397–1474) was one of the earliest composers of the
Burgundian School to make his career in Italy, where he spent his formative
years. He was also active at the court of Savoy in southeastern France, which
was noted for the brilliance of its art. He spent his last years in his native
Cambrai in northern France, where he continued to compose until his death.

In the music of Dufay and his Burgundian colleagues, the rhythmic complexities of fourteenth-century music were abandoned in favor of an uncom-
plicated, more accessible style. The meandering vocal lines of the past were
replaced by well-defined melodies and clear-cut rhythms. Harmony grew simpler and more consonant, foreshadowing a language based on triads and sense
of key. Eventually, Dufay expanded the standard musical texture from three
voices to four. He wrote music in all the genres current during his lifetime, including polyphonic masses, motets, hymns, and secular songs in French and
Italian. His output includes at least nine complete settings of the Ordinary of
the Mass as well as many individual mass movements. Four of his masses are
built on a cantus firmus taken from either a Gregorian chant or a popular song.

The *L'homme armé* Mass takes a catchy, popular tune as its basis. Although
often concealed in a web of polyphony, the tune is the structural framework
for each section of the mass and is usually sounded by the tenors in long notes.
The opening movement, the Kyrie, divides into three sections according to its
text (see Listening Guide 35). Dufay begins each of these sections with a reduced number of voices, then adds the tenor with different parts of the fixed
tune, filling out the harmonies. In this mass, one can hear at times the hollow-
sounding octaves and fifths of Medieval music and also the mellifluous thirds
and sixths that were growing in popularity.

Listening Guide 35

 C/S: 1A/9 C/S: 1/ 24 – 26

DUFAY: *L'homme armé* Mass, Kyrie

(3:41)

Date of work: 1460s
Basis: Cantus firmus, based on the tune *L'homme armé* (The Armed Man)
Medium: 4 voices, nonimitative polyphony
Movements from Ordinary of Mass:

Kyrie	Sanctus
Gloria	Agnus dei
Credo	

Cantus firmus—*L'homme armé* tune (**A-B-A** form):

A   L'hom-me, l'hom-me, l'homme ar - mé, l'homme ar-mé, l'homme ar - mé doibt on doub - ter, doibt on doub - ter.

B   On a fait par-tout cri - er   Que chas - cun se vien-gue ar - mer D'un hau-bre-gon de   fer.

A   L'hom-me, l'hom-me, l'homme ar - mé, l'homme ar-mé, l'homme ar - mé doibt on doub - ter, doibt on doub - ter.

The man at arms is to be feared.
Everywhere it has been proclaimed
That everyone must wear an iron coat of mail.
The man at arms is to be feared.

KYRIE: Prayer, with 9 invocations

	Text	Translation	Description
		Kyrie I	
24 0:00	Kyrie, eleison.	Lord, have mercy upon us.	3-voice opening, triple meter, melismatic. *L'homme armé* tune (**A**) enters in Tenor in slower notes.
	Kyrie, eleison.	Lord, have mercy upon us.	
	Kyrie, eleison.	Lord, have mercy upon us.	
		Christe	
25 1:14	Christe, eleison.	Christ, have mercy upon us.	2-voice opening, duple meter. *L'homme armé* tune (**B**) enters in Tenor, then bass voice enters.
	Christe, eleison.	Christ, have mercy upon us.	
	Christe, eleison.	Christ, have mercy upon us.	
		Kyrie II	
26 2:33	Kyrie, eleison.	Lord, have mercy upon us.	3-voice opening, triple meter, melismatic. *L'homme armé* tune (**A**) enters in Tenor; moves faster than in Kyrie I.
	Kyrie, eleison.	Lord, have mercy upon us.	
	Kyrie, eleison.	Lord, have mercy upon us.	

Dufay's music was highly esteemed in his own lifetime. And like the cathedrals in which it was first heard, it is music for the ages.

The Motet in the Renaissance

The Renaissance motet now became a sacred form with a single Latin text, for use in the Mass and other religious services. Motets in praise of the Virgin Mary were extremely popular because of the many religious groups all over Europe devoted to Marian worship. These works were in three or four voices, sometimes based on a chant or other cantus firmus.

One of the greatest masters of the Renaissance motet was the Franco-Flemish composer Josquin Desprez (c. 1440–1521). With him, the transition is complete from the anonymous composer of the Middle Ages, through the shadowy figures of the late Gothic, to the highly individual artist of the Renaissance.

Josquin Desprez

Josquin Desprez and the Motet

"He is the master of the notes. They have to do as he bids them; other composers have to do as the notes will."—MARTIN LUTHER

Josquin (as he is known) probably studied with the Flemish master Johannes Ockeghem, who exerted a powerful influence on several generations of composers (see p. 335). Josquin's varied career led him to Italy, where he served at several ducal courts—especially those of Galeazzo Sforza, Duke of Milan, and Ercole d'Este, Duke of Ferrara—as well as in the Papal Choir in Rome. During his stay in Italy, his northern art absorbed the classical virtues of balance and moderation, the sense of harmonious proportion and lucid form, that found their archetype in the radiant art of Raphael. After leaving Rome, he returned to his native France. His last appointment was as a canon at the collegiate church of Condé; he was buried in the choir of this church.

The older generation of musicians had been preoccupied with solving the technical problems of counterpoint—problems that fit the intellectual climate of the waning Middle Ages. Josquin appeared at a time when the humanizing influences of the Renaissance were being felt throughout Europe. The contrapuntal ingenuity that he acquired from Ockeghem he was able to harness to a higher end: the expression of emotion. His music is rich in feeling, in serenely beautiful melody, and in expressive harmony.

Josquin composed over one hundred motets, at least seventeen Masses, and numerous secular pieces. In all these, he used a variety of techniques; some works were based on preexistent models, both monophonic and polyphonic, while others were original throughout.

Josquin's *Ave Maria . . . virgo serena* is a fine example of how the composer utilized the motet to try out new techniques (see Listening Guide 36). The four-voiced composition sets a rhymed poem to the Virgin Mary, in which

Listening Guide 36

C/S: 1B/2
Sh: 1A/5

C/S: 1/ 32 – 38
Sh: 1/ 6 – 12

JOSQUIN: *Ave Maria . . . virgo serena*

(4:37)

Date of work: 1470s
Genre: 4-voice motet
Basis: Chant to Virgin Mary
Poem: Rhymed poem (a couplet, 5 quatrains, and a closing couplet)

Enjoyment of Music Josquin *Ave Maria*

		Text	Translation	Description
32	0:00	Ave Maria, gratia plena, Dominus tecum, virgo serena.	Hail Mary, full of grace, The Lord is with you, gentle Virgin.	4 voices in imitation (SATB); chant used; duple meter
33	0:44	Ave cujus conceptio Solemni plena gaudio Coelestia, terrestria, Nova replet laetitia.	Hail, whose conception, Full of solemn joy, Fills the heaven, the earth, With new rejoicing.	2 and 3 voices, later 4 voices; more homophonic texture
34	1:20	Ave cujus nativitas Nostra fuit solemnitas, Ut lucifer lux oriens, Verum solem praeveniens.	Hail, whose birth Was our festival, As our light-giving rising light Coming before the true sun.	Voice pairs (SA/TB), then 4 voices in imitation
35	1:58	Ave pia humilitas, Sine viro fecunditas, Cujus annuntiatio, Nostra fuit salvatio.	Hail, pious humility, Fertility without a man, Whose annunciation Was our salvation.	Voice pairs (SA/TB); a more homophonic texture
36	2:26	Ave vera virginitas, Immaculata castitas, Cujus purificatio Nostra fuit purgatio.	Hail, true virginity, Unspotted chastity, Whose purification Was our cleansing.	Triple meter; clear text declamation; homophonic texture
37	3:03	Ave praeclara omnibus Angelicis virtutibus, Cujus fuit assumptio Nostra glorificatio.	Hail, famous with all Angelic virtues, Whose assumption was Our glorification.	Imitative voice pairs; return to duple meter
38	3:58	O Mater Dei, Memento mei. Amen.	O Mother of God, Remember me. Amen.	Completely homophonic; text declamation in long notes, separated by simultaneous rests

Josquin experiments with different combinations of voices and textures. High voices are set in dialogue with low ones; imitative textures alternate with homophonic settings. The piece opens with a musical reference to a chant for the Virgin, but soon drops this melody in favor of a freely composed form that is highly sensitive to the text. The final couplet, a personal plea to the Virgin ("O Mother of God, remember me"), is set in a simple texture that emphasizes the words above all, proclaiming the emotional spirit of a new age—the humanism of the High Renaissance.

The High Renaissance Mass

Counter-Reformation

After the Protestant revolt led by Martin Luther (1483–1546), the Catholic Church responded with a reform movement focused on a return to true Christian piety. This movement became part of the Counter-Reformation, whereby the church strove to recapture the minds of its people. Among its manifestations were the activities of Franciscans and Dominicans with the poor; the founding of the Society of Jesus (Jesuits) by St. Ignatius Loyola (1491–1556); and the deliberations of the Council of Trent, which extended—with some interruptions—from 1545 to 1563.

Council of Trent

In its desire to regulate every aspect of religious discipline, the Council of Trent took up the matter of church music. The cardinals were much concerned over the corruption of the traditional chant by the singers, who added all manner of embellishments to the Gregorian melodies. The council members objected to the use of certain instruments in religious services, to the practice of incorporating popular songs in masses, to the secular spirit that was invading sacred music, and to the generally irreverent attitude of church

A choir and instruments participate in the celebration of Mass. An engraving by **Philip Galle** *after* **J. Stradanus,** *from* Encomium musices *of 1595.*

musicians. They pointed out that in polyphonic settings of the Mass, the sacred text was made unintelligible by the overelaborate contrapuntal texture. Certain zealots advocated abolishing counterpoint altogether and returning to Gregorian chant, but there were many music lovers among the cardinals who opposed so drastic a step.

The committee assigned to deal with the problem contented itself with issuing general recommendations. The authorities favored a pure vocal style that would respect the integrity of the sacred texts, that would avoid virtuosity and encourage piety. One composer who met the need for a reformed church music in exemplary fashion was Giovanni Pierluigi da Palestrina.

Palestrina and the Pope Marcellus Mass

"I have held nothing more desirable than that what is sung throughout the year, according to the season, should be more agreeable to the ear by virtue of its vocal beauty."

Giovanni Pierluigi da Palestrina (c. 1525–94), called Palestrina after his birthplace, worked as an organist and choirmaster at various churches, including St. Peter's in Rome. His patron, Pope Julius III (r. 1550–55), appointed him to the Sistine Chapel Choir even though, as a married man, he was ineligible for the semi-ecclesiastical post. He was dismissed by a later pope but ultimately returned to direct another choir at St. Peter's, where he spent the last twenty-three years of his life. The contemplative beauty of his music does not exclude intense emotion; but this is emotion directed to an act of faith.

Palestrina wrote over a hundred masses, of which the most famous is the Mass for Pope Marcellus, successor to Julius III. It is popularly believed that this mass was written to satisfy the new, strict demands placed on polyphonic church music by the Council of Trent. Since the papal choir sang without instrumental accompaniment at this time, the *Pope Marcellus* Mass was probably performed a cappella. It was written for six voice parts—soprano, alto, two tenors, and two basses, a typical setting for the all-male church choirs of the time. The highest voice was sung by boy sopranos or male falsettists, the alto part by male altos or countertenors (tenors with very high voices), and the lower parts were distributed among the normal ranges of the male voice.

The Gloria from the *Pope Marcellus* Mass exhibits Palestrina's conservative style. As was typical, the work begins with a monophonic intonation of the opening line, "Gloria in excelsis Deo" (Glory be to God in the highest), followed by a carefully constructed polyphonic setting of the remaining text. Notable is the way Palestrina balances the harmonic and polyphonic elements of his art so that the words of the sacred text are clear and audible, an effect desired by the Council of Trent. Shifts in register and voices heard vary the musical texture throughout. (See Listening Guide 37 for the text and analysis.)

Palestrina's style is representative of the pure a cappella style of vocal polyphony. A cappella, meaning "in the church style," indicates a vocal performance without instruments, hence a manner of writing that is focused above all on the beauty and capacity of the human voice. This was Palestrina's ideal of sound—pure, serene, and celestial.

A contemporary engraving that depicts Palestrina presenting his earliest printed work to Pope Julius III.

Listening Guide 37

C/S: 1B/4   C/S: 1/ 42 – 43
Sh: 1A/6   Sh: 1/ 13 – 14

PALESTRINA: *Pope Marcellus* Mass, Gloria   (6:15)

Date of work: Published 1567
Genre: Mass; Gloria, from setting of the Ordinary
Voices: 6 (SATTBB)
Characteristics: Frequent textural changes, reduction of voices

Opening of Gloria, showing 6 voice parts (4 singing at one time), in clear word declamation:

		Text	Translation	Voices
42	0:00	Gloria in excelsis Deo	Glory be to God on high,	1
		et in terra pax hominibus	and on earth peace to men	4
		bonae voluntatis.	of goodwill.	4
		Laudamus te.	We praise Thee.	4
		Benedicimus te.	We bless Thee.	4
		Adoramus te.	We adore Thee.	3
		Glorificamus te.	We glorify Thee.	4
		Gratias agimus tibi propter	We give Thee thanks for	5
		magnam gloriam tuam.	Thy great glory.	3
		Domine Deus, Rex caelestis,	Lord God, heavenly King,	4
		Deus Pater omnipotens.	God, the Father Almighty	3
		Domine Fili	O Lord, the only-begotten Son,	4
		unigenite, Jesu Christe.	Jesus Christ.	6/5
		Domine Deus, Agnus Dei,	Lord God, Lamb of God,	3
		Filius Patris.	Son of the Father.	6
43	2:42	Qui tollis peccata mundi,	Thou that takest away the sins of the world,	4
		miserere nobis.	have mercy on us.	4
		Qui tollis peccata mundi,	Thou that takest away the sins of the world,	4/5
		suscipe deprecationem nostram.	receive our prayer.	5/4
		Qui sedes ad dexteram Patris,	Thou that sittest at the right hand of the Father,	3
		miserere nobis.	have mercy on us.	3
		Quoniam tu solus sanctus.	For thou alone art holy.	4
		Tu solus Dominus.	Thou only art the Lord.	4
		Tu solus Altissimus.	Thou alone art most high.	4
		Jesu Christe, cum Sancto Spiritu	Jesus Christ, along with the Holy Spirit	6/3/4
		in gloria Dei Patris.	in the glory of God the Father.	5
		Amen.	Amen.	6

54

Renaissance Secular Music

*"We here in the West have in the last two hundred years recovered the
excellence of good letters . . . The sustained industry of many learned men
has led to such success that today this our age can be compared to the
most learned times that ever were."*—LOYS LE ROY

Music in Court and City Life

The secular music of the Renaissance was intended for both the professional
and the amateur. Court festivities included music performed by professionals
for the entertainment of noble guests and dignitaries. With the rise of the merchant class, music making in the home became increasingly popular. Most
prosperous homes had a lute (a plucked-string instrument with a rounded
body) or a keyboard instrument, and the study of music was considered part

Amateur music making

Music played an increasingly important role in the celebrations of sixteenth-century nobility. The Wedding at Cana *by* **Paolo Veronese** *(1528–88).* (Louvre, Paris; photo by Erich Lessing/Art Resource, N.Y.)

of the proper upbringing for a young girl or, to a lesser degree, boy. Women began to play a prominent part in the performance of music both in the home and at court. During the later sixteenth century in Italy, a number of professional women singers achieved great fame (see p. 341). In addition, dancing provided a popular outlet for music at all levels of society.

From the union of poetry and music arose two important secular genres: the chanson and the madrigal. In both of these, music was used to enhance the poetry of such major literary figures as Francesco Petrarch and Pierre de Ronsard. The intricate verse structures of French and Italian poetry in turn helped to shape the resulting musical forms.

Ockeghem and the Burgundian Chanson

The fifteenth-century *chanson* was the favored genre at the court of the dukes of Burgundy and the kings of France, who were great patrons of the arts. Chansons were usually written for three voices, with one or both lower voices played by instruments. They were set to the courtly love poetry of the French Renaissance, the poems being in the form of a *rondeau,* a *ballade,* or a *virelai.* These fixed text forms established the character of the setting and the musical repetition of sections. If there was a recurrent refrain of one or two lines, it was reflected in the music.

Text forms

Johannes Ockeghem (c. 1410–97) was born in Flanders. He became a singer at the Church of Our Lady in Antwerp, then entered the service of Charles I, Duke of Bourbon. He ultimately joined the French court, where he served for many years. His settings of the Mass include a Requiem; he also wrote motets and about twenty chansons in fixed forms.

His piece *L'autre d'antan* (The Other Year) is in a more popular style of poetry than many of the court chansons. This informal love song tells in a simple, direct manner how the lover was first conquered, then rejected. The fair one's glance that pierced his defenses was "forged in Milan"—a reference to the town that made the best armor and swords. One line from the chanson, "Puis apres nostre amour cessa" (And then our love ended), echoes a sentiment that resounds through popular poetry and song down to our day.

The work illustrates one of the most widespread poetic forms of the late fifteenth century, the rondeau. This example features a six-line refrain for the opening stanza; the refrain returns in part in the middle of the poem and in full at the end. The musical setting fits this intricate scheme, consisting of two sections that are repeated according to the repetition in the poem. (See Listening Guide 38 for the text and musical structure.)

Ockeghem's chanson opens with imitative counterpoint, and the setting is largely syllabic, with some melismas near the end of phrases. In our recording, two parts are sung, and the bottom one is played on a bowed-string instrument. The two voices in this chanson sing in the same range, with much crisscrossing of parts. The music is in a much older style than Palestrina's, as is indicated by the hollow-sounding cadences on intervals of the fifth and octave

Johannes Ockeghem and the singers of his chapel.

Listening Guide 38

C/S: 1B/1   C/S: 1/ 27 – 31

OCKEGHEM: *L'autre d'antan*

(2:39)

Date of work: Late 15th century
Genre: Burgundian chanson, 3 voices
Poem: Rondeau (anonymous)
Musical form: 6-line refrain (in italics, rhyming *a-a-b-b-a-a*); 2 musical sections, **A** and **B**,
  repeated as follows: **A-B-a-A-a-b-A-B** (capital letters = refrain text)

Opening of chanson—brackets show imitation in all parts:

L'autre d'antan

			Text	Rhyme Scheme	Musical Form	Translation
27	0:00	Refrain	*L'autre d'antan, l'autrier passa,*	*a*	**A**	The other year, the other day, she passed by
			Et en passant me tresperça	*a*		And, in passing, pierced me through
	0:16		*D'ung regard forgié a Melan*	*b*	**B**	With a glance forged in Milan
			Qui me mist en l'arriere ban,	*b*		That knocked me into the rear ranks,
			Tant maulvais brassin me brassa.	*a*		So rude a blow she dealt me.
			L'autre d'antan, l'autrier passa.	*a*		The other year, the other day, she passed by.
28	0:38	Verse	Par tel façon me fricassa	a	a	She destroyed me so thoroughly
			Que de ses gaiges me cassa;	a		That she dismissed me from her troops;
			Mais, par Dieu, elle fist son dan.	b		But, by God, she did her damage.
29	0:57	Partial refrain	*L'autre d'antan, l'autrier passa,*	*a*	**A**	The other year, the other day, she passed by
			Et en passant me tresperça	*a*		And, in passing, pierced me through
			D'ung regard forgié a Melan.	*b*		With a glance forged in Milan.
30	1:17	Verse	Puis aprés nostre amour cessa,	a	a	And then our love ended,
			Car, oncques puis qu'elle dansa	a		For, ever since she did her dance,

		L'autre d'antan, l'autre d'antan	*b*			The other year, the other year,
1:36		Je n'eus ne bon jour ne bon an,	*b*	b		I've had neither good day nor good year,
		Tout de mal enuy amassa.	*a*			So much bad luck has piled up.
		L'autre d'antan, l'autrier passa.	*a*			*The other year, the other day, she passed by.*
31 1:56	Refrain	*L'autre d'antan, l'autrier passa,*	*a*	**A**		*The other year, the other day, she passed by,*
		Et en passant me tresperça	*a*			*And, in passing, pierced me through*
		D'ung regard forgié a Melan	*b*			*With a glance forged in Milan*
2:15		*Qui me mist en l'arriere ban,*	*b*	**B**		*That knocked me into the rear ranks,*
		Tant maulvais brassin me brassa.	*a*			*So rude a blow she dealt me.*
		L'autre d'antan, l'autrier passa.	*a*			*The other year, the other day, she passed by.*

rather than on the more mellow third.

The Renaissance chanson continued as a favorite secular form throughout the sixteenth century, and culminated in the towering figure of Roland de Lassus (c. 1532–94). This Franco-Flemish master wrote about 150 chansons, most of them on the verses of such famous French poets as Pierre de Ronsard and Clément Marot. The texts, freed from the fixed forms of the previous century, cover a wide range of emotions from amorous to bawdy to religious. The sixteenth-century chanson is most often set for four voices, generally in a chordal or homophonic style. Typical of this genre is *Bon jour mon coeur* by Lassus, set with many musical subtleties to a poem by Ronsard.

Roland de Lassus

Instrumental Dance Music

The sixteenth century witnessed a remarkable flowering of instrumental dance music. With the advent of music publishing, printed dance music became readily available for solo instruments as well as small ensembles. Venice, Paris, and Antwerp took the lead as centers of the new publishing industry. The dances were often fashioned from vocal works such as madrigals and chansons, which were published in simplified versions that were played instead of sung.

The instruments to be used in these dance arrangements were left unspecified. As in Medieval performances, they were determined by the particular occasion. Outdoor performances called for loud instruments such as the shawm and sackbut (Medieval oboe and trombone). For certain civic occasions, on the other hand, soft instruments such as recorders and bowed strings were preferred. Although percussion parts were not written out in Renaissance music, the evidence suggests that they were improvised at the performance.

Instruments

A number of dance types became popular during the sixteenth century,

Dance types

A stylized sixteenth-century painting of four singers performing from music part books. The couple in back are beating time, as was customary. Concert in the Open Air, **Anonymous** *(Italian School).* (Bourges, Musée de Berry)

several of which survived into the Baroque era. The stately court dance known as the *pavane* often served as the first number of a set and was followed by one or more quicker dances, especially the Italian *saltarello* (jumping dance; see p. 315) and the French *galliard* (a more vigorous version of the saltarello). The *allemande,* or German dance, in moderate duple time, retained its popularity throughout the time of Bach and was adapted into the Baroque dance suite. Less courtly was the *ronde,* or round dance, a lively romp associated with the outdoors and performed in a circle.

SUSATO'S DANCES

One of the most popular dance collections of the sixteenth century was published in Antwerp in 1551 by Tielman Susato (c. 1515–67), a music printer who was also a prolific composer and instrumentalist. His collection, called *Danserye,* was described on its title page as "very cheerful and fit to play on all musical instruments." It contained pavanes, galliards, *basses danses* (an older version of the pavane), as well as allemandes, rondes, and *branles* (a quick dance of the follow-the-leader type). Many of the dances in Susato's collection were drawn from vocal models, these being identified above the music. One of the loveliest of the pavanes is *Mille regretz* (A Thousand Regrets), based on a widely known chanson of the same name by Josquin Desprez.

Two rondes   Our example presents two rondes, each with repeated sections. In this performance, soft instruments are featured. The first ronde is introduced by a drum, followed by a high recorder in the upper part and a regal or reed organ in the bass. The middle parts are filled in by various other recorders at each repetition.

The second ronde, based on a chanson entitled *Mon amy* (My Friend), is performed at a slower tempo on bowed-string instruments of the *viola da gamba* type. This Renaissance instrument had six or more strings and was fretted, like a guitar. Gambas were held between the legs like a cello. (Indeed, *gamba* is the Italian word for "leg.") The strings are accompanied by a harpsichord and lute, which support the harmonies. This set of dances closes with a restatement of the first ronde (see Listening Guide 39), a procedure we have observed already in the minuet-and-trio movements of the Classical era.

It was through dance pieces such as these that Renaissance composers explored the possibilities of purely instrumental forms. From these humble beginnings sprang the imposing structures of Western instrumental music.

Music printer Tielman Susato (far left) and his son present a music book to Queen Mary of Hungary.

Listening Guide 39

C/S: 1B/3   C/S: 1/ 39 – 41

SUSATO: Two Dances   (1:58)

Date of work: 1551 dance collection
Setting: 4 parts, played on soft instruments (in this recording)

39   0:00   **RONDE I**

Form: 2 sections, each repeated (**A-A-B-B**)
Tempo/Meter: Lively duple
Instrumentation: Recorders, regal organ, and drum

Opening of melody, **A** section:

40   0:28   **RONDE II ("Mon amy")**

Form: 3 sections, each repeated (**A-A-B-B-C-C**)
Tempo/Meter: Moderate duple
Instrumentation: Violas da gamba, accompanied by harpsichord and lute

Opening of melody, **A** section:

41   1:31   **RONDE I** (with repeats)

The Italian Madrigal

In the madrigal, the Renaissance found one of its chief forms of secular music. The sixteenth-century *madrigal* was an aristocratic form of poetry-and-music that flourished at the small Italian courts, where it was a favorite diversion of cultivated amateurs. The text was a short poem of lyric or reflective character, often including the emotional words for weeping, sighing, trembling, and dying that the Italian madrigalists learned to set with such a wealth of expression. Love and unsatisfied desire were by no means the only topics of the madrigal. Included too were humor and satire, political themes, and scenes and incidents of city and country life, with the result that the Italian madrigal literature of the sixteenth century presents a vivid panorama of Renaissance thought and feeling.

Instruments participated, duplicating or even substituting for the voices. Sometimes only the top part was sung while the other lines were played on instruments. During the first period of the Renaissance madrigal—the second quarter of the sixteenth century—the composer's chief concern was to give pleasure to the performers, often amateurs, without much thought to virtuosic display. In the middle phase (c. 1550–80), the Renaissance madrigal became an art form consciously directed toward the listener.

The final phase of the Italian madrigal (1580–1620) extended beyond the late Renaissance into the world of the Baroque. The form became the direct expression of the composer's personality and feelings. Certain traits were carried to the point of mannerism: rich chromatic harmony, dramatic declamation, vocal virtuosity, and vivid depiction of emotional words in music. Two of the greatest masters of the late madrigal were Luca Marenzio and Claudio Monteverdi. We will study Monteverdi later as an example of early Baroque style.

MARENZIO AND THE SINGING LADIES OF FERRARA

Luca Marenzio

The Italian madrigalist Luca Marenzio (1553–99) received his early musical training in northern Italy, but soon left for the south. Having established a reputation as a singer, he secured a position in Rome in the household of Cardinal Luigi d'Este. During his years there, he became internationally known as a composer, writing many volumes of madrigals that were published in Rome and northern Europe. Several of these collections were dedicated to members of the Este family, whom he met while visiting their home in Ferrara.

In 1588, Marenzio entered the service of another great Italian family, the Medici of Florence. Wishing to build a spectacular musical establishment, Grand Duke Ferdinando de'Medici hired Marenzio to organize and write music for a great wedding festivity in 1589. Shortly thereafter, the composer returned to Rome, where he remained until his death in 1599. He was buried at the Church of Saint Lawrence in Lucina, "not without grief from the musicians there, who did him honor for his compositions."

Marenzio is best remembered for his madrigals (he wrote over four hundred), for which he set texts ranging from light pastorals, typical of his early works, to serious sonnets, favored in his late publications. Although all his madrigals were reprinted many times, he was known in his day for his early works. The poet Guarini described him as a musician "who goes dispersing delight with his sweetness and lightness, determined above all not to offend the ear." Nevertheless, Marenzio's style is often marked by the expressive word painting and richly chromatic harmonies typical of the era.

One of Marenzio's most delightful early works is a madrigal for six voices entitled *Cantate Ninfe* (Sing, Nymphs), published in Rome in 1581 and dedicated to Alfonso II d'Este, his patron's brother. This madrigal makes reference to a famous ensemble of professional women singers at Ferrara, known as the *Concerto delle donne* (Ensemble of the Ladies). The singers included four sopranos—Laura Peperara, Tarquinia Molza, Anna Guarini, and Livia d'Arco—who were popular performers when Marenzio visited there. Another frequent visitor to Ferrara, the theorist Vincenzo Giustiniani, described their brilliant florid singing in some detail.

Concerto delle donne

> The ladies vied with each other . . . in the design of exquisite passages. . . . They moderated their voices, loud or soft, heavy or light, according to the demands of the piece they were singing; now slow, breaking off sometimes with a gentle sigh, now singing long passages legato or detached, now groups, now leaps, now with long trills, now short, or again with sweet running passages sung softly to which one sometimes heard an echo answer unexpectedly. They accompanied the music and the sentiment with appropriate facial expressions, glances and gesture. . . . They made the words clear in such a way that one could hear even the last syllable of every word.

Many composers wrote music for these famous singers in a new style that intermingled their high voices in sweet dissonance and elaborate ornamentation, accompanied by a bass instrument and harpsichord or lute. The contrast of high and low, without the middle range filled in with polyphonic writing, sounded the beginnings of the new Baroque style.

This sixteenth-century Venetian painting may have been an homage to the famous women singers from Ferrara. A Concert. (Courtesy of RCMI)

Cantate Ninfe opens with only the top three voices singing, clearly a musical as well as textual reference to the high timbres of the women's voices. This madrigal is written for two sopranos, two mezzo-sopranos, tenor, and bass. (See Listening Guide 40 for text.) Examples of word painting abound: the opening word "cantate" (sing) is drawn out in an arched, lyrical melisma; the word "leggiadrette" (graceful) is set in a light, fluidly moving style; the passion of "novelli ardori" (new ardors) is enhanced by chromaticism; the setting of "scherzate e ridete" (joke and laugh) evokes the gaiety of the moment and is repeated in an echo effect; and the command "gioite tutti" (rejoice together) is emphasized by a shift to a dancelike triple meter in homophonic texture. This madrigal presents the lighter side of love, evoking a rustic setting through references to Cupids, the countryside, and Phyllis, a symbolic name for a shepherdess that occurs in many madrigals. *Cantate Ninfe* displays the refinement of style for which Marenzio was famous. It reflects a more gracious time when courtiers could pursue the pleasures of life and art with wit and elegance.

Listening Guide 40

📼	C/S: 1B/5	💿	C/S: 1/ 44
	Sh: 1A/7		Sh: 1/ 15

MARENZIO: *Cantate Ninfe*   (1:25)

Date of work: Published 1581, *First Book of Madrigals for Six Voices*
Genre: Italian madrigal
Medium: 6 voices (SSAATB)
Poem: 6 lines (*a-b-b-a-c-c*), anonymous

	Text	*Translation*
44 0:00	Cantate Ninfe, leggiadrette e belle	Sing, graceful and lovely Nymphs,
	I miei novelli ardori,	Of my new ardors,
0:17	E scherzate e ridete insieme Amori	And Cupids, joke and laugh together
	Con la mia Filli in queste part'e in quelle.	With my Phyllis, everywhere in the countryside,
0:41	Cantate e di piacer gioite tutti,	Sing and be joyous everyone,
	C'ho d'amor colto i desiati frutti.	For I have reaped the desired fruits of love.

Examples of word painting:

Opening with three women's voices, in arched, melismatic line on text "Sing, Nymphs":

Musical laughter on "joke and laugh":

E scher - za - te, e scher - za - te, e scher - za - te e ri - de - - te

Voices sing together, in dancelike triple meter, on "be joyous everyone":

gio - i - te   tut - ti,   gio - i - te   tut - ti,

gio - i - te   tut - ti,   gio - i - te   tut - ti,

gio - i - te   tut - ti,   gio - i - te   tut - ti,

gio - i - te   tut - ti,   gio - i - te   tut - ti,

gio - i - te   tut - ti,   gio - i - te   tut - ti,

gio - i - te   tut - ti,   gio - i - te   tut - ti,

The English Madrigal

Just as Shakespeare and other English poets took over the Italian sonnet, so the composers of England adopted the Italian madrigal and developed it into a native art form. All the brilliance of the Elizabethan age is reflected in the school of madrigalists who flourished in the late sixteenth century during the reigns of Elizabeth I (1558–1603) and James I (1603–25). Among the most important figures were Thomas Morley (1557–1603), John Wilbye (1574–1638), and Thomas Weelkes (c. 1575–1623).

The first collection of Italian madrigals published in England appeared in 1588 and was called *Musica transalpina* (Music from Beyond the Alps). The madrigals, including some by Marenzio, were "Englished"—that is, the texts were translated. In their own madrigals, the English composers preferred simpler texts. New, humorous madrigal types were cultivated, some with refrain syllables such as "fa la la."

FAIR PHYLLIS BY JOHN FARMER

John Farmer was active in the 1590s in Dublin, where he was organist and master of the children at Christ Church. In 1599, he moved to London and

John Farmer was active in the 1590s in Dublin, where he was organist and master of the children at Christ Church. In 1599, he moved to London and published his only collection of four-part madrigals. One of these, *Fair Phyllis*, attained great popularity. He died in 1601.

Fair Phyllis is characteristic of the English madrigal in its pastoral text and gay mood. Typical are the repeated sections, the fragments of contrapuntal imitation that overlap and obscure the underlying meter, the changes from homophonic to polyphonic texture, and the cadences on the weaker pulse of the measure. The last line of the poem is set to chords, with a change to triple meter.

The English composers took over the word painting of the Italians. For example, the opening line, "Fair Phyllis I saw sitting all alone," is sung by a single voice. (See Listening Guide 41 for the text.) So too the statement that Phyllis's lover wandered up and down is rendered musically by a downward movement of the notes, which is repeated at various pitch levels and imitated in all the parts.

The Renaissance madrigal impelled composers to develop new techniques of combining music and poetry. In doing so, it prepared the way for one of the most influential forms of Western music—opera.

*In this woodcut from **Edmund Spenser's** The Shepheardes Calendar, Queen Elizabeth is shown in a pastoral setting, surrounded by her musical ladies-in-waiting.*

Listening Guide 41

FARMER: *Fair Phyllis*

(1:15)

Date of work: Published 1599
Genre: English madrigal, 4 voices
Poem: 6 lines (*a-b-a-b-c-c*), 10 or 11 syllables each
Musical style: Polyphonic, with varied textures

52   0:00

Text

Fair Phyllis I saw sitting all alone,
Feeding her flock near to the mountain side.
The shepherds knew not whither she was gone,
But after her lover Amyntas hied.
Up and down he wandered, whilst she was missing;
When he found her, o, then they fell a-kissing.

Examples of word painting:

"Fair Phyllis I saw sitting all alone"—sung by soprano alone:

Fair   Phyl - lis I saw   sit - ting all a - lone,

"Up and down"—descending line, repeated in all parts imitatively; shown in Soprano and Alto:

From Renaissance to Baroque

"The [Venetian] church of St. Mark was . . . so full of people that one could not move a step . . . a new platform was built for the singers, adjoining . . . there was a portable organ, in addition to the two famous organs of the church, and the other instruments made the most excellent music, in which the best singers and players that can be found in this region took part."—F. SANSOVINO

Polychoral Music in Venice

Venice was a major seaport in the sixteenth century and enjoyed a unique position at the crossroads of trade with the East. Its magnificent Basilica of St. Mark, famous throughout Europe as a specimen of Byzantine architecture,

Venetian painters captured the splendid pageantry of their city on canvas. Here, singers and instrumentalists take part in a religious ceremony. **Gentile Bellini** *(c. 1429–1507),* Procession in Piazza San Marco. *(Scala/Art Resource, N.Y.)*

Musicians performing in the singers' gallery of St. Mark's in Venice. Drawing by **Giovanni Antonio Canal** *(1697–1768), called* **Canaletto**. (Hamburg Kunsthalle)

"The [Venetian] church of St. Mark was . . . so full of people that one could not move a step . . . a new platform was built for the singers, adjoining . . . there was a portable organ, in addition to the two famous organs of the church, and the other instruments made the most excellent music, in which the best singers and players that can be found in this region took part."—F. SANSOVINO

Polychoral Music in Venice

Venice was a major seaport in the sixteenth century and enjoyed a unique position at the crossroads of trade with the East. Its magnificent Basilica of St. Mark, famous throughout Europe as a specimen of Byzantine architecture, was the musical center for an impressive line of choirmasters and organists. The chief characteristic of the Venetian school was *polychoral* singing, involving the use of two or three choirs that either answered each other antiphonally (making possible all kinds of echo effects) or sang together. (*Antiphonal* performance suggests groups singing in alternation and then together.) This antiphonal style was furthered by the fact that two organs were installed in St. Mark's, with a choir at each organ and also at other points in the church. The element of space thus became a factor in music, rather like the "surround-sound" of today. The result was an interplay of sound that was heightened by the use of strings and winds and found its counterpart in the dazzling colors and tumultuous scenes of the Venetian painters.

Polychoral singing

Antiphonal style

Dynamic contrast   take full advantage of the dynamic contrasts possible between a string and wind group, as in his famous *Sonata pian' e forte* (soft and loud). He was also one of the first to specify which instruments were to play a particular piece. He achieved a sonorous balance between voices and instruments that was without precedent in his time.

The polychoral motet *Plaudite, psallite* (Oh, Clap Your Hands and Sing), from the *Symphoniae sacrae* (Sacred Symphonies) published in 1597, is conceived in Gabrieli's grandest manner (see Listening Guide 42). Written for three four-voice choirs and organ, the motet sets a text drawn principally from Psalm 47 and from St. Paul's Letter to the Ephesians. This work is largely in duple meter but changes to triple each time the "Alleluia" refrain occurs. The choirs both alternate in antiphonal singing and join forces in mighty outpourings of polychoral sound. It is likely that this work was intended for performance on Ascension, one of the highest Christian feast days.

This music, belonging as it does to the final decades of the sixteenth century, leaves the world of the Renaissance behind. The splendor of its sound brings us into the next great style period—the Baroque.

A Comparison of Renaissance and Baroque Styles

Renaissance (1450–1600)	*Baroque (1600–1750)*
Dufay, Ockeghem, Josquin, Palestrina, Marenzio, Monteverdi (early works)	Monteverdi (late works), Purcell, Vivaldi, Handel, Bach, Jacquet de la Guerre
Modal harmony	Major and minor tonality
Imitative polyphony	New monodic or solo style; polyphony in late Baroque
A cappella vocal music	Concerted music (voices and instruments)
Religious vocal forms: mass and motet dominant	New religious vocal forms: oratorio, Lutheran cantata
Secular vocal forms: chanson, madrigal	Secular vocal forms: opera, cantata
Instrumental forms beginning, derived from vocal forms: dance music	Instrumental forms developing: sonata, concerto grosso, sinfonia, suite
Instruments unspecified	Specified instruments
Works built on preexistent melody (cantus firmus)	Freely composed works
Performances at church and court	Rise of public theaters

Listening Guide 42

 C/S: 1B/6   C/S: 1/ 45 – 46

GIOVANNI GABRIELI: *Plaudite, psallite* (4:06)

Date of work: 1597
Genre: Polychoral motet, for Ascension Day
Medium: 3 choirs (SATB), organ
Meter: Alternates duple and triple ("Alleluia" sections)
Text: Psalm 47 and St. Paul's Letter to the Ephesians

		Text	Translation
45	0:00	Plaudite, psallite,	Oh, clap your hands and sing,
		Jubilate Deo,	Rejoice in the Lord,
		Omnis terra:	All the earth:
	0:18	*Alleluja.	*Alleluia.
		Benedicant Dominum,	Let all the nations
		Omnes gentes,	Bless the Lord,
		Collaudantes eum:	Praising Him:
46	1:16	*Alleluja.	*Alleluia.
		Quia fecit nobiscum	For the Lord has shown
		Dominus misericordiam:	His mercy to us:
	2:14	*Alleluja.	*Alleluia.
		Et captivam duxit,	And led the captive woman
		Captivitatem, admirabilis	To her freedom, admirable
		Et gloriosus in saecula:	And glorious forever:
		*Alleluja.	*Alleluia.
			*Signifies change to triple meter.

Changing textures and alternations of choirs in motet opening, illustrated by the placement of words:

Choir I	Plau-di-te,		om-nis ter-ra:
Choir II		Plau-di-te,	Ju-bi-la-te De-o, om-nis ter-ra:
Choir III		Psal-li-te,	om-nis ter-ra:

Choir I		Al-le-lu-ja, Al-le-lu-ja.
Choir II		Al-le-lu-ja, Al-le-lu-ja, Al-le-lu-ja.
Choir III	Al-le-lu-ja,	Al-le-lu-ja.

PART SIX

The Baroque Era

"It is not enough to have a good mind; the main thing is to use it well."
—RENÉ DESCARTES

Peter Paul Rubens *(1577–1640),* The Lion Hunt. (Alte Pinakothek, Munich)

UNIT XVIII

The Baroque and the Arts

55

The Baroque Spirit

*"I do not know what I may appear to the world; but to myself I seem to
have been only like a boy playing on the seashore . . . whilst the great
ocean of truth lay all undiscovered before me."*
—SIR ISAAC NEWTON

The period of the Baroque stretched across a stormy century and a half of
European history. It opened shortly before the year 1600, a convenient sign-
post that need not be taken too literally, and may be regarded as having come
to a close with the death of Bach in 1750.

The term "baroque" was probably derived from the Portuguese *barroco*, a
pearl of irregular shape much used in the jewelry of the time. The period
1600–1750 was a time of change and adventure. The conquest of the New
World stirred the imagination and filled the coffers of western Europe. The
middle classes acquired wealth and power in their struggle against the aristocracy. Empires clashed for mastery of the world. Appalling poverty and
wasteful luxury, magnificent idealism and savage oppression—against contra-
dictions such as these unfolded the pomp and splendor of Baroque art, an art
vigorous, decorative, monumental.

The transition from the classically minded Renaissance to the Baroque was
foreshadowed in the art of Michelangelo (1475–1564). His turbulent figures,
their bodies twisted in struggle, reflect the Baroque love of the dramatic. In
like fashion, the Venetian school of painters—Titian, Tintoretto, Veronese—
captured the dynamic spirit of the new age. Their crowded canvases are
ablaze with color and movement.

Baroque art

The Baroque was the era of absolute monarchy. Rulers throughout Europe
took as their model the splendor of the French court at Versailles. Louis XIV's
famous "I am the State" summed up a way of life in which all art and culture

Politics and culture

353

The bold and vigorous Baroque style was fore-shadowed in this dramatic drawing by **Michelangelo** *(1474–1564),* Studies for the Libyan Sibyl. (Metropolitan Museum of Art, Purchase, 1924, Joseph Pulitzer Bequest)

served the ruler. Courts large and small maintained elaborate musical establishments including opera troupes, chapel choirs, and orchestras. Baroque opera, the favorite diversion of the aristocracy, centered on the gods and heroes of antiquity, in whom the occupants of the royal box and their courtiers found a flattering likeness of themselves.

Excluded from the salons of the aristocracy, the middle classes created a culture of their own. Their music making centered on the home, the church, and the university group known as *collegium musicum* (which still functions on many campuses today). For them, the comic opera and the prose novel, both of which were filled with keen and witty observation of life, came into being. For them, painting abandoned its grandiose themes and turned to intimate scenes of bourgeois life. The Dutch school, embodying the vitality of a new burgher art, reached its high point in Rembrandt (1606–69), a master whose insights penetrated the regions of the soul.

Under the leadership of merchant princes and financiers, the culture of the city came to rival that of the palace. These new art lovers vied with the court in their devotion to splendor; they responded to the beauty of brocade and velvet, marble and jewels. This aspect of the Baroque finds expression in the painting of Peter Paul Rubens (1577–1640), whose canvases exude a driving

Rembrandt *(1606–69), one of the greatest geniuses of the Baroque era, chose his subjects from the burgher class, abandoning the grandiose themes of the past.* Portrait of the Syndics of the Clothmaker's Guild. (Rijksmuseum, Amsterdam)

energy, a celebration of life. His voluptuous nudes established the seventeenth-century ideal of feminine beauty.

Scientific frontiers

The Baroque was also an age of reason. The findings of Kepler, Galileo, and Copernicus in physics and astronomy, of Descartes in mathematics and Spinoza in philosophy, were milestones in the intellectual history of Europe. The English physician William Harvey explained the circulation of the blood, and Sir Isaac Newton formulated the theory of gravity.

Religion

The Baroque was an intensely devout period. Religion was a rallying cry on some of the bloodiest battlefields in history. The Protestants were centered in England, Scandinavia, Holland, and the north German cities, all strongholds of the rising middle class. On the Catholic side were two powerful dynasties, the French Bourbons and the Spanish-Austrian Hapsburgs, who fought one another as fiercely as they did their Protestant foes. In the 1790s, after decades of struggle, the great Hapsburg empire was broken, and France emerged as the leading state on the Continent. Germany was in ruins, and England rose to world power. Europe was ready to advance to the stage of modern industrial society.

At the same time, religion and survival were the focus of life in the American colonies. Settled largely by Protestant refugees who emigrated from northern Europe during the seventeenth century, the colonies based their

The rapturous mysticism of the Counter-Reformation found expression in the eerie landscapes of **El Greco** *(1541–1614).* View of Toledo. (Metropolitan Museum of Art, H. O. Havemeyer Collection, Bequest of Mrs. H. O. Havemeyer, 1929)

new society on religious principles, which some zealots carried to an extreme. (See CP 5.)

Protestant culture was rooted in the Bible. John Milton (1608–74) in *Paradise Lost* produced the poetic epic of Protestantism, even as Dante three and a half centuries earlier had expressed the Catholic point of view in *The Divine Comedy.* The Catholic world answered Martin Luther's reforms with the Counter-Reformation, whose rapturous mysticism found expression in the canvases of El Greco (1541–1614). These paintings are the creations of a visionary mind that distorts the real in its search for a reality beyond.

The role of the artist   Artists played a variety of roles in Baroque society. Peter Paul Rubens and Anthony Van Dyck were not only famous painters but also ambassadors and friends of princes. Antonio Vivaldi was a priest, John Milton a political leader, George Frideric Handel an opera impresario. Artists usually functioned under royal or princely patronage, or, like Johann Sebastian Bach, they might be employed by a church or city administration. In all cases, artists were in direct contact with their public. A musical work of art was frequently created for a specific occasion—an opera for a royal wedding, a cantata for a religious service—and for immediate use. The composer wrote for a particular place and time, but the great ones created for the ages.

Cultural Perspective 13

Music and the American Religious Spirit

Music has always been an important vehicle for the expression of beliefs and a powerful, universal force in the dissemination of religion. What role, then, did music play in the establishment of various religions in the Americas? Early European settlers in the New World brought their faiths with them and, with the aid of music, converted some of the indigenous population. As a result, many people of modern-day Mexico, colonized by the Spanish, and of northeastern Canada, settled by the French, are Roman Catholics.

In the early seventeenth century, the Eastern Seaboard of what is today the United States was occupied by various Protestant groups from England, Germany, and the Netherlands. Music played an important role in the religious and social lives of these early colonists, consisting largely of the singing of Psalms from the Old Testament. (We learned of the importance of the Psalms to Christianity in CP 2.) Some early settlers brought Psalm books with them from Europe, and in 1640, the American colonies produced their first printed book: *The Whole Booke of Psalms* (also known as the *Bay Psalm Book*). This publication was reissued in many editions throughout the seventeenth and eighteenth centuries, eventually with tunes and syllables as an aid in reading them.

Even though Psalm books were increasingly available, not everyone had one, nor were all colonists literate. Hence, a singing style known as lining out was practiced, characterized by a slow drawn-out tempo, with a minister or member of the congregation chanting out the text line by line before it was sung by the congregation. Various people embellished the tune, resulting in dissonant heterophony. (This is a simultaneous statement of two or more versions of the same melody, typical of many world music cultures.) To our ears, the vocal tone they used would be rather strident and tense.

This practice eventually gave way to composed polyphonic settings of the Psalms. The foremost American composer in this genre was the Boston music teacher William Billings (1746–1800). He is remembered today for his fuging tunes, polyphonic Psalms or hymns in an overlapping, imitative setting (related to the fugue but not as strict in form). Billings's works were intended not for the church service but as sacred or devotional music, performed in the singing schools that had sprung up in New England.

Folklike devotional music was cultivated by African Americans and whites alike in the nineteenth and twentieth centuries. Known as spirituals and gospel hymns, these religious songs were sung at revivals and prayer meetings. In the twentieth century, gospel music has become an eclectic style of Protestant African-American sacred music, which has supplanted spirituals in popularity for worship and entertainment. In this modern style, vocalists, often accompanied by dancing and clapping, embellish simple melodies with complex rhythms, pitch alterations, and added phrases. Yet another devotional style popular among youth today is contemporary Christian music, a kind of sacred country rock exemplified by Amy Grant, among many others.

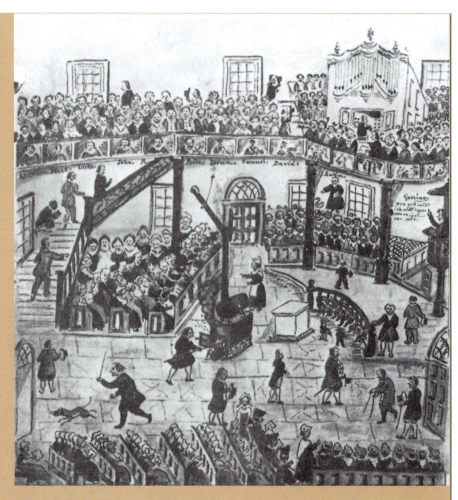

A church service at Reading, Pennsylvania, in the early 1800s. From a drawing by **Lewis Miller.**

Terms to Note:

lining out	spiritual
heterophony	gospel music
fuging tune	

Suggested Listening:

Early American hymn
Fuging tune (William Billings)
Spiritual (African-American or white)
Gospel music
Contemporary Christian music (Amy Grant)

56

Main Currents in Baroque Music

"The end of all good music is to affect the soul."—CLAUDIO MONTEVERDI

Origins of the Monodic Style

With the transition from Renaissance to Baroque came a great change: the shifting of interest from a texture of several independent parts to music in which a single melody stood out; that is, from polyphonic to homophonic texture. The new style, which originated in vocal music, was named *monody*— literally, "one song," music for one singer with instrumental accompaniment. (Monody is not to be confused with monophony, which is an unaccompanied vocal line; see p. 21.) The year 1600 is associated with the emergence of the monodic style. Like many such milestones, the date merely indicates the coming to light of a process that was long preparing.

Monody

The victory of the monodic style was achieved by a group of Florentine writers, artists, and musicians known as the Camerata, a name derived from the Italian word for "salon." Among them were Vincenzo Galilei, father of the astronomer Galileo Galilei, and the composers Giulio Caccini (c. 1545–1618) and Jacopo Peri (1561–1633). The members of the Camerata were aristocratic humanists. Their aim was to resurrect the musical-dramatic art of ancient Greece. Since almost nothing was known of ancient music, the Camerata instead came forth with an idea that was very much alive.

The Camerata

This idea was that music must heighten the emotional power of the text. "I endeavored," wrote Caccini in 1602, "the imitation of the conceit of the words, seeking out the chords more or less passionate according to the meaning." Thus came into being what its inventors regarded as the *stile rappresentativo* (representational style), consisting of a melody that moved freely over a foundation of simple chords.

Stile rappresentativo

The Camerata appeared at a time when it became necessary for music to free itself from the complexities of counterpoint. The year 1600 bristled with discussions about *le nuove musiche,* "the new music," and what its adherents proudly named "the expressive style." They soon realized that this representational style could be applied not only to a poem but to an entire drama. In this way, they were led to what many regard as the single most important achievement of Baroque music: the invention of opera.

Origins of the opera

New Harmonic Structures

The melody-and-chords of the new music was far removed from the intricate interweaving of voices of the older Renaissance style. Since musicians were familiar with the basic harmony, it was unnecessary to write the chords out in full. Instead, the composer put a numeral above or below the bass note, indicating the chord required, and the performer filled in the necessary harmonies. This system, known as *basso continuo* or *continuous bass,* required two instrumentalists for the accompaniment. One played the bass line on a cello or bassoon, and another filled in the harmonies on a chordal instrument, generally harpsichord or organ. Musicians of this period were able to "think with their fingers," that is, they could read and improvise on these figures (called *figured bass*) with ease. The resulting continuo provided a scaffolding over which a vocal or instrumental melody could unfold.

The Baroque witnessed one of the most significant changes in all music history: the establishment of major-minor tonality. As interest shifted from counterpoint to a simpler style based on a single-line melody, the harmonic system grew simpler too. With the development of the major-minor tonality, the thrust to the keynote, or tonic, became the most powerful force in music.

Now each chord could assume its function in relation to the key center. Composers of the Baroque soon learned to exploit the opposition between the chord of rest, the I (tonic), and the active chord, the V (dominant). So too the movement, or modulation, from home key to contrasting key and back became an important element in the shaping of musical structure. Composers developed larger forms of instrumental music than had ever been known before.

This transition to major-minor tonality was marked by a major technical advance. Because of a curious quirk of nature, keyboard instruments tuned according to the scientific laws of acoustics (first discovered by the ancient Greek philosopher Pythagoras) give a pure sound in some keys but increasingly out-of-tune intervals in others. As instrumental music acquired greater prominence, it became more and more important to be able to play in all the keys; thus a variety of tuning systems were developed. In the seventeenth century, a discovery was made: by slightly adjusting or tempering the intervals within the octave, and thereby spreading the discrepancy evenly among all the tones, it became possible to play in every major and minor key without experiencing unpleasant results. This tuning adjustment is known as *equal temperament.* It increased the range of harmonic possibilities that were available to the composer.

Although we are uncertain which of the many temperaments or tuning systems was preferred by Johann Sebastian Bach, this composer demonstrated that he could write in every one of the twelve major and twelve minor keys. The result, *The Well-Tempered Clavier,* is a two-volume collection, each containing twenty-four preludes and fugues, or one in every possible key. Equal temperament eventually transformed the major-minor system, making it a completely flexible medium of expression.

The growing harmonic sense brought about a freer handling of dissonance. Baroque musicians used dissonant chords for emotional intensity and color. In the setting of poetry, the composer heightened the impact of an expressive word through dissonance.

Basso continuo

Figured bass

Major-minor tonality

Tonic and dominant

Equal temperament

Use of dissonance

Baroque Musical Style

During the Baroque, the rhythmic freedom of the monodic style gave way to a vigorous rhythm based on regular accent. This new rhythm was carried by the bass part, whose relentless beat is a prime trait of many compositions of the late Baroque. Once under way, the steady pulsation never slackens until the goal is reached. This gives Baroque music its unflagging drive, producing the same effect of restless but controlled motion that we find in Baroque painting, sculpture, and architecture. Rhythm pervaded the musical conception of the Baroque, and helped it capture the drive and movement of a dynamic era.

Vigorous rhythm

The elaborate scrollwork of Baroque architecture found its musical equivalent in the principle of continuous expansion. A movement will start off with a striking musical figure that unfolds through a process of ceaseless spinning out. In vocal music, the Baroque melody heightened the impact of the words. Wide leaps and the use of chromatic tones helped create a melody that was extremely expressive.

Continuous melody

Baroque music does not know the constant fluctuation of volume that marks later styles. The music moves at a fairly constant level of sonority. A passage uniformly loud will be followed by one uniformly soft, creating the effect of light and shade. The shift from one level to the other, known as *terraced dynamics,* is a characteristic feature of the Baroque style. For greater volume of tone, Baroque composers wrote for a larger number of players rather than directing each instrument to play louder; they found a major source of expression in the contrast between a soft passage and a loud—that is, between the two terraces of sound rather than in the *crescendo*s of later styles. This con-

Terraced dynamics

The grand staircase of the Residenz, home of the Prince-Bishop of Würzburg, is a superb example of Baroque interior design, with its sculptural ornaments and elaborate decorations.

ception shapes the structure of the music, lending it a monumental simplicity.

It follows that Baroque composers were much more sparing of expression marks than those who came after. The music of the period carries little else than an occasional *forte* or *piano,* leaving it to the player to supply whatever else may be necessary.

The Rise of the Virtuoso Musician

The heightened interest in instruments in the Baroque era went hand in hand with the need to master their technique. There followed a dramatic rise in the standards of playing, which paralleled the improvements introduced by the great builders of instruments in Italy and Germany. This in turn made it possible for composers to write works that demanded a more advanced playing technique. Out of this development came the challenging harpsichord sonatas of Domenico Scarlatti and the virtuosic violin works of Arcangelo Corelli, to name only two masters of the period.

The castrato The emergence of instrumental virtuosity had its counterpart in the vocal sphere. The rise of opera saw the development of a phenomenal vocal technique. The advance in vocal virtuosity was much encouraged by the rise of the *castrato,* the artificial male soprano or alto who dominated the operatic scene of the early eighteenth century. Such singers were castrated during their boyhood in order to preserve the soprano or alto register of their voices for the rest of their lives. What resulted, after years of training, was an incredibly agile voice of enormous range, powered by breath control the like of which singers today cannot even begin to approach. The castrato's voice combined the power of the male with the brilliance of the upper register. Strange as it may seem to us, Baroque audiences associated it with heroic male roles. After the

Caricature of the famous castrato Farinelli by **Pier Leone Ghezzi** *(1674-1755). (Collection of Janos Scholz, N.Y.)*

French Revolution, this custom, so against human dignity, was abolished. When castrato roles are performed today, they are usually sung in lower register by a tenor or baritone, or in the original register by a woman singer in male costume.

Improvisation played a significant role in Baroque music. Singers and players alike added their own embellishments to what was written down (as is the custom today in jazz). This was their creative contribution to the work. The practice was so widespread that Baroque music sounded quite different in performance from what it looked like on the written page.

Improvisation

The Doctrine of the Affections

The *doctrine of the affections* related primarily to the union of music and poetry. The Baroque inherited from the Renaissance an impressive technique of text painting, in which the music vividly mirrored the words. It was generally accepted that music ought to arouse the emotions or affections—joy, anger, love, hate, fear, or exaltation. By the late seventeenth century, the practice had evolved of building an entire piece or movement, even of instrumental music, on a single affection. The opening motive established the mood of the piece, which pervaded it until the end. This procedure differs markedly from the practice of the Classical and Romantic eras, when music was based on two or more contrasting emotions.

Women in Baroque Music

We noted the prominence of women in the musical life of the Renaissance. They continued to play an active and expanded role in the music of the Baroque. With the establishment of opera houses throughout Europe, the opportunity for women to enter the ranks of professional musicians greatly increased. Some reached the level of superstars, such as the Italian sopranos Faustina Bordoni and Francesca Cuzzoni, between whom a notorious rivalry raged. Women also continued their role as patrons of the art and as hostesses of the salons where music was actively cultivated.

A few women gained renown as composers, much admired by their male colleagues. Principal among them was the French composer Elisabeth-Claude Jacquet de la Guerre, who achieved a reputation both for her harpsichord music and her cantatas. She was singled out for praise by no less a master than François Couperin, the leader of the French harpsichord school. We will consider her keyboard works in a later chapter.

Internationalism

The Baroque was a culturally international period. National styles existed—without nationalism. Jean-Baptiste Lully, an Italian, created the French lyric tragedy. Handel, a German, gave England the oratorio. There was free interchange among national cultures. The sensuous beauty of Italian melody, the

A performance at the Teatro Argentina in Rome, 1729, as portrayed by **Giovanni Paolo Pannini** *(1697–1765).* (Scala/Art Resource, N.Y.)

pointed precision of French dance rhythm, the luxuriance of German counterpoint, the freshness of English choral song—these nourished an all-European art that absorbed the best of each.

Exoticism
The great voyages of exploration during the Renaissance had opened up hitherto unknown regions of the globe. This in turn aroused the inhabitants of Europe to a vivid interest in remote cultures and far-off locales. Thus exoticism became a discernible element of Baroque music. A number of operas looked to faraway lands for their settings—Persia, India, Turkey, the Near East, Peru, and the American forest. In one such work, the popular opera-ballet *Les Indes galantes* by Jean-Philippe Rameau (1683–1764), each act was set in a different corner of the world. These operas gave opportunity for picturesque scenes, interesting local color, and dances that might not have been authentic but that delighted audiences through their appeal to the imagination. Thus an international spirit combined with an interest in the exotic to produce an art that flowed easily across national boundaries.

Vocal Music of the Baroque

57

Baroque Opera

Early Opera in Italy

Early opera, an outgrowth of Renaissance theatrical traditions and the musical experiments of the Florentine Camerata, lent itself to the lavish spectacles and scenic displays that graced royal weddings and similar ceremonial occasions. *Orfeo* (1607) and *Arianna* (1608) were composed by the first great master of the new genre, Claudio Monteverdi (1567–1643), in whom the dramatic spirit of the Baroque found its true spokesman. It was in his operas that the innovations of the Florentine Camerata reached artistic maturity.

Claudio Monteverdi: His Life and Music

> *"The modern composer builds upon the foundation of truth."*

Monteverdi spent twelve fruitful years at the court of the duke of Mantua. In 1613, he was appointed choirmaster of St. Mark's in Venice, and retained that prestigious post until his death thirty years later.

The madrigal holds a special place in his output, for through his collections, published between 1587 and 1634, unfolds the transition from the older polyphonic style of the Renaissance to the accompanied solo madrigal of the Baroque. Into his operas, ballets, madrigals, and religious works Monteverdi injected an emotional intensity that was new to music. He welded the new-born lyric drama of the Florentines into a coherent musical form and tightened their shapeless recitative into an expressive line filled with drama. He

Claudio Monteverdi

Principal Works

Operas, including *Orfeo* (1607), *Arianna* (1608, music lost), *Il ritorno d'Ulisse* (The Return of Ulysses, 1640), and *L'incoronazione di Poppea* (*The Coronation of Poppea,* 1642); other dramatic music, including *Combattimento di Tancredi e Clorinda* (The Combat of Tancredi and Clorinda, 1624)

Secular vocal music, including 9 books of madrigals, scherzi musicali, and canzonettas

Sacred vocal music, including Vespers (1610), masses, Magnificats, madrigali spirituali, motets, and psalms

originated what he called the *stile concitato* (agitated style) to express the hidden tremors of the soul, introducing such novel effects as the string tremolo and pizzicato as symbols of passion. Monteverdi aspired above all to make his music express the emotional content of poetry. "The text," he declared, "should be the master of the music, not the servant."

Monteverdi used dissonance and instrumental color for dramatic expressiveness, atmosphere, and suspense. He emphasized the contrast between characters by abrupt changes of key. He held that rhythm is bound up with emotion. A master of polyphonic writing, he retained in his choruses the great contrapuntal tradition of the past. There resulted a noble art, full of pathos and rooted in human emotions. The characters in his music dramas were neither puppets nor abstractions, but men and women who gave vent to their joy and sorrows through song. When his patron, the duke of Mantua, suggested a libretto on a mythological subject of the kind fashionable at the time—a dialogue of the winds—the composer protested:

> How shall I be able to imitate the speaking of the winds that do not speak; and how shall I be able to move the affections by such means? Arianna was moving because she was a woman, and likewise Orfeo was moving because he was a man and not a wind. The harmonies imitate human beings, not the noise of winds, the bleating of sheep, the neighing of horses.

THE CORONATION OF POPPEA

Although the earliest operas derived their plots from Greek mythology, Monteverdi's *Coronation of Poppea,* a late work from his Venetian period, instead turned to history. By this time, the first public opera houses had been opened in Venice. Opera was moving out of the palace to become a widely cultivated form of popular entertainment. In the early court operas, Monteverdi used a diverse orchestra consisting of those instruments that were readily available. But in writing for a theater whose repertory would include works by other composers, he adhered to, and helped evolve, a more standardized ensemble with strings at its core.

Coronation Scene from The Coronation of Poppea, *New York State Theater at Lincoln Center, March 7, 1973.* (Beth Bergman)

Monteverdi's final opera remained popular after his death; the composer Pietro Francesco Cavalli (1602–76) oversaw later productions of the work in Rome, featuring some revisions he made to the last act. It is with his reworkings that the opera is performed today. The libretto, by Giovanni Busenello, was based on an episode in Roman history. The Emperor Nero plots to depose his wife, Ottavia, in order to marry his mistress, the courtesan Poppea. His adviser, the philosopher Seneca, views this decision as an affront to the state and voices his objection. For this he is condemned to death. Once he is out of the way, Poppea triumphs and is crowned Empress of Rome.

The action calls for a varied cast of characters spread across the social spectrum from Emperor to commoners, with vivid characterization of the main personages and dramatic confrontations between them. The opera treats powerful emotions that find expression in recitatives and arias, choruses, and passages in arioso style (between aria and recitative). Also effective is Monteverdi's use of the "agitated style," in movements interspersed with instrumental sinfonias and ritornelli. A *ritornello,* a term related to the English "return," originally denoted an instrumental passage heard at the beginning and end of an aria, but, as we have seen, came to mean a passage that returned again and again in the manner of a refrain. Monteverdi established the love duet as an essential feature of the opera both in the first act and at the end. *Ritornello*

The characters in this historic drama are hardly admirable. Nero (a castrato role) is a spoiled, self-indulgent playboy; his wife, Ottavia, plots to poison her rival; his mistress, Poppea, is calculating and ambitious; and Seneca, despite his courage, is pompous and self-seeking. What gives them all their humanity is the moving music in which Monteverdi has clothed their emotions.

In the final scene of the opera, Nero achieves his purpose and leads Poppea to the throne. When the consuls and tribunes arrive to salute Poppea, we hear a chorus for tenors and basses with much imitation between the two lines. (For the complete text, see Listening Guide 43.)

A sinfonia sets the scene for the final love duet between Nero and Poppea, which closes the opera. In the duet, the opening section returns after the middle part, which has been repeated; the result is a pattern of **A-B-B-A** that foreshadows the da capo, or **A-B-A,** aria, which dominated later opera. The duet *Ground bass* unfolds over a four-note *ground bass* that is carried by various instruments, such as lute, harp, and harpsichord. A ground bass refers to a short phrase repeated over and over in the lower voice while the upper voices pursue their independent course. With each repetition, some aspect of the melody, harmony, or rhythm is changed. The lovers' voices intermingle in a tender dialogue. The emotional phrase "pur t'annodo" (I enchain you) is highlighted by melismatic treatment. (In a melisma, you will recall, a single syllable of text is extended over a group of notes.) Notable is Monteverdi's affective use of dissonance on such phrases as "più non peno" (no more grieving) and "più non moro" (no more sorrow or dying).

Listening Guide 43

C/S: 1B/7   C/S: 1/ 47 – 51

MONTEVERDI: *The Coronation of Poppea (L'incoronazione di Poppea),* Act III, Scene 7

(6:45)

Date of work: 1642
Genre: Opera, Italian
Basis: Roman history
Characters:
    Nero, Emperor of Rome
    Poppea, his mistress, soon to be Empress
    Ottavia, wife of Nero, to be deposed
    Seneca, sage and adviser to Nero
    Consuls and tribunes

ACT III, SCENE 7: CORONATION SCENE

Chorus—consuls and tribunes, crowning of Poppea

		Text	Translation	Description
47	0:00	A te, a te sovrana augusta,	O hail to thee our Empress, our ruler,	Two-part writing, imitative, recitative-like
		Con il consenso universal di Roma, Indiademiam la chioma.	By our unanimous consent, and that of all Romans, Now with this crown, we crown thee.	
	0:38	A te l'Asia, a te l'Africa s'atterra;	Now shall Asia, now shall Africa be humble before thee.	Fanfare-like passage

		Text	Translation	Description

| 48 | 1:01 | A te l'Europa, e'l mar che cinge e serra Quest'impero felice,

Ora consacra e dona Questa del mondo imperial corona. | And now let Europe, and all the seas which belong to This most fortunate empire,

Offer and consecrate in honor this the crown of the mighty Roman empire. | Dancelike melody begins with basses, imitated in tenors; closes with tremolo (repeated-note trill) on "imperial" |

Example from chorus, with dancelike meter, imitation between two voices, and melisma on "corona" (crown):

49	1:52	**Sinfonia**—orchestral section, moving bass line, jubilant in character; sets up love scene between Nero and Poppea

Duet—Nero and Poppea

Form: **A-B-B-A; A** section with 4-note ground bass

		Text	*Translation*	*Description*
		A		
50	2:28	Pur ti miro, pur ti stringo, pur ti godo, pur t'annodo più non peno, più non moro, O mia vita, o mio tesoro.	I adore you, I embrace you, I desire you, I enchain you, no more grieving, no more sorrow, O my dearest, O my beloved.	4-note ground bass in opening; imitation between 2 voices
			B	
51	4:01	Io son tua, speme mia dillo dì l'idol mio, tu sei pur, sì mio ben, sì mio cor, mia vita, sì.	I am yours, O my love, tell me so, you are mine, mine alone, O my love. Feel my heart, see my love, see.	Middle section, free bass; short motives imitated
			B	
	4:23	Io son tua, etc.	I am yours, etc.	Entire middle section repeated; repeat of opening section
			A	
	4:59	Pur ti miro, etc.	I adore you, etc.	

Opening of duet (ground bass shown in brackets):

Dissonance on words "moro" (death) and "peno" (grieving):

With Monteverdi, Italian opera took on the basic shape it was to maintain for the next several hundred years. The powerful musical portrayal of human passions captured in *The Coronation of Poppea* was echoed in the soaring melodies of Giuseppe Verdi's masterworks two centuries later.

Opera in France

Tragédie lyrique

By the turn of the eighteenth century, Italian opera had gained wide popularity in the rest of western Europe. Only in France was the genre not accepted. Rather, French composers set out to fashion a national style, drawn from their strong traditions of court ballet and classical tragedy. The result was the *tragédie lyrique,* which combined colorful, sumptuous dance scenes and spectacular choruses in tales of courtly love and heroic adventure. The most important composer of the tragédie lyrique was Jean-Baptiste Lully (1632–87), whose operas won him favor with the French royal court under Louis XIV. Lully was the first to succeed in adapting the recitative to the inflections of the French language, and he exerted a major influence in shaping the French overture (see p. 387). With such masterpieces as *Amadis* (1684) and *Armide* (1686), French opera was born.

Opera in England

The masque

During the reigns of the first two Stuart kings, James I (r. 1603–25) and Charles I (r. 1625–49), the English *masque* emerged into prominence. This was a type of aristocratic entertainment that combined vocal and instrumental music with poetry and dance. Many masques were presented privately in the homes of the nobility.

In the period of the Commonwealth that followed (1649–60), stage plays were forbidden; the Puritans regarded the theater as an invention of the devil. However, a play set to music could be passed off as a "concert." The "semi-operas" that flourished during the rule of Oliver Cromwell (1653–58) were essentially plays with a liberal mixture of solo songs, ensembles, and choral numbers interspersed with instrumental pieces. Since the dramatic tradition in England was much stronger than the operatic, it was inevitable that in these works the spoken word took precedence over the sung. However, in the 1680s, an important step toward opera was taken when John Blow presented his *Venus and Adonis,* which was sung throughout. This paved the way for the first great English opera, *Dido and Aeneas,* by Blow's pupil Henry Purcell.

Henry Purcell: His Life and Music

"As Poetry is the harmony of Words, so Musick is that of Notes; and as Poetry is a Rise above Prose and Oratory, so is Musick the exaltation of Poetry."

Henry Purcell

Henry Purcell (1659–95) occupies a special niche in the annals of his country. He was a leading figure in the illustrious line of composers that, stretching back to pre-Tudor times, won for England a foremost position in the world of music.

Purcell's brief career unfolded at the court of Charles II (r. 1660–85), extending through the turbulent reign of James II (r. 1685–88) and into the period of William and Mary (r. 1689–1702). He held various posts as singer, organist, and composer. Purcell's works cover a wide range of genres. Yet this national artist realized that England's music must be part of the European tradition. It was his historic role to assimilate the achievements of the Continent—the dynamic instrumental style, the movement toward major-minor tonality, the recitative and aria of Italian opera, and the pointed rhythms of the French—and to acclimate these to his native land.

Purcell's court odes and religious anthems are solemn ceremonial music of

Principal Works

Dramatic music, including *Dido and Aeneas* (1689) and *The Fairy Queen* (1692); incidental music for plays

Sacred vocal music, including a Magnificat, Te Deum, and anthems

Secular vocal music, including court odes and welcome songs

Instrumental music, including fantasias, sonatas, marches, overtures, In nomines, and harpsichord suites and dances great breadth and power. His instrumental music ranks with the finest achievements of the middle Baroque. His songs display the charm of his lyricism as well as his gift for setting the English language. In the domain of the theater, he produced, besides a quantity of music for plays, one of the gems of English opera.

DIDO AND AENEAS

Presented in 1689 "at Mr. Josias Priest's boarding school at Chelsy by young Gentlewomen . . . to a select audience of their parents and friends," *Dido and Aeneas* achieved a level of pathos for which there was no precedent in England. A school production imposed obvious limitations, to which Purcell's genius adapted itself in extraordinary fashion. Each character is projected in a few telling strokes. The mood of each scene is established with the utmost economy. The libretto by Nahum Tate provided Purcell—despite some inferior rhymes—with a serviceable framework. As in all school productions, this one had to present ample opportunities for choral singing and dancing. The opera took about an hour. Within that span, Purcell created a work of incredible concentration and power.

He based the work on an episode in Virgil's *Aeneid,* the ancient Roman epic that traces the adventures of the hero Aeneas after the fall of Troy. Both Purcell and his librettist could assume that their audience was thoroughly familiar with Virgil's classic. They could therefore compress the plot and suggest rather than fill in the details. Aeneas and his men are shipwrecked at Carthage on the northern shore of Africa. Dido, the Carthaginian Queen, falls in love with him; he returns her affection. But he cannot forget that the gods have commanded him to continue his journey until he reaches Italy; it is his destiny to be the founder of Rome. Much as he hates to hurt the Queen, he knows that he must depart; she too ultimately realizes that she must let him go. She prepares to meet her fate—death—in the moving lament that is the culminating point of the opera, "When I am laid in earth." (For the text, see Listening Guide 44.) In Virgil's poem, Dido mounts the funeral pyre, whose flames light the way for Aeneas's ships as they sail out of the harbor.

Following the brief recitative "Thy hand, Belinda," Dido's lament unfolds over a five-measure ground bass, or ostinato, that descends along the chromatic scale, always a symbol of grief in Baroque music. The opera closes with an emotional chorus mourning Dido's fate.

In *Dido and Aeneas,* Purcell struck the true tone of lyric drama. Yet this masterpiece did not inspire similar efforts until two centuries later. It remained as unique a phenomenon in history as its composer, whom his contemporaries called "the British Orpheus."

Handel and Late Baroque Opera

Opera in the late Baroque found its master in George Frideric Handel, who, although German by birth, dominated the operatic scene in London during the first decades of the eighteenth century. This was the London of the

Listening Guide 44

C/S: 1B/9   C/S: 1/ 53 – 54
Sh: 1A/9   Sh: 1/ 17 – 18

PURCELL: *Dido and Aeneas,* Act III, Dido's Lament (5:09)

Date of work: 1689
Genre: Opera, English
Basis: Aeneid, by Virgil
Characters:
　　Dido, Queen of Carthage
　　Aeneas, adventuring hero
　　Belinda, Dido's serving maid
　　Sorceress, Spirit, Witches

---

53 0:00   **Recitative:** "Thy hand, Belinda," sung by Dido

Introduces lament aria; sung over sparse accompaniment

Text

Thy hand, Belinda; darkness shades me.
On thy bosom let me rest;
More I would, but Death invades me;
Death is now a welcome guest.

54 0:54   **Aria:** "When I am laid in earth," Dido's lament

Basis: Ground bass, 5-measure pattern in slow triple meter, descending chromatic scale, repeated eleven times

Opening of aria, with
two statements of the
ground bass:

Setting	Statements of Ground Bass
Instrumental introduction	1
When I am laid in earth, may my wrongs create no trouble in thy breast.	2
	3
When I am laid . . .	4
no trouble . . .	5

Remember me, remember me, but ah, forget	6
my fate, remember me, but ah, forget my fate.	7
Remember me . . .	8
forget my fate . . .	9
Instrumental closing	10
Instrumental closing	11

Hanoverian kings George I (r. 1714–27) and George II (r. 1727–60). It was their taste that he managed to please and their aristocrats whom, as an opera impresario, he had to win over.

Handel was in every sense an international figure. His art united the beautiful vocal melody of the Italian school with the stately gestures of the French style and the contrapuntal genius of the Germans. To these elements he added the majestic choral tradition of the English. The result was perfectly suited to the London scene.

Julius Caesar Handel's dramatic works were in the vein of *opera seria,* or serious Italian opera, which projected heroic or tragic subjects. His opera about Julius Caesar, written in 1724, is one of his finest. In this work, Cleopatra, eager to conquer Caesar with her beauty, enchants him with a memorable love song, "V'adoro" (I adore you), establishing at the outset the single affection of the aria.

When opera seria declined in popularity, Handel turned his talents toward the *oratorio* (a music drama based on a religious subject), producing his famous masterwork *Messiah* in 1742. (Handel's life and works are discussed in Chapter 59.)

58

Bach and the Baroque Cantata

The Baroque inherited the great vocal polyphony of the sixteenth century. At the same time, composers pursued a new interest in solo song accompanied by instruments and in dramatic musical declamation. Out of the fusion of all these came a new Baroque form: the cantata.

Cantata The *cantata* (from the Italian *cantare,* "to sing"—that is, a piece to be sung) is a work for vocalists, chorus, and instrumentalists based on a poetic narrative of a lyric or dramatic nature. It is generally short and intimate, consisting of several movements including recitatives, arias, and ensemble numbers.

Cantatas, however, might be based on either secular or sacred themes. In the Lutheran tradition, to which the late-Baroque composer Johann Sebastian Bach belonged, the sacred cantata was an integral part of the church service, related, along with the sermon and prayers that followed it, to the Gospel for the day. Every Sunday of the church year required its own cantata. With extra works for holidays and special occasions, an annual cycle came to about sixty cantatas. Bach composed four or five such cycles, from which only two hundred works have come down to us. By the second quarter of the eighteenth century, the German cantata had absorbed the recitative, aria, and duet of the opera; the pomp of the French operatic overture; and the dynamic instrumental style of the Italians. These elements were unified by the all-embracing presence of the Lutheran chorale.

The Lutheran Chorale

A *chorale* is a hymn tune, specifically one associated with German Protestantism. The chorales served as the battle hymns of the Reformation. As one of his reforms, Martin Luther required that the congregation participate in the service. To this end, he inaugurated services in German rather than Latin, and allotted an important role to congregational singing. "I wish," he wrote, "to make German psalms for the people, that is to say sacred hymns, so that the word of God may dwell among the people also by means of song."

Chorale

Martin Luther

Luther and his fellow reformers created the first chorales. They adapted a number of tunes from Gregorian chant, others from popular sources and secular art music. Originally sung in unison, these hymns soon were written in four-part harmony to be sung by the choir. The melody was put in the soprano, where all could hear it and join in singing. In this way, the chorales greatly strengthened the trend to clear-cut melody supported by chords (homophonic texture).

In the elaborate vocal works that appeared in the Protestant church service, the chorale served as a unifying thread. When at the close of an extended work the chorale unfolded in simple four-part harmony, its granitic strength reflected the faith of a nation. The chorale nourished centuries of German music and came to full flower in the art of Bach.

Johann Sebastian Bach

"The aim and final reason of all music should be nothing else but the Glory of God and the refreshment of the spirit."

Johann Sebastian Bach (1685–1750) was heir to the polyphonic art of the past. He is the culminating figure of the Baroque style and one of the giants in the history of music.

HIS LIFE

Bach was born at Eisenach in Germany, of a family that had supplied musicians to the churches and town bands of the region for several generations. Left an orphan at the age of ten, he was raised in the town of Ohrdruf by an older brother, an organist who prepared him for the family vocation. From the first, he displayed inexhaustible curiosity concerning every aspect of his art. "I had

Johann Sebastian Bach

to work hard," he reported in later years, adding with considerably less accuracy, "Anyone who works as hard will get just as far."

Early years   He held posts as organist at Arnstadt (1703–07) and at Muhlhausen (1707–08), and at the age of twenty-three was appointed to his first important position: court organist and chamber musician to the duke of Weimar. The Weimar period (1708–17) saw the rise of his fame as an organ virtuoso and the composition of many of his most important works for that instrument. His first six children were born in this period. Bach's two marriages produced at least nineteen offspring, many of whom did not survive infancy. Four of his sons became leading composers of the next generation.

The Cöthen period   Disappointed because the duke had failed to promote him, Bach decided to accept an offer from the prince of Anhalt-Cöthen. Here he served a prince partial to chamber music. In his five years at Cöthen (1717–23), he produced suites, concertos, sonatas for various instruments, and a wealth of keyboard music; also the six concerti grossi dedicated to the margrave of Brandenburg. During this period, Bach's first wife died, and in late 1721, he remarried; his new wife, Anna Magdelena, was a young singer at court. Shortly after, Bach's patron married a woman who did not share the prince's love for music. When the composer's position at court gradually declined in importance, he sought employment elsewhere.

The Leipzig years   Bach was thirty-eight when he was appointed to one of the most important posts in Germany, that of cantor of St. Thomas's in Leipzig. Several candidates were considered before him, among them Georg Philipp Telemann (1681–1767), who at that time was much more famous than Bach, and who

An eighteenth-century engraving of St. Thomas's Church in Leipzig, where Bach worked from 1723 until he died, in 1750.

Principal Works

Sacred vocal works, including over 200 church cantatas; 7 motets; Magnificat (1723), *St. John Passion* (1724), *St. Matthew Passion* (1727), *Christmas Oratorio* (1734), Mass in B minor (1749)

Secular vocal works, including over 20 cantatas

Orchestral music, including 4 orchestral suites, 6 *Brandenburg Concertos,* concertos for 1 and 2 violins, and for 1, 2, 3, and 4 harpsichords

Chamber music, including 6 sonatas and partitas for unaccompanied violin, 6 sonatas for violin and harpsichord, 6 suites for cello, *The Musical Offering* (1747), flute sonatas, and viola da gamba sonatas

Keyboard music, including 2 volumes of *Das wohltemperirte Clavier (The Well-Tempered Clavier,* 1722, 1742), 6 *English Suites* (c. 1722), 6 *French Suites* (c. 1722), *Chromatic Fantasy and Fugue* (c. 1720), *Italian Concerto* (1735), *Goldberg Variations* (1741–42), and *Die Kunst der Fuge (The Art of Fugue,* c. 1745–50); suites, fugues, capriccios, concertos, inventions, sinfonias

Organ music, including over 150 chorale preludes, toccatas, fantasias, preludes, fugues, and passacaglias

declined the offer. One member of the town council reported, "Since the best man could not be obtained, lesser ones would have to be accepted." It was in this spirit that Leipzig received the greatest of her cantors.

Bach's duties at St. Thomas's were formidable. He supervised the music for the city's four main churches, selected and trained the choristers for these institutions, and wrote music for the church services as well as for special occasions such as weddings and funerals. In 1729, Bach was appointed to an additional post in Leipzig: director of the collegium musicum, a group of university students and musicians that gave regular concerts. Despite all this activity, his twenty-seven years in Leipzig (1723–50) saw the production of stupendous works.

The routine of his life was enlivened by frequent professional journeys, when he was asked to test and inaugurate new organs. His last expedition, in 1747, was to the court of Frederick the Great at Potsdam, where Bach's son Carl Philipp Emanuel served as accompanist to the flute-playing monarch. Frederick announced to his courtiers with some excitement, "Gentlemen, old Bach has arrived." He led the composer through the palace, showing him the new pianos that were beginning to replace the harpsichord. Upon Bach's invitation, the king gave him a theme on which he improvised one of his astonishing fugues. After his return to Leipzig, Bach further elaborated on the royal theme, added a trio sonata, and dispatched *The Musical Offering* to "a Monarch whose greatness and power, as in all the sciences of war and peace, so especially in music everyone must admire and revere."

The prodigious labors of a lifetime took their tolls; his eyesight failed. After an apoplectic stroke and several operations for cataracts, Bach was stricken

In The Flute Concert *by the nineteenth-century painter* **Adolf von Menzel,** *Frederick the Great plays the flute to the accompaniment of a chamber ensemble, with J. S. Bach's son Carl Philipp Emanuel at the harpsichord.* (Nationalgalerie, Berlin)

with blindness. He persisted in his final task, the revising of eighteen chorale preludes for the organ. The dying master dictated to a son-in-law the last of these, *Before Thy Throne, My God, I Stand.*

HIS MUSIC

Bach was one of the greatest religious artists. He believed that music must serve "the Glory of God." Through the Lutheran hymn tunes known as chorales, the most learned composer of the age was united with the living current of popular melody, to become the spokesperson of a faith.

Organ music   The prime medium for Bach's talents was the organ. In his lifetime, he was known primarily as a virtuoso organist. Since he was a devout Lutheran, the chorale prelude was central to his organ output. Short chorale preludes are found in his *Little Organ Book (Orgelbüchlein),* a collection he compiled in Weimar and Cöthen for his students. One of his most famous organ works is the extended chorale prelude on *A Mighty Fortress Is Our God,* which we will study in Chapter 62.

Solo and chamber music   In the field of keyboard music, his most important work is *The Well-Tempered Clavier.* As mentioned earlier, the forty-eight preludes and fugues in these two volumes have been called the pianist's Old Testament (the New being Beethoven's sonatas). Of the sonatas for various instruments, a special interest is attached to the six for unaccompanied violin. The master created for the four strings of the violin an intricate polyphonic structure that draws from the instrument forms and textures of which one would never have suspected it capable. The *Brandenburg Concertos* present various instrumental combinations pitted against one another. The four orchestral suites are appealingly lyrical.

The two-hundred-odd church cantatas that have reached us form the centerpiece of Bach's religious music. They constitute a personal document of spirituality; they project his vision of life and death. The drama of the Crucifixion inspired Bach to eloquence. His Passions are epics of the Protestant faith. (A *Passion* is a musical setting of the account of the Crucifixion according to one of the four Evangelists.) The monumental Mass in B minor, which occupied Bach for a good part of the Leipzig period, was inappropriate for the Catholic service because of its length, but it found its eventual home in the concert hall.

Religious music

Bach's last works reveal the master at the height of his contrapuntal wizardry; these include the *Musical Offering* and *The Art of Fugue.* The latter work constitutes his final summing-up of the procedures of counterpoint and was left unfinished at his death.

Last works

Bach's position in history is that of one who consummated existing forms rather than one who originated new ones. His sheer mastery of the techniques of composition has never been equaled.

CANTATA NO. 80: *A MIGHTY FORTRESS IS OUR GOD*

Bach's cantatas have anywhere from five to eight movements, of which the first, last, and usually one middle movement are choral numbers. These are normally fashioned from a chorale tune in one of various ways, ranging from simple hymnlike settings to elaborate choral fugues. Interspersed with the choruses are solo arias and recitatives, some of which may also be based on a chorale melody or its text. Bach's lyricism found its purest expression in his arias, elaborate movements with ornate vocal lines and expressive instrumental accompaniments.

The orchestral accompaniments abound in striking motives that combine contrapuntally with the vocal line to create the proper mood for the text and illustrate its meaning. In many cases, the aria is conceived as a kind of duet between the voice and a solo instrument, so that a single instrumental color prevails throughout the piece. This accorded with the doctrine of the "single affection."

In the cantata *A Mighty Fortress Is Our God,* Bach set Martin Luther's chorale of that name, for which the founder of Lutheranism probably composed the music as well as the words. Luther's words and melody are used in the first, second, fifth, and last movements. The rest of the text is by Bach's favorite librettist, Salomo Franck.

Bach took it for granted that the devout congregation of St. Thomas's knew Luther's chorale by heart. A majestic melody of imposing directness, it is today a familiar Protestant hymn tune. Except for an occasional leap, the melody moves stepwise along the scale. It is presented in nine phrases that parallel the nine lines of each stanza of Luther's poem (the first two phrases are repeated for lines three and four of the poem; see Listening Guide 45).

The cantata opens with an extended choral movement in D major, in which

First movement

A German cantata per-
formance with orchestra
and organ, as depicted in
J. G. Walther's Dictionary
(1732).

each line of text receives its own fugal treatment. (A *fugue* is a polyphonic composition based on imitation; the form will be discussed in detail in Chapter 62.) In this movement, each musical phrase is announced by one voice, then imitated in turn by the other three. Each phrase is an embellished version of the original chorale tune. The trumpets and drums we hear in this movement were added after the master's death by his son Wilhelm Friede-mann, who strove to enhance the pomp and splendor of the sound.

Second movement   The second number depicts Christ's struggle against the forces of evil. Strings in unison set up a leaping figure over a running bass. (We say that in-struments are playing *in unison* when they are all playing the same notes.) There follows a duet for soprano and bass soloists in D major; the combination of the soprano's variation on the original tune, the florid counterpoint of the bass, and the assured stride of the great chorale make one of Bach's most vivid musical pictures.

Middle movements   The middle movements of the cantata feature freely composed recitatives and arias grouped around an energetic Allegro for chorus that sets Luther's chorale. In this central choral movement, the orchestra creates the framework for the battle between good and evil that is suggested in the tenor recitative and arioso (a short aria-like passage) that follow. In each movement, Bach captures a single affection, as was typical of the era.

Final movement

The final number rounds off the cantata, with the chorale sung in D major by full chorus and orchestra. We now hear Luther's melody in hymnlike four-part harmonization, each vocal line doubled by instruments. The great melody of the chorale stands revealed in all its simplicity and grandeur.

Listening Guide 45

 C/S: 2B/2–5
Sh: 1A/10–12

 C/S: 2/ 38 – 50
Sh: 1/ 19 – 29

BACH: Cantata No. 80, *A Mighty Fortress Is Our God (Ein feste Burg ist unser Gott),* Nos. 1, 2, 5, 8
(13:46)

Date of work: 1715–24; revised for the Feast of the Reformation (October 31)
Form: 8 movements, for chorus, soloists, and orchestra
Basis: Chorale (hymn) tune by Martin Luther

OVERALL STRUCTURE

Movement	Medium	Use of chorale tune
1. Choral fugue	Chorus and orchestra	Embellished fugal chorale
2. Aria, Duet	Soprano and bass	Soprano line only
3. Recitative/Arioso	Bass solo	
4. Aria	Soprano solo	
5. Chorus	Chorus and orchestra	Unison chorale
6. Recitative/Arioso	Tenor solo	
7. Aria, Duet	Alto and tenor	
8. Chorale	Chorus and orchestra	4-part chorale

Original chorale tune:

Ein fe - ste Burg_ ist un - ser Gott, ein' gu - te Wehr und_ Waf - fen;
er hilft uns frei_ aus al - ler Not, die uns jetzt hat be - trof - fen.

Der al - te bö - se Feind, mit Ernst er's jetzt meint, gross Macht und viel

List sein grau - sam Rü - stung ist; auf Erd' ist nicht seins - gleich - en.

1. Choral fugue, D major, 4/4 meter   (4:52)

		Text	*Translation*	*First sung by*
38	0:00	Ein feste Burg ist unser Gott,	A mighty fortress is our God,	Tenors
		ein' gute Wehr und Waffen;	a good defense and weapon:	Sopranos
39	1:13	er hilft uns frei aus aller Not,	He helps free us from all the troubles	Tenors
		die uns jetzt hat betroffen.	that have now befallen us.	Sopranos
40	2:28	Der alte böse Feind,	Our ever evil foe,	Basses
41	2:58	mit Ernst er's jetzt meint,	in earnest plots against us,	Altos
42	3:23	gross Macht und viel List	with great strength and cunning	Tenors
43	3:44	sein grausam Rüstung ist;	he prepares his dreadful plans.	Sopranos
44	4:08	auf Erd' ist nicht seinsgleichen.	Earth holds none like him.	Tenors

Opening melody in tenors (notes of chorale marked with x):

Instrumental canon, based on chorale tune in augmentation:

2. Duet for soprano and bass, D major, 4/4 meter   (3:53)

		Soprano	
45	0:00	Mit unsrer Macht ist nichts getan,	With our own strength nothing is achieved,
		wir sind gar bald verloren.	we would soon be lost.
		Es streit't für uns der rechte Mann,	But on our behalf strives the Mighty One,
		den Gott selbst hat erkoren.	whom God himself has chosen.
46	1:48	Fragst du, wer er ist?	Ask you, who is He?
		Er heisst Jesus Christ,	He is called Jesus Christ,
		der Herre Zebaoth,	Lord of Hosts,
		und ist kein andrer Gott,	And there is no other God,
		das Feld muss er behalten.	He must remain master of the field.

		Bass	
45	0:00	Alles was von Gott geboren,	Everything born of God
		ist zum Siegen auserkoren,	has been chosen for victory.
46	1:48	Wer bei Christi Blutpanier	He who holds to Christ's banner,
		in der Taufe Treu' geschworen,	truly sworn in baptism,
		siegt im Geiste für und für.	his spirit will conquer forever and ever.

Opening of soprano line with second stanza of chorale (notes of chorale marked with x):

Mit uns - rer Macht_____ ist nichts ge - tan,

(Shorter recordings skip to movement 8.)

5. Chorale for unison chorus, D major, 6/8 meter   (3:31)

Text	*Translation*
47 0:00 Und wenn die Welt voll Teufel wär	Though the world were full of devils
und wollten uns verschlingen,	eager to devour us,
so fürchten wir uns nicht so sehr,	We need have no fear,
es soll uns doch gelingen.	as we will still prevail.
48 1:50 Der Fürst dieser Welt,	The Arch-fiend of this world,
wie saur er sich stellt,	no matter how bitter his stand,
tut er uns doch nicht,	cannot harm us,
das macht, er ist gericht't,	indeed he faces judgement,
ein Wörtlein kann ihn fällen.	one Word from God will bring him low.

Orchestral opening, with paraphrase of chorale melody:

Opening of unison chorale (all voices sing same tune):

Und wenn die Welt __ voll Teu - fel wär

8. Chorale, D major, 4/4 meter, full chorus and orchestra   (1:20)

49 0:00 Das Wort sie sollen lassen stahn	Now let the Word of God abide
und kein Dank dazu haben.	without further thought.
Er ist bei uns wohl auf dem Plan	He is firmly on our side
mit seinem Geist und Gaben.	with His spirit and strength.
50 0:34 Nehmen sie uns den Leib,	Though they deprive us of life,
Gut, Ehr', Kind und Weib,	wealth, honor, child and wife,
lass fahren dahin,	we will not complain,
sie haben's kein Gewinn;	it will avail them nothing;
das Reich muss uns doch bleiben.	for God's kingdom must prevail.

Opening of hymnlike setting of chorale, in 4 voices (instruments doubling voices) and continuo:

59

Handel and the Baroque Oratorio

The Oratorio

The *oratorio,* one of the great Baroque vocal forms, descended from the religious play-with-music of the Counter-Reformation. It took its name from the Italian word for "a place of prayer." The first oratorios were sacred operas, and were produced as such. However, toward the middle of the seventeenth century, the oratorio shed the trappings of the stage and developed its own characteristics as a large-scale musical work for solo voices, chorus, and orchestra, generally based on a biblical story. It was performed in a church or hall without scenery, costumes, or acting. The action usually unfolded with the help of a narrator, in a series of recitatives and arias, ensemble numbers such as duets and trios, and choruses. The role of the chorus was often emphasized. Bach's Passions represent a special type of oratorio, focusing on the final events of Christ's life. More typical of the genre are the oratorios of George Frideric Handel, perhaps the consummate master of this vocal form.

George Frideric Handel

"Milord, I should be sorry if I only entertained them. I wished to make them better."

George Frideric Handel

If Bach represents the spirituality of the late Baroque, Handel (1685–1759) embodies its worldliness. Born in the same year, the two giants of the age never met. The cantor of Leipzig had little point of contact with a composer who from the first was cut out for an international career.

HIS LIFE

Handel was born at Halle in Germany, the son of a prosperous barber-surgeon who did not regard music as a suitable profession for a young man of the middle class. After a year at the University of Halle, the ambitious youth went to Hamburg, where he gravitated to the opera house and entered the orchestra as a second violinist. He soon absorbed the Italian operatic style popular in Hamburg. His first opera, *Almira,* written when he was twenty, created a sensation. He spent the next three years in Italy, where his operas were received enthusiastically.

The early operas

At the age of twenty-five, Handel was appointed conductor to the elector of Hanover. He received the equivalent of fifteen hundred dollars a year at a time when Bach at Weimar was paid eighty. A visit to London in the autumn of 1710 brought him for the first time to the city that was to be his home for nearly fifty turbulent years. His opera *Rinaldo,* written in a mere fourteen days, conquered the English public with its fresh, tender melodies. A year later, Handel obtained another leave and returned to London, this time for good.

His great opportunity came with the founding in 1720 of the Royal Academy of Music. This enterprise, launched for the purpose of presenting Italian opera, was backed by a group of wealthy peers headed by the king. Handel was appointed one of the musical directors and at thirty-five found himself occupying a key position in the artistic life of England. For the next eight years, he was active in producing and directing his operas as well as writing them. His pace was feverish; he worked in bursts of inspiration, turning out a new opera in two to three weeks. To this period belongs *Julius Caesar,* one of his finest works in the new vein of opera seria, or serious opera.

The rise of the ballad opera

Despite Handel's productivity, the Royal Academy failed. The final blow came in 1728 with the sensational success of John Gay's *Beggar's Opera.* Sung in English, its tunes relating to the experience of the audience, this humorous *ballad opera* was the answer of middle-class England to the gods and heroes of the aristocratic opera seria. (See pp. 417–19 for a discussion of *The Beggar's Opera.*)

Rather than accept failure, Handel turned from opera to oratorio, quickly realizing the advantages of a type of entertainment that dispensed with costly foreign singers and lavish scenery. Among his greatest achievements in this new genre were *Israel in Egypt, Messiah, Judas Maccabaeus,* and *Jephtha,* one of his last works. The British public could not help but respond to the imagery of the Old Testament, set forth in Handel's heroic tone.

The final years   Handel suffered the same affliction as Bach—loss of his eyesight from cataracts. Like Bach and the poet John Milton, he dictated his last works, which were mainly revisions of earlier ones. He continued to appear in public, conducting his oratorios and displaying his legendary powers on the organ.

In 1759, shortly after his seventy-fourth birthday, Handel began his usual oratorio season, conducting ten major works in little over a month to packed houses. *Messiah* closed the series. He collapsed in the theater at the end of the performance and died some days later. The nation he had served for half a century accorded him its highest honor. A London paper recounted the following: "Last night about Eight O'clock the remains of the late great Mr. Handel were deposited at the foot of the Duke of Argyll's Monument in Westminster Abbey. . . . There was almost the greatest Concourse of People of all Ranks ever seen upon such, or indeed upon any other Occasion."

HIS MUSIC

Handel's rhythm has the powerful drive of the Baroque. One must hear a Handel chorus to realize what momentum can be achieved with simple 4/4 time. He leaned to diatonic harmony even as Bach's more searching idiom favored the chromatic. His melody, rich in mood and feeling, unfolds in great majestic arches. His thinking is based on massive pillars of sound—the chords—within which the voices interweave. Rooted in the world of the theater, Handel made use of tone color for atmosphere and dramatic expression.

Handel's more than forty operas center on stories of heroes and adventur-

Principal Works

Operas (over 40), including *Almira* (1705), *Rinaldo* (1711), *Giulio Cesare* (*Julius Caesar,* 1724), and *Orlando* (1733)

Oratorios, including *Esther* (1718), *Alexander's Feast* (1736), *Israel in Egypt* (1739), *Messiah* (1742), *Samson* (1743), *Belshazzar* (1745), *Judas Maccabaeus* (1747), *Solomon* (1749), and *Jephtha* (1752); other sacred vocal music, including *Ode for the Birthday of Queen Anne* (c. 1713), *Acis and Galatea* (masque, 1718), *Ode for St. Cecilia's Day* (1739), *Utrecht Te Deum* (1713), anthems, and Latin church music

Secular vocal music, including solo and duo cantatas; arias

Orchestral music, including the 12 Concerti Grossi, Op. 6 (1739), *Water Music* (1717), and *Music for the Royal Fireworks* (1749); concertos for oboe, organ, horn

Chamber music, including solo and trio sonatas

Keyboard music, including harpsichord suites, fugues, preludes, airs, and dances ers, in ingenious musical settings that not only appealed to the London public but enjoyed popularity in Germany and Italy as well. His arias run the gamut from a display of brilliant coloratura to poignant love songs.

The oratorios are choral dramas of overpowering vitality and grandeur. Their soaring arias and dramatic recitatives, stupendous fugues and double choruses, consummate the splendor of the Baroque. With the instinct of the born leader, Handel gauged the needs of his adopted country and created in the oratorio an art form steeped in the atmosphere of the Old Testament, ideally suited to the taste of England's middle class.

The oratorios

Handel made the chorus—the people—the center of the drama. Freed from the rapid pace imposed by stage action, he expanded to vast dimensions each scene and emotion. The chorus now touches off the action, now reflects upon it. As in Greek tragedy, it serves as both protagonist and spectator. The characters are drawn larger than life-size. Saul, Joshua, Deborah, Judas Maccabaeus, and Samson are creatures of destiny, regal in defeat as in victory.

Handel was prolific in the area of instrumental music; his most important works are his concertos and two memorable orchestral suites, the *Water Music* (1717) and *Music for the Royal Fireworks* (1749). We will consider a movement from the *Water Music* in a later chapter.

MESSIAH

In the spring of 1742, the city of Dublin witnessed the premiere of one of the world's most widely loved works, Handel's *Messiah.* Written down in twenty-four days, this oratorio is the product of Handel working as if possessed. His servant found him, after the completion of the "Hallelujah Chorus," with tears streaming from his eyes. "I did think I did see all Heaven before me, and the Great God Himself!"

The libretto is a compilation of biblical verses from the Old and New Testaments, set in three parts. The first part (the Christmas section) tells of the prophecy of the coming of Christ and His birth; the second (the Easter section), of His suffering, death, and the spread of His doctrine; and the third, of the redemption of the world through faith. With its impressive choruses, moving recitatives, and broadly flowing arias, the work has come to represent the Handelian oratorio in the public mind.

Handel's original orchestration was modest and clear in texture. He wrote mainly for strings and continuo; oboes and bassoons were employed to strengthen the choral parts. Trumpets and drums were reserved for special numbers.

The Overture—called "Sinfony" in the score—opens the Christmas section with a Grave (slow, solemn) in a somber E minor. The strings project an affection of intense drama. Handel here returned to the *French overture,* which had been developed a century earlier by the master of Baroque opera in France, Jean-Baptiste Lully. This form consists of two sections: a slow introduction in pompous style with dotted rhythms (this is often repeated), followed by an Allegro in imitative style on a short, striking subject. Handel's stately opening section leads into a sturdy fugue in three voices. In Baroque

Part I

French overture

A performance of Handel's Messiah *in 1784, from an eighteenth-century engraving.*

fashion, the brisk rhythm persists without a letup until the brief return to the slow dotted rhythm of the opening.

We have noted two kinds of recitative: *secco* ("dry," or unaccompanied), which is supported only by the continuo instruments; and *accompagnato* (accompanied by orchestra). The contrast between the two types is well illustrated by the recitative beginning "And there were shepherds abiding in the fields," which is heard in the Christmas section of *Messiah* (No. 14). Listening Guide 46 shows how Handel alternates between these two styles.

This recitative serves to introduce a vigorous four-part chorus, "Glory to God in the Highest." Here too we find an interesting contrast. The opening phrase is set to a passage of chords (homophonic texture). The next phrase, "Good will toward men," is sung by all four voices in imitative counterpoint (polyphonic texture). This jubilant chorus displays all the powerful resonance that gives Handel's music its pomp and majesty.

Da capo aria

The soprano aria "Rejoice greatly, O daughter of Zion" is in three-part, or **A-B-A,** form. In this type of aria, the composer generally did not write out the third part, since it duplicated the first. Instead he wrote the words *da capo* at the end of the second section, indicating that the performer was to repeat the first section, freely elaborating it with ornamentation. (*Da capo* is Italian for "from the head," that is, from the beginning.) Hence this kind of structure came to be known as a *da capo aria*. In "Rejoice greatly," Handel wrote out the last section with a few variations.

Violins present an energetic figure that will soon be taken up by the voice. Notable are the melismatic passages on the word "rejoice." The instruments exchange motives with the voice throughout and help provide an element of unity through the ritornellos that bring back certain passages.

The climax of the work comes in the second part, the Easter section, with the "Hallelujah" Chorus. The musical emphasis given the key word "Hallelujah" is one of those strokes of genius that resound through the ages.

"Hallelujah" chorus

Messiah was meant to be an "Entertainment," as its librettist described it. That is, it was intended for the commercial concert hall by a bankrupt impresario-composer eager to recoup his losses. That so exalted a conception could take shape in such circumstances testifies to the nature of the age whence it issued—and to the stature of the master whom Beethoven called "the greatest and ablest of all composers."

Listening Guide 46

C/S: 2A/6–8
Sh: 1A/13, 1B/1

C/S: 2/ 12 – 22
Sh: 1/ 30 – 35

HANDEL: *Messiah,* Nos. 1, 14, 15, 16, 44   (15:33)

Date of work: 1742
Genre: Oratorio, in 3 parts

(Shorter recordings include Nos. 16, 44.)

PART I: CHRISTMAS SECTION

1. Overture   (4:04)
Form: French overture, 2 parts (slow, fast), first repeated (**A-A-B**)

12 0:00 **A** section—Grave, E minor, played twice; stately, dotted rhythms:

Grave

etc.

13 1:27 **B** section—Allegro moderato, E minor, imitative polyphony in 3 voices; opening subject introduced by oboes and 1st violins:

Allegro moderato

tr

etc.

14. Recitative   (1:25)

Text	Description
Recitative (secco)	
14 0:00 There were shepherds abiding in the field, keeping watch over their flock by night.	Sustained chords in harpsichord

Recitative (accompagnato)

0:14 And lo, the angel of the Lord came upon them, and the glory of the Lord shone round about them, and they were sore afraid.

String accompaniment, with arpeggiated chords

Recitative (secco)

0:33 And the angel said unto them, fear not, for behold, I bring you good tidings of great joy, which shall be to all people; for unto you is born this day in the city of David a Saviour, which is Christ the Lord.

Sustained chords

Recitative (accompagnato)

15 1:07 And suddenly there was with the angels a multitude of the heavenly host, praising God, and saying:

Allegro, with rippling string figure

---

15. Chorus   (1:55)

Text	*Description*
16 1:25 Glory to God in the highest	4-voices, homophonic, with moving string accompaniment
and peace on earth,	Tenors and basses alone, descending octave leap in basses, homophonic
good will toward men.	Imitative, polyphonic treatment; fugue built from lowest to highest voice; antiphonal exchange of "good will"
(All text lines repeated)	Orchestral closing

---

17 ### 16. Soprano aria (A-B-A, da capo)   (4:10)

Instrumental introduction, vocal theme presented in violins, B♭ major

A

3:23 Rejoice greatly,
O daughter of Zion,
shout, O daughter of Jerusalem,
behold, thy King cometh unto thee.

Disjunct rising line, melismas on "rejoice"; melody exchanged between soprano and violin

Syncopated, choppy melody, ends in F major
Instrumental ritornello

B

18 4:50 He is the righteous Saviour and He shall speak peace unto the heathen.

Begins in G minor, slower and lyrical; modulates, returns to B♭ major

A'

19 5:53 Rejoice greatly . . .

Abridged instrumental ritornello; new melodic elaborations; longer melismas on "rejoice"

Extended melisma on "rejoice" from last section:

re - joice   great - ly,

PART II: EASTER SECTION

44. Chorus   (3:50)

		Text	*Description*
20	0:00		Short instrumental introduction
		Hallelujah!	4 voices, homophonic at opening
21	0:25	For the Lord God	Textural reductions, leading to imitation and overlapping of text, builds in complexity
		omnipotent reigneth.	
		The kingdom of this world	Homophonic treatment, simple accompaniment
		is become the Kingdom of our Lord	
		and of His Christ;	
22	1:38	and He shall reign for ever and ever.	Imitative polyphony, voices build from lowest to highest
		King of Kings	Women's voices introduce the text, punctuated by "Hallelujah"; closes in homophonic setting with trumpets and timpani
		and Lord of Lords.	
		Hallelujah!	

Opening of chorus, with refrain in homophonic style:

PART III: REDEMPTION SECTION

UNIT XX

Instrumental Music of the Baroque

60

The Baroque Concerto

The Rise of Instrumental Music

The Baroque was the first period in history in which instrumental music was as important as vocal. New instruments were being developed, and old instruments were perfected. The technique of playing reached new heights, and great virtuosos, such as Bach and Handel at the organ, Corelli and Tartini on the violin, and Scarlatti and Couperin on the harpsichord, appeared.

On the whole, composers still thought in terms of line rather than instrumental color, so that the same line of music might be played by a string, a woodwind, and a brass instrument. As we know, this was different from the practice of the Classical and Romantic periods, when color changed constantly. In the early Baroque, much music was still performed by those instruments that were available. However, late Baroque composers increasingly began to choose specific instruments according to their timbre. They also began to write more idiomatically for instruments: that is, they asked them to do what they could do best. As specifications became more precise, the art of orchestration was born.

Baroque Instruments

The seventeenth century saw a dramatic improvement in the construction of string instruments. Some of the finest violins ever built came from the workshops of Stradivarius, Guarneri, and Amati. The best of these now fetch sums unimagined a generation ago. The Stradivarius violin of the young concert artist Midori, for example, is now worth $3.5 million.

Strings　　The strings of Baroque instruments were made of gut rather than the steel used today. Gut produced a softer yet more penetrating sound. In general, the string instruments of the Baroque resemble their modern descendants except for certain details of construction. In addition, playing techniques have changed, especially in regard to bowing.

Woodwinds

The woodwind instruments were used increasingly for color in the late Baroque orchestra. The wooden flute, recorder, and oboe were especially effective in suggesting pastoral scenes, while the bassoon cast a darker hue. The great improvements in the fingering mechanisms of these instruments came later.

Brass

The trumpet developed from an instrument used for military signals to one with a solo role in the orchestra. It was still a "natural instrument"—that is, without the valves that enabled it to play in all keys; and it demanded real virtuosity on the part of the player. Trumpets contributed a bright sonority to the orchestral palette, to which the horns, also natural instruments, added their gentler, outdoor sound.

Organ

The three important keyboard instruments of the Baroque were the organ, the harpsichord, and the clavichord. In ensemble music, they provided the continuo (continuous bass), and were used extensively for solo performance as well. The *Baroque organ,* used both in church and in the home (see p. 410), had a pure, transparent timbre. The colors produced by the various stops contrasted sharply, so that the ear could distinguish the various lines of counterpoint. The use of multiple keyboards made it possible to achieve terraced levels of soft and loud.

Harpsichord

The *harpsichord* differed from the modern piano in two important respects. First, its strings were plucked by quills instead of being struck with hammers, and its tone could not be sustained like that of a piano. Second, the

An evening outdoor concert in 1744 by the Collegium Musicum of Jena, Germany, featuring an orchestra of strings, woodwinds, trumpets, and drums gathered around the harpsichord.

A two-manual harpsi-chord from about 1650, built by Jan Couchet of Antwerp. (Metropolitan Museum of Art, Crosby Brown Collection of Musical Instruments, 1889; photo by Sheldon Collins)

pressure of the fingers on the keys varied the tone only slightly, producing subtle dynamic nuances. Double keyboards were common, used to produce different sonorities and levels of sound.

Clavichord   The *clavichord* was a favorite instrument for the home. Its gentle tone was produced by the action of a metal tangent that exerted pressure on the string, and the tone continued for as long as the key was held down. This allowed for some delicate effects not available on the harpsichord. However, by the end of the eighteenth century, both the harpsichord and the clavichord had been supplanted in public favor by the piano.

In recent years, a new drive for authenticity has made the original sounds of eighteenth-century instruments familiar to us. Recorders and wooden flutes, restored violins with gut strings, and mellow-toned, valveless brass instruments are heard again, and the Baroque orchestra has recovered not only its smaller scale but also its transparent tone quality.

The clavichord was favored in home music making for its subtle tone and nuances. This German instrument was built in 1763 by Christian Kintzing. (Metropolitan Museum of Art; see p. iv)

Concerto Types

Contrast was as basic an element of Baroque music as unity. This twofold prin-ciple found expression in the *concerto,* an instrumental form based on the op-position between two dissimilar masses of sound. (The Latin verb *concertare* means "to contend with," or "to vie with.")

Baroque composers produced two types of concerto: the solo concerto and the concerto grosso. The concerto for solo instrument and an accompa-nying instrumental group lent itself to experiments in sonority and virtuoso playing, especially in the hands of the Italian master Antonio Vivaldi. The vio-lin was the most frequently used instrument for the solo concerto, which usu-ally consisted of three movements, in the familiar sequence Allegro-Adagio-Allegro. This flexible form prepared the way for the solo concerto of the Classic and Romantic periods.

Solo concerto

The *concerto grosso* was based on the opposition between a small group of instruments, the *concertino,* and a larger group, the *tutti,* or *ripieno* (Italian for "full"). One of the early contributors to this genre was the Italian composer and violinist Arcangelo Corelli (1653–1713). Among his Opus 6 Concerti Grossi, published posthumously in 1714, is the famous *Christmas Concerto.* Giuseppe Torelli (1658–1709), active in the northern Italian musical center of Bologna, contributed significantly to the development of both concerto types. His mature works feature the three-movement structure described above as well as unifying ritornellos (short recurring passages) in individual movements.

Concerto grosso

The concerto embodied what one writer of the time called "the fire and fury of the Italian style." Of the many Italian concerto composers, Vivaldi was the greatest and most prolific. The Italian style spread all over Europe and strongly influenced the German masters Bach and Handel, among others.

Antonio Vivaldi: His Life and Music

"Above all, he was possessed by music." —MARC PINCHERLE

For many years, interest in the Baroque centered on Bach and Handel to such an extent that other masters were neglected. None suffered more in this re-gard than Antonio Vivaldi (1678–1741), who has been rediscovered in the twentieth century.

Vivaldi was born in Venice, the son of a violinist. He was ordained in the church while in his twenties and came to be known as "the red priest," a ref-erence to the color of his hair. For the greater part of his career, Vivaldi was *maestro de' concerti,* or music master, at the most important of the four music schools for which Venice was famous. These schools were attached to chari-table institutions for the upbringing of orphaned girls, and they played a vital role in the musical life of the Venetians. Much of Vivaldi's output was written for concerts at the Conservatorio del'Ospedale della Pietà, which attracted

Antonio Vivaldi

In Concert in a Girls' School, **Francesco Guardi** *(1712–93) depicts a Venetian entertainment featuring an orchestra of young women (upper left) similar to the one directed by Vivaldi.* (Alte Pinakothek, Munich)

visitors from all over Europe. Judging by the music that Vivaldi wrote for them, the young women were expert performers.

In addition to his position in Venice, Vivaldi found work composing operas for other Italian cities. The end of his life is mysterious; a contemporary Venetian account states that "the Abbé Don Antonio Vivaldi, greatly esteemed for his compositions and concertos, in his day made more than fifty thousand ducats, but as a result of excessive extravagance he died poor in Vienna." He was buried in a pauper's grave, and to save expense, his funeral was given "only a small peal of bells."

Vivaldi was active during a period that was of crucial importance in the exploration of a new instrumental style, in which the instruments were liberated from their earlier bondage to vocal music. His novel use of rapid scale passages, extended arpeggios, and contrasting registers contributed decisively to the development of violin style and technique. He played a leading part in the history of the concerto, effectively exploiting the contrast in sonority between large and small groups of players.

THE FOUR SEASONS

Perhaps Vivaldi's best-known work is *The Four Seasons,* a group of four violin concertos. We have observed the fondness for word painting in Baroque vocal works, where the music is meant to portray the action described by the

Principal Works

Orchestral music, over 239 violin concertos, including *Le quattro stagioni (The Four Seasons,* Op. 8, Nos. 1–4, c. 1725); other solo concertos (bassoon, cello, oboe, flute, recorder), double concertos, ensemble concertos, sinfonias

Chamber music, including sonatas for violin, cello, and flute; trio sonatas

Vocal music, including oratorios (*Juditha triumphans,* 1716), mass movements (Gloria), Magnificat, psalms, hymns, and motets; secular vocal music, including solo cantatas and operas

words. In *The Four Seasons,* Vivaldi applies this principle to instrumental music. Each concerto is accompanied by a poem, presumably written by the composer, describing the joys of that particular season. Each line of the poem is printed above a certain passage in the score; the music at that point mirrors, as graphically as possible, the action described.

Of the four concertos, *Spring (La primavera)* is the least graphic; it evokes mood and atmosphere rather than specific actions. The solo violin is accompanied by an orchestra consisting of first and second violins, violas, and cellos, with the basso continuo realized (improvised from the figured bass) on harpsichord or organ. The poem is a sonnet whose first two quatrains (eight lines of text) are distributed throughout the first movement, an Allegro in E major. (See Listening Guide 47 for the text.)   *First movement*

Both poem and music evoke the birds' joyous welcome to spring and the gentle murmur of streams, followed by thunder and lightning. The image of birdcalls takes shape in staccato notes, trills, and running scales; the storm is portrayed by shuddering repeated notes answered by quickly ascending scales. Throughout, an orchestral *ritornello,* or refrain, returns again and again in alternation with the solo section. Ultimately, "the little birds return to their melodious warbling," and we return to the home key of E. A florid passage for the soloist leads to the final ritornello.   *Ritornello*

In the second movement, a Largo in 3/4, Vivaldi evokes an image from the poem of the goatherd who sleeps "in a pleasant field of flowers" with his faithful dog by his side. Over the bass line of the violas, which sound an ostinato rhythm of an eighth note followed by a quarter on the second beat of each measure, he wrote, "The dog who barks." This dog clearly has a sense of rhythm. The solo violin unfolds a tender, melancholy melody in the noblest Baroque style. The finale, an Allegro, is marked "Rustic Dance." Nymphs and shepherds dance in the fields as the music suggests the drone sound of bagpipes. Ritornellos and solo passages alternate in bringing the work to a happy conclusion.   *Second movement*   *Third movement*

Like Bach, Vivaldi was renowned in his day as a performer rather than a composer. Today, he is recognized as the "father of the concerto," having established ritornello form as its basic procedure, and as a herald of musical Romanticism.

Listening Guide 47

C/S: 2A/2–4
Sh: 1B/2

C/S: 2/ 3 – 8
Sh: 1/ 36 – 39

VIVALDI: *Spring,* from *The Four Seasons (La primavera, from Le quattro stagioni)*

(9:34)

Date of work: Published 1725

Genre: Programmatic concerto for solo violin from Op. 8 (*The Contest Between Harmony and Inspiration*), Nos. 1–4, each based on an Italian sonnet:

No. 1: *Spring (La primavera)*   No. 3: *Autumn (L'autunno)*
No. 2: *Summer (L'estate)*   No. 4: *Winter (L'inverno)*

OP. 8, NO. 1, *SPRING*

Movements: 3
Basis: Italian sonnet, translated below:

I. Allegro

> Joyful Spring has arrived,
> The birds greet it with their cheerful song,
> And the brooks in the gentle breezes
> flow with a sweet murmur.
>
> The sky is covered with a black mantle,
> And thunder and lightning announce a storm,
> When they fall silent, the birds
> Take up again their melodious song.

II. Largo

> And in the flower-rich meadow,
> To the gentle murmur of bushes and trees,
> The goatherd sleeps, his faithful dog at his side.

III. Allegro (Rustic Dance)

> To the festive sounds of a rustic bagpipe
> Nymphs and shepherds dance in their favorite spot
> When spring appears in its brilliance.

First movement: Allegro; in ritornello form, E major   (3:33)

Ritornello theme:

		Description	Program
3	0:00	Ritornello 1, in E major	Spring
	0:31	Solo 1; birdlike trills and high running scales, accompanied by violins	Birds
4	1:06	Ritornello 2	Spring
5	1:14	Solo 2; whispering figures like water flowing, accompanied by orchestra	Murmuring brooks

	1:39	Ritornello 3	Spring
	1:46	Solo 3 modulates; repeated notes, fast ascending scales, accompanied by orchestra	Thunder, lightning
	2:15	Ritornello 4, in relative minor (C sharp)	Spring
	2:23	Solo 4; trills and repeated notes	Birds
	2:43	Ritornello 5, returns to E major; brief solo passage interrupts	
6	3:11	Closing tutti	

(Shorter recordings stop here.)

7 **Second movement: Largo; 3/4 meter, C-sharp minor, orchestration reduced—for solo violin, two violins, and viola**   (2:29)

Opening of movement, with solo violin, slow and melodious, representing the sleeping goatherd ("Il capraro che dorme") and viola, with insistent rhythm, the dog barking ("Il cane che grida"):

8 **Third movement: Danza Pastorale (Rustic Dance), Allegro; in ritornello form, E major**

Opening of movement, with dance tune (ritornello) in upper strings; lilting, compound   (3:32)
meter; sustained notes (like bagpipe drone) in lower strings:

Bach and the Late Baroque Concerto

We have already studied Bach as a composer of vocal church music. During the six years he served as court composer at Cöthen (1717–23), Bach produced a large number of instrumental chamber works. In 1717, he had occasion to play before a royal visitor, Margrave Christian of Brandenburg. The nobleman was so impressed that he asked the composer to write some works for his orchestra. Several years later, Bach sent him the six pieces that have become known as the *Brandenburg Concertos,* with a dedication in flowery French that begged His Royal Highness "not to judge their imperfection by the strictness of that fine and delicate taste which all the world knows You have for musical works; but rather to take into consideration the profound respect and the most humble obedience to which they are meant to bear witness." It is not known how the margrave responded to the concertos that have immortalized his name.

Brandenburg Concertos

In these pieces, Bach captured the spirit of the concerto grosso, in which two groups vie with each other. The second of the set, in F major, has long been a favorite, perhaps because of the brilliant trumpet part. The solo group—the concertino—consists of trumpet, recorder (often played on modern flute), oboe, and violin, all of them instruments in the high register. The accompanying group—the tutti, or ripieno—includes first and second violins, violas, and double basses. The basso continuo is played by cello and harpsichord.

BRANDENBURG CONCERTO NO. 2

First movement

The opening movement of *Brandenburg Concerto* No. 2 is a sturdy Allegro, bright and assertive. The broad outlines of its form depend on well-defined areas of light and shade—the alternation of the tutti and the solo group. Recorder, oboe, and violin play the recurring, or ritornello, theme in unison with the first violin of the accompanying group, while the trumpet outlines the tonic triad. The contrapuntal lines unfold in a continuous, seamless texture, powered by a rhythmic drive that never flags from beginning to end. The movement modulates freely from the home key of F major to the neighboring major and minor keys. When its energies have been fully expanded, it returns to F for a vigorous cadence. (See Listening Guide 48.)

Second and third movements

The slow movement, an Andante in D minor, is a soulful dialogue among solo violin, oboe, and recorder. Each in turn enters with the theme. This moving Andante is infused with the poignant emotion of the Baroque. Third and last is an Allegro assai (very fast), in which trumpet, oboe, violin, and recorder enter successively with the jaunty subject of a four-voiced fugue. After much interchange resembling a lively conversation among four equals, the movement reaches its destination with the final pronouncement of the subject by the trumpet.

Listening Guide 48

C/S: 2B/1   C/S: 2/ 31 – 33

BACH: *Brandenburg Concerto* **No. 2 in F major, First Movement**   (4:52)

Date of work: 1717–18
Genre: Concerto grosso
Concertino: Violin, oboe, recorder (or flute), trumpet
Movements:
    I. Allegro
    II. Andante
    III. Allegro assai

FIRST MOVEMENT: Allegro; in ritornello form

Opening of ritornello theme:

		Section	Description	Key
31	0:00	Ritornello 1	Full ensemble; 8-measure statement	F major
	0:19	Solo 1	Solo violin; short statement	F major
	0:24	Ritornello 2	Full ensemble; short statement	F major
	0:28	Solo 2	Oboe and violin; short statement	F major
	0:33	Ritornello 3	Full ensemble; short statement	C major
	0:38	Solo 3	Recorder and oboe; short statement	F major
	0:43	Ritornello 4	Full ensemble; short statement	C major
	0:48	Solo 4	Trumpet and recorder	F major
	0:53	Ritornello 5	Full ensemble; 6-measure statement	C major
	1:08	Solo 5	Trumpet, violin, recorder, oboe; short statement	F major
32	1:12	Ritornello 6	Full ensemble; long statement with entries exchanged between instruments, ending with cellos	Various
	2:23	Solo 6	Recorder, violin, oboe, trumpet; each with short statement	Various
	2:42		Long modulatory tutti section; various exchanges between instruments	
33	4:07	Ritornello 7	Full ensemble; final statement	Returns to F major

61
The Baroque Suite

The suite of the Baroque era consisted of a series of varied dance movements, all in the same key. It was a natural outgrowth of earlier traditions that paired dances of contrasting tempos and character (a typical pair from the Renaissance was the pavane-galliard, the first slow and stately, the second quick and lively).

Dance types

The suite presented an international galaxy of dance types: the German *allemande,* in quadruple meter at a moderate tempo; the French *courante,* in triple meter at a moderate tempo; the Spanish *sarabande,* a stately dance in triple meter; and the English *jig* (gigue), in a lively 6/8 or 6/4. These had begun as popular dances, but by the time of the late Baroque, they had left the ballroom far behind and become abstract types of art music. Between the slow sarabande and fast gigue might be inserted a variety of optional numbers such as the *minuet,* the *gavotte,* the lively *bourrée,* or the *passepied.* These dances of peasant origin introduced a refreshing earthiness into their more formal surroundings. The suite sometimes opened with an *overture,* and might include a variety of other brief pieces with attractive titles.

Binary form

The standard form of each piece in the suite was a highly developed binary structure **(A-B)** consisting of two sections of approximately equal length, each being rounded off by a cadence. The first part usually moved from the home key (tonic) to a contrasting key (dominant), while the **B** part made the corresponding move back. The two parts often used closely related melodic material. The form was made apparent to the ear by the modulation and the full stop at the end of the first part. As a rule, each part was repeated, giving an **A-A-B-B** structure.

The essential element of the suite was dance rhythm, with its imagery of physical movement. The suite offered composers an elegant entertainment based on popular rhythms that could be transmuted into art.

The principle of combining dances into a suite could be applied to chamber, orchestral, and solo music. In the genre of chamber music, the Italian composer Corelli was noted for his sonatas in suite form, known as *sonatas da camera,* or *chamber sonatas.* (These were distinguished from *sonatas da chiesa,* or *church sonatas,* which were more serious, contrapuntal chamber works.) The suite was also a popular form for solo keyboard and lute works. Bach's French and English suites for solo harpsichord are splendid examples. In France, dance collections were known as *ordres* (orders), and often contained numerous miniature pieces. Among the composers of solo keyboard suites was the central figure of the French harpsichord school, François Couperin (1668–1733). Notable too was a woman recognized in her day as an extraordinary harpsichordist and composer: Elisabeth-Claude Jacquet de la Guerre (c. 1666–1729).

Elisabeth-Claude Jacquet de la Guerre: Her Life and Music

A child prodigy whose talents attracted attention in her earliest years, Elisabeth-Claude Jacquet enjoyed the patronage of Louis XIV; the Sun King himself supervised her education at court. One reviewer wrote of the young girl's remarkable abilities, "She sings at sight the most difficult music. She accompanies herself, and others who wish to sing, at the harpsichord, which she plays in an inimitable manner. She composes pieces and plays them in all keys asked of her . . . for four years she has been appearing with these extraordinary qualities, and she still is only ten years old."

Jacquet de la Guerre

The daughter of an organ builder, Elisabeth married Marin de la Guerre, organist of the Church of Saint-Chapelle, about 1684; their home became a center of music making in Paris. The French writer Titon du Tillet described these musical gatherings: "All the great musicians and fine connoisseurs went eagerly to hear her." During these years, she was productive as a composer of operas, cantatas, and chamber music. In 1694, the French Royal Academy presented one of her earliest works, a five-act opera entitled *Cephale and Procris.*

According to French composer François Couperin, a number of women achieved a high standard of performance as harpsichordists, among them his own daughter, who held a court position as a musician. In his treatise on keyboard playing, Couperin claimed that women such as Jacquet de la Guerre had a natural advantage over men in harpsichord playing because of their smaller hand size and nimble dexterity.

Elisabeth Jacquet de la Guerre retired from public performance in 1717, after the death of her husband and her son. Following her death in 1729, a French commemorative medal was struck in her honor.

A pioneer in several genres, Jacquet de la Guerre was active in all branches of her art. Her opera *Cephale and Procris,* a tragédie lyrique, follows in the tradition of Jean-Baptiste Lully. Her sacred cantatas, based on stories drawn from Scripture, are among the few examples of this genre in the French Baroque. In cantatas such as *The Parting of the Red Sea* and *The Deluge,* she led the way to a type of descriptive music that became popular, as we have seen, in a later age.

Vocal music

In 1687, Jacquet de la Guerre produced the first collection of solo harpsichord works ever published by a woman. Two decades later, she added a collection of fourteen pieces representing a new type of chamber music—for harpsichord with an optional violin part—that led the way to the duo sonata. These works combine the lyrical Italian style with the decorative and highly ornamented French keyboard style.

Keyboard music

PIECES FOR HARPSICHORD

The collection of works found in her Pieces for Harpsichord (1707) form two suites; the first, in D minor, presents a variety of dance types that include the four standard movements of the Baroque suite and a number of variations,

Principal Works

Keyboard works: 2 books of suites (*Les Pièces de Clavecin,* 1687, and *Pièces de Clavecin qui peuvent se jouer sur le viollon,* 1707)

Instrumental chamber music, including solo sonatas for violin with harpsichord; trio sonatas

Vocal works, including 2 operas (an opera-ballet, 1691, now lost; and *Cephale et Procris,* 1694); 3 collections of cantatas; a Te Deum; songs and airs

called *doubles.* The suite begins with an extended allemande entitled "La Flamande" (The Flemish Girl) and its double. This is followed by a courante and its double, a sarabande, and a gigue with double. After these come several added movements, including a final *chaconne,* an elaborate Baroque form based on a repeated harmonic progression.

The gigue, a light-hearted dance in a compound meter of six, features many melodic ornaments typical of French harpsichord style. Its disjunct line derives from a French Baroque lute style known as *stile brisé* (broken style). Like the other dances in this suite, this one is in a standard two-part, or binary, form **(A-A-B-B).** The first part moves from D minor to A major (the dominant); the second part moves back to D minor (see Listening Guide 49). Thus the piece traces the movement from tonic to dominant and back to tonic again that was, we saw, a basic organizing principle of the Classical style.

Listening Guide 49

C/S: 2A/1   C/S: 2/
Sh: 1B/3   Sh: 1/ 40 — 41

JACQUET DE LA GUERRE: Suite No. 1, 2nd Gigue, from Pieces for Harpsichord *(Pièces de Clavecin)*

(3:25)

Date of work: 1707

Genre: Gigue, 6/8 dance from Baroque suite

Medium: Solo harpsichord or harpsichord with violin

Form: Binary **(A-A-B-B)**

Order of works in first suite (D minor):

"La Flamande" (Allemande)*	Sarabande*	Double
Double	Gigue*	Rigaudon
Courante*	Double	2nd Rigaudon
Double	2nd Gigue	Chaconne
		*Standard movements of suite

2ND GIGUE

1 0:00 **A** section—lilting, disjunct theme in D minor, set in 4-measure phrases, with some embellishments; ends in **A** major:

0:35 **A** section repeated

2 1:12 **B** section—more conjunct line, highly ornamented, longer than **A** section; finally returns to D minor:

2:10 **B** section repeated

Handel and the Orchestral Suite

The two orchestral suites by Handel, the *Water Music* and *Music for the Royal Fireworks,* are memorable contributions to the genre. The *Water Music* was surely played (but probably not first composed) for a royal party on the Thames River in London on July 17, 1717. Two days later, the *Daily Courant* reported:

> On Wednesday Evening, at about 8, the King took Water at Whitehall in an open Barge, and went up the River towards Chelsea. Many other Barges with Persons of Quality attended, and so great a Number of Boats, that the whole River in a manner was cover'd; a City Company's Barge was employ'd for the Musick, wherein were 50 Instruments of all sorts, who play'd all the Way from Lambeth (while the Barges drove with the Tide without Rowing, as far as Chelsea) the finest Symphonies, compos'd express for this Occasion, by Mr. Handel; which his Majesty liked so well, that he caus'd it to be plaid over three times in going and returning.

WATER MUSIC

The twenty-two numbers of the *Water Music* were performed without continuo instruments, as it was not possible to bring a harpsichord aboard the barge. The conditions of an outdoor performance, in which the music would have to contend with the breeze on the river, birdcalls, and similar noises, led Handel to a music that unfolded in sweeping lines, marked by lively rhythms and catchy melodies.

In this imaginary depiction of Handel's Water Music, *the composer is seen perched on the edge of the front barge with King George I on his left; in the second barge, musicians seem to be playing Handel's work.* (Bettmann Archive)

The *Water Music* opens with a French overture and includes a variety of dance numbers, among them minuets in graceful 3/4 time, bourrées in fast 4/4, and hornpipes in lively triple meter. It does not follow the standard order of dance movements for the suite. Occasional echo effects exemplify the terraced dynamics of the Baroque. In these varied numbers, Handel combined the Italian string style of Corelli with the rhythmic vivacity of the French and the songfulness of Purcell to produce a style imprinted with his own robust personality and perfectly suited to the taste of an English audience.

No. 6   The work is divided into three suites, of which the first, in F major, is the most popular. We will study a minuet and trio, No. 6, from this suite. This movement opens with an introductory duet between the first and second horns, in which the first presents a fanfare outlining the F-major chord and the second imitates it two measures later. The fanfare then becomes the minuet theme played by the entire group. Section **A** is the minuet, a two-part dance form, and section **B** is the trio, another two-part dance (we studied minuet-and-trio form in Chapter 37). The contrast between them is underlined by a change of mode—from major to minor—and character. The **A** section is repeated without the introductory fanfare. (See Listening Guide 50.)

More than two and a half centuries after it was written, Handel's *Water Music* is still a favorite with the public. One has only to hear a few measures of it to understand why.

Listening Guide 50

C/S: 2A/5   C/S: 2/ 9 – 11

HANDEL: *Water Music,* First Suite, No. 6   (1:49)

Date of work: 1717 (first performance)
Form: Dance suite, beginning with French overture
Medium: Orchestra (2 horns, 2 oboes, bassoon, and strings)

FIRST SUITE, NO. 6: Minuet and Trio

9 0:00 Opening fanfare in French horns, 16-measure duet (first 8 measures shown):

0:12 **A** section—minuet, F major; begins with disjunct fanfare theme; two sections, each repeated (**a-a-b-b,** 8 measures each)

10 0:52 **B** section—trio, F minor; reduced orchestration, strings and bassoon only; two sections, each repeated (**c-c-d-d,** 8+8+16+16 measures; opening melody shown):

11 1:27 **A** section—minuet, F major; return of opening dance, without repeats

62

Other Baroque Instrumental Forms

Sonata, Passacaglia, and Overture

The sonata was widely cultivated throughout the Baroque. In its early stages, it consisted of either a movement in several sections or several movements that contrasted in tempo and texture. We have already noted the distinction *Chamber sonatas* that was drawn between the *sonata da camera,* or *chamber sonata,* which was usually a suite of stylized dances, and the *sonata da chiesa,* or *church* *Church sonatas* *sonata.* The latter was more serious in tone and more contrapuntal in texture. Its four movements, arranged in the sequence slow-fast-slow-fast, generally made little use of dance rhythms. The prolific output of the Italian composer Arcangelo Corelli emphasized the distinction between these two types, yet in practice they overlapped. Many church sonatas ended with one or more dancelike movements, while many chamber sonatas opened with an impressive introductory movement in the church-sonata style.

Sonatas were written for one to six or even eight instruments. The favorite Baroque combination for such works was two violins and continuo. Because of the three printed staffs in the music, such compositions came to be known *Trio sonatas* as *trio sonatas.* Yet the title is misleading, because it refers to the number of parts rather than to the number of players. As we saw, the basso continuo needed two performers—a cellist (or bass viol player or bassoonist) to play the bass line and a harpsichordist or organist to realize the harmonies indicated by the figures. Thus it takes four players to perform a trio sonata.

Sonatas for unaccompa- Some Baroque composers wrote sonatas for single, unaccompanied instru-
nied instruments ments. Notable among these was Bach, whose sonatas for unaccompanied violin and for unaccompanied cello are centerpieces of the repertory. Domenico Scarlatti (1685–1757) is known for his over five hundred sonatas for solo harpsichord, characterized by brilliant passagework, hand crossings, and other virtuoso techniques that helped lay the foundation for modern piano technique. Set in one-movement binary form, his works bear the seed that was to develop into the Classical sonata.

Passacaglia One of the most majestic forms of Baroque music is the *passacaglia,* which utilizes the principle of the ground bass. A melody is introduced alone in the bass, usually four or eight bars long, in a stately triple meter. The theme is repeated again and again, serving as the foundation for a set of continuous variations that exploit all the resources of polyphonic art. (We heard a passacaglia in the last movement of Brahms's Fourth Symphony, discussed in Chapter 23.) *Chaconne* A related type is the *chaconne,* in which the variations are based not on a melody but on a succession of harmonies repeated over and over. Passacaglia and chaconne exemplify the Baroque urge toward abundant variation and embellishment of a musical idea, and that desire to make "much out of little" which is the essence of the creative act.

A sonata for violin and harpsichord is being performed by Florentine Court Musicians *in a painting by* **Anton Domenico Gabbiani** *(1652–1726).* (Scala/Art Resource, N.Y.)

The operatic overture was an important genre of orchestral music. Two types were popular during this period. The *French overture,* of which we heard an example in Handel's *Messiah* (Listening Guide 46), generally followed the pattern slow-fast. Its fast section was in the loosely fugal style known as *fugato.* The *Italian overture* consisted of three sections: fast-slow-fast. The opening was not in fugal style; the middle section was lyrical; there followed a vivacious, dancelike finale. This pattern, expanded into three separate movements, was later adopted by the concerto grosso and the solo concerto. In addition, we have noted that the opera overture of the Baroque was one of the ancestors of the symphony of later eras.

Overtures: French and Italian

Keyboard Forms

The keyboard forms of the Baroque fall into two categories: free forms based on harmony, with a strong element of improvisation, such as the prelude and chorale prelude; and stricter forms based on counterpoint, such as the fugue. Bach's keyboard music shows his mastery of both types.

A *prelude* is a fairly short piece based on the continuous expansion of a melodic or rhythmic figure. It originated in improvisations performed on the lute and keyboard instruments. In the late Baroque, the prelude was used to introduce a group of dance pieces or a fugue. Since its texture was for the most part homophonic, it made an effective contrast with the contrapuntal texture of the fugue that followed it. Later in this chapter, we will study an example of a prelude and fugue from Bach's *Well-Tempered Clavier.*

Prelude

Church organists, in introducing the chorale to be sung by the congregation, fell into the practice of embellishing the traditional melodies. There grew

Chorale prelude   up a body of instrumental works—*chorale preludes* and *chorale variations*—in which organ virtuosity of the highest level was combined with the spirit of inspired improvisation.

BACH AND THE CHORALE PRELUDE

In his capacity as a church organist, Bach wrote more than 140 organ chorales. Some were short, with the tune stated in its original form. Others presented a longer elaboration of the tune, giving free rein to the imagination. Bach's chorale prelude on *A Mighty Fortress Is Our God,* a tune we heard in Cantata No. 80 (see Chapter 58), was composed in 1709, during the Weimar period. The work uses imitation, rearrangements of the tune, and cantus firmus technique (the melody is announced clearly in one part, while the other parts move in elaborate counterpoint against it).

The piece is written for an organ with three keyboards and pedals, to allow for different registrations and colors. (By registration, we mean the art of combining various registers and colors of the organ through use of the stops that control them.) The texture varies from one to three parts, played by both hands and the feet on the pedals. (See Listening Guide 51 for analysis.)

This two-manual Compenius organ at Frederiksborg Castle, Denmark, dates from the early seventeenth century.

Listening Guide 51

 C/S: 2A/9   C/S: 2/ 23 – 30

BACH: Chorale Prelude, *A Mighty Fortress Is Our God* (*Ein feste Burg ist unser Gott*)

(3:33)

Date of work: 1709, Weimar
Form: Chorale prelude
Medium: Organ
Basis: Lutheran chorale (hymn) tune, *Ein feste Burg ist unser Gott*

Original chorale tune, with 9 phrases:

Ein fe - ste Burg_ ist un - ser Gott, ein' gu - te Wehr und_ Waf - fen;
er hilft uns frei_ aus al - ler Not, die uns jetzt hat be - trof - fen.

Der al - te bö - se Feind, mit Ernst er's jetzt meint, gross Macht und viel

List sein grau - sam Rü - stung ist; auf Erd' ist nicht seins - gleich - en.

		Basis (Chorale Phrase)	Description	Measures
23	0:00	1	Solo elaboration in *fagotto* (bassoon) stop; higher register elaborates same phrase, now in 2-part texture	1–7
24	0:24	2	2-part texture; tune clearly stated in right hand over moving part	8–10
25	0:37	3	Tune now in lower part, with moving right-hand part above	12–15
26	0:50	4	Tune decorated in dotted notes in lower part; some imitation between parts	16–19
27	1:07	5	2-part imitation on decorated tune over moving pedal line; 3-part texture	20–23
28	1:22	6, 7	Tune in long notes in pedal, with 2 upper parts in imitation; extension of last note of phrase 7; solo line leads to phrase 8	24–32
29	2:00	8	Tune in short motives; imitated between upper parts over ostinato bass; solo line leads to phrase 9	35–39
30	2:25	9	Clear statement of last phrase in high register; 2-part texture; followed by coda featuring imitation and moving pedal line; closes with elaborations over sustained note in pedal	41–end

Opening of work, showing elaborated chorale tune (notes of tune marked with an x):

The Fugue and Its Devices

From the art and science of counterpoint issued one of the most exciting forms of Baroque music, the fugue. The name is derived from *fuga,* the Latin for "flight," implying a flight of fancy, or possibly the flight of the theme from one voice to the other. A *fugue* is a contrapuntal composition in which a theme of strongly marked character pervades the entire fabric, entering in one voice and then in another. The fugue consequently is based on the principle of imitation. Its main theme, the subject, constitutes the unifying idea, the focal point of interest in the contrapuntal web.

We have already encountered the fugue or fugal style in a number of works: at the beginning of the book, in Britten's *Young Person's Guide to the Orchestra (Variations and Fugue on a Theme of Purcell);* in Handel's overture and choruses of *Messiah;* in the opening movement of Bach's cantata *A Mighty Fortress Is Our God;* and in his organ chorale prelude of the same *Fugal voices* name. Thus a fugue may be written for a group of instruments, for a solo instrument, or for full chorus. Whether the fugue is vocal or instrumental, its several lines are called voices. In vocal and orchestral fugues, each line is sounded by a different performer or group of performers. In fugues for keyboard instruments, the ten fingers—on the organ, the feet as well—manage the complex interweaving of the voices.

Subject   The *subject,* or theme, is stated alone at the beginning in one of the voices—soprano, alto, tenor, or bass. It is then imitated in another voice—this *Answer* is the *answer*—while the first continues with a *countersubject,* or coun- *Countersubject* tertheme. Depending on the number of voices in the fugue, the subject will then appear in a third voice and be answered in the fourth, with the other voices usually weaving a free contrapuntal texture against these. (If a fugue is in three voices, there is, naturally, no second answer.) When the theme has been presented in each voice once, the first section of the fugue, the exposition, is at an end. From then on, the fugue alternates between sections that feature the entrance of the subject and less weighty interludes known as *Episodes* *episodes,* which serve as areas of relaxation, until it reaches its home key at the *recapitulation,* or restatement.

The subject of the fugue is stated in the home key, the tonic. The answer is given in a related key, that of the dominant, which lies five tones above the tonic. There may be modulation to foreign keys in the course of the fugue, which builds up tension against the return home. The Baroque fugue thus embodied the opposition between home and contrasting keys, which was one of the basic principles of the new major-minor system.

As the fugue unfolds, there must be not only a sustaining of interest but also the sense of mounting urgency that is proper to an extended artwork. Each recurrence of the theme reveals new facets of its nature. The composer manipulates the subject as pure musical material in the same way that the sculptor molds clay. Especially effective is the use of *stretto,* in which the theme is imitated in close succession. The effect is one of voices crowding upon each other, creating a heightening of tension that brings the fugue to its climax. The final statement of the subject, generally in a decisive manner, brings the fugue to an end.

Stretto

Fugal technique reached unsurpassed heights in the hands of Bach and Handel. In the Baroque and in later eras, compositions other than fugues employed fugal techniques through an imitative passage known as *fugato.*

Fugato

The Baroque fugue, then, was a form based on imitative counterpoint that combined the composer's technical skill with imagination, feeling, and exuberant ornamentation. There resulted a type of musical art that may well be accounted one of the supreme achievements of the era.

PRELUDE AND FUGUE IN C MINOR BY BACH

The Well-Tempered Clavier was described in Chapter 56 as the celebrated work that circumnavigated the tonal globe, a journey made possible by the new system of equal temperament for tuning keyboard instruments. It was this system that made it possible to play in all the keys. The first volume of the collection, completed in 1722 during the years Bach worked in Cöthen, contains a prelude and fugue in each of the twelve major and twelve minor keys. The second volume, also containing twenty-four preludes and fugues, appeared twenty years later.

The Prelude and Fugue in C minor is No. 2 in the first volume of *The Well-Tempered Clavier.* The prelude is a "perpetual motion" type of piece based on running sixteenth notes in both hands that never let up, outlining a single chord in each measure. We usually associate emotion in music with a beautiful melody. This prelude shows how deeply moving a series of harmonies can be. The music modulates from C minor to the relative major, E-flat major, then returns to the home key. Notable is the utter unity of mood, the "single affection" that gives this piece its unflagging momentum.

Prelude

The fugue, in three voices, is based on one of those short, incisive themes for which Bach had a special gift. First presented by the alto voice in the home key of C minor, it is answered by the soprano in G minor, the dominant. One last statement of the subject in the bass line closes the exposition.

Fugue

There are two countersubjects that serve to shed new light on the subject, whose successive entries are separated by episodes woven out of the basic idea. (See Listening Guide 52.) As in the prelude, the music is pervaded by a relentless drive. When the piece finally reaches the C-major chord at the end, we are left with the sense of a journey completed, an action happily consummated.

Listening Guide 52

C/S: 2A/10   C/S: 2/ 34 – 37
Sh: 1B/4   Sh: 1/ 42 – 45

BACH: Prelude and Fugue in C minor, from *The Well-Tempered Clavier, Book I*

(3:22)

Date of work: 1722
Medium: Harpsichord

34 0:00 **PRELUDE:** Free, improvisatory-style piece; establishes key of C minor; begins with fast, repeated sixteenth-note pattern through various harmonies; ends with cadenza-like passage

Opening of prelude, showing 2 sixteenth-note patterns (in C minor, then F minor), each repeated:

FUGUE: 3 voices (SAB), with 2-measure subject; features many episodes with fragments of subject

Subject:

Code for line graph: Subject/Answer: _____
                        Countersubject 1: – – – – – – – – – –
                        Countersubject 2: – · – · – · – · – · – ·
                        Episode: ∿∿∿∿∿∿∿

	EXPOSITION				
35 0:00	S	answer	bridge	– – – – – – – –	episode 1
	A	subject	– – – – – – –	– · – · – · – ·	∿∿∿∿∿∿
	B			_____	∿∿∿∿∿∿
	Measure: 1	3	5	7	9
	Statement in: C minor	G major		C minor	
36 0:28	S	_____	episode 2	– – – – – – – ·	episode 3
	A	– · – · – · – ·	∿∿∿∿∿∿	– – – – – – –	∿∿∿∿∿∿
	B	– – – – – – –	∿∿∿∿∿∿	_____	∿∿∿∿∿∿
	Measure: 11	13	15	17	
	Statement in: E♭ major	(relative major)	G major		
	RECAPITULATION				
37 1:02	S	_____	episode 4	– – – – – – – ·	cadential extension
	A	– – – – – – – ·	∿∿∿∿∿∿	– · – · – · – ·	free
	B	– · – · – · – ·	∿∿∿∿∿∿	_____	free
	Measure: 20	23	26	29	
	Statement in: C minor		C minor	C minor (C major)	

TRANSITION IV

To the Age of Enlightenment

The Rococo and the Age of Sensibility

In the reigns of Louis XIV (1643–1715) and Louis XV (1715–74), the old regime passed from high noon to twilight. With the death of Louis XV, the privileged minority at the top of the social pyramid exchanged their games of power for those of frivolity. Art moved from the monumentality of the Baroque to the caprice and intimacy of the Rococo.

The word derives from the French *rocaille,* "a shell," suggesting the decorative scroll- and shellwork characteristic of the style. The Rococo took shape as a reaction against the grandiose gesture of the Baroque. Out of the disintegrating world of the Baroque came a miniature, ornate art aimed at the enchantment of the senses and asserting the attractive doctrine that the first law is to enjoy oneself.

The greatest painter of the French Rococo was Jean Antoine Watteau (1684–1721). To the dream world of love and gallantry that furnished the themes of his art, Watteau brought the insights and the techniques of the Dutch school of Rubens. Watteau's intimate, pastoral scenes signaled the shift in French society.

The musical counterpart to Watteau was François Couperin (1668–1733), mentioned earlier as the greatest of the French keyboard school. Couperin was one of a family of distinguished musicians. His works, along with those of Elisabeth-Claude Jacquet de la Guerre, crystallize the miniature world of the Rococo. Their goal is to charm, to delight, to entertain.

François Couperin

The desire to systematize all knowledge, which characterized the coming Age of Enlightenment, also made itself felt on the musical scene. Jean-Philippe Rameau (1683–1764), the foremost French composer of the era, tried to establish a rational foundation for the harmonic practice of his time. Such works as the *Treatise on Harmony* (1722) set forth concepts that furnished the point of departure for modern musical theory.

Jean-Philippe Rameau

Jean Antoine Watteau *(1684–1721), with his dream world of love and gallantry, was the artistic counterpart of François Couperin.* La Gamme d'Amour (The Gamut of Love). (National Gallery, London)

The Rococo witnessed as profound a change in taste as has ever occurred in the history of music. In turning to a polished entertainment music, composers adopted a new ideal of beauty. Elaborate polyphonic texture yielded to a single melody line with a simple chordal accompaniment, in much the same way that the contrapuntal complexities of late Renaissance music gave way to the early Baroque ideal of monody. It is surely true that history repeats itself. This age desired its music above all to be simple and expressive of natural feel-

Empfindsamkeit ing. Thus was born the "sensitive" style of the *Empfindsamkeit* and the Age of Sensibility—an age that saw the first stirrings of that responsiveness to emotion that was to come to full flower with Romanticism.

The new style reached its apex in Germany in the mid-eighteenth century, a period that saw the activity of Bach's four composer sons—Wilhelm Friedemann, Carl Philipp Emanuel, Johann Christoph, and Johann Christian. Along with their contemporaries, these composers consummated the revolution in taste that resulted in the neglect of Bach's music for many years after his death.

This musical revolution saw the expansion of the major instrumental genres of the sonata and the concerto, and the enrichment of symphonic styles with elements drawn from the operatic aria and overture and from the tunes and rhythms of Italian comic opera. From all this was born a new thing—the idiom of the Classical sonata cycle, which was described in Chapter 37 and of which we have now heard numerous examples. The new art form was the collective achievement of several generations of musicians who were active in Italy, France, and Germany throughout the pre-Classical period (c. 1730–75).

One of the outstanding figures of the pre-Classical era was Carl Philipp Emanuel Bach (1714–88), the second son of Johann Sebastian. He deepened the emotional content of the abstract instrumental forms and played a decisive role in the creation of the modern piano idiom. His dramatic sonata style exerted a powerful influence upon the masters of the Classical era. And his theoretical treatise *Essay on the True Art of Playing Keyboard Instruments* (1753–62) throws much light on the musical practices of the mid-eighteenth century.

C. P. E. Bach

The Changing Opera

The vast social changes taking shape in the eighteenth century were bound to be reflected in the lyric theater. Grandiose Baroque opera, geared to an era of absolute monarchy, had no place in the shifting societal structure. Increasingly its pretensions were satirized all over Europe. The defeat of opera seria in London by *The Beggar's Opera* had its counterpart in Paris a quarter of a century later. In 1752, a troupe of Italian singers in the French capital presented Giovanni Battista Pergolesi's comedy with music *La serva padrona* (The Servant Mistress). There ensued the "War of the Buffoons" between those who favored the traditional French court opera and those who saw in the rising Italian comic opera, or *opera buffa,* a new, realistic art. The former camp was headed by the king, Madame de Pompadour, and the aristocracy; the latter was led by the queen and the Encyclopedists—Rousseau, d'Alembert, Diderot—who hailed the comic form for its expressive melody and natural sentiment and because it had thrown off what they regarded as the outmoded contrapuntal style. In the larger sense, the War of the Buffoons was a contest between the rising bourgeois art and a dying aristocratic art.

"War of the Buffoons"

THE BEGGAR'S OPERA

The Beggar's Opera by John Gay (1685–1712), a satirical play with songs, was presented in London in 1728, where it had enormous success. The plot presented a picture of life among London's lower classes. The characters—highwaymen, pickpockets, harlots, and their unsavory associates—were a far cry from the gods and heroes of Handel's works for the stage. *The Beggar's Opera* sounded the death knell of opera seria, whose traditions and singers were Italian, and ushered in a vogue of racy pieces in English with popular songs and dances, a trend that has persisted in the Broadway musicals of our own time.

The songs were chosen by Gay with the assistance of Johann Christoph Pepusch (1667–1752), who arranged them for performance. Included were some English and Scottish folk songs, along with popular tunes and dances from a variety of sources.

Solidly rooted in the eighteenth century, the piece was revived again and again throughout the nineteenth and twentieth centuries. The most famous of these revivals is the *Threepenny Opera* of Bertolt Brecht and Kurt Weill, twentieth-century collaborators who imposed a modern sensibility upon the old tale and a few of its tunes. This work was produced in Berlin in 1928, exactly two hundred years after Gay's original.

The Beggar's Opera is introduced by the Beggar—the author—and the Player, who serve as the vehicles for satirical commentary on Italian operatic traditions. The story involves two women, Polly Peachum and Lucy Lockit, both in love with the criminal Macheath, who has been jailed by their fathers, a bounty hunter and a jailer respectively. The second act ends with what is called the jealousy scene between the two women, a parody of a notorious real-life onstage quarrel between two operatic sopranos—Francesca Cuzzoni and Faustina Bordoni. Polly, now married to Macheath, arrives to see her husband and finds Lucy, pregnant by Macheath, visiting at the jail. The women express their jealousy in "Why how now, Madam Flirt," sung to a tune well-known to the London public. This is a strophic setting alternating between the women, set in a somewhat operatic style. When Polly's father Peachum arrives to take her away, she sings of her love for Macheath in "No pow'r on earth," on a tune by a little-known English composer. Lucy is then persuaded to help Macheath escape, knowing full well that she will lose him. Her lament, "I like the Fox shall grieve," is sung to a moving Scottish air (see Listening Guide 53). These attractive tunes make clear why the middle classes preferred this type of entertainment to the much more aristocratic opera.

Listening Guide 53

C/S: 2B/6   C/S: 2/ 51 – 53

GAY: *The Beggar's Opera,* end of Act II   (5:52)

Date of work: 1728

Genre: Ballad opera

Characters:
  Peachum
  Mrs. Peachum
  Polly Peachum, secretly married to Macheath
  Macheath, a highwayman
  Lockit, a jailer
  Lucy Lockit, in love with Macheath

51 0:00   **Air 38: "Why how now, Madam Flirt"**—duet, Lucy and Polly

Sung to the tune of *Good-morrow, Gossip Joan;* strophic setting, **A-A,** in E major; quick tempo, with embellishments in operatic style:

LUCY

A Why how now, Madam Flirt?
   If you thus must chatter;
   And are for flinging Dirt,
   Let's try who best can spatter;
   Madam Flirt!

POLLY

A Why how now, saucy Jade;
   Sure the Wench is Tipsy!
   How can you see me made
   The scoff of such a Gipsy!
   Saucy Jade!

Dialogue: Peachum enters and takes Polly off as she sings of her love for Macheath.

52 1:06   **Air 39: "No pow'r on earth"**—solo, Polly

Sung to *Irish Howl,* by George Vanbrughe; form **A-A-B-C,** in F major, slow tempo:

A No pow'r on earth can e'er divide
   The knot that sacred love hath ty'd.
A No pow'r . . .
B When parents draw against our mind,
   The true-love's knot they faster bind.
C Oh, oh ray, oh Amborah—oh, oh . . .

Dialogue: Macheath professes his love to Lucy and convinces her to help him escape by stealing the keys from the sleeping jailer. She knows that freeing him means losing him, and sings of her loss. She fetches the keys, and Macheath escapes.

53 3:58   **Air 40: "I like the Fox shall grieve"**—solo, Lucy

Sung to the tune of *The Lass of Patie's Mill;* binary form (**A-A-B-B**), D major, slow tempo:

A I like the Fox shall grieve,
   Whose mate hath left her side.
   Whom Hounds, from morn to eve,
   Chase o'er the country wide.
A I like the Fox . . .
B Where can my lover hide?
   Where cheat the weary pack?
   If Love be not his guide,
   He never will come back!
B Where can my lover hide . . .

Cultural Perspective 14

Crossover and the Growing Musical Audience

There is hardly a time in history when traditional and art musics did not influence each other in some way. Traditional music, sometimes called folk music, is generally transmitted by oral tradition, without the aid of notation. As a result, a song is constantly changing as it is passed along. Even when a traditional piece is finally written down, it continues to live on in oral tradition as well, since many people learn it only from listening.

A composer might well be the first person to write down a traditional song, and he or she can merge it with art music in one of two ways. First, a folk song may be set in a composed arrangement with accompaniment, where it remains easily recognizable. Many composers throughout history have been attracted to the tunefulness of folk songs; we will hear how the twentieth-century American composer Aaron Copland set cowboy songs in his ballet *Billy the Kid*. Second, and further removed from the source, is the emulation of a folk style, characterized by particular rhythmic, melodic, or harmonic patterns but providing only a hint of the original. This phenomenon is even more common; we heard an example of this treatment in a polonaise by Chopin, which was modeled on traits of a popular Polish dance.

We have noted that *The Beggar's Opera* made use of actual ballads (strophic folk songs with narrative texts) as well as famous tunes borrowed from Handel operas; John Gay wrote new words to these melodies, and his collaborator wrote simple accompaniments. In this case, the public loved the parody of serious opera and responded through immediate recognition of the well-known tunes; thus opera became a kind of crossover genre with more widespread appeal than ever. (The term "crossover" applies to a style, artist, or recording that is intended to appeal to a new audience.) The phenomenal success of *The Beggar's Opera* inspired others to write similar pieces. The German answer to ballad opera was Singspiel (a sung play), presented with spoken dialogue between the folklike tunes. Mozart's opera *The Magic Flute* (1791) is an artistic masterwork in this genre. It is from this tradition—a mixture of song and speech—that the European operetta evolved, which in turn gave way to the American musical theater of today.

Such mergers of styles often broaden the appeal of both traditional and art music, expanding the audience for each. Like composers, some modern performers whose reputations have been built in one musical style attempt to lure new audiences through crossover recordings in another style. This is extremely common in today's eclectic musical world; one style that has seen many successful crossover artists is country and western, a highly popular, mass-disseminated product of twentieth-century America. Among the singers who have broken down the distinctions between country/western and mainstream popular music are The Eagles (*Lyin' Eyes*), Kenny Rogers (*The Gambler*), Dolly Parton (*Workin' Nine to Five*), and Willie Nelson (*Mamas, Don't Let Your Babies Grow Up to Be Cowboys*). Other well-known works that have crossed over stylistic boundaries—this time between art music and rock—are the Who's rock opera *Tommy* (1969), Leonard Bernstein's *Mass* (1971), and, more recently, Paul McCartney's *Liverpool Oratorio* (1991).

A scene from The Beggar's Opera *of 1728, as drawn by* **William Hogarth** *(1697–1764).* (Tate Gallery, London/ Art Resource, N.Y.)

Terms to Note:	**Suggested Listening**
oral tradition	Ballad opera (*The Beggar's Opera*, by John Gay)
ballad	Rock opera *(Tommy,* by Pete Townshend of the Who)
crossover	Art/rock crossover (*Mass,* by Leonard Bernstein; *Liverpool Oratorio,* by Paul McCartney)
Singspiel	
musical theater	

Gluck and Opera Reform

It fell to a German-born composer trained in Italy to liberate serious opera from some of its outmoded conventions and bring it into harmony with the thought and feeling of the new era. Christoph Willibald Gluck (1714–87) found his way to a style that met the new need for dramatic truth and expressiveness. "I have striven to restrict music to its true office of serving poetry by means of expression and by following the situations of the story, without interrupting the action or stifling it with a useless superfluity of ornaments," he said. How well he realized the aesthetic needs of the new age: "Simplicity, truth and naturalness are the great principles of beauty in all forms of art."

A Comparison of Baroque and Classical Styles

Baroque (c. 1600–1750)	*Classical* (c. 1750–1825)
Monteverdi, Purcell, Scarlatti, Corelli, Vivaldi, Handel, Bach, Jacquet de la Guerre	Haydn, Mozart, Beethoven, Schubert
Continuous melody with wide leaps, chromatic tones for emotional effect	Symmetrical melody in balanced phrases and cadences; tuneful, diatonic, with narrow leaps
Single rhythm predominant; steady, energetic pulse; freer in vocal music	Dance rhythms favored; regularly recurring accents
Chromatic harmony for expressive effect; major-minor system established with brief excursions to other keys	Diatonic harmony favored; tonic-dominant relationship expanded, becomes basis for large-scale form
Polyphonic texture; linear-horizontal dimension	Homophonic textures; chordal-vertical dimension
Instrumental genres: fugue, concerto grosso, trio sonata, suite, chaconne, prelude, passacaglia	Symphony, solo concerto, solo sonata, string quartet, other chamber music ensembles
Vocal genres: opera, mass, oratorio, cantata	Opera, mass, solo song
Binary form predominant	Ternary form becomes important, sonata-allegro form developed
Religious music predominant	Secular music predominant
Terraced (contrasting) dynamics	Continuously changing dynamics through *crescendo* and *decrescendo*
Continuous tone color throughout one movement	Changing tone colors from one section to the next
String orchestra, with added woodwinds; organ and harpsichord in use	Orchestra standardized into four choirs; introduction of clarinet, trombone; rise of piano to prominence
Improvisation expected; harmonies realized from figured bass	Improvisation largely limited to cadenzas in concertos
Single affection; emotional exuberance and theatricality	Emotional balance and restraint

This conviction was embodied in the works he wrote for the Imperial Theater at Vienna, notably *Orpheus and Eurydice* (1762) and *Alceste* (1767), both collaborations with the poet Raniero Calzibigi. There followed the lyric dramas with which he conquered the Paris Opera; the most important were based on legends by the ancient Greek writer Homer—*Iphigenia in Aulis* (1774) and *Iphigenia in Taurus* (1778). In these works, Gluck successfully fused a number of elements: the monumental choral scenes and dances that had always been a feature of French lyric tragedy, the animated ensembles of comic opera, the vigor of the new instrumental style in Italy and Germany, and the broadly arching vocal line that was part of Europe's operatic heritage. The result was a music drama whose dramatic truth and expressiveness profoundly affected the course of operatic history.

PART SEVEN

The Twentieth Century

"The century of aeroplanes has a right to its own music. As there are no precedents, I must create anew."—CLAUDE DEBUSSY

Henri Matisse *(1869-1954),* The Cowboy, *from* Jazz. (Louis E. Stern Collection, Museum of Modern Art, N.Y.)

TRANSITION V

The Post-Romantic Era

"I came into a very young world in a very old time."—ERIK SATIE

The post-Romantic era extended from around 1890 to 1910. The composers of this period included radicals, conservatives, and those in between. Some continued on the traditional path; others struck out in new directions; still others tried to steer a middle course between the old and the new. During these years, several national schools continued to flourish, notably those of Spain, England, Finland, and the United States.

Two important movements ushered in the twentieth century: Impressionism, heralded by Claude Debussy and Maurice Ravel, and post-Romanticism. We have already encountered (in Chapter 32) the Italian post-Romantic concept of verismo, exemplified by Leoncavallo's *Pagliacci* and the operas of Giacomo Puccini and Pietro Mascagni. In this chapter, we will explore the Germanic post-Romantic style of Gustav Mahler and Richard Strauss.

Gustav Mahler: His Life and Music

"To write a symphony is, for me, to construct a world."

One of the striking phenomena of the current musical scene has been the upsurge of Gustav Mahler's popularity. For whatever reason, his troubled spirit seems to reach the musical public in a most persuasive way. "My time will come," he used to say. It has.

Gustav Mahler (1860–1911) was born and raised in Bohemia. His parents were quick to recognize the boy's talent. Piano lessons began when Gustav was six. He was sent to Vienna and entered the conservatory at fifteen, the university three years later. His professional career began modestly enough: at the age of twenty, he was engaged to conduct operettas at a third-rate summer theater. A dynamic conductor who found his natural habitat in the opera house, Mahler soon achieved a reputation that brought him more important posts,

Gustav Mahler

Vienna Opera

until at twenty-eight he was director of the Royal Opera at Budapest. From Budapest, Mahler went to Hamburg. Then, at thirty-seven, he was offered the most important musical position in the Austrian Empire—the directorship, with absolute powers, of the Vienna Opera. His ten years there (1897–1907) made operatic history. He brought to his duties a fiery temperament, unwavering devotion to ideals, and the inflexible will of the zealot. When he took over, the current fad was the unpretentious style of the French composer Jules Massenet. By the time his rule ended, he had taught a frivolous public to revere Mozart, Beethoven, and Gluck, and made them listen to uncut versions of Wagner's operas as well.

Conversion to Catholicism

Shortly before he was appointed to Vienna, Mahler, a Jew, converted to Catholicism. This step was motivated primarily by the desire to make his way in a city where anti-Semitism was rampant. Beyond that, Mahler belonged to a generation of Jewish intellectuals who had lost identification with their religious heritage and who sought roots in the Austro-German culture of which they felt themselves to be a part. "I am thrice homeless," he remarked. "As a Bohemian born in Austria. As an Austrian among Germans. And as a Jew throughout the world."

"Humanly I make every concession, artistically—none!" was Mahler's creed. Such obstinance was bound to create powerful enemies. Mahler's final years in Vienna were embittered by the intrigues against him, which flourished despite the fact that he had transformed the Imperial Opera into the premier lyric theater of Europe. The death of a little daughter left him grief-stricken. A second disaster followed soon after: he was found to have a serious heart ailment. When he finally was forced to resign his post, the blow was not unexpected.

New York Philharmonic

Mahler, now almost forty-eight (he had only three more years to live), accepted an engagement at New York's Metropolitan Opera. He hoped to earn enough to be able to retire at fifty, so that he finally might compose with the peace of mind that had never been granted him. His three years in New York were marked by the storms that his tempestuous personality inevitably provoked. In 1909, he assumed direction of the New York Philharmonic Orchestra. When the ladies of the Board once complained to Alma Mahler that her husband had ignored their wishes, she replied, "But in Vienna the Emperor himself did not dare to interfere!"

Principal Works

Orchestral music, including 10 symphonies

Song cycles with orchestra, including *Lieder eines fahrenden Gesellen* (*Songs of a Wayfarer,* 1885), *Des knaben Wunderhorn* (*The Youth's Magic Horn,* 1888), *Kindertotenlieder* (*Songs on the Death of Children,* 1904), and *Das Lied von der Erde* (*The Song of the Earth,* 1908); Lieder

In the middle of a taxing concert season with the Philharmonic, Mahler fell ill with a streptococcus infection and was taken to Paris, where a new serum treatment had been developed. But he took a turn for the worse, and set forth on his last journey, back to the scene of his greatest triumphs—the Vienna that he both loved and detested. On his deathbed, he conducted with one finger on the quilt, uttering a single word: "Mozart." He was buried, as he had requested, beside his daughter in a cemetery outside Vienna.

"The act of creation in me is so closely bound up with all my experience that when my mind and spirit are at rest I can compose nothing." In this identification of art with personal emotion, Mahler was entirely the Romantic.

The spirit of song pervades Mahler's art. He followed Schubert and Schumann in cultivating the song cycle, but with orchestral rather than piano accompaniment. *Songs of a Wayfarer,* composed in 1885, is a set of four songs filled with Schubertian longing. Mahler wrote the texts himself, inspired by a vision that appealed to his imagination: the rejected lover wandering alone over the face of the earth. His next cycle was inspired by a famous collection of German folk poetry, *The Youth's Magic Horn.* The moving *Songs on the Death of Children* is a cycle for voice and orchestra to the grief-laden poems of Rückert. The peak of his vocal writing is *The Song of the Earth,* which we will study.

Vocal music

Mahler was the last in the illustrious line of Viennese symphonists that extended from Haydn, Mozart, Beethoven, and Schubert to Brahms and Bruckner. His tonal imagery was filled with the jovial spirit of Austrian popular song and dance. His nine symphonies abound in lyricism, with long, flowing melodies and richly expressive harmonies. (The Tenth Symphony was left unfinished at his death, but recently has been edited and made available for performance.) Mahler's sense of color ranks with that of the great masters of orchestration. He contrasted solo instruments in the manner of chamber music, achieving his color effects through clarity of line rather than massed sonorities.

Symphonies

It was through musical texture that Mahler made his most important contribution to contemporary technique. In his orchestral style, which was based on counterpoint, two or more melodies could unfold simultaneously, each setting off the other. Mahler never abandoned the principle of tonality; he needed the key as a framework for his vast designs.

THE SONG OF THE EARTH

Regarded by many as Mahler's masterpiece, *The Song of the Earth* is an extended cycle of six songs for tenor, contralto (or baritone), and orchestra. It was written just after his daughter's death when Mahler learned that he had a heart ailment. From initial despair he progressed to a heightened awareness of life. "I see everything in a new light. I thirst for life more than ever before, and find the 'habit of existence' more sweet than it ever was." This mood spurred him to a work in which a fierce joy in the beauty of earthly things mingled with gentle resignation.

He found his text in Hans Bethge's *Chinese Flute,* a translation—more ac-

Cultural Perspective 15

Vienna at the Turn of the Century

Vienna was a city obsessed with the arts. There, writers, artists, and composers found an intellectual climate that nurtured a broad spectrum of ideas. In 1897, a group of young artists organized a movement known as the Viennese Secession, dedicated to the overthrow of what they perceived as conservative Viennese tastes. This artistic "declaration of independence" forged the way for new and sometimes radical styles, yet for a model they turned to the historical figure of Beethoven. Their 1902 exhibition featured as its centerpiece a large statue of Beethoven by Max Klinger and an enormous Beethoven frieze by painter Gustav Klimt, in front of which Mahler conducted the famous *Ode to Joy* from the Ninth Symphony.

An even more startling influence on the arts in turn-of-the-century Vienna came from the East Asian traditions of Japan and China. New trends in painting and architecture were shaped during these years—in particular, architect Adolf Loos's interpretation of a Japanese house led the way from the short-lived ornamentation of the Jugendstil (youth style) to the more modern and functional look of the Bauhaus (literally, building house). One of the most famous Bauhaus objects is the Barcelona chair, produced by Mies van der Rohe in 1929 and still popular—and expensive—today.

Viennese writers were drawn in particular to Chinese poetry, as was much of the rest of Europe. This genre charmed the West with images of nature and intriguing tales of the human condition. Earlier, the well-known German writer Johann Wolfgang von Goethe (1749–1832) had attempted to wed Eastern and Western traditions in his renditions of China's great poet Li Po. A member of a group called The Eight Immortals of the Wine Cup, Li focused his writings on wine, women, and nature—he is popularly believed to have drowned while attempting to kiss the moon's reflection in a pond. Goethe's unveiling of Chinese poetry to German-speaking Europe in turn inspired Hans Bethge's *Chinese Flute* (*Die Chinesische Flöte,* 1907), derived from the poetry of Li. Even women's fashions responded to the vogue for Eastern styles.

This was the environment in which Mahler produced his cycle *The Song of the Earth,* with its pentatonic melodic elaborations, accompanying harmonies that transcend the familiar mold of tonality, and transparent texture. Although the modernism of turn-of-the-century Vienna had not met with unqualified acceptance, the way was paved for the experiments in musical style of the so-called second Viennese school, led by composer Arnold Schoenberg (Chapter 68). Schoenberg's adventuresome spirit and influence is still heard in art music today.

Modern Vienna remains a thriving musical center, boasting some of the finest performance groups in the world—the Vienna Philharmonic Orchestra, which was conducted by Mahler at the turn of the century; the renowned Vienna Boy's Choir; and the great Vienna State Opera, to name only a few. As always, Viennese musical taste balances the old and the new: the city is an established center for the performance of early music and, at the same time, a leader in the contemporary music movement.

*Viennese architect **Adolph Loos** (1870–1933) helped move modern design toward more functional and less ornate forms. His interpretation of a Japanese house, a manifestation of Viennese interest in Far Eastern culture, illustrates this artistic trend.* (Austrian Cultural Institute)

Terms to Note:

Jugendstil
Bauhaus
pentatonic
second Viennese school

Suggested Listening:

Mahler: *The Song of the Earth,* Third
    Movement
Chinese music (with pentatonic scale)

curately, adaptation—of poems by Li Po, the eighth-century poet considered to be one of China's greatest. In their assertion that youth and happiness are fleeting and a bottle of wine brings the ultimate freedom, these verses are strikingly similar to the *Rubaiyat* of the Persian poet Omar Khayyám. The lyricist in Mahler responded to these eloquent images of joy and despair, while the symphonist expanded the material in the orchestra. *The Song of the Earth* was completed in 1911, just prior to Mahler's death. It received its premiere in Munich some six months later under the baton of his disciple Bruno Walter.

The third movement of the cycle, *Of Youth (Von der Jugend)*, for tenor and orchestra, delicately evokes its Chinese theme through pentatonic scale patterns, the use of triangle, and haunting woodwind instruments. The text evokes a faraway scene: "In the middle of the little pool stands a pavilion of green and of white porcelain" where friends, beautifully dressed, sit drinking tea, chatting, or writing verses, while watching their reflections in the water below. (For text and analysis, see Listening Guide 54.) Life here is peaceful, and eminently civilized. The bridge of jade that arches like a tiger over the pool has its musical counterpart in the arch form, **A-B-A,** of the movement. The dainty staccato notes of the first and third sections contrast with the smoother pattern of the middle part. The sound is extraordinarily transparent, achieved by a sparse orchestral texture that differs very much from the lush and sumptuous sound of the composer's later symphonies.

Third movement

In the early 1900s, all of Vienna responded to the vogue for Eastern effects. In Expectation *(1905–9), a painting by* **Gustav Klimt** *(1862–1918), the subject reflects this fashion.* (Austrian Museum of Applied Arts, Vienna)

Listening Guide 54   C/S: 6B/8   C/S: 6/ 48 — 50

MAHLER: *The Song of the Earth (Das Lied von der Erde), Third Movement*

(3:09)

Date of work: 1908–9

— *use of pentatonic scale*

Basis: The Chinese Flute by Hans Bethge

Medium: Song cycle for voice (tenor, alto/baritone) and orchestra

Movements:

   I. "Drinking Song of the Sorrow of the Earth" ("Das Trinklied vom Jammer der Erde")
  II. "The Lonely One in Autumn" ("Der Einsame in Herbst")
 III. "Of Youth" ("Von der Jugend")
 IV. "Of Beauty" ("Von der Schönheit")
  V. "The Drunkard in Spring" ("Der Trunkene im Frühling")
 VI. "The Farewell" ("Der Abschied")

III. "Of Youth" ("Von der Jugend"), tenor and orchestra (A-B-A form)

Opening woodwind line, based on a pentatonic scale:

Theme 1 (first strophe):

Mit - ten in dem klei - nen Tei - che steht ein Pa - vil - lon aus grü - nem und aus weis - sem Porzel - lan.

Theme 2 (second strophe):

Wie der Rücken ei - nes Ti - gers wölbt die Brücke sich aus Ja - de zu dem Pa - vil - lon hin - ü - ber.

		Text	Translation	Description
				A SECTION Introduction—woodwinds, French horn, and triangle; pentatonic theme
48	0:00	Mitten in dem kleinen Teiche steht ein Pavillon aus grünem und aus weissem Porzellan.	In the middle of the little pool stands a pavilion of green and of white porcelain.	Strophe 1—theme 1, B-flat major, dancelike, with staccato accompaniment
		Wie der Rücken eines Tigers wölbt die Brücke sich aus Jade zu dem Pavillon hinüber.	Like the back of a tiger arches the bridge of jade over to the pavilion.	Strophe 2—theme 2, more dramatic
	0:37			Interlude—woodwinds, with theme 1
				B SECTION
49	0:48	In dem Häuschen sitzen Freunde, schön gekleidet, trinken, plaudern, manche schreiben Verse nieder.	In the little house, friends are sitting beautifully dressed, drinking, chatting; several are writing verses.	Strophe 3—G major, then a g-minor variation of theme 2
	1:00			Interlude—woodwinds, very brief
		Ihre seidnen Ärmel gleiten rückwärts, ihre seidnen Mützen	Their silken sleeves slip backwards, their silken caps	Strophe 4—theme 2
				Interlude—with varied woodwinds, then strings
		hokken lustig tief im Nakken.	perch gaily on the back of their necks.	
		Auf des kleinen Teiches stiller Wasserfläche zeigt sich alles wunderlich im Spiegelbilde.	On the little pool's still surface everything appears fantastically in a mirror image.	Strophe 5—based on theme 2, slower and more chromatic

	2:06		Interlude—strings, chromatic, based on strophe 5
50	2:33		**A** SECTION Introduction—from the beginning, returns to B-flat major
		Alles auf dem Kopfe stehend	Everything is standing on its head	Strophe 6—theme 1
		in dem Pavillon aus grünem und aus weissem Porzellan;	in the pavilion of green and of white porcelain;	
		wie ein Halbmond scheint die Brükke umgekehrt der Bogen. Freunde, schön gekleidet, trinken, plaudern.	Like a half-moon stands the bridge, upside-down its arch. Friends, beautifully dressed, are drinking, chatting.	Strophe 7—theme 2

Mahler attempted to breathe vitality into the Romantic world of thought and feeling, which was rapidly disintegrating. This desire gives his music its nostalgia and fevered unrest. His highly personal vision of life and art has made him one of the major prophets of the twentieth century.

Richard Strauss: His Life and Music

"I work very long on melodies. The important thing is not the beginning of the melody but its continuation, its development into a fully completed artistic form."

Richard Strauss

Among the German opera composers who followed Wagner, Richard Strauss (1864–1949) was the most prominent. His operas remain indispensable works in the repertory, and are admired by an international public.

Strauss was born in Munich. His father was a virtuoso horn player who belonged to the court orchestra. His mother was the daughter of a successful Munich brewer. In this solid middle-class environment, a high value was placed on music and money. These remained Strauss's twin passions throughout his life.

Symphonic poems

His first works were in the Classical forms. At twenty-one, he found his true style in vivid program music, in which he emphasized "the poetic, the expressive in music." *Macbeth,* his first symphonic poem, was followed by *Don Juan,* an extraordinary achievement for a young man of twenty-four. Then came the series of symphonic poems that trumpeted his name throughout the civilized world: *Death and Transfiguration, Till Eulenspiegel's Merry Pranks, Thus Spake Zarathustra, Don Quixote,* and *A Hero's Life.*

Operas

In the early years of the twentieth century, Strauss conquered the operatic stage with *Salome, Elektra,* and *Der Rosenkavalier* (The Cavalier of the Rose). The international triumph of the last work on the eve of the First World

War marked the summit of his career. He collected unprecedented fees and royalties for his scores. Strauss was eager to dispel the romantic notion that the artist is better off starving in an attic. On the contrary, he insisted that "worry alone is enough to kill a sensitive man, and all thoroughly artistic natures are sensitive."

Strauss's collaboration with Hugo von Hofmannsthal, the librettist of *Elektra* and *Der Rosenkavalier,* continued until the latter's death in 1929. By this time, new concepts of modernism had surfaced; the onetime innovator, now entrenched as a conservative, was inevitably left behind. When the Nazis came to power in 1933, Strauss was confronted with a challenge and an opportunity. He was by no means reactionary in his political thinking; his daughter-in-law was Jewish, and the cosmopolitan circles in which he traveled were not susceptible to Hitler's ideology. Hence the challenge to speak out against the Third Reich arose—or to leave Germany, as many writers, musicians, and other intellectuals were doing. But the new regime was courting men of arts and letters. Strauss saw the road open to supreme power, and took advantage of the opportunity. In 1933, on the threshold of seventy, he was elevated to the official hierarchy as president of the Reichsmusikkammer (State Chamber of Music). But his reign was brief and uneasy. He declined to support the move to ban Mendelssohn's music. When his opera *The Silent Woman* was withdrawn after its premiere because the librettist, Stefan Zweig, was Jewish, Strauss resigned.

The war's end found the eighty-one-year-old composer the victim of a curious irony. He was living in near poverty because the huge sums he was owed for performances of his works in England and America had been impounded as war reparations. He was permitted to return to his villa at Garmisch, in the Bavarian Alps. To his friends, Strauss explained that he had remained in Nazi Germany because someone had to protect culture from Hitler's barbarians. Perhaps he even believed it. Speeches were given at the Bavarian Academy of Arts on the occasion of his eighty-fifth birthday. Shortly thereafter, he died.

Hugo von Hofmannsthal

Involvement with Nazis

Principal Works

Orchestral music: symphonic poems, including *Macbeth* (1888), *Don Juan* (1888–89), *Tod und Verklärung* (*Death and Transfiguration,* 1889), *Till Eulenspiegels lustige Streiche* (*Till Eulenspiegel's Merry Pranks,* 1895), *Also sprach Zarathustra* (*Thus Spake Zarathustra,* 1896), *Don Quixote* (1897), and *Ein Heldenleben* (*A Hero's Life,* 1898); 2 symphonies (*Domestic,* 1903; *Alpine,* 1915); 3 concertos (2 for horn, 1 for oboe)

15 operas, including *Salome* (1905), *Elektra* (1909), *Der Rosenkavalier* (The Cavalier of the Rose, 1911), and *Die schweigsame Frau* (The Silent Woman, 1935)

Choral works, with and without orchestra; chamber works

Strauss carried to its extreme limit the nineteenth-century appetite for story-and-picture music. His symphonic poems are a treasury of orchestral discoveries. In some, he anticipates modern sound effects—the clatter of pots and pans, the bleating of sheep, the gabble of geese, hoofbeats, wind, thunder, storm. Much more important, these works are packed with movement and gesture, with the sound and fury of a fiery temperament.

Strauss's operas continue to be widely performed. *Salome,* from Oscar Wilde's famous play, and *Elektra,* based on Hofmannsthal's version of the Greek tragedy, are long one-act operas. Swiftly paced, moving relentlessly to their climaxes, they are superb theater. *Der Rosenkavalier,* noted for its sensuous lyricism and some entrancing waltzes, remains the most popular of his operas.

DER ROSENKAVALIER

The action takes place in Vienna during the reign of the empress Maria Theresa (1717–80). The Princess of Werdenberg, a great lady of the court, is the wife of the Field Marshall and is therefore known as the Marschallin. Her youth is fading, and she tries to hold on to it by having an affair with a handsome young aristocrat, Octavian, who is considerably her junior. Her cousin, Baron Ochs, is a boorish fortune hunter with atrocious manners and morals. Herr von Faninal, a rich merchant of Vienna, is eager to crash high society and is convinced that if the Baron would become his son-in-law, all doors would be open. He therefore promises his beautiful young daughter Sophie to the Baron. The opera opens on the day of the betrothal. Sophie has not yet met her fiancé. When she does, she detests him.

It was customary among the Viennese nobility for a prospective bridegroom to send his lady love a silver rose. Baron Ochs delegates Octavian to deliver the rose to Sophie. Act II opens with the ceremonious scene of the Presentation of the Rose. For the two young people, it is love at first sight. The rest of the action details how the lovers overcome the obstacles that threaten to keep them apart. Sophie defies her father. After a duel between Octavian and the Baron in which Ochs is slightly wounded, Octavian begins a complicated intrigue to free Sophie from the dreadful engagement. His plot works. At the end of Act III, the Marschallin, realizing that time is against her, relinquishes Octavian to Sophie, and the lovers are united.

This is a glamorous opera about glamorous people, combining comedy, romance, and sentiment. Hugo von Hofmannsthal's libretto contributed to its spectacular success, as did Strauss's wonderfully lyrical writing. In its uncut version, *Der Rosenkavalier* is extremely long. It was first performed in Dresden in 1911 and soon triumphed throughout Europe and America. Strauss had to make some concessions, as some of the scenes were quite risqué for the time. He revised the scenes that took place in the Marschallin's bedroom and toned down the Baron's coarse language, sung in a slang Viennese dialect.

The role of the Marschallin has been associated with some of the greatest sopranos in the history of opera. As for the other characters, Baron Ochs's part

The touching trio that concludes Der Rosenkavalier *as sung by Gwyneth Jones, Tatiana Troyanos, and Kathleen Battle (right to left) in the 1985 Metropolitan Opera production.* (Courtesy of Winnie Klotz, Metropolitan Opera)

demands a singing actor of the highest caliber; Sophie is an unforgettable ingenue; and Octavian is a trouser role—that is, the part of a young man is sung by a woman. (You may remember that Cherubino in Mozart's *Marriage of Figaro* was also a trouser role.)

We will hear the Trio sung toward the end of the third act by the Marschallin, Sophie, and Octavian (see Listening Guide 55). The three women's voices intermingle in soaring melodies that mark one of the high points of the score. Notable is the sumptuous orchestration that frames this number. In this ensemble, the characters pour out their emotions. Sophie sings of her confused state of mind. Octavian is torn between his love for Sophie and his guilt over the pain he is causing the Princess. And the aging Marschallin resigns herself to the inevitable.

Don't ask on exam...

Listening Guide 55

 C/S: 7A/2   C/S: 7/ 5 – 6

STRAUSS: *Der Rosenkavalier* (The Cavalier of the Rose), Act III, Trio (5:20)

- *Date of work:* 1909–10
- *Setting:* 18th-century Vienna

— neo-classical style

, STRAUSS considered 'OLD', going back instead of forward.

- *Librettist:* Hugo von Hofmannsthal
- *Principal characters:*

Princess von Werdenberg, Marschallin, wife of the Field Marshall
Baron Ochs of Lerchenau, cousin to the Princess
Octavian, a young nobleman
Herr von Faninal, a rich merchant
Sophie von Faninal, his daughter
Valzacchi and Annina, an Italian couple who specialize in intrigue

ACT III, TRIO

Marschallin's opening motive
(taken from earlier scene):

Hab'⎯ mir's ge - lobt, ihn lieb ⎯ zu ha - ben

OCTAVIAN (*undecided, as if he wished to follow her*)

5 0:00   Marie Theres'!   Maria Theresa!

MARSCHALLIN (*to herself*)

Hab' mir's gelobt,	I swore I would cherish him
ihn lieb zu haben in der richtigen Weis',	in the right way,
dass ich selbst sein Lieb' zu einer	that I would even love his love
ander'n noch lieb hab'!	for another!
Hab' mir freilich nicht gedacht,	I certainly did not think
dass es so bald mir aufgelegt sollt'	that it would happen so soon.
werden! Es sind die mehreren Dinge	Most things in the world
auf der Welt, so dass sie ein's nicht	would be hard to believe
glauben tät', wenn man sie möcht erzählen hör'n.	if one were told about them.
Alleinig, wer's erlebt,	Only those who experience it believe it
der glaubt daran und weiss nicht wie—	and do not know how—

OCTAVIAN (*to himself*)

Es ist was kommen	Something has come
und ist was g'scheh'n.	and something has happened.
Ich möcht' sie fragen:	I want to ask her:
Darf's denn sein? Und grad' die Frag'	can it be? And just that question,
die spür' ich, dass sie mir verboten ist.	I feel, is forbidden.
Ich möcht' sie fragen:	I want to ask her:
Warum zittert was in mir?	Why am I trembling?
Ist denn ein grosses Unrecht gescheh'n?	Has there been a great injustice?
Und grad'an die	And she is the very one
darf ich die Frag' nicht tun.	I may not question.

SOPHIE (*to herself*)

Mir ist, wie in der Kirch'n,	I feel as if I were in church,
heilig ist mir und so bang	I am awed and so frightened

und doch ist mir unheilig auch!	And yet I also feel profane!
Ich weiss nicht, wie mir ist.	I do not know how I feel.
Ich möcht' mich niederknie'n dort	I want to kneel down
vor der Frau und möcht' ihr was	before the lady and appeal to her
antun. Denn ich spür, sie gibt mir ihn	because I sense that she gives him to me.
und nimmt mir was	And at the same time
von ihm zugleich.	takes something of him away.
Weiss garnicht, wie mir ist!	I know nothing of what I feel.

6 3:10   **Tempo primo** *(Return to opening theme)*

	MARSCHALLIN
Da steht der Bub, and da steh' ich,	There stands the boy, and here I stand,
und mit dem fremden Mädel dort	and with that strange girl there
wird er so glücklich sein, als wie halt	he will be as happy as men
Männer das Glücklichsein versteh'n.	who understand happiness can be.

	OCTAVIAN
Und dann seh' ich dich an,	And then I look at you,
Sophie, und seh' nur dich, und spür'	Sophie, and see only you, sense
nur dich, Sophie, und weiss von	only you, Sophie, and know of nothing
nichts als nur dich hab' ich lieb.	but that I love you.

	SOPHIE
Möcht' alles versteh'n	I want to understand everything,
und möcht' auch nichts versteh'n.	and I also do not want to understand.
Möcht' fragen und nicht fragen,	I wish to ask and not to ask,
wird mir heiss und kalt.	I'm getting hot and cold.

(looking into Octavian's eyes)

Und spür' nur dich und weiss nur eins:	And feel only you and know only one thing:
dich hab' ich lieb!	that I love you!

	MARSCHALLIN
In Gottes Namen.	In God's name.

The Impressionist and Post-Impressionist Eras

— first modern composer

VERY IMPORTANT! *must study*

63

Claude Debussy and Impressionism

"For we desire above all—nuance,
Not color but half-shades!
Ah! nuance alone unites
Dream with dream and flute with horn."—PAUL VERLAINE

The Impressionist Painters

In 1867, Claude Monet (1840–1926), rebuffed by the academic salons, nevertheless found a place to exhibit his painting *Impression: Sun Rising*. Before long, "Impressionism" had become a term of derision to describe the hazy, luminous paintings of this artist and his followers. A distinctly Parisian style, Impressionism counted among its exponents Camille Pissarro (1830–1903), Edouard Manet (1832–83), Edgar Degas (1834–1917), and Auguste Renoir (1841–1919). These artists, discarding those elements of the Romantic tradition that had became formulaic, strove to retain on canvas the freshness of their first impressions. They took painting out of the studio into the open air. What fascinated them was the continuous change in the appearance of things. They painted water lilies, a haystack, or clouds again and again at different hours of the day. Instead of mixing their pigments on the palette, they juxtaposed brush strokes of pure color on the canvas, leaving it to the eye of the beholder to do the mixing. An iridescent sheen bathes each painting; outlines shimmer and melt in a luminous haze.

The Impressionists abandoned the grandiose subjects of Romanticism. Their focus was not the human form, but light. They showed little interest in the drama-packed themes that had inspired centuries of European art. They

The Impressionists took painting out of the studio into the open air; their subject was light. **Claude Monet** *(1840-1926),* Impression: Sun Rising. (Musée Marmottan, Paris)

preferred "unimportant" material: still lifes, dancing girls, nudes; everyday scenes of middle-class life, picnics, boating and café scenes; nature in all its beauty, Paris in all its moods. Ridiculed at first—"Whoever saw grass that's pink and yellow and blue?"—they eventually succeeded in imposing their vision upon the age.

The Symbolist Poets

A parallel revolt against traditional modes of expression took place in poetry under the leadership of the Symbolists, who strove for direct poetic experience unspoiled by intellectual elements. They sought to suggest rather than describe, to present the symbol rather than state the thing. Symbolism as a literary movement gained prominence in the work of French writers Charles Baudelaire (1821-67), Stéphane Mallarmé (1842-98), Paul Verlaine (1844-96), and Arthur Rimbaud (1854-91). These poets were strongly influenced by the American Edgar Allan Poe (1809-49), whose writings were introduced into France by an admirer, Baudelaire. They were sensitive to the sound of a word as well as its meaning, and tried to evoke poetic images that affected all the senses.

Music and ballet provided **Edgar Degas** *(1834–1917) with many subjects, as in this painting,* The Dance Class. (Metropolitan Museum of Art, Bequest of Mrs. Harry Payne Bingham, 1986)

The Symbolists experimented in free verse forms that opened new possibilities in their art. They achieved in language an abstract quality that had once belonged to music alone. Characteristic was Verlaine's pronouncement: "Music above all!" And the essentially musical approach of the Symbolists was not lost upon the musicians. According to the composer Paul Dukas (1865–1935), it was the writers, not the musicians, who exerted the strongest influence on the greatest of the musical Impressionists, Claude Debussy.

Impressionism in Music

Impressionism came to the fore at a crucial moment in the history of European music. The major-minor system had served the art since the seventeenth century, but composers were beginning to feel that its possibilities had been exhausted. Debussy and his followers were attracted to other scales, such as the church modes of the Middle Ages, which gave their music an archaic sound. They began to emphasize the primary intervals—octaves, fourths, fifths, and the parallel movement of chords in the manner of Medieval organum. They were sympathetic to the novel scale structures introduced by nationalists such as the Russian composers Alexander Borodin and Musorgsky, or the Norwegian Edvard Grieg. They responded especially to the influence of non-Western music: the Moorish strain in the songs and dances of Spain, and the Javanese and Chinese orchestras that were heard in Paris during the World Exposition of 1889. Here they found a new world of sonority: rhythms, scales, and colors that offered a bewitching contrast to the traditional sounds of Western music (see CP 16).

The major-minor system, as we saw, is based on the pull of the active tones to the tonic, or rest tone. Impressionist composers regarded this as a formula that had become too obvious. In their works, we do not hear the triumphal final cadence of the Classical-Romantic period, in which the dominant chord is resolved to the tonic with the greatest possible emphasis. The time was ripe for more subtle harmonic relationships. Classical harmony looked upon dissonance as a momentary disturbance that found its resolution in the consonance. Composers now began to use dissonance as a value in itself, freeing it *Use of dissonance* from the need to resolve. They taught their contemporaries to accept tone combinations that had formerly been regarded as inadmissible, even as the Impressionist painters taught them to see colors in sky, grass, and water that had never been seen there before.

The whole-tone scale that figures prominently in Impressionist music de- *Whole-tone scale* rives from non-Western sources. This is a pattern built entirely of whole-tone intervals. It cannot be formed from the white or black keys alone on a piano keyboard, but by a combination of both (for example, the sequence C-D-E-F♯-G♯-A♯-C). In this scale, the seventh tone is not pulled to the eighth, the tonic, for the interval is not the usual half step but a whole step instead. There results a fluid scale pattern whose allure can be gauged only from hearing it played.

Turning from the grandiose subjects of Romanticism, the Impressionists derived their themes from the events of everyday life. **Pierre Auguste Renoir** *(1841–1919),* Lady at the Piano. (Art Institute of Chicago, Mr. and Mrs. Ryerson Collection)

Parallel chords

Several other procedures came to be associated with musical Impressionism. One of the most important is the use of parallel, or "gliding," chords, in which a chord built on one tone is duplicated immediately on a higher or lower tone. Such parallel motion was prohibited in the Classical system of harmony, but it was precisely these forbidden progressions that Impressionist composers found fascinating.

Ninth chords

The harmonic innovations identified with Impressionism led to the formation of daring new tone combinations. Characteristic was the use of the five-note combinations known as *ninth chords* (so-called because the interval between the lowest and highest tones of the chord was a ninth). These played so prominent a part in Debussy's opera *Pelléas and Mélisande* that the work came to be known as "the land of ninths." As a result of such procedures, Impressionist music wavered between major and minor without adhering to either. It floated in a borderland between keys, creating elusive effects that might be compared to the misty outlines of Impressionist painting.

Orchestral color

These floating harmonies demanded the most subtle colors. There was no room here for the lush, full sonority of the Romantic orchestra. Instead, one hears a veiled blending of timbres, a shimmer of pictorial quality: flutes and clarinets in their dark lower register, violins in their lustrous upper range, trumpets and horns discreetly muted; and over the whole, a silvery gossamer of harp, celesta, triangle, glockenspiel, muffled drum, and cymbal brushed with a drumstick. One instrumental color flows into another close by, as from oboe to clarinet to flute, in the same way that Impressionist painting moves from one color to another in the spectrum, as from yellow to green to blue.

Rhythm

Impressionist rhythm too shows the influence of non-Western music. The metrical patterns of the Classical-Romantic era were marked by a recurrent accent on the first beat of the measure. Such emphasis was hardly appropriate for the new dreamlike style. In many a work of the Impressionist school, the music glides across the bar line from one measure to the next in a floating rhythm that discreetly obscures the pulse.

Small forms

The Impressionists turned away from the large forms of the Austro-German tradition, such as symphony and concerto. They preferred short lyric forms—preludes, nocturnes, arabesques—whose titles suggested intimate lyricism or painting, such as Debussy's *Clair de lune* (Moonlight), *Nuages* (Clouds), and *Jardins sous la pluie* (Gardens in the Rain). The question arises: was Impressionism a revolt against the Romantic tradition or simply its final manifestation? Beyond question, Debussy and his followers rebelled against certain aspects of Romanticism, especially the symphony of Beethoven and the music drama of Wagner. Yet in a number of ways, Impressionism continued the fundamental tendencies of the Romantic movement in its love of beautiful sound; emphasis on program music, tone painting, and nature worship; addiction to lyricism; attempt to unite music, painting, and poetry; and emphasis on mood and atmosphere. In effect, the Impressionists substituted a thoroughly French brand of Romanticism for the Austro-German variety.

Characteristics of Musical Impressionism

1. Whole-tone scale (beginning on C):

2. Example from Debussy's *Pelléas and Mélisande,* illustrating use of whole-tone scales:

3. Parallel movement of chords (octaves and open fifths) in example of 9th-century organum:

4. Parallel movement of chords (fifths and octaves) from Debussy's *Sunken Cathedral:*

5. Structure of a ninth chord built on C:

6. Use of ninth chords in Debussy's *Pelléas and Mélisande:*

Claude Debussy

Claude Debussy: His Life and Music

"I love music passionately. And because I love it I try to free it from barren traditions that stifle it. It is a free art gushing forth, an open-air art boundless as the elements, the wind, the sky, the sea. It must never be shut in and become an academic art."

The most important French composer of the early twentieth century, Claude Debussy (1862–1918) was born near Paris in the town of St. Germain-en-Laye, where his parents kept a china shop. He entered the Paris Conservatory when he was eleven. Within a few years, he shocked his professors with bizarre harmonies that defied the rules. "What rules then do you observe?" inquired one of his teachers. "None—only my own pleasure!" "That's all very well," retorted the professor, "provided you're a genius." It became increasingly apparent that the daring young man was.

Early years

Debussy was twenty-two when his cantata *The Prodigal Son* won the Prix de Rome. Like Berlioz before him, he looked upon his stay in the Italian capital as a dreary exile from the boulevards and cafés that made up his world. By this time, he had already realized his future style. "The music I desire," he wrote a friend, "must be supple enough to adapt itself to the lyrical effusions of the soul and the fantasy of dreams."

Pelléas and Mélisande

The 1890s, the most productive decade of Debussy's career, culminated in the writing of *Pelléas and Mélisande*. Based on the symbolist drama by the Belgian poet Maurice Maeterlinck, this opera occupied him for the better part of ten years. He continued to revise the score up to the opening night, which took place on April 30, 1902, at the Opéra-Comique. *Pelléas* was attacked as being decadent, precious, and lacking in melody, form, and substance. Nevertheless, its quiet intensity and subtlety of nuance had a profound impact upon the musical public. It became an international success.

After *Pelléas,* Debussy was famous. He appeared in the capitals of Europe as conductor of his works and wrote articles that established his reputation as one of the wittiest critics of his time. In the first years of the new century, he exhausted the Impressionist vein and found his way to a new and tightly controlled idiom, a kind of distillation of Impressionism.

Later years

His energies sapped by the ravages of cancer, Debussy worked on with remarkable fortitude. The outbreak of war in 1914 robbed him of all interest in music. France, he felt, "can neither laugh nor weep while so many of our men heroically face death." After a year of silence, he realized that he had to contribute to the struggle in the only way he could, "by creating to the best of my ability a little of that beauty which the enemy is attacking with such fury." One of his last letters speaks of his "life of waiting—my waiting-room existence, I might call it—for I am a poor traveler waiting for a train that will never come any more."

Debussy died in March 1918 during the bombardment of Paris. The funeral procession made its way through deserted streets as the shells of the German guns ripped into his beloved city. It was just eight months before the victory was celebrated in France. And French culture has ever since celebrated

Principal Works

Orchestral music, including *Prélude à "L'après-midi d'un faune"* (*Prelude to "The Afternoon of a Faun,"* 1894), Nocturnes (1899), *La mer* (*The Sea,* 1905), *Images* (1912), incidental music

Dramatic works, including the opera *Pelléas et Mélisande* (1902) and the ballet *Jeux* (Games, 1913)

Chamber music, including a string quartet (1893) and various sonatas (cello, 1915; violin, 1917; flute, viola, and harp, 1915)

Piano music, including *Pour le piano* (For the Piano, 1901), *Estampes* (Prints, 1903), 2 books of preludes (1909–10, 1912–13)

Songs and choral music; cantatas, including *L'enfant prodigue* (*The Prodigal Son,* 1884)

Debussy as one of its most distinguished representatives.

For Debussy, as for Monet and Verlaine, art was primarily a sensuous experience. The epic themes of Romanticism were distasteful to his temperament as both a man and an artist. "French music," he declared, "is clearness, elegance, simple and natural declamation. French music aims first of all to give pleasure."

Debussy turned against the grand structure that was the supreme achievement of the Germans: sonata-allegro form. He regarded exposition-development-recapitulation as an outmoded formula. (At a concert once, he whispered to a friend, "Let's go—he's beginning to develop!") An even greater threat, he felt, was posed by the Wagnerian music drama, which at that time attracted the intellectuals of France. He found Wagner's grandiose *Ring* ponderous and tedious. "The idea of spreading one drama over four evenings! Is this admissible, especially when in these four evenings you always hear the same thing? . . . My God! how unbearable these people in skins and helmets become by the fourth night." In the end, however, he paid moving tribute to the master. Wagner "can never quite die," he wrote, and called him "a beautiful sunset that was mistaken for a dawn."

From the Romantic exuberance that left nothing unsaid Debussy sought refuge in an art of indirection, subtle and discreet. Instead of sonata structure, he preferred short, flexible forms. These mood pieces evoked the favorite images of Impressionist painting: gardens in the rain, sunlight through the leaves, clouds, moonlight, sea, mist.

Debussy worked slowly, and his fame rests on a comparatively small output; *Pelléas and Mélisande* is viewed by many as his greatest achievement. Among the orchestral compositions, the *Prelude to "The Afternoon of a Faun"* is firmly established in public favor, as are the three nocturnes (*Clouds, Festivals, Sirens*) and *La mer* (*The Sea*). His handling of the orchestra is inherently French, allowing individual instruments to stand out against the mass. In his scores, the lines are widely spaced, the texture light and airy.

Orchestral works

Debussy chose this Japanese print, The Hollow of the Wave off Kanagawa *by* **Katsushioka Hokusai** *(1760–1849), for the front cover of his orchestral work* La mer. *(Metropolitan Museum of Art; Bequest of Mrs. H. O. Havemeyer, 1929, The H. O. Havemeyer Collection)*

Piano works   Debussy was one of the important piano composers; he created a distinctive new style of writing for the instrument. The widely spaced chords with their parallel successions of seconds, fourths, and fifths form a sonorous halo. He exploited the resources of the instrument with infinite finesse—the contrast of low and high registers, the blending of sounds through the use of the pedal, the clash of overtones. His piano pieces form an essential part of the modern repertory. Among the best-known are *Clair de lune* (Moonlight, the most popular piece he ever wrote), *Evening in Granada, Reflections in the Water,* and *The Sunken Cathedral.* Many of his piano works demonstrate an interest in non-Western scales and instruments, which he first heard at the Paris Exhibition in 1889 (see CP 16).

Vocal and chamber music   Debussy was one of the most influential among the group of composers who established the French song as a national art form independent of the German Lied. His settings of the French Symbolists Baudelaire, Verlaine, and Mallarmé are marked by exquisite refinement. In chamber music, he achieved an unqualified success with his String Quartet in G minor. The three sonatas of his last years—for cello and piano; violin and piano; and flute, viola, and harp—reveal him as moving toward a more abstract and concentrated style.

PRELUDE TO "THE AFTERNOON OF A FAUN"

Debussy's best-known orchestral work was inspired by a pastoral of Stéphane Mallarmé that evokes a landscape of antiquity. The poem centers on the faun,

Cultural Perspective 16

The Paris World Exhibition of 1889: A Cultural Awakening

How and when did people from distant regions of the world interact before the era of jet travel and electronic communications? One kind of event that has long brought people from various cultures together is a world exposition. In the nineteenth century, an exhibition was a way of demonstrating European domination, where countries proudly organized exhibits from their colonies around the world. France hosted such a happening in 1867, at which the most popular exhibit was a large-scale model of the newly built Suez Canal, the waterway through Egypt that connects the Mediterranean and Indian oceans. One French writer described the many different musical instruments he heard at the exposition—from Mexico, Japan, Siam (now Thailand), and Brazil, and of various Native American tribes. His book also praised the Steinway Piano Company of New York, which provided pianos for the event far superior to any built in Europe.

In 1889, France presented another exposition, this one marking the centenary of the French Revolution. The Eiffel Tower was the French showcase for this world's fair. Musicians from around the world performed here for a receptive European public, who were impressed by the fine singing of Russian choirs, famous for their so-called Russian basses—men with extraordinarily low vocal ranges. One of the most popular of all the exhibits was that from the Indonesian island of Java; this featured dancers and a gamelan. (You will remember that a gamelan is an ensemble of mainly percussion instruments—including gongs, chimes, and drums, among others.) Many classical composers, including Claude Debussy, heard this game-

lan for the first time. Debussy wrote of its unique sound to a friend: "Do you not remember the Javanese music able to express every nuance of meaning, even unmentionable shades, and which makes our tonic and dominant seem like empty phantoms for the use of unwise infants?" He attempted to capture something of this sound—its pentatonic scale, unusual timbre, and texture—in a number of his compositions, including the famous orchestral tone poem *La Mer* (*The Sea,* 1905), the piano work *Pagodas* (from *Estampes,* 1903), and a number of his piano preludes.

Other events sparked the imagination of visitors to the Paris Exhibition. Evening festivities included a parade of musicians representing the African nations of Algeria, Senegal, and the Congo, as well as Java, Anam (now Vietnam), and New Caledonia (a Pacific island off the Australian coast). Performances included belly dancers and whirling dervishes from the Middle East (see p. 236); African-American cakewalk dancers from the southern United States (a cakewalk was a dance of nineteenth-century origin that featured rhythmic strutting and prancing arm in arm in a parody of white plantation owners' behavior); and dancing women from Cambodia. This last group inspired a watercolor drawing, *Cambodian Dancing Girl,* by the famous artist and sculptor Auguste Rodin and a poem by French writer Pierre Louÿs entitled *The Dancing Girl with Crotales* (a kind of small cymbal), which is the basis for a Debussy piano work of the same name (from a collection called *Six Antique Epigraphs,* 1914).

Folk and popular musics traversed cultural boundaries at the Paris Exhibition. It was

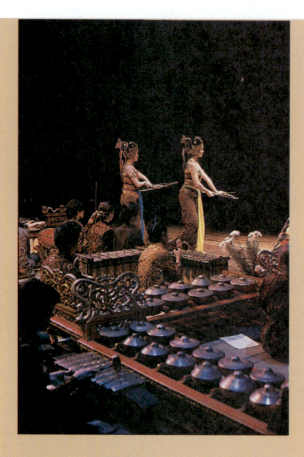

Visible standing in front of this gamelan orchestra from Java are two dancers holding bow and arrow as part of the work they are performing. (Photo by Jack Vartoogian)

there that Debussy was introduced to traditional Russian songs in settings by Rimsky-Korsakov as well as the music of Hungarian and Spanish Gypsies. Like Bizet, Debussy attempted to capture the rhythms of the habanera and the strumming style of flamenco guitars in several of his piano works (*The Interrupted Serenade* and *Evening in Granada*).

Today, world expositions more freely offer opportunities for cultural and artistic exchanges from across the globe. But we do not have to wait for such events to witness a performance from some distant region; we have only to tune in a PBS (Public Broadcasting System) special on, for example, Mexican mariachi bands or view a library video on Japanese Noh drama to broaden our cultural experiences and to stimulate our eyes, our ears, and our imagination.

Terms to Note:

Russian bass
gamelan
cakewalk

Suggested Listening:

Debussy: *La mer, Pagodas* (from *Estampes*),
    or *Evening in Grenada*
Javanese music (gamelan orchestra)

a mythological creature of the forest that is half man, half goat. This "simple sensuous passionate being" awakes in the woods and tries to remember. Was he visited by three lovely nymphs, or was this but a dream? He will never know. The sun is warm, the earth fragrant. He curls himself up and falls into a wine-drugged sleep.

The work is in sections that follow the familiar pattern of statement-departure-return. Yet the movement is fluid and rhapsodic. Almost every fragment of melody is repeated immediately, a trait that the composer carries to an extreme. Characteristic is the relaxed rhythm that flows across the bar line in a continuous stream. By weakening and even wiping out the accent, Debussy achieved that dreamlike fluidity that is a prime trait of Impressionist music.

We first hear a flute solo in the velvety lower register. The melody glides along the chromatic scale, narrow in range and languorous. (See Listening Guide 56 for themes and an excerpt from the poem.) Glissandos on the harp usher in a brief dialogue in the horns. This mixture of colors had never been heard before.

Next, a more decisive motive emerges, marked *en animant* (growing lively). This is followed by a third theme, marked *même movement et très soutenu* (same tempo and very sustained). It is an ardent melody that carries the composition to an emotional climax. The first melody then returns in an altered guise. At the close, antique cymbals are heard, *pianissimo.* (*Antique cymbals* are small disks of brass; the rims are struck together gently and allowed to vibrate.) "Blue" chords are heard on the muted horns and violins, sounding infinitely remote. The work dissolves into silence. It takes nine minutes to play. Rarely has so much been said in so brief a time.

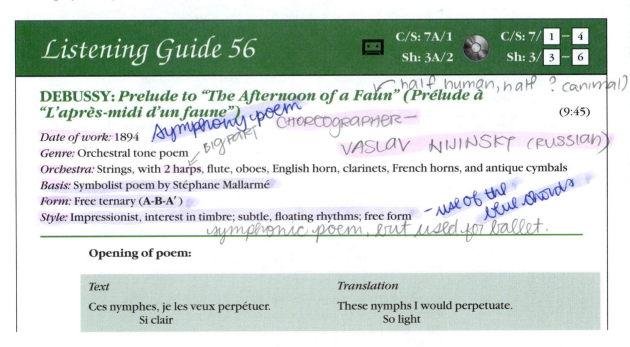

Listening Guide 56

C/S: 7A/1 Sh: 3A/2

C/S: 7/ 1 – 4 Sh: 3/ 3 – 6

DEBUSSY: *Prelude to "The Afternoon of a Faun" (Prélude à "L'après-midi d'un faune")*

(9:45)

half human, half ? (animal)

Date of work: 1894 *Symphony poem* *CHOREOGRAPHER — VASLAV NIJINSKY (Russian)* *big part*
Genre: Orchestral tone poem
Orchestra: Strings, with 2 harps, flute, oboes, English horn, clarinets, French horns, and antique cymbals
Basis: Symbolist poem by Stéphane Mallarmé
Form: Free ternary (**A-B-A′**)
Style: Impressionist, interest in timbre; subtle, floating rhythms; free form *— use of the blue chords*

symphonic poem, but used for ballet.

Opening of poem:

Text	Translation
Ces nymphes, je les veux perpétuer.	These nymphs I would perpetuate.
Si clair	So light

7s - flute (1st instru.)
21s - harp (2nd instrument)
27s - french horn (3rd instrument)S
muted Sound of brass

Leur incarnat léger, qu'il voltige dans l'air
Assoupi de sommeils touffus.
      Amais-je un rêve?
Mon doute, amas de nuit ancienne, s'achève
En maint rameau subtil, qui, de meuré les vrais
Bois mêmes, prouve, hélas! que bien seul je
    m'offrais
Pour triomphe la faute idéale de roses.
 	
Réfléchissons . . . ou si les femmes dont tu
    gloses
Figurent un souhait de tes sens fabuleux!
	their gossamer embodiment, floating on the air
	inert with heavy slumber.
	      Was it a dream I loved?
	My doubting harvest of the bygone night ends
	in countless tiny branches; together remaining
	a whole forest, they prove, alas, that since I am
	    alone,
	my fancied triumph was but the ideal imperfec-
	    tion of roses.
	
	Let us reflect . . . or suppose those women that
	    you idolize
	were but imaginings of your fantastic lust!

1 0:00   **A** SECTION
Opening chromatic melody in flute; passes from one instrument to another, accompanied by muted strings and vague beat:

2:45   **B** SECTION
Clarinet introduces more animated idea, answered by rhythmic figure in cellos

2 3:15   New theme, more animated rhythmically in solo oboe, builds in *crescendo*:

3 4:33   Contrasting theme in woodwinds, then strings, with syncopated rhythms, builds to climax:

4 6:21   **A′** SECTION
Abridged return, in varied setting

64

Ravel and Post-Impressionism

"I did my work slowly, drop by drop. I tore it out of me by pieces."

Maurice Ravel was a post-Impressionist whose instinctive need for order and clarity of organization impelled him to return to basic conceptions of form. Thus his art unfolded between the ideals of Impressionism and Neo-classicism.

His Life

Maurice Ravel (1875–1937) was born in Ciboure, near St.-Jean-de-Luz, in the Basses-Pyrénées region at the southwestern tip of France. The family moved to Paris shortly after Maurice was born. His father, a mining engineer who had aspired to be a musician, was sympathetic to the son's artistic talents. Maurice entered the conservatory when he was fourteen, and remained there for sixteen years—an unusually long apprenticeship.

Ravel's artistic development was greatly stimulated by his friendship with a group of avant-garde poets, painters, and musicians who believed in his gifts long before those were recognized by the world at large. Youthful enthusiasts, they called themselves the *apaches* (the French word for "ruffians" or "common criminals"). In this atmosphere, the young composer found the intellectual companionship he needed. Ravel's career more or less followed the same course as that of many leaders of the modern movement in art. At first, his music was hissed by the audiences and denounced by the critics. Only a few recognized the special quality of his work, but their number steadily grew. Ultimately the tide turned, and he found himself famous.

In the years after the First World War, Ravel came into his own. He was acknowledged to be the foremost composer in France and was much in demand to conduct his works throughout Europe. In 1928, he was invited to tour the United States. Before he would consider the offer, he had to be assured of a steady supply of his favorite French wines and cigarettes. Ravel and America took to one another, although he tired first. "I am seeing magnificent cities, enchanting country," he wrote home, "but the triumphs are fatiguing. Besides, I was dying of hunger."

Toward the end of his life, Ravel was tormented by restlessness and insomnia. He found comfort in the hectic atmosphere of the Parisian nightclubs, where he would listen for hours to American jazz. As he approached sixty, he fell victim to a rare brain disease that attacked the centers of speech and motor coordination. It gradually became impossible for him to read notes, to remember tunes, or to write. So as not to watch himself "go piece by piece," as he put it, he decided to submit to a dangerous operation. This was performed toward the end of 1937. He never regained consciousness.

Maurice Ravel

Early years

American trip

Last years

His Music

Like Debussy, Ravel was a national artist to the core. He was drawn, along with Debussy, to the images that fascinated the Impressionist painters: daybreak, the sea, the interplay of water and light. He too exploited Spanish dance rhythms, worshipped the old French harpsichordists, and was attracted to the scales of Medieval as well as foreign musics.

But the differences in the music of the two composers are as pronounced as the similarities. Ravel's music has an enameled brightness that contrasts with the twilight softness of Debussy's. His rhythms are more incisive and marked by a drive that Debussy rarely strives for. His sense of key is firmer, his harmony is more dissonant, and his melodies are broader in span. Unlike

Comparison with Debussy

Principal Works

Orchestral music, including *Rapsodie espagnole* (*Spanish Rhapsody,* 1908), *Pavane pour une infante défunte* (Pavane for a Dead Princess, 1910), *Le tombeau de Couperin* (1919), Piano Concerto for the Left Hand (1930), and Piano Concerto in G (1931)

Ballets, including *Ma mère l'oye* (*Mother Goose,* 1911), *Daphnis et Chloé* (1912), *La valse* (1920), and *Boléro* (1928)

2 operas: *L'heure espagnole* (The Spanish Hour, 1911) and *L'enfant et les sortilèges* (The Child and the Enchantments, 1925)

Chamber music, including a string quartet (1903) and sonatas (violin and violin/cello)

Piano music, including *Pavane pour une infante défunte* (1908, later orchestrated), *Jeux d'eau* (Water Games, 1901), *Gaspard de le nuit* (Gaspard of the Night, 1908), *Ma mère l'oye* (4 hands, 1910; later orchestrated), and *Le tombeau de Couperin* (1917, later orchestrated)

Songs with instruments, including *Shéhérazade* (1903) and *Chansons madécasses* (*Songs of Madagascar,* 1925–26); songs with piano

Debussy's, Ravel's orchestration derives from the nineteenth-century masters; he stands in the line of descent from Berlioz, Rimsky-Korsakov, and Richard Strauss. Where Debussy aimed to "decongest" sound, Ravel handled the huge orchestra of the post-Romantic period with brilliant virtuosity. And he was drawn to the Classical forms much earlier in his career than Debussy, who turned to them only toward the end.

One of the outstanding piano composers of the twentieth century, Ravel extended the heritage of Liszt even as Debussy became the disciple of Chopin. He was a master of the French art song. Among his most impressive works in this genre are two exotic song cycles: *Shéhérazade,* which is loosely connected with *The Arabian Nights,* and the powerful *Songs of Madagascar,* which we will study.

It was, however, through his orchestral works that Ravel won the admiration of the international public. The *Spanish Rhapsody, Mother Goose,* and the concert versions of the ballets *Daphnis and Chloé, La valse,* and *Boléro* have remained among the most frequently performed works of our century. Widely admired too are the classically oriented Piano Concerto in G and the dramatic Concerto for the Left Hand, a masterpiece.

Ravel, like Debussy, has become immensely popular in the United States. His harmonies and orchestration held a particular attraction for jazz arrangers and Hollywood composers. As a result, his idiom—somewhat altered, to be sure—became part of the daily listening experience of millions of Americans.

Cultural Perspective 17

A Composer's World of Musical Styles

While some composers focus on developing their own national musical styles, others exhibit a passion for those of foreign cultures. Few composers, however, were as broad-ranging in their interests as Maurice Ravel. In addition to his attraction to Africa (as seen in *Songs of Madagascar*), Ravel's tastes leaned toward East Asian, Spanish, Basque, Greek, Hebrew, and African-American musics.

Born in the Basque region of southern France (in the Pyrénées, a mountain range that separates Spain from France), Ravel did not quickly forget the modal melodies and harmonies of his youth, which echo in much of his music. His fascination for Spanish dances is manifested in several pieces. Rich with Iberian color, his *Spanish Rhapsody* (*Rapsodie espagnole,* 1907) sounds the rhythms of the malaguena (one of many types of flamenco music that feature guitar strumming) and the habanera (with its characteristic rhythmic ostinato; see pp. 165, 171), which we have already heard in Bizet's *Carmen.* Ravel's most famous work, the hypnotic *Boléro* for orchestra, was originally a one-act ballet built on the characteristic bass and accompanying percussion figures of a popular Spanish dance form. Often thought of as an erotic work, *Boléro* is based on an insistent rhythmic pattern that is altogether memorable.

One of Ravel's last works was *Don Quixote to Dulcinea* (1933), a song cycle based on the writings of Miguel de Cervantes that was intended for a film of *Don Quixote.* This three-movement piece features three distinct rhythmic styles: a guajira (of Cuban origin), with shifting 3/4 and 6/8 meters; a Basque zortziko, in a rapid quintuple meter; and a jota, a leaping dance from northern Spain. His violin work *Tzigane* (1924), which means "Gypsy," is a showy concert rhapsody with many exciting and exotic effects.

Like Debussy, Ravel attended the 1889 World Exhibition in Paris, and heard there the sounds of the Far East. Not surprisingly, one of his early works, the orchestral song cycle *Shéhérazade* (1903), includes what he believed was a Persian melody and was inspired by the Arabian folk tales of *The Thousand and One Nights* (sometimes called *Arabian Nights* and the source for the stories of Aladdin and Ali Baba). Included in his *Mother Goose Suite* (originally for piano) is the piece *Laideronnette, Empress of the Pagodas,* based on a fairy tale about an empress who is serenaded during her bath by creatures playing string instruments made from nut shells. Here Ravel uses a pentatonic scale (this one formed by the black keys on the piano) along with grace-note melodic inflections and percussive effects, characteristics that the composer associated with music of East Asia.

Finally, we can see the full breadth of Ravel's interests by turning to several other of his works. One song collection features arrangements of five popular Greek melodies (1904–6), and another originally contained arrangements of Hebrew, Scottish, Italian, Flemish, Russian, Spanish, and French tunes (*Chansons populaires,* 1910). Ravel also drew on American popular music, especially the African-American styles of ragtime, blues, and jazz, heard in his stage work *The Child and the Enchantments,* his Violin Sonata (the second movement is entitled "Blues,") and his two piano concertos. In short, Ravel

Just as **Henri Rousseau** *(1844–1910) found his subject matter in the images of distant places, so did Ravel seek inspiration in the world's musics.* The Sleeping Gypsy *(1897).* (Museum of Modern Art, N.Y., gift of Mrs. Simon Guggenheim)

tried his hand at a global range of styles. Although he did not have first-hand knowledge of each of the cultures he emulated, he held a vision of the universality of music that was far ahead of his time.

Suggested Listening:

Ravel works (*Songs of Madagascar, Boléro, Rapsodie espagnole, Shéhérazade, Tzigane*)

SONGS OF MADAGASCAR

The text for this song cycle was drawn from a collection of poems by Evariste-Désiré de Parny (1753–1814). In his preface, the poet tried to describe the people of the African nation of Madagascar, even though he had never visited the island and did not know the language. The poems, consequently, were mostly of his own invention, although he claimed that they were derived from the folk songs he had collected.

Ravel was always attracted to unusual subjects; in this case, the language and imagery of Parny's poetry captured his imagination. The spark was provided by the American patron Elizabeth Sprague Coolidge, who in 1925 commissioned Ravel to write a song cycle. The choice of poetry was left to the composer, but Mrs. Coolidge specified an accompaniment of flute, cello, and piano. Ravel described the resulting work as "a sort of quartet in which the voice has the role of the leading instrument." He thought the cycle introduced "a new—even erotic—element stemming from the subject matter of Parny's songs." It dealt with three subjects—love, war, and idleness.

The second song, "Do Not Trust the White Men" ("Méfiez-vous des blancs"), describes the arrival on the African island of white men, who came uttering friendly words and eventually slaughtered the natives. This poem is a passionate outcry against the evils of colonialism. Ravel's song provoked a scandal at its premiere in Paris. At the time, France was fighting to regain control of its African empire, and patriotic Frenchmen regarded the sentiments of the song as treason.

The song opens with a wild cry of outrage—"Aoua!"—followed by a warning, "Don't trust the white men, inhabitants of these shores." (For the text and analysis, see Listening Guide 57.) Clangorous dissonances underline the danger. Then, against a darkly sinister background, the voice traces the deceit and cruelty that the Europeans inflicted on the natives. The anger builds gradually, unstoppable, until it explodes in a shattering climax. The music subsides to the final "Aoua!" and a repetition of the basic warning, now *pianissimo*. Ravel rightly considered *Songs of Madagascar* to be among his greatest works.

Listening Guide 57

C/S: 7A/6   C/S: 7/ 19 – 20

RAVEL: *Songs of Madagascar (Chansons madécasses)*, Second Movement

(3:42)

Date of work: 1925–26
Genre: Song cycle with chamber ensemble
Medium: Mezzo-soprano, flute, cello, piano
Basis: Poems by Evariste-Désiré de Parny
Movements:
    I. "Nahandove"
    II. "Do Not Trust the White Men" ("Méfiez-vous des blancs")
    III. "It Is Good to Lie Down" ("Il est doux de se coucher")

II. "Do Not Trust the White Men" ("Méfiez-vous des blancs")

	Text	Translation	Description
19 0:00	Aoua! Aoua! Méfiez-vous des blancs, habitans du rivage.	Aoua! Aoua! Do not trust the white men, those who live on these shores.	*Fortissimo* opening cry, dissonant piano accompaniment; recitative-like style; small range, conjunct, un-
	Du temps de nos pères, des blancs descendirent dans cette île;	From our father's time, white men have descended upon this island;	

	on leur dit: Voilà des terres; que vos femmes les cultivent.	they were told: "Here is the soil; have your women cultivate it.		dulating; soft, sinister accompaniment
	Soyez justes, soyez bons, et devenez nos frères.	Be fair, be kind, and become our brothers."		
	Les blancs promirent, et cependant ils faisaient des retranchements.	The white men promised, and yet they built entrenchments.		
	Un fort menaçant s'éleva; le tonnerre fut renfermé dans des bouches d'airain;	A menacing fort was erected; thunder was enclosed in brass mouths;		
1:40	leurs prêtres voulurent nous donner un Dieu que nous ne connaissons pas;	their priests wished to give us a God we did not know;		Builds up speed, volume, and drama
	ils parlèrent enfin d'obéissance et d'esclavage; plûtot la mort!	they finally spoke of obedience and slavery; what's more, of death!		
	Le carnage fut long et terrible; mais, malgré la foudre qu'ils vomissaient,	The carnage was long and terrible; but, in spite of the lightning they belched forth,		
	et qui écrasait des armées entières, ils furent tous exterminés.	annihilating whole armies, they were all destroyed.		
2:13	Aoua! Aoua! Méfiez-vous des blancs!	Aoua! Aoua! Do not trust the white men!		Opening cry heard again—loud, in high range, more rhythmic, accented style
2:20	Nous avons vu de nouveaux tyrans, plus forts et plus nombreux,	We have seen new tyrants, stronger and more numerous,		
	planter leur pavillon sur le rivage; le ciel a combattu pour nous;	raise their tents on the shore; the heavens waged war for us,		
	il a fait tomber sur eux les pluies, les tempêtes, et les vents empoisonnés.	unleashing rains, storms, and poisonous winds.		Builds to climax on high note
	Ils ne sont plus, et nous vivons, et nous vivons libres.	They are gone, and we live, and we live freely.		Slower, more deliberate
2:52	Aoua! Aoua! Méfiez-vous des blancs, habitans du rivage.	Aoua! Aoua! Do not trust the white men, those who live on these shores.		Adagio, soft statement of opening cry

20 2:20

Opening vocal cry:

Aoua!＿＿ Aoua!＿＿ Méfi‐ez‐vous des blancs, ha‐bi‐ tans du ri‐va‐ ge.

Recitative-like vocal line; conjunct, with small range:

Du temps de nos pè‐res, des blancs de‐scen‐ di‐rent dans cette î‐le;

UNIT XXII

■

The Early Twentieth Century

65

Main Currents in Early Twentieth-Century Music

"The entire history of modern music may be said to be a history of the gradual pull-away from the German musical tradition of the past century." —AARON COPLAND

The Reaction Against Romanticism

As the quotation from Aaron Copland implies, the new generation of composers had to fight not only the Romantic past but the Romanticism in themselves. The new attitudes took hold just before the outbreak of the First World War. European art sought to escape its overrefinement and tried to capture the spontaneity and the freedom from inhibition that was associated with primitive life. Composers turned to the dynamism of non-Western rhythm even as the fine arts discovered the abstraction of African sculpture and the monumental simplicity of the exotic paintings of Paul Gauguin and Henri Rousseau. Fresh concepts were sought in the musics of Africa, Asia, and eastern Europe. Out of the unspoiled, vigorous traditional music in these areas came powerful rhythms of an elemental fury, as in Bartók's *Allegro barbaro* (1911) and Stravinsky's *Rite of Spring* (1913).

The powerful abstraction of African sculpture helped European art overcome its overrefinement. A bronze musician from Nigeria. (Photo by Lee Boltin)

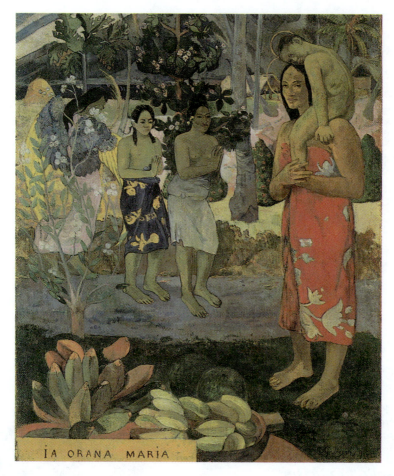

IA ORANA MARIA

Parisian painter **Paul Gauguin** *(1848–1903) was drawn to the simplicity of Tahitian life and the emotional directness of his native subjects. His attention to primitive elements, as seen in* Orana Maria *(1891), has influenced nearly every school of twentieth-century art.* (Metropolitan Museum of Art, bequest of Sam A. Lewisohn, 1951)

New Trends in the Arts

We have seen that changing currents in art and literature nearly always have parallels in music. In the years immediately preceding the First World War, the Italian movement known as Futurism attracted musicians who aspired to an "art of noise" that foreshadowed the music of Edgard Varèse and the electronic music in the 1950s. Another influential movement was Dadaism, which was founded in Switzerland and after 1918 spread to other major art centers.

Dadaism   The Dadaists, principally writers and artists who reacted to the horrors of the bloodbath that had engulfed Europe, rejected the concept of Art with a capital A—that is, something to be put on a pedestal and reverently admired. To make their point, they produced works of absolute absurdity. They also reacted against the excessive complexity of Western art and tried to recapture the simple way in which a child views the world.

Following their example, the French composer Erik Satie led the way toward a simple, "everyday" music, and exerted an important influence—along with the writer Jean Cocteau—on the group called *Les Six* (see Chapter 71).

Marcel Duchamp
(1887-1968), in Nude Descending a Staircase, No. 2, *organized the indiscipline of Dada into a visionary art.* (Philadelphia Museum of Art, Louise and Walter Arensberg Collection)

Several decades later, this influence was clearly apparent in the work of the American composer John Cage, who will be discussed in a later chapter.

The Dada group, which included artists like Hans Arp and Marcel Duchamp, subsequently merged into the school of Surrealism, as exemplified by Salvador Dali, who exploited the world of dreams. Other styles of modern art included Cubism, the Paris-based style of painting embodied in the work of Pablo Picasso, Georges Braque, and Juan Gris, which encouraged the painter to construct a visual world in terms of geometric patterns; and Expressionism, which we will see had a significant impact on music of the early twentieth century.

Subsequent styles

Expressionism

Expressionism was the German answer to French Impressionism. Whereas the French genius rejoiced in luminous impressions of the outer world, the Germanic temperament preferred digging down to the depths of the soul. As with Impressionism, the impulse for the movement came from painting. Wassily Kandinsky (1866-1944), Paul Klee (1879-1940), and Oskar Kokoschka (1886-1980) influenced Arnold Schoenberg and his followers even

Expressionist values

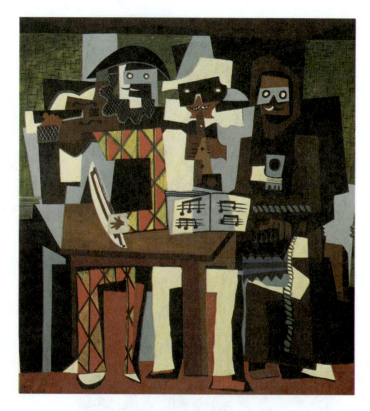

Pablo Picasso *(1881-1974) constructs a visual world of Cubist patterns in* Three Musicians. (Philadelphia Museum of Art, A. E. Gallatin Collection)

as the Impressionist painters influenced Debussy. Expressionism is familiar to Americans not only through the paintings of Kandinsky and Klee, but also in the writings of Franz Kafka (1883–1924). Expressionism in music triumphed first in the Germanic central European area and reached its full tide in the dramatic works of the second Viennese school.

The language of Expressionism

The musical language of Expressionism favored a hyperexpressive harmonic language linked to inordinately wide leaps in the melody and to the use of instruments in their extreme registers. Expressionist music soon reached the boundaries of what was possible within the major-minor system. Inevitably, it had to push beyond.

The New Classicism

One way of rejecting the nineteenth century was to return to the eighteenth. The "back to Bach" movement assumed impressive proportions in the early 1920s. There was no question here of duplicating the music of the Baroque master; the slogan implied rather a revival of certain principles that appeared to have been best understood in his time. Instead of revering Beethoven and Wagner, as the Romantics had done, composers began to emulate the great musicians of the eighteenth century—Bach, Handel, Scarlatti, Couperin, Vivaldi—and the detached, objective style that is often associated with their music.

The New Classicism (also called Neoclassicism) tried to rid music of the story-and-picture meanings favored in the nineteenth century. The New Classicists turned away from the symphonic poem and the Romantic attempt to bring music closer to poetry and painting. They preferred absolute to program music, and they focused attention on craftsmanship and balance, a positive affirmation of the Classical virtues of objectivity and control.

Absolute music

66

New Elements of Musical Style

"Music is now so foolish that I am amazed. Everything that is wrong is permitted, and no attention is paid to what the old generation wrote as composition."—SAMUEL SCHEIDT

The New Rhythmic Complexity

Twentieth-century music turned away from the standard rhythmic patterns of duple, triple, or quadruple meter. Rather, composers explored the possibilities of nonsymmetrical patterns based on odd numbers: five, seven, eleven, thirteen beats to the measure. In nineteenth-century music, a single meter customarily prevailed through an entire movement or section. Now the metrical flow shifted constantly, sometimes with each measure. Formerly, one rhythmic pattern was used at a time. Now composers turned to *polyrhythm*— the simultaneous use of several rhythmic patterns. As a result of these innovations, Western music achieved something of the complexity and suppleness of Asian and African rhythms.

Polyrhythm

The new generation of composers preferred freer rhythms that were flexible in the highest degree, of an almost physical power and drive. Indeed, the revitalization of rhythm is one of the major achievements of early twentieth-century music.

The New Melody

Rhythm was not the only element in which symmetrical structure was abandoned; melody was affected too. Twentieth-century composers did not develop the neatly balanced phrase repetitions that prevailed formerly. Their ideal was a direct, forward-driving melody from which all nonessentials had been cut away. They assumed a quicker perception on the part of the hearer than did composers in the past.

Nineteenth-century melody was fundamentally vocal in character; composers tried then to make the instruments "sing." Early twentieth-century melody was neither unvocal nor antivocal; it was simply not conceived in re-

Instrumental melody

lation to the voice. It abounded in wide leaps and dissonant intervals. Besides, much twentieth-century music lacked a melodic orientation. Sometimes no melody is to be found because the composer had other goals in mind. Twentieth-century composers have greatly expanded our notion of what a melody is. As a result, many patterns are accepted as melodies today that would hardly have been considered as such a century ago.

The New Harmony

Polychords and polyharmony

No single factor sets off early twentieth-century music from that of the past more decisively than the new conceptions of harmony that emerged in the twentieth century. The triads of traditional harmony, we saw, were formed by combining three tones, on every other degree of the scale, or in thirds: 1-3-5 (for example, C-E-G), 2-4-6 (D-F-A), and so on. Traditional harmony also employed four-note combinations, with another third piled on top of the triad, known as seventh chords (1-3-5-7), and, as we saw in the music of the Impressionists, five-note combinations known as ninth chords (1-3-5-7-9). Twentieth-century composers added more "stories" to such chords, forming highly dissonant *polychords* of six and seven notes. The emergence of these complex "skyscraper" chords brought greater tension to music than had existed before, and allowed the composer to play two or more streams of harmony against each other, creating *polyharmony.*

NEW CONCEPTIONS OF TONALITY

The new sounds of twentieth-century music necessarily burst the confines of traditional tonality and called for new means of organization, extending or replacing the major-minor system. These approaches, in general, followed four principal paths—expanded tonality, polytonality, atonality, and twelve-tone music.

The widespread use of chromatic harmony in the late nineteenth century led, in the early twentieth, to the free use of all twelve tones around a center. Although this approach retained the basic principle of traditional tonality—gravitation to the tonic—it wiped out the distinction between diatonic and chromatic and between major and minor modes. The expansion of tonality was encouraged by the increased interest in the music of non-Western cultures as well as in the Medieval church modes, as we have already noted.

Polytonality

From the development of polyharmony, a further step followed logically: heightening the contrast of two keys by presenting them simultaneously, or *polytonality.* Confronting the ear with two keys at the same time meant a radical departure from the basic principle of traditional harmony, a single central key. Polytonality came into prominence with the music of Stravinsky; one of the earliest works to use this harmonic system is the ballet *Petrushka,* which we will study. Toward the end of a piece, one key was generally permitted to assert itself over the others. In this way, the impression was restored of orderly progression toward a central point.

Atonality

The concept of total abandonment of tonality is associated with the composer Arnold Schoenberg, whom we shall meet later. He advocated doing away with the tonic by giving the twelve tones of the chromatic scale equal importance—thus achieving *atonal* music. Atonality was much more of an innovation than polytonality, for it entirely rejected the framework of key. Consonance, according to Schoenberg, was no longer capable of making an impression; atonal music moved from one level of dissonance to another, functioning always at maximum tension, without areas of relaxation.

THE TWELVE-TONE METHOD

Having accepted the necessity of moving beyond the existing tonal system, Schoenberg sought a unifying principle that would take the place of the system of tonality. He found this in a strict technique that he had worked out by the early 1920s. He named it "the method of composing with twelve tones"— that is, with twelve equal tones, no one of which is more important than any other. Each composition that uses Schoenberg's method, known as *serialism,* is based on an arrangement of the twelve chromatic tones called a *tone row.* This row is the unifying idea for that particular composition, and serves as the source of all the musical events that take place in it. (The term *dodecaphonic,* the Greek equivalent of *twelve-tone,* is sometimes also used for Schoenberg's method; the term *serial music,* an allusion to the series of twelve tones, has come to refer in more recent decades to postwar extensions of the technique.)

Serialism

The tone row

A tone row thus establishes a series of pitches from which a composer builds themes, harmonies, and counterpoint. Schoenberg provided flexibility and variety in this seemingly confining system through alternative forms of the tone row. Its *transposition* involves beginning the row on other notes. In its *inversion,* the movement of the notes is in the opposite direction, up instead of down and vice versa, so that the row appears upside down. Its *retrograde* is an arrangement of the pitches in reverse order, so that the row comes out backward, and its *retrograde inversion* turns the row upside down and backward. (You will remember that these same techniques were discussed as contrapuntal devices in earlier music, especially in the Baroque fugue.)

Forms of the row

THE EMANCIPATION OF DISSONANCE

The history of music, we have seen, has been the history of a steadily increasing tolerance on the part of listeners. Throughout this long evolution, one factor remained constant: a clear distinction was drawn between dissonance, the element of tension, and consonance, the element of rest. Consonance was the norm, dissonance the temporary disturbance. In many contemporary works, however, tension becomes the norm. Therefore, a dissonance can serve even as a final cadence, provided it is less dissonant than the chord that came before. In relation to the greater dissonance, it is judged to be consonant. Twentieth-century composers emancipated dissonance by freeing it from the obligation to resolve to consonance. Their music taught listeners to accept tone combinations whose like had never been heard before.

Texture: Dissonant Counterpoint

The nineteenth century was preoccupied with harmony; the early twentieth emphasized counterpoint. The new style swept away the sounds of both the Romantic cloudburst and Impressionistic haze. In their place came an airy linear texture that fit the New Classical ideal of craftsmanship, order, and detachment.

Consonance unites the constituent tones of harmony or counterpoint; dissonance separates them and makes them stand out against each other. Composers began to use dissonance to set off one line against another. Instead of basing their counterpoint on the agreeable intervals of the third and sixth, they turned to astringent seconds and sevenths. Or they might heighten the independence of the voices by putting them in different keys.

Orchestration

The rich sonorities of nineteenth-century orchestration gave way to a leaner sound, one that was hard and bright, played by a smaller orchestra. The decisive factor in the handling of the orchestra was the change to a linear texture. Color came to be used in the new music not so much for atmosphere as for bringing out the lines of counterpoint and of form. The string section lost its traditional role as the heart of the orchestra; its tone was felt to be too warm. Attention was focused on the more penetrating winds. There was a movement away from a radiant sound in favor of darker instruments—viola, bassoon, trombone. The emphasis on rhythm brought the percussion group into greater prominence than ever before, and the piano, which in the Romantic era was preeminently a solo instrument, found a place in the orchestral ensemble.

New Conceptions of Form

The first quarter of the century saw the final expansion of traditional forms in the gigantic symphonies and symphonic poems of Mahler and Strauss. What had been a concise, twenty-five-minute structure in the hands of Haydn and Mozart now took over an hour and a half to play. Music could hardly go further in this direction. A reaction took shape as composers began to move toward the Classical ideals of tight organization and succinctness. In addition, they revived a number of older forms such as toccata, fugue, passacaglia and chaconne, concerto grosso, theme and variations, and suite, as well as the traditional symphony, sonata, and concerto. The tendency to elevate formal *Formalism* above expressive values is known as *formalism.* The New Classicism, like the old, strove for purity of line and proportion.

Popular styles   Composers also vitalized their music through materials drawn from popular styles. Ragtime piano music, with its sprightly syncopations, traveled across the Atlantic to Europe. The rhythmic freedom of jazz captured the ears of many composers, who strove to achieve something of the spontaneity of the popular style. (We will look into the origins of jazz and its influence on other styles in a later chapter.)

67

Stravinsky and the Revitalization of Rhythm

"I hold that it was a mistake to consider me a revolutionary. If one only need break habit in order to be labeled a revolutionary, then every artist who has something to say and who in order to say it steps outside the bounds of established convention could be considered revolutionary."

Certain artists embody the most significant impulses of their time and affect artistic life in the most powerful fashion. Such an artist was Igor Stravinsky, the Russian composer who for half a century reflected the main currents in twentieth-century music.

Igor Stravinsky

His Life

Igor Stravinsky (1882–1971) was born in Oranienbaum, a summer resort not far from St. Petersburg, where his parents lived. He grew up in a musical environment; his father was the leading bass at the Imperial Opera. Although he was taught to play the piano, his musical education was kept on the amateur level; his parents wanted him to study law. He enrolled at the University of St. Petersburg and began his legal education, meanwhile continuing his musical studies. At twenty, he submitted his work to Rimsky-Korsakov, with whom he subsequently worked for three years.

Success came early to Stravinsky. His music attracted the notice of Serge Diaghilev, the legendary impresario of the Paris-based Russian Ballet, who commissioned Stravinsky to write the score for *The Firebird,* which was produced in 1910. Stravinsky was twenty-eight when he arrived in Paris to attend the rehearsals. Diaghilev pointed him out to the ballerina Tamara Karsavina with the words "Mark him well—he is a man on the eve of fame."

Serge Diaghilev

The Firebird was followed a year later by *Petrushka.* Presented with dancers Vaslav Nijinsky and Tamara Karsavina in the leading roles, this production secured Stravinsky's position in the forefront of the modern movement. In the spring of 1913, the third and most spectacular of the ballets Stravinsky wrote for Diaghilev, *The Rite of Spring,* was staged. The opening night was one of the most scandalous in modern musical history; the revolutionary score touched off a near riot. People hooted, screamed, slapped each other, and were convinced that what they were hearing "constituted a blasphemous attempt to destroy music as an art." However, a year later, when the work was presented at a symphony concert under Pierre Monteux, it was received with enthusiasm and established itself as a masterpiece.

The Rite of Spring

The outbreak of war in 1914 brought to an end the whole way of life on which Diaghilev's sumptuous dance spectacles depended. Stravinsky, with his wife and children, took refuge in Switzerland, their home for the next six years. The difficulty of assembling large bodies of performers during the war worked hand in hand with his evolution as an artist: he moved away from the grand scale of the first three ballets to works more intimate in spirit and modest in dimension.

American years

The Russian Revolution had severed Stravinsky's ties with his homeland. In 1920, he settled in France, where he remained until 1939. During these years, Stravinsky concertized extensively throughout Europe, performing his own music as pianist and conductor. He also paid two visits to the United States. In 1939, he was invited to deliver the Charles Eliot Norton lectures at Harvard University. When the Second World War broke out, he decided to settle in California, outside Los Angeles; in 1945, he became an American citizen. In his later years, Stravinsky's worldwide concert tours made him the most celebrated figure in twentieth-century music, and his caustically witty books of "conversations" written with his disciple Robert Craft are full of musical wisdom and footnotes to history. He died in New York on April 6, 1971, at the age of eighty-nine.

His Music

Stravinsky's style evolved continuously throughout his career. This evolution led from the post-Impressionism of *The Firebird* and the primitivism of *The Rite of Spring* to the controlled classicism of his mature style.

Early works

Stravinsky was a leader in the revitalization of European rhythm. His first success was won as a composer of ballet, where rhythm is allied with body movement and expressive gesture. His was a rhythm of unparalleled dynamic power, furious yet controlled. In harmony, Stravinsky reacted against the restless chromaticism of the Romantic period, but no matter how daring his harmony, he retained a sense of key. His subtle sense of sound makes him one of

Principal Works

Orchestral music, including Symphonies of Wind Instruments (1920), Concerto for Piano and Winds (1924), *Dumbarton Oaks Concerto* (1938), Symphony in C (1940), Symphony in Three Movements (1945), and *Ebony Concerto* (1945)

Ballets, including *L'oiseau de feu* (*The Firebird,* 1910), *Petrushka* (1911), *Le sacre du printemps* (*The Rite of Spring,* 1913), *Les noces* (*The Wedding,* 1923), and *Agon* (1957)

Operas, including *The Rake's Progress* (1951); opera-oratorio *Oedipus Rex* (1927); other dramatic works, including *Histoire du soldat* (*The Soldier's Tale,* 1918)

Choral music, including *Symphony of Psalms* (1930), *Canticum sacrum* (1955), *Threni* (1958), and *Requiem Canticles* (1966)

Chamber music; piano music (solo and for two pianos); songs

the great orchestrators. His sonority is marked by an enameled brightness and a texture so clear that, as Diaghilev remarked, "one can see through it with one's ears."

The national element predominates in his early works, as in *The Firebird* and *Petrushka*, in which he found his personal style. *The Rite of Spring* recreates the rites of ancient Russia. The decade of the First World War saw the turn toward simplification of means. *The Soldier's Tale,* a dance-drama for four characters, is an intimate theater work accompanied by a seven-piece band. The most important work of the years that followed is *The Wedding,* a stylization of a Russian peasant wedding.

Stravinsky's Neoclassical period culminated in several major compositions. *Oedipus Rex* is an "opera-oratorio"; the text is a translation into Latin of Jean Cocteau's adaptation of the Greek tragedy by Sophocles. The *Symphony of Psalms,* for chorus and orchestra, is regarded by many as the chief work of Stravinsky's maturity; it was composed, according to the composer, "for the glory of God." Equally admired is *The Rake's Progress,* an opera on a libretto by W. H. Auden and Chester Kallman, after Hogarth's celebrated series of engravings. Written as the composer was approaching seventy, this radiantly melodious score, which uses the set forms of Mozartean opera, is the essence of Neoclassicism. *Neoclassical period*

Stravinsky had still another surprise in store for his public. In the works written after he was seventy, he showed an increasing receptiveness to the serial procedures of the twelve-tone style, which in earlier years he had opposed. This preoccupation revealed itself in a number of works dating from the middle 1950s, of which the most important are the ballet *Agon* and the choral work *Threni: Lamentations of the Prophet Jeremiah.* *Twelve-tone works*

PETRUSHKA

One of the best-known of all ballet scores, *Petrushka* presents the ill-fated adventures of a puppet who suddenly comes to life. The clown with a broken heart (we met the type in Leoncavallo's opera) is known in various locales as Pierrot, Pagliaccio, and Petrushka. Stravinsky called him "the immortal and unhappy hero of every fair in all countries."

The setting—a street fair during Carnival week (called Shrovetide) in St. Petersburg in the 1830s—allowed the composer to evoke the colorful atmosphere of the city he loved. With its liberal use of folk tunes, the work is a legitimate offspring of the Russian national school, and has found an important place in the concert hall as well as in the theater (see CP18).

The opening tableau, or scene, shows the crowds milling about the booths of the fairgrounds. People of all classes mingle; a group of drunkards pass by as children cluster around a peepshow. A man with a hurdy-gurdy appears, accompanied by a dancer. Just as she begins her routine, a man with a music box and another dancer set up on the other side of the stage. Both rivals continue for a short while, then give up and withdraw. Suddenly a drum roll summons the crowd to the little marionette theater in the center of the stage, and the Showman plays his flute. The curtain rises, revealing three puppets— *First tableau*

The original backdrop for the first tableau of Petrushka *established the mood for the entire ballet. The sets and costumes were designed by* **Alexandre Benois,** *who had worked extensively with the Diaghilev company.* (Ella Gallup Sumner and Mary Catlin Sumner Collection; © Wadsworth Athenaeum, Hartford, Conn.)

Petrushka, the Ballerina, and the Moor. The Showman touches the dolls with his flute, whereupon they spring to life. At first, they dance on their hooks in the little theater. Then, to the delight of the audience, they step down and break into the tumultuous Russian dance.

Second and third tableaux   The second tableau, set in Petrushka's room, focuses on the little clown's unhappy love for the Ballerina. She is put off by his appearance and rejects him. The third tableau takes place in the Moor's room. He is brutal and stupid, but the Ballerina is charmed by his good looks and his magnificent uniform. Petrushka, mad with jealousy, interrupts their lovemaking. The Moor throws him out.

Final tableau   In the final tableau, we are back in the fairground. The crowd is festive. Coachmen, grooms, and nursemaids dance merrily. Suddenly there is a commotion in the puppet theater. Petrushka rushes out from behind the curtain, pursued by the Moor, who overtakes him and strikes him with his sword. Petrushka falls, mortally wounded. To the horror of the crowd, he dies. The Showman attempts to reassure the bystanders by shaking the little puppet, showing them that it is only a doll stuffed with sawdust. As he begins to drag the puppet to his room, he catches sight of Petrushka's ghost high above him, grimacing and menacing. He had not foreseen that his creation, through suffering, would develop a soul. Stricken with fear, the Showman drops the doll and steals away.

The opening measures of *Petrushka* evoke the sound of the folk music that surrounded Stravinsky in his childhood. The orchestra teems with movement and excitement. A solo flute, supported by a second flute, presents a synco-pated melody in high register that captures the agitation of this crowd scene. (See Listening Guide 58.) This tune returns as a unifying element throughout.

The music displays the drive and energy of Stravinsky's rhythm, which was based on new concepts involving irregular meters and polyrhythms. These presented unprecedented difficulties for the dancers. As the choreographer for the ballet noted, "It was necessary to explain the musical counts to the dancers. At times it was especially difficult to remember the rapid changes of the beats." Stravinsky's opening passage, for example, alternates 3/4 and 4/4.

Stravinsky drew his melodic inspiration from the folk music of his country. One tune heard in this opening tableau is called the *Song of the Volochebniki* (Singing Beggars), and is a Russian Easter carol. It is set in a narrow range and rooted in the key, moving stepwise along the scale.

This tableau consists of three sections, the first and third of which are ron-dos. Between them is a flute cadenza played by the Showman that leads to the rise of the curtain in the puppet theater and the boisterous Russian Dance, which begins the third section.

The percussive harmony in *Petrushka* became a hallmark of Stravinsky's style. He used a variety of means to achieve his ends: simple diatonic chords to accompany popular tunes; pentatonic, whole-tone, and modal harmonies; and chromatic progressions. This ballet provides a famous example of this polyharmony, where Stravinsky juxtaposes two independent streams of chords clashing against each other. Called the "Petrushka chord," this har-mony consists of a C-major arpeggio superimposed on one built on F-sharp major. These were absolutely new sounds, and they foreshadowed the direc-tion in which harmony would move in the twentieth century and stamped Stravinsky quite early in his career as one of the great innovators.

It was Stravinsky's historic role to sound the spirit of a new era, one that still resounds in our own time. In the closing lines of his autobiography, he wrote: "I live neither in the past nor in the future. I am in the present. I cannot know what tomorrow may bring forth. I can only know what the truth is for me today."

Listening Guide 58

C/S: 7B/1
Sh: 3A/3

C/S: 7/ 25 – 40
Sh: 3/ 7 – 15

STRAVINSKY: *Petrushka*, First Tableau   (9:56)

Date of work: 1911 (revised in 1947)
Genre: Ballet, often performed as concert piece for orchestra
Setting: Admiralty Square, St. Petersburg, in the 1830s, during Shrovetide (Carnival)
Form: 4 tableaux (scenes)
Characters: 3 puppets (Petrushka, Ballerina, Moor), Showman

FIRST TABLEAU: 3 sections

Scenario: *Crowds of people are strolling about the scene—common people, gentlefolk, a group of drunkards arm-in-arm, children clustering round the peepshow, women round the stalls. A street musician appears with a hurdy-gurdy. He is accompanied by a dancer. Just as she starts to dance, a man with a music box and another dancer turn up on the opposite side of the stage. After performing simultaneously for a short while, the rivals give up the struggle and retire. Suddenly the Showman comes out through the curtains of a little theater on the stage. The curtains are drawn back to reveal three puppets on their stands: Petrushka, the Ballerina, and the Moor. The Showman charms them into life with his flute, and they begin to dance—at first they jig on their hooks on the little stage, but then, to everyone's astonishment, they step down and dance among the public.*

SECTION 1: Vivace; rondo form (**A-B-A-C-A-B-A**)

25	0:00	**A**—crowd scene, syncopated, pentatonic flute melody in shifting meters; portrays agitation:	
		Repeated-note figure dominates:	
26	0:53	**B**—Russian folk song, *Song of the Volochebniki;* full orchestra, homophonic texture, accented:	
27	1:35	**A**—crowd scene music returns from opening, in woodwinds with brass interruptions	
28	1:43	**C**—hurdy-gurdy player and 2 dancers Dance tune 1, in 3/4, clarinet:	
29	2:24	Dance tune 2, in 2/4, flutes and triangle:	

30	2:47	Dance tune 1 returns, combined with celesta
31	3:44	**A**—crowd scene music
32	3:57	**B**—*Song of the Volochebniki* in full orchestra
33	4:39	**A**—crowd scene music extended and developed, builds to climax and drum roll

SECTION 2: Lento; through-composed

34	5:26	Drum roll followed by mysterious chords

35	6:08	Flute cadenza (played by Showman), accompanied by chromatic passages in winds and gently moving strings and harp:

Mysterious noises as puppet theater curtain opens

(Shorter recordings stop here.)

SECTION 3: Allegro, Russian Dance; rondo form (A-B-A-B-A)

36	7:35	**A**—dance theme, full orchestra with piano and xylophone in 2/4:

37	7:43	**B**—fragment of Russian folk song for St. John's Eve, in oboe and strings, punctuated by piano
38	8:09	**A**—dance theme returns, slows down in various instruments, including piano
39	8:17	**B**—folk song for St. John's Eve heard in various instruments; oboe, then piano:

40	9:15	**A**—dance theme in piano then orchestra, comes to sudden ending; stage goes dark; long trumpet note

Cultural Perspective 18

Petrushka and **Russian Folk Traditions**

What are the native folk traditions and songs that attracted the composer Igor Stravinsky when writing his ballets? And what is particularly Russian about them? Stravinsky followed in the footsteps of his friend and mentor Nicolai Rimsky-Korsakov in his use of Russian folklore and traditional melodies. In his first ballet, *The Firebird,* Stravinsky explores a native folk legend, drawing several memorable themes from his country's rich arsenal of traditional songs.

As in many countries, the festivities celebrated in the Russian countryside combine Christian and older rites. Thus Stravinsky's setting for his second ballet, *Petrushka,* is Shrovetide, or Carnival (known in Russia as Maslenitza, or Butterweek). This is a pre-Lenten celebration marked by merrymaking and feasting, celebrated throughout the Christian world in preparation for the penitential Easter season. Among the five traditional songs the composer used in *Petrushka* were one for Easter and one for St. John's Eve (Midsummer Night).

Stravinsky learned several of these songs from a collection compiled by Rimsky-Korsakov entitled *100 Russian Folk Songs.* Among these was the Easter carol *Song of the Volochebniki,* heard in the first tableau of *Petruskha.* This folk song concerns a group of singing beggars who went from house to house offering Easter greetings. The traditional greeting "For Jesus Christ is arisen" was exchanged not only by beggars but by family and friends as well; the standard reply, "He is indeed risen," was accompanied by kissing on each cheek. The text details the beggars' demands from a farmer—some eggs,

a chicken pie, a hunk of beef.

Like many folk songs, this one is strophic but with every other line repeating the traditional Easter refrain. The tune, spanning only the range of a fifth, is enlivened by occasional shifts from duple to triple meter (Example 1).

Another Russian traditional tune heard in the first part of *Petrushka* is the *Song for St. John's Eve,* which evokes the spirit typical of Midsummer Night celebrations. Associated with festivities surrounding the summer solstice (which marks the longest day of the year by the sun's position), Midsummer Night is, on the Christian calendar, preparatory to the popular religious feast of St. John the Baptist (June 24). Traditional celebrations involved excited dancing around a ritual bonfire coupled with wanton behavior. You may remember tales of this eve from Shakespeare's play *A Midsummer Night's Dream,* in which groups of lovers spend the night in the forest, victims of fairies' pranks and enchantments. The *Song for St. John's Eve* is told by a girl who plans to party the whole night with her boyfriend, and is set to a more elaborate tune than the last—a wavering melodic line with disjunct leaps and several short melismas (Example 2).

Today, both the pre-Lenten Carnival and the summer solstice (June 21) remain occasions for festivities and music making. Famous carnival celebrations are held in New Orleans and Rio de Janeiro with spectacular parades, masked balls, mock ceremonials, and street dancing, and the solstice is observed in the coastal city of Santa Barbara, California, where a free-spirited, zany parade and revelry honor the arrival of summer.

Example 1:

Ding - a - ling, ding - a - ling, from each one beg an egg, For Je - sus

Christ is a - ris - en, God's own Son! Ho - ho! my good mas - ter, is

etc.

no one at home? For Je - sus Christ is a - ris - en, God's own Son!

Example 2:

I am run - ning, run - ning in _____ the sun - shine _____

through the har - vest _____ field _____ run - ning I _____ reach a shrine. _____

Russian village life and customs come alive in The Easter Procession *(1915) by* **Boris Kustodiev** *(1878-1927), a painter known for his colorful folk-print style.*

Suggested Listening:

Stravinsky: *The Firebird* and *Petrushka*
Russian folk songs

68

Schoenberg and the Second Viennese School

"I personally hate to be called a revolutionist, which I am not. What I did was neither revolution nor anarchy."

Arnold Schoenberg

The German Expressionist movement was manifested in the music of Arnold Schoenberg and his followers. Schoenberg's pioneering efforts in the breakdown of the traditional tonal system and the development of the twelve-tone method revolutionized musical composition. His innovations were further developed by his most gifted students, Alban Berg and Anton Webern, both of whom we will study. These three composers are often referred to as the second Viennese school (the first being Haydn, Mozart, and Beethoven).

His Life

Early years

Arnold Schoenberg (1874–1951) was born in Vienna. He began to study the violin at the age of eight, and soon afterward made his initial attempts at composing. Having decided to devote his life to music, he left school while in his teens. For a time, he earned his living working in a bank and meanwhile continued to compose, working entirely by himself. Presently he became acquainted with a young musician, Alexander von Zemlinsky, who for a few months gave him lessons in counterpoint. This was the only musical instruction he ever had.

Through Zemlinsky, young Schoenberg was introduced to the advanced musical circles of Vienna, which at that time were under the spell of Wagner's operas. In 1899, when he was twenty-five, Schoenberg wrote the string sextet *Transfigured Night*. The following year, several of his songs were performed in Vienna and created a scene. "And ever since that day," he once remarked with a smile, "the scandal has never ceased."

In 1901, after his marriage to Zemlinsky's sister, Schoenberg moved to Berlin and obtained a post in a theater, conducting operettas and music-hall songs. The composer's early music already displayed certain traits of his later style. A publisher to whom he brought a quartet observed, "You must think that if the second theme is a retrograde inversion of the first theme, that automatically makes it good!"

Return to Vienna

Upon his return to Vienna, Schoenberg became active as a teacher and soon gathered about him a band of disciples that included Alban Berg and Anton Webern. The devotion of these innovative young musicians sustained him in the fierce battle for recognition that still lay ahead. With each new work, Schoenberg moved closer to taking as bold a step as any artist has ever taken—the rejection of tonality.

The First World War interrupted Schoenberg's creative activity. Although he was past forty, he was called up for military service in the Vienna garrison. By then, he had reached a critical point in his development. There followed a silence of seven years, between 1915 and 1923, during which he clarified his position in his own mind and evolved a set of structural procedures to replace tonality. The goal once set, Schoenberg pursued it with great determination. His "method of composing with twelve tones" caused much bewilderment in the musical world. All the same, he was now firmly established as a leader of contemporary musical thought.

This period in Schoenberg's life ended with the coming to power of Hitler in 1933. Like many Austrian-Jewish intellectuals of his generation, he had grown away from his Jewish origins and ultimately converted to Catholicism. But after he left Germany, he found it spiritually necessary to return to the Hebrew faith. He arrived in the United States in the fall of 1933. After a short *Move to the United States* period of teaching in Boston, he joined the faculty of the University of Southern California and shortly afterward was appointed professor of composition at the University of California in Los Angeles. In 1940, he became an American citizen. He taught until his retirement at the age of seventy, and continued his musical activities until his death in 1951.

His Music

Schoenberg's early works may be described as representative of post-Wagnerian Romanticism; he still used key signatures and remained within the boundaries of tonality. The best-known work of this era is *Transfigured Night*. Schoenberg's second period, the atonal-Expressionist, got under way with the *Atonal-Expressionism* Three Piano Pieces, Opus 11, in which he abolished the distinction between

Principal Works

Orchestral music, including Five Pieces for Orchestra (1909), *Verklärte Nacht* (*Transfigured Night,* 1917), Variations for Orchestra (1928), and concertos for violin (1936) and piano (1942)

Operas, including *Die glückliche Hand* (The Blessed Hand, 1913) and *Moses und Aron* (incomplete, 1932)

Choral music, including *Gurrelieder* (1911), *Die Jakobsleiter* (Jacob's Ladder, 1922), and *A Survivor from Warsaw* (1947); smaller choral works, including *Friede auf Erden* (Peace on Earth, 1907)

Chamber music, including 4 string quartets, serenade, wind quintet, and string trio

Vocal music, including *Pierrot Lunaire* (Moonstruck Peter, 1912)

Piano music, including Three Piano Pieces, Op. 11 (1909)

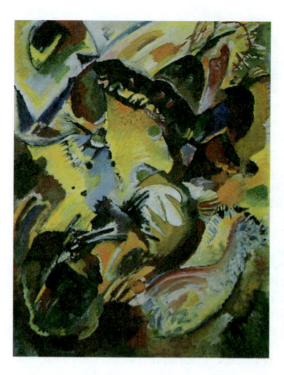

Atonal-Expressionism found its counterpart in the canvases of Expressionist painters who defied the traditional notions of beauty in order to define the artist's inner self. **Wassily Kandinsky** *(1886–1944),* Painting No. 199. (Museum of Modern Art, N.Y., Nelson A. Rockefeller Fund)

consonance and dissonance as well as the sense of a home key. The high points of this period are the Five Pieces for Orchestra, Opus 16, and *Pierrot lunaire,* which we shall study.

Twelve-tone and American periods

Schoenberg's third style period, that of the twelve-tone method, reached its climax in the Variations for Orchestra, Opus 31, one of his most powerful works. In the fourth and last part of his career—the American phase—he carried the twelve-tone technique to further stages of refinement. Several among the late works present the twelve-tone style in a manner markedly more accessible than earlier pieces, often with tonal implications. Among those are the brilliant Piano Concerto and the cantata *A Survivor from Warsaw.*

Schoenberg was a tireless propagandist for his ideas. His essays conveyed his ideas in a penetrating style. Among his observations are the following: "Genius learns only from itself, talent chiefly from others"; "Creation to an artist should be as natural and inescapable as the growth of apples to an apple tree"; "The twelve tones will not invent for you."

PIERROT LUNAIRE

One of Schoenberg's preoccupations was the attempt to bring spoken word and music as close together as possible. He solved the problem through *Sprechstimme* (spoken voice), a new style in which the vocal melody is spoken rather than sung on exact pitches and in strict rhythm. As Schoenberg explained it, the reciter sounded the written note at first but abandoned it by rising or falling in pitch immediately after. The result was a weird, strangely effective vocal line, which he brought to perfection in his most celebrated work, *Pierrot lunaire.*

Sprechstimme

In 1884, the Belgian poet Albert Giraud, a disciple of the Symbolists, published a cycle of fifty short poems under the title that Schoenberg later adopted. His Pierrot was the poet-rascal-clown whose chalk-white face, passing abruptly from laughter to tears, enlivened every puppet show and pantomime in Europe. (We have already met him in Russia as Petrushka and in Italy as Pagliaccio.) Giraud's poems were liberally spiced with those elements of the macabre and the bizarre that suited the end-of-century taste for decadence. Translated into German by Otto Erich Hartleben, the poems, with their abrupt changes of mood from guilt and depression to atonement and playfulness, fired Schoenberg's imagination. He picked twenty-one, arranged them in three groups of seven, and set them for a female reciter and a chamber music ensemble of five players using eight instruments: piano, flute/piccolo, clarinet/bass clarinet, violin/viola, and cello. The work, he explained, was conceived "in a light, ironical, satirical tone."

Giraud's short poems enabled Schoenberg to create a series of miniatures for which Sprechstimme served as a unifying element. This unity was balanced by the utmost variety from one piece to the next of structure, texture—from dense to sparse—and instrumentation. The result was a perfect musical expression of the bizarre images in the text. Schoenberg also experimented with what he called *Klangfarbenmelodie* (tone-color melody), in which each note of a melody is played by a different instrument, creating a shifting effect that evokes the moonbeams of which the poet spoke. Each of the poems is a *rondeau,* a fifteenth-century verse form in which the opening lines return as a refrain in the middle of the poem and at its end.

Klangfarbenmelodie

We will focus on two of the poems. No. 18 is "The Moonfleck" ("Der Mondfleck"; see Listening Guide 59 for the text). Pierrot, out for fun, is disturbed by a white spot—a patch of moonlight—on the collar of his jet-black jacket. He rubs and rubs but cannot get rid of it. His predicament inspired Schoenberg to contrapuntal complexities of a spectacular kind. The piano introduces a three-voice fugue, while the other instruments unfold such devices

No. 18

Schoenberg conducting a performance of Pierrot lunaire *with soprano Erica Stiedry-Wagner at Town Hall, New York, on November 17, 1940. A sketch by* **Benedict Fred Dolbin** *(1883–1971).*

as strict canons in diminution (smaller note values) and retrograde (backward). Schoenberg was obviously fascinated by such constructions, which recall the wizardry of the Renaissance contrapuntists.

No. 21   The last poem, No. 21, is "O Scent of Fabled Yesteryear" ("O alter Duft aus Märchenzeit"), in which Schoenberg brings in all eight instruments. Pierrot revels in the fragrant memories of old times, looking out serenely on a world bathed in sunlight. This return to an earlier, more innocent time leads Schoenberg to sound the gentle thirds and consonant triads of the harmonic system he had abandoned. Pierrot's Sprechstimme dies away in a *pianissimo*. Thus ends the work that Stravinsky called "the solar plexus as well as the mind of early twentieth-century music."

Certain creative spirits capture the mood of their time and place. Rarely has a musician done so as completely as Schoenberg in *Pierrot lunaire*.

Listening Guide 59

C/S: 7A/3–4   C/S: 7/ 7 – 10
Sh: 3A/4–5   Sh: 3/ 16 – 19

SCHOENBERG: *Pierrot lunaire,* Nos. 18 and 21   (2:44)

Date of work: 1912
Genre: Song cycle
Medium: Solo voice and 5 instrumentalists (violin/viola, cello, flute/piccolo, clarinet/bass clarinet, piano)
Text: 21 poems from Albert Giraud's *Pierrot lunaire,* all in rondeau form; in 3 parts

Part I:
  1. "Moondrunk"
  2. "Columbine"
  3. "The Dandy"
  4. "Pale Washerwoman"
  5. "Valse de Chopin"
  6. "Madonna"
  7. "The Sick Moon"

Part II:
  8. "Night"
  9. "Prayer to Pierrot"
  10. "Theft"
  11. "Red Mass"
  12. "Gallows Ditty"
  13. "Beheading"
  14. "The Crosses"

Part III:
  15. "Homesickness"
  16. "Vulgar Horseplay"
  17. "Parody"
  18. "The Moonfleck"
  19. "Serenade"
  20. "Homeward Journey"
  21. "O Scent of Fabled Yesteryear"

Pierrot, sad clown figure, is obsessed with the moon, having drunk moonwine; his loves, fantasies, and frenzies are exposed.

Pierrot becomes obsessed with guilt and atonement.

Pierrot climbs from the depths of depression to a more playful mood, but with fleeting thoughts of guilt; then he becomes sober.

18. "The Moonfleck" ("Der Mondfleck")   (0:56)

Medium: Voice, piccolo, clarinet in B♭, violin, cello, piano

Tempo: Sehr rasche (very quickly)

Voice in Sprechstimme against fast and dissonant accompaniment; canonic treatment veiled in flickering effect of instruments (italics below indicate repeated text of rondeau form)

Text	Translation
7 0:00 *Einen weissen Fleck des hellen Mondes* *Auf dem Rücken seines schwarzen Rockes,* So spaziert Pierrot im lauen Abend, Aufzusuchen Glück und Abenteuer.	*With a fleck of white—from the bright moon—* *On the back of his black jacket,* Pierrot strolls about in the mild evening Seeking his fortune and adventure.
Plötzlich stört ihn was an seinem Anzug, Er beschaut sich rings und findet richtig— **8** 0:26 *Einen weissen Fleck des hellen Mondes* *Auf dem Rücken seines schwarzen Rockes.*	Suddenly something strikes him as wrong, He checks his clothes and sure enough finds *A fleck of white—from the bright moon—* *On the back of his black jacket.*
Warte! denkt er: das ist so ein Gipsfleck! Wischt und wischt, doch—bringt ihn nicht herunter!	Damn! he thinks: that's a spot of plaster! Wipes and wipes, but—he can't get it off.
Und so geht er, giftgeschwollen, weiter, Reibt und reibt bis an den frühen Morgen— *Einen weissen Fleck des hellen Mondes.*	And so goes on his way, his pleasure poisoned, Rubs and rubs till the early morning— *A fleck of white—from the bright moon.*

Opening, for voice and instruments:

21. "O Scent of Fabled Yesteryear" ("O alter Duft aus Märchenzeit")   (1:48)

Medium: Voice, flute, piccolo, clarinet in A, bass clarinet in B♭, violin, viola, cello, piano

Tempo: Bewegt (with motion)

Melancholy mood in simpler setting, dissonant, with musical refrain on words "O alter Duft aus Märchenzeit" (shown in italics)

Text	*Translation*
[9] 0:00	
O alter Duft aus Märchenzeit,	*O scent of fabled yesteryear,*
Berauschest wieder meine Sinne!	*Intoxicating my senses once again!*
Ein närrisch Heer von Schelmerein	A foolish swarm of idle fancies
Durchschwirrt die leichte Luft.	Pervades the gentle air.
Ein glückhaft Wünschen macht mich froh	A happy desire makes me yearn for
Nach Freuden, die ich lang verachtet:	Joys that I have long scorned:
[10] 0:43 *O alter Duft aus Märchenzeit,*	*O scent of fabled yesteryear,*
Berauschest wieder mich!	*Intoxicating me again.*
All meinen Unmut geb ich preis:	All my ill humor is dispelled:
Aus meinem sonnumrahmten Fenster	From my sun-drenched window
Beschau ich frei die liebe Welt	I look out freely on the lovely world
Und träum hinaus in selge Weiten . . .	And dream of beyond the horizon . . .
O alter Duft aus Märchenzeit!	*O scent of fabled yesteryear!*

Opening, for piano and voice in Sprechstimme:

69
Berg and Early Twentieth-Century Opera

"When I decided to write an opera, my only intention was to give to the theater what belongs to the theater. The music was to be so formed that at each moment it would fulfill its duty of serving the action."

It was the unique achievement of Berg to humanize the abstract procedures of the Schoenbergian technique and to infuse them with this feeling. He imprinted the stamp of a great lyric imagination upon this new, difficult idiom.

His Life

Alban Berg

Alban Berg (1885–1935) was born in Vienna. He came from a well-to-do family and grew up in an environment that fostered his artistic interests. At nineteen, he made the acquaintance of Arnold Schoenberg, who was sufficiently impressed with the youth's manuscripts to accept him as a pupil. During his six years with Schoenberg (1904-9), Berg acquired the consummate mastery of technique that characterizes his later work. Schoenberg was not only an exacting master, but also a devoted friend and mentor who shaped Berg's whole outlook on art.

The outbreak of war in 1914 hurled Berg into a period of depression. "The urge 'to be in on it,'" he wrote to Schoenberg, "the feeling of helplessness at being unable to serve my country, prevented any concentration on work." A few months later, he was called up for military service, despite his uncertain health (he suffered from asthma and a nerve ailment). He was presently transferred to the War Ministry in Vienna. At this time, an opera, *Wozzeck,* occupied his thoughts, but he could not begin writing the music until the war was over. In December 1925, *Wozzeck* was presented at the Berlin State Opera. Suddenly, Berg was lifted from comparative obscurity to international fame.

In the decade that remained to him, he produced only a handful of works, but each was a significant contribution to his total output. During these years, he was active as a teacher. He also wrote about music, propagandizing tirelessly on behalf of Schoenberg and his school. With the coming to power of Hitler, the works of the twelve-tone composers were banned in Germany as alien to the spirit of the Third Reich. The resulting loss of income was a source of worry to Berg, as was, in far greater degree, the rapid spread of Nazism in Austria. Schoenberg's departure for the United States was a bitter blow.

Exhausted and ailing after the completion of his Violin Concerto, Berg went to the country for a short rest before resuming work on his opera *Lulu.* An insect bite brought on an abscess, and the infection spread. Upon his return to Vienna, he was stricken with blood poisoning and died on Christmas Eve 1935, seven weeks before his fifty-first birthday.

Principal Works

2 operas: *Wozzeck* (1917-22) and *Lulu* (unfinished, 1935)

Orchestral music, including Three Orchestral Pieces, Op. 6 (1915), Chamber Concerto (1925), Three Pieces from *Lyric Suite* (1928), and Violin Concerto (1935)

Chamber music, including String Quartet (1910) and *Lyric Suite* (1926)

Piano music, including Piano Sonata, Op. 1 (1908)

Songs, including Four Songs, Op. 2 (1910)

His Music

Berg's style was rooted in the world of German Romanticism—the world of Schumann, Brahms, Wagner, Richard Strauss, and Mahler. The Romantic streak in his temperament tied him to this heritage even after he had adopted the twelve-tone style. His imagination was that of the musical dramatist. For him, the musical gesture was bound up with character and action, mood and atmosphere. Yet, like his teacher, he leaned toward the formal patterns of the past—fugue and invention, passacaglia, variations, sonata, and suite.

Berg's most widely known composition, after the opera *Wozzeck,* is the *Lyric Suite.* The work is in six movements; the first and last follow strictly "the method of composing with twelve tones." Originally written for string quartet, the *Lyric Suite* achieved such popularity that the composer arranged the three middle movements for string orchestra.

Lulu   Berg spent the last seven years of his life working on the opera *Lulu,* which is based on a single twelve-tone row. The composer fashioned the libretto himself from two dramas by Frank Wedekind—*Earth Spirit* (1893) and *Pandora's Box* (1901). Lulu is the eternal type of *femme fatale* "who destroys everyone because she is destroyed by everyone." Berg was in the midst of orchestrating *Lulu* when he interrupted the task to write his Violin Concerto. The opera remained unfinished for many years, but recently the orchestration was completed by the Austrian composer Friedrich Cerha, and now *Lulu* has taken its place alongside *Wozzeck* as one of the challenging works of the modern lyric theater.

Alban Berg is probably the most widely admired master of the twelve-tone school. His premature death robbed contemporary music of a major figure.

WOZZECK

In 1914, Berg saw the play that urged him to the composition of *Wozzeck*. The author, Georg Büchner (1813–37), belonged to a generation of intellectuals stifled by the political repressions that were imposed upon Europe after the defeat of Napoleon. In the character of Wozzeck, Büchner created an archetype of "the insulted and injured" of the earth.

Berg's libretto tightened the original play. He shaped the material into three acts, each containing five scenes. The scenes are linked by brief orchestral interludes whose motivic structure serves to round off what has preceded as well as to introduce what follows. As a result, Berg's "opera of protest and compassion" has an astonishing unity of texture and mood.

The action centers on Wozzeck's unhappy love for Marie, by whom he has had an illegitimate child. Wozzeck, a common soldier, is the victim of the sadistic Captain and the Doctor, a coldly scientific gentleman who uses Wozzeck for his experiments—to which the soldier submits because he needs the money. (Wozzeck is given to hallucinations. The Doctor is bent on proving his theory that mental disorder is related to diet.) Marie is hopelessly infatuated with the handsome Drum Major. Wozzeck slowly realizes that she has been unfaithful to him. Ultimately he kills her. Driven back to the death scene by guilt and remorse, he drowns himself.

Harmonically, the greater part of the opera is cast in an atonal-Expressionist idiom. Berg anticipates certain twelve-tone procedures; he also looks back to the tonal tradition, writes a number of passages in major and minor keys, and uses leitmotifs in the Wagnerian manner.

We will study the final two scenes of the opera. In scene 4 of Act III, *Act III, scene 4*
Wozzeck comes back to the path near the pond where he has killed Marie, and stumbles against her body. Poignantly, he asks, "Marie, what's that red cord around your neck?" (See Listening Guide 60 for the text.) He finds the knife with which he committed the murder, throws it into the pond, and, driven by his delusions, follows it into the water. His last words as he drowns—"I am washing myself in blood—the water is blood . . . blood!"—usher in a series of ascending chromatic scales that pass in a ghostly *pianissimo* from strings to woodwinds to brass. The Doctor appears, followed by the Captain. We see the haunted scene through their eyes as, terrified, they run away.

The final scene opens with a symphonic interlude in D minor, a passionate *Act III, scene 5*
lament for the life and death of Wozzeck. This inspired fantasy indicates how

Wozzeck deliriously searches for the body of Marie in a scene from Act III of a 1989 Metropolitan Opera production with Gottfried Hornik in the title role. (Winnie Klotz, Metropolitan Opera)

richly Berg's art was nourished by the Romanticism of Mahler. The scene takes place in the morning in front of Marie's house. Children are playing. Marie's little boy rides a hobbyhorse. Other children rush in with news of the murder, but Marie's son does not understand. The children run off as he continues to ride and sing. Then, noticing that he has been left alone, he calls "Hop, hop" and rides off on his hobbyhorse, to the sound of clarinet, drum, xylophone, and strings playing *pianissimo*. For sheer heartbreak, the final curtain has few to equal it in the contemporary lyric theater.

Wozzeck envelops the listener in a hallucinated world in which the hunters are as driven as the hunted. It could only have come from central Europe in the 1920s. But its characters reach out beyond time and place to become eternal symbols of the human condition.

Listening Guide 60

C/S: 7B/2   C/S: 7/ 44 – 47

BERG: *Wozzeck,* Act III, Scenes 4 and 5   (9:56)

Date of work: 1922
Genre: Opera, in three acts
Basis: Expressionist play by Georg Büchner

(handwritten notes: styll – atonal expressionism — use of leading lmotive – like Wagner — w/ 5 scenes in each — use of sprechstimme)

ACT III, SCENE 4: By the pond

Characters: Wozzeck, Doctor, Captain

WOZZECK

44 0:00	Das Messer? Wo ist das Messer? Ich	The knife? Where is the knife? I left it there.

Das Messer? Wo ist das Messer? Ich
hab's dagelassen. Näher, noch näher.
Mir graut's . . . da regt sich was.
Still! Alles still und tot.

The knife? Where is the knife? I left it there.
Around here somewhere.
I'm terrified . . . something's moving.
Silence. Everything silent and dead.

(shouting)

Mörder! Mörder!   Murderer! Murderer!

(whispering again)

Ha! Da ruft's. Nein, ich selbst.   Ah! Someone called. No, it was only me.

(still looking, he staggers a few steps further and stumbles against the corpse)

Marie! Marie! Was hast du für eine rote Schnur
um den Hals?
Hast dir das rote Halsband verdient,
wie die Ohrringlein, mit deiner Sünde!
Was hängen dir die schwarzen Haare
so wild? Mörder! Mörder! Sie werden
nach mir suchen. Das Messer verrät mich!

Marie! Marie! What's that red cord around
your neck?
Was the red necklace payment for your sins,
like the earrings?
Why's your dark hair so wild about you?
Murderer! Murderer! They will come and
look for me. The knife will betray me!

(looks for it in a frenzy)

Da, da ist's.   Here! Here it is!

(at the pond)

So! Da hinunter!   There! Sink to the bottom!

(throws knife into the pond)

Es taucht ins dunkle Wasser wie ein Stein.	It plunges into the dark water like a stone.

(The moon appears, blood-red, from behind the clouds. Wozzeck looks up.)

Aber der Mond verrät mich, der Mond ist blutig. Will denn die ganze Welt es ausplaudern! Das Messer, es liegt zu weit vorn, sie finden's beim Baden oder wenn sie nach Muscheln tauchen.	But the moon will betray me: the moon is bloodstained. Is the whole world going to incriminate me? The knife is too near the edge: they'll find it when they're swimming or diving for snails.

(wades into the pond)

Ich find's nicht. Aber ich muss mich waschen. Ich bin blutig. Da ein Fleck— und noch einer. Weh! Weh! Ich wasche mich mit Blut— das Wasser ist Blut . . . Blut . . .	I can't find it. But I must wash myself. There's blood on me. There's a spot here— and another. Oh, God! I am washing myself in blood— the water is blood . . . blood . . .

(drowns)

Wozzeck's last words before drowning, accompanied by very soft ascending chromatic scales in strings:

Weh!   Ich wa-sche mich mit   Blut___   das   Was-ser ist Blut..._____   Blut..._____

(The Doctor appears, followed by the Captain.)

45 3:02

CAPTAIN

Halt!	Wait!

DOCTOR *(stops)*

Hören Sie? Dort!	Can you hear? There!

CAPTAIN

Jesus! Das war ein Ton!	Jesus! What a ghastly sound!

(stops as well)

DOCTOR *(pointing to the pond)*

Ja, dort!	Yes, there!

CAPTAIN

Es ist das Wasser im Teich. Das Wasser ruft. Es ist schon lange niemand ertrunken. Kommen Sie, Doktor! Es ist nicht gut zu hören.	It's the water in the pond. The water is calling. It's been a long time since anyone drowned. Come away, Doctor. It's not good for us to be hearing it.

(tries to drag the Doctor away)

DOCTOR *(resisting and continuing to listen)*

Das stöhnt, als stürbe ein Mensch. Da ertrinkt Jemand!	There's a groan, as though someone were dying. Somebody's drowning!

CAPTAIN

Unheimlich! Der Mond rot, und die Nebel grau. Hören Sie? . . . Jetzt wieder das Ächzen.	It's eerie! The moon is red, and the mist is grey. Can you hear? . . . That moaning again.

DOCTOR

Stiller, . . . jetzt ganz still.	It's getting quieter . . . now it's stopped altogether.

CAPTAIN

Kommen Sie! Kommen Sie schnell!   Come! Come quickly!

(He rushes off, pulling the Doctor along with him.)

---

46   4:43   **Orchestral Interlude in D minor**
Chromatic, lush strings; Adagio tempo; leads to dissonant climax in brass and woodwinds,
with timpani

---

47   8:29   **ACT III, SCENE 5: Children playing in front of Marie's house**
Melody of children's song, distorted:

CHILDREN

Ringel, Ringel, Rosenkranz, Ringelreih'n   Ring-a-ring-a-roses,
Ringel, Ringel, Rosenkranz, Ring . . .   A pocket full of . . .

(Their song and game are interrupted by other children bursting in.)

ONE OF THE NEWCOMERS

Du, Käthe! Die Marie!   Hey, Katie! Have you heard about Marie?

SECOND CHILD

Was ist?   What's happened?

FIRST CHILD

Weisst' es nit? Sie sind schon Alle 'naus.   Don't you know? They've all gone out there.

THIRD CHILD *(to Marie's little boy)*

Du! Dein' Mutter ist tot!   Hey! Your mother's dead!

MARIE'S SON *(still riding)*

Hopp, hopp! Hopp, hopp! Hopp, hopp!   Hop, hop! Hop, hop! Hop, hop!

SECOND CHILD

Wo ist sie denn?   Where is she, then?

FIRST CHILD

Drauss' liegt sie, am Weg, neben dem Teich.   She's lying out there, on the path near the pond.

THIRD CHILD

Kommt, anschaun!   Come and have a look!

(All the children run off.)

MARIE'S SON *(continuing to ride)*

Hopp, hopp! Hopp, hopp! Hopp, hopp!   Hop, hop! Hop, hop! Hop, hop!

(He hesitates for a moment and then rides after the other children.)

Child on hobbyhorse, with *pianissimo* accompaniment:

70

Webern and Serial Technique

"With me, things never turn out as I wish, but only as is ordained for me—as I must."

In the 1950s and 1960s, the music of Anton Webern came into its own. His works are brief, subtle, fleeting; yet they hold a firm place in our musical life, and they have decisively influenced the thinking of many younger composers.

His Life

Anton Webern (1883–1945) was born in Vienna. His musical gifts were obvious at an early age. He was twenty-one when he met Schoenberg and, with Alban Berg, formed the nucleus of the group of students who gathered around the master. He also studied musicology and received his doctorate in this field.

After leaving the university, Webern conducted at various German provincial theaters and in Prague. But Vienna was the hub of his world. He directed the Vienna Workers' Symphony Concerts organized by the authorities of the then socialist city, but as the years passed, he found public activity less and less congenial to his retiring personality. After the First World War, he settled in Mödling, a suburb of Vienna, where he lived quietly, devoting himself to composition and teaching.

Webern suffered great hardship after Austria became part of the Third Reich. The Nazis regarded his music as *Kulturbolshevismus* (cultural Bolshevism), forbade its performance, and burned his writings. He was permitted to teach only a few pupils, and had to give his lectures—in which he

Anton Webern

explained the Schoenbergian point of view—in secret. In order to avoid forced labor during the war, he worked as proofreader for a Viennese publisher. To escape the Allied bombings of Vienna, Webern and his wife sought refuge at the home of their son-in-law in a small town near Salzburg. But fate awaited him there. On September 15, 1945, as he stepped out of his house in the evening to smoke a cigarette (the war had ended five months before, but the town was still under a curfew), he failed to understand an order to halt and was shot by a trigger-happy sentry of the American occupying forces. "The day of Anton Webern's death," wrote his most celebrated admirer, Igor Stravinsky, "should be a day of mourning for any receptive musician. We must hail not only this great composer but also a real hero. Doomed to total failure in a deaf world of ignorance and indifference, he inexorably kept on cutting his dazzling diamonds, of whose mines he had such a perfect knowledge."

His Music

Webern responded to the radical aspects of Schoenberg's doctrine, just as Berg exploited its more conservative elements. Of the three masters of the modern Viennese school, he was the one who cut himself off most completely from the tonal past. The Schoenbergians, we saw, favored short forms. Webern carried this urge for brevity much further than either of his colleagues. His scores call for the most unusual combinations of instruments. Each tone is assigned its specific function in the overall scheme. The instruments are often used in their extreme registers; they frequently play one at a time, and very little. This technique confers upon the individual sound an importance it never had before.

In the works of Webern's maturity, the twelve-tone technique was used with unprecedented strictness. Schoenberg had contented himself with an organization based upon fixed series of pitches. Webern extended this concept to include timbres and rhythms, moving toward complete control of all the elements—in other words, total serialization. His disciples carried the implications of his music still further. As a result, Webern emerged as the dominant influence on the compositional process of the mid-twentieth century.

Principal Works

Orchestral music, including Passacaglia, Op. 1 (1908); Five Pieces for Orchestra, Op. 10 (1913); Symphony, Op. 21 (1928); and Variations, Op. 30 (1940)

Chamber music, including Five Movements for String Quartet (1909) and other string quartets

Choral music, including cantatas; many songs

Piano music, including Variations, Op. 27 (1936)

In this pointillistic painting, **Georges Seurat** *(1859–1891) uses dots of pure color to create a shimmering effect in the same way Webern and Schoenberg use changing instrumental timbres.* Study for "A Sunday on La Grande Jatte." (Metropolitan Museum of Art, Bequest of Sam A. Lewisohn, 1951)

SYMPHONY, OPUS 21

The Symphony, Opus 21—for clarinet, bass clarinet, two horns, two harps, violins, violas, and cellos—ushered in the most important phase of Webern's career, when his desire for absolute purity of language led him to his own completely original style. With this work, he became the first of the modern Viennese school to undertake the grand form of the Classical period. (As we saw, neither Schoenberg nor Berg wrote symphonies.) However, Webern's piece is far removed from the expansion-and-development techniques traditionally associated with symphonic style. It is equally far from the tonic-dominant opposition that made the symphony the embodiment of tonal thinking.

Webern's Symphony takes just under ten minutes to play, and shows the same concentration of thought and sparseness of writing as do his other scores. In the matter of color, Webern expanded Schoenberg's device of Klangfarbenmelodie (tone-color melody), in which each note of a melodic line was played by a different instrument; he assigned two, three, or four notes to each. There resulted the exact tonal equivalent of pointillism in painting, in which dots of pure color were juxtaposed to create a shimmering effect.

The symphony abounds in those complex contrapuntal procedures, such as double canon and retrograde (backward) motion, that fascinated composers from the late Middle Ages to the Baroque era. It is in two movements. The first, based on a tone row, is in a sonata form with canonic structures; the second is a theme with seven variations and a coda, all derived from the tone row of the first movement (see Listening Guide 61). The symmetrical organization shows the workings of Webern's mind: Variations 1 and 7 are double canons, 2 and 6 are trios, 3 and 5 are pointillistic in effect, and the 4th occupies the central position and serves as the turning point of the movement.

Listening Guide 61

 C/S: 7A/8   C/S: 7/ 41 – 43

WEBERN: Symphony, Op. 21, Second Movement
(2:55)

Date of work: 1928
Medium: Chamber orchestra
Movements (both 12-tone):

*[handwritten annotations: * serialism (control) * pointilism — less than 10 min * 2nd mvmt — based on theme + variation]*

   I. Ruhig schreitend (moving quietly); sonata form, with double canon for 4 voices
   II. Variationen (Theme and Variations)

SECOND MOVEMENT: Theme and Variations

Basis: 11-measure theme, based on the inversion and retrograde inversion of tone row
   from first movement; inverted tone row heard in harp and French horn; retrograde
   inversion of same row heard in clarinet and bass clarinet

Character: Pointillistic, disjunct

Forms of tone row used:

| 41 | 0:00 | **Theme:** Sehr ruhig (very quiet) |

    Gentle statement in clarinets, with muted horns and harps
   Variation 1: lebhafter (livelier)
    Muted string; 4-part double canon in contrary motion; alternation of pizzicato and
    bowed notes; second half of variation is retrograde of first half
   Variation 2: sehr lebhaft (very lively)
    Clarinet, bass clarinet, and horn, with harp and occasional strings
   Variation 3: wieder mässiger (again more moderately)
    Ensemble, in pointillistic style

| 42 | 1:05 | **Variation 4:** äusserst ruhig (extremely quiet) |

    Ensemble, in slowest section with dense counterpoint
   Variation 5: sehr lebhaft (very lively)
    Strings and harp, in ostinato that builds in volume
   Variation 6: marschmässig (marchlike)
    Clarinet, bass clarinet, and horn; canons in woodwinds with sustained horn notes

| 43 | 2:07 | **Variation 7:** etwas breiter (somewhat broader) |

    Ensemble, double canon in contrary motion
   Coda:
    Theme and retrograde form in clarinet, harp, violin, and cello; closes with harp notes

---

The creator of this remarkable music was content to go his way, overshadowed by those who made a bigger noise in the world. He had no way of knowing that little over a decade after his death, many avant-garde musicians in
Europe and America would think of themselves as belonging to "the Age of
Webern."

UNIT XXIII

The Nationalism of the Twentieth Century

71

The European Scene

"The art of music above all other arts is the expression of the soul of a nation. The composer must love the tunes of his country and they must become an integral part of him."—RALPH VAUGHAN WILLIAMS

Twentieth-century nationalism differed from its nineteenth-century counterpart in one important respect. Composers approached traditional music with a scientific spirit, prizing the ancient tunes precisely because they departed from the conventional mold. By this time, the phonograph had been invented. The new students of folklore took recording equipment into the field in order to preserve the songs exactly as the village folk sang them, and the composers who used those songs in their works tried to retain their traditional flavor.

National Schools

French composers in the generation after Debussy and Ravel tried to recapture the wit and spirit that are part of their national heritage. One group in particular, called *Les Six* after its six members, followed the example of Erik Satie (1866–1925) in their efforts to develop a style that combined objectivity and understatement with the New Classicism and the even newer concepts of harmony. Of this group, Darius Milhaud (1892–1974) is remembered today mainly for his ballet *The Creation of the World* (1923) and as a leader in the development of polytonality. Arthur Honegger (1892–1955), born in France of Swiss parents, shocked the world with *Pacific 231,* a symphonic poem glorifying the locomotive. Germaine Tailleferre (1892–1983), the only woman in

French school

Les Six

this select group of composers, furthered the cause of the New Classicism, writing in most genres with fluency.

Francis Poulenc (1899-1963) has emerged as the most significant figure of this group. He was one of the outstanding art song composers of his day, and his piano pieces are thoroughly Parisian. Two of his best-known operas—*Dialogues of the Carmelites* (1953-56) and *The Human Voice* (1958), the latter based on a one-act play by Jean Cocteau—found a wide audience in the United States in English versions by the present writer, Joseph Machlis.

Russian school

In the post-Romantic period, the Russian school produced two composers of international fame. The piano works of Sergei Rachmaninoff (1873-1943) are enormously popular with the concertgoing public, especially his Second Piano Concerto and Variations on a Theme of Paganini. Alexander Scriabin (1872-1915), a visionary artist whose music is wreathed in a subtle lyricism, was one of the leaders in the twentieth-century search for new harmonies. In the next generation, two important figures emerged: Sergei Prokofiev, whom we will study later in this chapter; and Dmitri Shostakovich (1906-75), the first Russian composer of international repute who was wholly a product of Soviet musical culture.

English school

England had produced no major composer for two hundred years until Edward Elgar and Frederick Delius appeared upon the scene. They were followed by two figures who were of prime importance in establishing the modern English school—Ralph Vaughan Williams (1872-1958) and Benjamin Britten (1913-76). Britten's works for the stage have established his reputation as one of the foremost opera composers of the era. Among his works are *Peter Grimes* (1945), an opera about an English fishing village based on George Crabbe's poem *The Borough,* and *Billy Budd* (1951), after Herman Melville's story. Widely admired too are the lovely Serenade for tenor solo, horn, and string orchestra (1943) and the deeply moving *War Requiem* (1961). You will recall that Britten's *Young Person's Guide to the Orchestra* was discussed earlier in the book (see Chapter 9).

German school

Among the composers who came into prominence in Germany in the years after the First World War, Paul Hindemith (1895-1963) was the most significant. He left Germany when Hitler came to power—his music was banned from the Third Reich as "cultural Bolshevism"—and spent two decades in the United States, during which he taught at Yale University and at Tanglewood, Massachusetts, where many young Americans came under his influence.

Carl Orff (1895-1982) took his point of departure from the clear-cut melodies and vigorous rhythms of Bavarian folk song. He is best-known in North America for his cantata *Carmina burana* (1937). Kurt Weill (1900-50) was one of the most arresting figures to emerge from Germany in the 1920s. For the international public, his name is indissolubly linked with *The Threepenny Opera* (1928), which he and the poet Bertolt Brecht adapted from John Gay's *Beggar's Opera.* Frequent revivals have made this one of the century's most famous theater pieces.

Other nationalists

Hungarian nationalism found two major representatives in Béla Bartók, whom we shall study, and Zoltán Kodály (1882-1967). Kodály was associated with Bartók in the collection and study of traditional songs, and he made the folk element prominent in his music. Czechoslovakia's national school is well represented by Leoš Janáček (1854–1928), whose operas *Jenůfa* (1904) and *The Cunning Little Vixen* (1924) have found great favor with the American public. Spain contributed two important nationalists of the post-Romantic era—Isaac Albéniz (1860–1909) and Enrique Granados (1867–1916), both of whom paved the way for the major figure of the modern Spanish school, Manuel de Falla (1876–1946).

Finland's Jean Sibelius (1865–1957) was an important figure during the 1920s and 1930s, especially in England and the United States. His Second Symphony, Violin Concerto, and tone poem *Finlandia* remain popular. Carl Nielsen (1865–1931), a Danish composer, wrote six symphonies that have slowly established themselves in our concert life. Ernest Bloch (1880–1959), a native of Switzerland, was one of the few Jewish composers who consciously identified himself musically with his cultural origins. In *Schelomo*—the biblical name of King Solomon—he produced a "Hebrew Rhapsody" for cello and orchestra that gave eloquent expression to his heritage, much as Arnold Schoenberg did a generation later in *A Survivor from Warsaw.*

Sergei Prokofiev: His Life and Music

> *"The cardinal virtue (or, if you like, vice) of my life has always been the search for originality. I hate imitation. I hate hackneyed methods. I do not want to wear anyone else's mask. I want always to be myself."*

Sergei Prokofiev (1891–1953) was one of those fortunate composers who achieved popularity with both the general public and professional musicians. He appeared at a twilight moment in the history of Russian music, infusing it with a fresh but traditional air. Prokofiev entered the St. Petersburg Conservatory at the age of thirteen. He arrived for the entrance examination armed with the manuscripts of four operas, two sonatas, a symphony, and a number of piano pieces; Rimsky-Korsakov, who was one of the examiners, exclaimed, "Here is a pupil after my own heart!"

Sergei Prokofiev

Years outside Russia

At nineteen, Prokofiev made his first public appearance in St. Petersburg playing a group of his piano pieces. The dynamism of this music at once revealed a distinctive personal style. The works that followed—especially the Second Piano Concerto, the Second Piano Sonata, and the *Sarcasms* for piano—established the young composer as the "naughty boy" of Russian music, a role he thoroughly enjoyed.

The Revolution of 1917 caught Prokofiev unaware, since politics lay outside his sphere of interest. As living conditions grew more difficult, he decided to emigrate to the United States, where he would be able to work in peace. It became clear, however, that the conquest of the New World was not going to be as easy as he had imagined.

> I wandered through the enormous park in the center of New York and, looking up at the skyscrapers that bordered it, thought with cold fury of the marvelous American orchestras that cared nothing for my music, of the critics who balked so violently at anything new, of the managers who arranged long tours for artists playing the same old hackneyed programs fifty times over.

There was nothing to do but admit defeat and look elsewhere.

In 1920, Prokofiev made Paris his home, with frequent journeys to the musical centers of Europe and the United States to perform his music. Yet the sense of being uprooted grew within him. "I've got to talk to people who are of my own flesh and blood, so that they can give me back something I lack here—their songs, my songs," he wrote a friend.

Soviet years

The years of wandering were followed by nineteen years in Russia (except for professional trips abroad). During this period, he consolidated his position as the leading composer of the Soviet school. As one who had voluntarily rejoined the Soviets when he might have made a career elsewhere, he was laden with honors by the regime and reaped considerable financial rewards. In 1943, he received the Stalin Prize for his Seventh Piano Sonata. The following year, he was awarded the Order of the Red Banner of Labor for outstanding service in the development of Soviet music.

Nevertheless, of all the Soviet composers, Prokofiev was the one who, because of his long residence abroad, was most closely associated with the Western influences that the regime considered opposed to socialist art. When the Central Committee of the Communist Party in 1948 accused the leading Soviet composers of "bourgeois formalism"—the conventional term for non-Soviet trends in art—Prokofiev was one of the main targets. The government showed its displeasure by ordering his works to be removed from the repertory, along with those of Shostakovich, Aram Khachaturian, and Nikolai Miaskovsky. However, as these men happened to be the Big Four of Soviet music, the prohibition could not be maintained. After a few months, Prokofiev's works—first his ballets, then his symphonies—began to be performed again.

He died on March 5, 1953, at the age of sixty-two. His death came one day after that of Joseph Stalin. The Soviet government withheld the news for forty-eight hours, presumably so that the one event would not overshadow the other.

Classical elements

Prokofiev himself has provided us with the best analysis of the elements of his style. "The first is Classical, originating in my early childhood when I heard my mother play Beethoven sonatas. It assumes a Neoclassical aspect in my sonatas or concertos, or imitates the Classical style of the eighteenth century." In the *Classical* Symphony, composed "as Haydn might have written it had he lived in our day," Prokofiev came as close as anyone in the twentieth century to recapturing the spirit of Haydn's effortless Allegros. The second element in his style he identified as the search for innovation. "At first this consisted in the quest for an individual harmonic language but was later transformed into a medium for the expression of strong emotions."

Search for innovation

Motor and lyrical elements

"The third is the element of the toccata, or motor element, probably influenced by Schumann's Toccata, which impressed me greatly at one time." The toccata is associated with a strong rhythmic drive, generally of the "perpetual motion" type, which is favored in the music of our century. "The fourth element is lyrical. Since my lyricism has for a long time been denied appreciation, it has grown but slowly. But at later stages I paid more and more attention to lyrical expression."

Principal Works

Orchestral works, including 7 symphonies (No. 1, *Classical,* 1917); *Scythian Suite* (1915); *Peter and the Wolf* (with narrator, 1936); 5 piano concertos; 2 violin concertos; and 1 cello concerto

Operas, including *The Love for Three Oranges* (1921), *The Flaming Angel* (1923), and *War and Peace* (1943)

Ballets, including *The Prodigal Son* (1929), *Romeo and Juliet* (1938), and *Cinderella* (1945)

Choral music, including *Alexander Nevsky* (1939, cantata adapted from film score)

Chamber music, including string quartets and sonatas

Piano music, including 9 sonatas

Film music, including *Lieutenant Kije* (1933) and *Alexander Nevsky* (1938); incidental music; songs

"I should like to limit myself to these four elements, and to regard the fifth, that of the grotesque which some critics try to foist on me, as merely a variation of the others. In application to my music, I should like to replace the word 'grotesque' with 'Scherzo-ness' or with the three words giving its gradations: 'jest,' 'laughter,' 'mockery.'" Prokofiev stood in the forefront of those who attempted to broaden musical expression to include the comic and the mischievous. In his later years, this mellowed into a compassionate humor.

The comic and mischievous

Prokofiev became one of the most popular of twentieth-century composers, and a number of his works, among them the concert suites from the ballet *Romeo and Juliet,* have become "classics." In his later symphonies, he sought to recapture the heroic affirmation of the Beethovenian symphony. Of his operas, two in particular have found favor outside Russia: *The Love for Three Oranges* and *War and Peace.* The latter, based on Tolstoy's novel, is considered his masterpiece for the lyric theater.

ALEXANDER NEVSKY

The decade preceding the outbreak of the Second World War was a period of mounting tension throughout Europe as the Soviet Union was increasingly threatened by Hitler's Germany. Thus a film based on the life of a folk hero who defeated the Germans was bound to have a morale-raising effect on the Russian people. In 1938, the great director Sergei Eisenstein produced such a film about Alexander Nevsky, the Grand Duke of Novgorod who in 1240 defeated an attacking Swedish army on the river Neva, and in 1242 defeated the German attackers in a battle on the frozen surface of Lake Chudskoye. Prokofiev wrote the film score, which he later shaped into a cantata. That the project had the full support of the Soviet government is indicated by the fact that members of the Russian army served as extras for the film.

Alexander's triumphant return to Pskov as depicted in Sergei Eisenstein's great film Alexander Nevsky. (Museum of Modern Art Film Stills Archive, N.Y.)

The cantata, for chorus, mezzo-soprano, and orchestra, is in seven movements. (See Listening Guide 62 for their titles.) We will hear the final movement, "Alexander's Entry into Pskov." The Grand Duke and his troops return triumphant from the decisive battle. The folk-song-like tune of the fourth movement reappears against brilliant orchestration. Throughout this seventh movement, percussion punctuates the choral parts, which often separate into women's and men's voices. Prokofiev here anticipated the mood of the final scene of *War and Peace,* in which Marshall Kutuzov and his soldiers celebrate their victory over Napoleon's invading army.

Despite his subsequent difficulties with the Soviet government and its official doctrine of "socialist realism" (as opposed to the "bourgeois formalism" of the West), Prokofiev appears to have remained faithful to the aesthetic he adopted upon his return to Russia. A year before his death, he wrote the following lines:

> When I was in the United States and England I often heard discussions on the subject of whom music ought to serve, for whom a composer ought to write, and to whom his music should be addressed. In my view the composer, just as the poet, the sculptor, or the painter, is in duty bound to serve man, the people. He must beautify human life and defend it. He must be a citizen first and foremost, so that his art may consciously extol human life and lead man to a radiant future. Such, as I see it, is the immutable goal of art.

Listening Guide 62

PROKOFIEV: *Alexander Nevsky,* Seventh Movement (4:42)

[handwritten: — nationalism]
[handwritten: — use of folk-like melody or (from film score)]

Date of work: 1939
Genre: Cantata for chorus, mezzo-soprano, and orchestra, in 7 movements
Basis: Film score for *Alexander Nevsky* (1938), directed by Sergei Eisenstein
Movements:

I. "Russia Beneath the Yoke of the Mongols" (orchestral prelude)—portrays the desolation of the country under the foreign invaders

II. "Song About Alexander Nevsky"—celebrates Alexander's earlier victory over the Swedes

III. "The Crusaders in Pskov" (chorus)—depicts the brutal treatment of the people of Pskov by the Germans

IV. "Arise, People of Russia" (chorale)—rallies the people to rise up and defend the Motherland

V. "The Battle on the Ice"—spectacular orchestral movement, with choral chants; depicts the victory of the Russians as the Germans sink under the cracking ice

VI. "The Field of the Dead" (mezzo-soprano solo)—laments the fate of a fallen knight

VII. "Alexander's Entry into Pskov"

SEVENTH MOVEMENT: "Alexander's Entry into Pskov"

Text	Translation	Description
CHORUS OF RUSSIANS		
48 0:00 Na vyliki boi vykhodila Rus'.	Russia marched out to mighty battle.	Loud and stately chorus with orchestra, punctuated with percussion
Voroga pobyedila Rus'.	Russia overcame the enemy.	
Na rodnoi zyemlye nye byvat' vragu.	On our native soil, let no foe exist.	
Kto pridyot, budyet nasmyert' bit.	Whoever invades will be killed.	
WOMEN		
Vyesyelisya, poi, mat'rodnaya Rus'!	Be merry, sing, mother Russia!	Quicker tempo, with bells and xylophone; folklike melody sung by women's voices
Na rodnoi Rusi nye byvat' vragu.	In our native Russia, let no foe exist.	
Nye vidat' vragu nashikh russikh syol.	Let no foe see our native villages.	
Kto pridyol na Rus', budyet nasmert' bit.	Whoever invades Russia will be killed.	

Opening of women's verse:

Sopranos *f* Vye - sye - lis - ya, poi, mat' - rod - na - ya Rus'! Na - rod - noi Ru - si nye by - vat' vra - gu. *etc.*
Altos *f*

	MEN		
	Nye vidat' vragu nashikh, russikh syol.	Let no foe see our native villages.	Men's voices answer the women; violins forecast Motherland Russia theme soon to be sung
	Kto pridyot na Rus', budyet nasmert' bit.	Whoever invades Russia will be killed.	
	Na Rusi rodnoi, na Rusi bol'shoi nye byvat' vragu.	In our native Russia, in great Russia, let no foe exist.	The Motherland Russia theme, in 3 lower voices
			An orchestral interlude; quick, imitative exchanges between the instruments; woodwinds featured
49 2:36	Na Rusi rodnoi, na Rusi bol'shoi nye byvat' vragu. Vyesyelisya, poi, mat' rodnaya Rus'!	In our native Russia, in great Russia, let no foe exist. Be merry, sing, mother Russia!	Motherland theme in unison, stately, with an animated orchestral accompaniment
	Na vyelikii prazdnik sobralasya . Rus'. Vyesyelisya, Rus'! rodnaya mat'!	At the mighty festival, all Russia has gathered together, Be merry, Russia, mother of ours!	Chorale-like, very slow; stately brass, with much percussion; a grandiose ending

Altos **Motherland theme, in altos and basses:**

mf dolce   *etc.*

Na   Ru - si   rod - noi,   na   Ru - si   bol' - shoi   nye by - vat'   vra - gu.

Basses *mf dolce*

Béla Bartók: His Life and Music

Béla Bartók

Study of folklore

"What is the best way for a composer to reap the full benefits of his studies in peasant music? It is to assimilate the idiom of peasant music so completely that he is able to forget all about it and use it as his musical mother tongue."

It was the mission of Béla Bartók (1881–1945) to reconcile the traditional songs of his native Hungary with the main currents of European music. In the process, he created an entirely personal language and revealed himself as one of the major artists of our century.

Bartók was born in a small Hungarian town in which his father served as director of an agricultural school. He studied at the Royal Academy in Budapest, where he came in contact with the nationalist movement aimed at shaking off the domination of German musical culture. His interest in folklore led him to realize that what passed for Hungarian in the eyes of the world—the idiom romanticized by Liszt and Brahms and kept alive by café musicians—was really the music of Romany, or Gypsies. The true Hungarian idiom, he decided, was to be found only among the peasants. In company with his fellow composer Zoltán Kodály, he toured the remote villages of the country, determined to collect the native songs before they died out forever. "Those days I spent in the villages among the peasants," he wrote later, "were among the happiest of my life. In order to feel the vitality of this music one must, so to speak, have lived it. And this is possible only when one comes to know it by direct contact with the peasants."

With the performance at the Budapest Opera of his ballet *The Wooden Prince,* Bartók came into his own. The fall of the Hapsburg monarchy in 1918 released a surge of national sentiment that created a favorable climate for his music. In the following decade, Bartók became a leading figure in the musical life of his country.

The alliance between the Hungarian government and Nazi Germany on the eve of the Second World War confronted the composer with issues that he faced squarely. He protested the performances of his music on the Berlin radio and at every opportunity took an anti-Fascist stand. To go into exile meant surrendering the position he enjoyed in Hungary, but he would not compromise. "He who stays on when he could leave may be said to acquiesce tacitly in everything that is happening here." Bartók's friends, fearing for his safety, urged him to leave the country while there was still time. He came to the United States in 1940 and settled in New York City.

Emigration to America

The last five years of his life were not happy ones. Sensitive and retiring, he felt uprooted, isolated in his new surroundings. He made some public appearances, playing his music for two pianos with his wife and onetime pupil, Ditta Pásztory-Bartók, but these barely provided for their needs.

In his final years, Bartók suffered from leukemia and was no longer able to appear in public. Friends appealed for aid to the American Society of Composers, Authors, and Publishers (ASCAP), which granted funds that provided the composer with proper care in nursing homes and enabled him to continue writing to the end. A series of commissions from various sources spurred him to the composition of his last works. They rank among his finest. "The trouble is," he remarked to his doctor shortly before the end, "that I have to go with so much still to say." He died in the West Side Hospital in New York City at the age of sixty-four.

Final years

The tale of the composer who spends his last days in poverty and embitterment only to be acclaimed after his death would seem to belong to the Romantic past, to the legend of Mozart and Schubert. Yet it happened in this century. Bartók had to die in order to succeed in the United States. Almost immediately, there was an upsurge of interest in his music.

Like Stravinsky, Bartók was careful to disclaim the role of revolutionary. "In art there are only fast or slow developments. Essentially it is a matter of evolution, not revolution." Despite the newness of his musical language, he was rooted in the Classical heritage. "In my youth my ideal was not so much the art of Bach or Mozart as that of Beethoven." He adhered to the logic and beauty of Classical form and to Beethoven's vision of music as an embodiment of human emotion.

Principal Works

Orchestral works, including *Music for Strings, Percussion, and Celesta* (1936), Concerto for Orchestra (1943), 2 violin concertos (1908, 1938), and 3 piano concertos (1926, 1931, 1945)

1 opera: *Bluebeard's Castle* (1918)

2 ballets: *The Wooden Prince* (1917) and *The Miraculous Mandarin* (1926)

Chamber music, including 6 string quartets (1908–39); *Contrasts* (for violin, clarinet, and piano, 1938); sonatas, duos

Piano music, including *Allegro barbaro* (1911) and *Mikrokosmos* (6 books, 1926–39)

Choral music, including *Cantata profana* (1930); folk song arrangements

Songs, including folk song arrangements

Melody and harmony

Bartók found Eastern European traditional music to be based on ancient modes, unfamiliar scales, and nonsymmetrical rhythms. These freed him from what he called "the tyrannical rule of the major and minor keys," and brought him to new concepts of melody, harmony, and rhythm.

Classical and Romantic elements intermingle in Bartók's music. His Classicism shows itself in his emphasis on construction. His harmony can be bitingly dissonant. Polytonality abounds in his work; but despite an occasional leaning toward atonality, he never wholly abandoned the principle of key.

Rhythmic innovations

Bartók's is one of the great rhythmic imaginations of modern times. His pounding, stabbing rhythms constitute the primitive aspect of his art. Like Stravinsky, Bartók changes meter at almost every bar and frequently uses syncopations and repeated patterns (ostinatos). He, along with Stravinsky, played a major role in the revitalization of European rhythm, infusing it with earthy vitality and tension.

Form

Bartók was more traditional in respect to form, for his model was the sonata of Beethoven. In his middle years, he came under the influence of Baroque music and turned increasingly from harmony to linear thinking. His complex texture is a masterly example of modern dissonant counterpoint. It sets forth his development toward greater abstraction, tightness of structure, and purity of style.

Orchestration

Bartók departed from the orchestral sound of Strauss and Debussy and found his way to a palette all his own. His orchestration ranges from brilliant mixtures to threads of pure color that bring out the intertwining melody lines; from a hard, bright glitter to a luminous haze. A virtuoso pianist himself, he is one of the masters of modern piano writing. He typifies the twentieth-century use of the piano as an instrument of percussion and rhythm. His six string quartets may well rank among the finest achievements of our century. Bartók

Cultural Perspective 19

Bartók—a Roving Collector of Folk Songs

What kinds of music did the Hungarian composer Béla Bartók hear in the Eastern European villages he visited? What are the essential ingredients of the traditional music of his native Hungary and neighboring regions? Bartók, along with fellow composer Zoltán Kodály (1882–1967), searched out and wrote down folk songs in an attempt to identify the national musics of various Eastern European cultures. The two did not take on this project as composers but as folklorists who wanted to study traditional music scientifically. (Today, we would call them ethnomusicologists. The comparative study of musics of the world, focusing on the cultural context of performance, is known as ethnomusicology.) Their fieldwork, in the villages and countrysides of Eastern Europe, centered not on the music of a single culture but on numerous distinct groups: Slovak, Romanian, Bulgarian, Serbian, Croatian, and Arab, as well as Hungarian. The many thousands of songs they collected reflect the very essence of these peoples—their social rituals (weddings, matchmaking, and dancing) and their religious ceremonies.

Bartók drew extensively in his compositions from the melodies, rhythms, and poetic structures of this rich body of traditional music. He was partial to modal scales, especially those typical of Slovak and Romanian melodies, and adopted certain Croatian melodic inflections such as the glissando as a hallmark of his style. (A glissando, you will remember, is a slide from one pitch to another, often used with string instruments.) But rhythm was the primary attraction of this body of folk music and dance. Bartók tried at times to imitate the vocal style of Hungarian music, which is based on free speech-rhythms and follows the natural inflection of the language. At other times, he used the irregular folk dance rhythms typical of Bulgarian music. These propelling rhythms were driven by additive meters built from unit groups of 2, 3, or 4. Thus instead of dividing a 9/8 meter into regular divisions of 3, he might build it from irregular groups of 2 and 3 (2 + 3 + 2 + 2, for example; see the discussion of additive meters on p. 16). From this folk legacy Bartók fashioned a unique musical style.

One type of music collected by Bartók was that of the Romanies, or Gypsies, a word that conjures up Hollywood-style images of traveling caravans full of roguish and colorful entertainers. In reality, this little-understood and itinerant group has a long and esteemed musical history. Believed to have originated in northern India, Romany peoples eventually settled throughout Europe and America. One of the most important and well-documented groups is the Hungarian Romanies, who were especially famous for their dance music, played by violinists and bagpipers. Bartók soon understood that theirs was not the traditional music he sought to collect but rather an urban, commercial style cultivated by professional performers. Beginning in the late eighteenth century, Romany bands were usually made up of two violins, a cimbalom (a zither-like instrument whose strings are struck), and a double bass. The Hungarian composer Franz Liszt, who also drew inspiration and themes from this music, publicly recognized the skill and musicianship of these performers in his book *The Gypsy in Music*. Gypsy ensembles remain popular in modern-day Hungary, and consist of professionally trained musicians playing all styles of music—art, traditional, and popular.

Béla Bartók as a young man recording folk songs in a Transylvanian mountain village. (The photograph was taken in the 1900s by fellow composer Zoltán Kodály.)

Terms to Note:

ethnomusicology
fieldwork
glissando
additive meter

Suggested Listening:

Bartók: *Music for Strings, Percussion, and Celesta,* Fourth Movement
Liszt: *Hungarian Rhapsody* No. 2
Folk songs collected by Bartók
Gypsy (Romany) music

is best-known to the public by the three major works of his last period. The *Music for Strings, Percussion, and Celesta* is regarded by many as his masterpiece. Tonal richness and warmth characterize the Concerto for Orchestra, a favorite with American audiences. The master's final effort, the Third Piano Concerto, is an impassioned and broadly conceived work.

Bartók's music encompasses the diverse trends of his time, polytonality and atonality, Expressionism and Neoclassicism, folk dance and machine music, the lyric and the dynamic. It reaches from the primitive to the intellectual, from program music to the abstract, from nationalism to the universal.

MUSIC FOR STRINGS, PERCUSSION, AND CELESTA

This work was a landmark in the development of twentieth-century chamber music textures. Bartók's instrumentation called for two string groups to frame the percussion and celesta. He carefully specified the arrangement of the players on the stage:

	Double bass I	Double bass II	
Cello I	Timpani	Bass drum	Cello II
Viola I	Side drums	Cymbals	Viola II
Violin II	Celesta	Xylophone	Violin IV
Violin I	Piano	Harp	Violin III

The first movement, marked Andante tranquillo, is a fugue based on a single *crescendo* that grows from *pianissimo* to a *fortissimo* climax and then works back to a softer *pianississimo* (**ppp**). The second movement is an Allegro. The main idea of this closely knit sonata form is a taut, imperious subject whose chromatic character relates it to the subject of the preceding movement. The third movement, an Adagio, is a "night piece" that reveals Bartók's gift for evoking a magical nocturnal landscape through instrumental color. The movement is an arch form, proceeding to a high point and then retracing its path back to the beginning.

First movement

Middle movements

We will hear the fourth movement, an Allegro molto in rondo form, which combines the passionate abandon of Eastern European folk dance and contrapuntal processes tossed off with true virtuosity. The asymmetrical, dancelike rhythm of the central idea alternates with the propulsive, jazzy animation in the contrasting sections. Each recurrence of the rondo theme brings fresh variation. (See Listening Guide 63 for analysis.)

Fourth movement

Listening Guide 63

C/S: 7A/7   C/S: 7/ 21 – 24
Sh: 3A/6   Sh: 3/ 20 – 23

BARTÓK: *Music for Strings, Percussion, and Celesta,* Fourth Movement

Date of work: 1936   (6:42)

Medium: Double string orchestra, percussion, piano, and celesta

Movements:
  I. Andante tranquillo; fugue
  II. Allegro; sonata form
  III. Adagio; "Night Music"
  IV. Allegro molto

[handwritten annotations: — use of sonata allegro form — rondo-like form — hungarian folksong influence — quotation from — shifting meter]

FOURTH MOVEMENT: Allegro molto

Form: Rondo (**A-B-A-C-B-D-A**)

Basis: Folk dance tunes, the first a transformed version of the opening-movement fugue subject

21   0:00   **A** section—pizzicato chords in strings, resembling folk instruments, and timpani; modal theme, with Bulgarian dance rhythm (8 eighth notes grouped in 2 + 3 + 3), irregular rhythm:

22   0:26   **B** section—timpani solo intro-
            duces humorous piano tune:

     0:43   **A** section—first theme returns;
            stops abruptly with wavering
            string line; piano enters with
            main theme, answered by strings

23   1:27   **C** section—Più mosso (more mo-
            tion); simple, folklike tune in
            strings, played staccato, accom-
            panied by piano:

     2:34   **B** section—piano tune returns,
            very dissonant, builds in volume
            and tempo (Vivacissimo, with
            strings)

24   3:15   **D** section—strings enter with
            melody treated in inversion (up-
            side down) and stretto (overlap-
            ping statements) in a fugue:

     5:22   **A** section—first theme returns,
            inverted; accented in strings;
            brief celesta solo, then strings
            and piano:

Bartók's prime characteristic both as musician and man was the uncompromising integrity that informed his every act—what a compatriot of his has
called "the proud morality of the mind." He was one of the great spirits of the
century.

72

The American Scene: Art Music

"Music [is] the favorite passion of my soul."—THOMAS JEFFERSON

The Beginnings of American Nationalism

We have already explored various aspects of early American music and concert life in Cultural Perspectives (pp. 213, 357), noting several styles that were unique to the United States. These included the fuging tune, illustrated in works by the eighteenth-century composer William Billings; the popular ballad, by such writers as Stephen Foster; and the moving spiritual of the African-American and rural white communities.

By 1850, a substantial concert life had grown up in major U.S. and Canadian cities, dominated by European composers and musicians. Young Americans who were attracted to a musical career, whether as composers or performers, went abroad to complete their studies. When they returned home, they brought the European traditions with them. One of the first to use American song and dance as a source of inspiration was Louis Gottschalk (1829-69), a charismatic pianist and composer born in New Orleans and trained in Paris, who made his American debut in 1853. Some of Gottschalk's original piano pieces, such as *The Banjo* and *Bamboula,* incorporated features of an African-American musical idiom. It was only gradually that American musicians shook off the influence of German music. This development was consummated in the music of Charles Tomlinson Griffes (1884-1920), who turned for inspiration to France and the music of the Impressionists rather than to Germany, where he was trained. Meanwhile an unknown New Englander was working in isolation to find a vital way of expressing the American spirit in music— Charles Ives, whom history has revealed as the first major prophet of North America's musical coming of age.

In this century, American composers of art music have not followed any one style, but each has distilled a personal, innovative synthesis from the available possibilities. The extraordinary emigration of composers and other musicians from Europe on the eve of the Second World War added a further element to the mix. Since the Second World War, the United States has been the birthplace of many of the most significant new developments in art music. After a long period in search of "American music," composers have discovered that there is no such thing, but many different American musics—every one of them impossible to imagine as the product of any other culture.

Early history

The beginnings of American nationalism

Charles Ives

Career in business

Renown as composer

Charles Ives: His Life and Music

"Beauty in music is too often confused with something that lets the ears lie back in an easy chair. Many sounds that we are used to do not bother us, and for that reason we are inclined to call them beautiful. Frequently, when a new or unfamiliar work is accepted as beautiful on its first hearing, its fundamental quality is one that tends to put the mind to sleep."

Charles Edward Ives (1874–1954) waited many years for recognition. Today he stands as the first great American composer of the twentieth century, and one of the most original spirits of his time.

Ives was born in Danbury, Connecticut. His father had been a bandmaster in the Civil War and continued his profession in civilian life. Charles at thirteen held a job as church organist and arranged music for the various ensembles conducted by his father. At twenty, he entered Yale, where he studied composition with Horatio Parker. Ives's talent for music was evident throughout his four years at Yale; yet when he had to choose a career, he decided against a professional life in music. He suspected that society would not pay him for the kind of music he wanted to compose. He was right.

Ives therefore entered the business world. Two decades later, he was head of the largest insurance agency in the country. The years it took him to achieve this success—roughly from the age of twenty-one to forty-two—were the years when he also wrote his music. He composed at night, on weekends, and during vacations, working in isolation, concerned only to set down the sounds he heard in his head.

The few conductors and performers whom he tried to interest in his compositions pronounced them unplayable. After a number of these rebuffs, Ives gave up showing his manuscripts. When he felt the need to hear how his music sounded, he hired a few musicians to run through a work. Except for these rare and quite inadequate performances, Ives heard his music only in his imagination. He pursued this path undeflected and alone, piling up one score after another in his barn in Connecticut. When well-meaning friends suggested that he try to write music that people would like, he could only retort, "I can't do it—I hear something else!"

Ives's double life as a business executive by day and composer by night finally took its toll. In 1918, when he was forty-four, he suffered a physical breakdown that left his heart damaged. The years of unrewarded effort had taken more out of him emotionally than he had suspected. Although he lived almost forty years longer, he produced nothing further of importance.

When Ives recovered, he faced the realization that the world of professional musicians was irrevocably closed to his ideas. He felt that he owed it to his music to make it available to those who might be less conservative. He therefore had the *Concord* Sonata for piano privately printed, also the *Essays Before a Sonata,* a kind of elaborate program note that presented the essence of his views on life and art. These were followed by the *114 Songs.* The three volumes, which were distributed free of charge to libraries, music critics, and whoever else asked for them, did not cause a ripple as far as the public was concerned. But they gained Ives the support of other experimental com-

Principal Works

Orchestral music, including 4 symphonies (1898, 1902, 1904, 1916), *Three Places in New England* (1914), *The Unanswered Question* (1908), and *The Fourth of July* (from *A Symphony: New England Holidays,* 1913)

Chamber music, including 2 string quartets and 4 violin sonatas

Piano music, including 2 sonatas (No. 2, *Concord,* 1915)

Choral music and many songs, including *General William Booth Enters into Heaven* (1914)

posers who were struggling to make their way in an indifferent world. The tide finally turned when the American pianist John Kirkpatrick, at a recital in New York's Town Hall in January 1939, played the *Concord* Sonata. Ives was then sixty-five. The piece was repeated several weeks later by Kirkpatrick and scored a triumph. The next morning, the critic Lawrence Gilman hailed the *Concord* Sonata as "the greatest music composed by an American."

Ives had already begun to exert an influence upon the younger generation of composers, who found in his art a realization of their own ideals. Now he was "discovered" by the general public and proclaimed as the grand old man of American music. In 1947, his Third Symphony was performed and won a Pulitzer Prize. This story of delayed recognition was carried by newspapers throughout the country. Ives awoke at seventy-three to find himself famous. He died in New York City at the age of eighty.

Both as man and artist, Ives was rooted in the New England tradition of plain living and high thinking that came to flower in the idealism of such American writers as Nathaniel Hawthorne, Louisa May Alcott, Ralph Waldo Emerson, and Henry David Thoreau. The sources of his tonal imagery are to be found in the music of his childhood: hymn tunes and traditional songs, the town band at holiday parades, the fiddlers at Saturday night dances, patriotic songs and sentimental parlor ballads, the melodies of Stephen Foster, and the medleys heard at country fairs and in small theaters.

This wealth of American music had attracted other musicians besides Ives. But they, acknowledging European taste, proceeded to smooth out and "correct" these well-known tunes. Ives was as free from subservience to the European tradition as Walt Whitman. His keen ear caught the sound of untrained voices singing a hymn together—some, in their eagerness, straining and sharpening the pitch, others just missing it and flatting, so that in place of the single tone there was a cluster of tones that made a deliciously dissonant chord. Some voices were a trifle ahead of the beat, others lagged behind; consequently the rhythm sagged and turned into a jumble of polyrhythms. Ives heard the pungent clash of dissonance when two bands in a parade, each playing a different tune in a different key, came close enough together to overlap;

Cultural Perspective 20

Music and the Patriotic Spirit

Have you ever been moved to tears by a patriotic song—perhaps your national anthem? Music has often fueled emotions, inciting acts of heroism and patriotism that are remembered for generations through song. We have heard several traditional songs of the Civil War echoing through the twentieth-century compositions of Charles Ives. Other tunes well-known to most of us had their origins in wartime as well. The colonial troops of the American Revolution marched to the fife-and-drum strains of *Yankee Doodle. Dixie* ("I wish I was in the land of cotton," written, ironically, by a Northerner) was a rallying cry of the Civil War's Confederacy sounded against the North's *Battle Hymn of the Republic* (a poem by author Julia Ward Howe, sung to the tune of *John Brown's Body*).

In the early twentieth century, songwriter George M. Cohan was so moved by the U.S. declaration of war against Germany in 1917 that he wrote *Over There* ("Send the word, over there, that the Yanks are coming"), a catchy song that caught on immediately with the American public and soldiers during the First World War. Likewise, songwriter Irving Berlin joined with singer Kate Smith in a 1938 radio broadcast to build patriotic support just prior to U.S. involvement in the Second World War. The song that captured the hearts of millions was *God Bless America,* now thought of by many as the country's "second national anthem."

The national anthems of many countries, including the United States, were the direct result of wartime emotions. The lyrics of *The Star-Spangled Banner* were written in 1814 by a Baltimore attorney named Francis Scott Key during the English bombardment of Fort McHenry (a famous battle during the War of 1812). Key was aboard a small ship in Chesapeake Bay, nervously watching the flag over the fort and knowing that if it went down, so too would his beloved Baltimore. Thus the flag-inspired lyrics—"Oh, say, can you see, by the dawn's early light, what so proudly we hailed at the twilight's last gleaming? Whose broad stripes and bright stars through the perilous fight"—which he adapted to the disjunct tune of an English drinking song that everyone finds difficult to sing. (This song was not adopted as the U.S. national anthem until 1931.) France's *Marseillaise* is another example of a revolutionary anthem ("Allons, enfants de la patrie! Le jour de gloire est arrivé," or "Arise, children of the homeland! The day of glory has arrived"), as is Mexico's *Mexicanos, al grito de guerra* (Mexicans, to the War Cry), a spirited song of independence.

Happily, the patriotic spirit is alive in peacetime as well. It has produced such notable anthems as Britain's *God Save the Queen* (or *King*)—the same tune to which we sing *America* ("My country 'tis of thee") and the stately *Emperor's Hymn* by Haydn. The latter was originally adopted as the Austrian anthem but serves today as the national song of recently unified Germany, with the text "Einigkeit und Recht und Freiheit," or "Unity and right and liberty." Canada also recently adopted an anthem that draws together its multiethnic population—*O Canada,* written in 1880 by the French-Canadian Calixa Lavallée, was named the country's national hymn (in French and English) in 1980. The universality of music is illustrated in Israel's anthem, *Hatikvah* (The Hope), a moving poem of the Jewish people

Sheet music cover for Over There *by George M. Cohan, written to inspire American troops fighting in the First World War. The cover design is by the famous American artist* **Norman Rockwell.**

returning to their ancient homeland in the late nineteenth century, set to the melody of a haunting Bohemian folk song. In times of national crisis or pride, whether responding to a war or an Olympic victory, these memorable songs resound deep in the soul of a people.

Suggested Listening:

National anthems (U.S., France, Mexico, Canada, Israel, Great Britain, Germany)

he heard the effect of quarter tones (an interval half the size of a half step) when fiddlers at a country dance brought excitement into their playing by going a bit off pitch. He remembered the wheezy harmonium at church accompanying the hymns a trifle out of tune.

All these, Ives realized, were not departures from the norm; they were the norm of traditional American musical speech. Thus he found his way to such conceptions as polytonality, atonality, polyharmony, chord clusters based on intervals of a second, and polyrhythms. And this occurred in the last years of the nineteenth century, when Schoenberg was still writing in a post-Wagnerian idiom, and neither Stravinsky nor Bartók had begun his career. This singular musician, isolated from the public and his fellow composers, developed conceptions far ahead of his time and accurately forecast the paths that twentieth-century music would follow. *Polytonality and polyrhythm*

The central position in Ives's orchestral music is held by the four symphonies. Among his other orchestral works are *Three Places in New England, The Unanswered Question,* and a cycle of four tone poems entitled *A Symphony: New England Holidays,* from which we will study *The Fourth of July.* The Sonata No. 2 for piano— "Concord, Mass., 1840–1860"—which occupied him from 1909 to 1915, reflects various aspects of New England's cul- *Orchestral and other works* ture. Its four movements are named after distinctive American authors: "Emerson," "Hawthorne," "The Alcotts," and "Thoreau." Ives also wrote a variety of songs, as well as chamber, choral, and piano compositions.

THE FOURTH OF JULY

The Fourth of July is the third movement of Ives's *New England Holidays.* His program note for the work presents a nostalgic picture of a scene from his youth:

> It's a boy's Fourth—no historical orations—no patriotic grandiloquence by grown-ups—no program in his yard! But he knows what he's celebrating—better than some of the country politicians. And he goes at it in his own way, with a patriotism nearer kin to nature than jingoism. It starts in the quiet of midnight before and grows raucous with the sun. Everybody knows what it's like—cannon on the green, village band on Main St., firecrackers under tin cans, lost-finger, fifes, clam chowder, a prize-fight, burnt shins, parades (in and out of step), saloons all closed (more drunks than usual), baseball game (Danbury All-Stars vs. Beaver Brook Boys), pistols, mobbed umpire, Red White and Blue, runaway horse—and the day ends with the sky-rocket over the church steeple, just after the annual explosion sets the Town Hall on fire. All this is not in the music—now now!

Ives's way of weaving patriotic and popular tunes into the fabric of the music—a phrase here, a fragment there, sometimes buried in the orchestral hubbub—is entirely his own. At times, the ear readily identifies the melody; at other times, all we hear are a few notes that quickly disappear. Sometimes Ives unfolds two tunes simultaneously, and in different keys at that. The harmonic language is highly dissonant and builds to several explosions of sound that have all the brilliance of aural fireworks. This makes us hear what sound very much like wrong notes. Ives had to caution his copyist about this: "Mr. Price, please don't try to make things nice! All the notes are right. Just copy as I have—I want it that way."

The meter shifts continually in the opening measures, alternating between 4/4 and 7/8. It is obvious from several works by Ives, including this one, that the tune that most completely symbolized America to him was *Columbia, the Gem of the Ocean,* also known as *The Red, White, and Blue.* (It must be remembered that *The Star-Spangled Banner* did not officially become the U. S. national anthem until 1931.) In *The Fourth of July,* Ives quotes *Columbia, the Gem of the Ocean* almost in its entirety. Sounded by the brass, it becomes a basic element of the march section (see Listening Guide 64).

High-dissonance tension, bitonality and polytonality, polymeters and polyrhythms, and wonderful passages of orchestral noise place this piece in the mainstream of international modernism. But its fundamental building blocks are as unmistakably American as apple pie. Ives's final comment in the score is "not evenly, but as a falling rocket."

The works of Charles Ives are now firmly established in contemporary concert life. Like the writers he admired most—Emerson, Hawthorne, Thoreau—he has become an American classic.

Listening Guide 64

 C/S: 7A/5   C/S: 7/ 11 – 18

IVES: *The Fourth of July,* from *A Symphony: New England Holidays*   (6:04)

Date of work: 1911–13

Medium: Large orchestra

Movements:

    I. *Washington's Birthday*

    II. *Decoration Day*

    III. *The Fourth of July*

    IV. *Thanksgiving and Forefathers' Day*

THIRD MOVEMENT: *The Fourth of July*

Principal tune heard: *Columbia, the Gem of the Ocean:*

11	0:00	Begins soft and slow (Adagio molto); violin plays opening of *Columbia, the Gem of the Ocean* over sustained chord
	0:55	Double basses and tuba play opening of *Columbia* against dissonant strings; tempo picks up—shifting meters with dissonant strings and woodwinds, punctuated by double basses and timpani
12	2:05	Faster (Allegretto); flutes, piccolo, and violin play fragments of *Columbia* over repeated-note ostinato in double basses
	2:22	Trumpet plays a phrase from *Marching Through Georgia*
13	2:36	Explosive chord, marked "like a gun shot"; Più Allegretto: woodwinds present fragments of *Sailor's Hornpipe* and other dance tunes, changing meters
14	3:00	Violins and woodwinds, followed by brass with fragments of *Battle Hymn of the Republic;* dissonance builds
	3:20	*Reveille* bugle call sounded in horns, then trumpets:

	3:30	Trombones play phrase of *Columbia,* quick-step time, marked più moto
15	3:40	March begins, adds fifes to orchestra, which plays a phrase of *The Girl I Left Behind Me;* suggestion of *London Bridge* in fifes
16	4:01	Dissonant explosion of sound—marked con furore (with furor), then quieter; a tempo—xylophone presents two tunes, *Garryowen* and *St. Patrick's Day in the Morning* over dissonant strings; trombone plays phrase of *Columbia*

17	4:52	Quick-step, Allegro con spirito; main tune, *Columbia,* heard nearly in entirety in brass, chaotic and dissonant, with other tunes played at same time:
		        xylophone plays *Yankee Doodle*
		        flute plays *The Battle Hymn of the Republic*
		        piccolo plays *Katy Darling*

18	5:28	Loud combination of tunes suddenly stops; bells, then drum roll
		Final explosion of sound, dying away to lyrical, dissonant strings "not evenly, but as a falling rocket"

Ruth Crawford: Her Life and Music

"Serious music is a cooperation of head and heart, of feeling and thinking."—CHARLES SEEGER on RUTH CRAWFORD

Ruth Crawford

Ruth Crawford (1901–53) was born in East Liverpool, Ohio, and grew up "in that traditional cradle of Americanism, a minister's household." She composed along traditional lines until, in her late twenties, she went to New York. There she studied with her future husband, the musicologist-folklorist Charles Seeger, who, along with the composer Henry Cowell and others, was active in what was then the avant-garde. Crawford's compositions took a boldly experimental turn, and she produced a series of strikingly original works. She was the first woman to hold a Guggenheim Fellowship in composition, which gave her a year of study in Berlin. It was during this time that she wrote her most important work, the String Quartet (1931).

There was, however, no audience in America for what Crawford had to say. The public had ears only for the European masterpieces of the past. And she faced the additional challenge of being a woman in a field that was traditionally male-dominated. Like other avant-garde composers, notably Charles Ives, she gave up composing when she should have been at the height of her creativity. After her marriage to Charles Seeger, she collaborated with him in editing collections of American folk songs. This activity played a part in determining the career of her stepson, the talented folk singer Pete Seeger. Crawford died in Chevy Chase, Maryland, at the age of fifty-two, her music practically forgotten. It is only in recent years that she has been recognized as one of the few innovative American composers who in wholly remarkable fashion anticipated developments that became current several decades later.

Ruth Crawford's String Quartet (1931) is a concise, arresting work that displays her style at its best. The fourth movement, an Allegro possibile (as fast as

> ## Principal Works
>
> Instrumental works, including 1 orchestral piece; numerous chamber pieces, including String Quartet (1931) and several suites
>
> Piano music, including several sets of preludes
>
> Songs, including several sets on poems by Carl Sandburg (Five Songs, 1929; Three Songs, 1932); choral music

possible), is remarkable in its anticipation of present-day procedures. Serial technique is used not only for the notes, but also for its rhythmic and phrase structure. What we have here is an attempt to achieve total control over all elements. In this movement, Crawford was introducing ideas that, outside a narrow circle, were completely unknown in America. At the same time, she foreshadowed the serial techniques that became the major preoccupation of composers in the years after the Second World War.

RAT RIDDLES

Rat Riddles is the first of a set of three songs on poems by the American poet Carl Sandburg, whom Ruth Crawford met when she was his daughters' piano teacher. She helped prepare his poem anthology, which appeared in 1927, and published her Three Songs on his texts five years later. Sandburg described her work as "mystic and elfin with a quality akin to Emily Dickinson."

The scoring for *Rat Riddles* is unusual: alto singer and a chamber ensemble of three groups. The main group is called, in Baroque fashion, *concertanti* and consists of the solo voice, oboe, piano, and four percussionists playing a variety of instruments (Chinese block, triangle, tambourine, cymbals, and bass drum). The song can be performed with this group alone. The other two groups, called ostinati, one of winds and one of strings, supply rhythmic punctuation.

The texture is contrapuntal and heterophonic. The term *heterophony* indicates a texture of two or more voices each of which goes its own way, so that they are not only interdependent but also unusually independent of one another. Charles Seeger described her style of heterophony as "together-soundingness in which separate-soundingness predominates."

Heterophony

Sandburg's poem contains two distinct elements—couplets of narration spoken by the poet and passages of dialogue with the rat. Crawford's setting closely follows the literary form. A kind of Baroque *ritornello* (recurring passage) opens the work and returns in variation for each couplet of narration. Interspersed with these are passages of dialogue that are more animated and wider in range. (See Listening Guide 65 for the text.)

Wit, imagination, and originality abound in *Rat Riddles*. We can only conjecture in what direction this gifted musician would have continued if the time and place had been ready for her.

Listening Guide 65

C/S: 8A/3   C/S: 8/ 12 – 15

CRAWFORD: *Rat Riddles,* from Three Songs (1933)   (3:26)

Date of work: 1930

Text: Carl Sandburg

Medium: Alto voice with chamber ensemble, divided into 3 groups:

Concertanti (principal group): voice, oboe, piano, 4 percussionists (playing Chinese block, triangle, tambourine, cymbals, bass drum)

Ostinati 1 (wind instruments): clarinet, bassoon, trumpet, French horn, trombone

Ostinati 2 (string instruments): violin I, violin II, viola, cello, double bass

Tempo: Moderato ritmico (moderate, rhythmic)

		Text	*Description*
12	0:00		**Ritornello**—opens with percussion, then piano and disjunct oboe line, with trills punctuated by *ostinati*
		There was a gray rat looked at me with green eyes out of a rathole.	Vocalist—small intervals, growing more disjunct
		"Hello, rat," I said, "Is there any chance for me to get onto the language of the rats?"	More animated, wider range, and more disjunct
13	0:57		**Ritornello**—instruments, oboe featured
		And the green eyes blinked at me, blinked from a gray rat's rathole.	Variation of first couplet
		"Come again, rat," I said, "slip me a couple of riddles; there must be riddles among the rats."	Irregular rhythmic groupings; voice over long oboe trill and active piano part
14	1:40		**Ritornello**—instruments, oboe prominent
		And the green eyes blinked at me and a whisper came from the gray rathole:	Variation of opening couplet
		"Who do you think you are and why is a rat? Where did you sleep last night and why do you sneeze on Tuesdays?	Recitative-like, over bass drum roll, dramatic; climax on "sneeze"
		And why is the grave of a rat no deeper than the grave of a man?"	More lyrical, sustained accompaniment
15	2:59		**Ritornello**—instruments, returns to opening tempo
		And the tail of a green-eyed rat whipped and was gone at a gray rathole.	Variation of opening couplet, percussion and piano at close

Opening of vocal line in first couplet:

There was   a   gray   rat   looked at me with green eyes

Aaron Copland: His Life and Music

"I no longer feel the need of seeking out conscious Americanism. Because we live here and work here, we can be certain that when our music is mature it will also be American in quality."

Aaron Copland

Aaron Copland (1900–90) has been generally recognized as the representative figure among contemporary American composers. In his music, he achieves the clarity and sense of balance that is regarded as the essence of the Classical temperament.

Copland was born "on a street in Brooklyn that can only be described as drab. . . . Music was the last thing anyone would have connected with it." During his early twenties, he studied in Paris with the famous teacher Nadia Boulanger, her first full-time American pupil. When Boulanger was invited to give concerts in New York, she asked Copland to write a work for her. This was the Symphony for Organ and Orchestra. Contemporary American music was still a novelty to New York audiences. After the first performance, in 1925, conductor Walter Damrosch found it necessary to calm down his subscribers. "If a young man at the age of twenty-five," he announced from the stage of Carnegie Hall, "can write a symphony like that, in five years he will be ready to commit murder." Damrosch's prophecy was not fulfilled.

In his growth as a composer, Copland mirrored the dominant trends of his time. After his return from Paris, he turned to the jazz idiom, a phase that culminated in his brilliant Piano Concerto. There followed a period during which the Neoclassicist experimented with the abstract materials of his art and produced the Piano Variations, *Short Symphony,* and *Statements for Orchestra.* "During these years I began to feel an increasing dissatisfaction with the relations of the music-loving public and the living composer. It seemed to me that we composers were in danger of working in a vacuum," Copland wrote. He realized that a new public for contemporary music was being created by the radio, phonograph, and film scores. "It made no sense to ignore them and to

Jazz idiom

Neoclassical period

Principal Works

Orchestral music, including 3 symphonies, Piano Concerto (1926), *Short Symphony* (1933), *Statements for Orchestra* (1933–35), *El salón México* (1936), *A Lincoln Portrait* (1942), *Fanfare for the Common Man* (1942), and *Connotations for Orchestra* (1962)

3 ballets: *Billy the Kid* (1938), *Rodeo* (1942), *Appalachian Spring* (1944)

Film scores, including *The City* (1939), *Of Mice and Men* (1939), *Our Town* (1940), *The Red Pony* (1948), and *The Heiress* (1948)

Piano music, including Piano Variations (1930)

Chamber music; choral music and songs

continue writing as if they did not exist. I felt that it was worth the effort to see if I couldn't say what I had to say in the simplest possible terms." In this fashion, Copland was led to what became a most significant development after the 1930s: the attempt to simplify the new music so that it would communicate to a large public.

The 1930s and 1940s saw the creation of the works that established Copland's popularity. *El salón México* (1936) is an orchestral piece based on Mexican melodies and rhythms. The three ballets, *Billy the Kid, Rodeo,* and *Appalachian Spring,* continue to delight an international audience. Among his film scores are *Quiet City, Of Mice and Men, Our Town, The Red Pony,* and *The Heiress,* which brought him an Academy Award. Two important works written in time of war are *A Lincoln Portrait,* for speaker and chorus, drawn from Lincoln's own speeches, and the Third Symphony. In *Connotations for Orchestra,* Copland demonstrated that he could handle twelve-tone techniques.

BILLY THE KID

For the ballet based on the saga of *Billy the Kid,* Copland produced one of his freshest scores. In it are embedded in whole or in part several classic cowboy tunes. They are not quoted literally. Rather, Copland uses these melodies as a point of departure for his own creations; they flavor his music but are assimilated into his personal style.

Billy the Kid—the Brooklyn-born William Bonney—had a brief but intense career as a desperado, in the course of which he became one of the legends of the Wild West. The ballet touches on the chief episodes of his life. We see him first as a boy of twelve; when his mother is killed by a stray bullet in a street brawl, he stabs the man responsible for her death. Later, during a card game, he is accused of cheating and kills the accuser. Captured after a gun battle, he is put in jail. He then murders his jailer and gets away. A romantic interlude ensues when he rejoins his Mexican sweetheart in the desert. But there is no escaping. At the close, we hear a lament on the death of the notorious outlaw.

The concert suite Copland put together contains about two-thirds of the ballet. *The Open Prairie,* which serves as a prologue, evokes a remote and spacious landscape. This is transformed into a poetic symbol of all that is vast and unchanging. We will hear the first scene, *Street in a Frontier Town.* In this scene, as Copland explained, he used tunes of the Wild West such as the cowboy songs *Goodbye, Old Paint; The Old Chisholm Trail; Git Along, Little Dogies;* and *Great Grand-Dad.* (See Listening Guide 66 for details.) The composer adapted these melodies to his needs, decking them out with polyrhythms, polytonal harmonies, and dissonances made more striking because they fall on accented beats. The result is a music of powerful rhythmic thrust and vigorous physical activity, bursting with energy and excitement as it mounts to a *fortissimo* climax.

Music has a glorious way of leaping over barriers of race, religion, and nation. And so it was given to the son of Russian-Jewish immigrants growing up on the streets of Brooklyn to create a musical image of the American West, the prairie, and the cowboy that is heard and recognized worldwide.

Fernando Bujones dancing the title role in the American Ballet Theater produc-tion of Billy the Kid. *This scene, from* Street in a Frontier Town, *shows the frightened boy just after his mother is accidentally killed.* (©Martha Swope)

Listening Guide 66

C/S: 8A/2	C/S: 8/ 9 – 11
Sh: 3A/7	Sh: 3/ 24 – 26

COPLAND: *Billy the Kid,* Scene 1, *Street in a Frontier Town*   (6:22)

Date of work: 1938 (ballet first performed); 1939 (orchestral suite)

Genre: Orchestral suite from ballet

Basis: Actual story of outlaw William Bonney (called Billy the Kid)

Sections of orchestral suite:

    The Open Prairie

  1. *Street in a Frontier Town*

  2. *Prairie Night (Card Game at Night)*

  3. *Gun Battle*

  4. *Celebration* (after Billy's Capture)

  5. *Billy's Death*

Copland's notes on the ballet: *The ballet begins and ends on the open prairie. The first scene is a street in a frontier town. Cowboys saunter into town, some on horseback, others on foot with their lassos; some Mexican women do a jarabe, which is interrupted by a fight between two drunks. Attracted by the gathering crowd, Billy is seen for the first time, a boy of twelve, with his mother. The brawl turns ugly, guns are drawn, and in some unaccountable way, Billy's mother is killed. Without an instant's hesitation, in cold fury, Billy draws a knife from a cowhand's sheath and stabs his mother's slayers. His short but famous career has begun. In swift succession we see episodes in Billy's later life—at night, under the stars, in a quiet card game with his outlaw friends, hunted by a posse led by his former friend Pat Garrett, in a gun battle. A drunken celebration takes place when he is captured. Billy makes one of his legendary escapes from prison. Tired and worn out in the desert, Billy rests with his girl. Finally the posse catches up with him.*

***Street in a Frontier Town;* Moderato**

9 0:00   Piccolo solo, with tune *Great Grand-Dad:*

           Other woodwinds join in dialogue

0:21   New tune in oboe and trumpet, almost in
        unison, with dissonance on strong beat (x):

0:44   *Great Grand-Dad* heard in piccolo, while
        strings enter with dissonant tune from
        above

0:57   Alternation of two tunes—the first in
        woodwinds and strings, second in trom-
        bones

1:08   Trumpet, with new, shifting-meter tune (4
        + 3 + 4 + 3), with accompaniment in op-
        posite meter (3 + 4 + 3 + 4):

1:15   Strings take up shifting-meter tune; brass
        and strings return to dissonant tune, which
        dies out

1:47   Large chords played *fortissimo* in full or-
        chestra, punctuated by bass drum

10 1:57   Quick dance tune in strings in 4/4, accom-
           panied by syncopated woodblock:

2:18   Horns enter with new tune in triplets

2:28   Dance tune continues, with interjections
        of earlier dissonant tune in oboe and trum-
        pet

2:56   Opening tune heard in piccolo and clar-
        inet, more animated, with grace notes and
        harmonics in strings and sleigh bells, fol-
        lowed by slower, legato melody in low
        strings

11 3:26   Mexican dance (Jarabe) and finale; trum-
           pet, with melody in 5/8 meter, accompa-
           nied by woodblock and gourd (accents
           shown with x's):

4:14	Violins enter with tune *Goodbye, Old Paint* in legato, 3/4 meter; alternate with oboe playing verse of same cowboy song:	
5:23	*Goodbye, Old Paint* continues in fabric of complex polyphony; full orchestra plays tune, alternating chorus and verse; transformed as it builds to climax	
5:56	3 loud chords, followed by 2 low notes (gunshots), end section	

Cultural Perspective 21

Copland Looks to the Wild West and South of the Border

We have seen that composer Aaron Copland was inspired by songs of the Western frontier, although he was born and raised in Brooklyn, New York. There is a wide repertory of traditional tunes of the West that have come down to us today. Some tell of famous outlaws such as Billy the Kid and Jesse James or of high-stakes gamblers like Wild Bill Hickok; others are work songs (*Git Along, Little Dogie*) or laments of death on the trail or in gunfights (*The Streets of Laredo*). In short, they narrate the way of life of the American cowboy. Traditional songs such as *Goodbye, Old Paint* suggest that one's horse was not only a tool of the trade, but a trusted companion as well. ("Old paint" refers to a pinto horse, *pinto* being Spanish for "spotted"; see p. 27 for tune and words.)

The Hollywood image of the American cowboy, with John Wayne always winning the fights against the bad guys, is somewhat distorted. Many of those roving the American frontier were Southerners—whites and African Americans—who lost their homes

and families in the Civil War. It is through an ex-slave named Charley Willis that the song *Goodbye, Old Paint* is preserved today; he taught it to a ranch hand who, in old age, recorded it for folk song collector John Lomax. Other cowboys were Native Americans, and many were Chicanos (called *vaqueros* after the Spanish word for "cowboys"). Several commonly used words derive from the early days of Spanish colonization in the West: lariat (a rope) comes from *la reata,* and chaps (leather leg coverings) is short for *chaparreras.*

What of women in the West? Several were legendary: the expert markswoman Annie Oakley was originally from Cincinnati, at the edge of the frontier, and traveled as part of a Wild West show, while Calamity Jane was from the Dakota Territory (the Dakotas were not yet states) and reportedly could outshoot any man. (You may know that Annie Oakley inspired the well-known 1946 Broadway musical *Annie Get Your Gun,* by Irving Berlin.) Another heroine of frontier days was

Copland's music for Billy the Kid *is as firmly rooted in uniquely American traditions as the cowboy bronzes of* **Frederic Remington** *(1861–1909), like* Bronco Buster. *(Amon Carter Museum, Fort Worth, Texas)*

Emily West, an African-American woman who played a key role in the Battle of San Jacinto, in which the Texans defeated the Mexican army of General Antonio Lopez de Santa Ana. It is she, not a flower, who is the subject of *The Yellow Rose of Texas* ("the yellow rose of Texas beats the belles of Tennessee"—the allusion to "yellow" refers to the fact that she was of mixed Caucasian and African-American ancestry). Many more unnamed women braved the long and difficult trip west to establish a new life for their families. The familiar song *Sweet Betsy from Pike* praises one such courageous woman ("Oh, don't you remember Sweet Betsy from Pike, who crossed the big mountains with her lover Ike?").

Cowboy songs have been preserved for us today through folk song collectors, as described above, who published volumes of traditional music in the early twentieth cen-

tury. But the well-known tunes have been widely disseminated by the media as well: singing cowboys were popular in 1930s and 1940s movies (Gene Autry, Roy Rogers, and Tex Ritter), country/western recording artist Johnny Cash's recent release *Cash* (1994) includes an arrangement of the traditional song *Oh, Bury Me Not on the Lone Prairie,* and another artist, Chris Ledoux, is making a name for himself singing newly composed cowboy songs.

The lore of the West has intrigued artists as well, and several have left us vivid images of life of this earlier era. Most famous are the American painters Winslow Homer (1836–1910) and Frederic Remington (1861–1909), the latter well-known for his rough-and-tumble cowboys and cavalrymen and for his much-prized bronze sculptures like *Bronco Buster.*

Aaron Copland also looked to Latin

America for traditional music. He toured Mexico and South America, visiting with such native composers as Carlos Chávez (1899–1978) and Alberto Ginastera (1916–83), both of whom combined indigenous musics with European styles in their own compositions. Copland's orchestral work *El salón México* (1936) draws on the colorful sounds of Mexican dance music, as does his ballet suite *Billy the Kid*. This latter work incorporates the jarabe, a rural Mexican dance and musical form that has various sections in different tempos and meters. An exhibition dance, the jarabe is performed by a couple attired in gala dress—the man with wide-brimmed hat and chaps, the woman in a multicolored, sequined skirt and shawl. Today, the jarabe is an urban form, accompanied by mariachi groups (with trumpets, violins, guitar, and guitarron, or bass guitar). Mariachi bands, originally from western Mexico, can be heard today throughout that country as well as in parts of the United States.

Terms to Note:

jarabe
mariachi

Suggested Listening:

Copland: *Street in a Frontier Town* from
    Billy the Kid, or *El salón México*
Traditional songs of the Old West
Mexican music (mariachi band, jarabe)
Works by Carlos Chávez or Alberto Ginastera

UNIT XXIV

Popular Styles

73

Blues and Early Jazz

"Music is your own experience, your thoughts, your wisdom. If you don't live it, it won't come out of your horn."—CHARLIE PARKER

We have seen that a diversity of cultures met in the great melting pot that is America. Blues and jazz, rooted in the music of African Americans, were part and parcel of the American scene, and captured the imagination of the world.

Jazz refers to a music created mainly by African Americans in the early twentieth century as they blended elements drawn from African musics with the popular and art traditions of the West. One of the most influential early *Ragtime* styles was *ragtime,* so-called for its "ragged" rhythm marked by highly syncopated melodies. Primarily a piano style, ragtime gained popularity in instrumental ensemble arrangements by Scott Joplin (1868–1917), an African-American composer known as the "king of ragtime." Fame came to Joplin in 1899 with the publication of his *Maple Leaf Rag,* a piano piece that sold thousands of copies. It has since been arranged for all kinds of ensembles; this work, along with his rag *The Entertainer,* were included in the soundtrack of the movie *The Sting* (1974).

Blues *Blues* is a truly American form of folk music based on a simple, repetitive poetic-musical structure. Its text typically consists of a three-line stanza of which the first two lines are identical. Its vocal style was derived from the work songs of Southern blacks. The term "blues" refers to a mood as well as a harmonic progression, which is usually twelve or sixteen bars in length. Characteristic is the *blue note,* a slight drop in pitch on the third, fifth, or seventh tone of the scale.

New Orleans jazz Blues is a fundamental form in jazz. The music we call jazz was born in New Orleans through the fusion of such African-American elements as ragtime and

Twelve-Bar Blues Progression

Chord	I	IV	I	V	I
	Tonic	Subdominant	Tonic	Dominant	Tonic
Bars	4	2	2	2	2 = 12

Blue notes on the scale:

Blues vocal form (3-line strophe, first 2 repeated): from *Empty Bed Blues* (recorded in 1928 by Bessie Smith)

> I woke up this morning with an awful aching head.
> I woke up this morning with an awful aching head.
> My new man had left me, just a room and an empty bed.

blues with other traditional styles—spirituals, work songs, and shouts. (For more on the roots of jazz, see CP 22.) Basic to these elements was the art of improvisation. Performers made up their parts as they went along, often with a number of them improvising at the same time. They were able to do this because all the players knew the basic rules—the tempo, the form, the harmonic progression, and the order in which instruments were to be featured. A twelve-bar blues progression followed the standard harmonic pattern included in the chart above.

New Orleans jazz depended upon the players' multiple improvisation, which created a polyphonic texture. Each instrument had its role. The trumpet or cornet played the melody or an embellished version; the clarinet was often featured in a countermelody above the main tune; the trombone improvised below the trumpet and signaled the chord changes; and the rhythm section—consisting of string bass or tuba, guitar or banjo, and drums—provided rhythmic and harmonic support. Among the "greats" of New Orleans jazz were Joseph "King" Oliver (cornet), Sidney Bechet (soprano saxophone), Ferdinand "Jelly Roll" Morton (piano), and Louis "Satchmo" Armstrong (trumpet).

Louis Armstrong and the Blues

During the 1920s, New Orleans musicians traveled throughout the country—to New York, Chicago, Denver, and points west—spreading their new sound. One well-known musician, Louis "Satchmo" Armstrong (c. 1898–1971), settled in Chicago in 1922, joining the ten-piece New Orleans style ensemble

The Hot Five in 1925: (left to right) Louis Armstrong, trumpet; Johnny St. Cyr, banjo; Johnny Dodds, clarinet; Kid Ory, trombone; and Lil Hardin Armstrong, piano.

known as the King Oliver Creole Jazz Band. The young Armstrong, playing cornet, made his first recordings in 1923 with this ensemble, and went on to revolutionize jazz.

Armstrong was unquestionably the most important single force in the development of early jazz styles. He was a great improviser who expanded the capacities of his instrument in range and tone colors through the use of various mutes. To distinguish his unique melodic-rhythmic style of performance, his admirers coined the term "swing," which became a standard description of

Scat singing
jazz. His 1926 recording of *Heebie Jeebies* introduced *scat singing*, a jazz style that sets syllables without literal meaning (vocables) to an improvised vocal line. Ella Fitzgerald later brought this technique to a truly virtuosic level.

Armstrong's style of jazz introduced a number of new features: stop-time choruses (solos accompanied by spaced staccato chords); double-time choruses, in which each beat of each measure was subdivided; a simple two- or four-beat meter based on evenly accented pulses; and solo rather than ensemble choruses. Through these innovations, jazz was transformed into a solo art that presented improvised fantasias on chord changes rather than on a repeated melody.

West End Blues is a twelve-bar blues recorded in 1928 by Armstrong and the Savoy Ballroom Five. It features Satchmo on trumpet and in a vocal, along with Fred Robinson on trombone, Jimmy Strong on clarinet, Mancy Cara on banjo, Zutty Singleton on drums, and the great Earl "Fatha" Hines on piano. This number opens with an unaccompanied trumpet solo by Armstrong in double time. There follow five choruses on the tune over the repeating

Chorus
twelve-bar progression mentioned earlier. (In jazz, a *chorus* refers to a single statement of the harmonic-melodic pattern; see analysis in Listening Guide 67.) In the first chorus, we hear a solo trumpet melody set to a fairly simple

chordal accompaniment. The second chorus brings in the mellow voice of the trombone, supported by a percussive accompaniment. The third chorus features clarinet against Satchmo's scat singing in a call-and-response pattern, while the fourth highlights Hines's so-called trumpet-style piano playing. In the last chorus, a trumpet and clarinet duet is heard over the insistent chords, beginning with a sustained note—a high B flat—on the trumpet, followed by a double-time melody. This chorus is extended with a brief *tag* (the jazz term for a short coda). Throughout the selection, we hear many blue, or bent, notes.

Louis Armstrong's sound summed up an era. It has remained one of the high points of the American jazz style.

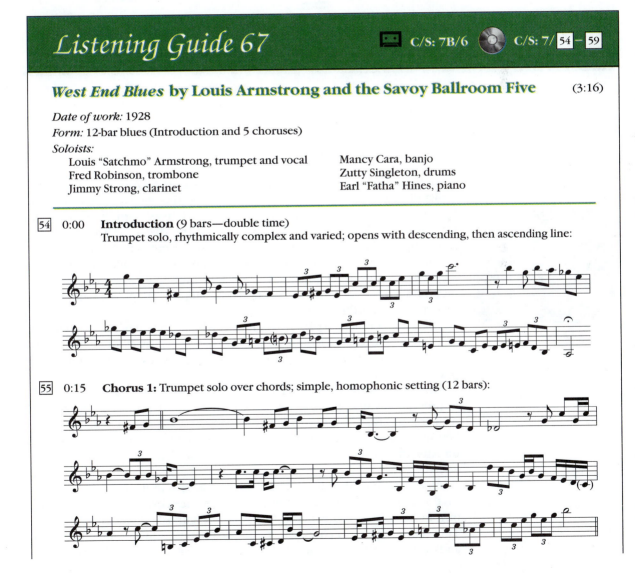

Listening Guide 67

C/S: 7B/6   C/S: 7/ 54 – 59

West End Blues by Louis Armstrong and the Savoy Ballroom Five   (3:16)

Date of work: 1928
Form: 12-bar blues (Introduction and 5 choruses)
Soloists:

Louis "Satchmo" Armstrong, trumpet and vocal
Fred Robinson, trombone
Jimmy Strong, clarinet

Mancy Cara, banjo
Zutty Singleton, drums
Earl "Fatha" Hines, piano

54 0:00 **Introduction** (9 bars—double time)
Trumpet solo, rhythmically complex and varied; opens with descending, then ascending line:

55 0:15 **Chorus 1:** Trumpet solo over chords; simple, homophonic setting (12 bars):

56 | 0:49 | **Chorus 2:** Trombone solo over chords, with percussion accompaniment (12 bars)

57 | 1:23 | **Chorus 3:** Clarinet and vocal solos (scat singing); motives exchanged in imitation

58 | 1:58 | **Chorus 4:** Piano solo; simple chordal accompaniment (12 bars)

59 | 2:31 | **Chorus 5:** Trumpet and clarinet duet (8 bars); polyphonic texture begins with high held note for 4 bars, then trumpet with double-time movement:

2:55 | **Piano solo** (4 bars)

Tag (2-bar coda): Full ensemble

Duke Ellington and the Big Band Era

Duke Ellington

From the inspired, improvisational style of Louis Armstrong, we turn to the brilliantly composed jazz of Duke Ellington and the big band, or swing, era. Edward Kennedy "Duke" Ellington (1899–1974) was born in Washington, D.C., and was playing in New York jazz clubs in the 1920s. He became famous as a composer in the following decade. With the advent of the big bands, there was a greater need for arranged or written-down music. Ellington played a major role in this development. A fine pianist himself, he was an even better orchestrator. As one of his collaborators remarked, "He plays piano, but his real instrument is the orchestra."

Ellington's orchestral palette was much richer than that of the New Orleans band. It included two trumpets, one cornet, three trombones, four saxophones (some doubling on clarinet), two string basses, guitar, drum, vibraphone, and piano.

One of his best-known and most unpretentious works is *Ko-Ko*, originally written for his unfinished opera *Boola*. First recorded in 1940, *Ko-Ko*, like Armstrong's *West End Blues*, is a twelve-bar blues, expressively set in a minor key. In this work, Ellington drew inspiration from the drum ceremonies based on African religious rites that used to take place in New Orleans's Congo Square.

Ko-Ko opens with a distinctive rhythmic pattern in the tom-tom and baritone saxophone that is persistent throughout the score (see Listening Guide 68). In both form and content, this is an accomplished jazz "composition." Throughout its seven choruses, it continually builds in dynamic, harmonic, and textural intensity. Solo choruses feature valve trombonist Juan Tizol, backed by the orchestra in a call-and-response exchange; trombonist Joe Nanton, with his characteristic plunger-mute style; Ellington on piano, with imaginative figurations that superimpose dissonant harmonies over the established E-flat minor tonality; and bassist Jimmy Blanton, heard against the full ensemble divided into choirs of varying tone colors. The final chorus displays a fullness of orchestration that suggests more instruments than are actually playing. A rounded binary form of **A-B-A** is alluded to by a coda that recapitulates the opening.

Ellington made a many-faceted contribution to the world of jazz. As a composer, he brought his art to new heights and a newfound legitimacy; as an arranger, he left a rich legacy of works for a wide range of jazz groups; as a band leader, he served as teacher and model to a whole generation of jazz musicians. He occupies an important place in America's cultural heritage.

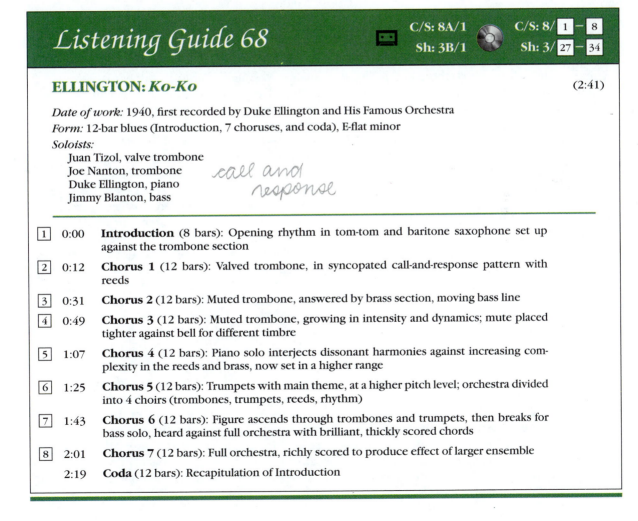

Listening Guide 68

C/S: 8A/1
Sh: 3B/1

C/S: 8/ 1 – 8
Sh: 3/ 27 – 34

ELLINGTON: *Ko-Ko*   (2:41)

Date of work: 1940, first recorded by Duke Ellington and His Famous Orchestra
Form: 12-bar blues (Introduction, 7 choruses, and coda), E-flat minor
Soloists:
  Juan Tizol, valve trombone
  Joe Nanton, trombone
  Duke Ellington, piano
  Jimmy Blanton, bass

call and response

1	0:00	**Introduction** (8 bars): Opening rhythm in tom-tom and baritone saxophone set up against the trombone section
2	0:12	**Chorus 1** (12 bars): Valved trombone, in syncopated call-and-response pattern with reeds
3	0:31	**Chorus 2** (12 bars): Muted trombone, answered by brass section, moving bass line
4	0:49	**Chorus 3** (12 bars): Muted trombone, growing in intensity and dynamics; mute placed tighter against bell for different timbre
5	1:07	**Chorus 4** (12 bars): Piano solo interjects dissonant harmonies against increasing complexity in the reeds and brass, now set in a higher range
6	1:25	**Chorus 5** (12 bars): Trumpets with main theme, at a higher pitch level; orchestra divided into 4 choirs (trombones, trumpets, reeds, rhythm)
7	1:43	**Chorus 6** (12 bars): Figure ascends through trombones and trumpets, then breaks for bass solo, heard against full orchestra with brilliant, thickly scored chords
8	2:01	**Chorus 7** (12 bars): Full orchestra, richly scored to produce effect of larger ensemble
	2:19	**Coda** (12 bars): Recapitulation of Introduction

Cultural Perspective 22

The Roots of Jazz

Jazz has been viewed by many as a truly American art form, but in reality it draws together traditions from West Africa, Europe, and the Americas. Much has been written about the African origins of jazz and how this musical style developed in the United States. This subject evokes an earlier episode of American history: the slave trade from Africa. Many of the slaves brought to America came from the west coast of Africa, often called the Ivory or Gold Coast, and represented different tribes—the Yoruba, Fanti, Ashanti, and Ibo, among others. It is not surprising, then, that studies comparing the musical traditions in sub-Saharan Africa with those in certain isolated regions of black America have confirmed many similarities. These include singing styles (call-and-response patterns and various vocal inflections) and storytelling techniques, traits that have remained alive for several centuries in both regions through oral tradition.

Black music in nineteenth-century America included various kinds of ritual and ceremonial dancing and the singing of work songs (communal songs that synchronized the rhythm of group tasks) and spirituals (a kind of religious folk song, often with a refrain). West African religious traditions mingled freely with the Protestant Christianity adopted by some slaves. One practice was the ring shout, an ecstatic dance that featured a shuffle step to the lively singing of spirituals accompanied by hand clapping (certain dance steps were prohibited by slave owners, as was drumming). Thus some African rhythms were perpetuated in the New World. The art of storytelling through music, typical of many west African tribes, and praise singing (glorifying deities or royalty) were other traditions retained by slaves that would contribute to spirituals and blues. Both men and women were involved in singing, both as soloists and in ensembles—the leader in a call-and-response ceremonial song could be either a man or a woman—but the musical storyteller, called the griot, was always a man, whose position was to preserve and transmit the history, stories, and poetry of the people.

The city of New Orleans fueled the early sounds of jazz. There, in Congo Square, slaves met in the pre–Civil War era to dance to the accompaniment of all types of instruments, including drums, gourds, mouth harps, and banjos. Their music featured a strong underlying pulse over which syncopations and polyrhythmic elaborations took place. Melodies featured African-derived techniques such as rhythmic interjections, vocal glides, and percussive sounds made with the tongue and throat, and were often set in a musical scale with blue notes (lowered scale degrees on the third, fifth, or seventh of a major scale). Evidence supporting this style has been found recently in isolated communities on islands off the Eastern Seaboard of the United States; these island inhabitants, called Gullahs, are descendants of ex-slaves and speak a dialect that combines English with African languages.

In the years after the Civil War and the Emancipation Proclamation (1863), a new style of music arose in Southern logging camps—country or rural blues, performed by a raspy-voiced male singer and, by the turn of the century, accompanied by an acoustic steel-string guitar. This music voiced the difficulties of everyday life in a continuation of the storyteller, or griot, tradition. The

The Bamboula, *danced in Congo Square, New Orleans, to the accompaniment of drums and singing, according to artist* **E. V. Kemble** *in 1885.*

vocal lines featured melodic pitch bending, or blue notes, sung over repeated bass patterns. One of the greatest of the Mississippi blues singers was Charlie Patton.

Dance music also flourished among Southern blacks, and one type in particular, ragtime, strongly influenced early jazz. Ragtime was the first African-American music to experience widespread popularity. This catchy style was soon heard across the country and in Europe, both as accompanied song and as solo piano music; one important composer in this genre was Scott Joplin (see p. 524). The rhythmic vitality of ragtime fascinated such art music composers as Debussy, who captured its spirit in *Golliwog's Cakewalk,* and Stravinsky, in *Ragtime for Eleven Instruments* (1918), *Piano-Rag-Music* (1919), and a dance in *The Soldier's Tale* (1918).

Terms to Note:

ring shout	blue note
spiritual	ragtime
call and response	

Suggested Listening:

African-American spirituals or work songs
Rural blues (Charlie Patton)
Ragtime (Scott Joplin)
New Orleans jazz (*West End Blues*)

Later Jazz Styles and Performers

By the end of the 1940s, musicians had become disenchanted with big band jazz. Their rebellion took shape in bebop and cool-style jazz. *Bebop* (also known as *bop*) was an invented word whose two syllables suggested the two-

Bebop

note phrase that was the trademark of this style. Dizzy Gillespie, Charlie Parker, Bud Powell, and Thelonious Monk developed bebop in the 1940s. In the next two decades, the term came to include a number of substyles such as *Cool jazz* — *cool jazz* (the "cool" suggesting a restrained, unemotional manner), West Coast jazz, hard bop, and soul jazz. The principal exponent of cool jazz was trumpeter Miles Davis; this laid-back style is characterized by lush harmonies, lowered levels of volume, moderate tempos, and a new lyricism.

West Coast Jazz — *West Coast jazz* is essentially a small-group, cool-jazz style featuring mixed timbres (one instrument for each color, without piano) and contrapuntal improvisations. Among the important West Coast ensembles that sprang up in the 1950s are the Dave Brubeck Quartet (with Paul Desmond on saxophone) and the Gerry Mulligan Quartet (with Chet Baker on trumpet). Mulligan's group is noted for its use of walking bass lines (plucked on the string bass) and riffs backing up the solo instrument—in this case, either Baker on trumpet or Mulligan on baritone saxophone. (A *riff* is a short melodic ostinato frequently heard in jazz; it derives from West African call-and-response patterns.) Representative of this style is the Gerry Mulligan Quartet 1953 recording of *My Funny Valentine*, a well-known tune from a Broadway show of the 1930s that Mulligan revived to national popularity. (See Listening Guide 69 in Chapter 74 for an analysis of both the original show tune and the West Coast jazz style version.)

In 1957, the composer Gunther Schuller, in a lecture delivered at Brandeis University, put forth the idea that any kind of music could profit by being combined with another kind; art music could learn from jazz, and vice versa. *Third stream jazz* — He coined the term *third stream*, holding that classical music was the first stream, jazz the second, and the third combined the other two. Although the designation referred mainly to the instruments used, it was soon extended to include other elements as well, such as the adoption by jazz performers of classical forms and tonal devices.

Schuller's idea was taken over by a number of jazz musicians, among them John Lewis (b. 1920), who formed his Modern Jazz Quartet in answer to the growing demand for jazz on college campuses across the country. The ensemble played concerts that "swung" but also featured serious, composed works. Lewis's *Sketch*, a work recorded in 1959, combined the foursome of his jazz ensemble with the Beaux Arts Quartet, one of the finest string quartets in the country.

By the 1960s, new experiments were in the making. A free-style avant-garde jazz emerged, with tenor saxophonist John Coltrane as its leading proponent. Also heard for the first time was a hybrid style known as *fusion*, *Fusion* — which combined jazz improvisation with amplified instruments and the rhythmic pulse of rock. Trumpeter Miles Davis was an important catalyst in the advent of this style, and performers such as guitarist Jerry Garcia (from the Grateful Dead) and vibraphone player Gary Burton are modern-day exponents of the fusion sound. Each of these three jazz musicians—Davis, Garcia, and Burton—has also recorded an arrangement of the show tune *My Funny Valentine*, demonstrating the familiar song's adaptability and timelessness.

Among the many outstanding performers in the world of jazz, two women—both African Americans—made an indelible mark. Bessie Smith (1894–1937) was arguably the greatest blues singer of all time. She began her professional career singing in cabarets and minstrel shows, and made her first blues recording in 1923, establishing herself as the most successful African-American recording artist of her era. She sang with the "greats"—Louis Armstrong, Benny Goodman, Fletcher Henderson, and many more. Her career was damaged by the Great Depression and her addiction to alcohol; the circumstances surrounding her premature death remain obscure. Her style was intense and emotionally charged, her range wide and expressive. She set the standard by which all other blues singers have been measured.

Billie Holiday (1915–59) was an equally outstanding jazz singer. A native of Baltimore, Holiday began to sing professionally in New York in 1929. Her first recording, in 1933, was with clarinetist Benny Goodman, with whom she made many recordings. Affected too by the Depression of the 1930s, Holiday suffered from a hopeless drug addiction. She was an original, noted for her melodic nuances and blues style, a languid, behind-the-beat rhythm. Among her most famous performances are renditions of *God Bless the Child*, *All of Me*, *These Foolish Things*, and *Strange Fruit*.

74

Musical Theater and Jazz

The Development of American Musical Theater

The American musical theater of today developed from the comic opera, or *operetta*, tradition of Johann Strauss, Jacques Offenbach, and other Europeans. This genre was revamped to the American taste by a number of composers, chief among them Victor Herbert (1850–1924), whose works include such charming items as *Babes in Toyland* (1903), *Mlle. Modiste* (1905), and *Naughty Marietta* (1910). The Broadway musical (or musical comedy) gradually evolved in the 1920s, with such works as Sigmund Romberg's *Student Prince* (1924), set in a glamorized Old Heidelberg, and Jerome Kern's *Show Boat* (1927), a tale of Mississippi River life. In the ensuing decades, the musical established itself as America's unique contribution to world theater.

Early musicals

The genre was dependent on romantic plots in picturesque settings enlivened by comedy, appealing melodies, choruses, and dances. Within the framework of a thoroughly commercial theater, a group of talented composers and writers created a body of works that not only enchanted audiences of their time but lasted well beyond it. Among these were Burton Lane's *Finian's Rainbow* (1947), Cole Porter's *Kiss Me, Kate* (1948), Frank Loesser's

Guys and Dolls (1950), Harold Rome's *Fanny* (1954), and Lerner and Loewe's *My Fair Lady* (1956).

Sources of plots

Originally, the plots of musicals were contrived and silly; their main function was to serve as scaffolding for the songs and dances. Gradually, the emphasis changed to present a more convincing treatment of character and situation. Decisive in this regard was the fact that composers began to turn to sophisticated literary sources for their plots. *Show Boat* was based on an Edna Ferber novel, *Kiss Me, Kate* on Shakespeare's *Taming of the Shrew, Guys and Dolls* on the stories of Damon Runyon, *Fanny* on Marcel Pagnol's trilogy, and *My Fair Lady* on George Bernard Shaw's *Pygmalion.* As their approach grew more serious, the genre outgrew its original limitations.

This had already happened with what became the most enduring work of American lyric theater, George Gershwin's masterpiece *Porgy and Bess* (1935), based on the novel and play by DuBose and Dorothy Heyward. This "American folk opera," as Gershwin called it, was so far ahead of its time that, despite its focus on African-American folk idioms, it did not establish itself with any degree of success until its European tour in the 1950s. The work paved the way for such musicals as Leonard Bernstein's *West Side Story* (1957), one of the first to have a tragic ending, and Jerry Bock's *Fiddler on the Roof* (1964), based on stories by the great Jewish humorist Sholem Aleichem. Both works won worldwide success, and both would have been unthinkable twenty years earlier.

The composer Richard Rodgers collaborated with two talented lyricists during his long career to produce some of the best-loved musicals of the era. Along with Lorenz Hart, he created a string of successful Broadway shows, including *Babes in Arms* (1937), which we will study. After the death of Hart in 1943, Rodgers teamed up with Oscar Hammerstein II to produce such unforgettable musicals as *Oklahoma!* (1943), *Carousel* (1945), *South Pacific* (1949), *The King and I* (1951), and *The Sound of Music* (1959). Here too the literary sources were of a high order. *Carousel* was based on Ferenc Molnár's *Liliom, Oklahoma!* on Lynn Riggs's *Green Grow the Lilacs, South Pacific* on the stories of James Michener, *The King and I* on *Anna and the King of Siam* by Margaret Landon, and *The Sound of Music* on the moving memoir of Baroness Maria von Trapp.

Rodgers and Hammerstein

Stephen Sondheim

In the 1970s and 1980s, Stephen Sondheim brought the genre to new levels of sophistication in a series of works that included *A Little Night Music* (1973), *Sweeney Todd* (1979), *Sunday in the Park with George* (1983), and *Into the Woods* (1988). Sondheim continues to attract Broadway audiences of the 1990s, most recently with *Passion* (1994).

Andrew Lloyd Webber

A new era opened with the advent of rock musicals such as Galt MacDermot's *Hair* (1968), the Who's *Tommy* (1969; music and lyrics by Peter Townshend), and Andrew Lloyd Webber's *Jesus Christ Superstar* (1971). Suddenly the romantic show tunes to which millions of young Americans had learned to dance and flirt went completely out of fashion. After a while, however, melody returned. The British Lloyd Webber conquered the international stage with *Evita* (1978), *Cats* (1981), *The Phantom of the Opera* (1986), and *Sunset Boulevard* (1993)—works in which song and dance were combined with dazzling scenic effects, as in the court operas of the Baroque. Together with Frenchman Claude-Michel Schonberg's *Les Misérables* (1987) and *Miss Saigon* (1988, in collaboration with Alain Boublil), these pieces represented a new phenomenon. What had been almost exclusively an American product was now taken over by Europeans.

Recently, many "classic" musicals have enjoyed successful revivals on Broadway: among these are *My Fair Lady, Guys and Dolls, Carousel, Show Boat,* and 1992 Tony Award winner *Crazy for You,* an adaptation of Gershwin's *Girl Crazy* (1930). Other recent American productions of note are *The Kiss of the Spider Woman* (1993), by John Kander and lyricist Fred Ebb (whose earlier collaboration produced the 1966 musical *Cabaret*), and the Disney studio's *Beauty and the Beast* (1994), based on the animated film. With this work, Disney has not only reversed the standard order of a hit musical generating a film, but has opened up a new world of source material and writers.

From the many great American stage works mentioned above, we will consider two representative examples: Rodgers and Hart's *Babes in Arms* and Bernstein's *West Side Story.* Through these, we will see not only the musical growth of the Broadway tradition, but the significant interaction between jazz and the American musical theater.

Rodgers and Hart and the American Musical Stage

One of the most gifted songwriting teams of the Broadway stage, Richard Rodgers and Lorenz Hart wrote nearly thirty shows between 1926 and 1943. In so doing, they single-handedly elevated the level of lyrics in musical comedy from clichés to serious poetry, leaving the world such favorite songs as *My Funny Valentine* and *Bewitched,* among many others.

Richard Rodgers at the piano, Lorenz Hart to his right. (Courtesy of Culver Pictures)

Richard Rodgers (1902–79) was largely self-taught in music. Attracted to the musical stage works of Victor Herbert and Jerome Kern, he began writing music and lyrics for some off-Broadway productions. In 1918, he met Lorenz Hart (1895–1943) at Columbia University, where Hart was studying journalism. Their first big hit occurred in 1925, with the musical revue *Garrick Gaieties*. Soon they turned their attention to more serious musical plays that merged songs with drama and character development. Their most successful collaborations include *The Girl Friend* (1926), *A Connecticut Yankee* (1927), *On Your Toes* (1936), *Babes in Arms* (1937), *I Married an Angel* (1938), *The Boys from Syracuse* (1938), and *Pal Joey* (1940). Rodgers and Hart also tried their hand at writing songs for film scores, and film versions were made of many of their stage works. Their career together was the subject of a 1948 film entitled *Words and Music*.

Rodgers and Hart songs typically feature sophisticated texts with multisyllabic rhymes (where more than the last syllable rhymes) and occasional internal rhymes; these are set to lyrical, small-ranged melodies accompanied by simple harmonies. *Babes in Arms* is one of their most appealing shows. It is set in a fictional actors' colony called Seaport, and focuses on a group of adolescents left behind when their parents go on tour and thus forced to make it on their own. The plot deals with all aspects of life—love, finance, politics, and morality. The young people set out to produce a show of their own, to demonstrate that they are capable of taking care of themselves. *My Funny Valentine,* a sentimental ballad, is sung by an itinerant traveler, Billie Smith, after she has her first lovers' quarrel with Val LaMar over whether two African-American youths should take part in the show. The rhythmic *Johnny One Note* spins a tale of a singer with a limited vocal range as a part of the show within the show, and later, when Billie decides to return to the road, she sings the catchy tune *The Lady Is a Tramp*.

Babes in Arms drew immediate praise from critics, who found the cast "as nice a group of youngsters as ever dove into an ice cream freezer at a birthday party." Its success was ensured shortly after its opening when all the competing shows closed, leaving it the only musical on Broadway in the summer of 1937. This sophisticated Rodgers and Hart score has inspired many pop and jazz arrangements, particularly of its most famous ballad, *My Funny Valentine*. (See Chapter 73 for a discussion of jazz arrangements of the song.) We will hear both the original version of this memorable song and a West Coast jazz rendition by the Gerry Mulligan Quartet (see Listening Guide 69).

Listening Guide 69

C/S: 7B/4–5
Sh: 3B/2

C/S: 7/ 50 – 53
Sh: 3/ 35 – 36

RODGERS: *My Funny Valentine*

Date of work: First performance on April 14, 1937
Text: Lorenz Hart
Genre: Musical theater song (solo voice and orchestra)
Form: Verse and refrain (**A-B-A′**)

(Shorter recordings begin with version 2.)

VERSION 1: Vocal selection from *Babes in Arms* (4:05)

		Text	*Description*
		VERSE (Moderately)	
50	0:00	Behold the way our fine-feathered friend His virtue doth parade. Thou knowest not, my dim-witted friend, The picture thou hast made. Thy vacant brow and thy tousled hair Conceal thy good intent. Thou noble, upright, truthful, sincere, And slightly dopey gent—you're . . .	Speechlike vocal line doubled by solo oboe; phrase endings punctuated by woodwinds and celesta
		REFRAIN (Slowing, with much expression)	
51	1:03	My funny Valentine, Sweet comic Valentine, You make me smile with my heart.	**A**—lyrical, conjunct with orchestra and celesta; C minor (8 measures)
		Your looks are laughable, Unphotographable, Yet you're my favorite work of art.	Variation of opening of refrain; C minor, transition to E-flat major (8 measures)
		Is your figure less than Greek? Is your mouth a little weak? When you open it to speak, Are you smart?	**B**—more leaps in melody; in E-flat major (8 measures)
		But don't change a hair for me. Not if you care for me. Stay, little Valentine, stay. Each day is Valentine's Day.	**A′**—variation of opening of refrain; return to C minor (12 measures)
		REFRAIN repeated	Orchestral statement of **A** section; melody in low strings, accompanied by woodwinds and celesta
		Is your figure less than Greek . . .	Voice reenters with repeated text (**B** and **A′**); solo violin obbligato accompanies voice; climax on "Stay, little Valentine, stay"; orchestral closing with celesta leads to final chord

Opening melody of refrain:

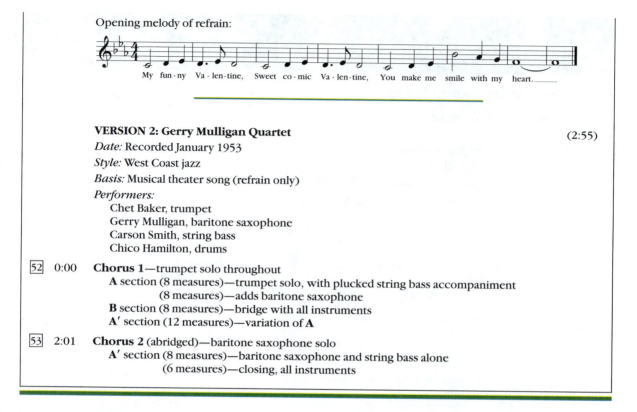

My fun-ny Va-len-tine, Sweet co-mic Va-len-tine, You make me smile with my heart._____

VERSION 2: Gerry Mulligan Quartet   (2:55)
Date: Recorded January 1953
Style: West Coast jazz
Basis: Musical theater song (refrain only)
Performers:
    Chet Baker, trumpet
    Gerry Mulligan, baritone saxophone
    Carson Smith, string bass
    Chico Hamilton, drums

52 0:00   **Chorus 1**—trumpet solo throughout
        A section (8 measures)—trumpet solo, with plucked string bass accompaniment
            (8 measures)—adds baritone saxophone
        B section (8 measures)—bridge with all instruments
        A′ section (12 measures)—variation of **A**

53 2:01   **Chorus 2** (abridged)—baritone saxophone solo
        A′ section (8 measures)—baritone saxophone and string bass alone
            (6 measures)—closing, all instruments

Leonard Bernstein and the Broadway Musical

Leonard Bernstein

Conductor

In the same decade that West Coast jazz came to prominence, the composer-conductor Leonard Bernstein attempted another important union of jazz with musical theater. The result was *West Side Story,* a stage work that has achieved the status of a classic.

As a composer, conductor, educator, pianist, and television personality, Bernstein (1918–90) had one of the most spectacular careers of our time. He was born in Lawrence, Massachusetts, the son of Russian-Jewish immigrants. At thirteen, he was playing with a jazz band. He entered Harvard when he was seventeen and studied composition with Walter Piston. He attended the Curtis Institute in Philadelphia, then became one of the band of disciples whom the conductor Serge Koussevitsky gathered around him. In 1943, when he was twenty-five, Bernstein was appointed Artur Rodzinski's assistant at the New York Philharmonic. A few weeks later, Bruno Walter, the guest conductor, was suddenly taken ill, and Rodzinski was out of town. Bernstein, at a few hours' notice, took over the Sunday afternoon concert and coast-to-coast broadcast, and gave a spectacular performance. Overnight he became famous. Thereafter his career proceeded apace until, in 1958, at the age of forty, he was appointed director of the New York Philharmonic, the first American-born conductor (and the youngest) to occupy the post.

Principal Works

Orchestral works, including the *Jeremiah Symphony* (1942); Symphony No. 2, *The Age of Anxiety* (piano and orchestra, 1949); Serenade (violin, strings, and percussion, 1954); and Symphony No. 3, *Kaddish* (1963)

Works for chorus and orchestra, including *Chichester Psalms* (1965) and *Songfest* (1977)

Operas, including *A Quiet Place* (1983)

Musicals, including *On the Town* (1944), *Wonderful Town* (1953), *Candide* (1956), and *West Side Story* (1957)

Other dramatic music, including the ballet *Fancy Free* (1944), the film score *On the Waterfront* (1954), and *Mass* (1971)

Chamber and instrumental music; solo vocal music

Composer

As a composer, Bernstein straddled the worlds of serious and popular music. He was thus able to bring to the Broadway musical a compositional technique and knowledge of music that few of its practitioners had possessed. In his concert works, he speaks the language of contemporary music with enormous fluency—not as an experimenter but as one who, having inherited the great tradition, sets upon it the stamp of his own personality. The composer possessed a genuine flair for orchestration; the balance and spacing of sonorities, the use of the brass in the high register, and the idiomatic writing that shows off each instrument to its best advantage all bespeak a master. His harmonic idiom is spicily dissonant, his jazzy rhythms have great vitality, and his melodies soar.

Bernstein's feeling for the urban scene—specifically the New York scene—is vividly projected in his theater music. In *On the Town* (a full-length version of his ballet *Fancy Free*), *Wonderful Town*, and *West Side Story*, he achieves a sophisticated kind of musical theater that explodes with movement, energy, and sentiment. His death in October 1990 aroused universal mourning. He was truly a world figure.

WEST SIDE STORY

West Side Story, with book by Arthur Laurents and lyrics by Stephen Sondheim, updated the Romeo and Juliet saga to a modern-day setting of rival gangs of youths on the streets of New York. The hostility between the Jets and the Sharks becomes the modern counterpart of the feud of the Capulets and the Montagues in Shakespeare's play. Tony, one of the Jets, falls in love with Maria, whose brother leads the Sharks. The tale of the star-crossed lovers unfolds in scenes of great tenderness, whence come memorable songs like *Tonight* and *Maria*, alternating with electrifying dances choreographed by Jerome Robbins, as it mounts inevitably to Tony's tragic death.

Chita Rivera, who played Anita in the original 1957 production of West Side Story, *dancing to* America *with the other Shark girls.* (© Martha Swope)

Bernstein subsequently adapted the music for a set of Symphonic Dances in eight episodes. (See Listening Guide 70.) These are based on motives drawn from the chief songs, especially *Maria* and *Somewhere,* which here receive the kind of symphonic expansion not possible in the theater. The score displays the composer's colorful orchestration as well as his imaginative handling of jazz and Latin-American rhythms. It calls for an expanded woodwind and percussion section, including the piano. The music of the *Cool* fugue builds to several climaxes, with fugal textures that become increasingly dense and polyphonic before they grow gentle and relaxed. This section of the score is from a dance sequence by the Jets, prior to the final fight, or rumble, with the Sharks. Fleeting references to the lyrical ballads of the play resonate through the score, which demands much of our ears, especially our tolerance of high levels of dissonance. It was Bernstein's intent to bring the mood and atmosphere of the drama into the concert hall. He succeeded.

Leonard Bernstein is regarded today not only as one of the foremost American conductors, but as a composer whose creative activity extended over an unusually wide spectrum. Beyond that, he will be remembered as one of the most extraordinary musical personalities of our century.

Listening Guide 70

BERNSTEIN: Symphonic Dances from *West Side Story*, excerpts   (5:30)

Date of work: 1961

Basis: Dance sequences from the musical *West Side Story* (1957)

Overview of Symphonic Dances:

Prologue (Allegro moderato)—the rivalry grows between the two teenage gangs, the Jets and the Sharks.

Somewhere (Adagio)—in a visionary dance sequence, the gangs are united in friendship.

Scherzo (Vivace leggiero)—in the same dream, they break through the city walls and suddenly find themselves in a world of space, air, and sun.

"Mambo" (Presto)—reality again; competitive dance between the two gangs.

"Cha-cha" (Andantino con grazia)—the star-crossed lovers see each other for the first time and dance together.

Cool, Fugue (Allegretto)—an elaborate dance sequence in which the Jets practice controlling their hostility.

"Rumble" (Molto allegro)—climactic gang battle during which the two gang leaders are killed.

Finale (Adagio)—love music developing into a procession, which recalls, in tragic reality, the vision of *Somewhere.*

Cool, Fugue (Allegretto)

Based largely on several short rhythmic motives:

Melody of *Cool* is drawn from opening of *Maria* (rising augmented fourth, going to a fifth):

21	0:00	Allegretto—grows out of rhythmic patterns shown above, adding instruments and increasingly syncopated; alternating woodwinds and strings
	0:41	Muted trumpet solo (from *Somewhere*):

Regular rhythmic brush pattern on cymbals, punctuated by 3-note motive (vibraphone, piano):

22	1:03	Fugue subject, with dotted rhythms, begins in flute, against constant brush in cymbals; then heard in clarinet and piano, marked "with jazz feel":

| 1:36 | 3-note dotted pattern returns and builds, against long notes in strings: | |

2:23   Solo percussion break followed by homophonic syncopated chords

Second solo percussion break followed by
unison section based on 3-note motive

[23] 2:52   Brass featured in syncopated jazz section,
with shakes on high notes, accompanied
by syncopated patterns in strings and
woodwinds:

3:19   Rhythmic pattern from opening returns,
builds to climax

"Rumble" (Molto Allegro)

[24] 4:00   Syncopations, rhythmic vitality, and complexity build to loud, homophonic chords
in orchestra, irregularly spaced

4:48   Fugal section grows out of quiet 3-note pattern, instruments added, building to regular pulse on eighth notes; marked
crescendo, rising chromatic pattern leads
to final glissando and closing chords (*fff*)

Cultural Perspective 23

Latin-American Dance Music

The energetic rhythms of Leonard Bernstein's *West Side Story* do not sound particularly foreign to us, yet they are based on dances from a variety of Latin-American countries. Some dances, like the Brazilian samba and the Cuban rumba, began as rural music that was later popularized by urban bands. In the 1950s and 1960s, Americans and Europeans alike were dancing to the distinctive rhythms of the Cuban cha cha cha and mambo and the Brazilian bossa nova, all derived from earlier traditional styles. We noted previously that the Argentinian tango, a heated couple dance that had its origins in the poor neighborhoods of Buenos Aires, has remained popular through much of the twentieth century. The Afro-Cuban conga is a favorite Latin-American Carnival dance whose name is also applied to a long, single-headed drum used in much Latin-American popular music. (You will hear this drum in the Latin rock example *Black Magic Woman/Gypsy Queen,* performed by Santana.) The collective term "salsa" (Spanish for "sauce," as in "spicy") is sometimes used to label various contemporary styles loosely based on Afro-Cuban dance music.

Although these are the dances of an earlier generation, there are more recent Latin-American types that have achieved international prominence. In the 1960s, a popular Jamaican style appeared called ska, characterized by quick, off-the-beat rhythms and represented by such artists as the Skalites and Millie Small (whose hit song *My Boy Lollipop*

Jamaican reggae star Bunny Wailer (Livingston), who sang with the original Bob Marley and the Wailers, performing at Madison Square Garden in 1986. (Photo courtesy of Ebet Roberts)

had some success in the United States and Canada). This led the way for reggae, a Jamaican style music that slows down the quick beat of ska and emphasizes the role of the bass, placing it in a complex rhythmic relationship with the other parts (see p. 551).

Music of Latin America and the Caribbean has enjoyed continued popularity, in part because of its potential as "dance-floor dynamite." The current rage for world beat music, which has opened the Western market to a myriad of new styles, has changed the sounds and rhythms of popular music forever, and has brought Latin American music into our everyday experience.

Terms to Note:

samba	bossa nova	ska
rumba	tango	reggae
cha cha cha	conga	world beat
mambo	salsa	

Suggested Listening:

Bernstein: *West Side Story*
Latin-American dance music
Ska or reggae
Bob Marley and the Wailers

75

Rock and the Global Scene

"Nobody likes rock and roll but the public."—BILL HALEY

The rise of *rock and roll* (and its offspring, *rock*) is one of the most important phenomena of the second half of the twentieth century. Economically, it has grown into a multibillion-dollar industry; socially, it has had a far-reaching impact on the way people live, dress, talk, and even think; musically, it has dominated the popular scene for some forty years, and influenced virtually every other style of music—classical, jazz, country/western, and contemporary world beat.

Rhythm and blues

Rock and roll was first heard in the 1950s, born of a union of African-American rhythm and blues with country/western and pop music. *Rhythm and blues,* popular from the late 1940s through the early 1960s, is a predominantly vocal genre, featuring a solo singer accompanied by a small group including piano, guitar (electric or acoustic), acoustic bass, drums, and tenor saxophone. Its harmonies and structure are clearly drawn from twelve-bar blues and thirty-two-bar pop song form. As the name implies, the style is characterized by a strong, driving beat, usually in a quadruple meter. Among the many great rhythm and blues performers were four African Americans: Bessie Smith (whom we encountered earlier as a blues singer), Big Bill Broonzy, B. B. King, and Joe Turner.

Rock and roll

In the mid-1950s, *rock and roll* emerged as a form of rhythm and blues that crossed racial lines: white singers like Bill Haley (*Rock Around the Clock,* with the Comets, 1954), Elvis Presley (*Heartbreak Hotel* and *Hound Dog/Don't Be Cruel,* both from 1956), and Jerry Lee Lewis (*Whole Lotta Shakin' Going On* and *Great Balls of Fire,* both from 1957) drew on elements of the black style. At the same time, African Americans like Chuck Berry (*Roll Over, Beethoven,* 1956), Fats Domino (*Blueberry Hill,* 1956), and Little Richard (*Long Tall Sally,* 1956) caught the attention of a white audience. The preferred vocal quality was somewhat raspy, belted out in a lively manner. The styles of Chuck Berry and Little Richard clearly derived from gospel music, and that of Jerry Lee Lewis was much influenced by country/western singers. The new sounds of rock and roll revolutionized the music industry's concept of markets, appealing to wide audiences across racial lines.

Soft rock

As hard-driving rock and roll declined in popularity around 1960, a gentler, more lyrical style—*soft rock*—found an audience. The medium of radio furthered the crooning styles of white singers Bobby Darin (*Splish, Splash,* 1958; *Dream Lover,* 1959), Neil Sedaka (*Calendar Girl,* 1960–61; *Breaking Up Is Hard to Do,* 1962), and Bobby Vinton (*Roses Are Red,* 1962; *Mr. Lonely,* 1964). Meanwhile, black America was listening to the sound of *soul* and *Motown* (from Motortown, or Detroit—a fusion of gospel, pop, and rhythm and blues). Top recording artists included Diana Ross and the Supremes (*Where Did Our Love Go,* 1964), James Brown (*Papa's Got a Brand New Bag,* 1965), Gladys

The irrepressible Chuck Berry, seen in three typical positions.

Knight and the Pips (*I Heard It Through the Grape Vine,* 1967), Aretha Franklin (*Respect,* 1967), and Stevie Wonder (*You Are the Sunshine of My Life,* 1973). Ray Charles (*I've Got a Woman,* 1965) is often considered to be the "father" of soul.

In the early 1960s, rock and roll was revitalized with the popularity of a new dance, the twist, and with the emergence of new groups, notably the Beach Boys in the United States and the Beatles, the Rolling Stones, and the Who in Britain. It was the Beatles who provided direction amid a variety of styles. In 1964, this group from Liverpool, England, took America by storm, performing at Carnegie Hall in New York, at the Washington Coliseum, and on the *Ed Sullivan Show.* In 1964, the top five tunes on the Billboard chart were theirs (*Can't Buy Me Love, Twist and Shout, She Loves You, I Want to Hold Your Hand,* and *Please Please Me*). This foursome—Paul McCartney on electric bass, George Harrison and John Lennon on amplified acoustic guitars, and Ringo Starr on drums—featured a strong rhythm section and a hard-driving beat, with John and Paul doing unison and two-part vocals in a high range, almost a falsetto.

The Beatles

The Beatles' success story continued because they had the creativity to experiment. With Paul McCartney's lyrical ballad *Yesterday* (1965), the Beatles moved from rock and roll to a pop sound combined with string quartet; and with the albums *Rubber Soul* (1965) and *Revolver* (1966), the group adopted a new style, with more expressive lyrics, complex harmonies, and sophisticated recording techniques. George took up the Indian sitar (*Norwegian Wood,* 1965), which he had heard in the folk-rock style of a California group, the Byrds. With these new sounds, the old rock and roll was gone, and the more expressive style known as rock emerged.

In the late 1960s, the Beatles continued to show their individuality as well as their newfound interest in Eastern philosophy. *Hey Jude* (1968) was their biggest-selling single of all time; and the albums *Sgt. Pepper's Lonely Hearts*

The Beatles performing in 1968. (Courtesy of Apple Corps Ltd.)

Club Band (1967) and *Abbey Road* (1969) were both stunning musical achievements that showcased their various songwriting abilities. Notable among the selections on these albums are John Lennon's *Lucy in the Sky with Diamonds,* Paul McCartney's *When I'm Sixty-Four,* and George Harrison's *Here Comes the Sun.* In 1970, the group broke up, each of its members going on to successful solo careers.

The Byrds

Many of the expressive features of rock were molded by California bands, especially the Byrds. One of the most creative rock groups, the Byrds originated in Los Angeles in 1964 and soon became caught up in the politics of the San Francisco scene—the free speech movement and the protest of American involvement in the Vietnam War (1957–75). Their music combined the folk style of protest singers Bob Dylan and Joan Baez with the new sounds of rock, *Folk rock* thereby creating *folk rock.* Their first release was their biggest hit: *Mr. Tambourine Man* (1965), set to words and music by Bob Dylan. This was followed in the same year by *Turn, Turn, Turn,* a Pete Seeger song with lyrics from the Old Testament. *Eight Miles High* (1966), one of the first recordings banned because of its drug references, was highly adventuresome in its harmonic language.

The Byrds' sound combined group vocals sung in close harmony with acoustic guitar and an electric twelve-string instrument (adopted from the Beatles), coupled with a brittle amplified tambourine as part of the rhythm section. In their version of *Mr. Tambourine Man* (see Listening Guide 71), the refrain is heard twice, with Roger (Jim) McGuinn singing solo verses from Dylan's original text. McGuinn expressed the group's concept of their sound on the album notes: "The sound of the airplane in the Forties was a *rrrrrrr-rooooooaaaaaaaahhhhhhhhhh* sound and Sinatra and other people sang like that, with those sorts of overtones. Now we've got the *krrrriiiis-sssssssshhhhhhhhhhhhhh* jet sound, and the kids are singing up in there now. It's the mechanical sound of the era."

Listening Guide 71

 C/S: 8B/5 C/S: 8/ 43

DYLAN: *Mr. Tambourine Man* by the Byrds (2:27)

Date of work: 1965
Text and music: Bob Dylan
Genre: Folk rock
Meter: Quadruple (4/4)
Performers:

Roger (Jim) McGuinn, 12-string guitar, vocal
David Crosby, acoustic guitar
Gene Clark, tambourine

Chris Hillman, electric bass
Michael Clarke, drums

Text	Description
43 0:00	**Introduction** (4 measures)—solo guitar, joined by bass, tambourine, and drums
0:09 Hey, Mr. Tambourine Man, play a song for me. I'm not sleepy and there ain't no place I'm goin' to. Hey, Mr. Tambourine Man, play a song for me. In the jingle, jangle mornin' I'll come followin' you.	**Chorus** (refrain)—sung in closed harmony, with all instruments, strong beat in percussion
0:42 Take me for a trip upon your magic, swirling ship, All my senses have been stripped, And my hands can't feel to grip, And my toes too numb to step Wait only for my boot heels to be wanderin.'	**Verse**—vocal (McGuinn); strong beat continues, punctuated by sharp, syncopated chords in guitar
I'm ready to go anywhere I'm ready for to fade Into my own parade Cast your dancing spell my way I promise to go under it.	
1:32 Hey, Mr. Tambourine Man, play a song for me. I'm not sleepy and there ain't no place I'm goin' to. Hey, Mr. Tambourine Man, play a song for me. In the jingle, jangle mornin' I'll come followin' you.	**Chorus** (refrain)
	Instrumental closing (12 measures)—short repeated ostinato in electric guitar and bass, fades out

Opening of chorus (refrain):

Hey! Mis-ter Tam-bou-rine Man play a song for me, I'm not

sleep-y and there is no place I'm go-in' to.

Woodstock   The rock of the 1960s peaked in the Woodstock Festival, held in upstate New York in August 1969, where over 300,000 music fans gathered for four days of "peace, love, and brotherhood." Important performances were given there by the Who (*Summertime Blues,* with Peter Townshend's famous guitar-smashing routine), Joe Cocker (singing the Beatles' *With a Little Help from My Friends*), Country Joe and the Fish (with the antiwar song *What Are We Fighting For?*), Jimi Hendrix (known for his psychedelic blues-style rendition of *The Star-Spangled Banner*), Richie Havens (with the spiritual *Sometimes I Feel Like a Motherless Child*), and a then unknown group named Santana (*Soul Sacrifice*), who went on to develop Latin rock. Other performers included the North Indian sitarist Ravi Shankar and folk singers Joan Baez and Arlo Guthrie. On the twenty-fifth anniversary of this festival, nostalgic re-creations took place in Bethel and Saugerties, New York, featuring some of the same performers.

The British invasion   Meanwhile, the success of the Beatles in America had sparked a British invasion of rock groups—the Dave Clark Five (*Over and Over,* 1965), the Animals (*The House of the Rising Sun,* 1964), and especially the Rolling Stones (*I Can't Get No Satisfaction,* 1965). The Stones soon became the "bad boys" of rock: their lyrics, most by Mick Jagger, and their public behavior condoned sexual freedom, drugs, and violence. Open sexual innuendo (*Let's Spend the Night Together*) and tales of an LSD trip (*Something Happened to Me Yesterday*) are typical themes. Their concert tours sparked violence wherever they went: at the Altamont Festival of 1969 (California's answer to Woodstock), a person was murdered in the crowd as Jagger sang *Sympathy for the Devil* to an out-of-control audience. Despite the negative image the group acquired, the Rolling Stones opened the path more than any other group for new styles of the 1970s and 1980s: hard rock, punk rock, and heavy metal.

Acid rock   America's answer to this British invasion was *acid rock*—a San Francisco style of music that focused on drugs, extremely high volume levels, instrumental improvisations, and new sound technologies. The Jefferson Airplane (*White Rabbit,* 1967), featuring female lead singer Grace Slick, made no pretense about their psychedelic lyrics, and the Grateful Dead (with Jerry Garcia on lead guitar) performed lengthy instrumental improvisations at deafening volume levels. The music world was shaken in 1970–71 by the alcohol- and drug-related deaths of three superstars: the phenomenal blues guitarist Jimi Hendrix, the raspy-voiced Janis Joplin, and the lead singer of the Doors, Jim Morrison. Each was only twenty-seven years old.

The Eclecticism of the 1970s

Jazz rock   Two eclectic styles of rock were developing at this time: *jazz rock* (later called *fusion*), featuring traditional jazz-style instruments (trumpet, trombone, sax-
Art rock   ophone, and flute) along with long, improvised melodic lines; and *art rock,* which used large forms, complex harmonies, and sometimes quotations from classical music. One of the most important jazz rock groups was Blood, Sweat, and Tears, whose 1969 album launched three hits—*You've Made Me So Very*

Happy, And When I Die, and *Spinning Wheel,* the last of which epitomized the style with its improvised solos and walking bass line. More rock-oriented was the group Chicago (*Does Anybody Really Know What Time It Is?* 1971), known for its horn lines and vocal improvisations.

Art rock (sometimes called *progressive rock*) was largely a British style, pioneered by the Moody Blues with their 1968 album *Days of Future Passed,* recorded with the London Symphony Orchestra. In 1969, the Who premiered its rock opera *Tommy,* written by Peter Townshend. In 1972, keyboardist Keith Emerson together with Greg Lake and Carl Palmer produced a major art rock work with *Pictures at an Exhibition,* based on the Musorgsky suite that we have studied. One American who experimented with art rock's large forms was Frank Zappa (and the Mothers of Invention), who invited listeners to dissect his music: "These things are so carefully constructed that it breaks my heart when people don't dig into them and see all the levels that I put into them."

Among the fusion bands that have remained popular is Santana, named after its leader-guitarist. This group started out as a California blues band to which Carlos Santana, son of a Mexican mariachi musician, added Latin and African percussion instruments. The resulting sound electrified the Woodstock audience with a new style, *Latin rock.* Santana's distinctive sound came from their instrumentation—conga drums (of African-Cuban origin, played with bare hands), maracas (Latin-American rattles), and timbales (small kettledrums of Cuban origin)—their polyrhythmic drumming style, and their tight, Latin-style rhythms. A fine jazz guitarist, Carlos Santana has also recorded with many jazz artists.

Latin rock

Santana enjoyed international popularity in the early 1970s with such hit songs as *Evil Ways* (1969), *Black Magic Woman/Gypsy Queen* (1970), and *Guajira* (1971). Carlos arranged *Black Magic Woman,* written by Peter

Guitarist Carlos Santana, who has remained a popular Latin rock and jazz musician for some twenty-five years, performing in Mexico City, 1993. (Paul Freehauf/Courtesy of Santana Management)

Green (of Fleetwood Mac fame), and *Gypsy Queen,* by guitarist Gabor Szabo, as a single number: the first as a strophic song interspersed with jazzlike guitar and keyboard improvisations, the second as a double time, hard-driving guitar solo. (See Listening Guide 72.)

Listening Guide 72

C/S: 8B/6   C/S: 8/ 44 — 45
Sh: 3B/4   Sh: 3/ 41 — 42

Black Magic Woman/Gypsy Queen by Santana   (5:18)

Date of work: 1970
Text and music: Peter Green/Gabor Szabo
Genre: Latin rock
Meter: Quadruple (4/4)
Performers:

Carlos Santana, vocal, guitar	David Brown, bass
Alberto Gianquinto	Michael Schrieve, drum set
Rico Reyes, vocal	José "Chepito" Areas, percussion (timbales)
Coke Escovedo, percussion (timbales)	Michael Carabello, percussion (congas)
Greg Rolie, vocal, keyboard	

Black Magic Woman

		Text	*Description*
44	0:00		**Introduction** (20 measures)—keyboard ostinato figure heard with bass, punctuated with percussion; lead guitar enters with another idea; ostinato continues against regular beat; texture becomes thicker, polyphonic treatment against guitar, shimmering brush on cymbals
	0:41		Lead guitar (Santana, 12 measures)—instrumental verse in improvised style, against Latin-style percussion
	1:07		Electric keyboard (8 measures)—partial verse improvised against thicker texture
	1:23	Got a black magic woman, Got a black magic woman, I've got a black magic woman, Got me so blind I can't see That she's a black magic woman She's trying to make a devil out of me.	**Verse 1** (12 measures)—chords change every 2 measures; steady rhythmic beat
	1:46	Don't turn your back on me, baby, Don't turn your back on me, baby, Yes, don't turn your back on me, baby, Stop messin' 'round with your tricks. Don't turn your back on me, baby, You just might pick up my magic sticks.	**Verse 2** (12 measures)—same style, with denser accompaniment

2:10	**Verse 3**—an instrumental double verse (24 measures): solo guitar; beat on cymbal hit with drum stick; volume level increases
2:55	Got your spell on me, baby,	**Verse 4** (12 measures)
	Got your spell on me, baby,	
	Yes, you've got your spell on me, baby,	
	Turnin' my heart into stone.	
	I need you so bad, magic woman,	
	I can't leave you alone.	
3:18	**Instrumental closing**—return of opening ostinato, in lower range; leads directly into *Gypsy Queen*

45 3:38 ***Gypsy Queen* (instrumental)**

Oscillating tones on guitar marks beginning of new instrumental number; double time (twice as fast); guitar with fast-paced accompaniment; hard-driving tempo and beat, ends with decay on distorted electric guitar note

The 1970s and 1980s were characterized by a fragmentation of musical styles and a continuous procession of new groups. Mainstream rock was represented by America (*A Horse with No Name*, 1972), the Eagles (*Hotel California*, 1972), and the Doobie Brothers (*Listen to the Music*, 1972), among others. The British once again invaded, this time with *heavy metal rock*, featuring simple, repetitive motives and loud, distorted instrumental solos. Led Zeppelin (*Whole Lotta' Love*, 1969) and Black Sabbath were the most important heavy metal bands of the 1970s. *Glitter rock*, a showy, theatrical style of performance, was best represented by Britain's outrageous David Bowie (*Diamond Dogs* album, 1974) and later by the talented keyboardist Elton John (*Bennie and the Jets*, from *Goodbye, Yellow Brick Road*, 1973). The ultimate rebellion came in the form of *punk rock*, a return to the basics of rock and roll—simple, repetitive, and loud—coupled with offensive lyrics and shocking behavior. Britain's Sex Pistols (*Anarchy in the U.K.* and *God Save the Queen*, both from 1977), featuring lead singer Johnny Rotten, was the first major punk group. They were followed by the Clash, who focused their music on the central issues of the punk rebellion: unemployment (*Career Opportunities*), violence (*Hate and War*), racism (*White Riot*), and police brutality (*Police and Thieves*). The last work is a *cover* (a recording that remakes an earlier, successful recording) of a reggae hit.

Other reactions to the difficult times of the 1970s included the commercial dance music known as *disco*, and *reggae*, a Jamaican style with offbeat rhythms and chanted vocals that reflected the beliefs of a Christian religious movement known as Rastafarianism. Representative reggae artists include Bob Marley and the Wailers and Black Uhuru. The style was especially popular in Britain, where Eric Clapton's cover of Bob Marley's *I Shot the Sheriff* (1974) met with great success. A return to soft rock was yet another rejection of

Heavy metal rock

Glitter rock

Punk rock

Cover

Disco and reggae

heavy metal and punk rock and was epitomized by such artists as the Carpenters (*We've Only Just Begun,* 1970) and Olivia Newton-John (*I Honestly Love You,* 1975), among others.

New wave   *New wave* was a direct outgrowth of punk rock, and it has been popular among British and American groups since the late 1970s. Rejecting heavy metal and art rock, new wave bands led the way to a simpler, 1950s-based music. In Britain, the rock scene was led by Elvis Costello (backed up by the Attractions in *This Year's Model,* 1978) and Police with lead singer Sting (*Roxanne,* 1978; *Every Breath You Take,* 1986). The New York City scene developed around a number of clubs in lower Manhattan, including CBGBs (Country, Blue Grass, and Blues), where Blondie debuted in 1975. Named for their attractive blond singer Deborah Harry, this group achieved commercial success with its album *Parallel Lines* (1978), and later turned to disco (*Heart of Glass,* 1980) and reggae styles (*The Tide Is High,* 1980). America's most influential new wave group was the Talking Heads, with songwriter-singer David Byrne and producer Brian Eno. Their lyrics filled with social commentary and their style influenced by third-world musics, the Talking Heads made significant musical contributions to the rock sound of the 1980s.

The 1980s and the Video Generation

The single most important development in the 1980s was the music video. Now, instead of the radio, the visual medium (and especially MTV, or Music Television, which premiered in August 1981 and launched its network of stars in January 1983) was the principal means of presenting music to the public. New and colorful performers like Duran Duran came on the scene, and an image- and fashion-conscious aesthetic soon dominated rock. One giant in the video arena was Michael Jackson, who had gained fame as a member of the Jackson Five (a group that carried on the Motown sound) and who then became a superstar in the 1980s. Jackson's album *Thriller* (1982–83) broke all previous sales figures; hit songs included *The Girl Is Mine* (sung with Paul McCartney), *Billie Jean,* and *Beat It* (his version of the rumble scene from Bernstein's *West Side Story*). His fast dance style, combined with his ability as a ballad singer, accounts for his continued popularity. Other superstars of the 1980s include Bruce Springsteen (*Born in the USA,* 1984) and Madonna, who launched her first big hit with *Like a Virgin* (1984), which she followed with the eclectic album *True Blue* (1986). She has had great success and a film career based on her carefully developed image as a sex object.

Among the important groups in the late 1980s, two stand out. The Irish group U2 sounded a unified voice of political activism and personal spirituality in their collection *The Unforgettable Fire* (1984). Following a series of concerts for Live Aid and Amnesty International, the group achieved stardom with the 1987 Grammy-winning album *The Joshua Tree* (which included two Number One hits, *With or Without You* and *I Still Haven't Found What I'm Looking For*). The Los Angeles band Guns N' Roses, featuring outspoken lead

The Irish group U2, in concert at Zooropa in Rotterdam, the Netherlands, 1993. (Peter Stone)

singer Axl Rose and guitarist Slash, transcended their metal roots in *Appetite for Destruction* (1987) and *Use Your Illusion* (I and II, both from 1991), revealing an accessible style that is heavily derivative of many of rock's greatest performers.

Rap

The technological developments of the early 1980s, including the use of synthesizers and other electronic devices, paved the way for *rap,* a highly rhythmic style of musical patter that had been popular with New York audiences in the 1970s and later developed wider appeal. The group Run DMC (*Raising Hell,* 1986) was largely responsible for the commercialization of rap; their collaboration with Aerosmith on the cover recording of the 1977 hit song *Walk This Way* brought the style to white audiences. Public Enemy, a group from Long Island, New York, produced several highly influential rap albums (*It Takes a Nation of Millions to Hold Us Back,* 1988; *Apocalypse 91: The Enemy Strikes Black,* 1991), and female rapper Queen Latifah voiced a strong case against the genre's frequent female bashing in *All Hail the Queen* (1989).

Rap, in its diversified forms, has continued as one of the most popular types of African-American music and has been imitated by white groups, such as the Beastie Boys and Vanilla Ice. *Gangsta rap* of the 1990s has further disseminated the style through graphic descriptions of the realities of inner-city life. Leading groups in this style include N.W.A. (Niggas with Attitude), whose 1991 album *Efil4zaggin* ("Niggaz 4 Life" backward) hit the top of the charts, and former N.W.A. rapper Ice Cube (*Death Certificate,* 1991).

Grunge rock

The late 1980s and early 1990s also saw the rise of a Seattle-based hybrid of punk and 1970s metal known as *grunge rock* (so-called after its harsh guitar sounds). Popular groups to come out of the grunge scene were Soundgarden,

Nirvana, and Pearl Jam. Pearl Jam's *Ten* and Nirvana's *Nevermind* (1991) had huge commercial appeal, attracting widely diverse audiences.

This overview of rock has highlighted a mere handful of groups, citing those whose influence is difficult to challenge. Rock is unquestionably here to stay, but popularity in this genre is fleeting; only time will tell which current artists and styles will be remembered tomorrow.

World Beat

One of today's most eclectic musical movements promises to bring a new global perspective to the music listener. Not really a single style, this movement promotes popular music of the third world, ethnic and traditional music from all regions, and collaborations between Western and non-Western musicians. The so-called *world beat,* or *ethno-pop,* has been around for some time. In the 1950s, the television-watching world heard African-Cuban music played by Desi Arnaz in *I Love Lucy,* and enjoyed Harry Belafonte's vocal calypsos, a mixture of Jamaican and American styles. In the 1960s, the Brazilian bossa nova found favor *(The Girl from Ipanema),* and Ravi Shankar, along with the Beatles, brought Indian sitar music to the West.

Graceland

One of the most famous and successful collaborations of differing musical cultures resulted in Paul Simon's album *Graceland* (1986), which featured various styles of South African music. Simon was especially attracted to a style known as "township jive," the street music of Soweto, and to the musicality of South Africa's popular vocal group Ladysmith Black Mambazo. The album was politically controversial, since it violated commercial sanctions against South Africa's apartheid policy; in the end, however, it did much to further the cause of blacks there. It was truly an international venture, using musicians from all over, including the popular Senegalese singer Youssou N'Dour. The album

Joseph Shabalala, founder and leader of the popular South African vocal group Ladysmith Black Mambazo. (Jack Vartoogian)

also served to introduce the a cappella vocal group Ladysmith Black Mambazo to the American public; the ensemble went on to win the Grammy Award for the best traditional folk recording of 1988.

The South African choral singing heard on *Graceland* exemplifies a traditional style developed by Zulu migrant workers known as *mbube* (meaning "lion"). This style was first introduced to the Western world in 1961 with the Tokens' *The Lion Sleeps Tonight* (also called *Wimowea*), and is now familiar to many through the recordings of Ladysmith Black Mambazo. Originally a style sung in labor camps to alleviate loneliness, mbube has become a music of social protest linked to anti-apartheid. The music features the call-and-response pattern typical of many African cultures, with the a cappella choral responses set in rich, close-knit harmonies. Irregular phrasing and syncopated rhythms enliven the musical movement, and special effects such as trilled vocal glides and blues-style interjections are typical. *That's Why I Choose You*, despite its English text, is an example of mbube singing style, featuring leader Joseph Shabalala and the nine-member Ladysmith Black Mambazo.

Mbube

Listening Guide 73

C/S: 8B/7
Sh: 3B/5

C/S: 8/
Sh: 3/

That's Why I Choose You by Ladysmith Black Mambazo   (2:51)

Date of work: 1992
Text and music: Joseph Shabalala
Genre: World beat, South African mbube
Singing style: Call and response; chorus in close harmony
Special effects: Trilled vocal glides; some nonlexical vocables
Medium: A cappella male vocal group (9 members); Joseph Shabalala, leader

46 0:00   Leader: The man . . .

           Chorus: The man is allowed to choose what he likes,
                    The woman she's allowed to agree what she likes,
                    Everybody is free to do what they like,
                    Everybody is free, do what you like.
                       (repeated throughout, following solo)

           Leader: And the lovers lay,
                    You can do what you like, my friend.

           Chorus: See me now, see me no more.

           Leader: Why don't you touch me? Because you see me now,
                    Now you are appointed,

           Chorus: Try by your own means to conduct me,
                    somehow, somewhere. *(repeated)*

47 0:54   Leader: I feel your hands . . .

           Chorus: . . . are soft and nice,

Leader: I see your eyes . . .

Chorus: . . . are full of love,   Ye! (solo)

Leader: I feel your hands . . .

Chorus: . . . are soft and nice,   Ye! (solo)

Leader: I see your eyes . . .

Chorus: . . . are full of love,   Oh yes! it is warm. (solo)

Leader: That's why . . .

Chorus: I choose you now.
         You're going to be my household doll.
             (exchange repeated many times with various interjections)
         Boom, boom . . .
         Baby, baby, baby, baby, baby . . . (solo)
             (vocal glide and other sounds)

Leader: I feel your hands is soft and nice, and *shuphuluzi* (person you tickle), they
         nice, oh yes!

Chorus: Ta, la, la, la, la, la, tu, lu, lu,
         I choose you now.
         You're gonna be my household doll,
         That's why I choose you now.
             (repeated with interjections of Ye! *and* Baby!*)*

48 2:13 Leader: I'm warnin' you.

Chorus: I'm warnin' you, don't let a good time passes you.

Leader: Why don't you touch me? *(Echo singer repeats line)*

Chorus: Why don't you touch me?

Leader: Hold me.

Chorus: Hold me.

Leader: I feel your hands are soft and nice,
         I see your eyes are full of love.

Chorus: Why don't you touch me, hold me,
         Why don't you touch me?

Leader: You should be illumined.

Chorus: I'm warnin' you, don't let a good time passes you.

Cultural Perspective 24

The Sounds of World Beat

World beat is a significant trend in popular music today. You might test this for yourself: visit your nearest CD store and browse through the international or world section. You are likely to find an overwhelming selection from all corners of the earth—chants by Tibetan monks, Bolivian panpipe ensembles, Javanese gamelan orchestras, folk songs from Bosnia and Herzegovina, Russian balalaika ensembles, ceremonial music from Ghana, and Navajo dance music, to name only a few possibilities. It seems that America is as hungry for world music as it is for pizza, couscous, and sushi.

Where did a listening audience with such international tastes come from? It would be easy to suggest that, as a multi-ethnic population, people are in search of their musical roots. This may be true to some degree, but it is not only African Americans, for example, who listen to reggae, jazz, or music of sub-Saharan Africa. This global awakening began with the wars of the mid-twentieth century, in which thousands of Americans were transported to far-off places (South Pacific islands, Vietnam, Iraq), and the public at home was made increasingly aware of these locales through the media. Global communications brought us vivd, next-day images from Vietnam and, some years later, live pictures from Kuwait. Important too was the raised sociopolitical consciousness of the 1960s, and such historical events as Woodstock, where hundreds of thousands were moved by the performance of Indian sitarist Ravi Shankar playing a music to which they had had little prior exposure. Today, we can experience world musics first-hand through a

The Gyütö monks from Tibet, famous for their extraordinary style of chanting Buddhist Tantras.

transportation network that allows fast travel to all regions of the globe; meanwhile, at home, the media—radio, TV, and movies—continually feed our appetite for new sounds. Recording companies are responding to increased consumer demand for world musics, producing all kinds of specialty collections as well as samplers for those who want a varied multicultural listening experience.

Does a recording of modern world music capture the essence of a culture's tradition? There are a number of historical field recordings by anthropologists and ethnomusicologists that carefully preserve particular traditional musics and ceremonies (as they existed at the time of the recording). You can probably find some of these collections in your college or university library (the Nonesuch Explorer series and Folkways recordings are fairly standard). But music is a living art. Thus, despite efforts to preserve "authentic" musics of certain cultures, what we hear today is often a fusion of styles—traditional, art, and pop—from around the world. Some of these popular musics reflect the strong impact of Western rock, such as we hear in the recordings of Senegalese singer Youssou N'Dour. Other styles, such as the South African music of Ladysmith Black Mambazo, cultivate more indigenous sounds, setting them in a contemporary idiom for today's avid listeners.

Suggested Listening:

South African music (Ladysmith Black Mambazo)
Irish music (The Chieftains)
Tibetan music (Gyütö monks)
Senegalese music (Youssou N'Dour)

The New Music

76

New Directions

"From Schoenberg I learned that tradition is a home we must love and forgo."—LUKAS FOSS

The term "new music" has been used throughout history. Practically every generation of creative musicians has produced sounds and styles that were never heard before. All the same, the second half of the twentieth century has heard such far-reaching innovations in the art that we are perhaps more justified than any previous generation in applying the label to the music of the present. In effect, we have witnessed nothing less than the birth of a new world of sound.

The Arts Since Mid-Century

The increasing social turmoil since the Second World War has brought about a restlessness of spirit; this is inevitably reflected in the arts, which are passing through a period of violent experimentation with new media, new materials, and new techniques. Artists are freeing themselves from every vestige of the past in order to explore new areas of thought and feeling.

The trend away from objective painting led to Abstract Expressionism in the United States during the 1950s and 1960s. In the canvases of such painters as Robert Motherwell and Jackson Pollock, space, mass, and color were freed from the need to imitate objects in the real world. The urge toward abstraction was felt equally in sculpture, as is evident in the work of such artists as Henry Moore and Isamu Noguchi. (See illustration on p. 561.) *Abstract Expressionism*

At the same time, a new kind of realism appeared in the art of Jasper Johns, Robert Rauschenberg, and their colleagues, who owe some of their inspiration to the Dadaists of four decades earlier. Rauschenberg's aim, as he put it,

In Abstract Expressionism, space and mass become independent values, liberated from the need to express reality. Elegy to the Spanish Republic No. 18 *by* **Robert Motherwell** *(b. 1915).* (Museum of Modern Art, N.Y., Charles Mergentime Fund)

Pop Art

was to work "in the gap between life and art." This trend culminated in Pop Art, which drew its themes and techniques from modern urban life: machines, advertisements, comic strips, movies, commercial photography, and familiar objects connected with everyday living. A similar aim motivated Andy Warhol's *Four Campbell's Soup Cans,* Jim Dine's *A Nice Pair of Boots,* and Rauschenberg's own *First Landing Jump* (see p. 562).

Post-Modernism

Today, the term "Post-Modernism"—implying a movement away from formalism—is applied to a variety of styles, including conceptual art, minimalism, and environmental art. One of the most successful proponents of Post-Modernism is the architect Michael Graves, whose Humana Building in Louisville, Kentucky (see p. 563), features a monumental entrance and a lobby reminiscent of an ancient temple. Environmental art, sometimes called earthworks, is one manifestation of the minimalist movement, which advocates a bareness and simplicity (we will read about minimalism in music in Chapter 80). The artist Robert Smithson is well-known for *Spiral Jetty,* an environmental sculpture in the Great Salt Lake, in Utah (see p. 564).

Feminist and ethnic art

The feminist movement has affected mainstream developments in the art world since the late 1960s, by focusing attention on a lesser-known body of works and artists and on issues of gender. The collaborative projects led by Judy Chicago, carried out by teams of women artists, have contributed much to this movement. Recently, serious attention has also been given to the artistic achievements of America's diverse ethnic communities, especially African-American and Native American art.

Poetry

In the field of literature, poetry has lent itself to the most widespread experimentation. Many poets face the contemporary world with a profound sense of alienation. Modern American poetry ranges over a wide gamut from intellectualism to the Whitmanesque exuberance of the "beat generation." Freedom of verse forms and a wit tinged with bitterness have characterized many poets.

Drama and the novel

Although drama and the novel are by their very nature based on an imitation of life, they have not remained indifferent to the new trends. The theater moved away from the social and psychological concerns that permeated the work of Arthur Miller and Tennessee Williams in the 1950s, turning instead to the "theater of the absurd," whose leading European proponents—Samuel Beckett, Eugene Ionesco, and Jean Genet—viewed the world with a vast disillusionment, placing metaphysical absurdity at the core of human existence. The spirit of the absurd also penetrated the novel; witness such works as *Catch 22* by Joseph Heller and *Giles Goat-Boy* by John Barth, to name only two that captured the pulse of the 1960s.

Performance art

Linked to developments in modern theater is performance art, which combines visual stimuli with theater and music in a multimedia event. The term "happening" was coined in the 1950s to describe this semi-improvised event, which was often highly dependent on audience participation. The experimental composer John Cage was intrigued by this art form, as is Laurie Anderson, who combines popular music, storytelling, comic routines, and high-tech equipment as a forum in which to address social issues (see p. 565).

Literary criticism

Several recent trends have changed the way we look at literature—deconstruction is a practice of reading, or more correctly, a mode of textual analysis. Developed in the early 1970s, it is based on the concept that any text can be understood to say something quite different from what it first appears to mean; a deconstructive interpretation focuses only on the text itself, without concern for external influences, such as its context. Another new way of understanding literature is through feminine criticism. Popular since the late 1960s, this movement questions long-standing male attitudes and interpretations of texts and attempts to describe women's experience as depicted in literature.

New-wave cinema

Finally, the cinema—of all the arts the one most securely chained to storytelling of a popular kind—has also responded to the twin impulses of exper-

The urge toward abstraction has been felt by sculptors such as **Henry Moore** *(b. 1898). Recumbent Figure. (Tate Gallery/Art Resource, N.Y.)*

The themes and techniques of Pop Art are drawn from modern urban life while incorporating incongruities into each work. A construction by **Robert Rauschenberg** *(b. 1925),* First Landing Jump. (Museum of Modern Art, N.Y., Gift of Philip Johnson)

imentation and abstraction. Among the "new wave" directors may be mentioned Michelangelo Antonioni (*Blowup*, 1966; *The Passenger*, 1975), Jean-Luc Godard (*Breathless*, 1959), and Federico Fellini (*La Strada*, 1959; *8½*, 1963; *Amarcord*, 1974; *The Ship Sails On*, 1983). In films like Alain Resnais's *Last Year at Marienbad* (1962) and Ingmar Bergman's *Persona* (1966), the Abstract Expressionist urge was realized on the screen.

These are only a few landmarks in the second half of the twentieth century, but they are enough to indicate that art has become increasingly intellectual, experimental, and abstract.

Toward Greater Organization in Music

When Schoenberg based his twelve-tone method on the use of tone rows, he was obviously moving toward a much stricter organization of sound material. It remained for later generations to extend the tone-row principle to the elements of music other than pitch. The arrangement of the twelve tones in a series might be paralleled by similar groupings of durations (time values), dynamic values (degrees of loudness), or timbres. Other factors too might be brought under serial organization: the disposition of registers and densities, types of attack, or sizes of intervals. By extending the serial principle in all possible directions, a composer could achieve a totally organized fabric, controlled by the basic premise: the generating power of the series.

Total serialism   This move toward *total serialism* resulted in an extremely complex, ultra-rational music. The composers who embraced this idea, such as Pierre Boulez

The Humana Building *in Louisville, Kentucky, designed by architect* **Michael Graves,** *is a perfect example of postmodern style, with its monumental entrance and grandiose window treatment.* (John Nation)

and Karlheinz Stockhausen, pushed some of the new ways of hearing and experiencing music to unprecedented limits.

Toward Greater Freedom in Music

The urge toward a totally controlled music had its counterpart in the desire for greater, even total, freedom from all predetermined forms and procedures. Music of this type emphasizes the antirational element in artistic experience: intuition, chance, the spur of the moment. Composers who wish to avoid the rational ordering of musical sound may rely on the element of chance and allow, say, a throw of dice to determine the selection of their material, or perhaps build their pieces around a series of random numbers generated by a computer. They may let the performer choose the order in which the sections are to be played, or indicate the general course of events in regard to pitches, durations, and registers but leave it up to the performer to fill in the details. The performance thus becomes a musical "happening" in the course of which the piece is recreated afresh each time it is played.

Such indeterminate music is known as *aleatoric* (from *alea,* the Latin word for "dice," which from ancient times have symbolized the whims of chance). In aleatory music, the overall form may be clearly indicated, but the details are left to choice or chance. On the other hand, some composers, among them John Cage, will indicate the details of a composition clearly enough but leave its overall shape to choice or chance; this type of flexible structure is known

Aleatoric music

The Spiral Jetty, *built in 1970 by* **Robert Smithson,** *is an environmental sculpture in the Great Salt Lake, Utah. It exemplifies the principles of bareness and simplicity that characterize the minimalist movement.* (Courtesy of John Weber Gallery; photo by Gian Franco Gorgoni)

Open form

as *open form*. Related to these tendencies is the increased reliance on improvisation—a technique common in music of the Baroque and earlier eras and reintroduced, in the 1950s and 1960s, in the domain of jazz. Traditionally, improvisation consists of spontaneous invention within a framework and a style that have been clearly established, so that player and listener have fairly well-defined ideas of what is "good" and what is "bad." In the more extreme types of aleatory music, no such criteria are set; anything that happens is acceptable to the composer.

A representative figure of this new freedom is Lukas Foss (b. 1922), whose *Time Cycle* (1960) and *Echoi* (1961–63) established his place in the forefront of those who were experimenting with indeterminacy, group improvisation, and fresh approaches to sound. Foss was also a leader in the trend toward collage, whereby composers use for their own purpose material from the past. This orientation is evident in the *Baroque Variations for Orchestra* (1967).

Microtonality

Contemporary attitudes have liberated not only forms but all the elements of music from the restrictions of the past. The concept of a music based on the twelve pitches of the chromatic scale has been left far behind. Electronic instruments make possible the use of sounds that lie "in the cracks of the piano keys"—the microtonal intervals, such as quarter tones, that are smaller than semitones—and very skilled instrumentalists and vocalists have now mastered these novel scales.

The Internationalism of the New Music

The Second World War and the events leading up to it disrupted musical life in Europe much more than in North America, with the result that the United States forged ahead in certain areas. For example, the first composer to apply serial organization to dimensions other than pitch was the American Milton Babbitt, who will be discussed in a later chapter. The experiments of John Cage anticipated and influenced similar attempts abroad. Earle Brown (b.

1926) was the first to use open form; Morton Feldman (1926–87) was the first to write works that gave the performer a choice. Once the war was over, the Europeans quickly made up for lost time. Intense experimentation went on in Italy, Germany, France, England, Holland, and Scandinavia. This has gradually spread eastward; serial and electronic music have also taken root in Japan, while the music of the East has in turn influenced Western composers.

A number of Europeans have achieved international reputations. Luciano Berio (b. 1925) is a leading figure among the radicals of the post-Webern generation in Italy. He was one of the founders of the electronic studio in Milan, which became a center of avant-garde activity, and for several years taught composition at the Juilliard School in New York. Berio's music exemplifies three major trends in the contemporary scene—serialism, electronic technology, and indeterminacy. A characteristic work is his well-known homage to Martin Luther King, Jr., *Sinfonia* (1969), for orchestra, organ, harps, piano, chorus, and reciters. The Greek composer Iannis Xenakis (b. 1922), who was trained as an engineer, expresses the close ties between music and science characteristic of our time. Xenakis's music derives its very special sound from massed sonorities, prominent use of glissandos, and a texture woven out of individual parts for each instrument in the orchestra. Krzysztof Penderecki (b. 1933) is the foremost composer of Poland. His search for new sonorities and new ways of producing them has resulted in the inclusion in his scores of such noises as the sawing of wood and the clicking of typewriters. His choral music includes special effects such as hissing, shouting, whistling, articulating rapid consonants, and the like. In this area, he has been much influenced by Xenakis.

The German composer Karlheinz Stockhausen (b. 1928) assumed leadership in the 1950s of an international group of composers who worked at an avant-garde studio at the Cologne, Germany, radio station. His works pursue the possibilities of serialism, aleatory technique, improvisation, and electronic manipulation of prerecorded tape. Pierre Boulez, the most important

Luciano Berio

Iannis Xenakis

Krzysztof Penderecki

Karlheinz Stockhausen

Pierre Boulez

Mixed-media artist **Laurie Anderson,** *whose face is magnified in this scene from her film* Home of the Brave *(1986), is accompanied by two backup singers and a saxophonist.* (Photo © Talk Normal Productions, Inc.)

Sophia Gubaidulina

composer of the French avant-garde, is widely known for his activities as a conductor and as head of IRCAM (the French government's institute for composition and acoustics). We will study a work by Boulez in a later chapter. The Soviet composer Sophia Gubaidulina (b. 1931) stands as a leader among women on the international scene. Her modernist tendencies draw upon eclectic techniques instilled with a strong spiritual element. In some vocal works, she gives the voice nontextual and highly emotional utterances. Her reputation has been established by her violin concerto, entitled *Offertorium* (1980), which parodies J. S. Bach's *Musical Offering* in a Webernesque setting similar to Klangfarbenmelodie.

Other Aspects of the New Music

George Perle

Several composers have tried to reconcile serial procedures with tonality. None has played a more important role in this area than George Perle (b. 1915). Using a language based on the twelve-tone scale, he has retained the concept of tonal centers. Perle had to wait until his seventies to be recognized as one of the important composers of his generation. In 1986, he won the Pulitzer Prize for his Wind Quintet IV as well as a "genius" grant from the MacArthur Foundation. Before then, he was known chiefly for his books, including *Serial Composition and Atonality* (1962) and *Twelve-Tone Tonality*

Charles Wuorinen

(1978). Charles Wuorinen (b. 1938) started out from the sound world of Stravinsky, Schoenberg, and Edgard Varèse (see p. 590), and found his way to the twelve-tone system in the 1960s. He freely adapts the procedures of serialism to the needs of the particular piece he is writing. A prolific composer, he has received his share of awards and honors, among them a Pulitzer Prize and

Ralph Shapey

a MacArthur Fellowship. Ralph Shapey (b. 1921) directs the Contemporary Chamber Players at the University of Chicago. A disciple of the French composer Edgard Varèse, Shapey defines music as "an object in Time and Space: aggregate sounds structured into concrete sculptural forms." His output is mostly instrumental; but he was one of the first American composers to treat the voice as an instrument "using syllables in organized sound-structures."

Louise Talma

Among women composers, Louise Talma (b. 1906), who studied with the French teacher Nadia Boulanger, is an important exponent of serialism. Much influenced by Stravinsky, Talma retains tonal qualities in her music, using serial techniques such as combinatoriality and intersecting rows as added unifying procedures. She is known for her choral works, including *La Corona* (1955) and an opera, *The Alcestiad* (1955–58), a collaboration with writer

Barbara Kolb

Thornton Wilder. Barbara Kolb (b. 1939), the first American woman to win the prestigious Prix de Rome, has developed a personal style of serialism. Her piano work *Appello* (1976) is based on Pierre Boulez's *Structures* (1952), but achieves much more expressive serialism than the sparse pointillism of her model.

It is impossible to name all the composers who have contributed to the myriad of contemporary styles and procedures. In the following chapters, we will explore a number of representative men and women who have helped shape and give expression to modern musical ideas.

Cultural Perspective 25

Canada's Vision for a Global Culture

What significant contemporary musical trends are found in Canada, and how does this country's musical life compare with that of the United States? A huge, multi-ethnic country, Canada has attempted to establish a national identity despite its linguistic and cultural divisions and its relative youth as a nation (it achieved independence in 1867). Thus while the traditional musics of Canada are widely varied—representing the French, British, Native American, and Inuit (Eskimo) cultures—its modern art music has presented a more unified and mainstream front.

Canadian composers are notable for their interest in avant-garde techniques, and the country in general for the promotion of new music. With the advent of electronic music in the 1950s, Canada was quick to respond with studios around the country—in Ottawa, Toronto, Montreal, and Vancouver. Composer John Weinzweig (b. 1913) first championed twelve-tone technique in Canada; he, along with Jean Papineau-Couture of the French-Canadian community, actively sought support for new music through an organization they headed, the Canadian League of Composers. The country also boasts one of the best music information centers in the world, devoted exclusively to the promotion and dissemination of music by Canadians.

Most contemporary Canadian composers have felt the influence of one of the country's important thinkers, Marshall McLuhan (1911–80), who early on saw the far-reaching consequences of electronic communication. McLuhan prophesied the coming of what he called a "global village," achieved through the mass media of radio, TV, films, and computers—in short, a new way of experiencing the world. He firmly believed, however, that the means of communication—the medium—had more influence than the actual message. (The commonly heard phrase "The medium is the message" is the title of a book by McLuhan.) His writings had a significant impact on composer John Cage, who included phrases from them in a verbal collage he created (published under the title *I-VI*, 1988–89).

One Canadian composer who has responded to the ideas of both McLuhan and Cage is R. Murray Schafer (b. 1933). His early interest in new techniques of sound, notation, and mixed media, especially theater, has led him to a worldwide study of acoustic ecology. This project, known as World Soundscapes, explores the relationship between people and the sounds of the environment. Echoing McLuhan's concern for the impact of technology, Schafer has been actively recording and preserving the sounds of the world. One of his recent works, *Ra* (1983), is based on the Egyptian legend of the sun god passing through the night. Envisioned as a total environment, this is a work of musical theater—with actors, dancers, masks, and audience participation—that lasts from sunset to sunrise. Schafer also draws on the natural resources and native culture of his homeland, as in *The Princess of the Stars* (1981), a drama based on a Native American legend that is performed outdoors, at dawn, on the shore of a lake. Both works expand our established notions of performance ritual—that is, the place, time, and conventions of a concert.

Schafer has also influenced the arts in Canada as an educator. He has taught at universities on both coasts, in Newfoundland

A Native American legend is the theme of R. Murray Schafer's Princess of the Stars, *performed at dawn at Two Jack Lake in the Canadian Rockies.* (Photo by Ed Ellis; courtesy of Banff Centre for the Arts)

and British Columbia, and has worked extensively with children in order to develop their general awareness and receptiveness to sounds. Like McLuhan, Schafer has achieved a global view of sound through his inventory of worldwide soundscapes, which he hopes will change the relationship between humanity and the acoustic environment.

77
New Sounds on Traditional Instruments

The New Virtuosity

Musical styles so different from all that went before need a new breed of instrumentalists and vocalists to cope with their technical demands. One has only to attend a concert of avant-garde music to realize how far the art of piano playing or singing has moved from the world of Chopin or Verdi. The piano keyboard may be brushed or slammed with fingers, palm, or fist; or the player may reach inside to hit, scratch, or pluck the strings directly. A violinist may tap, stroke, and even slap the instrument. Vocal music runs the gamut from whispering to shouting, including all manner of groaning, moaning, or hissing along the way. Wind players have learned to produce a variety of double stops, subtle changes of color, and microtonal progressions; and the percussion section has been enriched by an astonishing variety of noisemakers and special effects. In every important musical center, groups of players and singers are springing up who have a genuine affinity with the new music.

VIRTUOSO WOMEN SINGERS OF THE TWENTIETH CENTURY

Among the extraordinary virtuosos of the new music are four American women singers who have made a significant mark on the development of contemporary styles. Bethany Beardslee (b. 1927), a soprano who is widely admired for the silvery quality and wide range of her voice, presented the American premieres of works by Schoenberg, Stravinsky, and Berg. In 1964, she was awarded a grant from the Ford Foundation to commission a composition from Milton Babbitt. This ground-breaking work, *Philomel,* for soprano and prerecorded tape, is based on the Roman poet Ovid's tale of a princess who was raped by the King and subsequently had her tongue cut out. She was transformed into a nightingale so she could sing of her suffering. This violent story, really an antirape statement, is heard through Beardslee's virtuosic distortions and fragmentation of the human voice.

Bethany Beardslee

Equally noted for her vocal virtuosity was Cathy Berberian (1928–83), a singer who gained fame with her 1958 performance of *Aria* by John Cage. In this work, she had to create her own melody from the composer's purposely vague indications, singing a text in five languages and changing between numerous vocal styles, including jazz, contralto, Sprechstimme, Marlene Dietrich, coloratura soprano, folk, Oriental, baby, and nasal. She was married for some years to the Italian composer Luciano Berio, who wrote a large number of works for her, including *Circles* (1960). Berberian was a composer as well, and wrote with her own voice in mind.

Cathy Berberian

Phyllis Bryn-Julson (b. 1945) attracted the attention of her teacher Gunther Schuller with her phenomenal sight-reading ability and *perfect pitch* (the ability to sing any note without the aid of a pitch reference). She is noted for her ability to sing *quarter tones* (an interval halfway between a half step), a technique called for in certain non-Western-inspired compositions. Her performance in 1966 of the suite from Alban Berg's opera *Lulu,* with the Boston Symphony Orchestra, showed off the ease with which she could sing the difficult intervals found in twelve-tone music.

Phyllis Bryn-Julson

The clear and versatile voice of the mezzo-soprano Jan DeGaetani (1933–89) can be heard on recordings of early music, Schubert Lieder, Stephen Foster songs, and many contemporary pieces. She premiered, among other works, the challenging song cycle *Ancient Voices of Children,* written by George Crumb in 1970. (See Chapter 78 for a discussion of this work.) In 1973, she was appointed to the faculty of the Eastman School of Music in Rochester, New York, and made her first appearance with the New York Philharmonic Orchestra. She sang regularly with the Contemporary Chamber Ensemble, the group with whom she made a famous recording of Schoenberg's *Pierrot lunaire.* As a singer and teacher, she has greatly influenced the next generation of performers.

Jan DeGaetani

Each of these women gained fame through her remarkable ability to sing avant-garde music. Indeed, in this arena, the talents of women musicians, especially sopranos, far exceeded those of men. This placed certain female singers in great demand in contemporary music, and allowed them a venue for showing off their flexible voices and adventuresome spirits.

Elliott Carter: A Modern American Master

"I like music to be beautiful, ordered, and expressive of the more important aspects of life."

Elliott Carter

Of the composers who have come into prominence in recent years, none is more widely admired by his fellow musicians than Elliott Carter (b. 1908). His works are not of the kind that achieve easy popularity; but their profundity of thought and maturity of workmanship indicate a musical intellect of the first order.

Carter started out with a musical idiom rooted in diatonic-modal harmony, but gradually assimilated a dissonant chromaticism that places him (if one must attach a label) among the Abstract Expressionists. He employs fluctuating tempo as a form-building element, through the use of a novel technique that he calls "metrical modulation," whereby the speed of the rhythmic pulse is subtly modified. When several instruments are playing together, each with its own pulse and each changing that pulse independently in a different direction, there results an original and powerful kind of texture.

In the works of Carter's maturity, he explores the possibilities of this technique in a variety of ways. The three string quartets are bold, uncompromising works that constitute the most significant contribution to this medium since Bartók; both the Second and Third brought the composer Pulitzer Prizes.

Eight Etudes and a Fantasy

Carter's impeccable craftsmanship is apparent in Eight Etudes and a Fantasy (1950), a piece that grew directly out of his activity as a teacher. He

Principal Works

Orchestral works, including Variations for Orchestra (1955), Double Concerto (harpsichord and piano, 1961), Concerto for Orchestra (1969), *A Symphony of Three Orchestras* (1976), and *Penthode* (1985)

Chamber and solo works, including 3 string quartets (1951, 1960, 1971); Eight Etudes and a Fantasy (1950); and various sonatas and quintets; piano music, including *Night Fantasies* (1980)

Vocal music, including *A Mirror on Which to Dwell* (1976) and *Syringa* (1978)

2 ballets

had asked his students to bring in examples illustrating the use of woodwind instruments, and had invited four woodwind players in the class to perform them. Disappointed in what the class had written, he sketched some passages on the blackboard for the woodwind players to try. These he later developed into the Eight Etudes and a Fantasy, in which he explores the possibilities of flute, oboe, clarinet, and bassoon in imaginative ways.

We will study his Sonata for Flute, Oboe, Cello, and Harpsichord, a work commissioned by harpsichordist Sylvia Marlowe and the Harpsichord Quartet of New York in 1952 (see Listening Guide 74). The composer explained that his idea "was to stress as much as possible the vast and wonderful array of tone-colors available on the modern harpsichord. . . . It seemed very important to have the harpsichord speak in a new voice, expressing characters unfamiliar to its extensive Baroque repertory." In this work, Carter departs from his earlier Neoclassical style; the three movements of the sonata do not have traditional forms, but are freer, with an improvisational character.

Sonata for Flute, Oboe, Cello, and Harpsichord

The first movement, marked Risoluto (determined), opens, according to the composer, "with a splashing dramatic gesture whose subsiding ripples form the rest of the movement." It is in two sections, the first energetic and highly rhythmic, the second calmer and more lyrical. In the second part, the composer emphasizes its lyricism by indicating the outline of the melody above the harpsichord part. We find in this movement a rarefied texture in which each note stands out against the sound mass. The use of pizzicato in the cello and staccato in the flute points up this quality of extreme clarity. The instrumental lines are spaced wide apart, giving a sense of musical expanse. In several places, one instrument carries on the musical line where another left off, so that we get the impression of smooth, uninterrupted movement.

First movement

The second movement, a Lento, is "an expressive dialogue between the harpsichord and the others." The final movement is in 6/8 meter, reminiscent of the *forlana,* a dance of the Venetian gondoliers. The composer explains that the characteristic rhythmic cell of this dance gave birth to all sorts of rhythmic changes.

Second and third movements

Carter's works are oriented toward the most serious aspects of musical art. They offer a continual challenge to the listener and confirm his position as one of the most important composers in America.

Pierre Boulez and the French Avant-Garde

"I think that music should be magic and collective hysteria."

Pierre Boulez (b. 1925) is the most important French composer of the avant-garde. He is also well-known because of his widespread activities as a conductor, in which capacity he has propagandized tirelessly on behalf of contemporary music. The American public grew familiar with his name and work through his five-year stint as music director of the New York Philharmonic.

Pierre Boulez

Listening Guide 74

C/S: 8A/4   C/S: 8/ 16 – 17

CARTER: Sonata for Flute, Oboe, Cello, and Harpsichord, First Movement

(3:17)

Date of work: 1952
Movements:
    I. Risoluto
    II. Lento
    III. Allegro

FIRST MOVEMENT: Risoluto (determined)

16 0:00 Harpsichord, then cello, flute, and oboe enter; they engage in frenzied, contrapuntal interplay, shifting meters (5/4–4/4–3/4)

     0:22 Harpsichord and flute have disjunct, staccato line in eighth notes; other instruments interject short motives

            Builds to climax in quicker notes; harpsichord has fast chords that alternate between hands; reaches *fortissimo* dynamic level, then dies down

17 1:21 Next section—slower, lyrical melody in harpsichord; marked Tempo giusto (moderate); other instruments elaborate on melody:

            Harpsichord continues with melody at various pitch levels; other instruments respond with short motives

            Ripples die out as music softens and slows; ends with harpsichord alone on widely spaced dissonant chord

---

Boulez studied at the Paris Conservatory, where the composer Olivier Messiaen (1908-92) exerted a powerful influence on him. He subsequently fell under the spell of Debussy, Stravinsky, and later, Webern, whose impact was at its height just after the Second World War. Taking Webern's later works as his point of departure, Boulez extended serial techniques to control not only pitch but rhythm, dynamics, texture—in short, a total serialism of the elements. Especially interested in rhythm, Boulez wrote of one early work that he tried "for the first time to articulate rhythmic structures, of which Messiaen had revealed to me the possibilities, upon classical serial structures."

The emotional content of Boulez's music extends from a gentle lyricism to a furious Expressionism. From Messiaen, he has taken over a fondness for bell and percussion sounds that evoke the Balinese *gamelan,* an orchestra made up largely of gongs and other metalophones (see illustration on p. 450).

Among his chief early works are three piano sonatas, *The Hammer Without a Master,* and *Fold upon Fold,* the latter two for voice and chamber ensemble. More recently, Boulez has worked in combined media, such as orchestra with electronic equipment; one such piece, *Répons,* has undergone several recent revisions.

Principal Works

Orchestral works, including *Rituel* (1975) and *Répons* (orchestra and digital equipment, 1981–)

Chamber works, including *Le marteau sans maître* (*The Hammer Without a Master,* 1954) and *Pli selon pli* (*Fold upon Fold,* 1962, which includes 3 *Improvisations on Mallarmé*)

Piano music, including 3 piano sonatas (1946, 1948, 1957) and *Structures I* and *II* for two pianos (1952, 1961)

Boulez's best-known work, *The Hammer Without a Master,* presents the chief traits of his style within a compact frame. It is a suite of nine movements based on three short poems by René Char. We will study three movements—the setting of the first poem, *Furious Artisans* (No. 3), and the Prelude (No. 1) and Postlude (No. 7) to this poem (see Listening Guide 75 for analysis and text).

The Hammer Without a Master

The piece is for contralto singer and six instruments, of which alto flute, guitar, and viola are most in evidence. These are supported by xylophone and a varied group of percussion played by a single performer. The full group never plays together; instead, each movement presents a different combination of instruments from the ensemble.

The overall sound, of the bell and percussion variety, is limpid and brilliant, evoking the music of several non-Western cultures. Boulez himself has commented on these influences: "the xylophone representing the African balaphone, the vibraphone the Balinese gender, and the guitar recalling the Japanese koto." Maracas and bongo drums further suggest the sounds of Latin-American music.

The vocal line shows the wide leaps we associate with twelve-tone music. Boulez does not attempt to make the words of the poem clear in his setting; "if you want to 'understand' the text," he says, "read it!" Char's poetry is thoroughly surrealist in the violence of its images. The reader may find the translation more than a little mystifying.

The Prelude, entitled *Before "Furious Artisans,"* is scored for alto flute, vibraphone, guitar, and viola. The tense, plucked-string sound of the guitar is prominent, reminiscent of the mandolin in certain works by Schoenberg and Webern. The dark hue of the viola contrasts with the lighter timbre of the flute. Boulez's serial technique, with its emphasis on dissonant intervals, makes for a highly integrated texture.

Furious Artisans, a duet between the voice and flute, unfolds in a free, improvisational manner, both ornate and rhapsodical, in the manner of certain musics from East Asia. The words dissolve in music, an effect heightened by the fact that vowels are frequently extended over several notes. The voice is treated here as an instrument, asked to sing an enormously wide range with devilishly difficult intervals. The flute part, also very virtuosic, includes a technique known as *flutter tonguing* (in which the tongue is "fluttered" against the roof of the mouth), heard prominently at several points in the movement.

The brief Postlude, *After "Furious Artisans,"* relates to the Prelude in both its interval structure and sound texture. Here, Boulez calls upon three rather than four instruments, omitting the viola. Since it does not directly follow *Furious Artisans,* it serves rather as a reminiscence.

Witold Lutosławski and Aleatoric Music

> "I . . . realized that I could compose music different from that of my past."

Witold Lutosławski

The Polish composer Witold Lutosławski (1913–94) was one of the most prominent members of the European avant-garde. Yet he found ways to combine contemporary procedures with elements drawn from more traditional styles.

Lutosławski's serial period began with *Funeral Music* (1958), written in a unique style that blended twelve-tone elements with chromatic harmony in elaborately contrapuntal textures abounding in canonic devices. He next fell under the influence of John Cage. It occurred to him while listening to Cage's Concerto for Piano and Orchestra (1960) that "I could progress toward the whole not from the small detail but the other way around—I could start out from chance and create order in it gradually." Lutosławski coined the term "aleatoric counterpoint" to indicate a type of music in which the pitches for all the parts are written out, but the rhythms are improvised within given rules. ("Aleatoric," you will recall, refers to indeterminate or random music in which certain elements are deliberately left to chance.)

Principal Works

Orchestral works, including 3 symphonies (1947, 1967, 1983), Concerto for Orchestra (1954), *Funeral Music* (1958), *Jeux vénitiens* (*Venetian Games,* 1961)

Vocal music, including *Three Poems of Henri Michaux* (with orchestra, 1963)

Chamber music, including String Quartet (1964)

Piano music, including *Bucolics* (1952)

Listening Guide 75

 C/S: 8A/9   C/S: 8/ 28 – 30

BOULEZ: *The Hammer Without a Master (Le marteau sans maître),*
Nos. 1, 3, 7

(5:14)

Date of work: 1953–54; revised 1957

Medium: Alto voice, alto flute, viola, guitar, vibraphone, xylophone, and unpitched percussion

Text: 3 poems by René Char, surrealist poet

Structure: 9 movements, with serial organization (indentations line up related movements)

    1. *Before "Furious Artisans" (Avant "L'artisanat furieux")*
        2. Commentary I on *Hangmen of Solitude (Bourreaux de solitude)*
    3. *Furious Artisans (L'artisanat furieux)*
        4. Commentary II on *Hangmen of Solitude*
            5. *Lovely Building and Forebodings (Bel edifice et les pressentiments), version première*
    6. *Hangmen of Solitude*
    7. *After "Furious Artisans" (Après "L'artisanat furieux")*
        8. Commentary III on *Hangmen of Solitude*
            9. *Lovely Building and Forebodings, double*

---

28 0:00   **1. *Before "Furious Artisans" (Avant "L'artisanat furieux")***   (1:46)

Medium: Alto flute, vibraphone, guitar, and viola

Tempo: Rapide (quickly)

Description:
    Dialogue between 4 instruments, disjunct, with wide leaps; individual notes stand out;
    meter constantly shifting; viola alternates bowing and pizzicato

Opening of first movement, showing exchanges between instruments:

29 0:00 **3. *Furious artisans (L'artisanat furieux)*** (2:27)

Medium: Alto voice and flute

Tempo: Modéré sans rigueur (moderate, without strictness)

Text	*Translation*
La roulotte rouge au bord du clou	The red caravan at the prison's edge
Et cadavre dans le panier	And the corpse in the basket
Et chevaux de labours dans le fer à cheval	And the work horses in the horseshoe
Je rêve la tête sur la pointe de mon couteau le Pérou	I dream of Peru with my head on the point of my knife

Description:

Solo flute introduction, with wide-ranging leaps

Voice enters, unaccompanied, in chromatic, disjunct line, followed by flute with flutter tonguing on sustained note:

Voice has grace notes on "du clou"; builds to climax with melody that reverses that of opening

Dialogue continues with imitation; voice enters on sustained pitch (C), flute enters on dissonant tone (C sharp); duet transposes the 12-tone row

Closes with flutter tonguing on flute

30 0:00 **7. *After "Furious Artisans" (Après "L'artisanat furieux")*** (1:01)

Medium: Flute, vibraphone, and guitar

Tempo: Rapide (quickly)

Opening texture and intervals related to first movement, but more polyphonic:

Brief pause, then acceleration of rhythm

Another pause, then constant rhythm set in vibraphone

Closes abruptly with 2 guitar notes

Venetian Games derives its title from the Festival of Contemporary Music in Venice, for which it was written. We will hear the first movement, which has a distinct architectural structure in which aleatoric sections alternate with notated ones. The orchestra is divided into two groups, winds and percussion pitted against the strings, one group alternating with the other. (See Listening Guide 76 for analysis.) The wind sections are written out; they often begin and end with a loud percussion chord. The music is very active rhythmically, with a piano part added to the winds toward the end of the movement. The string sections throughout are aleatoric; in these sections, the composer strives for maximum freedom of choice. They feature dissonant chord clusters, with loud entries on particular pitches, some pizzicato. There are eight sections, labeled from A to H in the scores. The woodwind-and-percussion sound at the beginning of the movement is balanced by string sound at the end. Four percussion chords shape the final cadence, each softer than the one before.

The second movement ends with a passage for piano *ad libitum* (an indication that gives the performer the liberty to include or omit that particular part). The third movement includes a free solo part for flute, with the entries of the other instruments decided by the conductor. There are fixed time frames for passages that are otherwise free. In the fourth movement, the opening and closing sections are notated, while the middle part is aleatoric.

Lutosławski's music shows how avant-garde elements can combine with older styles. He established himself as one of the most interesting personalities on the contemporary scene.

Venetian Games

Listening Guide 76 C/S: 8A/5 C/S: 8/ 18 – 19

LUTOSŁAWSKI: *Venetian Games (Jeux vénitiens)*, **First Movement**   (3:16)

Date of work: 1961
Movements: 4

FIRST MOVEMENT

Timed sections (A–H) alternate winds/percussion (A, C, E, G) and strings (B, D, F, H);
string sections very free (aleatoric)

		Sections	*Length*	*Description*
18	0:00	A	(13")	Woodwinds and percussion; closes with percussive chord
	0:13	B	(33")	Strings—individual entries on pitches; closes with high violin pitch
	0:46	C	(21")	Woodwind and percussion, with timpani added; percussive chord begins and ends section
19	1:07	D	(28")	Strings—high, repeated notes, dissonant clusters
	1:35	E	(7")	Woodwind, percussion, timpani, with brass added; begins with percussive chord
	1:42	F	(2")	Strings
	1:44	G	(28")	Woodwinds, brass, percussion, timpani, with piano added; begins with percussive chord
	2:12	H	(64")	Strings; closes with 4 percussion chords, each softer than the last

78

Modern Composers and Non-Western Styles

Throughout the course of history, the West has felt the influence of other cultures. This has been especially true in music. Twentieth-century composers, as we have seen, found inspiration not only in African musics but also in the strong rhythmic features of the songs and dances from the borderlands of Western culture—southeastern Europe, Asiatic Russia, the Near East, and parts of Latin America. We have also encountered the strong impetus toward primitivism that came from African styles developed by American musicians, in which the powerful rhythmic impulse of their heritage was combined with the major-minor tonality of Western art music. Out of this amalgam grew the rich literature of spirituals, work songs, and shouts, and ultimately ragtime, blues and jazz, swing, and rock.

A number of contemporary composers have responded in particular to the philosophy of the Far East, notably Zen Buddhism and Indian thought. Among them are three Californians whose work has attracted much notice: Henry Cowell, Harry Partch, and especially John Cage, whose name was associated with the avant-garde scene for over fifty years.

Important Experimenters

Henry Cowell (1897–1965) was drawn toward a variety of non-Western musics. His studies of the music of Japan, India, and Iran as well as rural Ireland and America led him to combine Asian instruments with traditional Western ensembles, as in his two koto concertos (1962 and 1965). (The koto, illustrated on p. 35, is a Japanese zither with thirteen strings stretched over bridges and tuned to one of a variety of pentatonic scales.) He also experimented with the use of foreign scales, which he harmonized with Western chords. The piano provided Cowell with an outlet for a number of his innovations: these include *tone clusters,* groups of adjacent notes that are sounded with the fist, palm, or forearm, and plucking of the piano strings directly with the fingers.

Henry Cowell

Tone clusters

The piano also lent itself to experiments with new tuning systems. One of the first to attempt microtonal music for the piano was Charles Ives, who wrote for pianos tuned a quarter tone apart. But perhaps the most serious proponent of this technique was Harry Partch (1901–74), who single-mindedly pursued the goal of a microtonal music. In the 1920s, he evolved a scale of forty-three microtones to the octave and built instruments with this tuning, adapting Hindu and African instruments to meet his purpose. Among his idiophones are cloud-chamber bowls (made of glass), cone gongs (made of

Harry Partch

Harry Partch with two of his remarkable musical instruments: a gourd tree and a cone gong. (Courtesy of BMI Archives)

metal), diamond marimba (made of wood), and tree gourds. His performance group, called the Gate 5 Ensemble, played his works from memory, producing a music whose interest lay not in harmony but in melody and in timbre. One work that espouses his vision is *The Delusion of Fury* (1969), a large-scale ceremonial piece that employs elements of Japanese Noh drama in its first part, "On a Japanese Theme," and demands that its instrumentalists make choral-voice sounds in its second part, entitled "On an African Theme."

The Music of John Cage

"I am more like a hunter or inventor than a lawmaker."

John Cage

John Cage (1912–92) represents the type of eternally questing artist who no sooner solves one problem than he presses forward to another. Born in Los Angeles, Cage attended Pomona College, then left school to travel in Europe. He exhibited an early interest in non-Western scales, which he learned from his mentor Henry Cowell. As a student of Arnold Schoenberg, Cage explored compositions with fixed tone rows, but was eventually persuaded that future advance lay through rhythm rather than pitch. This abiding interest in rhythm led him to explore the possibilities of percussion instruments. He soon realized that the traditional division between consonance and dissonance had given way to a new opposition between music and noise, as a result of which the boundaries of the one were extended to include more of the other. In 1937, the young composer prophesied that "the use of noise to make music will continue and increase until we reach a music produced through the aid of electrical instruments, which will make available for musical purposes any and all sounds that can be heard."

Prepared piano

Cage's exploration of percussive rhythm led him to invent, in 1938, what he called the "prepared piano." The preparation consisted of inserting nails, bolts, nuts, screws, and bits of rubber, wood, or leather at crucial points in the strings of an ordinary grand piano. There resulted a myriad of sounds whose overall effect resembled that of a Javanese *gamelan* (an ensemble made up of various kinds of gongs, xylophones, drums, bowed and plucked strings, cymbals, and sometimes singers). He wrote a number of works for the prepared piano, notably the set of *Sonatas and Interludes* (1946–48). The music reflects the composer's preoccupation with East Asian philosophy. "After reading the work of Ananda K. Coomaraswamy, I decided to attempt the expression in music of the 'permanent emotions' of Indian tradition: the heroic, the erotic, the wondrous, the mirthful, sorrow, fear, anger, the odious, and their common tendency toward tranquility." The striving for tranquillity was a pervasive element in Cage's life and work.

Indeterminacy

His interest in indeterminacy led to compositions in which choices were made by throwing dice. He also relied on the *I Ching* (Book of Changes), an ancient Chinese method of throwing coins or marked sticks for chance numbers, from which he derived a system of charts and graphs governing the series of events that could happen within a given structural space. One final frontier he conquered was the transfer of indeterminacy to tape. This problem he solved in *Fontana Mix* (1958), which became the first taped work to establish conditions whose outcome could not be foreseen. These experiments established John Cage as a decisive factor in the artistic life of the mid-twentieth century.

Cage was intensely interested in the role of silence in regard to sound. "In this new music," he declared, "nothing takes place but sounds: those that are notated and those that are not." Those that are not notated appear in the written music as silence, opening the listener's ears to the sounds that happen to be in the environment. "There is no such thing as an empty space or an empty time. There is always something to see, something to hear. In fact, try as we may to make a silence, we cannot."

Out of this profound observation came a piece, entitled *4'33"*, without any musical content at all, consisting of four minutes and thirty-three seconds of silence. During this period, listeners are expected to become aware of the sounds in the hall or outside it, the beating of their hearts or the sounds floating around in their imagination. The piece was first "performed" by the pianist David Tudor in 1952. He came out onstage, placed a score on the piano rack, sat quietly for the duration of the piece, then closed the piano lid and walked off the stage.

Some critics considered this a hoax or a not-so-clever trick. Yet Cage viewed this as one of the most radical statements he had made (and he made many) against the traditions of Western music, one that raised profound questions. What is music, and what is noise? And what does silence contribute to music? In any case, *4'33"* is a piece that can be performed by anyone on any instrument, and it will certainly make the listener more aware of the surroundings in a new way.

4'33"

Multicultural Influences in Contemporary Society

This impulse toward a world music sound has continued with such composers as Alan Hovhaness (b. 1911), Lou Harrison (b. 1917), Philip Glass, Terry Riley, and Steve Reich (on the last three composers, see pp. 600–2). In this category also belong several composers who combined their Asian heritage with the traditions of the West; these include Chou Wen-Chung (b. 1923), Toru Takemitsu (1930–96), and Yuji Takahashi (b. 1909). The result of all this activity has been to open up to the West a new world of styles, techniques, and instruments.

We have in past chapters traced how artistic impulses from disparate cultures have steadily grown closer together. Having received powerful impetus during the Second World War, this trend has been further strengthened through worldwide air travel and the media—radio, television, and the press—all of which have made the earth a smaller place. The result is that artists in general and musicians in particular are subject to multicultural influences to a degree undreamed of in earlier times.

We will study two modern representatives of this awakening: the American composer George Crumb, whose settings of the Spanish poet Federico García

Lorca are enhanced by flamenco and East Asian music; and the Hungarian György Ligeti, whose piano études assume the rhythmic complexity of certain African musics.

George Crumb's Ancient Voices of Children

George Crumb

Federico García Lorca

In recent years, George Crumb (b. 1929) has forged ahead to a notable position among the composers of his generation. He owes this preeminence partly to the emotional character of his music, allied to a highly developed sense of the dramatic. His kind of romanticism is most unusual among the advanced composers of his generation. Crumb uses contemporary techniques for expressive ends that make an enormous impact in the concert hall. He has won numerous honors and awards and is currently professor of composition at the University of Pennsylvania.

Crumb has shown an extraordinary affinity for the poetry of Federico García Lorca, the great poet who was killed by the Fascists during the Spanish Civil War. Besides *Ancient Voices of Children,* his Lorca cycle includes four other works: *Night Music I*; four books of madrigals; *Songs, Drones, and Refrains of Death*; and *Night of the Four Moons.* "In *Ancient Voices of Children,* as in my earlier Lorca settings," the composer states, "I have sought musical images that enhance and reinforce the powerful yet strangely haunting imagery of Lorca's poetry. I feel that the essential meaning of this poetry is concerned with the most primary things: Life, death, love, the smell of the earth, the sounds of the wind and the sea." These concepts, Crumb goes on to explain, "are embodied in a language which is primitive and stark, but which is capable of infinitely subtle nuance."

Principal Works

Orchestral music, including *Echoes of Time and the River* (1967) and *A Haunted Landscape* (1984)

Vocal music based on Lorca poetry, including *Night Music I* (1963); four books of madrigals (1965–69); *Songs, Drones, and Refrains of Death* (1968); *Night of the Four Moons* (1969); and *Ancient Voices of Children* (1970)

Chamber music, including *Black Angels* (1970), for electrified string quartet; *Lux aeterna* (Eternal Light, 1971), for voice and chamber ensemble (including sitar); and *Vox balaenae* (The Voice of the Whales, 1971), for amplified instruments

Music for amplified piano, including 2 volumes of *Makrokosmos* (1972, 1973) and *Music for a Summer Evening* (1974); piano music (*Processional*, 1984)

Ancient Voices of Children is a cycle of songs for soprano, boy soprano, oboe, mandolin, harp, electric piano, and percussion (see Listening Guide 77). Endowed with an aural imagination of remarkable vividness, Crumb tirelessly explores new ways of using voice and instruments. Like many contemporary composers, he uses the voice like an instrument, in a vocal style he describes as ranging "from the virtuosic to the intimately lyrical." He found his ideal interpreter in the mezzo-soprano Jan DeGaetani, whose recording of the work remains as a model for all other interpreters.

Ancient Voices of Children

The score abounds with unusual effects, many inspired by musics of distant cultures. The soprano opens with a fanciful *vocalise* (a wordless melody, in this case based on purely phonetic sounds) that is reminiscent of a rhapsodic East Asian melody. She sings into an electrically amplified piano, arousing a shimmering cloud of sympathetic vibrations. The pitch is "bent" to produce microtones, also typical of some styles of Asian music. Included in the score are a toy piano, harmonica, and musical saw as well as a rich array of percussion instruments, many borrowed from other cultures, such as Tibetan prayer stones, Japanese temple bells, tuned tom-toms (high-pitched drums of African origin), Latin-American claves (wooden clappers), and maracas (a kind of rattle). Also heard are marimba, vibraphone, sleigh bells, glockenspiel plates, and tubular bells. The composer described this combination of styles: "I was conscious of an urge to fuse unrelated stylistic elements . . . a suggestion of Flamenco with a Baroque quotation, or a reminiscence of Mahler with the Orient."

The first song from this cycle, *The Little Boy Is Looking for His Voice (El niño busca su voz)*, is very free and fantastic in character. The soprano part offers a virtuoso exhibition of what the voice can do in the way of cries, sighs, whispers, buzzings, trills, and percussive clicks. There are even passages marked "fluttertongue"—an effect we have hitherto associated only with instruments. Throughout, Crumb captures the improvisational spirit of flamenco song. The passion is here, the sense of mystery and wonder—but in a thoroughly twentieth-century setting.

First song

In *Ancient Voices,* Crumb found the right music for the dark intimations of Lorca's poetry. The work has justly established itself as a prime example of contemporary imagination and feeling.

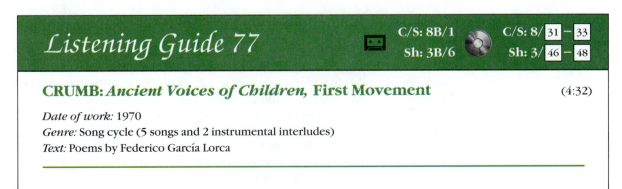

Listening Guide 77

C/S: 8B/1
Sh: 3B/6

C/S: 8/ 31 – 33
Sh: 3/ 46 – 48

CRUMB: *Ancient Voices of Children,* First Movement

(4:32)

Date of work: 1970
Genre: Song cycle (5 songs and 2 instrumental interludes)
Text: Poems by Federico García Lorca

1. *The Little Boy Is Looking for His Voice (El niño busca su voz)*
Medium: Soprano, electric piano, harp, tam-tam, other percussion

		Text	Translation	Description
31	0:00			Opens with an elaborate vocalise for soprano, including cries, trills, other vocal gymnastics; she sings into piano with pedal down for resonance
32	2:47	El niño busca su voz. (La tenía el rey de los grillos.) En una gota de agua buscaba su voz el niño.	The little boy is looking for his voice. (The king of the crickets had it.) In a drop of water the little boy looked for his voice.	Strophe 1—sung by soprano alone with turns, trills, hisses; she continues with low-pitched recitation
33	3:32	No la quiero para hablar; me haré con ella un anillo que llevará mi silencio en su dedo pequeñito.	I don't want it to speak with; I will make a ring of it so that he may wear my silence on his little finger.	Strophe 2—overlaps strophe 1; boy soprano sings offstage, through cardboard tube; folklike character to melody

Vocal line, at beginning of strophe 1:

György Ligeti

György Ligeti's Etudes for Piano

György Ligeti (b. 1923), a native Hungarian, settled in Vienna and then Stockholm. He was also active in Germany, at the electronic music studio in Cologne as well as in summer courses at Darmstadt. In Darmstadt, he worked closely with other leaders of the European avant-garde such as Stockhausen and Boulez (to whom the piece we will study is dedicated). Ligeti belongs to the circle of composers who have tried to broaden the Schoenberg heritage by making it responsive to more recent currents. He was especially interested in achieving with traditional instruments the finer gradations of sound made familiar by electronic music. Through tone clusters and amalgams of sound that create a flow of shifting densities and colors, Ligeti has gone beyond fo-

Principal Works

Orchestral works, including *Apparitions* (1958–59), *Atmosphères* (1961), *Lontano* (1967), and Piano Concerto (1983)

Chamber works, including Chamber Concerto (1970) and Trio for Violin, Horn, and Piano (1982)

Theater works, including *Aventures* (1962), *Nouvelles aventures* (1962–65), and *Le grand macabre* (1976)

Choral works, including *Lux aeterna* (Eternal Light, 1966) and *Magyar Etüdök* (Hungarian Studies, 1983)

Keyboard music, including Etudes for Piano (1985)

cusing on fixed, recognizable pitches to working with large clusters of tones.

One of Ligeti's major preoccupations has been the interweaving of many separate strands into a complex polyphonic fabric, deriving the shape and momentum of the music from barely perceptible changes in timbre, dynamics, density, and texture rather than from more easily recognized external events. The result is a shimmering current of sound, to which he applied the term "micropolyphony." This phase of Ligeti's development reached its fullest expression in his works of the early 1960s. He subsequently moved toward a style with more transparent textures and more clear-cut melodic, harmonic, and rhythmic contours.

Atmosphères, "for large orchestra without percussion," established Ligeti's position as a leader of the European avant-garde. Together with his choral work *Lux aeterna,* it was included in the soundtrack of the Stanley Kubrick film *2001: A Space Odyssey* (1968), making the composer's name familiar to an international public. In *Atmosphères,* Ligeti explored the region that lies between instrumental and electronic music. Although the score interweaves more than sixty individual lines, what the listener hears is a murmurous continuum. As he put it, he was composing with blocks of sound—except that the blocks all merged into a continuous flow. *(margin: Atmosphères)*

Ligeti's Etudes for Piano illustrate another of his interests—the manipulation of rhythm. In these pieces, he experimented with illusionary rhythm, where, for example, the listener perceives a work to be much slower than it is actually played because of the recurrence of certain accented notes. Inspiration for this rhythmic treatment came from a variety of sources. The composer had long held a fondness for paradoxes and mathematical puzzles, and also had studied the musics of certain sub-Saharan African cultures. Around 1980, he became aware of the player piano works written by Conlon Nancarrow (b. 1912), an American expatriate living in Mexico, who was able to achieve levels of virtuosity in rhythm and polyphony that were unknown in live performance. By punching holes in piano rolls in a certain precise way, Nancarrow could superimpose elaborate rhythmic ratios that were automatically played on the mechanical instrument. Ligeti sought to achieve a similar *(margin: Etudes for piano)* effect on the regular piano with a live person performing.

The first étude from Book I is entitled *Disorder* (*Désordre*) and is the most rhythmically contorted of the set. Here, Ligeti combines two distinct musical processes: an additive metric pattern (5 + 3 or 3 + 5) and a simultaneous sounding of triple and duple patterns (making a 3:2 ratio) in the pianist's right and left hands. (See Listening Guide 78 for analysis.) These techniques make for "disorder" in the piece—the hands do not always coincide in their accents, with one hand falling behind the other, then catching up again, then lagging once more. All this is taken at a very lively tempo, vigorous and strongly accented. Thus the music whizzes by at a speed at which the ear cannot possibly disentangle the complexities involved. What you will hear is a rhythmic drive and texture of extraordinary force and energy that builds to a furious climax in the upper register of the instrument, then vanishes.

Ligeti's careful mathematical planning throughout the work, and his borrowing of African concepts of additive meter and polyrhythms, are obscured by the overall perception of chaos. At the same time, this work presses the pianist's virtuosic ability to new heights.

Listening Guide 78

C/S: 8A/8   C/S: 8/ 25 – 27
Sh: 3B/7   Sh: 3/ 49 – 51

LIGETI: *Disorder (Désordre),* from Etudes for Piano, Book I   (2:41)

Date of work: 1985
Medium: Solo piano
Form: Cycles of order and disorder, achieved through a mathematical system of accents
Tempo: Molto vivace, vigoroso, molto ritmico (very fast, vigorous, and rhythmical)

---

25   0:00   Hands begin synchronized, with movement in eighth notes in groups of 8 (accents in patterns of 3 + 5 or 5 + 3), played legato, accents played *forte;* right hand gradually gets ahead of left by dropping one eighth note every 4 measures; dissonance increases

Opening 7 measures, showing accents and divergence of parts:

0:37   Hands finally come together again with same accents; after 4 measures, same process begins with eighth notes in right hand

0:50   Shift in rhythmic patterns: both hands begin shortening patterns at different rates; hands and accents synchronize in pattern of 4 eighths per measure (accented 1 + 3 or 3 + 1), then diverge again as groupings change

26   0:58   Both hands converge, then begin patterns of 3, but not coordinated or accented the same; builds to *crescendo;* bass part (left hand) drops one octave lower

       Hands continue to diverge in range, at *fortissimo;* briefly synchronize, then diverge

       1:32   Hands converge again at *fff* marking with all notes heavily accented; piece reaches climax

27   1:33   Intensity and volume let down; both hands in treble range synchronized for a long time, then diverge to more rhythmic complexity and increasingly dense texture

       Piece ends with hands ascending to upper end of keyboard and off

79

Technology and Music

"I have been waiting a long time for electronics to free music from the tempered scale and the limitations of musical instruments. Electronic instruments are the portentous first step toward the liberation of music."—EDGARD VARÈSE

Perhaps the single most important musical development of the 1950s and 1960s was the emergence of electronic music. This was foreshadowed, during the earlier part of the century, by the invention of a variety of electronic instruments of limited scope. From such instruments as the electronic organ and the *ondes Martenot*—an instrument producing sounds by means of an electronic oscillator—a future was predicted that was quickly realized by the booming revolution of technology.

The Technological Revolution

The postwar emergence of electronic music falls into three stages. The first stage came with the use of magnetic tape recording, which was much more flexible as a medium for storing sounds than the lacquer-disk recording that had been used previously. Around 1947, a group of technicians at a Paris radio station, led by Pierre Schaeffer, had already begun to experiment with what *Musique concrète* they called *musique concrète,* a music made up of natural sounds and disc recordings that were then altered by changing the playback speed. Their activities took on a new impetus when they began to use tape, which gave them a wider range of possibilities in altering the sounds they used as source material, and enabled them to cut and splice the sounds into new combinations.

The possibility of using not only natural but also artificially generated sounds soon presented itself. A wide variety of equipment for generating and altering sounds came into use. Significant in this regard were the experiments carried on by Otto Luening and Vladimir Ussachevsky at Columbia University, and by Herbert Eimert and Karlheinz Stockhausen in Cologne. These men began their work around 1951. Within a few years, there were studios for the production of tape music in many of the chief musical centers of Europe and America. With the raw sound (either naturally or electronically produced) as a starting point, the composer could isolate its components, alter its pitch, volume, or other dimensions, play it backward, add reverberation (echo), filter out some of the overtones, or add other components by splicing and overdubbing. Even though all these operations were laborious and time-consuming—it might take many hours to process only a minute of finished music—composers hastened to avail themselves of the new medium.

The second step in the technological revolution came with the develop- *Synthesizers* ment of *synthesizers,* which are essentially devices combining sound generators and sound modifiers in one package with a unified control system. The first elaborate device was the RCA Electronic Music Synthesizer, unveiled in 1955; a more sophisticated model was installed four years later at the Columbia-Princeton Electronic Music Center in New York City. The synthesizer is capable of generating completely new sounds or combinations of sounds, with an infinite variety of pitches, durations, timbres, dynamics, and rhythmic patterns. This complex machine represented an enormous step forward in electronic music composition, since the composer was now able to control many of the characteristics beforehand and thus could bypass some of the time-consuming manual production techniques associated with tape-recorder music. The German composer Karlheinz Stockhausen (b. 1928), working in the Cologne studio, wrote two *Electronic Studies* (1953–54), built entirely from electronic sounds, and later produced his electronic masterpiece *Song of the Youths* (*Gesang der Jünglinge,* 1956) for vocal and recorded synthesized sounds. This work marked the beginning of a long-lasting fascination with the electronic exploration of language.

Because of its size and cost, the RCA machine at Columbia has remained unique; but advances in technology resulted in various smaller synthesizers that encompassed many of the features of the RCA machine as well as adding

Cultural Perspective 26

Music and the World of Technology

From the advent of the electric guitar in the 1930s to the digital sound synthesis of today, art and popular music have become highly dependent on electronic technology. Each new stage of development seems revolutionary until it becomes first familiar, then obsolete, and this occurs quickly in the modern world of electronics.

The ability to synthezise sounds has been crucial to both the popular performer and the electronic music composer. Commercial musicians continue to use keyboard synthesizers and samplers (devices that digitize, store, and play back sounds) in popular music and in film and TV scores. These electronic instruments produce "real instrument" as well as new sounds. One of the most significant developments in digital electronics has been the adoption of MIDI (musical instrument digital interface) standards. This technology allows electronic musical instruments and computers to communicate or to be "networked." In a MIDI system, the per-

former or composer can control a number of instruments either directly or through a computer, which becomes part of the musical process. (You can see an example of this in the instrument setup for Tod Machover's *Bug-Mudra* on p. 596.) The computer is capable of recording input, reordering, transposing, superimposing, synchronizing, and playing back musical ideas in performance. Sources for MIDI input are not only keyboards but guitars, winds, and percussion instruments as well. In this way, composers and performers can interact with the computer and electronic musical instruments in live performance as well as in the studio.

We are all reaping the benefits of new music technologies. The quality and convenience of recordings we listen to has improved radically over the years. We have progressed from LPs to cassettes to various digital formats including CDs (compact discs) and, most recently, DATs (digital audio tapes), DCCs (digital compact cassettes), and

A small commercial studio with Macintosh computer, MIDI keyboard, mixing console, video monitor, and other equipment used to produce TV soundtracks. (Photo by Yvette Roberts)

MDs (minidisks). We now have "intelligent" interactive media at our fingertips, notably the world of CD-ROM (compact disk–read only memory), which contains a mixture of sounds, words, and images. This technology allows us to explore a wide variety of subjects—musical and otherwise—choosing our own path, and at our own pace. It too will be joined and perhaps eclipsed by multimedia on-demand services such as Internet (a worldwide network of computer systems) and cable delivery services, which will provide us access to interactive materials from all over the world.

It is already possible for performers on a world tour to record their parts in a new release via satellite link, without returning to the studio. Soon, rather than buying the latest CD issued by your favorite recording group, you will be able to order a selection through an on-line service, download it to your system, hear it through your computer, and even remix the instrumentation and voices yourself. The world of technology promises more exciting media than we have yet to imagine possible to enhance our listening pleasure and our ability to experience music actively.

Terms to Note:

synthesizer	DAT
sampler	DCC
MIDI	MD
CD	interactive technology

Suggested Listening:

Computer music (Machover: *Bug-Mudra*)

---

a few of their own. The reduced size and cost of these synthesizers put them within the reach of even small studios and individual composers. The best-known of these pioneering machines were the Moog, Buchla, and ARP.

Computer music

The third stage of development involves the "digital revolution" sweeping the electronic world. Digital circuits developed for computer systems have been adapted and refined for use in music. Digital technologies include MIDI communications standards, synthesis, sampling, and signal processing. Composers now have the ability to store all aspects of any sound—pitch, timbre, duration, and volume—in binary numbers (as a series of 0's and 1's). A microcomputer records, stores, and allows retrieval and manipulation of this new world of sounds in a fast and efficient manner. To actually hear the sounds, however, the string of numbers must be converted into an electrical signal that can be pushed through speakers, using a process known as digital-to-analog conversion. These technological advances have given composers even more control over their music and its performance, and have impacted commercial music enormously. (See CP 26, "Music and the World of Technology.")

Important Figures in Electronic Music

Edgard Varèse

One of the pioneers of electronic music was the French composer Edgard Varèse (1883–1965), who turned to this new medium relatively late in his life.

His only completely electronic composition is *Poème electronique* (1958), a work commissioned for a sound and light show in a Brussels World Fair pavilion. The pavilion design, by the architect Le Corbusier, called for music to accompany projected images, so that visual and audio elements worked together to build a total environment. The music was composed on three channels, most of it created directly on tape. Varèse combined sounds of the human voice, treated electronically, with percussion and synthetic sounds created by an oscillator and several filters. A pulse generator was used to make drum sounds. Written when the composer was seventy-three, this landmark work heralded the musical sounds of the future.

Electronic music has two novel aspects. The most immediately obvious one is the creation of "new sounds," and this has impelled many musicians to use the new medium. Equally important, perhaps, is the fact that the composer of electronic music is able to work directly with the sounds and can produce a finished work without the help of an intermediary—the performer.

However, the combination of electronic sounds with live music has also proved to be a fertile field, especially since many younger composers have been working in both media. Works for soloist and recorded tape have become common, even "concertos" for tape recorder (or live-performance synthesizer or computer) and orchestra. One important composer working in this mixed medium is Mario Davidovsky, formerly professor of composition at Columbia University and director of the Columbia-Princeton Electronic Music Center; he now teaches at Harvard University. Among his works for tape and live performer is a series known as *Synchronisms* (1963–74). These are dialogues for solo instrument and prerecorded tape; No. 1, for flute and tape, is particularly effective because of the flute's purity of tone, wide range of dynamics, and agility in pitch and articulation. "The attempt here has been made," Davidovsky writes, "to preserve the typical characteristics of the conventional instruments and the electronic medium respectively—yet to achieve integration of both into a coherent musical texture."

Mario Davidovsky

One of the more experimental of contemporary women composers is Pauline Oliveros (b. 1932), who helped found the San Francisco Tape Center and became its director in 1966. She has explored mixed media and the possibilities of multichannel tape interacting with live performers and theatrical forms; she is also known for her experiments with live electronic music, in which sounds are generated and manipulated during the performance. In the 1970s, Oliveros became involved with Asian culture and philosophy as well as the feminist movement; one major composition from this era is *Sonic Meditations* (1971–74), consisting of twenty-five pieces with verbal descriptions that suggest ways to make, hear, and think about sounds. Her recent works look back to earlier techniques. *The Roots of the Moment* (1988) combines an interactive electronic environment with her favorite instrument, the accordion. A forerunner in the field of electronic music, Oliveros has strongly influenced the younger generation of composers.

Pauline Oliveros

Electronic music has permeated the commercial world of music making in a big way. Much of the music we hear today as movie and TV soundtracks is electronically generated, although some effects are so like conventional instruments that we are not always aware of the new technology. Popular music groups have been "electrified" for some years, but now regularly feature synthesizers that simulate conventional rock band instruments as well as altogether new sounds.

In this chapter, we will consider the works of two contemporary composers of different generations who have made important contributions to the merger of technology and music. Milton Babbitt, one of the stalwarts of an older generation, has experimented with combining live performers—in this case, singers—with electronic tape; and Tod Machover, a leader among the younger musicians, explores the world of artificial intelligence, where performers interact with computers that are capable of making intelligent musical responses.

Milton Babbitt and Electronic Music

"Anyone who hears well can be educated to appreciate my music. The more you listen to serial music, the better able you are to recognize its grammar, its configurations, its modes of procedure."

Milton Babbitt

Just as composers of the nineteenth century related their music to Romantic poetry and painting, several of the avant-garde composers of our time tend to relate their work to the exact sciences, thereby raising the intellectual element in art over the emotional one. A leading proponent of this ultrarational attitude is Milton Babbitt (b. 1916). "Some people say my music is 'too cerebral,'" he states. "Actually, I believe in cerebral music—in the application of intellect to relevant matters. I never choose a note unless I know precisely why I want it there and can give several reasons why it and not another."

At the age of twenty-two, Babbitt was invited by his mentor Roger Sessions to join the graduate music faculty at Princeton University, where he taught for many years. Given his kind of mind, he was inevitably attracted to the almost scientific logic of the twelve-tone method, which for him represented a revolution in musical thought "whose nature and consequences can be compared only with those of the mid-nineteenth-century revolution in theoretical physics."

Serialism

Babbitt is one composer who has realized the possibilities for further development inherent in Schoenberg's system. It became his conviction that "the twelve-tone set must dominate every aspect of the piece." He applied the principle of the series not only to pitch but also to rhythm, dynamics (including not only the softness and loudness but also the attack and decay of the sound), and timbre. He thus developed the premises of Schoenberg's method into an all-inclusive system in which the basic row totally controlled the relationships and processes within a particular piece.

Electronic music

By the same token, Babbitt was one of the first to evaluate the possibilities of electronic music, not because of the new sonorities it made possible, but because it offered the composer complete control over the final result. At the Columbia-Princeton Electronic Music Center in New York City, he was able to work out his ideas on the RCA Synthesizer. All the same, it has never been

Babbitt's intention that the synthesizer should replace the live musician. "I know of no serious electronic composer who ever asserts that we are supplanting any other form of music or any other form of musical activity. We're interested in increasing the resources of music." The next step, Babbitt saw, was to combine electronic music with live performers. This new area he explored in a number of pathbreaking works.

Babbitt has been especially partial to the combination of soprano voice and tape. *Phonemena* is one of three works he wrote in this medium. The title comes from the word "phoneme," the smallest unit of speech, and points up the composer's interest in words as pure sound material quite apart from their meaning.

Phonemena

Phonemena is based on twenty-four consonant and twelve vowel sounds (see Listening Guide 79). Every note or attack is sung to a consonant and

Listening Guide 79

C/S: 8A/6   C/S: 8/ 20

BABBITT: *Phonemena*

(4:14)

Date of work: 1969–70
Medium: Soprano and piano; revised for soprano and prerecorded tape
Character: Very disjunct vocal line, with some florid passagework
Text: Based on phonemes (smallest units of speech); 24 consonant and 12 vowel sounds
Form: Highly structured serialism (including pitches, rhythms, dynamics, use of phonemes)

20   0:00   Opening of work (with piano):

Principal Works

Orchestral works, including *Relata I* (1965), *Relata II* (1968), *Ars combinatoria* (1981), Piano Concerto (1985)

Chamber works, including Three Compositions for Piano (1947), Composition for Four Instruments (1948), *Arie da Capo* (1978), *A Solo Requiem* (1977), *Four Play* (1984), and 5 string quartets

Synthesizer works, including Composition for Synthesizer (1960–61) and Ensembles for Synthesizer (1962–64)

Works for live performers and tape, including *Vision and Prayer* (soprano and tape, 1961), *Philomel* (soprano and tape, 1963), *Correspondences* (string orchestra and tape, 1966–68), *Phonemena* (soprano and tape, 1969–70), and *Reflections* (piano and tape, 1975)

vowel, or just a vowel. Pitchless phonemes enter twice, the second time as a whispered sound; this sound closes the piece. The vocal line ranges over two octaves that contain many leaps. This disjunct style occasionally becomes florid, with quick passagework articulated in a number of ways.

The significant artist is one whose work projects the forward-moving impulses of his time. Milton Babbitt belongs to this category. His music embodies important intellectual currents of the contemporary scene.

Tod Machover and New Technologies in Music

Tod Machover (b. 1952) received his training at the Juilliard School, where he studied composition with Elliott Carter and Roger Sessions. He spent five fruitful years as director of the departmental media facility at Pierre Boulez's IRCAM in Paris, the French government center for contemporary music. His opera *Valis* received its premiere in Paris at the Centre Pompidou and was produced in Tokyo in 1990; the recording of the opera was singled out as "best of the year" by the *New York Times.* He is currently working on an opera project with the dynamic director Peter Sellars.

Machover is one of a growing number of composers who understand and use the computer in their music. Most of his works involve computers in live interactive performances with acoustical instruments; in such pieces, he is able to contrast the two sonorities. He has a marked interest in soloistic virtuosity and rhythmic vitality, and has written works for "hyper-instruments," which he explains "are designed to augment and expand performance virtuosity in real time, using intelligent, interactive machines." He has combined acoustic instruments such as guitar and percussion with hyper-instruments, and has written similar works for such professional musicians as the cellist Yo-Yo Ma, the violist Kim Kashkashian, and the St. Paul Chamber Orchestra.

Composer Tod Machover posing with the FXOS Dexterous Hand Master. (Photo by Peter Menzel)

Machover has also provided a connection to the hyper-instrument system through a special electronic glove—the FXOS Dexterous Hand Master—which is worn by a performer or conductor. This glove measures nuances of movements and, through the computer system, influences the overall sound.

Bug-Mudra (1990), commissioned by the Fromm Music Foundation of Harvard University, was recorded live in Tokyo by the Bunkamura Cocoon Theater. The piece is for two guitars, percussion, and live computer electronics (see Listening Guide 80). The *Bug* in the title refers to a computer "bug"— that is, a glitch in the software or hardware. *Mudra* is the word for hand gestures in classical Indian dance, and refers here to the conductor's hand movements, measured by the electronic glove. Energized by amplified dynamics, the piece, according to the composer, "forms a regular V, starting with a bang, moving toward a moment of agitated stillness at its center, and building up gradually to first recapitulate its opening, and then to intensify, ending with an even greater bang" on "an affirmative unison." Machover's description of his goal in this work is helpful:

Bug-Mudra represents my ideas about diversity and unification of musical materials. While homogeneous in its form, mood, and sonic quality, the work manages to combine many quite distinct elements. Electric and acoustic guitar are brought together integrating different "styles" of guitar playing (folk-like strumming, rock rhythms and melodies, improvisatory jazz-like riffs, classical cantabile, "new music" figurations, etc.), and classical form and developmental procedures are applied to "riffs" that suggest rock music.

The sound is light and of an almost chamber music delicacy, powered by propulsive, self-generating rhythms that give the impression of boundless exuberance. This is a music of great physical activity that, except for its "moment of agitated stillness," never flags. Miniature explosions punctuate the texture and keep it moving.

Tod Machover is one of a generation of composers who are exploring new paths in music technology and the possibilities of interactive performance. We can only imagine to what new regions they will lead their art.

Bug-Mudra

Listening Guide 80

C/S: 8B/4
Sh: 3B/8

C/S: 8/ 40 — 42
Sh: 3/ 52 — 54

MACHOVER: *Bug-Mudra,* excerpt

(5:11)

Date of work: 1989–90

Medium: 2 guitars (1 acoustic, 1 electric), percussion (suspended cymbals, electronic mallet controller), hyper-instrument system (connected to FXOS Dexterous Hand Master worn by conductor)

Hyper-instrument setup for *Bug-Mudra:*

Structure: 6 sections (our recording includes only parts 1–3; quotes are from composer's description)

40	0:00	1.	"Rapid, syncopated and contrapuntal song."
41	2:04	2.	Development of rhythm and harmony of section 1.
42	3:48	3.	"A virtuosic electric bass melody, over which acoustic guitar tremolos and electronic percussion washes build up interchanging harmonies and harmonic spectra."
		4.	"Melodic and lyrical . . ."
		5.	"A vivid fantasy . . ."
		6.	"A recapitulation of Section 1 . . ."

80

Other Recent Trends

The New Romanticism

Serial, or twelve-tone, music, with its emphasis on the intellectual and con-
structivist aspects of art, has lost some momentum in recent decades in favor
of a more eclectic synthesis of familiar styles known as the New Romanticism.
A number of composers began to feel that the time had come to close the gap
between themselves and the public by restoring music to its former position
as "the language of the emotions," complete with appealing melodies, regular
rhythms, lush harmonies, and rich orchestral colors.

This New Romanticism has taken a variety of forms. Some composers have
combined the general harmonic language of the Romantic era with other current trends, such as the New Virtuosity. Others have used the Romantic style
or the works of a particular composer more literally. As often happens in art,
there are no clear dividing lines. Many works that are labeled as examples of
the New Romanticism share techniques with serial and aleatoric music and
employ the new instrumental possibilities that have opened up since the middle of the century.

The New Romanticism had an important precursor in Samuel Barber *Samuel Barber*
(1910–81). His music, suffused with feeling, leans toward the grand gestures
of nineteenth-century tradition. Several of his works achieved enormous popularity, among them the light-hearted Overture to *The School for Scandal*
(1932) and the elegiac *Adagio for Strings* (1936). Although his later works,
from the 1940s on, feature more "modern" harmony and scoring, his successful opera *Vanessa* (1958), on a libretto by Gian Carlo Menotti, was praised as
"highly charged with emotional meaning."

Ned Rorem (b. 1923) is one of the distinguished composers of his genera- *Ned Rorem*
tion. He has written widely in all genres, from chamber and orchestral music
to opera. His songs are in the great line of descent from the great French art
song of the post-Romantic period. His works are stamped with an aristocratic
refinement. Rorem is a talented writer as well and has published several books
of criticism and memoirs in the form of diaries.

Thea Musgrave (b. 1928), a Scottish-born composer, is one of the leading *Thea Musgrave*
exponents of the New Romanticism. She is best-known for her stage works—
operas and ballets. *Mary, Queen of Scots* (1977) is a highly accessible and
tonal opera that draws on the history of the composer's native land. Musgrave
selected a figure from American history as the heroine in her opera *Harriet,
the Woman Called Moses* (1985), the story of Harriet Tubman, who escaped
from slavery and helped establish the Underground Railroad. In addition to
her accomplishments as a composer, Musgrave has conducted numerous orchestras and opera companies in the performances of her own works.

Of a younger generation of composers interested in the New Romanticism,
David Del Tredici (b. 1937) stands out for the broad lyric appeal of his music. *David Del Tredici*

As a result, he is one of the most widely performed composers of his age group. In recent years, he has focused on large works for soprano and orchestra inspired by *Alice's Adventures in Wonderland* and *Through the Looking Glass* by the nineteenth-century writer Lewis Carroll. These compositions have found favor with the public, especially *Final Alice* (1976) and *In Memory of a Summer Day* (1980).

John Corigliano

Among the most accessible works of the New Romantic idiom are those of John Corigliano (b. 1938), whose music displays an imaginative use of contemporary techniques. His major works include *The Naked Carmen* (1970), an "eclectic rock opera" fashioned after Bizet, and *The Ghosts of Versailles* (1991), commissioned by the Metropolitan Opera in New York. The latter work, with a highly original libretto by William Hofmann, was a resounding success at its premiere.

Ellen Taaffe Zwilich

Amid the varied experiments and styles of late twentieth-century music, Ellen Taaffe Zwilich (b. 1939) has chosen to continue the great tradition of the symphony. In 1975, Zwilich became the first woman to earn a doctorate in composition from the Juilliard School. She was also the first woman to win the Pulitzer Prize in composition, granted to her in 1983 for the Symphony No. 1 (1982). Her return to traditional forms and her reaffirmation of tonality have endeared her to concert audiences and musicians alike.

Tobias Picker

Tobias Picker (b. 1954) belongs to that fortunate breed of artists to whom recognition comes early enough to be enjoyed. His First Symphony was commissioned by the San Francisco Symphony in 1982, when he was twenty-eight. *Keys to the City* (1982), really his second Piano Concerto, was written for the one-hundredth anniversary of the Brooklyn Bridge; a performance of this work, with the composer as soloist, was broadcast on national television. Picker's style is marked by grand gesture, sweeping melodies, expressive harmonies, and virtuoso instrumental writing, all of which rank him with the New Romantics.

Joan Tower and Quotation Music

Joan Tower

Joan Tower (b. 1938) was born in New Rochelle, New York, and grew up in South America. After studying piano at Bennington College and Columbia University, she founded the Da Capo Players in 1969, a performance group dedicated to new music. In 1985, she was appointed composer-in-residence of the St. Louis Symphony, for whom she wrote her first large orchestral work, *Silver Ladders* (1986). This composition earned her the Grauemeyer Award (she was the first American to receive this honor), and she went on to win a Guggenheim Fellowship and grants from the Koussevitzky Foundation and the National Endowment for the Arts. Since 1972, she has taught at Bard College in Annandale-on-Hudson, New York.

Tower's music has been strongly influenced by that of Beethoven and Stravinsky. In her Piano Concerto (1985), she paid homage to Beethoven, making prominent use of three of his piano sonatas, and as we will see, her chamber work *Petroushskates* was inspired by Stravinsky.

Petroushskates

Commissioned by the Da Capo Players and the New York State Council on the Arts to celebrate the tenth anniversary of the ensemble, *Petroushskates* received its premiere in New York's Alice Tully Hall in 1980. The piece is written for a chamber ensemble of flute, clarinet, violin, cello, and piano—a combination that in our time almost rivals the string quartet in importance. *Petroushskates* was inspired by Stravinsky's *Petrushka* (Tower retains the "ou" of the French spelling), combined with the imagery of figure skating. The composer explains:

> In an attempt to understand why figure skating, especially pair skating, was so beautiful and moving to me I discovered a musical corollary I had been working on for a while—the idea of a seamless action. . . . I also always loved *Petrushka* and wanted to create an homage to Stravinsky and that piece in particular. As it turned out, the pairs of figure skaters became a whole company of skaters [in the piece], thereby creating a sort of musical carnival on ice.

Stravinsky often parodied other composers: Pergolesi, Bach, and Tchaikovsky come to mind. Here, he himself is the object of parody. Like many of his works, *Petrushka* is an essentially balletic piece—a piece that is inspired by body motion. As we have seen (in Chapter 67), it exhibits the rhythmic energy that is of the essence in ballet music.

The opening measures of Tower's piece evoke in a remarkable way the opening of Stravinsky's ballet (see Listening Guide 81). The buzzing patterns that are repeated over and over, the fragments of melody thrust almost randomly at the listener, and the frequent changes of meter are all reminiscent of Stravinsky, as are the vivid contrasts between high and low registers and the predominantly C-major sound of the music. When the dynamic forward movement lets up, it becomes almost listless, but this is only in preparation for the next takeoff. We are dealing with a motoric music of a high energy level, a high dissonance content, above all high spirits.

The bunched-up chords in the bass, which impose their powerful accents on the musical fabric, recall the growling sound in Stravinsky's *Rite of Spring*. The ear is titillated by images of physical activity. This is an "homage to" rather than an imitation of Stravinsky. This technique of parodying another work or works is known as *quotation music,* yet throughout, Tower asserts her own personality and her own sound.

Quotation music

Principal Works

Orchestral music, including *Sequoia* (1981), *Silver Ladders* (1986), and *For the Uncommon Woman* (1993); concertos for flute, clarinet, cello, and piano (*Homage to Beethoven,* 1985)

Chamber music, including *Hexachords* (1972) for solo flute and *Wings* (1981) for solo clarinet; *Breakfast Rhythms I* and *II* (1974–75), *Petroushskates* (1980), *Noon Dance* (1982), and 3 *Fanfares for the Uncommon Woman* (1987–91) for chamber ensembles

The final gesture, a downward run on flute, clarinet, and violin followed by a single octave in the bass on the cello and piano, has the proper devil-may-care impudence. Tower's piece, like its title, is very much of our time.

Listening Guide 81

C/S: 8B/2   C/S: 8/ 34 – 37
Sh: 3B/9   Sh: 3/ 55 – 58

TOWER: *Petroushskates*

(5:39)

Date of work: 1980
Medium: Chamber ensemble (flute, clarinet, violin, cello, piano)
Basis: Parody of Stravinsky's *Petrushka* (see LG 58), combined with skating idea

34 0:00 Opening parodies *Petrushka* with reduced texture; quick rhythm with trills in woodwinds against wavering motive in piano; interval of second important

    0:27 Builds to high register, then suddenly shifts to low; dies down, and tempo slackens

35 0:55 Skating theme introduced in clarinet and flute (marked *dolce*); slower tempo; flute plays with interval of minor second and irregular rhythmic groupings:

         Builds in dynamics, range, and dissonance; flute and clarinet alternate with quick runs

36 2:05 Suddenly slow and expressive (Sostenuto); mysterious sounding, then grows more dissonant in high woodwinds

37 2:41 Returns to frantic rhythm of opening; strings with quick sixteenth-note pattern, interrupted by piano chords; then woodwinds take over quick notes, followed by piano in loud, pounding rhythms

    4:40 Returns to opening sounds, with piano trills; builds with rhythmic accents; piano and woodwinds have ascending trill figures that lead to closing, a quick descending pattern

Untitled (Monument for V. Tatlin, 1964)
by **Dan Flavin,** *an eight-foot structure of
cool, white fluorescent light, is a distinctive
example of imaginative minimalism.*
(Pace Wildenstein Gallery; photo by Ella
Page Wilson; © 1995 Dan Flavin Artists
Rights Society [ARS], N.Y.)

Minimalism and Post-Minimalism

Independently of the New Romantics, another group of young composers
found their own way to simplification of the musical language. They stripped
their compositions down to the barest essentials in order to concentrate the
listener's attention on a few basic details. This urge toward a minimal art first
found expression in painting and sculpture. It became a significant force in
contemporary music during the 1970s.

The salient feature of *minimalist music,* as it has come to be known, is the
repetition of melodic, rhythmic, and harmonic patterns with very little variation. The music changes so slowly that the listener is forced to focus a maximum of attention on a minimum of detail. Such concentration can have a
hypnotic effect, and indeed the term "trance music" has attached itself to
some works of the minimalists. But it is a label they reject because, as they
point out, their material is selected most carefully and worked out in highly
disciplined procedures. One can say, however, that in minimalist music, time
moves at a different pace from what most of us are accustomed to.

By simplifying melody, rhythm, and harmony within an unwavering tonality, the minimalists turn away from the complex, highly intellectual style of the
serialists. They reject the heritage of Schoenberg and Webern just as they do
the cerebral preoccupations of Boulez and Babbitt. Instead, they open themselves to modes of thought emanating from the third world, especially the
contemplative art of India and the quasi-obsessive rhythms of some African

Cultural Perspective 27

The Non-Western Roots of Minimalist and New-Age Music

Unlike nineteenth-century composers, whose exotic musical interests were rarely supported by actual knowledge or experience, many modern composers have devoted serious study to musics of other cultures. Some have made extended visits to foreign countries in order to assimilate musical styles within the context of the culture and to hear the native instruments and tuning systems first-hand.

One basic concept that has intrigued many contemporary composers is the use of highly repetitive structures, a feature common to musics of various Asian and African cultures and quite different from Western practice. This is apparent in the work of early minimalist composers such as Steve Reich, who was particularly interested in Indonesian gamelan music and drumming styles from the West African nation of Ghana. "I studied Balinese and African music because I love them," he said, "and also because I believe that non-Western music is presently the single most important source of new ideas for Western composers and musicians."

In 1970, Reich achieved a long-standing goal: to study music in Ghana. "I was overwhelmed by their music, [it was] like being in front of a tidal wave." Reich learned that in Ghanaian drumming (and especially that of the Ewe tribe that he visited), a basic rhythm called a "timeline" holds the ensemble together, over which each musician plays a repeated rhythmic pattern, the most complex performed by the group leader or master drummer. The essential organization is thus multilinear—each line contributes a simple pattern resulting in a complex fabric of parts. On his return, Reich wrote *Drumming* (1971), a work for percussion ensemble, including drums, bells, and maracas (rattles made from gourds), that draws heavily on the cyclic structures and polyrhythms he heard in Ghana. *Drumming* is set in a cycle of 12 beats, which can be divided variously (4 groups of 3, 3 groups of 4, or 6 groups of 2). As in the traditional style of Ghana, the pace of the rhythm is quick, but the changes in the patterns occur slowly.

The non-Western-inspired works of minimalist Philip Glass have had wide appeal with popular-music audiences, in part because this music is more accessible to the listener. The style generally presents fewer minute details on which to concentrate, and thus promotes perception of a composition as a whole. Minimalism can also be linked directly to rock and, to a lesser extent, to jazz, both musical styles being based on repetition of a limited amount of harmonic material. Rock groups of the 1970s, such as Pink Floyd and the Talking Heads (with minimalist composer Brian Eno), led the way for the new-age music of today, which offers a soothing audio environment. Like minimalist music, the trancelike quality of the new-age style is generated by repetitive structures and constantly shifting variation techniques that we have previously associated with certain world musics. Truly an international phenomenon, this musical style—represented by pianist George Winston, electric violinist Jean-Luc Ponty, and multi-instrumentalist Kitaro, among others—can be heard on traditional, ethnic, acoustic, electric, and electronic instruments.

An Aulo-Ewe drum ensemble from east coastal Ghana, noted for its highly complex rhythmic organizations. The instruments are (left to right): rattles (axaatse), double bell (gankogui), and three barrel drums—master drum (atsimewu), sogo, and kidi.

Terms to Note:

minimalism
new age

Suggested Listening:

Minimalist music (Steve Reich, Philip Glass)
African drumming (Ghana)
new-age music

cultures, as well as to jazz, pop, and rock. Although influenced by the early ideas of John Cage, for the most part minimalists reject his interest in indeterminacy and chance. They prefer to control their sounds.

There are several kinds of minimalist music. In some works, the pulse is repeated with numbing regularity. Others are very busy on the surface, though the harmonies and timbres change very slowly. Terry Riley (b. 1935) introduced the element of pulse and the concept of tiny motivic cells that repeat in his ninety-minute masterwork entitled *In C* (1964). Influenced by the music of the Far East, by ragtime and jazz, and by the theories of John Cage, Riley has employed elements of performer choice in electronic music, along with improvisation. The music of Steve Reich (b. 1936) moves so slowly that it seems to come out of a time sense all his own; this is particularly true of his works on tape. Reich describes his sense of time as "a musical process happening so gradually that listening resembles watching the minute hand of a watch—you perceive it moving only after you stay with it for a while." This contemplative quality is his answer to the pace of our fast-moving society.

The most widely known minimalist is Philip Glass (b. 1937), whose career began conventionally enough with attendance at the University of Chicago

Terry Riley

Steve Reich

Philip Glass

and the Juilliard School, after which he went off to Paris on a Fulbright Scholarship to study with Nadia Boulanger. It was she who imparted to him, as he put it, "the skills that make music go." Even more decisive was his contact with the Indian sitar player Ravi Shankar (see illustration on p. 51). Glass was fascinated with non-Western music. "And, of course, I was also hearing the music of Miles Davis, of John Coltrane, and the Beatles." When he returned to New York, he became convinced that "modern music had become truly decadent, stagnant, uncommunicative. Composers were writing for each other and the public didn't seem to care." It was out of this conviction that Glass evolved his own style, drawing upon the musical traditions of India and Africa as well as the techniques of rock and progressive jazz. His most important works include *Glassworks* (1983) and his operas, *Einstein on the Beach* (1976), *Satyagraha* (1980), and *Akhnaten* (1984).

John Adams and Post-Minimalism

John Adams

Although both minimalism and the New Romanticism sought above all to escape the overly intellectual world of serialism, they did so by completely different paths. There was bound to appear a composer who, by seeking to expand the expressive gamut of minimalist music, would respond to the emotional impulses emanating from the New Romantics. Such a one was John Adams (b. 1947), the best-known among the post-minimalists, who was educated at Harvard and in 1972 began teaching at the San Francisco Conservatory of Music. Strongly influenced by Steve Reich, Adams's is a subtle music marked by warm sonorities and much energy. At the same time, he presents a more personal approach to music than either Glass or Reich.

Adams attracted much attention with his opera *Nixon in China* (1987), which takes place in Peking (Beijing) during the three days of President Nixon's visit in November 1972. The works that followed show Adams increasingly receptive to the sumptuous orchestral palette and expressive harmonies of the New Romanticism. They fully justify his description of himself as "a very emotional composer, one who experiences music on a very physical level. My music is erotic and Dionysian, and I never try to obscure those feelings when I compose." *Nixon in China* was followed by *The Death of Klinghoffer* (1991), which handled a more explosive issue—the killing of an elderly Jewish tourist by Arab terrorists.

Nixon in China

Nixon in China was the product of a fruitful collaboration between Adams, the imaginative director Peter Sellars, and the poet Alice Goodman. As portrayed in the opera, the President is a complex but interesting character who is human in his insecurities and his hopes that he has chosen the right course. The public was attracted by the political currency of the subject; the opera was received enthusiastically and played to sold-out houses.

Act I opens with an orchestral prelude, which is followed by a chorus of troops ready to welcome the President when Air Force I lands in Peking. Introductions are made, the President airs his hopes and fears, and he meets the legendary Chairman Mao, whose discourse is enlivened by several philo-

A toast of friendship between the president and Pat Nixon, Chou En-lai, and Henry Kissinger from Act I of the Brooklyn Academy of Music's production of Nixon in China. *(© Martha Swope)*

sophical observations. The action then leads steadily to the formal banquet at which Premier Chou En-lai toasts his guest and the President responds.

Act II focuses on the First Lady, Pat Nixon, who is guided around Peking accompanied by journalists. In the evening, the Nixons attend a performance of *The Red Detachment of Women,* a revolutionary ballet devised by Chairman Mao's wife, the powerful Chiang Ching. (In the political upheavals that followed Mao's death, she was denounced as a member of the Gang of Four and ended her life in prison.)

Act III depicts the Nixons' last night in Peking. Everyone is exhausted, but the main characters consider how they came to participate in this extraordinary event. The final words reflect the melancholy thoughts of Chou.

We will hear an excerpt from scene 3 of Act I, the banquet for the Nixons. Formality breaks down as the evening progresses, and we see Nixon at his best as a messenger of peace between the two nations. Considering that he had previously denounced Communist Russia, we see him also as an astute diplomat. (See Listening Guide 82 for text.)

Nixon's speech follows the toast of Premier Chou. What is striking is the utter simplicity with which Adams sets English, allowing the vocal line to bring out the natural inflections of the language. Words that you might never suppose would be sung, such as "satellite technology" or "telecommunications," spin out with musical ease. He keeps the orchestra in the background with a discreet twittering that never disrupts the text. Range, repetition, and rhythmic energy serve to emphasize important words. A gradual orchestral *crescendo* accompanies an era of peace and friendship. The climactic sentence, "We must seize the hour and seize the day," receives powerful weight through repetition.

The voices of the other guests interweave in a passage of approval for Nixon's remarks, and the scene ends with an instrumental postlude that affirms the vision of a peaceful future.

Listening Guide 82   C/S: 8B/3   C/S: 8/ 38 – 39

ADAMS: *Nixon in China,* Act I, Scene 3, Finale   (6:18)

Date of work: 1987
Medium: Opera
Librettist: Alice Goodman
Setting: China, February 21–25, 1972
Characters:
> Richard Nixon, President of the United States (1969–74)
> Pat Nixon, the First Lady
> Henry Kissinger, National Security Adviser to the Nixon administration
> Mao Tse-tung, Chairman of the People's Republic of China
> Chiang Ching, politician and wife of Mao
> Chou En-lai, Premier of China

ACT I, SCENE 3

It is evening of the first day. The Americans are being feted in the Grand Hall of the People. Outside, the roof is outlined with strings of lights, inside there are tables set for nine hundred. Against the far wall a small dais supports a bank of microphones. The American and Chinese flags are pinned against the wall. The President and First Lady sit on either side of the Premier, their backs to the flags, and gaze across the snowy field of table linen. There is their party, there the newsmen, there the important Chinese. In the distance the vision begins to blur. The atmosphere is convivial; in that huge hall the President feels strangely joyful and lightheaded, as if this were the evening of arrival in heaven. And so the conversation rises and falls throughout the courses of the banquet.

After the third course is finished, Premier Chou rises to toast his American guests. President Nixon rises to respond.

		NIXON
38	0:00	Mr. Premier, distinguished guests	Solo voice against insistent rhythm; woodwind quips and loud interjections by brass; recitation style

NIXON

Mr. Premier, distinguished guests	Solo voice against insistent rhythm; woodwind
I have attended many feasts	quips and loud interjections by brass; recitation
But never have I so enjoyed	style
A dinner, nor have I heard played	
Better the music that I love	
Outside America. I move	
A vote of thanks to one and all	More lyrical vocal style; low instruments enter
Whose efforts made this possible.	with sharp notes interrupting the voice
No one who heard could but admire	
Your eloquent remarks, Premier.	
And millions more hear what we say	
Through satellite technology	
Than ever heard a public speech	
Before. No one is out of touch.	
Telecommunication has	
Broadcast your message into space.	
Yet soon our words won't be recalled	

While what we do can change the world.
We have at times been enemies,
We still have our differences, God knows.
But let us, in these next five days,
Start a long march on new highways,
In different lanes, but parallel
And heading for a single goal.
The world watches and listens. We
Must seize the hour and seize the day.

Reaches climax, followed by brief instrumental interlude; piano enters with pounding chords; wavering wind parts

Low instruments drop out

Repeated text interrupted by chorus

President Nixon and Premier Chou toast each other, then Mrs. Nixon. Caught up in the spirit of friendship, the banqueters go from table to table toasting one another.

39   2:37

CHORUS
Cheers

Chorus repeats word against insistent rhythm and brass chords; various soloists alternate with chorus

NIXON
This is the hour!

CHOU
Your health!

PAT
And yours!

CHOU
To Doctor Kissinger!

NIXON
Cheers!

KISSINGER
Cheers!
New friends and present company!

NIXON
To Chairman Mao!

CHOU
The U.S.A.!

PAT
Have you forgotten Washington?

Woodblock enters to keep up rhythm

CHOU
Washington's birthday!

Repeated by chorus and brass

NIXON
Everyone
Listen, just let me say one thing.
I opposed China. I was wrong.

Interrupted by chorus with "Cheers"

KISSINGER
Bottoms up, Mr. President.

PAT

What did you say, Sweetheart? I can't
Catch every word in all this noise.

CHOU

Mr. President, look down and see what the
Chinese people have done to earn this praise.

CHORUS 1

We have at times been enemies.

CHORUS 2

The Chinese people are renowned.

NIXON

Ideas we have entertained—

PAT

"America the Beautiful!"

CHORUS 1

We must broadcast seeds of goodwill

CHORUS 2

Comrades and friends—

NIXON

—in former years
Grow in a night to touch the stars.

CHORUS

Look down and think what the Chinese
People have done to earn this praise.

PAT

Spring is here. I love you, dear.

CHOU

Comrades and friends, brothers again.

KISSINGER

You won't believe how moved I am.

CHORUS

We marvel now.

NIXON

It's like a dream.

Much repeated text accompanied by brass and
woodblock

Instrumental close with brass on disjunct line

Coda

These pages have included a variety of facts—historical, biographical, and technical—that have entered into the making of music and that must enter into an intelligent listening to music. Like all books, this one belongs to the domain of words, and words have no power over the domain of sound. They are helpful only insofar as they lead us to enjoy the music.

The enjoyment of music depends upon perceptive listening. And perceptive listening (like perceptive anything) is something that we achieve gradually, with practice and effort. By acquiring a knowledge of the circumstances out of which a musical work issued, we prepare ourselves for its multiple meanings; we lay ourselves open to that exercise of mind and heart, sensibility and imagination, that makes listening to music so unique an experience. But in the building up of our musical perceptions—that is, of our listening enjoyment—let us always remember that the ultimate wisdom resides neither in dates nor in facts. It is to be found in one place only: the sounds themselves.

APPENDIX I

Musical Notation

The Notation of Pitch

Musical notation presents a kind of graph of the sounds with regard to their duration and pitch. These are indicated by symbols called *notes,* which are written on the *staff,* a series of five parallel lines with four spaces between:

Staff

The positions of the notes on the staff indicate the pitches, each line and space representing a different degree of pitch.

    A symbol known as a *clef* is placed at the left end of the staff and determines the group of pitches to which that staff refers. The *treble clef* (𝄞) is used for pitches within the range of the female singing voices, and the *bass clef* (𝄢) for a lower group of pitches, within the range of the male singing voices.

Clefs

    Pitches are named after the first seven letters of the alphabet, from A to G; the lines and spaces are named accordingly. (From one note named A to the next is the interval of an octave.) The pitches on the treble staff are named as follows:

Pitch names

And those on the bass staff:

For pitches above and below these, short extra lines called *ledger lines* can be added:

Middle C—the C that, on the piano, is situated approximately in the center of the keyboard—comes between the treble and bass staffs. It is represented by either the first ledger line above the bass staff or the first ledger line below the treble staff, as the following example makes clear. This combination of the two staffs is called the *great staff* or *grand staff*:

Accidentals

There are also signs known as *accidentals,* which are used to alter the pitch of a written note. A *sharp* (♯) before the note indicates the pitch a half step above; a *flat* (♭) indicates the pitch a half step below. A *natural* (♮) cancels a sharp or flat. Also used are the *double sharp* (×) and *double flat* (♭♭), which respectively raise and lower the pitch by two halftones—that is, a whole tone.

In many pieces of music, where certain sharped or flatted notes are used consistently throughout the piece, these sharps or flats are written at the be-
Key signature
ginning of each line of music, in the *key signature*. This may be seen in the following example of piano music. Notice that piano music is written on the great staff, with the right hand usually playing the notes written on the upper staff and the left hand usually playing the notes written on the lower:

The Notation of Rhythm

Note values

The duration of each musical tone is indicated by the appearance of the notes placed on the staff. These notes use a system of relative values. For example, in the following table, each note represents a duration half as long as the preceding one:

| whole note | half note | quarter note | eighth note | sixteenth note | thirty-second note | sixty-fourth note |

In any particular piece of music, these note values are related to the beat of the music. If the quarter note represents one beat, then a half note lasts for two beats, a whole note for four; two eighth notes last one beat, as do four sixteenths. The following chart makes this clear:

Note   *Beats*

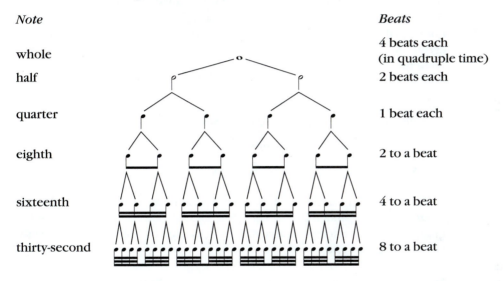

whole — 4 beats each (in quadruple time)

half — 2 beats each

quarter — 1 beat each

eighth — 2 to a beat

sixteenth — 4 to a beat

thirty-second — 8 to a beat

When a group of three notes is to be played in the time normally taken up by only two of the same kind, we have a *triplet:*   *Triplet*

It is possible to combine successive notes of the same pitch, using a curved line known as a *tie:*   *Tie*

beats: 4 + 4 = 8   2 + 4 = 6 $1 + \frac{1}{2} = 1\frac{1}{2}$

A *dot* after a note enlarges its value by half: *Dot*

beats: 2 + 1 = 3 $1 + \frac{1}{2} = 1\frac{1}{2}$ $\frac{1}{2} + \frac{1}{4} = \frac{3}{4}$

Rests

Time never stops in music, even when there is no sound. Silence is indicated by symbols known as *rests,* which correspond in time value to the notes:

whole rest	half rest	quarter rest	eighth rest	sixteenth rest	thirty-second rest	sixty-fourth rest

Time signature

The metrical organization of a piece of music is indicated by the *time signature,* which specifies the meter. This consists of two numbers, written as in a fraction. The upper numeral indicates the number of beats within the measure; the lower one shows which unit of value equals one beat. Thus, the time signature 3/4 means that there are three beats to a measure, with the quarter note equal to one beat. In 6/8 time, there are six beats in the measure, each eighth note receiving one beat. Following are the most frequently encountered time signatures:

duple meter	2/2	2/4	
triple meter	3/2	3/4	3/8
quadruple meter		4/4	
sextuple meter		6/4	6/8

Measures and bar lines

The following examples show how the system works. Notice that the *measures* are separated by a vertical line known as a *bar line;* hence a measure is sometimes referred to as a *bar.* As a rule, the bar line is followed by the most strongly accented beat, the ONE.

Sur le pont d'Avignon, French children's song (round)

Sur le pont d'A - vi - gnon, l'on y dan - se l'on y dan - se,

Sur le pont d'A - vi - gnon, l'on y dan - se tout en rond.

Clef: Treble
Key signature: None = key of C major
Meter: Duple (2/4)
Other features: Begins with pick-up note (upbeat)

Home on the Range, American song of the West

Oh, give me a home where the buf - fa - lo roam, where the

deer   and the   an - te - lope   play,   where

sel - dom   is   heard   a   dis - cour - ag - ing   word   and   the

skies   are   not   clou - dy   all   day.

Clef: Bass
Key signature: 1 flat (B♭) = key of F major
Meter: Triple (3/4)
Other features: Pick-up note, dotted rhythms, and ties

Auld Lang Syne, Scottish traditional song

Should   auld   ac - quain - tance   be   for - got,   and— nev - er brought to   mind,   Should

auld   ac - quain - tance   be   for - got   and— days   of   auld   lang   syne?

Clef: Treble
Key signature: 1 sharp (F♯) = key of G major
Meter: Quadruple (4/4)
Other features: Pick-up note, dotted rhythms

Greensleeves, English traditional song

A - las,   my   love,— you   do   me   wrong— to   cast   me   off— dis - cour - teous - ly,   Though

I   have   loved— you   oh   so   long— de - light - ing   in — your   com - pa - ny.

Clef: Treble
Key signature: 1 sharp (F♯) = key of E minor
Meter: Sextuple (6/8)
Other features: Pick-up note, dotted rhythms, and accidentals (D♯ and C♯)

APPENDIX II

Glossary

absolute music Music that has no literary, dramatic, or pictorial program. Also *pure music*.

a cappella Choral music performed without instrumental accompaniment.

accelerando Getting faster.

accent The emphasis on a beat resulting in that beat's being louder or longer than another in a measure.

accompagnato Accompanied; also a *recitative* that is accompanied by orchestra.

acid rock Genre of American rock that emerged in the late 1960s, often associated with psychedelic drugs. Its style featured heavy amplification, instrumental improvisation, new sound technologies, and light shows.

adagio Quite slow.

additive meter Patterns of beats that subdivide into smaller, irregular groups (e.g., 2 + 3 + 2 + 3 = 10); common in certain Eastern European musics.

ad libitum Indication that gives the performer the liberty to omit a section or to improvise.

aerophone Instrument that produces sound by using air as the primary vibrating means, such as a flute, whistle, or horn.

agitato Agitated or restless.

Agnus Dei A section of the Mass; the last musical movement of the *Ordinary*.

aleatory Indeterminate music in which certain elements of performance (such as pitch, rhythm, or form) are left to choice or chance.

allegro Fast, cheerful.

allemande German dance in moderate duple time, popular during the Renaissance and Baroque periods; often the first movement of a Baroque *suite*.

alto Lowest of the female voices. Also *contralto*.

andante Moderately slow or walking pace.

answer Second entry of the subject in a *fugue*, usually pitched a fourth below or a fifth above the subject.

anthem A religious choral composition in English; performed liturgically, it is the Protestant equivalent of the *motet*.

antiphonal Performance style in which an ensemble is divided into two or more groups, performing in alternation and then together.

antique cymbals Small disks of brass, held by the player one in each hand, that are struck together gently and allowed to vibrate.

arabesque Decorative musical material or a composition based on florid *embellishment*.

aria Lyric song for solo voice with orchestral accompaniment, generally expressing intense emotion; found in *opera*, *cantata*, and *oratorio*.

arioso Short, aria-like passage.

arpeggio Broken chord in which the individual tones are sounded one after another instead of simultaneously.

Ars Antiqua French sacred polyphonic musical style from the period c. 1160–1320.

Ars Nova Fourteenth-century French polyphonic musical style that transformed the art increasingly from religious to secular themes.

art rock Genre of rock that uses larger forms and more complex harmonies than other popular styles; occasionally quotes examples from classical music. Also *progressive rock*.

a tempo Return to the previous tempo.

atonality Total abandonment of *tonality* (centering in a key). Atonal music moves from one level of dissonance to another, without areas of relaxation.

augmentation Statement of a melody in longer note values, often twice as slow as the original.

bagpipe Wind instrument popular in Eastern and Western Europe that has several tubes, one of which plays the melody while the others sound the *drones,* or sustained notes.

balalaika Guitar-like instrument of Russia with a triangular body, fretted neck, and three strings; often used in traditional music and dance.

ballade French poetic form and chanson type of the Middle Ages and Renaissance with courtly love texts. Also a Romantic genre, especially a lyric piano piece.

ballad opera English comic opera, usually featuring spoken dialogue alternating with songs set to popular tunes.

ballet A dance form featuring a staged presentation of group or solo dancing with music, costumes, and scenery.

banjo Plucked-string instrument with round body in the form of a single-headed drum and a long, fretted neck; brought to the Americas from Africa by early slaves.

baritone Male voice of moderately low range.

baritone horn See *euphonium.*

bas Medieval category of soft instruments, used principally for indoor occasions, as distinct from *haut,* or loud, instruments.

bass Male voice of low range.

bass clarinet Woodwind instrument of the clarinet family with the lowest range.

bass drum Percussion instrument played with a large, soft-headed stick; the largest orchestral drum.

basse danse Graceful court dance of the early Renaissance; an older version of the *pavane.*

basso continuo Italian for "continuous bass." See *figured bass.* Also refers to performance group with a bass, chordal instrument (harpsichord, organ), and one bass melody instrument (cello, bassoon).

bassoon Double-reed woodwind instrument with a low range.

bass viol See *double bass.*

beat Regular pulsation; a basic unit of length in musical time.

bebop Complex jazz style developed in the 1940s. Also *bop.*

bel canto "Beautiful singing"; elegant Italian vocal style characterized by florid melodic lines delivered by voices of great agility, smoothness, and purity of tone.

bell tree Long stick with bells suspended from it, adopted from *Janissary music.*

bent pitch See *blue note.*

big band Large jazz ensemble popular in 1930s and 1940s, featuring sections of trumpets, trombones, saxophones (and other woodwinds), and rhythm instruments (piano, double bass, drums, and guitar).

binary form Two-part (A-B) form with each section normally repeated. Also *two-part form.*

blue note A slight drop of pitch on the third, fifth, or seventh tone of the scale, common in blues and jazz. Also *bent pitch.*

blues African-American form of secular folk music, related to jazz, that is based on a simple, repetitive poetic-musical structure.

bop See *bebop.*

bossa nova Brazilian dance related to the *samba,* popular in the 1950s and 1960s.

bourrée Lively French Baroque dance type in duple meter.

branle Quick French group dance of the Renaissance, related to the *ronde.*

brass instrument Wind instrument with a cup-shaped mouthpiece, a tube that flares into a bell, and slides or valves to vary the pitch. Most often made of brass or silver.

brass quintet Standard chamber ensemble made up of two trumpets, French horn, trombone, and tuba.

bridge Transitional passage connecting two sections of a composition; also *transition.* Also the part of a string instrument that holds the strings in place.

bugle Brass instrument that evolved from the earlier military, or field, trumpet.

Burgundian chanson Fifteenth-century French composition, usually for three voices, some or all of which may be played by instruments. Also *chanson.*

cadence Resting place in a musical phrase; music punctuation.

cadenza Virtuosic solo passage in the manner of an improvisation, performed near the end of an aria or a movement of a concerto.

cakewalk Syncopated, strutting dance of nineteenth-century origin; developed among Southern slaves in a parody of white plantation owners.

call and response Performance style with a singing leader who is imitated by a chorus of followers. Also *responsorial singing.*

canon Type of polyphonic composition in which one musical line strictly imitates another at a fixed distance throughout.

cantabile Songful, in a singing style.

cantata Vocal genre for solo singers, chorus, and instrumentalists based on a lyric or dramatic poetic narrative. It generally consists of several movements including recitatives, arias, and ensemble numbers.

cantor Solo singer or singing leader in Jewish and Christian liturgical music.

cantus firmus "Fixed melody," usually of very long notes, often based on a fragment of Gregorian chant that served as the structural basis for a polyphonic composition, particularly in the Renaissance.

capriccio Short lyric piece of a free nature, often for piano.

carol English Medieval strophic song with a *refrain* repeated after each stanza; now associated with Christmas.

cassation Classical instrumental genre related to the *serenade* or *divertimento* and often performed outdoors.

castanets Percussion instruments consisting of small wooden clappers that are struck together. They are widely used to accompany Spanish dancing.

castrato Male singer who was castrated during boyhood to preserve the soprano or alto vocal register, prominent in seventeenth- and early eighteenth-century opera.

celesta Percussion instrument resembling a miniature upright piano, with tuned metal plates struck by hammers that are operated by a keyboard.

cello See *violoncello.*

chaconne Baroque form similar to the *passacaglia,* in which the variations are based on a repeated chord progression.

chamber choir Small group of up to about twenty-four singers, who usually perform *a cappella* or with piano accompaniment.

chamber music Ensemble music for up to about ten players, with one player to a part.

chamber sonata See *sonata da camera.*

chanson French polyphonic song, especially of the Middle Ages and Renaissance, set to either courtly or popular poetry. See also *Burgundian chanson.*

chimes Percussion instrument of definite pitch that consists of a set of tuned metal tubes of various lengths suspended from a frame and struck with a hammer. Also *tubular bells.*

Chinese block Percussion instrument made from a hollowed rectangular block of wood that is struck with a beater.

choir A group of singers who perform together, usually in parts, with several on each part; often associated with a church.

chorale Baroque congregational hymn of the German Lutheran church.

chorale prelude Short Baroque organ piece in which a traditional chorale melody is embellished.

chorale variations Baroque organ piece in which a chorale is the basis for a set of variations.

chord Simultaneous combination of three or more tones that constitute a single block of harmony.

chordophone Instrument that produces sound from a vibrating string stretched between two points; the string may be set in motion by bowing, striking, or plucking.

chorus   Fairly large group of singers who perform together, usually with several on each part. Also a choral movement of a large-scale work. In jazz, a single statement of the melodic-harmonic pattern.

chromatic   Melody or harmony built from many if not all twelve semitones of the octave. A *chromatic scale* consists of an ascending or descending sequence of semitones.

church sonata   See *sonata da chiesa.*

clarinet   Single-reed woodwind instrument with a wide range of sizes.

clavecin   French word for "harpsichord." See *harpsichord.*

clavichord   Stringed keyboard instrument popular in the Renaissance and Baroque that is capable of unique expressive devices not possible on the harpsichord.

clavier   Generic word for keyboard instruments, including harpsichord, clavichord, piano, and organ.

coda   The last part of a piece, usually added to a standard form to bring it to a close.

codetta   In sonata form, the concluding section of the *exposition.* Also a brief coda concluding an inner section of a work.

collegium musicum   An association of amateur musicians, popular in the Baroque era. Also a modern university ensemble dedicated to the performance of early music.

comic opera   See *opéra comique.*

commedia dell'arte   Type of improvised drama popular in sixteenth- and seventeenth-century Italy; makes use of stereotyped characters.

common time   See *quadruple meter.*

compound meter   Meter in which each beat is divisible by three rather than two.

computer music   A type of electro-acoustic music in which computers assist in creating works through sound synthesis and manipulation.

con amore   With love, tenderly.

concertante   Style based on the principle of opposition between two dissimilar masses of sound; concerto-like.

concert band   Instrumental ensemble ranging from forty to eighty members or more, consisting of wind and percussion instruments. Also *wind ensemble.*

concertino   Solo group of instruments in the Baroque *concerto grosso.*

concerto   Instrumental genre in several movements for solo instrument (or instrumental group) and orchestra.

concerto form   Structure commonly used in first movements of concertos that combines elements of Baroque *ritornello* procedure with *sonata-allegro form.* Also *first-movement concerto form.*

concerto grosso   Baroque concerto type based on the opposition between a small group of solo instruments (the *concertino*) and orchestra (the *ripieno*).

concert overture   Single-movement concert piece for orchestra, typically from the Romantic period and often based on a literary program.

conductor   Person who, by means of gestures, leads performances of musical ensembles, especially orchestras, bands, or choruses.

con fuoco   With fire.

conga   Afro-Cuban dance performed at Latin-American Carnival celebrations. Also a single-headed drum of Afro-Cuban origin, played with bare hands.

conjunct   Smooth, connected melody that moves principally by small intervals.

con passione   With passion.

consonance   Concordant or harmonious combination of tones that provides a sense of relaxation and stability in music.

continuous imitation   Renaissance polyphonic style in which the motives move from line to line within the texture, often overlapping one another.

contrabass   See *double bass.*

contrabassoon   Double-reed woodwind instrument with the lowest range in the woodwind family. Also *double bassoon.*

contralto   See *alto.*

cool jazz   A substyle of *bebop,* characterized by a restrained, unemotional performance with lush harmonies, moderate volume levels and tempos, and a new lyricism; often associated with Miles Davis.

cornet   Valved brass instrument similar to the trumpet but more mellow in sound.

cornetto   Early instrument of the brass family with woodwind-like finger holes. It developed from the cow horn, but was made of wood.

Council of Trent   A council of the Roman Catholic Church that convened in Trent, Italy, from 1543 to 1565 and dealt with Counter-Reformation issues, including the reform of liturgical music.

counterpoint   The art of combining in a single texture two or more melodic lines.

countermelody   An accompanying melody sounded against the principal melody.

countersubject   In a fugue, a secondary theme heard against the subject; a countertheme.

country-western   Genre of American popular music derived from traditional music of the rural South, usually vocal with an accompaniment of banjos, fiddles, and guitar.

courante   French Baroque dance, a standard movement of the *suite,* in triple meter at a moderate tempo.

cover   Recording that remakes an earlier, often successful, recording with a goal of reaching a wider audience.

Credo   A section of the Mass; the third musical movement of the *Ordinary.*

crescendo   Growing louder.

crossover   Recording or artist that appeals primarily to one audience but becomes popular with another as well (e.g., a rock performer who makes jazz recordings).

crumhorn   Early woodwind instrument, whose sound is produced by blowing into a capped double reed and whose lower body is curved.

cymbals   Percussion instruments consisting of two large circular brass plates of equal size that are struck sidewise against each other.

da capo   An indication to return to the beginning of a piece.

da capo aria   Lyric song in ternary, or **A-B-A,** form, commonly found in operas, cantatas, and oratorios.

decrescendo   Growing softer.

development   Structural reshaping of thematic material. Second section of *sonata-allegro form;* it moves through a series of foreign keys while themes from the exposition are manipulated.

diatonic   Melody or harmony built from the seven tones of a major or minor scale. A *diatonic scale* encompasses patterns of seven whole tones and semitones.

Dies irae   Chant from the *Requiem Mass* whose text concerns Judgment Day.

diminuendo   Growing softer.

diminution   Statement of a melody in shorter note values, often twice as fast as the original.

disco   Commercial dance music popular in the 1970s, characterized by strong percussion in a quadruple meter.

disjunct   Disjointed or disconnected melody with many leaps.

dissonance   Combination of tones that sounds discordant and unstable, in need of resolution.

divertimento   Classical instrumental genre for chamber ensemble or soloist, often performed as light entertainment. Related to *serenade* and *cassation.*

Divine Offices   Cycle of daily services of the Roman Catholic Church, distinct from the *Mass.*

doctrine of the affections   Baroque doctrine of the union of text and music.

dodecaphonic   Greek for "twelve-tone"; see *twelve-tone music.*

dolce   Sweetly.

dolente   Sad, weeping.

dominant   The fifth scale step, *sol.*

dominant chord   Chord built on the fifth scale step, the V chord.

double bass   Largest and lowest-pitched member of the bowed string family. Also called *contrabass* or *bass viol.*

double bassoon   See *contrabassoon.*

double exposition   In the concerto, twofold statement of the themes, once by the orchestra and once by the soloist.

double-stop   Playing two notes simultaneously on a string instrument.

downbeat   First beat of the measure, the strongest in any meter.

drone   Sustained sounding of one or several tones for harmonic support, a common feature of some folk musics.

dulcimer   Early folk instrument that resembles the *psaltery;* its strings are struck with hammers instead of being plucked.

duple meter   Basic metrical pattern of two beats to a measure.

duplum   Second voice of a polyphonic work, especially the Medieval *motet.*

duration   Length of time something lasts; e.g., the vibration of a musical sound.

dynamics   Element of musical expression relating to the degree of loudness or softness, or volume, of a sound.

embellishment   Melodic decoration, either improvised or indicated through *ornamentation* signs in the music.

embouchure   The placement of the lips, lower facial muscles, and jaws in playing a wind instrument.

encore   "again"; an audience request that the performer(s) repeat a piece or perform another.

Empfindsamkeit   German "sensitive" style of the mid-eighteenth century, characterized by melodic directness and homophonic texture.

English horn   Double-reed woodwind instrument, larger and lower in range than the oboe.

episode   Interlude or intermediate section in the Baroque *fugue,* which serves as an area of relaxation between statements of the subject.

equal temperament   Tuning system based on the division of the octave into twelve equal half steps; the normal system used today.

espressivo   Expressively.

ethnomusicology   Comparative study of musics of the world, with a focus on the cultural context of music.

ethno-pop   See *world beat.*

étude   Study piece that focuses on a particular technical problem.

euphonium   Tenor-range brass instrument resembling the tuba. Also *baritone horn.*

exoticism   Musical style in which rhythms, melodies, or instruments evoke the color and atmosphere of far-off lands.

exposition   Opening section. In the *fugue,* the first section in which the voices enter in turn with the subject. In *sonata-allegro form,* the first section in which the major thematic material is stated. Also *statement.*

falsetto   Vocal technique whereby men can sing above their normal range, producing a lighter sound.

fantasia   Free instrumental piece of fairly large dimensions, in an improvisational style; in the Baroque, it often served as an introductory piece to a fugue.

figured bass   Baroque practice consisting of an independent bass line that continues throughout a piece and often includes numerals indicating the harmony required of the performer. Also *thorough-bass.*

film music   Music that serves either as background or foreground for a film.

first-movement concerto form.   See *concerto form.*

first-movement form   See *sonata-allegro form.*

flat sign   Musical symbol (♭) that indicates lowering a pitch by a semitone.

fluegelhorn   Valved brass instrument resembling a bugle with a wide bell, used in jazz and commercial music.

flute   Soprano-range woodwind instrument, usually made of metal and held horizontally.

flutter tonguing   Wind instrument technique in which the tongue is fluttered or trilled against the roof of the mouth.

folk music.   See *traditional music.*

folk rock   Popular music style that combines folk music with amplified instruments of rock.

form   Structure and design in music, based on repetition, contrast, and variation; the organizing principle of music.

formalism   Tendency to elevate formal above expressive value in music, as in Neoclassical music.

forte (*f*)   Loud.

fortissimo (*ff*)   Very loud.

French horn   Medium-range valved brass instrument that can be played "stopped" with the hand as well as open. Also *horn.*

French overture   Baroque instrumental introduction to an opera, ballet, or suite, in two sections: a slow opening followed by an Allegro, often with a brief return to the opening.

fugato   A fugal passage in a nonfugal piece, such as in the development section of a *sonata-allegro form.*

fuging tune   Polyphonic, imitative setting of a *hymn* or *psalm,* popular in Great Britain and the United States from the eighteenth century.

fugue   Polyphonic form popular in the Baroque era in which one or more themes are developed by imitative counterpoint.

fusion   Style that combines jazz improvisation with amplified instruments of rock.

gagaku   Traditional court music of Japan.

galliard   Lively, triple-meter French court dance.

gamelan   Musical ensemble of Java or Bali, made up of gongs, chimes, metallophones, and drums, among other instruments.

gavotte   Duple-meter Baroque dance type of a pastoral character.

genre   Category or repertory of music.

gigue   Popular English Baroque dance type, a standard movement of the Baroque *suite,* in a lively compound meter.

gioioso   Joyous.

glee club   Specialized vocal ensemble that performs popular music, college songs, and more serious works.

glissando   Rapid slide through pitches of a scale.

glitter rock   Theatrical, flamboyant rock style popular in the 1970s.

glockenspiel   Percussion instrument with horizontal, tuned steel bars of various sizes that are struck with mallets and produce a bright metallic sound.

Gloria   A section of the Mass; the second musical movement of the *Ordinary.*

Goliard song   Medieval Latin-texted secular song, often with corrupt or lewd lyrics; associated with wandering scholars.

gong   Percussion instrument consisting of a broad circular disk of metal, suspended in a frame and struck with a heavy drumstick. Also *tam-tam.*

gospel music   Twentieth-century sacred music style associated with Protestant African Americans.

grace note   Ornamental notes, often printed in small type and not performed rhythmically.

Gradual   Fourth item of the *Proper* of the Mass, sung in a *melismatic* style, and performed in a *responsorial* manner in which soloists alternate with a choir.

grand opera   Style of Romantic opera developed in Paris, focusing on serious, historical plots with huge choruses, crowd scenes, elaborate dance episodes, ornate costumes, and spectacular scenery.

grave   Solemn; very, very slow.

Gregorian chant   Monophonic melody with a freely flowing, unmeasured vocal line; liturgical chant of the Roman Catholic Church. Also *plainchant* or *plainsong.*

ground bass   A repeating melody, usually in the bass, throughout a vocal or instrumental composition.

grunge rock   Contemporary Seattle-based rock style characterized by harsh guitar chords; hybrid of *punk rock* and *heavy metal.*

guitar   Plucked-string instrument originally made of wood with a hollow resonating body and a fretted fingerboard; types include acoustic and electric.

habanera   Moderate duple-meter dance of Cuban origin, popular in the nineteenth century; based on characteristic rhythmic figure.

half step   Smallest interval used in the Western system, in which the octave divides into twelve such intervals. Also *semitone.*

harmonics   Individual pure sounds that are part of any musical tone; in string instruments, crystalline tones in the very high register, produced by lightly touching a vibrating string at a certain point.

harmony   The simultaneous combination of notes and the ensuing relationships of intervals and chords.

harp   Plucked-string instrument, triangular in shape with strings perpendicular to the soundboard.

harpsichord   Early Baroque keyboard instrument in which the strings are plucked by quills instead of being struck with hammers like the piano. Also *clavecin.*

haut   Medieval category of loud instruments, used mainly for outdoor occasions, as distinct from *bas,* or soft, instruments.

heavy metal   Rock style that gained popularity in the 1970s, characterized by simple, repetitive ideas and loud, distorted instrumental solos.

heptatonic scale   Seven-note scale; in non-Western musics, often fashioned from a different combination of intervals than major and minor scales.

heterophonic   Texture in which two or more voices (or parts) elaborate the same melody simultaneously, often the result of improvisation.

homophonic   Texture with principal melody and accompanying harmony, as distinct from *polyphony.*

horn   See *French horn.*

hornpipe   Country dance of British Isles, often in a lively triple meter; optional dance movement of solo and orchestral Baroque suite.

hymn   Song in praise of God; often involves congregational participation.

idée fixe   "Fixed idea"; term coined by Berlioz for a recurring musical idea that links different movements of a work.

idiophone   Instrument that produces sound from the substance of the instrument itself by being struck, blown, shaken, scraped, or rubbed. Examples include bells, rattles, xylophones, and cymbals.

imitation   Melodic idea presented in one voice and then restated in another, each part continuing as others enter.

improvisation   Creation of a musical composition while it is being performed, seen in Baroque ornamentation, cadenzas of concertos, jazz, and some non-Western musics. See also *embellishment.*

incidental music   Music written to accompany dramatic works.

instrument   Mechanism that generates musical vibrations and transmits them into the air.

interlude   Music played between sections of a musical or dramatic work.

intermezzo   Short, lyric piece or movement, often for piano. Also a comic interlude performed between acts of an eighteenth-century *opera seria.*

interval   Distance and relationship between two pitches.

inversion   Mirror or upside-down image of a melody or pattern, found in fugues and twelve-tone compositions.

isorhythmic motet   Medieval and early Renaissance motet based on a repeating rhythmic pattern throughout one or more voices.

Italian overture   Baroque overture consisting of three sections: fast-slow-fast.

Janissary music   Music of the military corps of the Turkish sultan, characterized by percussion instruments such as triangle, cymbals, bell tree, and bass drum as well as trumpets and double-reed instruments.

jarabe   Traditional Mexican dance form with multiple sections in contrasting meters and tempos, often performed by *mariachi* ensembles.

jazz   A musical style created mainly by African-Americans in the early twentieth century that blended elements drawn from African musics with the popular and art traditions of the West.

jazz band   Instrumental ensemble made up of reed (saxophones and clarinets), brass (trumpets and trombones), and rhythm sections (percussion, piano, double bass, and sometimes guitar).

jig   Vigorous English Renaissance dance that may be the predecessor of the Baroque *gigue.*

jongleurs   Medieval wandering entertainers who played instruments, sang and danced, juggled, and performed plays.

jongleuresses   Female *jongleurs,* or wandering entertainer/minstrels.

karaoke   "Empty orchestra"; popular nightclub style from Japan where customers sing the melody to accompanying prerecorded tracks.

kettledrums   See *timpani.*

key   Defines the relationship of tones with a common center or tonic. Also a lever on a keyboard or woodwind instrument.

keyboard instrument   Instrument sounded by means of a keyboard (a series of keys played with the fingers).

keynote   See *tonic.*

key signature Sharps or flats placed at the beginning of a piece to show the key of a work.

Klangfarbenmelodie Twentieth-century technique in which the notes of a melody are distributed among different instruments, giving a pointillistic texture.

koto Japanese plucked-string instrument with a long rectangular body, thirteen strings, and movable bridges or frets.

lamentoso Like a lament.

largo Broad; very slow.

Latin rock Subgenre of rock featuring Latin and African percussion instruments (*maracas, conga drums, timbales*).

legato Smooth and connected; opposite of *staccato*.

Leitmotif "Leading motive," or basic recurring theme, representing a person, object, or idea, commonly used in Wagner's operas.

libretto Text, or script, of an opera, prepared by a librettist.

Lied German for "song"; most commonly associated with the solo art song of the nineteenth century, usually accompanied by piano.

Lieder Plural of *Lied*.

lute Plucked-string instrument, of Middle Eastern origin, popular in western Europe from the late Middle Ages to the eighteenth century.

lyric opera Hybrid form combining elements of *grand opera* and *opéra comique* and featuring appealing melodies and romantic drama.

madrigal Renaissance secular work originating in Italy for voices, with or without instruments, set to a short, lyric love poem; also popular in England.

madrigal choir Small vocal ensemble that specializes in *a cappella* secular works.

maestoso Majestic.

Magnificat Biblical text on the words of the Virgin Mary, sung polyphonically in church from the Renaissance on.

major scale Scale consisting of seven different tones that comprise a specific pattern of whole and half steps. It differs from a minor scale primarily in that its third degree is raised half a step.

mambo Dance of Afro-Cuban origin with a characteristic quadruple-meter rhythmic pattern.

mandolin Plucked-string instrument with a rounded body and fingerboard; used in some folk musics and in *country-western* music.

maracas Latin-American rattles (*idiophones*) made from gourds or other materials.

march A style incorporating characteristics of military music, including strongly accented duple meter in simple, repetitive rhythmic patterns.

marching band Instrumental ensemble for entertainment at sports events and parades, consisting of wind and percussion instruments, drum majors/majorettes, and baton twirlers.

mariachi Traditional Mexican ensemble popular throughout the country, consisting of trumpets, violins, guitar, and bass guitar.

marimba Percussion instrument that is a mellower version of the *xylophone*; of African origin.

masque English genre of aristocratic entertainment that combined vocal and instrumental music with poetry and dance, developed during the sixteenth and seventeenth centuries.

Mass Central service of the Roman Catholic Church.

mazurka Type of Polish folk dance in triple meter.

mbube "Lion"; *a cappella* choral singing style of South African Zulus, featuring call-and-response patterns, close-knit harmonies, and syncopation.

measure Rhythmic group or metrical unit that contains a fixed number of beats, divided on the musical staff by bar lines.

melismatic Melodic style characterized by many notes sung to a single text syllable.

melody Succession of single tones or pitches perceived by the mind as a unity.

membranophone Any instrument that produces sound from tightly stretched membranes that can be struck, plucked, rubbed, or sung into (setting the skin in vibration).

meno Less.

mesto Sad.

metallophone Percussion instrument consisting of tuned metal bars, usually struck with a mallet.

meter Organization of rhythm in time; the grouping of beats into larger, regular patterns, notated as *measures*.

metronome Device used to indicate the tempo by sounding regular beats at adjustable speeds.

mezzo forte (*mf*) Moderately loud.

mezzo piano (*mp*) Moderately soft.

mezzo-soprano Female voice of middle range.

micropolyphony Twentieth-century technique encompassing the complex interweaving of all musical elements.

microtone Musical interval smaller than a semitone, prevalent in some non-Western musics and in some twentieth-century art music.

MIDI Acronym for musical instrument digital interface; technology standard that allows networking of computers with electronic musical instruments.

minimalist music Contemporary musical style featuring the repetition of short melodic, rhythmic, and harmonic patterns with little variation.

Minnesingers Late Medieval German poet-musicians.

minor scale Scale consisting of seven different tones that comprise a specific pattern of whole and half steps. It differs from the major scale primarily in that its third degree is lowered half a step.

minuet and trio An A-B-A form (A = minuet; B = trio) in a moderate triple meter; often the third movement of the Classical *sonata cycle*.

misterioso Mysteriously.

modal Characterizes music that is based on modes other than major and minor, especially the early church *modes*.

mode Scale or sequence of notes used as the basis for a composition; major and minor are modes.

moderato Moderate.

modulation The process of changing from one key to another.

molto Very.

monody Vocal style established in the Baroque, with a solo singer and instrumental accompaniment.

monophonic Single-line texture, or melody without accompaniment.

monothematic Work or movement based on a single theme.

morality play Medieval drama, often with music, intended to teach proper values.

motet Polyphonic vocal genre, secular in the Middle Ages but sacred or devotional thereafter.

motive Short melodic or rhythmic idea; the smallest fragment of a theme that forms a melodic-harmonic-rhythmic unit.

movement Complete, self-contained part within a larger musical work.

MTV Acronym for music television, a cable channel that presents nonstop *music videos*.

musical Genre of twentieth-century musical theater, especially popular in the United States and Great Britain; characterized by spoken dialogue, dramatic plot interspersed with songs, ensemble numbers, and dancing.

music drama   Wagner's term for his operas.

music video   Video tape or film that accompanies a recording, usually of a popular or rock song.

musique concrète   Music made up of natural sounds and sound effects that are recorded and then manipulated electronically.

mute   Mechanical device used to muffle the sound of an instrument.

nakers   Medieval percussion instruments resembling small kettledrums, played in pairs; of Middle Eastern origin.

neumatic   Melodic style with two to four notes set to each syllable.

neumes   Early musical notation signs; square notes on a four-line staff.

new age   Style of popular music of the 1980s and 1990s, characterized by soothing timbres and repetitive forms that are subjected to shifting variation techniques.

New Orleans jazz   Early jazz style characterized by multiple improvisations in an ensemble of cornet (or trumpet), clarinet (or saxophone), trombone, piano, string bass (or tuba), banjo (or guitar), and drums; repertory included *blues, ragtime,* and popular songs.

new wave   Subgenre of rock popular since the late 1970s, highly influenced by simple 1950s-style *rock and roll;* developed as a rejection of the complexities of *art rock* and *heavy metal.*

ninth chord   Five-tone chord spanning a ninth between its lowest and highest tones.

nocturne   "Night piece"; common in the nineteenth century, often for piano.

nonmetric   Music lacking a strong sense of beat or meter, common in certain non-Western cultures.

non troppo   Not too much.

oboe   Soprano-range, double-reed woodwind instrument.

octave   Interval between two tones seven diatonic pitches apart; the lower note vibrates half as fast as the upper and sounds an octave lower.

ode   Secular composition written for a royal occasion, especially popular in England.

offbeat   A weak beat or any pulse between the beats in a measured rhythmic pattern.

ondes Martenot   Electronic instrument that produces sounds by means of an oscillator.

open form   Indeterminate contemporary music in which some details of a composition are clearly indicated, but the overall structure is left to choice or chance.

opera   Music drama that is generally sung throughout, combining the resources of vocal and instrumental music with poetry and drama, acting and pantomime, scenery and costumes.

opera buffa   Italian comic opera, sung throughout.

opéra comique   French comic opera, with some spoken dialogue.

opera seria   Tragic Italian opera.

oral tradition   Music that is transmitted by example or imitation and performed from memory.

oral transmission   Preservation of music without the aid of written notation.

oratorio   Large-scale dramatic genre originating in the Baroque, based on a text of religious or serious character, performed by solo voices, chorus, and orchestra; it is similar to opera but without scenery, costumes, or action.

orchestra   Performing group of diverse instruments in various cultures; in Western art music, an ensemble of multiple strings with various woodwind, brass, and percussion instruments.

Ordinary   Sections of the Roman Catholic Mass that remain the same from day to day throughout the church year, as distinct from the *Proper,* which changes daily according to the liturgical occasion.

ordre   See *suite.*

organ   Wind instrument in which air is fed to the pipes by mechanical means; the pipes are controlled by two or more keyboards and a set of pedals.

organal style   *Organum* in which the Tenor sings the melody (original chant) in very long notes while the upper voices move freely and rapidly above it.

organum   Earliest kind of polyphonic music, which developed from the custom of adding voices above a plainchant; they first ran parallel to it at the interval of a fifth or fourth and later moved more freely.

ornamentation   See *embellishment.*

ostinato   A short melodic, rhythmic, or harmonic pattern that is repeated throughout a work or a section of one.

overture   An introductory movement, as in an opera or oratorio, often presenting melodies from arias to come. Also an orchestral work for concert performance.

panpipe   Wind instrument consisting of a series of small vertical tubes or pipes of differing length; sound is produced by blowing across the top.

part song   Secular vocal composition, unaccompanied, in three, four, or more parts.

partita   See *suite.*

pas de deux   A dance for two that is an established feature of classical ballet.

passacaglia   Baroque form (similar to the *chaconne*) in moderately slow triple meter, based on a short, repeated bass-line melody that serves as the basis for continuous variation in the other voices.

passepied   French Baroque court dance type; a faster version of the *minuet.*

passion   Musical setting of the Crucifixion story as told by one of the four Evangelists in the Gospels.

pastorale   Pastoral, country-like.

pavane   Stately Renaissance court dance in duple meter.

pentatonic scale   Five-note pattern used in some African, Far Eastern, and Native American musics; can also be found in Western music as an example of exoticism.

percussion instrument   Instrument made of metal, wood, stretched skin, or other material that is made to sound by striking, shaking, scraping, or plucking.

performance art   Multimedia art form involving visual as well as dramatic and musical elements.

phrase   Musical unit; often a component of a melody.

pianissimo (*pp*)   Very soft.

piano (*p*)   Soft.

piano   Keyboard instrument whose strings are struck with hammers controlled by a keyboard mechanism; pedals control dampers in the strings that stop the sound when the finger releases the key.

pianoforte   Original name for the *piano.*

piano quartet   Standard chamber ensemble of piano with violin, viola, and cello.

piano quintet   Standard chamber ensemble of piano with two violins, viola, and cello.

piano trio   Standard chamber ensemble of piano with violin and cello.

piccolo   Smallest woodwind instrument, similar to the flute but sounding an octave higher.

pitch   Highness or lowness of a tone, depending on the frequency (rate of vibration).

pizzicato   Performance direction to pluck a string of a bowed instrument with the finger.

plainchant   See *Gregorian chant.*

plainsong   See *Gregorian chant.*

poco   A little.

polka   Lively Bohemian dance; also a short, lyric piano piece.

polonaise   Stately Polish processional dance in triple meter.

polychoral   Performance style developed in the late sixteenth century involving the use of two or more choirs that alternate with each other or sing together.

polyharmony   Two or more streams of harmony played against each other, common in twentieth-century music.

polyphonic   Two or more melodic lines combined into a multivoiced texture, as distinct from *monophonic.*

polyrhythm   The simultaneous use of several rhythmic patterns or meters, common in twentieth-century music and in certain African musics.

polytonality   The simultaneous use of two or more keys, common in twentieth-century music.

portative organ   Medieval organ small enough to be carried or set on a table, usually with only one set of pipes.

positive organ   Small single-manual organ, popular in the Renaissance and Baroque eras.

prelude   Instrumental work intended to precede a larger work.

prepared piano   Piano whose sound is altered by the insertion of various materials (metal, rubber, leather, and paper) between the strings; invented by John Cage.

presto   Very fast.

program music   Instrumental music endowed with literary or pictorial associations, especially popular in the nineteenth century.

program symphony   Multimovement programmatic orchestral work, typically from the nineteenth century.

progressive rock   See *art rock.*

Proper   Sections of the Roman Catholic Mass that vary from day to day throughout the church year according to the particular liturgical occasion, as distinct from the *Ordinary,* in which they remain the same.

Psalms   Book from the Old Testament of the Bible; the 150 Psalm texts, used in Jewish and Christian worship, are often set to music.

psaltery   Medieval plucked-string instrument similar to the modern zither, consisting of a soundbox over which strings were stretched.

punk rock   Subgenre of rock popular since the mid-1970s, characterized by loud volume levels, driving rhythms, and simple forms typical of earlier rock and roll; often characterized by shocking lyrics and offensive behavior.

pure music   See *absolute music.*

quadruple meter   Basic metrical pattern of four beats to a measure. Also *common time.*

quadruple stop   Playing four notes simultaneously on a string instrument.

quadruplum   Fourth voice of a polyphonic work.

quartal harmony   Harmony based on the interval of the fourth as opposed to a third; used in twentieth-century music.

quotation music   Music that parodies another work or works, presenting them in a new style or guise.

raga   Melodic pattern used in music of India; prescribes pitches, patterns, ornamentation, and extramusical associations such as time of performance and emotional character.

ragtime   Late nineteenth-century piano style created by African Americans, characterized by highly syncopated melodies; also played in ensemble arrangements. Contributed to early jazz styles.

range   Distance between the lowest and highest tones of a melody, an instrument, or a voice.

rap   Subgenre of rock in which rhymed lyrics are spoken over rhythm tracks; developed by African Americans in the 1970s and widely disseminated in the 1980s and 1990s.

rebec   Medieval bowed-string instrument, often with a pear-shaped body.

recapitulation   Third section of *sonata-allegro form,* in which the thematic material of the *exposition* is restated, generally in the tonic. Also *restatement.*

recitative   Solo vocal declamation that follows the inflections of the text, often resulting in a disjunct vocal style; found in opera, cantata, and oratorio.

recorder   End-blown woodwind instrument with a whistle mouthpiece, generally associated with early music.

refrain   Text or music that is repeated within a larger form.

regal   Small Medieval reed organ.

reggae   Jamaican popular music style characterized by offbeat rhythms and chanted vocals over a strong bass part; often associated with the Christian religious movement Rastafarianism.

register   Specific area in the range of an instrument or voice.

relative key   The major and minor key that share the same key signature; for example, D minor is the relative minor of F major, both having one flat.

repeat sign   Musical symbol (𝄇) that indicates repetition of a passage in a composition.

Requiem Mass   Roman Catholic Mass for the Dead.

resolution   Conclusion of a musical idea, as in the progression from an active chord to a rest chord.

response   Short choral answer to a solo *verse;* an element of liturgical dialogue.

responsorial singing   Singing, especially in Gregorian chant, in which a soloist or a group of soloists alternates with the choir. See also *call and response.*

restatement   See *recapitulation.*

retrograde   Backward statement of melody.

retrograde inversion   Mirror image and backward statement of a melody.

rhythm   The controlled movement of music in time.

rhythm and blues   Popular African-American music style of the 1940s through 1960s featuring a solo singer accompanied by a small instrumental ensemble (piano, guitar, acoustic bass, drums, tenor saxophone), driving rhythms, and blues and pop song forms.

ring shout   Religious dance performed by African-American slaves, performed with hand clapping and a shuffle step to spirituals.

ripieno   The larger of the two ensembles in the Baroque *concerto grosso.* Also *tutti.*

ritardando   Holding back, getting slower.

ritornello   Short, recurring instrumental passage found in both the aria and the Baroque concerto.

rock and roll   American popular music style first heard in the 1950s; derived from the union of African-American *rhythm and blues, country-western,* and pop music.

rock band   Popular music ensemble that depends on amplified strings, percussion, and electronically generated sounds.

romance   Originally a ballad; in the Romantic era, a lyric instrumental work.

ronde   Lively Renaissance "round dance," associated with the outdoors, in which the participants danced in a circle or a line.

rondeau   Medieval and Renaissance fixed poetic form and chanson type with courtly love texts.

rondo   Musical form in which the first section recurs, usually in the tonic. In the Classical sonata cycle, it appears as the last movement in various forms, including **A-B-A-B-A, A-B-A-C-A,** and **A-B-A-C-A-B-A.**

round   Perpetual canon at the unison in which each voice enters in succession with the same melody (for example, *Row, Row, Row Your Boat*).

rounded binary   Compositional form with two sections, in which the second ends with a return to material from the first; each section is usually repeated.

rubato   "Borrowed time," common in Romantic music, in which the performer hesitates here or hurries forward there, imparting flexibility to the written note values. Also *tempo rubato.*

rumba   Latin-American dance of Afro-Cuban origin, in duple meter with syncopated rhythms.

rural blues   American popular singing style with raspy-voiced male singer accompanied by acoustic steel-string guitar; features melodic *blue notes* over repeated bass patterns.

sackbut   Early brass instrument, ancestor of the trombone.

salsa   "Spicy"; collective term for Latin-American dance music, especially forms of Afro-Cuban origin.

saltarello   Italian "jumping dance," often characterized by triplets in a rapid 4/4 time.

samba   Afro-Brazilian dance, characterized by duple meter, responsorial singing, and polyrhythmic accompaniments.

sampler   Electronic device that digitizes, stores, and plays back sounds.

Sanctus   A section of the Mass; the fourth musical movement of the Ordinary.

sarabande   Stately Spanish Baroque dance type in triple meter, a standard movement of the Baroque *suite.*

saxophone   Family of single-reed woodwind instruments commonly used in the concert and jazz band.

scale   Series of tones in ascending or descending order; may present the notes of a key.

scat singing   A jazz style that sets syllables without meaning (*vocables*) to an improvised vocal line.

scherzo   Composition in **A-B-A** form, usually in triple meter; replaced the *minuet and trio* in the nineteenth century.

secco   Operatic *recitative* that features a sparse accompaniment and moves with great freedom.

secular music   Nonreligious music; when texted, usually in the vernacular.

semitone   Also known as a *half step,* the smallest interval commonly used in the Western musical system.

sequence   Restatement of an idea or motive at a different pitch level.

serenade   Classical instrumental genre that combines elements of chamber music and symphony, often performed in the evening or at social functions. Related to *divertimento* and *cassation.*

serialism   Method of composition in which various musical elements (pitch, rhythm, dynamics, tone color) may be ordered in a fixed series. See also *total serialism.*

seventh chord   Four-note combination consisting of a triad with another third added on top; spans a seventh between its lowest and highest tones.

sextuple meter   Compound metrical pattern of six beats to a measure.

sforzando (sf)   Sudden stress or accent on a single note or chord.

shamisen   Long-necked Japanese *chordophone* with three strings.

sharp sign   Musical symbol (♯) that indicates raising a pitch by a semitone.

shawm   Medieval wind instrument that was the ancestor of the oboe.

side drum   See *snare drum.*

simple meter   Grouping of rhythms in which the beat is divisible by two, as in duple, triple, and quadruple meters.

sinfonia   Short instrumental work, found in Baroque opera, to facilitate scene changes.

Singspiel   Comic German drama with spoken dialogue; the immediate predecessor of Romantic German opera.

sitar   Long-necked plucked *chordophone* of northern India, with movable frets and a rounded gourd body; used as solo instrument and with *tabla.*

ska   Jamaican urban dance form popular in the 1960s that was influential in *reggae.*

slide trumpet   Medieval brass instrument of the trumpet family.

snare drum   Small cylindrical drum with two heads stretched over a metal shell, the lower head having strings across it; played with two drumsticks. Also *side drum.*

soft rock   Lyrical, gentle rock style that evolved around 1960 in response to hard-driving *rock and roll.*

sonata   Instrumental genre in several movements for soloist or small ensemble.

sonata-allegro form   The opening movement of the sonata cycle, consisting of themes that are stated in the first section (*exposition*), developed in the second section (*development*), and restated in the third section (*recapitulation*). Also *sonata form* or *first-movement form.*

sonata cycle   General term describing the multimovement structure found in sonatas, string quartets, symphonies, concertos, and large-scale works of the eighteenth and nineteenth centuries.

sonata da camera   Baroque chamber sonata, usually a suite of stylized dances. Also *chamber sonata.*

sonata da chiesa   Baroque instrumental work intended for performance in church; in four movements, frequently arranged slow-fast-slow-fast. Also *church sonata.*

sonata form   See *sonata-allegro form.*

song cycle   Group of songs, usually *Lieder,* that are unified musically or through their texts.

soprano   Highest-ranged voice, normally possessed by women or boys.

sousaphone   Brass instrument adapted from the tuba with a forward bell that is coiled to rest over the player's shoulder for ease of carrying while marching.

spiritual   Folklike devotional genre of the United States, sung by African Americans and whites.

Sprechstimme   A vocal style in which the melody is spoken at approximate pitches rather than sung on exact pitches; developed by Arnold Schoenberg.

staccato   Short, detached notes, marked with a dot above them.

statement   See *exposition.*

stile concitato   Baroque style developed by Monteverdi, which introduced novel effects such as rapid repeated notes as symbols of passion.

stile rappresentativo   A dramatic *recitative style* of the Baroque period in which melodies moved freely over a foundation of simple chords.

stopping   On a string instrument, altering the string length by pressing it on the fingerboard. On a horn, playing with the bell closed by the hand or a mute.

string instruments   Bowed and plucked instruments whose sound is produced by the vibration of one or more strings. Also *chordophone.*

string quartet   Chamber music ensemble consisting of two violins, viola, and cello. Also a multimovement composition for this ensemble.

string quintet   Standard chamber ensemble made up of either two violins, two violas, and cello or two violins, viola, and two cellos.

string trio   Standard chamber ensemble of two violins and cello or violin, viola, and cello.

strophic form   Song structure in which the same music is repeated with every stanza (strophe) of the poem.

Sturm und Drang   "Storm and stress"; late eighteenth-century movement in Germany toward more emotional expression in the arts.

style   Characteristic manner of presentation of musical elements (melody, rhythm, harmony, dynamics, form, etc.).

subdominant   Fourth scale step, *fa.*

subdominant chord   Chord built on the fourth scale step, the IV chord.

subject   Main idea or theme of a work, as in a fugue.

suite   Multimovement work made up of a series of contrasting dance movements, generally all in the same key. Also *partita* and *ordre.*

syllabic   Melodic style with one note to each syllable of text.

symphonic poem   One-movement orchestral form that develops a poetic idea, suggests a scene, or creates a mood, generally associated with the Romantic era. Also *tone poem.*

symphony   Large work for orchestra, generally in three or four movements.

syncopation   Deliberate upsetting of the meter or pulse through a temporary shifting of the accent to a weak beat or an offbeat.

synthesizer   Electronic instrument that produces a wide variety of sounds by combining sound generators and sound modifiers in one package with a unified control system.

tabla   Pair of single-headed, tuned drums used in north Indian classical music.

tabor   Cylindrical Medieval drum.

tala   Fixed time cycle or meter in Indian music, built from uneven groupings of beats.

tambourine   Percussion instrument consisting of a small round drum with metal plates inserted in its rim; played by striking or shaking.

tam-tam   See *gong.*

Te Deum   Song of praise to God; a text from the Roman Catholic rite, often set polyphonically.

tempo   Rate of speed or pace of music.

tempo rubato   See *rubato.*

tenor   Male voice of high range. Also a part, often structural, in polyphony.

tenor drum   Percussion instrument, larger than the snare drum, with a wooden shell.

ternary form   Three-part (A-B-A) form based on a statement (A), contrast or departure (B), and repetition (A). Also *three-part form.*

terraced dynamics   Expressive style typical of Baroque music in which volume levels shift based on the playing forces used.

tertian harmony   Harmony based on the interval of the third, particularly predominant from the Baroque through the nineteenth century.

texture   The interweaving of melodic (horizontal) and harmonic (vertical) elements in the musical fabric.

thematic development   Musical expansion of a theme by varying its melodic outline, harmony, or rhythm. Also *thematic transformation.*

thematic transformation   See *thematic development.*

theme   Melodic idea used as a basic building block in the construction of a composition. Also *subject.*

theme and variations   Compositional procedure in which a theme is stated and then altered in successive statements; occurs as an independent piece or as a movement of a *sonata cycle.*

theme group   Several themes in the same key that function as a unit within a section of a form, particularly in *sonata-allegro form.*

third   Interval between two notes that are two diatonic scale steps apart.

third stream   Jazz style that synthesizes characteristics and techniques of classical music and jazz; term coined by Gunther Schuller.

thorough-bass   See *figured bass.*

three-part form   See *ternary form.*

through-composed   Song structure that is composed from beginning to end, without repetitions of large sections.

timbales   Shallow, single-headed drums of Cuban origin, played in pairs; used in much Latin-American popular music.

timbre   The quality of a sound that distinguishes one voice or instrument from another. Also *tone color.*

timpani   Percussion instrument consisting of a hemispheric copper shell with a head of plastic or calfskin, held in place by a metal ring and played with soft or hard padded sticks. A pedal mechanism changes the tension of the head, and with it the pitch. Also *kettledrums.*

toccata   Virtuoso composition, generally for organ or harpsichord, in a free and rhapsodic style; in the Baroque, it often served as the introduction to a *fugue.*

tom-tom   Cylindrical drum without snares.

tone   A sound of definite pitch.

tonal   Based on principles of major-minor tonality, as distinct from *modal.*

tonality   Principle of organization around a tonic, or home, pitch, based on a major or minor scale.

tone cluster   Highly dissonant combination of pitches sounded simultaneously.

tone color   See *timbre.*

tone poem   See *symphonic poem.*

tone row   An arrangement of the twelve chromatic tones that serves as the basis of a *twelve-tone* composition.

tonic   The first note of the scale or key, *do.* Also *keynote.*

tonic chord   Triad built on the first scale tone, the I chord.

total serialism   Extremely complex, totally controlled music in which the twelve-tone principle is extended to elements of music other than pitch.

traditional music   Music that is learned by *oral transmission* and is easily sung or played by most people; may exist in variant forms. Also *folk music.*

transition   See *bridge.*

transposition   Shifting a piece of music to a different pitch level.

tremolo   Rapid repetition of a tone; can be achieved instrumentally or vocally.

triad   Common chord type, consisting of three pitches built on alternate tones of the scale (e.g., steps 1–3–5, or *do-mi-sol*).

triangle   Percussion instrument consisting of a slender rod of steel bent in the shape of a triangle, struck with a steel beater.

trill   Ornament consisting of the rapid alternation between one tone and the next above it.

trio sonata   Baroque chamber sonata type written in three parts: two melody lines and the *basso continuo;* requires a total of four players to perform.

triple meter   Basic metrical pattern of three beats to a measure.

triple-stop   Playing three notes simultaneously on a string instrument.

triplum   Third voice in early polyphony.

tritonic   Three-note scale pattern, used in the music of some sub-Saharan African cultures.

trobairitz   Female *troubadours,* composer-poets of southern France.

trombone   Tenor-range brass instrument that changes pitch by means of a movable double slide; there is also a bass version.

troubadours   Medieval poet-musicians in southern France.

trouvères   Medieval poet-musicians in northern France.

trumpet   Highest-pitched brass instrument that changes pitch through valves.

tuba   Bass-range brass instrument that changes pitch by means of valves.

tubular bells   See *chimes.*

tutti   "All"; the opposite of solo. See also *ripieno.*

twelve-bar blues   Musical structure based on a repeated harmonic-rhythmic pattern that is twelve measures in length (I-I-I-I-IV-IV-I-I-V-V-I-I).

twelve-tone music   Compositional procedure of the twentieth century based on the use of all twelve chromatic tones (in a *tone row*) without a central tone, or "tonic," according to prescribed rules.

two-part form   See *binary form.*

unison   Interval between two notes of the same pitch; the simultaneous playing of the same note.

upbeat   Last beat of the measure, a weak beat, which anticipates the downbeat.

verismo   Operatic "realism," a style popular in Italy in the 1890s, which tried to bring naturalism into the lyric theater.

verse   In poetry, a group of lines constituting a unit. In liturgical music for the Catholic Church, a phrase from the Scriptures that alternates with the *response.*

Vespers   One of the *Divine Offices* of the Roman Catholic Church, held at twilight.

vibraphone   A percussion instrument with metal bars and electrically driven rotating propellers under each bar that produces a *vibrato* sound, much used in jazz.

vibrato   Small fluctuation of pitch used as an expressive device to intensify a sound.

vielle   Medieval bowed-string instrument; the ancestor of the violin.

viola   Bowed-string instrument of middle range; the second highest member of the violin family.

viola da gamba   Family of Renaissance bowed-string instruments that had six or more strings, was fretted like a guitar, and played held between the legs like a modern cello.

violin   Soprano, or highest-ranged, member of the bowed-string instrument family.

violoncello   Bowed-string instrument with a middle-to-low range and dark, rich sonority; lower than a viola. Also *cello.*

virelai   Medieval and Renaissance fixed poetic form and chanson type with French courtly texts.

virtuoso   Performer of extraordinary technical ability.

vivace   Lively.

vocable   Nonlexical syllables, lacking literal meaning.

vocalise   A textless vocal melody, as in an exercise or concert piece.

volume   Degree of loudness or softness of a sound. See also *dynamics.*

waltz   Ballroom dance type in triple meter; in the Romantic era, a short, stylized piano piece.

West Coast jazz   Jazz style developed in the 1950s, featuring small groups of mixed timbres playing contrapuntal improvisations; similar to *cool jazz.*

whole step   Interval consisting of two half steps, or *semitones.*

whole-tone scale   Scale pattern built entirely of whole-step intervals, common in the music of the French Impressionists.

wind ensemble   See *concert band.*

woodwind   Instrumental family made of wood or metal whose tone is produced by a column of air vibrating within a pipe that has holes along its length.

woodwind quintet   Standard chamber ensemble consisting of one each of the following: flute, oboe, clarinet, bassoon, and French horn (not a woodwind instrument).

word painting   Musical pictorialization of words from the text as an expressive device; a prominent feature of the Renaissance madrigal.

work song   Communal song that synchronized group tasks.

world beat   Collective term for popular third-world musics, ethnic and traditional musics, and eclectic combinations of Western and non-Western musics. Also *ethno-pop.*

xylophone   Percussion instrument consisting of tuned blocks of wood suspended on a frame, laid out in the shape of a keyboard and struck with hard mallets.

APPENDIX III

About the Listening Guides

Refer to Listening Guide 13 on page 629 as you read the following explanations.

1. The green bar at the top contains symbols to help you locate each work in the various recording sets:

    📼 : cassettes

    💿 : compact discs

    C/S: 8 recordings for the Chronological and Standard versions

    Sh: 3 recordings for the Shorter version

    (MW): Norton CD-ROM Masterworks, vol. 1

Following the cassette symbol: a numeral indicates the individual cassette within the set; a letter indicates the A or B side of the cassette; after a diagonal slash, a numeral indicates the selection number on that cassette side.

Following the CD symbol: a numeral indicates the individual CD within the set; after a diagonal slash, a boxed number or numbers indicate the track or tracks on that CD devoted to the work.

The CD-ROM icon indicates that the selection is included in the Norton CD-ROM Masterworks, vol. 1. Individual track numbers are generally unnecessary for this resource; however, they do appear on the CD-ROM case.

2. The title of the work is followed by some basic information about it.

3. The total duration of a piece is given in parentheses to the right of the title. (In multimovement works, the duration of each movement is also given to the right of the movement title.)

4. The far left column provides boxed numbers corresponding to the CD tracks. In the Chronological and Standard versions of the book, these relate to the 8-CD package; in the Shorter version of the book, they relate to the Shorter 3-CD package.

5. The next column gives cumulative timings, starting at zero for each movement. Listeners using cassettes may set tape counters to 0:00 at the start of the movement and use these timings for orientation while listening.

6. The Listening Guides often provide musical examples. Even if you cannot read music notation well, these may give you some idea of the shape of the line you will hear. If the examples are not helpful, focus on the accompanying descriptions and the timings to identify the musical event in question.

7. For vocal works, the Listening Guides provide texts that are sung and translations for those not in English. Both text and translation are printed on a light green background.

NOTE: In cases where the Shorter recordings include only an excerpt of the work (one or several movements of a larger piece or an abridged version), this is noted within the Listening Guide at the relevant movement(s).

Listening Guide 13

BRAHMS: *A German Requiem,* Fourth Movement   (5:46)

Date of work: 1868
Genre: Requiem, for Protestant church
Medium: 4-part chorus, soloists, and orchestra
Movements: 7
Language: German

FOURTH MOVEMENT: Mässig bewegt (moderately agitated)

Text: Psalm 84
Form: Rondo (**A-B-A′-C-A′**)
Character: Lilting triple meter, marked *dolce* (sweetly)

Opening melody: clarinets and flutes begin in inversion of first phrase in chorus:

		Text	Translation	Description
42	0:00	Wie lieblich sind deine Wohnungen, Herr Zebaoth!	How lovely is Thy dwelling place, O Lord of hosts!	**A**—flowing, arched melody, SATB homophonic setting, answers orchestral opening, E-flat major; text repeated in Tenors, joined by other voices
43	1:24	Meine Seele verlanget und sehnet sich nach den Vorhöfen des Herrn; mein Leib und Seele freuen sich in dem lebendigen Gott.	My soul longs and even faints for the courts of the Lord; my flesh and soul rejoice in the living God.	**B**—shift to minor, builds fugally with word repetition from lowest to highest voices; sudden accents on first beat of measures, with plucked strings; text repeated, climax on "lebendigen"
44	2:38	Wie lieblich . . . Wohl denen, die in deinem Hause wohnen,	How lovely . . . Blessed are they that live in Thy house,	**A′**—opening returns in E-flat major, new text and varied setting
45	3:49	die loben dich immerdar!	that praise Thee evermore!	**C**—martial quality, faster movement in polyphonic setting
46	4:42	Wie lieblich . . .	How lovely . . .	**A′**—coda-like return, reminiscent of opening; soft orchestral closing, in E-flat major

APPENDIX IV

■

Attending Concerts

Despite the many ways now available to hear fine-quality recorded music, nothing can equal the excitement of a live concert. The crowded hall, the visual as well as aural stimulation of a performance, even the element of unpredictability—of what might happen on a particular night—all contribute to the unique, communicative powers of people making music. There are, however, certain traditions surrounding concerts and concertgoing—how to choose seats, the way performers dress, the appropriate moments to applaud, are but a few. These conditions differ somewhat between concerts of art music and of popular styles. Understanding the various concert traditions can contribute to your increased enjoyment of the musical event.

Choosing Concerts, Tickets, and Seats

Widely diversified musical events, performed by groups ranging from professional orchestras and college ensembles to church choirs, can be found in most parts of the country. It may take some ingenuity and research to discover the full gamut of concerts available in your area. Both city and college newspapers usually publish a calendar of upcoming events; these are often announced as well on the local radio stations. Bulletin boards on campus and in public buildings and stores are good places to find concert announcements. Often a music or fine arts department of a college will post a printed list of future events featuring both professional and student performers.

Ticket prices will vary considerably, depending on the nature of the event and the geographical location of the theater. Many fine performances can be heard for a small admission price, especially at college and civic auditoriums. For an orchestra concert or an opera in a major metropolitan area, you can expect to pay anywhere from $20 to $75 for a reserved seat. The first rows of the orchestra section, located at stage level, and of the first balcony or loge are usually the most expensive. Although many consider it desirable to sit as close as possible to the performers, these are often not the best seats for acoustical reasons. To hear a proper balance, especially of a large ensemble, you are better off sitting in the middle of the hall. Today, most new concert halls are constructed so that virtually all seats are satisfactory. For the opera, many people bring opera glasses or binoculars if they are sitting some distance from the stage.

Concert tickets may be reserved in advance as well as purchased at the door. Often, reduced prices are available for students and senior citizens. Tickets reserved by telephone, or charged to a credit card, are generally not refundable; they are held at the box office in your name.

Preparing for the Concert

You may want to find out what specific works will be performed at an upcoming concert so that you can read about them and their composers in advance. If this book does not provide enough background, visit your campus or local public library or ask your instructor for assistance. If you plan to attend an opera, it is especially helpful to read an overview of the plot, since productions are usually sung in the original language of the work. Fortunately, many large opera houses today have monitors that run simultaneous English translations above the stage, a practice that can increase our comprehension and enjoyment enormously.

Suitable attire for a concert depends somewhat on the degree of formality and the location of the event. Although strict traditions of concert dress have long since broken down, you will not feel out of place if you are neatly dressed. If you are attending an opening night of an opera, a musical, or an orchestra season, or if you have seats in a box or founder's circle, you will find most people wearing evening dress. But more usually, dress will be fairly informal.

Arriving at the Concert

Plan to arrive at a concert at least fifteen minutes before it is scheduled to begin. This is particularly important if the seating is open—that is, nonreserved by seat number—so that you can choose your location. The time before a performance is often when people meet with friends, have a beverage at the lobby bar, and are "seen."

Concert programs are generally passed out (and sometimes sold) in the lobby or handed to you by the usher showing you to your seat. The program provides important information about the pieces being performed and about the people performing them. Often you will find English translations of vocal texts as well.

Should you arrive after the performance has begun, you may not be able to enter the hall until the first break in the music. This may occur after the first piece, or following the first movement of a large-scale work. Being late can mean missing as much as twenty minutes or more of a concert. When you finally do enter the hall, it is considerate to take a seat as quickly and quietly as possible.

The Concert Program

The following is a sample program for an orchestra concert such as you might find at your college or in your community. When laid out in the traditional manner, the program provides the audience with a good deal of information about the concert and, for the informed listener, sets certain expectations for the upcoming sequence of musical events.

PROGRAM

Overture to *A Midsummer Night's Dream*   Felix Mendelssohn
                                                                              (1809–1847)

Symphony No. 41 in C major, K. 551 (*Jupiter*)   W. A. Mozart
    Allegro vivace   (1756–1791)
    Andante cantabile
    Menuetto (Allegretto) & Trio
    Finale (Molto allegro)

INTERMISSION

Concerto No. 1 for Piano and Orchestra   P. I. Tchaikovsky
  in B-flat minor, Op. 23   (1840–1893)
    Allegro non troppo e molto maestoso;
      Allegro con spirito
    Andante simplice; Prestissimo; Tempo I
    Allegro con fuoco

Barbara Allen, piano

The University Symphony Orchestra
Eugene Castillo, conductor

A glance at the program before the concert begins confirms that three works will be performed. The concert will open, as is often the case, with an overture. The title of this work implies that it has a literary basis: Shakespeare's well-known play *A Midsummer Night's Dream*. In other words, this is a programmatic piece. Since no subdivisions or internal tempo markings are noted, you can expect it to be a one-movement work. The program also provides dates for the composer, Felix Mendelssohn, which establish him as an early Romantic master. (Since we study Mendelssohn and this particular piece in the book, you could read about the work in advance.)

The concert will continue with a symphony by the eighteenth-century composer Mozart. The work's title suggests that Mozart wrote many symphonies; what we would not know without reading about him is that this is his last. You can further note that the symphony is in the key of C major and has a catalog number of 551 (assigned by a bibliographer named Köchel).

The program reveals that the symphony is in four sections, or movements, with contrasting tempo indications for each movement. The tempo pattern of fast (Allegro vivace)–slow (Andante cantabile)–moderate dance (Menuetto &

Trio)–fast (Molto allegro) given for the different movements matches the plan for the sonata cycle; thus, the work is typical in its overall structure. (You can read more about the sonata cycle and the forms you can expect in the individual movements in Chapter 28.)

The second half of the concert will be devoted to a single multimovement work—a piano concerto by the late nineteenth-century composer Tchaikovsky. (You may notice different spellings for Tchaikovsky and other Russian composers on some programs, owing to varied ways of transcribing their names.)

This concerto appears to be a three-movement work, falling again into a standard format (fast-slow-fast). The tempo markings for each movement are, however, much more descriptive than those for the Mozart symphony, using words like "maestoso" (majestic), "con spirito" (with spirit), and "con fuoco" (with fire). This is typical of the Romantic era, as is the work's somber minor key. In the concerto, your interest will be drawn sometimes to the soloist, performing virtuoso passages and cadenzas, and at other times to the orchestra.

In addition to the works to be performed, the printed program may well provide other information. This could include short notes about each composition and biographical sketches of the musical careers of the soloist and the conductor. Traditionally, the names of all the ensemble members are also listed, along with upcoming concert dates.

During the Performance

Certain concert conventions come into play when the performance begins. The house lights will generally go down for the entrance of the performers or the opening of the curtain. Large ensembles, such as an orchestra or chorus, will usually be on stage at this time. The orchestra takes this opportunity to tune their instruments, cued by the *concertmaster* or *concertmistress* (the first chair, first violinist) asking for a pitch from the oboe player. It is customary to applaud the entrance of the conductor or any soloists. There will then be a moment's pause for complete quiet before the concert begins.

Knowing when to applaud during a concert is important. Generally, one applauds after complete works, such as at the close of a symphony, a concerto, a sonata, or a song cycle; it is inappropriate to clap between movements of a multimovement work. Sometimes, short works are grouped together on the program, suggesting that they are a set. In this case, applause is suitable at the close of the group. If you are unsure, follow the lead of others in the audience. This is also sound advice for performances in a church, where people often feel reluctant to applaud until the close of a performance. One notable exception to the rule of avoiding applause during a work is at the opera, where it is traditional to interrupt the drama with applause after a particularly fine delivery of an aria or an ensemble number.

Most concerts have an intermission, which is indicated on the program. (At the opera, there may be two or more, one after each act.) This is the only time that it is appropriate to leave one's seat or the theater. After about fifteen minutes, the theater manager will signal the audience to return to their seats, by either flashing the lights or ringing a bell.

The Performers

Newcomers to the concert hall are often surprised at the way the performers are dressed. For many years, it has been traditional to wear black—long dresses for the women, tuxedos or tails for the men. While this may seem overly formal, it is still customary, since dark, uniform clothing will minimize visual distraction.

The behavior of the performers on the stage is often as formal as their dress. The entire orchestra generally stands at the entrance of the conductor, who shakes the hand of the first violinist before beginning. A small group, such as a string quartet, will often bow to the audience in unison. The only time a performer will directly address the audience is if, at the close of the program, an additional piece or two is demanded by the extended applause and appreciation. In this case, the *encore* (French for "again"), or extra work, is generally announced.

It may surprise you to see that some musicians perform from memory. This is particularly common for pianists, singers, and other soloists. To perform without music requires intense concentration and necessitates many arduous hours of study and practice.

This brief explanation is intended to remove some of the mystery surrounding concertgoing. The best advice that can be given is to take full advantage of the opportunities available—try something completely unfamiliar, perhaps the opera or the symphony, and continue enjoying concerts of whatever music you already like!

APPENDIX V

■

Chronological List of Composers, World Events, and Principal Figures in Literature and the Arts, 1100–1994

WORLD EVENTS	COMPOSERS	PRINCIPAL FIGURES
	HILDEGARD OF BINGEN (1098–1179)	Eleanor of Aquitaine (c. 1122–1204) Queen of France and England
1260 *Kublai Khan founds Yuan dynasty in China.*	PEROTIN (fl. c. 1200) COUNTESS OF DIA (fl. c. 1210)	Kublai Khan (1214–94) Emperor of China Dante Alighieri (1265–1321)
1270 *Last Crusade to the Holy Land.*	MONIOT D'ARRAS (fl. 1213–39)	Italian poet Francesco Petrarch (1304–74)
1271 *Marco Polo embarks for China.*	GUILLAUME DE MACHAUT (c. 1300–77) FRANCESCO LANDINI (c. 1325–97)	Italian poet and scholar Giovanni Boccaccio (1313–75)
1337 *Beginning of the Hundred Years' War between England and France.*		Italian writer Geoffrey Chaucer (c. 1345–1400) English poet
1415 *John Huss burned for heresy. Henry V defeats French at Agincourt.*	JOHN DUNSTABLE (c. 1390–1453)	Donatello (c. 1386–1466) Florentine sculptor
1431 *Joan of Arc executed.*	GUILLAUME DUFAY (C. 1397–1474)	
1453 *Fall of Constantinople to Turks.*	ANTOINE BUSNOIS (d. 1492)	François Villon (1431–c. 65) French poet Leonardo da Vinci (1452–1519)
1456 *Gutenberg Bible printed.*	JOHANNES OCKEGHEM (c. 1420–c. 95)	Italian painter and scientist Desiderius Erasmus (c. 1466–1536)
1492 *Columbus discovers the New World.*		Dutch humanist and scholar Niccolò Machiavelli (1469–1527)
1501 *First book of printed music published by Petrucci in Florence.*	JOSQUIN DESPREZ (c. 1440–1521) JACOB OBRECHT (c. 1457–1505)	Italian statesman Albrecht Dürer (1471–1528)
1506 *St. Peter's begun by Pope Julius II.*		German painter Nicolas Copernicus (1473–1543) Polish astronomer
1509 *Henry VIII becomes king of England.*		Isabella d'Este (1474–1539) Italian patroness of the arts
1513 *Ponce de León discovers Florida. Balboa reaches Pacific.*	MARCHETTO CARA (c. 1465–1525)	Michelangelo (1475–1564) Italian sculptor, painter, architect, and poet
1517 *95 Theses of Martin Luther.*	BARTOLOMEO TROMBONCINO (c. 1470–1535)	Martin Luther (1483–1546) German religious reformer Raphael (1483–1520)
1519 *Cortéz begins conquest of Mexico.*	CLEMENT SERMISY (1490–1562)	Italian painter

WORLD EVENTS	COMPOSERS	PRINCIPAL FIGURES
1534 *Henry VIII head of Church of England.*	THOMAS TALLIS (c.1505-85)	
1541 *De Soto discovers the Mississippi.*	JACOB ARCADELT (c. 1505-c. 1560) TIELMAN SUSATO (c. 1515-68) GIOVANNI DA PALESTRINA (c.1525-94) ROLAND DE LASSUS (c. 1532-94)	Pierre de Ronsard (1524-85) French poet Pieter Brueghel (1525-69) Flemish painter
1545 *Council of Trent begins.* **1556** *Worst earthquake death toll (830,000 in northeastern China).*	WILLIAM BYRD (1543-1623) GIULIO CACCINI (1545-1618) TOMÁS LUIS DE VICTORIA (c. 1549-1611) LUCA MARENZIO (1553-99)	El Greco (c. 1541-1614) Italian painter Miguel de Cervantes (1547-1616) Spanish novelist
1558 *Elizabeth I becomes queen of England.*	GIOVANNI GABRIELI (c. 1557-1612) THOMAS MORLEY (1557-1603) CARLO GESUALDO (1560-1613)	Edmund Spenser (1552-99) English poet Galileo Galilei (1564-1642) Italian astronomer
1572 *St. Bartholomew's Eve Massacre.*	JACOPO PERI (1561-1633) CLAUDIO MONTEVERDI (1567-1643)	William Shakespeare (1564-1616) English dramatist
1587 *Mary Queen of Scots executed.*	JOHN WILBYE (1574-1638) THOMAS WEELKES (c. 1575-1623)	John Donne (1573-1631) English metaphysical poet
1588 *Drake defeats Spanish Armada.*	ORLANDO GIBBONS (1583-1625) HEINRICH SCHÜTZ (1585-1672) FRANCESCA CACCINI (1587-1630)	Ben Jonson (1573-1637) English dramatist
1590 *First three books of Spenser's* Faerie Queene *published.*		Peter Paul Rubens (1577-1640) Flemish painter René Descartes (1596-1650) French mathematician and philosopher Anthony van Dyck (1599-1641) Flemish painter
1601 *Shakespeare,* Hamlet.		
1606 *William Jansz discovers Australia.*	GIACOMO CARISSIMI (1605-74)	Rembrandt van Rijn (1606-69) Dutch painter
1607 *First European settlement in America founded at Jamestown, Virginia.*		Pierre Corneille (1606-84) French dramatist John Milton (1608-74) English poet
1609 *Henry Hudson explores the Hudson River.*		
1611 *King James Version of Bible.*	BARBARA STROZZI (1619-c. 63)	
1620 *Mayflower Compact. Plymouth settled.*	JEAN-BAPTISTE LULLY (1632-87) DIETRICH BUXTEHUDE (1637-1707)	Jan Vermeer (1632-75) Dutch painter
1636 *Harvard established as first college in America.*		Jean Racine (1639-99) French playwright
1640 *The* Bay Psalm Book, *first book printed in American colonies.*		
1642 *Puritan Revolution begins in England. French found Montreal.*		
1643 *Reign of Louis XIV begins.*	ARCANGELO CORELLI (1653-1713) HENRY PURCELL (1659-95) ELISABETH-CLAUDE JACQUET DE LA	
1664 *New Amsterdam becomes New York.*	GUERRE (c. 1666-1729) FRANÇOIS COUPERIN (1668-1733) ANTONIO VIVALDI (1678-1741)	Joseph Addison (1672-1719) English essayist Richard Steele (1672-1719)
1682 *Reign of Peter the Great begins.*	GEORG PHILLIP TELEMANN (1681-1767) JEAN-PHILIPPE RAMEAU (1683-1764)	Irish-born playwright Jean Antoine Watteau (1684-1721)
1684 *Newton's theory of gravitation.*	JOHN GAY (1685-1712) JOHANN SEBASTIAN BACH (1685-1750) DOMENICO SCARLATTI (1685-1757) GEORGE FRIDERIC HANDEL (1685-1759)	French painter Alexander Pope (1688-1744) English poet and satirist Voltaire (1694-1778) French poet and satirist

WORLD EVENTS	COMPOSERS	PRINCIPAL FIGURES
1702 *Start of War of the Spanish Succession.*		
1714 *Queen Anne succeeded by George I, Handel's patron.*	GIOVANNI BATTISTA PERGOLESI (1710–36) WILHELM FRIEDEMANN BACH (1710–84) CHRISTOPH WILLIBALD GLUCK (1714–87) CARL PHILLIP EMANUEL BACH (1714–88)	Jean Jacques Rousseau (1712–78) Swiss-born French philosopher and composer
1715 *First Opéra Comique founded.*		Thomas Gray (1716–71)
1715 *Reign of Louis XV begins.*	JOHANN STAMITZ (1717–57)	English poet
1719 *Herculaneum and Pompeii redis-covered. Classical revival.*		Joshua Reynolds (1723–92) English portrait painter
1732 *Linnaeus's* System of Nature. *George Washington born.*	JOSEPH HAYDN (1732–1809)	Pierre-Augustin Caron de Beaumarchais (1732–99), French playwright
1737 *San Carlo Opera, Naples, opened.*	JOHANN CHRISTIAN BACH (1735–82)	
1743 *Thomas Jefferson born.*	WILLIAM BILLINGS (1746–1800)	Francisco Goya (1746–1828) Spanish painter Jacques-Louis David (1748–1825)
1752 *Franklin's discoveries in electricity.*	MUZIO CLEMENTI (1752–1832)	French painter Johann Wolfgang von Goethe
1756 *Opening of Seven Years' War (in America, the French and Indian War).*	WOLFGANG AMADEUS MOZART (1756–91)	(1749–1832), German poet Evariste-Désiré de Parny (1753–1814) French poet William Blake (1757–1827)
1759 *Wolfe captures Quebec.*	MARIA THERESIA VON PARADIS (1759–1824)	English poet and painter Robert Burns (1759–96)
1762 *Catherine the Great crowned empress of Russia.*	LUIGI CHERUBINI (1760–1842)	Scottish poet Friedrich von Schiller (1759–1805) German dramatist
1769 *Watt's steam engine.*		
1771 *First edition,* Encyclopaedia Britannica.	LUDWIG VAN BEETHOVEN (1770–1827) GASPARO SPONTINI (1774–1851)	William Wordsworth (1770–1850) English poet
1775 *American Revolution begins.*		J. M. W. Turner (1775–1851) English painter
1776 *Adam Smith's* The Wealth of Nations. *Declaration of Independence signed.*		E. T. A. Hoffmann (1776–1822) German writer
1778 *La Scala Opera opened in Milan.*	NICCOLÒ PAGANINI (1782–1840)	
1787 *Constitutional Convention.*	CARL MARIA VON WEBER (1786–1826) GIACOMO MEYERBEER (1791–1864)	Jean Ingres (1780–1867) French painter Lord Byron (1788–1824)
1789 *French Revolution begins.*	GIOACCHINO ROSSINI (1792–1868) LOWELL MASON (1792–1872)	English poet Alphonse Lamartine (1790–1869)
1791 *Bill of Rights.*		French poet Percy Bysshe Shelley (1792–1822)
1793 *Eli Whitney's cotton gin.*		English poet John Keats (1795–1821)
1796 *Jenner introduces vaccination.*	GAETANO DONIZETTI (1797–1848) FRANZ SCHUBERT (1797–1828)	English poet Jean Baptiste Corot (1796–1875) French landscape painter Heinrich Heine (1797–1856) German poet Alexander Pushkin (1799–1837) Russian poet and novelist Honoré de Balzac (1799–1850) French novelist

WORLD EVENTS	COMPOSERS	PRINCIPAL FIGURES
1800 *Laplace's mechanistic view of the universe.*	VINCENZO BELLINI (1801–35)	Alexander Dumas (1802–70) French novelist Victor Hugo (1802–85)

1803 *Louisiana Purchase.*	HECTOR BERLIOZ (1803–69)
	JOHANN STRAUSS (father) (1804–49)
	MIKHAIL GLINKA (1804–57)
	FANNY MENDELSSOHN HENZEL (1805–47)
		French writer
		Prosper Mérimée (1803–70)
		    French writer
		Ralph Waldo Emerson (1803–82)
		    American poet and philosopher
		Aurore Dudevant, alias George Sand
		    (1804–76), French novelist
		Henry Wadsworth Longfellow (1807–82)
		    American poet
		Honoré Daumier (1808–79)
		    French painter

	FELIX MENDELSSOHN (1809–47) FRÉDÉRIC CHOPIN (1810–49) ROBERT SCHUMANN (1810–56) FRANZ LISZT (1811–86)	Edgar Allen Poe (1809–49) American poet and writer

1812 *Napoleon invades Russia.*	RICHARD WAGNER (1813–83)	Georg Büchner (1813–37)
		    German playwright
		Charlotte Brontë (1816–55)
		    English novelist

1815 *Battle of Waterloo, Congress of Vienna.*	GIUSEPPE VERDI (1813–1901) CHARLES GOUNOD (1818–93) JACQUES OFFENBACH (1819–80)	Henry David Thoreau (1817–62) American naturalist and poet Emily Brontë (1818–48)

1819 *First steamship to cross Atlantic.*	CLARA SCHUMANN (1819–96)	English novelist
		Marius Petipa (1818–1910)
		    French choreographer
		Walt Whitman (1819–92)
		    American poet

1821 *First women's college in America established.*	PAULINE VIARDOT-GARCIA (1821–1910)
	CÉSAR FRANCK (1822–90)
	ÉDOUARD LALO (1823–92)
		Charles Baudelaire (1821–67)
		    French poet
		Feodor Dostoevsky (1821–81)
		    Russian novelist

1823 *Monroe Doctrine.*	BEDŘICH SMETANA (1824–84) JOHANN STRAUSS (son) (1825–99)	Alexander Dumas the younger (1824–95) French writer
1824 *Bolívar liberates South America.*	STEPHEN COLLINS FOSTER (1826–64) WILLIAM MASON (1829–1908)	Henrik Ibsen (1828–1906) Norwegian poet and playwright
1829 *Independence of Greece.*	LOUIS MOREAU GOTTSCHALK (1829–69)	Leo Tolstoi (1828–1910) Russian novelist

1830 *First railroad, Liverpool-Manchester. July Revolution in France.*		Emily Dickinson (1830–86)
		    American poet
		Camille Pissarro (1830–1903)
		    French painter

1832 *Morse invents telegraph.*	JOHANNES BRAHMS (1833–97) ALEXANDER BORODIN (1834–87)	Edouard Manet (1832–83) French painter
1833 *Slavery outlawed in British Empire.*		James Whistler (1834–1903) American painter
1834 *McCormick patents mechanical reaper.*	CAMILLE SAINT-SAËNS (1835–1921)	Edgar Degas (1834–1917) French painter
1837 *Queen Victoria ascends the throne.*	LÉO DELIBES (1836–91) MILY BALAKIREV (1837–1910)	Mark Twain (1835–1910) American author

1839 *Daguerreotype invented. New York Philharmonic Society and Vienna Philharmonic founded.*	GEORGES BIZET (1838–75)
	MODEST MUSORGSKY (1839–81)
	PETER ILYICH TCHAIKOVSKY (1840–93)
		H. H. Richardson (1838–86)
		    American architect
		Paul Cézanne (1839–1906)
		    French painter
		Auguste Rodin (1840–1917)
		    French sculptor
		Claude Monet (1840–1926)
		    French painter
		Thomas Hardy (1840–1928)
		    English novelist and poet

WORLD EVENTS	COMPOSERS	PRINCIPAL FIGURES
	ANTONÍN DVOŘÁK (1841–1904)	Pierre Auguste Renoir (1841–1919)
	JULES MASSENET (1842–1912)	French painter
	EDVARD GRIEG (1843–1907)	Stéphane Mallarmé (1842–98)
	NIKOLAI RIMSKY-KORSAKOV (1844–1908)	French Symbolist poet
	GABRIEL FAURÉ (1845–1924)	Henry James (1843–1916)
		American novelist
		Paul Verlaine (1844–96)
		French poet
		Friedrich Nietzsche (1844–1900)
1846 *Repeal of Corn Laws. Famine in Ireland.*		German philosopher
		Henri Rousseau (1844–1910)
		French painter
		Mary Cassatt (1845–1926)
1848 *Revolution throughout Europe. Gold Rush in California. Marx's Communist Manifesto.*		American painter
		Paul Gauguin (1848–1903)
		French painter
	VINCENT D'INDY (1851–1931)	Vincent van Gogh (1853–90)
1852 *Second Empire under Napoleon III. Stowe's Uncle Tom's Cabin.*	ARTHUR FOOTE (1853–1937)	Dutch painter
	LEOŠ JANÁČEK (1854–1928)	Louis H. Sullivan (1856–1924)
	GEORGE CHADWICK (1854–1931)	American architect
1854 *Commodore Perry opens Japan to the West. Crimean War.*		George Bernard Shaw (1856–1950)
		Irish dramatist and critic
1855 *Charge of the Light Brigade.*	ERNEST CHAUSSON (1855–99)	
	EDWARD ELGAR (1857–1934)	
1857 *Dred Scott decision.*	RUGGERO LEONCAVALLO (1857–1919)	
	GIACOMO PUCCINI (1858–1924)	
1858 *Covent Garden opened as opera house.*		Anton Chekhov (1860–1904)
		Russian writer
		Maurice Maeterlinck (1862–1949)
1859 *Darwin's Origin of Species. John Brown raids Harper's Ferry.*		Belgian poet and dramatist
		Gabriele D'Annunzio (1862–1938)
	HUGO WOLF (1860–1903)	Italian poet and dramatist
1861 *Serfs emancipated in Russia. American Civil War begins.*	ISAAC ALBÉNIZ (1860–1909)	Henri de Toulouse-Lautrec (1864–1901)
	GUSTAV MAHLER (1860–1911)	French painter
	EDWARD MACDOWELL (1861–1908)	Rudyard Kipling (1865–1936)
1863 *Emancipation Proclamation.*		English novelist and poet
	CLAUDE DEBUSSY (1862–1918)	Wassily Kandinsky (1866–1944)
1865 *Civil War ends. Lincoln assassinated.*	FREDERICK DELIUS (1862–1934)	Russian painter
		H. G. Wells (1866–1946)
	PIETRO MASCAGNI (1863–1945)	English novelist
	RICHARD STRAUSS (1864–1949)	Luigi Pirandello (1867–1936)
		Italian dramatist
1866 *Transatlantic cable completed.*	PAUL DUKAS (1865–1935)	Frank Lloyd Wright (1867–1959)
		American architect
1867 *Marx's Das Kapital (vol. I). Alaska purchased.*	JEAN SIBELIUS (1865–1957)	Maxim Gorky (1868–1936)
		Russian writer
	ERIK SATIE (1866–1925)	Henri Matisse (1869–1954)
1869 *Suez Canal completed.*	AMY MARCY BEACH (1867–1944)	French painter
	SCOTT JOPLIN (1868–1917)	Marcel Proust (1871–1922)
	ALBERT ROUSSEL (1869–1937)	French novelist
1870 *Franco-Prussian War. Vatican Council proclaims papal infallibility.*	WILL MARIAN COOK (1869–1944)	Theodore Dreiser (1871–1945)
		American novelist
		Sergei Diaghilev (1872–1929)
		Russian impresario
1871 *William I of Hohenzollern becomes German emperor. Paris Commune. Unification of Italy. Stanley and Livingston in Africa.*		Piet Mondrian (1872–1946)
		Dutch painter
	RALPH VAUGHAN WILLIAMS (1872–1958)	Willa Cather (1873–1947)
	MAX REGER (1873–1916)	American novelist
1873 *Dynamo developed.*	SERGEI RACHMANINOFF (1873–1943)	Gertrude Stein (1874–1946)
	DANIEL GREGORY MASON (1873–1953)	American poet
1875 *New Paris Opera opened.*	ARNOLD SCHOENBERG (1874–1951)	W. Somerset Maugham (1874–1965), English novelist and playwright
	CHARLES IVES (1874–1954)	

WORLD EVENTS	COMPOSERS	PRINCIPAL FIGURES
1876 *Telephone invented. Bayreuth theater opened.*	MAURICE RAVEL (1875-1937) MANUEL DE FALLA (1876-1946) CARL RUGGLES (1876-1971)	Rainer Maria Rilke (1875-1926) German poet
1877 *Phonograph invented.*	OTTORINO RESPIGHI (1879-1936) ERNEST BLOCH (1880-1959)	Isadora Duncan (1878-1927) American dancer Paul Klee (1879-1940)
1880 *Irish insurrection.*		Swiss painter
	BÉLA BARTÓK (1881-1945)	Pablo Picasso (1881-1973)

1881 *Czar Alexander II assassinated. President Garfield shot. Panama Canal begun. Boston Symphony founded.*	GEORGES ENESCO (1881-1955)
	NATHANIEL DETT (1882-1943)
	IGOR STRAVINSKY (1882-1971)
	ZOLTÁN KODÁLY (1882-1967)
		Spanish artist
		Virginia Woolf (1882-1941)
		   English novelist
		Georges Bracque (1882-1963)
		   French painter

1882 *Berlin Philharmonic founded. Koch discovers tuberculosis germ.*		Franz Kafka (1883-1924) Bohemian writer Amadeo Modigliani (1884-1920)
1883 *Brooklyn Bridge opened. Metropolitan Opera opened. Amsterdam Concertgebouw founded.*	EDGARD VARÈSE (1883-1965) ANTON WEBERN (1883-1945)	Italian painter and sculptor Sinclair Lewis (1885-1951) American novelist
1884 *Pasteur discovers inoculation against rabies.*	CHARLES T. GRIFFES (1884-1920) ALBAN BERG (1885-1935) JELLY ROLL MORTON (1885-1941)	Diego Rivera (1886-1951)
1886 *Statue of Liberty unveiled in New York Harbor.*	WALLINGFORD RIEGGER (1885-1961)	Mexican painter Juan Gris (1887-1927) Spanish painter

1887 *Daimler patents high-speed internal combustion machine. Artistic Secession movement in Vienna.*		Marcel Duchamp (1887-1968)
		   French-born American painter
		Georgia O'Keeffe (1887-1986)
		   American painter

1888 *Eiffel Tower. Brazil becomes a republic.*	HEITOR VILLA-LOBOS (1887-1959) FLORENCE PRICE (1888-1953)	Hans Arp (1888-1966) French sculptor Jean Cocteau (1889-1963)
1889 *Paris World Exhibition.*	BOHUSLAV MARTINU (1890-1959) SERGE PROKOFIEV (1891-1952)	French writer and film director Vaslav Nijinsky (1890-1950)
1890 *Journey around world completed in 72 days.*	ARTHUR HONEGGER (1892-1955) DARIUS MILHAUD (1892-1974) GERMAINE TAILLEFERRE (1892-1983)	Russian dancer Joan Miró (1893-1983) Spanish painter
1892 *Duryea makes first American gas buggy.*	LILI BOULANGER (1893-1918) DOUGLAS MOORE (1893-1969) BESSIE SMITH (1894-1937)	Martha Graham (1894-1991) American choreographer Aldous Huxley (1894-1963)
1894 *Nicholas II, last czar, ascends throne.*	WALTER PISTON (1894-1976)	English novelist Robert Graves (1895-1985) English poet

1895 *Roentgen discovers X-rays. Marconi's wireless telegraphy. First African American awarded Harvard Ph.D.*	PAUL HINDEMITH (1895-1963)
	WILLIAM GRANT STILL (1895-1978)
	CARL ORFF (1895-1982)
	HOWARD HANSON (1896-1981)
	ROGER SESSIONS (1898-1985)
		F. Scott Fitzgerald (1896-1940)
		   American novelist
		Sergei Eisenstein (1898-1948)
		   Russian film director
		Ernest Hemingway (1898-1961)

1897 *Queen Victoria's Diamond Jubilee.*	VIRGIL THOMSON (1896-1989) HENRY COWELL (1897-1965)	American novelist Henry Moore (1898-1986)
1898 *The Curies discover radium. Spanish-American War.*	GEORGE GERSHWIN (1898-1937) ROY HARRIS (1898-1979) LOUIS ARMSTRONG (c. 1898-1971)	English sculptor Federico García Lorca (1899- 1936), Spanish poet and
1899 *Boer War. First International Peace Conference at the Hague.*	E. K. ("DUKE") ELLINGTON (1899-1974) RANDALL THOMPSON (1899-1984) FRANCIS POULENC (1899-1963)	playwright Thomas Wolfe (1900-38) American novelist
1900 *Boxer Insurrection in China.*	AARON COPLAND (1900-90) ERNST KRENEK (1900-91)	John Steinbeck (1902-68) American novelist Langston Hughes (1902-67)
1901 *Queen Victoria dies. Edward VII succeeds.*	KURT WEILL (1900-50) RUTH CRAWFORD (1901-53) HARRY PARTCH (1901-74)	American poet and playwright Isamu Nuguchi (1904-88)
1903 *Wrights' first successful airplane flight.*	WILLIAM WALTON (1902-83) LUIGI DALLAPICCOLA (1904-75)	American sculptor Salvador Dali (1904-89) Spanish painter

WORLD EVENTS	COMPOSERS	PRINCIPAL FIGURES
1905 *Sigmund Freud founds psycho-analysis. First Russian Revolution.*	MARC BLITZSTEIN (1905–64) LOUISE TALMA (1906–) DMITRI SHOSTAKOVICH (1906–75)	George Balanchine (1904–83) Russian choreographer Jean-Paul Sartre (1905–80)
1906 *San Francisco earthquake and fire.*	MIRIAM GIDEON (1906–) ELLIOTT CARTER (1908–)	French philosopher and novelist
1908 *Model-T Ford produced.*	OLIVIER MESSIAEN (1908–92)	W. H. Auden (1907–73) English poet and dramatist
1909 *Peary reaches North Pole. National Association for the Advancement of Colored People (NAACP) founded.*	YUJI TAKAHASHI (1909–) SAMUEL BARBER (1910–82) ALAN HOVHANESS (1911–)	Richard Wright (1908–60) American novelist Agnes de Mille (1909–93) American choreographer Jean Genet (1910–86) French writer
1911 *Amundsen reaches South Pole.*	VLADIMIR USSACHEVSKY (1911–90)	Marshall McLuhan (1911–80) Canadian writer Tennessee Williams (1911–83) American playwright Eugene Ionesco (1912–)
1912 *China becomes republic.* Titanic *sinks.*	JOHN CAGE (1912–92)	Rumanian-born French dramatist Dylan Thomas (1914–53)
1914 *Panama Canal begins. World War I begins.*	WITOLD LUTOSŁAWSKI (1913–94) BENJAMIN BRITTEN (1913–76) BILLIE HOLIDAY (1915–59) DAVID DIAMOND (1915–)	Welsh poet and playwright
1917 *U.S. enters World War I. Russian Revolution. Prohibition Amendment.*	GEORGE PERLE (1915–) MILTON BABBITT (1916–) ALBERTO GINASTERA (1916–83)	Arthur Miller (1915–) American playwright Ingmar Bergman (1918–) Swedish filmmaker
1918 *Kaiser abdicates. World War I ends in armistice.*	LOU HARRISON (1917–) LEONARD BERNSTEIN (1918–90)	J. D. Salinger (1919–) American novelist Federico Fellini (1920–93)
1919 *Treaty of Versailles. Mussolini founds Italian Fascist Party.*	CHARLIE PARKER (1920–55) RALPH SHAPEY (1921–) LUKAS FOSS (1922–)	Italian filmmaker Denise Levertov (1923–) American poet
1920 *Women's suffrage: Nineteenth Amendment passed.*	IANNIS XENAKIS (1922–)	Norman Mailer (1923–) American novelist Robert Rauschenberg (1925–)
1922 *Discovery of insulin. First woman U.S. senator.*	GYÖRGY LIGETI (1923–)	American artist Andy Warhol (1926–87) American pop artist and
1923 *USSR established.*	CHOU WEN-CHUNG (1923–) NED ROREM (1923–) LUIGI NONO (1924–90)	film director John Ashbery (1927–) American poet
1927 *Lindbergh's solo flight across Atlantic.*	JULIA PERRY (1924–79) LUCIANO BERIO (1925–) PIERRE BOULEZ (1925–) GUNTHER SCHULLER (1925–) EARLE BROWN (1926–) MORTON FELDMAN (1926–87) BETSY JOLAS (1926–) THEA MUSGRAVE (1928–) KARLHEINZ STOCKHAUSEN (1928–) GEORGE CRUMB (1929–)	Günter Grass (1927–) German novelist Adrienne Rich (1929–) American poet Claes Oldenburg (1929–) American artist Jean-Luc Godard (1930–) French filmmaker Jasper Johns (1930–) American painter
1930 *The planet Pluto discovered.*	TORU TAKEMITSU (1930–96) DAVID BAKER (1931–)	Harold Pinter (1930–) English dramatist
1931 *Japan invades Manchuria. Empire State Building is completed.*	LUCIA DLUGOSZEWSKI (1931–) SOFIA GUBAIDULINA (1931–) PAULINE OLIVERAS (1932–)	Alvin Ailey (1931–89) American choreographer Yevgeny Yevtushenko (1933–)
1933 *Franklin D. Roosevelt inaugurated. Hitler dictator of Germany.*	KRZYSZTOF PENDERECKI (1933–) MARIO DAVIDOVSKY (1934–) PETER MAXWELL DAVIES (1934–)	Soviet poet Inamu Amiri Baraka (Le Roi Jones) (1934–) American poet
1936 *Spanish Civil War. Sulfa drugs introduced in the U.S.*		

WORLD EVENTS	COMPOSERS	PRINCIPAL FIGURES

1937 *Japan invades China. Amelia Earhart disappears over Pacific.*	TERRY RILEY (1935–)
	 STEVE REICH (1936–)
	 DAVID DEL TREDICI (1937–)
	 PHILIP GLASS (1937–)
		Michael Graves (1934–)
		    American postmodern architect
		 Jim Dine (1935–)
		    American artist

1939 *World War II starts. Germany invades Poland, Britain and France declare war on Germany, Russia invades Finland.*	JOAN TOWER (1938–)
	 CHARLES WUORINEN (1938–)
	 JOHN CORIGLIANO (1938–)
	 ELLEN TAAFFE ZWILICH (1939–)
	 BARBARA KOLB (1939–)
		Frank Stella (1936–)
		    American artist
		 Tom Stoppard (1937–)
		    Czech-born English playwright
		 Lanford Wilson (1937–)
		    American playwright
		 David Hockney (1937–)
		    British painter
		 Alan Ayckbourn (1939–)
		    British dramatist

1940 *Roosevelt elected to third term. Churchill becomes British prime minister.*		
1941 *U.S. attacked by Japan, declares war on Japan, Germany, Italy.*		

1943 *Germans defeated at Stalingrad and in North Africa. Italy surrenders.*		Sam Shepard (1943–)
		    American playwright and actor
		 Rainer Werner Fassbinder (1946–82)
		    German film and stage director

1944 *D-Day. Invasion of France.*		
1945 *Germany surrenders. Atom bomb dropped on Hiroshima. Japan surrenders. Roosevelt dies.*		
1948 *Gandhi assassinated. Nation of Israel established.*	LAURIE ANDERSON (1947–) JOHN ADAMS (1947–)	
1949 *Communists defeat Chiang Kai-shek in China. USSR explodes atom bomb.*		
1950 *North Korea invades South Korea.*		Wendy Wasserstein (1950–) American playwright
1952 *Eisenhower elected president. Elizabeth II crowned queen of England.*	OLIVER KNUSSEN (1952–) TOD MACHOVER (1953–)	Peter Sellars (1958–) American stage director
1955 *Warsaw Pact signed. Salk serum for infantile paralysis.*	TOBIAS PICKER (1954–)	
1957 *First underground atomic explosion. Russians launch first satellite, Sputnik I.*		
1959 *Alaska becomes 49th state. Castro victorious in Cuba. Hawaii becomes 50th state.*		
1960 *Kennedy elected president.*		
1963 *Cuban missile crisis. Algeria declared independent of France.*		
1963 *Kennedy assassinated. Lyndon Johnson becomes president.*		

WORLD EVENTS

1964 *Passage of Civil Rights Act.*

1965 *First walk in space. Alabama civil rights march.*

1966 *Indira Gandhi elected prime minister of India.*

1967 *Israeli-Arab Six-Day War. First successful heart transplant.*

1968 *Richard M. Nixon elected President. Martin Luther King Jr. and Robert F. Kennedy assassinated.*

1969 *American astronauts walk on moon. Woodstock Festival.*

1970 *U.S. intervention in Cambodia. Nobel Prize in Literature to Solzhenitsyn.*

1971 *26th Amendment gives 18-year-olds the right to vote.*

1972 *Richard Nixon reelected.*

1973 *Vietnam War ends. "Watergate Affair" begins. Vice President Agnew resigns. Roe vs. Wade decision on abortion rights.*

1974 *President Nixon resigns. First home computers sold.*

1975 *Francisco Franco dies. Vietnam War ends.*

1976 *Viking spacecraft lands on Mars. Mao Zedong dies. Jimmy Carter elected President.*

1977 *New Panama Canal Treaty signed. Menachem Begin named Israeli prime minister.*

1978 *John Paul II first Polish pope.*

1979 *Shah of Iran deposed. Major nuclear accident at Three-Mile Island.*

1980 *Ronald Reagan elected president.*

1981 *First woman appointed to Supreme Court. Egyptian President Sadat assassinated. First AIDS cases reported.*

1983 *First woman astronaut into space. U.S. invades Grenada.*

1984 *Reagan reelected president. AIDS virus identified. Bishop Tutu wins Nobel Peace Prize.*

1985 *Reagan-Gorbachev summit meeting.*

1986 *Space shuttle* Challenger *crew dies in launching disaster. Iran-Contra scandal revealed.*

1988 *George Bush elected president. Mikhail Gorbachev named Soviet president.*

1989 *Polish Solidarity trade union legalized. Berlin Wall dismantled. Chinese military massacre in Tiananmen Square. Exxon Valdez oil spill in Alaska.*

1990 *Reunification of Germany.*

1991 *Soviet Union dissolved; Commonwealth of Independent States formed. Persian Gulf War. Pan Am flight 103 explodes over Lockerbie, Scotland.*

1992 *Bill Clinton elected president. Rodney King beating sets off Los Angeles riots. Hurricane Andrew devastates coasts of Florida and Louisiana.*

1993 *North American Free Trade Agreement (NAFTA) ratified. Bombing of New York World Trade Tower. Middle East peace accord on Palestinian self-rule.*

1994 *First free elections in South Africa.*

PHOTOGRAPHS:

Collaert/Stradanus engraving: The Metropolitan Museum of Art.

Michelangelo drawing: The Metropolitan Museum of Art, Purchase, 1924, Joseph Pulitzer Bequest (24.197.2).

El Greco, *View of Toledo*. The Metropolitan Museum of Art, Bequest of Mrs. H. O. Havemeyer, 1929; The H. O. Havemeyer Collection, 1929 (29.100.6).

Clavichord. The Metropolitan Museum of Art, Purchase, Gift of George Bashlow, Helen C. Lanier, Mr. and Mrs. Jason Berger in honor of Angna Enters, Mrs. Harold Krechmer, Miss Erida D. White, Burt N. Pederson, Risa and David Bernstein, Miss Alice Getty, John Solum, Carroll C. Beverly and Garry S. Bratman, The Crosby Brown Collection of Musical Instruments by exchange, The Barrington Foundation Inc. Gift, and Rogers Fund, 1986 (1986.239). Photography by Sheldon Collins.

Harpsichord: The Metropolitan Museum of Art, The Crosby Brown Collection of Musical Instruments, 1889 (89.4.2363). Photography by Sheldon Collins.

Portrait of Vivaldi: The Metropolitan Museum of Art.

Honoré Daumier, *The Third Class Carriage:* The Metropolitan Museum of Art, Bequest of Mrs. H. O. Havemeyer, 1929; The H. O. Havemeyer Collection (29.100.129).

Erard Grand Piano: The Metropolitan Museum of Art, Gift of Mrs. Henry McSweeny, 1959 (59.76). Photography by Sheldon Collins.

Henri Matisse, *The Cowboy:* Plate XIV from *Jazz* by Henri Matisse. Paris, E. Tériade, 1947. Pochoir, comp: (irreg.) 16 1/2" x 25 1/2". The Louis E. Stern Collection. Photograph © 1994, The Museum of Modern Art, New York.

Edgar Degas, *The Dance Class*. The Metropolitan Museum of Art, Bequest of Mrs. Harry Payne Bingham, 1986 (1987.47.1).

Katsushioka Hokusai. *The Great Wave at Kanagawa*. The Metropolitan Museum of Art, Bequest of Mrs. H. O. Havemeyer, 1929; The H. O. Havemeyer Collection (JP 1847).

Henri Rousseau, *Repast of the Lion:* The Metropolitan Museum of Art, Bequest of Sam Lewisohn, 1951 (51.112.5).

Vasily Kandinsky, *Painting No. 199:* 1914. Oil on canvas, 64 1/8" x 48 3/8". The Museum of Modern Art, New York, Nelson A. Rockefeller Fund (by exchange).

Georges-Pierre Seurat, *Study for A Sunday on La Grande Jatte":* The Metropolitan Museum of Art, Bequest of Sam Lewisohn, 1951.

Robert Motherwell, *Elegy to the Spanish Republic,* 108: (1965–67). Oil on canvas, 6'10" x 11'6 1/4". The Museum of Modern Art, New York, Charles Mergentime Fund.

Robert Rauschenberg, *First Landing Jump:* 1961. Combine painting: cloth, metal, leather, electric fixture, cable, and oil paint on composition board; overall, including automobile tire and wooden plank on floor, 7'5 1/8" x 6' x 8 7/8". Gift of Philip Johnson. Photograph © 1994. The Museum of Modern Art, New York.

MUSIC:

Wolfgang Amadeus Mozart, *The Marriage of Figaro (Le nozze di Figaro)*. Copyright © 1959 (renewed) by G. Schirmer, Inc. (ASCAP). International copyright secured. All rights reserved. Reprinted by permission.

Richard Wagner, *Die Walküre*. Reprinted by permission of G. Schirmer, Inc. (ASCAP).

Arnold Schoenberg, *Pierrot lunaire,* Op. 21. Copyright 1914 by Universal Edition. Copyright renewed. All rights reserved. Used in the world excluding the U.S. by permission of European American Music Distributors Corporation, sole Canadian agent for Universal Edition. Used in the U.S. by permission of Belmont Music Publishers, Pacific Palisades, CA 90272.

Alban Berg, *Wozzeck*. Libretto. Copyright 1923, 1931 by Universal Edition A.G., Wien. Copyright renewed. All rights reserved. Used by permission of of European American Music Distributors Corporation, sole U.S. and Canadian agent for Universal Edition A.G., Wien. Full score copyright 1926 by Universal Edition A.G., Vienna. Full score copyright renewed. Pocket score copyright 1955 by Universal Edition A.G., Vienna. Pocket score copyright renewed. All rights reserved. Used by permission of of European American Music Distributors Corporation, sole U.S. and Canadian agent for Universal Edition A.G., Vienna.

Charles Ives, *The Fourth of July*. Copyright © 1932 (renewed) by Associated Music Publishers, Inc. (BMI). International copyright secured. All rights reserved. Reprinted by permission.

Ruth Crawford, *Rat Riddles,* from Three Songs. © 1933 New Music Edition. Used by permission of the publisher. Theodore Presser Company.

Mr. Tambourine Man, words and music by Bob Dylan. Copyright © 1964, 1965 Warner Bros. Inc. Copyright renewed 1992, 1993 Special Rider Music. International copyright secured. All rights reserved. Reprinted by permission.

Peter Green, *Black Magic Woman*. © Copyright 1968 and 1970 by King Publishing Co., Ltd. All rights controlled by Murbo Music Publishing, Inc., and Bourne Music Ltd., London. Used by permission of Murbo Music Publishing, Inc., and Bourne Company, Music Publisher. All rights reserved. International copyright secured.

Elliott Carter, Sonata for Flute, Oboe, Cello, and Harpsichord: Copyright © 1960 (renewed) by Associated Music Publishers, Inc. (BMI). International copyright secured. All rights reserved. Reprinted by permission.

Pierre Boulez, *Le marteau sans maître*. © Copyright 1954 by Universal Edition (London) Ltd., London. Final version: © Copyright 1957 by Universal Edition (London) Ltd., London. Copyright renewed. Poems de Réné Char: © Copyright 1964 by Jose Corti Editeur, Paris. Copyright renewed. All rights reserved. Used by permission of European American Music Distributors Corporation, sole U.S. and Canadian agent for Universal Edition (London) Ltd., London.

George Crumb, *Ancient Voices of Children*. © 1971 by C. F. Peters Corporation. Used by permission.

György Ligeti, *Etudes pour Piano,* Premier Livre. © 1986 B. Schott's Söhne, Mainz. All rights reserved. Used by permission of European American Music Distributors Corporation, sole U.S. and Canadian agent for B. Schott's Söhne, Mainz.

Milton Babbitt, *Phonemena*. © 1979 by C. F. Peters Corporation. Used by permission.

Joan Tower, *Petroushskates* for Flute, Clarinet, Violin, Cello, and Piano. Copyright © 1983 (renewed) by Associated Music Publishers, Inc. (BMI). International copyright secured. All rights reserved. Reprinted by permission.

Modest Musorgsky/Maurice Ravel, *Pictures at an Exhibition*. © Copyright 1929 by Boosey & Hawkes, Inc. Copyright renewed. Reprinted by permission of Boosey & Hawkes, Inc. (pp. 114–15)

Richard Strauss, *Der Rosenkavalier*. ©1911 by Adolph Furstner for Germany, Italy, Portugal, and the former countries of Russia. Copyright renewed 1940 by Furstner, Ltd., London. Copyright assigned 1943 to Boosey & Hawkes, Ltd., London, for all other countries except Germany, Danzig, Italy, and Portugal. Reprinted by permission of Boosey & Hawkes, Inc. (pp. 438–39)

Maurice Ravel, *Chansons Madecasses*. © 1926 by Durand S. A. Editions Musicales. Joint publication, Editions A.R.I.M.A. & S. A. Editions Musicales. Used by permission of the publisher. Sole representative in the U.S.A., Theodore Presser Company.

Igor Stravinsky, *Petrushka*. © Copyright by Edition Russe de Musique. © Copyright assigned to Boosey & Hawkes, Inc. Revised edition © copyright 1947, 1948 by Boosey & Hawkes, Inc.: Copyright renewed.

Sergei Prokofiev. *Alexander Nevsky*. © Copyright 1945, 1949, 1966 by MCA Music Publishing, a division of MCA, Inc. Copyright renewed. International copyright secured. All rights reserved.

Béla Bartók, *Music for Strings, Percussion, and Celesta*. © Copyright 1937 by Universal Edition, renewed 1964. © Copyright and renewal assigned to Boosey & Hawkes, Inc., for the USA. Reprinted by permission of Boosey & Hawkes, Inc. Used in the world excluding the U.S. by permission of European American Music Distributors Corporation, agent for Universal Edition. (pp. 505–6)

Aaron Copland, *Billy the Kid*. © Copyright 1941 by the Aaron Copland Fund for Music, copyright renewed. Reprinted by permission of Boosey & Hawkes, Inc., sole agent. (pp. 519–21)

Joe Oliver and Clarence Williams, *West End Blues*. © Copyright 1928 by MCA Music Publishing, a division of MCA, Inc. Copyright renewed. International copyright secured. All rights reserved.

Richard Rodgers, Lorenz Hart, *My Funny Valentine*. Copyright © 1937 by Chappell & Co. Copyright renewed. Rights on behalf of the estate of Lorenz Hart administered by W.B. Music Corp. The interest of Richard Rodgers for the extended term of copyright in the U.S. assigned to Williamson Music. International copyright secured. All rights reserved. Used by permission. (pp. 537–38)

Leonard Bernstein, *West Side Story*. © Copyright 1951 by the Estate of Leonard Bernstein. Copyright renewed. Reprinted by permission of Boosey & Hawkes, Inc., Sole agent.

Tod Machover, *Bug-Mudra*. © Copyright by Edition Ricordi, Paris. Reprinted by permission of Hendon Music, Inc., agent. (p. 596)

John Adams, *Nixon in China*. © Copyright 1987 by Hendon Music, Inc. Reprinted by permission of Hendon Music, Inc.

TRANSLATIONS:

Where not otherwise specified, all translations are by the author.

Moniot d'Arras, *Ce fut en mai*. Translated by W. D. Snodgrass.

Johannes Ockeghem, *L'autre d'antan*. Leeman Perkins and Howard Garey, eds., *The Mellon Chansonnier*. © 1979 Yale University Press.

Giovanni Gabrieli: *Plaudite, psallite*. Translated by Alejandro E. Planchart.

Wolfgang Amadeus Mozart, *The Marriage of Figaro (Le nozze di Figaro)*. Translated by Lionel Salter.

Johannes Brahms: *Futile Serenade (Vergebliches Ständchen)*. Translated by Philip Miller. From *Ring of Words: An Anthology of Song Texts*. Philip Miller, ed. New York: Norton, 1973.

Richard Wagner: *Die Walküre*. Translated by William Mann.

Igor Stravinsky: *Petrushka*. Translation reprinted from *Notes*, March 1945, by permission of the Music Library Association.

Alban Berg: *Wozzeck*. Translated by Sarah E. Soulsby.

Sergei Prokofiev: *Alexander Nevsky*. Translated by Steven Ledbetter.

Federico García Lorca: *Selected Poems*. Copyright 1955 by New Directions Publishing Corporation. Used by permission of New Directions Publishing Corporation. Translated by W. S. Merwin.

INDEX

*Included in *The Norton CD-ROM Masterworks*, Volume I.

(Continued)